DEVELOPING READING SKILLS

DEVELOPING READING SKILLS
second edition

Deanne K. Milan
City College of San Francisco

RANDOM HOUSE   NEW YORK

Second Edition
987654321
Copyright © 1983, 1987 by Random House, Inc.

Library of Congress Cataloging-in-Publication Data

Milan, Deanne K.
   Developing reading skills.

   Includes index.
   1. Reading (Higher education)   2. Reading
comprehension.   I. Title.
LB1050.42.M55   1987   428.4′07′11   86-21949
ISBN 0-394-36241-1

Manufactured in the United States of America

Photo Credits
p. 232, left: Courtesy of Apple Computer Company; p. 232, right: Courtesy of John Deere & Company; p. 235, top left: Randy Matusow/Monkmeyer; p. 235, top right: Freda Leinwand/Monkmeyer; p. 235, below: Courtesy of Guerlain, Inc.

PERMISSIONS ACKNOWLEDGMENTS

George Orwell, from *Shooting an Elephant and Other Essays,* by George Orwell. Copyright 1950 by Sonia Brownell Orwell; renewed 1978 by Sonia Pitt-Rivers. Reprinted by permission of Harcourt Brace Jovanovich, Inc., the estate of Sonia Brownell Orwell, and Martin Secker & Warburg Ltd.

A. J. Liebling, from *Liebling at Home,* by A. J. Liebling. Copyright 1938, 1941, 1952, 1962, renewed 1966, 1969, 1980 by A. J. Liebling. Reprinted by permission of Russell & Volkening, Inc., as agents for the author.

John Bleibtreu, from *The Parable of the Beast,* by John N. Bleibtreu. Copyright © 1968 by John N. Bleibtreu. Reprinted with permission of Macmillan Publishing Company.

Andrea Lee, from *Russian Journal,* by Andrea Lee. Copyright © 1979, 1980 by Andrea Lee. Reprinted by permission of Random House, Inc.

Irving Howe, from *World of Our Fathers,* by Irving Howe. Copyright © 1976 by Irving Howe. Reprinted by permission of Harcourt Brace Jovanovich, Inc.

Peter Farb, from *Word Play: What Happens When People Talk,* by Peter Farb. Copyright © 1973 by Peter Farb. Reprinted by permission of Alfred A. Knopf, Inc.

Michael Arlen, from *The Camera Age,* by Michael Arlen. Copyright © 1976, 1977, 1978, 1979, 1980, 1981 by Michael Arlen. Reprinted by permission of Farrar, Straus and Giroux, Inc.

Marchette Chute, from *Shakespeare of London,* by Marchette Chute. Copyright 1949 by E. P. Dutton, renewed 1977 by Marchette Chute. Reprinted by permission of the publisher, E. P. Dutton, a division of New American Library.

Richard Rodriguez, "Does America Still Exist?" by Richard Rodriguez. Copyright © 1984 by *Harper's Magazine.* Reprinted from the March 1984 issue by special permission.

Marie Winn, from *Children Without Childhood,* by Marie Winn. Copyright © 1981, 1983 by Marie Winn. Reprinted by permission of Pantheon Books, a Division of Random House, Inc.

Jonathan Schell, from *The Fate of the Earth,* by Jonathan Schell. Copyright © 1982 by Jonathan Schell. Reprinted by permission of Alfred A. Knopf, Inc.

Katherine Mansfield, "Miss Brill" from *The Short Stories of Katherine Mansfield.* Copyright 1922 by Alfred A. Knopf, Inc., and renewed 1950 by John Middleton Murry. Reprinted by permission of Alfred A. Knopf, Inc.

John Updike, "Separating" from *Problems and Other Stories* by John Updike. Copyright © 1975 by John Updike. Reprinted by permission of Alfred A. Knopf, Inc.

Flannery O'Connor, "Good Country People" from *A Good Man Is Hard to Find,* by Flannery O'Connor. Copyright 1955 by Flannery O'Connor; renewed 1983 by Regina O'Connor. Reprinted by permission of Harcourt Brace Jovanovich, Inc.

For

M. M. and C. M.

PREFACE

The second edition of *Developing Reading Skills* proceeds from the same premise that governed the first edition: good reading and clear thinking go hand in hand. The book is organized around the principle that students can best improve their comprehension and thinking skills first by intensive, analytical practice with short reading passages, followed by the application of these skills to longer and increasingly difficult essays and articles. As in the first edition, the reprinted selections represent a variety of topics intended to appeal to students and general readers alike. The emphasis, then, remains on helping students develop two kinds of skills: first, the ability to comprehend accurately the sort of prose that they can expect to encounter in their college courses and in the world at large, and, second, the ability to read this material critically and analytically.

Developing these skills requires concentration and an intense engagement with the text. Accordingly, the second edition of *Developing Reading Skills,* like its predecessor, deliberately excludes discussing speed techniques. The wisdom of this decision has been borne out as the nation's teachers have become increasingly concerned in the past few years about the inability of students at all levels of education to read perceptively or to think critically. This concern is similarly reflected by the inclusion of critical reading and thinking skills in the nation's elementary and high school curricula and in the proliferation of required critical reading and critical thinking courses in the college curriculum.

The second edition of *Developing Reading Skills* thus retains the underlying principles that made the first edition successful, while making some changes that should make the book more useful and appealing for both students and teachers. For an author, a second edition gives one the opportunity to undo mistakes, to clarify what was not clear the first time around, and to respond to and implement the many comments and suggestions one has gathered along the way.

Content and Organization Within this general framework, the chapters and their accompanying exercises are directed at improving these specific skills:

- Finding or identifying the main idea in a paragraph and the thesis of an essay
- Determining the author's purpose
- Discerning methods of development, patterns of organization, and logical relationships between ideas
- Making accurate inferences and judgments

- Determining the author's tone
- Recognizing irony and its various shades and subtleties
- Understanding and analyzing connotative and figurative language
- Distinguishing between fact and opinion
- Finding unstated assumptions, determining appeals, and evaluating arguments
- Identifying common logical fallacies
- Improving vocabulary, with particular emphasis on using context clues

This edition begins with a considerably expanded prefatory section. "The Reading Process" includes a discussion of the skills requisite for good comprehension and for making accurate inferences and judgments. "Improving Your Vocabulary" adds new material, in particular a more complete explanation of context clues, dictionary pronunciation symbols, usage labels in the dictionary, and other hints for using the dictionary profitably.

The main text is divided into five parts. Part 1, "Reading Paragraphs," consists of six chapters, each concerned with some aspect of the skills fundamental to good reading. In response to questions and comments from students over the past few semesters, I have clarified and simplified the explanations in these six chapters. Each chapter contains a brief explanation of the particular topic under discussion, followed by a paragraph or two exemplifying it. The most important change in Part 1, however, is the division of Chapter 5 (Tone and Language in the first edition) into two chapters. Chapter 5 now takes up language, with an expanded section on analyzing metaphors and similes. Chapter 6 discusses tone, with a more detailed discussion of irony, wit, sarcasm, and satire.

At the end of each chapter are exercises in the form of paragraphs for analysis, including questions on comprehension, vocabulary, and inference. In addition, Chapters 5 and 6 contain separate exercises for analyzing figurative language and determining tone. Another new feature of this edition is the inclusion of a short Practice Essay at the end of each chapter in Part 1. Intended to give students an opportunity to apply their skills to a sustained piece of writing, these selections are both readable and unintimidating in terms of length and subject matter. Instructors should consult the teacher's manual for a detailed explanation of the exercise material throughout the text.

Part 2, "Reading Critically: Evaluating What You Read," now (more logically) follows Part 1. Instructors will find the treatment of critical reading skills in the second edition considerably expanded, with a fuller and better organized discussion of argument, unstated assumptions, deductive and inductive reasoning, and logical fallacies. Throughout the discussion is an emphasis on evaluating evidence. In addition to exercises on valid arguments and logical fallacies, Part 2 ends with five short persuasive articles or editorials for analysis and evaluation and a Practice Essay.

Part 3, "Reading and Studying Textbook Material," includes the earlier discussion of the SQ3R study skills method, along with new sections on taking notes and on preparing for and taking objective and subjective tests.

Before students begin working through Part 4, "Reading Articles and Essays," they should be directed to read the new introductory section on how to read an essay. Using Alexander Petrunkevitch's classic essay, "The Spider and the Wasp," as its point of departure, this discussion helps students learn what to look for when they are assigned to read a college-level essay, and it provides them with a list of questions to use during their analysis. The remainder of Part 4 consists of twenty essays arranged into four groups. Of the twenty selections, eleven are new to the second edition. I have retained those that my students over the past three years have particularly enjoyed reading or that I have found useful for teaching and demonstrating certain problems in reading longer works. The premise underlying the choice of readings remains the same: students need to practice with first-rate material, not only because good writing is easier to read (by virtue of its clarity and organization) but also because it is usually good writing that unnecessarily intimidates the student. Instructors should find their old favorites, such as George Orwell's "Shooting an Elephant"; Helen Keller's "My First Meeting with Miss Sullivan"; Barry Lopez's "The Wolf"; and Bruno Bettelheim's "The Three Little Pigs" (along with the original fairy tale). In this edition, however, there is more emphasis on "human interest" reading material, with such selections as Russell Baker's autobiographical piece from *Growing Up*; Calvin Trillin's essay on the tragic death of a rebel teenager, "It's Just Too Late"; A. J. Liebling's humorous piece, "The Jollity Building"; and Susan Allen Toth's "Girlfriends." The exercises following each selection in Part 4 are more extensive than those in Part 1, particularly in terms of testing for inference, structure, and vocabulary in context. The teacher's manual contains a brief synopsis of each selection in Part 4 and an explanation of their arrangement according to readability levels.

The four stories in Part 5 are followed by discussion questions on content and structure, as well as by multiple-choice vocabulary exercises. I have included these stories, three of them new to the second edition, because they are a good way to get students involved with reading imaginative literature, because they sharpen interpretive skills, and because they provide enjoyment (and perhaps a respite) for both students and instructors.

A packet of tests is available for instructors who adopt the second edition.

Acknowledgments   The following people deserve special thanks for their contributions: MeMe Riordan, Michael Hulbert, Robert Stamps, Donald Cunningham, all of City College of San Francisco; Denise Dinwiddie, of Diablo Valley College; and Marcia Schneider, of the San Francisco Public Library. A number of Random House staff members also deserve thanks for their work on the text, especially C. Steven Pensinger and Anna Marie Muskelly.

DEANNE MILAN
San Francisco, California

TO THE STUDENT

Learning to read well is a difficult task but not an impossible one. You are undoubtedly aware that as a college student you are required to do an immense amount of reading for your courses. But reading involves more than merely decoding print. In fact, we might redefine "reading" and describe it as a process of decoding print that requires internal translation. In other words, you must take the author's words and internalize them—not only for what they mean on the surface but for what they suggest beyond that. Rather than reading passively, sitting back and letting the author do all the work, you must learn to read actively. When you read, you enter into a peculiar kind of relationship with the writer, a two-way process of communication. Although the writer is physically absent, the words on the page are nonetheless there to be analyzed, interpreted, questioned, perhaps even challenged. In this way, the active reader engages in a kind of silent dialogue with the writer.

The first step is to understand accurately the content of what you read—the surface meaning. But the next step is just as essential for the college reader—learning to read critically and analytically, that is, learning to read beyond the superficial in order to see relationships between ideas, to determine the author's purpose and tone, to make accurate inferences and judgments, to distinguish between facts and opinions.

While the bulk of your required reading will be expository—that is, prose writing that explains, shows, and informs (the kind of writing usually found in textbooks)—you will also be reading newspaper and magazine articles, biographies, and short stories. The purpose of *Developing Reading Skills* is to help you accomplish what is expected of you. What we will be concerned with, then, is a variety of interesting readings and accompanying exercises to give you intensive practice both in comprehension and in analytical skills.

The chapters and readings are arranged in a way that will help you tackle successively harder reading tasks, one at a time. Following the process of *accretion,* each portion of the text contains questions and exercises building on the skills you have already mastered. The text begins with two introductory sections, "The Reading Process" and "Improving Your Vocabulary." You should read both of these carefully before you begin work in the main portion of the text. Then, in Part 1, the paragraph is treated extensively with both explanations, illustrative passages, and exercises for you to practice with.

While at first it may seem odd—or at least artificial—to devote so much time to single paragraphs (which, after all, are seldom read in isolation), forcing you to concentrate on short passages both promotes and ensures careful reading on your part. The paragraph is the basic unit of writing; studying its structure and examining the author's ideas allow you to slow down and analyze on a small scale what he or she is trying to accomplish.

Entirely too much importance has been placed on building up one's reading speed, on skimming and scanning, on zooming through material simply to get the "drift" of what the author is saying. These techniques are useful and appropriate in certain circumstances—for example, for the busy executive who must wade through a stack of correspondence each day, for the sports page reader who wants to find out which team won, for the student looking through the library's card catalog for likely research sources, or for the reader of "Dear Abby." But they are inappropriate for the major part of the reading you will have to do in college. Finally, intensive practice of newly acquired critical skills is easier and less intimidating with a one-hundred-word paragraph than with a five-page essay.

As you work through Part 1, you will be introduced to key terms in rhetoric, the study of written prose. Each term is followed by an example paragraph or two and an explanation of how the author employs the particular device or technique under discussion. At the end of each chapter, you will be asked to read additional paragraphs and work through a series of exercises. In this fashion, you will learn to analyze the structure of what you read at the same time that you improve your comprehension. You will see that writers normally impose a pattern on their ideas; that they use particular methods to develop and support those ideas; that the structure of a passage can determine meaning and emphasis as well as reveal the writer's purpose and point of view. In other words, it is as important to understand the way a writer expresses his or her ideas—the methods used and the words chosen—as it is to understand the ideas themselves.

To show you how this works, let's examine a sentence from John Knowles's essay, "Everybody's Sport," which appears as the Practice Essay at the end of Chapter 4:

> Surf swimming is perhaps the most elemental of all athletic experiences: you give your being to the action of the waves, currents, tides—things titanic and even cosmic.

The first part of the sentence sets up a general statement to be proved: the subject "surf swimming" is limited by the controlling idea, "the most elemental of all athletic experiences." The second part, following the colon, is a specific explanation of that controlling idea. The relationship between the two parts, then, is between general and specific, or statement and explanation.

Further, in the second part, Knowles classifies "waves, currents, tides" by putting these things into a general category, "things titanic and even cosmic." "Titanic" means huge or colossal; "cosmic" is an adjective describing the entire universe. In addition, these words explain and reinforce the word "elemental" in the first part. Knowles thus builds the sentence appropriately to a climax, implying by his choice and arrangement of words that even the strongest swimmer is helpless against the immense power of the ocean.

This approach—emphasizing the relationship between content and form in paragraphs, essays, and short stories—may seem difficult or tedious at first, but it should eventually accomplish two results. The first result will be an improvement in your own writing. There is much evidence to support a connection between good reading skills and good writing skills. When you understand how professional writers structure, develop, and support their ideas, you will find yourself more aware of how to deal with your own writing assignments.

But more important, you will improve your ability to think and read logically and critically. For example, you will be able to read two articles on IQ tests and see that while one writer relies on unsupported generalizations, emotional statements, and unfounded assertions to back up the claim that intelligence tests should be abolished, the other writer cites statistics, facts, and specific illustrations of how IQ tests have been misused, thereby allowing readers to draw their own conclusions on the basis of the evidence presented. You will have learned to read critically and with greater enjoyment.

CONTENTS

INTRODUCTION

A. THE READING PROCESS

Steps to Good Comprehension This introduction will explore and illustrate some of the fundamentals involved in the reading process: What exactly are the attributes of a good reader? What distinguishes a good reader from a merely competent one?

The following is an explanation of the steps required for good comprehension, the key to which is careful and thoughtful reading. The good reader is actively involved with the text through thinking, questioning, and evaluating. But these steps must be preceded by a more fundamental activity—decoding—meaning the process of recognizing the individual words on the page. You must first pronounce the words as you read (to yourself, of course), and if you are unsure about the meaning of any unfamiliar words, look them up in the dictionary.

Once you have decoded the words, you can begin the comprehension step. Good comprehension requires more than simply knowing what each word means. The real meaning of any text lies in the relationship that the words have with one another. First, ask yourself, what is the author saying? What is the main idea of the passage? What does he or she want me to understand about the main idea? Try to paraphrase (put into your own words) what each sentence says. Then look at the relationship between the words and sentences. Do you see a pattern? How is the main idea supported? Once you have asked these questions, then you can begin the final step—evaluating what the author has said. Do the ideas seem reasonable to you? Has the writer provided sufficient support? What other information do you need before you can intelligently accept or reject the ideas? How do the author's ideas fit with what you know about the subject? Is there any evidence of bias? Of an underlying, but unstated motive? To repeat: The good reader is an *active* reader, thinking and questioning all the way through the text. The explanatory material and the exercises in the first six chapters will give you ample practice with these skills.

To illustrate what the good reader does subconsciously, let us practice with a short paragraph.

Marriage was not designed as a mechanism for providing friendship, erotic experience, romantic love, personal fulfillment, continuous lay psychotherapy, or recreation. The Western European family was not designed to carry a lifelong load of highly emotional romantic freight. Given its present structure, it simply has to fail when asked to do so. The very idea of an irrevocable contract obligating the parties concerned to a lifetime of romantic effort is utterly absurd.

Mervyn Cadwallader,
"Marriage as a Wretched Institution," *Atlantic Monthly*

As you read through the paragraph, first determine if there are any words whose meaning you are not sure of. Three words, in particular, might cause some difficulty. The first, *lay,* in the phrase "lay psychotherapy" is used as an adjective, so you can skip the verb definitions in the dictionary. Of these three adjective definitions, which appears to be the most appropriate?

1. pertaining to, coming from, or serving the laity; secular: *a lay preacher.*
2. practicing psychoanalysis but not having a medical degree: *a lay analyst.* 3. of, or typical of, the average or common man: *lay opinion.*

Definition 2 best fits the context, judging from the context clue "psychotherapy." The second word, *freight,* in sentence 2 is used in an unusual way. Since nowhere in the paragraph is there any mention of a railroad, we can infer that *freight*—as it is used in the phrase "a lifelong load of highly emotional romantic freight"—refers metaphorically to a burden. The third problematic word occurs in the last sentence: *irrevocable.* Here you might try to break the word into its constituent parts to see if you can determine its meaning before you reach for the dictionary. Embedded in the middle is the root *revoke,* meaning "to annul or cancel." The prefix *ir-* means "not," and the suffix *-able* is self-evident, "able to." Putting all of this together, then, yields a definition something like this—"not able to be annulled or canceled"—a perfectly acceptable definition for this context. The pronunciation, however, is a bit tricky. *Irrevocable* is not pronounced (ĭ-rĭ vōk′ ə-bəl), as one might expect, but (ĭ-RĔV′ ə-kə-bəl), with the accent on the second syllable. Finally, if any other words in the paragraph caused you difficulty, look them up before continuing.

The next step is to go through the passage one sentence at a time, paraphrasing each to yourself. To give yourself some practice, try your own hand at this step. Using a sheet of paper, paraphrase Cadwallader's paragraph before comparing your version with the one provided here.

Sentence 1 says that marriage is not designed as a system to provide friendship, sexual experience, romantic love, personal fulfillment for one's ambitions, constant amateur psychological therapy, or play. The second sentence can be paraphrased to say that in the Western European family marriage partners were not intended to be burdened with a lifelong commitment to romantic love. The third sentence suggests that marriage, according to the way the institution works now, can only fail when partners are asked to make that lifelong commitment. (Note that the phrase "when asked to do so" refers to the phrase in the second sentence about marriage "carrying a lifelong load of highly emotional romantic freight." This technique, omitting a word or phrase from a previous statement, is called an *ellipsis,* and it can confuse the unwary reader. The author assumes that the reader sees the connection between the first idea and the unstated second one.) The final sentence can be paraphrased to say that it is ridiculous to expect marriage to be an irrevocable contract which requires the partners to commit themselves to a lifelong romantic effort. Obviously this paraphrase is not as elegant as the original, but it is nonetheless an accurate restatement of the original.

Now that you have restated the author's ideas, you can briefly summarize the paragraph. Cadwallader is concerned with the subject of marriage, specifically the Western European version of this institution, and since American marriage patterns are based on the European, we can assume that he means his ideas to pertain to the marriage custom of the United States as well. The author wants us to understand that the institution of marriage is destined to fail because people hold the erroneous expectation that romantic love can be sustained for a lifetime.

Each sentence in the paragraph builds to his conclusion: Sentences 1 and 2 state what marriage was *not* designed to do. Sentence 3 draws a conclusion from the first two sentences; sentence 4 restates the main idea and ends with an emphatic statement of opinion, that our high expectations for marriage are utterly absurd. What support for these observations does Cadwallader present? Since he concentrates on what the institution of marriage was not designed to do, there is little in the way of support for the main idea. Indeed, the paragraph presents only the author's subjective opinion. Although there are no facts or explanations to support the main idea, we must remember that this paragraph comes from a larger context (a magazine article); therefore, it is probably fair to expect that support for this opinion will be provided in the body of the article. Since the paragraph has a negative tone (emphasizing what marriage was not intended to do), we need to ask what marriage *can* do. Thus, the good reader anticipates, and we can expect the author to strengthen his argument by presenting us with a reasoned explanation of what marriage *can* accomplish. Furthermore, the good reader asks questions. How do other cultures view marriage, if it is not intended to perpetuate romantic love? What are the reasons that impel people in other cultures to marry? Are we wrong to hold the expectation that romantic love will endure for a lifetime? A glance at the title of the article, "Marriage as a Wretched Institution," confirms that the author's position will be from a critical viewpoint.

In the everyday world, it is obviously impractical to write a paraphrase of every sentence you read, yet sometimes the practice of restating the author's meaning in your own words is useful if the ideas are complex or if you want to ensure that you are coming away with an accurate understanding of the original. (The statement that you haven't really understood an idea if you can't put it into your own words is true not only for your writing but for your reading, as well.) If these steps seem unduly tedious, remember that with practice you will get better and faster. As you work through this book, you will be able to deal with much longer passages than this, accomplishing just as much in a short period of time, because the process will have become automatic. Intensive reading of short pieces is the best way to promote critical and analytical reading, and that is the aim of everything in this text.

Making Accurate Inferences and Judgments   Before you begin Chapter 1, one other
basic skill must be introduced—drawing accurate inferences and judgments
from what you read. This technique might be used by someone who receives
a love letter, as they examine the fine meanings of each word, try to see just
what emotion (and intention) lies behind each phrase, and make predictions
about the sender's future actions. An *inference* is a conclusion that one can
reasonably draw from a situation or a series of facts. The legal definition is
perhaps more instructive and precise:

> A presumption of fact or an inference is nothing more than a probable
> or natural explanation of facts . . . and arises from the commonly ac-
> cepted experiences of mankind and the inferences which reasonable men
> would draw from these experiences.
>
> *American Jurisprudence*, Vol. 29, 2d Evidence, Section 161

For example, you infer that a woman wearing a ring on the fourth finger
of her left hand is married. You infer that an older man cashing a Social
Security check at the bank is retired. You infer that a library book with a
shabby cover and torn pages is frequently borrowed. If a yard contains a
sandbox and a swing set, you infer that children are among the residents of
the house. Notice that in each case these inferences derive from our "commonly accepted experiences," although none of them is *necessarily* true. The
woman wearing the wedding ring may be a widow; the man at the bank
may be receiving disability payments; the library book may be worn simply
because the library staff does not have the time or funds to repair tattered
books. As for the play equipment in the yard, perhaps the owners of the
house operate a day-care center and do not have any children of their own.
In other words, inferences are merely *reasonable* conclusions that may be
drawn from a situation or, as concerns us here, conclusions we can draw
from what we read. In reading, unlike real life, making inferences (sometimes called "reading between the lines") requires more careful attention—
not only to what the author states explicitly or directly, but also to what he
or she implies by word choice, arrangement of words, selection of details,
and the author's apparent attitude toward the subject. To give you a notion
of how the inference process works, read this paragraph on the origin of
Coca-Cola and the explanation of inferences that follows it:

> [1]The man who invented Coca-Cola was not a native Atlantan, but on
> the day of his funeral every drugstore in town testimonially shut up shop.
> [2]He was John Styth Pemberton, born in 1833 in Knoxville, Georgia,
> eighty miles away. [3]Sometimes known as Doctor, Pemberton was a phar-
> macist who, during the Civil War, led a cavalry troop under General Joe
> Wheeler. [4]He settled in Atlanta in 1869, and soon began brewing such
> patent medicines as Triplex Liver Pills and Globe of Flower Cough Syrup.
> [5]In 1885, he registered a trademark for something called French Wine
> Coca—Ideal Nerve and Tonic Stimulant; a few months later he formed
> the Pemberton Chemical Company, and recruited the services of a book-
> keeper named Frank M. Robinson, who not only had a good head for

figures but, attached to it, so exceptional a nose that he could audit the composition of a batch of syrup merely by sniffing it. [6]In 1886—a year in which, as contemporary Coca-Cola officials like to point out, Conan Doyle unveiled Sherlock Holmes and France unveiled the Statue of Liberty— Pemberton unveiled a syrup that he called Coca-Cola. [7]It was a modification of his French Wine Coca. [8]He had taken out the wine and added a pinch of caffeine, and, when the end product tasted awful, had thrown in some extract of cola (or kola) nut and a few other oils, blending the mixture in a three-legged iron pot in his back yard and swishing it around with an oar. [9]He distributed it to soda fountains in used beer bottles, and Robinson, with his flowing bookkeeper's script, presently devised a label, on which "Coca-Cola" was written in the fashion that is still employed. [10]Pemberton looked upon his concoction less as a refreshment than as a headache cure, especially for people whose throbbing temples could be traced to overindulgence. [11]On a morning late in 1886, one such victim of the night before dragged himself into an Atlanta drugstore and asked for a dollop of Coca-Cola. [12]Druggists customarily stirred a teaspoonful of syrup into a glass of water, but in this instance the factotum on duty was too lazy to walk to the fresh-water tap, a couple of feet off. [13]Instead, he mixed the syrup with some charged water, which was closer at hand. [14]The suffering customer perked up almost at once, and word quickly spread that the best Coca-Cola was a fizzy one.

E. J. Kahn,
The Big Drink

From sentence 1 we can infer that the man who invented Coca-Cola was well-respected for his role in inventing the drink, suggested by the fact that shopkeepers in Atlanta closed their shops on the day of Pemberton's funeral. ("Testimonially" is a key word here, meaning that they paid Pemberton an important tribute.) We can infer from sentence 3 that the title by which Pemberton was sometimes called, "Doctor," was a nickname, since his real profession was pharmacy, not medicine. From sentences 4, 5, and 6, we can infer that Pemberton produced several concoctions before hitting on the formula that was eventually to become the successful Coca-Cola. In addition, we can infer from sentence 6 that Coca-Cola officials are proud that their drink is a century old. From sentences 7 and 8, we can infer that the original version of Coca-Cola contained alcohol, and that adding some extract of cola nut and "other oils" improved the flavor, although Pemberton apparently did not use exact measurements. This is suggested by Kahn's choice of words, "thrown in." Furthermore, sentence 8 suggests that the Pemberton Chemical Company was not exactly the nineteenth-century version of a contemporary "high tech" industry, judging from the makeshift contraptions (the iron pot and oar) Pemberton used to mix his concoctions. (Notice, however, that we cannot infer from this paragraph that the original Coca-Cola contained cocaine—a common assumption. An unabridged dictionary is worth consulting here: The cola tree is quite different from the coca tree, the leaves of which are used in making cocaine. The cola nut, however, does yield a stimulant, which probably accounts for the persisting notion that the original Coca-Cola was addictive because it contained cocaine rather than caffeine.) From sentence 10 we can infer that Pemberton considered his drink to be more a therapeutic substance (to cure hangovers) than a refreshment. Most important, from the brief incident recounted in sentences 11 through 14, we can infer the main idea of the paragraph, which the author has not stated explicitly: that the making of the Coca-Cola we know today was a pure accident, the result of a soda jerk's laziness. Finally, we can infer from the last sentence that Coca-Cola's success was rapid.

What judgment can we make about the invention of Coca-Cola from the way Kahn has described it? I think it is fair to say that Kahn suggests that the whole affair was rather haphazard, an accident of circumstances instead of a calculated action stemming from years of market research, as is now the case when a company introduces a new product.

In several of the exercises in this book, you will be asked to label inference statements as follows: An *accurate* inference is one that the reader can reasonably make from the passage, whereas an *inaccurate* inference cannot reasonably be made, either because the statement in the exercise is worded incorrectly or because it represents a misinterpretation of the original. The final answer, *insufficient evidence,* means that there is not enough information provided in the original from which you can draw any sort of inference. You saw an example of an inference based on insufficient evidence in the Coca-Cola passage about the question of whether cocaine was present in the original beverage. In other inference exercises, the questions will be open-ended, meaning that you will be referred to a sentence in the passage from which you must draw your own inference. Above all, remember that you may be asked to justify your answer by pointing to the phrase or sentence that led you to it.

B. IMPROVING YOUR VOCABULARY

A good reading vocabulary is probably the single most important requirement for good reading. Every other skill—comprehension, retention, making inferences, evaluating—depends on your knowledge of words and their meanings in particular settings. After all, if you don't know the meaning of the words on the page, you can hardly understand what the writer is trying to say. Sometimes it is possible to "wing it," meaning that you can get the gist of the writer's main idea, even if some words remain unfamiliar. Most often, however, and especially with the careful reading you will be asked to do in this text, your accurate understanding of a passage may depend solely on the meaning of a single word, a situation where guessing is hazardous.

To demonstrate how imperative your understanding of a new word can be, consider the following sentences which appeared in an article from *Psychology Today* titled "Cocaine: A Social History": "Cocaine is rapidly attaining unofficial respectability the way marijuana did in the 1960s. It is accepted as a relatively *innocuous* stimulant, casually used by those who can afford it to brighten the day or the evening." Clearly, the adjective *innocuous* carries a lot of weight in this sentence, representing a popular judgment of cocaine. Here is a case where a hazy notion or an ill-considered guess can lead to a complete misinterpretation. While the context may give you a clue that the word has a positive connotation (its emotional association), you are much safer consulting a dictionary if you are in doubt. *Innocuous* means "having no adverse [negative] effect; harmless." Now that you have an accurate definition of this pivotal word, you can better evaluate what the authors say, meaning that you can consider the worth of their statement. The message is: When in doubt, look it up.

So the task of improving your vocabulary is inescapable; and while, at first, learning dozens of new words may appear to be a staggering task, it *is* possible. Everyone has to start somewhere, and everyone's vocabulary can be improved since the number of words in the English language is sufficiently vast to make even the best reader reach for the dictionary, at least occasionally. (Modern unabridged dictionaries generally have about 600,000 entries, but it has been estimated that the English language has well over 1,000,000 words.)

Learning New Words   An exhaustive treatment of vocabulary acquisition is not within the scope of this book, and any number of excellent vocabulary guides are available. Therefore, what follows are simply some suggestions to enable you to start on an active program to learn the new words that you encounter in your reading.

First, you should have two dictionaries—an abridged (shortened) paperback edition for class, and an unabridged or complete edition to keep at home. There are several excellent dictionaries, both abridged and unabridged, on the market. Ask your instructor to recommend one, or choose an unabridged edition from this list of some of the best known:

> *The Random House Dictionary of the English Language*
> *The American Heritage Dictionary of the English Language*
> *Webster's New World Dictionary*
> *Merriam Webster's Collegiate Dictionary*
> *The Oxford American Dictionary*

However, since language changes constantly, be sure that your dictionary is a current edition. You may save a little money by using your father's old school dictionary, but the definitions will not reflect up-to-date usage. In the next section, you will find some helpful suggestions for using the dictionary.

Second, develop an interest in language. When you look words up in an unabridged dictionary, look at the etymology, since many words have unusual origins. In the dictionary, the etymology of a word is given in brackets following the definitions; it explains and traces the derivation of the word and gives the original meaning. For instance, the dictionary traces the history of the word *nice* as follows: [Middle English, foolish, wanton, shy, from Old French, silly, from Latin *nescius*, ignorant, from *nescire*, to be ignorant]. You can easily see how radically this ordinary (and now nearly meaningless) word has changed over the centuries. Another example is the word *maudlin,* meaning "effusively sentimental." This word is a corruption of the name Mary Magdalene, the prostitute who was present at Christ's crucifixion. According to the New Testament, Christ had cured her of evil spirits. Mary annointed Christ's feet as He carried the cross, and later became identified with tearful repentance. Note that the word's connotation has changed, so that it now has strongly negative overtones. A final example is the common word *denim,* which represents another corruption, this time from the French phrase *serge de Nîmes* ("serge from Nîmes"). Serge, a kind of cloth, was manufactured in Nîmes, a city in southern France, but the fabric eventually came to be called "de Nîmes" ("denim").

Paying attention to a word's etymology when you look it up in the dictionary will give you a sense of the language's complexity, and in the case of *maudlin,* knowing the word's etymology may help you remember the meaning when you next encounter it in your reading.

Third, do not memorize long lists of words in isolation. This is a tempting, but inefficient, way of proceeding; you won't remember many words, and you will have no idea of the subtleties in their meanings or the ways the words are used in context. New words are best learned (and retained) when they occur as part of your reading.

Next, devise a system for learning important words you look up. Write new words and their meanings (and the context, if necessary) in a small notebook or on index cards. Reviewing these words periodically will ensure your mastery of them.

Finally, try to think of words that share similar meanings and origins as belonging to groups or families. The word *dormant,* for example, which means "inactive" (from the French verb *dormir,* "to sleep") might also suggest *dormitory* ("a place where one sleeps"), or *dormer* ("a window under a sloping roof, usually in a bedroom"). Similarly, several related words derive from the Latin root verb *adhaerere* ("to stick to"): *adhere* ("to stick fast or together"); *adherent* ("sticking or holding fast" as an adjective, or "a supporter" as a noun); *adhesion* ("attachment or devotion, as to a cause or individual"); and *adhesive* ("tending to adhere," "sticky"—as in adhesive tape). From the Latin root *fides,* we derive *fidelity* (faithfulness), its negative form *infidelity* (lack of religious faith; also adultery), and the stereotyped name for a dog, *Fido.* A knowledge of common Latin and Greek prefixes, roots, and suffixes is a good way to build your stock of vocabulary.

Using the Dictionary   You have already seen that the dictionary can provide the curious reader with information about a word's history, that is, how it came into the English language. But more central for your purposes are the other reasons that the dictionary can quickly become the most thumbed-through book on your desk. The dictionary is most often referred to for (1) correct spelling; (2) correct pronunciation; and (3) the best definition according to the context, that is, the way the word is used in a passage. Our concern here is with the second and third uses.

Pronunciation. Every dictionary contains a detailed key listing the pronunciation symbols in its front matter—the pages preceding the first definition on the *A* page. Rather than referring to the front matter every time you need to see how a word is pronounced, however, it is easier to look at the brief pronunciation key provided at the bottom of each page in the dictionary. If you are uncertain about the marks over the vowels (called diacritical marks), for example, you will find sample words illustrating each symbol: ă pat/ā pay means that ă (short *a*) is pronounced as in the word "pat," and ā (long *a*) is pronounced as it is in the word "pay." If you are unfamiliar with these pronunciation symbols, it would be a good idea to spend a few minutes looking at the bottom of both the lefthand and righthand pages of your dictionary until you can pronounce all of them without hesitation.

Second, and equally crucial for the correct pronunciation of new words, are stress or accent marks. Stress, the relative degree of loudness with which syllables in a word are pronounced, is indicated in three different ways. Primary stress, which is the louder, is indicated by a boldface (′) mark, while secondary stress is indicated by a similar mark in regular type (′), and unstressed syllables are unmarked. Thus, the word *apparatus* is printed in pronunciation symbols like this: (ăp′ ə-ră′ təs). The first syllable receives secondary stress; the second syllable is unstressed (the funny-looking upside-down *e* symbol is called a schwa and is always unstressed and pronounced "uh"); the third syllable receives primary or heaviest stress; the final syllable is also unstressed. The secret to correct pronunciation of English words is to locate the syllable with the primary stress first; then the rest of the word usually falls into place.

Here are some difficult words for you to practice pronouncing. First, locate the accented or stressed syllable (one-syllable words will not have any stress mark), then pronounce the rest of the word, referring to the brief pronunciation guide in your dictionary, if necessary.

coup	(ko͞o)
ribald	(rĭb′ əld)
blackguard	(blăg′ ərd)
vapid	(văp′ ĭd)
flaccid	(flăk′ sĭd)
gamin	(găm′ ĭn)
tropism	(trō′ pĭz əm)
nuclear	(no͞o klē-ər)
strophe	(strō′ fē)
schism	(sĭz′ əm) or (skĭz′ əm)
antithesis	(ăn-tĭth′ ə-sĭs)
charisma	(kə-rĭz′ mə)
chameleon	(kə-mēl′ yən)
inchoate	(ĭn-kō′ ĭt)
thermography	(thər-mŏg′ rə-fē)
onomatopoeia	(ŏn′ ə-măt′ ə-pē′ ə)
ersatz	(ĕr-zäts′)

amanuensis   (ə-măn′ yōō-ĕn′ sĭs)
chiton   (kīt′n)
apotheosis   (ə-pŏth′ ē-ō′ sĭs)

Order of Definitions. Be certain that you know the order in which your dictionary lists multiple definitions, which information can be found in the front matter. *The American Heritage Dictionary,* for example, uses a method the editors call "synchronic semantic analysis," meaning that "the first definition is the central meaning about which the other senses may be most logically organized." In *The Random House Dictionary,* "the most common part of speech is listed first, and the most frequently encountered meaning appears as the first definition for each part of speech." In contrast, *Merriam Webster's Collegiate Dictionary* and *Webster's New World Dictionary* both order definitions chronologically, so that the first definition is the earliest, the next definition is the next in historical usage, and so on. This system provides the reader with a good historical sense of a word's evolution, but it also means that you must be sure to read past the first definitions of a word to find its current meanings.

Whatever method your dictionary uses, it is critical that you pay attention to the word's *context*—what comes before and after the word in question or, in other words, the specific environment in which the word occurs. The context will help you choose the word's most appropriate definition if it has several senses. As an illustration, here are the four definitions for the adjective *barren* from *The Random House Dictionary:*

1. not producing, or incapable of producing, offspring: *a barren woman.*
2. unproductive; unfruitful: *barren land; a barren effort.* 3. without features of interest; dull: *a barren period in American architecture.* 4. destitute; bereft; lacking (usually followed by *of*): *barren of tender feelings.*

Which meanings would you assign the word *barren* in these three sentences?

_____ The Kalahari Desert, a vast area in southern Africa, is a *barren,* inhospitable region.

_____ During his later years, F. Scott Fitzgerald, the American fiction writer, endured a *barren* period when he could no longer write.

_____ The walls in the mayor's office are *barren,* reflecting his interest in cutting excessive government spending for unnecessary items.

You should have chosen definition 2 for the first two sentences, and definition 3 for the third sentence.

A knowledge of grammar also helps when you look up unfamiliar words in the dictionary, since words in English often fall into more than one grammatical category. (If your knowledge of grammar is shaky, refer to any grammar handbook to review the parts of speech.) The dictionary labels parts of speech with abbreviations (n. = noun; v. = verb; adj. = adjective; adv. = adverb, and so forth). The word *obscure* is one example of a word that crosses over grammatical lines; the first eight definitions in *The American Heritage Dictionary* define the word as a verb, whereas the next six definitions refer to the adjective form. Look up the word *obscure* in your dictionary, consider the definitions in the two grammatical categories, then write the part of speech and the best definition for the word as it is used in these two sentences:

1. The worst airplane disaster in history occurred in 1977, on Tenerife in the Canary Islands, when heavy fog *obscured* the runway and two jets collided during takeoff.

Part of speech _____

Meaning _____

2. From his beginnings in the *obscure* town of Plains, Georgia, Jimmy Carter launched a grassroots campaign for the American presidency.

Part of speech _____

Meaning _____

Even seemingly easy words may pose difficulties when you consult the dictionary. For example, in conversation, the word *fine* usually means "pleasant" or "agreeable," but *The American Heritage Dictionary* shows fourteen meanings for this adjective. Look up *fine* in your dictionary. Which is the best definition for the way the word is used in the following context?

The professor made a *fine* distinction between negligence and neglect.

Meaning _____

The best meaning is "subtle" or "precise," as in "a fine shade of meaning."

Shades of Meaning. Some dictionaries, notably those of *Random House* and *American Heritage,* provide extremely useful notes on synonyms to help you determine subtle differences in meaning between related words. For example, if you look up the word *impetuous* in *The American Heritage Dictionary,* you will find these synonyms and a detailed explanation of each following the last definition:

impetuous, heedless, hasty, headlong, sudden: These adjectives describe persons and their actions and decisions when marked by an abruptness or lack of deliberation. *Impetuous* suggests impulsiveness, impatience, or lack of thoughtfulness. *Heedless* implies carelessness or lack of a sense of responsibility or proper regard for the consequences of action. *Hasty* and *headlong* both stress hurried action, the latter especially implying recklessness. *Sudden* is applied to action, or to personal attributes such as moods, that make themselves apparent abruptly or unexpectedly. In the following sentence, then, the word *headlong* means not only abruptness, but also strongly implies recklessness:

Mary's *headlong* decision to marry astonished her family.

Notice that if the sentence is rewritten with *sudden* substituted for *head-long,* a different, more positive, implication results.

If you are unsure about the exact connotation of a word, consulting the notes on synonyms, when the dictionary provides them, for related words is extremely useful. Taking this extra step will serve you well, since you will develop a facility for understanding the subtleties underlying a cluster of related words which, on the surface, may seem to be synonymous.

One last word on using the dictionary: Frequently you will have to consult the dictionary (especially an abridged edition) more than once to get the precise meaning of a word. Let's suppose that you don't know the meaning of the word *beleaguered* as it is used in this sentence:

All around the *beleaguered* city of Phnom Penh homeless children wandered.

The abridged edition of *The American Heritage Dictionary* defines *beleaguer* as "to besiege"—not much help if you don't know the root *siege. Besiege* is defined as "to lay siege to"—still not much help. If you look up the word *siege,* you will find that it means "the surrounding and blockading of a town or fortress by any army bent on capturing it." *Beleaguered,* then, means "surrounded by troops." This flipping of pages to find one definition may seem like an annoying and tiresome process, but the search does have its rewards in that it gives you both an accurate definition and it adds three new words to your vocabulary stock. (Incidentally, consulting an unabridged dictionary would have yielded a clear definition the first time.)

Using Context Clues. A good dictionary is clearly an indispensable possession. Yet good readers can often determine the meaning of a word, or at least a satisfactorily close meaning, by paying attention to the context, defined earlier as the way the word is used in a sentence or passage, or the accompanying words or phrases that clarify the meaning of an unfamiliar word. Context is particularly useful when it is not essential that you have a precise definition. Here are three of the most common kinds of context clues.

First, a writer may provide a *synonym* for an unfamiliar word:

No matter how much Sarah tried to cut unnecessary words from her essays, her instructor always commented that her papers were *verbose.*

Here *verbose* clearly means "using unnecessary words."

Another kind of context clue is a *key word* or *key phrase*—one that is not a synonym but that nevertheless reveals the meaning of an unfamiliar word:

Spencer's attention to most tasks was *dilatory* at best; however, when it came time to wash and wax his Mazda RX7, he never put it off or made excuses.

The transitional word "however" signals a contrast, suggesting that *dilatory* means "putting off" or "seeking to delay." This definition is also suggested by the example in the last part of the sentence.

Finally, a *series of examples*, or the general situation described, may provide a good context clue:

> Professor Simon's taste in reading is *catholic:* He enjoys modern French poetry, chronicles of the Civil War, Shakespeare's tragedies, the mystery novels of Agatha Christie, and *Popular Computing* magazine.

From the five examples of reading material, you can deduce that *catholic* does not refer to a religion (in which case it would have been capitalized), but to a taste that is broad and all-inclusive.

To test your ability to use context clues, here are some exercises. First, read the passage carefully, paying attention to any clues that suggest the meaning for the italicized word. Underline the clue, and then choose the best definition for the italicized word from the choices given. (The name of the author who wrote each passage is provided in parentheses.)

1. Tide pools contain mysterious worlds within their depths, where all the beauty of the sea is subtly suggested and portrayed in miniature. Some of the pools occupy deep *crevices* or fissures; at their seaward ends these crevices disappear under water. (Rachel Carson)
   _____ *crevices:* (a) deep, wide holes; (b) narrow cracks; (c) earthquake faults; (d) unexplored areas.

2. Physically, the Bushmen are a handsome people . . . because of the extreme grace in their way of moving, which is strong and *deft* and *lithe*; and to watch a Bushman walking or simply picking up something from the ground is like watching part of a dance. (Elizabeth Marshall Thomas)
   _____ *deft:* (a) powerful; (b) clumsy; (c) gentle; (d) naturally skilled.
   _____ *lithe:* marked by (a) effortless grace; (b) slightness of stature; (c) meekness, mildness; (d) a long life.

3. The past, present, and future cannot be separately *discerned.* Much of what we perceive as new tends to support the ancient wisdom that the more things change the more they remain the same. (Lew Dietz)
   _____ *discerned:* (a) discussed; (b) foretold; (c) imagined; (d) perceived.

4. One day the wolves killed a caribou close to home and this convenient food supply gave them an opportunity to take a holiday. They did not go hunting at all that night, but stayed near the den and rested. The next morning dawned fine and warm, and a general air of contented *lassitude* seemed to overcome all three. Angeline lay at her ease on the rocks overlooking the summer den, while George and Albert rested in sandy beds on the esker ridge. The only signs of life from any of them through the long morning were occasional changes of position, and lazy looks about the countryside. (Farley Mowat)
   _____ *lassitude:* (a) anxiety; (b) peacefulness; (c) hunger; (d) inactivity.

5. Termites make *percussive* sounds to each other by beating their heads against the floor in the dark, resonating corridors of their nests. The sound has been described as resembling, to the human ear, sand falling on paper, but spectrographic analysis of sound records has recently revealed a high degree of organization in the drumming; the beats occur in regular, rhythmic phrases. (Lewis Thomas)

   _____ *percussive:* (a) produced by striking together; (b) clearly audible; (c) communicating; (d) nearly imperceptible.

6. The self-marking of invertebrate animals in the sea, who must have perfected the business long before evolution got around to us, was set up in order to permit creatures of one kind to locate others, not for predation but to set up *symbiotic* households. The anemones who live on the shells of crabs are precisely finicky; so are the crabs. Only a single species of anemone will find its way to only a single species of crab. They sense each other exquisitely, and live together as though made for each other. (Lewis Thomas)

   _____ *symbiotic:* describing a relationship between two organisms based on (a) mutual dislike and hostility; (b) close, probably beneficial association; (c) indifference; lack of interest and attention; (d) predation, in which one stalks the other for food.

7. The history of the word "creole" itself dates back to the slave trade. After slaves had been gathered from many parts of Africa, they were imprisoned in West African camps, *euphemistically* called "factories," for "processing" before being shipped out to "markets." (Peter Farb)

   _____ *euphemistically:* describing words that (a) accurately and fairly depict reality; (b) are less offensive substitutions for others considered offensive; (c) represent abstract or general qualities; (d) are substitutions for words that are too difficult to understand. (Hint: Why does the author use quotation marks around certain words in the last sentence?)

8. It is quite clear that Spanish is still the language of high prestige, and a Guarani [the Indian language of Paraguay] speaker, coming to market in the city, quickly feels his inferiority. Probably all bilingual situations equally *stigmatize* those who use low-prestige languages. (Peter Farb)

   _____ *stigmatize:* to mark as (a) inferior; (b) illiterate; (c) prestigious; (d) peculiar.

9. In an increasingly complex society it was no longer possible for children simply to melt into the adult world and function as somewhat inferior but nevertheless useful versions of adults. This had worked in past centuries, when children served as agricultural helpers or as workers in cottage industries or as apprentices to craftsmen. In such an economy the *attributes* required to carry out their assigned tasks successfully were persistence, perseverance, courage, and independence, virtues more readily acquired if a child is set loose early from intimate ties with those who nurtured him in infancy. (Marie Winn)

   _____ *attributes:* (a) facial features; (b) distinctive characteristics; qualities; (c) occupational skills; (d) descriptive terms.

10. The sheer magnitude of immigration from Europe during the last third of the nineteenth century made it certain that old-stock Americans, even if favoring in principle an open door for aliens, would begin to feel uncomfortable. From the vantage point of distance, what seems remarkable is not the extent of antiforeign sentiment that swept the country but the fact that until the First World War it did not seriously *impede* the flow of immigration. (Irving Howe)

_____ *impede:* (a) encourage; (b) increase; (c) obstruct; (d) favor.

So that you can check your work, here are the answers (given in parentheses) along with the context clues which point to the right definition:

1. *crevices* (b). Context clue: "fissures"
2. *deft* (d); and *lithe* (a). Context clues: "extreme grace in their way of moving"; "watching part of a dance"
3. *discerned* (d). Context clue: "perceive"
4. *lassitude* (d). Context clues: "stayed near the den and rested"; "Angeline lay at her ease"; "George and Albert rested"; "the only signs of life"
5. *percussive* (a). Context clues: "beating"; "drumming"; "beats occur in regular, rhythmic phrases"
6. *symbiotic* (b). Context clue: the last sentence
7. *euphemistically* (b). Context clue: "factories," for example, is a less harsh word than "slave camp"
8. *stigmatize* (a). Context clues: "inferiority" and "low-prestige language"
9. *attributes* (b). Context clue: "virtues"
10. *impede* (c). Context clue: the situation described and the logical progression of ideas

The above exercises show that context can be useful. However, when you are in doubt about the meaning of a word, it is far safer to consult the dictionary, especially if you suspect that the writer may be using the word in an unusual fashion or in an ironic sense. *Irony* refers to the use of a word to convey the opposite of the word's literal meaning. When you stumble into a table and your friend teases you by saying "How graceful!" he or she is being ironic. Writers also employ irony to good advantage, usually to heighten the meaning, to make the real underlying idea more emphatic. In this passage, the author uses two words ironically—*insinuating* and *insidious*—for humorous effect.

Ours is an age of escalation. Take, for example, walking. Only yesterday, it seems, going for a walk was as simple and natural as breathing; it was the most elementary form of recreation known to man, for thousands of years a pastime beyond improvement: pure, changeless, satisfying. But into this blameless tradition crept a tiny flaw. Going for a walk got to be known in elegant circles as "taking one's constitutional," *insinuating* the notion that walking might be done for reasons of health. Thus the *insidious* idea spread around that it was good for you, and ruin set in rapidly. From the premise that walking was good for the body the conclusion was drawn, with pristine American logic, that more of it, at a faster pace, would be better.

Ronald Jager,
"The End of Walking," *Harper's*

In its usual sense, *insinuate* means "to suggest in an underhanded way," and it implies that what is suggested is unpleasant. *Insidious* means "stealthy" or "treacherous." Here, Jager uses both words ironically, since the idea Jager "insinuates" is an idea most people readily accept. In addition, a good idea can't really be "insidious," since most people, in fact, believe that walking *is* good exercise, even confirmed nonwalkers. If the irony still escapes you, consult your dictionary. The etymology for *insidious* and the notes on synonyms for *insinuate* (located at the word *suggest*) should help.

Vocabulary Exercises. Each exercise in the text is intended to promote a good reading vocabulary. If you follow the suggestions outlined at the beginning of this introductory section (keeping a notebook, religiously looking words up, and so forth), you soon will be pleasantly surprised. New words will start to recur in your reading; words you have skipped over will begin to look familiar. (Don't expect your vocabulary to improve by magic, however; if you seldom read, you'll make little improvement. But even reading for pleasure thirty minutes a day can quickly result in impressive gains.)

In the exercises, the number of the sentence or paragraph in which the word occurred is provided in brackets. This enables you to locate the word in the selection easily and to study its fuller context before choosing the best definition. In Part 4, Reading Essays and Articles, other kinds of vocabulary exercises are included in addition to the usual multiple-choice questions.

All the skills explained here—seeing individual words as parts of larger groups, getting interested in the etymology of words, using the dictionary properly, and paying attention to context clues—will result not only in building your vocabulary, but also in enhancing your enjoyment of reading—the very reason you enrolled in this course.

part 1 ‖ READING PARAGRAPHS

chapter 1 ‖ THE FUNDAMENTALS OF READING PARAGRAPHS

A. THE MAIN IDEA

The paragraph, the form we will study and analyze in this chapter, is the fundamental unit of written thought. Simply defined, a paragraph is a group of sentences that develops and supports one idea. A paragraph may be any length as long as it keeps to that one idea. Although it may appear anywhere in the paragraph, the main idea is a general statement that most often appears at or near the beginning of the paragraph. Most books use the term *topic sentence* to describe the main idea of a paragraph, but since in adult prose a writer may not express the subject in a single explicit topic sentence, we will call this general statement the *main idea* rather than the topic sentence. Indeed, you may have to formulate the main idea yourself from bits and pieces of information presented in the first two or three sentences. In the exercises in this text, you will be asked to choose the sentence that expresses the main idea or, in some cases, to write a sentence expressing the main idea if the author has not provided an explicit one.

A well-constructed sentence that expresses the main idea consists of two parts: the *subject,* and the *controlling idea*—usually a word or phrase that limits, qualifies, or narrows down the subject so that it is manageable. Another way of looking at the structure of the main idea is to remember the two questions you learned in the introductory section on the reading process when you read the paragraph on marriage: What is the topic? What does the author want me to understand about that topic? The answers to these two questions will usually give you the paragraph's subject and controlling idea. Diagrammed, the standard main-idea sentence might look like this:

Main idea = Subject + Controlling idea

Consider this sentence: "The American presidency is a grueling and increasingly unrewarding job." In this example, the subject is "The American presidency," and the controlling idea or limiting phrase is "a grueling and increasingly unrewarding job." Here is another example:

17

SUBJECT

Learning to write on a word processor offers

CONTROLLING IDEA

great rewards for any writer, even the most inexperienced.

Note that the subject is underlined once and the controlling idea is underlined twice. Again, remember the two basic questions: What is the author's subject? (learning to write on a word processor). What does the author want me to understand about that subject? (that it offers any writer great rewards).

Irrelevant information in a main idea sentence should not be labeled. Read the following illustration:

Although considered by many to be a foolish luxury, an increasingly popular status symbol in suburban America is the hot tub.

The first clause does not properly have anything to do with the main idea. The author mentions that many find hot tubs foolish only to concede a truth; therefore, the first part should not be underlined. What, then, is the author's topic? (the hot tub). What does the author want you to understand about the hot tub? (that it is an increasingly popular status symbol . . .). Even more important, notice that in this example the order in which the subject and controlling idea appear is reversed, a common occurrence. The subject is the hot tub, *not* status symbols.

Here is a short exercise to give you practice in labeling main ideas. For each, underscore the subject with one line, and the word or phrase that acts as the controlling idea with two.

1. Letter writing is becoming a lost art.
2. The common garden snail is a terrible pest.
3. The most tragic effect of overpopulation is the threat of overpopulation in the world's poor countries.
4. Once out of fashion in the nation's schools, the study of Latin is becoming more popular, even in the elementary grades.
5. Psychologists agree that children who watch too much television may have difficulty distinguishing between fantasy and reality.
6. My cat, Vladimir, exhibits some very bizarre traits.
7. The most useful book a college student can own is an unabridged dictionary.
8. Many critics are now urging that the practice of plea bargaining be abolished for violent crimes.
9. Iowa is a state of great contrasts: frigid winters and broiling hot summers, verdant farmlands and modern cities.
10. Ann Beattie's stories reveal the themes of loneliness and the inability to communicate.

11. A frequent criticism of American automobiles is that they are designed to be obsolete within a few years of purchase.
12. One of the most serious problems in international affairs today is the threat of terrorism.
13. One couldn't hope for more delicious appetizers at a party than Chinese dim sum.
14. There is a tremendous difference in the directing styles of Francis Ford Coppola and George Lucas.
15. Serious gardeners may disagree, but an easy, maintenance-free ground cover is the often-maligned English ivy.

Now that you have had some practice separating the constituent parts of main idea sentences, let us move to the paragraph as a whole. As you read through the following paragraph, label each sentence with either a *G* (for general statements) or an *S* (for specific or supporting statements). Then try to discern a pattern for these statements. Which sentences represent main idea, support, and conclusion? For the purposes of this exercise, the sentences are printed in list form.

_____ 1. Language originates in magic.
_____ 2. The first "words" of a baby are not words at all, but magic incantations, sounds uttered for pleasure and enjoyed indiscriminately to bring about a desired event.
_____ 3. Sometime in the last quarter of the first year the baby makes the sounds "mama" or "dada."
_____ 4. The baby is surprised and pleased at the excitement he creates in his parents and can easily be induced to repeat this performance dozens of times a day.
_____ 5. Unfortunately, he doesn't know who or what "mama" is.
_____ 6. He will look right into your eyes and say "mama" and you melt at the lovely sound, and he will look right into his father's eyes and say "mama" and his father, embarrassed, corrects him.
_____ 7. He will pursue the dog's tail chanting "mama," and he will reach for a cookie yelling "mama" and he will lie in his crib murmuring "mamamamamamamama"—and he hasn't a thought in his head for M–O–T–H–E–R and the million things she gave him.
_____ 8. He doesn't connect the word and the person at this point.

Selma H. Fraiberg, *The Magic Years*

Let's see how you did. You should have marked sentences 1, 2, and 8 as general statements and the remaining sentences as specific. The pattern these sentences form is a fairly standard one: Sentence 1 makes a broad generalization; sentence 2 explains the first sentence and narrows down the generalization to a manageable topic. The sentences in the body of the paragraph (3–7) provide specific illustrations of a baby's speech and the parents' reactions to it, while sentence 8 presents the reader with a conclusion based on the foregoing evidence—that the baby cannot yet connect the word "mama" with his mother.

B. THE DIRECTION OF PARAGRAPHS

A paragraph does not simply consist of a topic sentence followed by a group of sentences written at random. As you saw in the preceding example by Selma Fraiberg, the paragraph makes a point; it proves what it sets out to prove; it has a *direction*. As you read the following paragraph, first try to pick out the topic sentence and determine both the specific subject and the controlling idea. Then determine the extent to which the writer supports that topic.

Physically and psychically women are by far the superior of men. The old chestnut about women being more emotional than men has been forever destroyed by the facts of two great wars. Women under blockade, heavy bombardment, concentration camp confinement, and similar rigors withstand them vastly more successfully than men. The psychiatric casualties of civilian populations under such conditions are mostly masculine, and there are far more men in our mental hospitals than there are women. The steady hand at the helm is the hand that has had the practice at rocking the cradle. Because of their greater size and weight, men are physically more powerful than women—which is not the same thing as saying that they are stronger. A man of the same size and weight as a woman of comparable background and occupational status would probably not be any more powerful than a woman. As far as constitutional strength is concerned, women are stronger than men. Many diseases from which men suffer can be shown to be largely influenced by their relation to the male Y-chromosome. More males die than females. Deaths from almost all causes are more frequent in males of all ages. Though women are more frequently ill than men, they recover from illnesses more easily and more frequently than men.

Ashley Montagu,
The Natural Superiority of Women

In this paragraph, Montagu begins with the topic sentence. His topic is that women are superior to men; the controlling idea—the words that restrict this broad assertion—are the adverbs "physically and psychically." In setting up the paragraph this way, Montagu leads the reader to expect proof for both parts of the controlling idea with explanations and examples, which indeed the body of the paragraph does. Notice that the first half of the paragraph provides evidence for the statement that women are "psychically" stronger, while the second part (beginning with sentence 6) supports the statement that women are "physically" stronger. The paragraph's direction, then, follows the established form—main idea + support— that we have come to expect as the standard paragraph pattern.

Here is another example of a paragraph whose main idea comes in the first sentence:

We've never been so self-conscious about our selves as we seem to be these days. The popular magazines are filled with advice on things to do with a self: how to find it, identify it, nurture it, protect it, even, for special occasions, weekends, how to lose it transiently. There are instructive books, best sellers on self-realization, self-help, self-development. Groups of self-respecting people pay large fees for three-day sessions together, learning self-awareness. Self-enlightenment can be taught in college electives.

Lewis Thomas,
The Medusa and the Snail

In the next paragraph, however, the first sentence serves only to introduce the reader to the general subject, and the main idea, that all species of lichens in the world are slow-growing, is reserved for the second sentence. The rest of the paragraph offers support in the form of a single, dramatic example.

There are some 16,000 species of lichens in the world. All are slow-growing, but those that encrust the rocks of mountain peaks are particularly so. At high altitudes, there may be only a single day in a whole year when growth is possible and a lichen may take as long as sixty years to cover just one square centimetre. Lichens as big as plates, which are very common, are therefore likely to be hundreds if not thousands of years old.

David Attenborough,
The Living Planet

Another common instance where statement of the main idea of a paragraph is delayed is illustrated in the next paragraph. In this case, the writer begins the paragraph with a statement that she intends to disprove, a common misconception that is explained in sentences 1 and 2. Sentence 3 contains the topic sentence, and the remaining sentences offer specific examples as evidence.

The aging process has been accused of causing the many prolonged illnesses that are prevalent among older people. It must be emphasized that this is not the case. Chronic illnesses begin to establish themselves in the organism much earlier, but for a long time they remain dormant, displaying no symptoms. I have in mind the various metabolic diseases, such as diabetes, stone formations, intestinal ulcers, arthritis. Other such illnesses are due to the changes that occur in the vascular system—among them, heart conditions, high blood pressure, hardening of the arteries, and many more. All these afflictions can be precipitated and aggravated by stress—including aging itself and its psychological impact on the aging person.

Olga Knopf,
Successful Aging

Chapter 4, Patterns of Paragraph Organization, will provide you with other, more sophisticated, ways of organizing information. For now, suffice it to say that the main idea of a paragraph *usually* comes at or near the paragraph's beginning, although it is perfectly common for a writer to delay presenting the main idea for several sentences or even to omit a topic sentence altogether, in which case you have to determine the main idea for yourself. If you keep in mind the two basic questions—What is this paragraph about? and, What does the writer want me to understand about the subject?—you should quickly succeed in developing the single most important skill involved in the reading process: finding the main idea of what you read.

C. LEVELS OF SUPPORT

Now we can turn our attention to the supporting part of the paragraph—the body sentences. Another useful skill in analytical reading is the ability to distinguish between *major* supporting statements and *minor* ones. Briefly, *major* statements directly relate to, and develop, the main idea, while *minor* ones further explain, illustrate, or otherwise develop the major ones. Analysis of levels of support trains you to think logically because you must assign ideas to categories and weigh their relative importance. Diagrammed, using an ideal model paragraph, the supporting statements might look like this:

Main Idea (topic sentence)
   Major Support
      Minor Support
      Minor Support
   Major Support
      Minor Support
      Minor Support
   Conclusion

The following paragraph nicely exemplifies the model above. Notice that each minor supporting sentence is printed in parentheses, with each parenthetical sentence serving to state the author's opinion of each type of book owner.

[1]There are three kinds of book owners. [2]The first has all the standard sets and best-sellers—unread, untouched. [3](This deluded individual owns wood-pulp and ink, not books.) [4]The second has a great many books—a few of them read through, most of them dipped into, but all of them as clean and shiny as the day they were bought. [5](This person would probably like to make books his own, but is restrained by a false respect for their physical appearance.) [6]The third has a few books or many—every one of them dog-eared and dilapidated, shaken and loosened by continual use, marked and scribbled in from front to back. [7](This man owns books.)

Mortimer Adler,
"How to Mark a Book," *Saturday Review*

The next paragraph is reprinted from an essay at the beginning of Part 4. The first two sentences describe the tarantula's body, while sentence 3 is the topic sentence. Read the remainder of the paragraph carefully and label the sentences according to whether they represent *major* (MA) support or *minor* (MI) support:

> [1]The entire body of a tarantula, especially its legs, is thickly clothed with hair. [2]Some of it is short and woolly, some long and stiff. [3]Touching this body hair produces one of two distinct reactions. [4]When the spider is hungry, it responds with an immediate and swift attack. [5]At the touch of a cricket's antennae the tarantula seizes the insect so swiftly that a motion picture taken at the rate of 64 frames per second shows only the result and not the process of capture. [6]But when the spider is not hungry, the stimulation of its hairs merely causes it to shake the touched limb. [7]An insect can walk under its hairy belly unharmed.
>
> Alexander Petrunkevitch,
> "The Spider and the Wasp"

You should have marked sentences 4 and 6 as *major* and sentences 5 and 7 as *minor*. The paragraph is beautifully constructed so that the supporting statements are balanced. Diagrammed, Petrunkevitch's paragraph would look like this:

Sentences 1 and 2:	Descriptive Details
Sentence 3:	Topic Sentence
Sentence 4:	Major Support
Sentence 5:	Minor Support
Sentence 6:	Major Support
Sentence 7:	Minor Support

Unhappily, not every paragraph works out as well as this one does. At the end of this chapter, a few of the exercises will ask you to distinguish between major supporting ideas (those that directly reinforce the topic), and minor ones (those that merely add to, or explain, the major details).

D. THE AUTHOR'S PURPOSE: MODES OF DISCOURSE

In addition to determining the main idea of the paragraph, its general direction, and classifying its supporting details, a good reader must also learn to establish the author's *purpose* in writing. You must learn to ask yourself *why* the author wrote. Ascertaining the purpose will help you accomplish other, more difficult skills that you will learn later in this text (such as detecting bias, understanding why the author chose one method of support over another, why the author chose one specific word with a peculiar connotation over another, and so on). The traditional term, *modes of discourse*, actually refers to the various kinds of prose writing: narration, description, exposition, and persuasion. But in simple terms, mode of discourse can be understood as the author's purpose in writing. In other words, the choice of one *mode* over another reflects the author's *purpose* in writing.

Narration

The first and most easily recognized mode of discourse is narration, which is simply telling a story. A writer employs narration because his or her *purpose* is to relate events, either real or imagined, in chronological order. One of the simplest forms of narration is the fable, a short tale written or told to illustrate a moral truth, as in this fable by Aesop:

THE FOX AND THE GRAPES

One hot summer's day a Fox was strolling through an orchard till he came to a bunch of Grapes just ripening on a vine which had been trained over a lofty branch. "Just the thing to quench my thirst," quoth he. Drawing back a few paces, he took a run and a jump, and just missed the bunch. Turning round again with a One, Two, Three, he jumped up, but with no greater success. Again and again he tried after the tempting morsel, but at last had to give it up, and walked away with his nose in the air, saying: "I am sure they are sour."

"IT IS EASY TO DESPISE WHAT YOU CANNOT GET."
Folk-Lore and Fable: Aesop, Grimm, Andersen

This fable is the source of the expression, "sour grapes," meaning, as the fable says, the practice of criticizing what you cannot have.

Typically, however, narration is used along with the other modes (description, exposition, or persuasion) to support an idea or to illustrate a theory, as Lewis Thomas does in the following paragraphs:

We may be about to rediscover that dying is not such a bad thing to do after all. Sir William Osler took this view: he disapproved of people who spoke of the agony of death, maintaining that there was no such thing.

In a nineteenth-century memoir on an expedition in Africa, there is a story by David Livingston about his own experience of near-death. He was caught by a lion, crushed across the chest in the animal's great jaws, and saved in the instant by a lucky shot from a friend. Later, he remembered the episode in clear detail. He was so amazed by the extraordinary sense of peace, calm, and total painlessness associated with being killed that he constructed a theory that all creatures are provided with a protective physiologic mechanism, switched on at the verge of death, carrying them through in a haze of tranquillity.

Lewis Thomas,
"The Long Habit," *Lives of a Cell*

Description

This mode of discourse refers to writing that shows what someone or something looks like or what something feels like. The writer's purpose is to paint a picture in words. Description always relies on sensory details, that is, words and phrases that appeal to the reader's senses. While description may be used alone and for its own sake—to set the scene or to evoke a mood —it most often appears, at least in longer pieces, in combination with other modes, usually narration or exposition. In the next paragraph, Gerald Durrell describes a mountain in Africa by using concrete details that appeal primarily to the reader's sense of sight. Durrell conveys, by means of these visual details, a dominant impression of N'da Ali as an inhospitable, brooding monster.

> N'da Ali was the largest mountain in the vicinity. It crouched at our backs, glowering over the landscape, the village, and our little hill. From almost every vantage point you were aware of the mountain's mist-entangled, cloud-veiled shape brooding over everything, its heights guarded by sheer cliffs of gnarled granite so steep that no plant life could get a foothold. Every day I had looked longingly at the summit, and every day I had watched N'da Ali in its many moods. In the early morning it was a great mist-whitened monster; at noon it was all green and golden glitter of forest, its cliffs flushing pink in the sun; at night it was purple and shapeless, fading to black as the sun sank. Sometimes it would go into hiding, drawing the white clouds around itself and brooding in their depths for two or three days at a time. Every day I gazed at those great cliffs that guarded the way to the thick forest on its ridged back, and each day I grew more determined that I would go up there and see what it had to offer me.
>
> Gerald Durrell,
> *The Overloaded Ark*

The next example of descriptive writing is from Mark Twain's *Huckleberry Finn*. Twain describes a summer thunderstorm from Huck's point of view. Notice in particular the informal language, the concrete details referring to colors, sights, and sounds, and the imaginative description of thunder at the end.

> We spread the blankets inside for a carpet, and eat our dinner in there. We put all the other things handy at the back of the cavern. Pretty soon it darkened up and begun to thunder and lighten; so the birds was right about it. Directly it begun to rain, and it rained like all fury, too, and I never see the wind blow so. It was one of these regular summer storms. It would get so dark that it looked all blue-black outside, and lovely; and the rain would thrash along by so thick that the trees off a little ways looked dim and spider-webby; and here would come a blast of wind that would bend the trees down and turn up the pale underside of the leaves; and then a perfect ripper of a gust would follow along and set the branches to tossing their arms as if they was just wild; and next, when it was just about the bluest and blackest—*fst!* it was as bright as glory and you'd have a little glimpse of tree-tops a-plunging about, away off yonder in the storm, hundreds of yards further than you could see before; dark as sin

again in a second, and now you'd hear the thunder let go with an awful crash and then go rumbling, grumbling, tumbling down the sky towards the under side of the world, like rolling empty barrels downstairs, where it's long stairs and they bounce a good deal, you know.

Mark Twain,
Huckleberry Finn

Exposition

Exposition, or expository writing, is the most common mode of discourse you will encounter in your college reading. It is essentially factual writing with a straightforward purpose: to explain, to make clear, to discuss, or to set forth. In this first example of expository writing, the noted anthropologist, Margaret Mead, explains the differences in the way babies are perceived in three different cultures.

Every people has a quite definite image of what a child is at birth. Russians, for example, see the newborn as so strong that they swaddle it firmly to protect it from harming itself. The French, in contrast, see the baby as fragile and vulnerable to anything harmful in the environment—and they softly swaddle the infant to keep it quietly safe.

In Bali a baby is not given a human name at birth. Until it seems clear it will live, the Balinese refer to it as a caterpillar or a mouse. At three months, when it is given a name, it becomes a participating human being whose mother, speaking for it, says the words of polite social response. But if the baby dies before this, people reproach it, saying "You didn't stay long enough. Next time stay and eat rice with us." For the Balinese believe in reincarnation. They believe the "soul," without any specific personality, is reborn every fourth generation within the same family.

Margaret Mead,
"A New Understanding of Childhood"

In this next example, Eugene Kinkead's subject is a particular species of snail darter discovered on the site of the Tellico Dam in Tennessee. Because the darter was on the list of endangered species, construction of the dam was halted for several years while environmentalists and dam supporters fought the issue in court. David Etnier, an ichthyologist who discovered the snail darter at the dam site, was responsible for naming the new species. This paragraph explains how new species are named, using Etnier's find as the primary example. You will see that the author's sole purpose is to explain; he relies only on *facts*—verifiable truths—as opposed to *opinions*, which are statements reflecting one's subjective or personal point of view.

In scientific nomenclature, the name of the discoverer of a new species is placed after the generic and specific names. Scientific practice omits the final name, so the new darter is usually known to ichthyologists as *Percina tanasi* or *P. tanasi*. Etnier had no choice about the name *Percina*, because his darter was obviously a member of that genus. But the selection of the specific term was his. *Tanasi* was the Cherokee name of a village on the Little Tennessee River which until 1725 was the capital of the Cherokee nation. (The name Tennessee is a corruption of *tanasi,* and was first used in 1762, on maps and reports of Lieutenant Henry Timberlake, a Virginian serving with a combined force of British regulars and colonial militia stationed in the area.) *P. tanasi's* common name, which derives from its main food—aquatic snails of two species—has become widely familiar: it is the snail darter.

Eugene Kinkead,
"Tennessee Small Fry"

Persuasion   This last mode of discourse is sometimes called *argumentation,* though technically there is a difference. *Argumentation* traditionally refers to the setting up of logically valid arguments that can be used in defense of a specific issue. *Persuasion* is an attempt to change another person's feelings or opinions by any effective means. In other words, the persuasive mode reflects the writer's attempt to *convince* the reader that a particular idea or opinion is worth holding, to win the reader over to a certain point of view, or to get the reader to change his or her mind. We see persuasive writing most often (and often at its worst) in advertisements, political speeches, newspaper or magazine editorials, voting pamphlets, or other writing in which the writer seeks to make us change our minds or to clarify our notions about controversial issues.

By its very nature, persuasive writing relies more on opinion than on fact since, by definition, it represents a subjective or personal point of view. In Part 2, Reading Critically, you will encounter a fuller discussion of persuasive writing. For now, it is enough to know that the two essential components of persuasive writing are *appeals to reason* and *appeals to the emotions,* either alone or in combination. In this first example, Marie Winn seeks to convince us that the supposed rise in illegitimate teenage pregnancies is not necessarily the result of increased sexual activity. For evidence, she cites an authoritative study on the subject, some general statistics, and her own explanation of the phenomenon. Therefore, she appeals to our *reason* rather than to our subjective feelings. (Note that the first sentence contains a key word, *precocity*; if you are unsure of its meaning, refer to your dictionary.)

The belief in extensive sexual precocity among pre-teenagers and teenagers these days may also be traced to certain well-publicized statistics about sexuality. There is, for instance, the dramatically increased number of teenagers having illegitimate babies during the last twenty years. Most people assume that this automatically proves teenagers are also more sexually active now—after all, you have to "do it" to get pregnant. But the authors of the study *Teenage Sexuality, Pregnancy and Childbearing* have an alternative explanation. They propose that the teenager who became pregnant two decades ago was far more likely to legitimize her baby by getting married than today's teenager for whom illegitimacy no longer bears the same stigma. Statistics gathered by the authors of the study confirm this hypothesis: great numbers of babies born to teenage mothers in the 1950s and 1960s followed within seven or eight months of marriage. Perhaps a few of these babies were premature, but most of the weddings it is clear, were helped along by a "shotgun." Seen from this perspective, a rise in teenage pregnancies does not necessarily prove a huge increase in teenage sexual activity.

Marie Winn,
Children Without Childhood

The aim to persuade by appealing to our emotions is also evident in this next example by John Steinbeck, who relies on charged language— words that convey a strong (in this case, negative) emotional impact. As you read the paragraph, mark these charged words or phrases.

I have often wondered at the savagery and thoughtlessness with which our early settlers approached this rich continent. They came at it as though it were an enemy, which of course it was. They burned the forests and changed the rainfall; they swept the buffalo from the plains, blasted the streams, set fire to the grass, and ran a reckless scythe through the virgin and noble timber. Perhaps they felt that it was limitless and could never be exhausted and that a man could move on to new wonders endlessly. Certainly there are many examples to the contrary, but to a large extent the early people pillaged the country as though they hated it, as though they held it temporarily and might be driven off at any time.

John Steinbeck,
America and Americans

You should have marked "savagery," "thoughtlessness," "blasted," "ran a reckless scythe," and "the virgin and noble timber." (In the case of the last phrase, the emotional feeling suggested is a positive one, in contrast to the others.) What neutral words or phrases could be substituted for these emotional ones?

E. MULTIPLE PURPOSES

Thus far, each of the paragraphs you have read in this chapter has reflected one dominant purpose; that is, each has demonstrated only one mode of discourse. But prose writers often have more than one purpose in mind, as does Beth Gutcheon in the following paragraph from the introduction to a book on how to make patchwork quilts:

People talk a surprising amount of twaddle about the romance of patchwork, especially lately. ("My, don't you wish some fairy would set those patches talkin'—what a tale they could tell!") My foot. They could tell a tale of days and months of mindless, thankless tedium, cooking food of a depressing sameness, washing and sewing and mending clothes that were forever being worn out or outgrown, frustrating days and sleepless nights with a whining child ill or dying of some disease that could have been cured by one shot of pencillin. For every block of patchwork sewn in a cheerful, sunlit kitchen while fresh pies cooled on the window sill and happy children warbled in the front yard, many more were sewn in the last numb, tired hour before sleep, when the babies were in bed and the older children could be set to help with the sewing as the last chore of their care-full day, when the heat and the light from the fire were insufficient for other work, when hands and bodies were stiff with cold and fatigue, when all had been snowbound for weeks, when the stillness of the work and of the night and of the long, deadly boring white winter brought homesickness for places and people never to be seen again, whether they were back home in Connecticut, or in Sweden or Slovakia.

Beth Gutcheon,
The Perfect Patchwork Primer

It is hard to pin down a single mode of discourse here. Although her dominant purpose seems to be to persuade us that our notions about the "romance of patchwork" are a lot of "twaddle," two other modes of discourse are also evident, resulting from her need to support her assertion with proof. As a result, she uses exposition to explain the day-to-day drudgery of the pioneer housewife, and description to counter romantic notions of pioneer life and show us the grim reality.

EXERCISES

Besides measuring your skill in determining the author's purpose, these exercises will also test your ability to ascertain the main idea, to make inferences and to define vocabulary words in context. For words that are not part of your active reading vocabulary, try first to determine the best meaning for the italicized word from its *context*, the way in which the particular word is used in the passage. (Refer to pp. 12–16 for a more detailed explanation of context.) Often you will be able to choose the best meaning in this way. However, if you are unsure, or if referring to the original context does not provide a sufficiently useful clue—as may often be the case—then you should turn to the dictionary rather than merely making a blind stab at the meaning. It is not cheating to look up words you don't know, even while you are working through exercises. You should follow this procedure for all the multiple-choice vocabulary exercises in this book.

Selection 1   [1]The long June twilight faded into night. [2]Dublin lay enveloped in darkness but for the dim light of the moon that shone through fleecy clouds, casting a pale light as of approaching dawn over the streets and the dark waters of the Liffey. [3]Around the beleaguered Four Courts the heavy guns roared. [4]Here and there through the city, machine guns and rifles broke the silence of the night, spasmodically, like dogs barking on lone farms. [5]Republicans and Free Staters were waging civil war.

Liam O'Flaherty,
"The Sniper," *Spring Sowing*

A. Vocabulary   For each italicized word from the paragraph, choose the best definition according to the context in which it appears.

1. *beleaguered* [sentence 3]: (a) conquered; (b) besieged; (c) betrayed; (d) heavily populated.

2. *spasmodically* [4]: (a) continually; (b) loudly; (c) intermittently; (d) annoyingly.

3. *waging* [5]: (a) pledging; (b) fighting; (c) threatening; (d) engaging in.

B. Content and Structure   Choose the best answer.

1. The topic sentence of this paragraph is expressed in sentence _____.

2. In the first two sentences of this paragraph, the mode of discourse is (a) narration; (b) description; (c) exposition; (d) persuasion.

3. The Liffey, mentioned in sentence 2, probably refers to (a) an ocean; (b) a river; (c) a public swimming pool; (d) a little pond.

4. We can infer from the weapon activity O'Flaherty mentions that (a) the Republicans were the stronger faction; (b) ammunition and weapons were in short supply; (c) outbursts of fighting occurred even at night; (d) most of the fighting took place in the countryside.

Selection 2   [1]The history of Florida is measured in freezes. [2]Severe ones, for example, occurred in 1747, 1766, and 1774. [3]The freeze of February, 1835, was probably the worst one in the state's history. [4]But, because more growers were affected, the Great Freeze of 1895 seems to enjoy the same sort of status in Florida that the Blizzard of '88 once held in the North. [5]Temperatures on the Ridge on February 8, 1895, went into the teens for much of the night. [6]It is said that some orange growers, on being told what was happening out in the groves, got up from their dinner tables and left the state. [7]In the morning, it was apparent that the Florida citrus industry had been virtually wiped out. [8]The groves around Keystone City, in Polk County, however, went through the freeze of 1895 without damage. [9]Slightly higher than anything around it and studded with sizable lakes, Keystone City became famous, and people from all over the Ridge came to marvel at this Garden of Eden in the middle of the new wasteland. [10]The citizens of Keystone City changed the name of their town to Frostproof.

John McPhee,
Oranges

A. Vocabulary   For each italicized word from the paragraph, choose the best definition according to the context in which it appears.

1. *status* [4]: (a) high standing; prestige; (b) state of affairs; situation; (c) popularity; (d) notoriety; ill fame.

2. *virtually* [7]: (a) tragically; (b) essentially; (c) surprisingly; (d) normally.

3. *studded* [9]: (a) constructed; (b) fortified; (c) blessed; (d) dotted; decorated.

4. *marvel* [9]: (a) admire; wonder at; (b) praise highly; (c) visit; remain for a long time in; (d) write about; describe.

B. Content and Structure

Choose the best answer.

1. According to sentence 1, "the history of Florida is measured in freezes." Who do you think measures Florida's history in this way? (a) McPhee; (b) all Americans; (c) citrus growers; (d) weather officials.

2. Which *two* modes of discourse are most evident throughout the paragraph? (a) narration; (b) description; (c) exposition; (d) persuasion.

3. In relation to the rest of the paragraph, sentences 1–4 represent (a) a justification; (b) a gradual narrowing down of the topic; (c) an illustration intended to get the reader's attention; (d) a description.

4. Which of the first four sentences represents the main idea of the entire paragraph? Sentence _____.

5. In sentence 9, McPhee compares Keystone City to the Garden of Eden, by which he means to suggest that the area represented (a) an area unspoiled by pollution or development; (b) a paradise where luscious fruit can grow; (c) a place of punishment for humanity's sins and errors in judgment; (d) a place from which human beings were banished forever.

C. Inferences

On the basis of the evidence in the paragraph, mark these statements as follows: *A* for accurate inferences, *I* for inaccurate inferences, and *IE* for insufficient evidence.

_____ 1. The freeze that occurred in February 1835 affected more growers than the Great Freeze of 1895.

_____ 2. During the Freeze of 1895, some growers left the dinner table and the state on hearing the news because they were financially ruined.

_____ 3. High elevations offer little protection to citrus groves from freezes.

_____ 4. The citrus industry is not particularly important to Florida's economy.

_____ 5. The motivation for the citizens of Keystone City to change the name of their town to Frostproof was a sense of pride in their groves' ability to escape the Great Freeze.

_____ 6. Frostproof is still a popular Florida tourist attraction.

_____ 7. John McPhee, the author of this paragraph, is a citrus grower.

Selection 3

[1]The settlement of the continent, once the Eastern coast ranges were crossed, proceeded with unparalleled speed, and so the naming of the new rivers, lakes, peaks and valleys, and of the new towns and districts, strained the inventiveness of the pioneers. [2]The result is the vast duplication of names that shows itself in the Postal Guide. [3]No less than eighteen imitative *Bostons* and *New Bostons* still appear, and there are nineteen

Bristols, twenty-eight *Newports*, and twenty-two *Londons* and *New Londons*. [4]Argonauts starting out from an older settlement on the coast would take its name with them, and so we find *Philadelphias* in Illinois, Mississippi, Missouri and Tennessee, *Richmonds* in Iowa, Kansas and nine other Western States, and *Princetons* in fifteen. [5]Even when a new name was hit upon it seems to have been hit upon simultaneously by scores of scattered bands of settlers; thus we find the whole land bespattered with *Washingtons, Lafayettes, Jeffersons* and *Jacksons,* and with names suggested by common and obvious natural objects, *e.g., Bear Creek, Bald Knob* and *Buffalo.* [6]The Geographic Board, in its fourth report made a belated protest against this excessive duplication. [7]"The names *Elk, Beaver, Cottonwood* and *Bald,*" it said, "are altogether too numerous." [8]Of postoffices alone there are fully a hundred embodying *Elk*; counting in rivers, lakes, creeks, mountains and valleys, the map of the United States probably shows at least twice as many such names.

H. L. Mencken,
American Language

A. Vocabulary

For each italicized word from the paragraph, choose the best definition according to the context in which it appears.

1. *unparalleled* [1]: (a) impressive; (b) unforeseen; (c) incomprehensible; (d) unequaled.
2. *strained* [1]: (a) stretched tight; pulled; (b) exerted; taxed to the utmost; (c) injured; impaired; (d) altered the relations between parts.
3. *embodying* [8]: (a) making part of a united whole; (b) imitating; (c) representing; (d) listing.

B. Content and Structure

Choose the best answer.

1. In your own words, write the main idea and the controlling idea of this paragraph:
   Main idea _____
   Controlling idea _____
   _____
2. The relationship between sentences 1 and 2 is best described as (a) statement and an example of it; (b) contrast, or statements of an opposite nature; (c) statement and a reason to explain it; (d) statement of cause and effect.
3. The mode of discourse in the paragraph is (a) narration; (b) description; (c) exposition; (d) persuasion.
4. To support the main idea, Mencken relies primarily on (a) definitions of key terms; (b) short examples; (c) opinions from authorities; (d) quotations from published sources.
5. Which word in sentence 5 is a synonym for *Argonauts* as it is used in sentence 4? _____

6. Label these statements derived from the paragraph according to whether they are *major* (MA) or *minor* (MI) supporting details with respect to the main idea.

    a. _____ There is a vast duplication of place names in the United States.

    b. _____ There are eighteen *Bostons* and *New Bostons,* twenty-eight *Newports,* twenty-two *Londons* and *New Londons.*

    c. _____ Settlers moving from an old location on the coast took their old names with them.

    d. _____ There are *Philadelphias* in Illinois, Mississippi, Missouri, and Tennessee, *Richmonds* in Iowa, Kansas, and nine other Western states, and *Princetons* in fifteen states.

    e. _____ It was common for new locations to be named for common and obvious natural objects.

    f. _____ Some new areas were named *Bear Creek, Bald Knob,* and *Buffalo.*

7. We can infer that the Geographic Board protested the excessive duplication of place names in the United States because (a) it showed that the pioneers weren't very imaginative; (b) it showed that the pioneers cared more about their original homes than about their new settlements; (c) such duplication was potentially confusing, especially for post office workers; (d) travelers would find it difficult to find their way around the country.

8. What inference can you make about Mencken's opinion concerning the duplication of place names? (a) He probably thinks the settlers imitated the names of their original homes because they were homesick. (b) He probably thinks that such duplication is foolish. (c) He probably thinks that the Geographic Board was getting concerned about an essentially trivial matter. (d) His opinion is not evident from the paragraph.

Selection 4

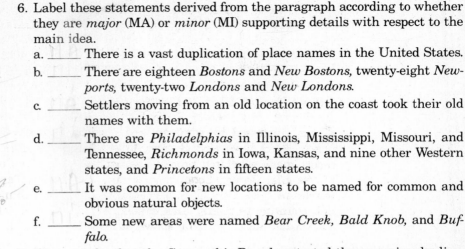

[1]I had a farm in Africa, at the foot of the Ngong Hills. [2]The Equator runs across these highlands, a hundred miles to the North, and the farm lay at an altitude of over six thousand feet. [3]In the day-time you felt that you had got high up, near to the sun, but the early mornings and evenings were limpid and restful, and the nights were cold.

[4]The geographical position, and the height of the land combined to create a landscape that had not its like in all the world. [5]There was no fat on it and no luxuriance anywhere; it was Africa distilled up through six thousand feet, like the strong and refined essence of a continent. [6]The colours were dry and burnt, like the colours in pottery. [7]The trees had a light delicate foliage, the structure of which was different from that of the trees in Europe; it did not grow in bows or cupolas, but in horizontal layers, and the formation gave to the tall solitary trees a likeness to the palms, or a heroic and romantic air like fullrigged ships with their sails

clewed up,* and to the edge of a wood a strange appearance as if the whole wood were faintly vibrating. [8]Upon the grass of the great plains the crooked bare old thorn-trees were scattered, and the grass was spiced like thyme and bog-myrtle; in some places the scent was so strong, that it smarted in the nostrils. [9]All the flowers that you found on the plains, or upon the creepers and liana in the native forest, were diminutive like flowers of the downs,**–only just in the beginning of the long rains a number of big, massive heavy-scented lilies sprang out on the plains. [10]The views were immensely wide. [11]Everything that you saw made for greatness and freedom, and unequalled nobility.

Isak Dinesen,
"The Ngong Farm," *Out of Africa*

A. Vocabulary

For each italicized word from the paragraph, choose the best definition according to the context in which it appears.

1. *limpid* [3]: (a) transparent; (b) calm; (c) hot; (d) predictable.
2. *distilled* [5]: (a) purified; refined; (b) elevated; (c) described; depicted; (d) extracted in small drops.
3. *diminutive* [9]: (a) large; (b) ordinary; (c) inferior; (d) tiny.

B. Content and Structure

Choose the best answer.

1. The mode of discourse in this passage is (a) narration; (b) description; (c) exposition; (d) persuasion.
2. Which two sentences best express the dominant impression of the Ngong farm? Sentences _____ and _____.
3. In the passage, Dinesen relies extensively on words that appeal to the reader's (a) emotions and feelings; (b) own experience in the region; (c) senses of sight, smell, and touch; (d) intellectual curiosity.
4. In sentence 5, Dinesen says, referring to the landscape, "there was no fat on it." What does she mean by this phrase?

   _____

   _____

5. The "colours in pottery" mentioned in sentence 6 probably refer to shades of (a) gray; (b) blue and yellow; (c) brown; (d) green.
6. The landscape Dinesen refers to is primarily (a) high mountains; (b) swampland; (c) grassland; (d) dense forest.
7. Which sentence contains a *metaphor* (an imaginative comparison between two unlike things)? Sentence _____.
   What two things are being compared? _____

   _____

8. The impression Dinesen conveys of this region in Africa is characterized by (a) gloom and dreariness; (b) loneliness; (c) barrenness; (d) openness.

---

*That is, with the lower corners raised up and tied.
**Grassy, rolling uplands, characteristic of southern England.

Selection 5*

[1]We tend to think of our selves as the only wholly unique creations in nature, but it is not so. [2]Uniqueness is so commonplace a property of living things that there is really nothing at all unique about it. [3]A phenomenon can't be unique and universal at the same time. [4]Even individual, free-swimming bacteria can be viewed as unique entities, distinguishable from each other even when they are the progeny of a single clone. [5]Spudich and Koshland have recently reported that motile microorganisms of the same species are like solitary eccentrics in their swimming behavior. [6] When they are searching for food, some tumble in one direction for precisely so many seconds before quitting, while others tumble differently and for different, but characteristic, periods of time. [7]If you watch them closely, tethered by their flagellae to the surface of an antibody-coated slide, you can tell them from each other by the way they twirl, as accurately as though they had different names.

Lewis Thomas,
The Medusa and the Snail

A. Vocabulary

For each italicized word from the paragraph, choose the best definition according to the context in which it appears.

1. *property* [2]: (a) characteristic trait or peculiarity; (b) special capability or power; virtue; (c) quality serving to define or describe an object or substance; (d) characteristic attribute possessed by all members of a class.

2. *phenomenon* [3]: (a) an event that can be perceived by the senses; (b) an unusual, significant, or unaccountable fact or occurrence; a marvel; (c) a person outstanding for some extreme quality or achievement; (d) any unexplainable event in nature.

3. *entities* [4]: Things existing (a) in a state of harmony; (b) in a dangerous environment; (c) independently; separate from one another; (d) inseparably from one another.

4. *progeny* [4]: (a) representations; (b) offspring; (c) exact replicas; clones; (d) parents.

5. *motile* [5]: Capable of (a) reproducing; (b) perceiving through sense organs; (c) moving spontaneously; (d) existing independently.

6. *tethered* [7]: (a) guided; (b) tied; restricted; (c) powered; (d) kept motionless.

B. Content and Structure

Choose the best answer.

1. The primary mode of discourse in this paragraph is (a) narration; (b) description; (c) exposition; (d) persuasion.

2. Which of the following best states the main idea of this paragraph? (a) Even free-swimming bacteria display unique characteristics when

---

*Note: Some of the scientific names in this paragraph are excluded from the following vocabulary exercise (e.g., *clone, microorganisms, flagellae, antibody*), so, if you are unsure of their meanings, be sure to look them up before you do the exercises.

searching for food. (b) Human beings are unique creatures in the universe. (c) Uniqueness is a quality universal to all living things. (d) Human beings are arrogant to think that they are the only unique organisms in the universe.

3. The primary purpose of sentence 1 is to (a) establish the main idea; (b) disprove an erroneous idea; (c) provide us with a dramatic opening statement to stimulate our interest; (d) criticize us for being self-centered.

4. The relationship between the words *unique* and *universal,* as they are used in sentence 3, is (a) antonyms or opposites; (b) synonyms; (c) steps in a process; (d) words with the same etymology.

5. To support the main idea, Thomas relies primarily on (a) definitions of key scientific terms; (b) a single illustration; (c) steps in a process; (d) a discussion of reasons to explain the phenomenon.

6. What Thomas wants us to understand about free-swimming bacteria is that (a) they are used often in laboratory experiments; (b) each organism behaves in a solitary and strange manner; (c) each organism displays unique characteristics in its swimming behavior; (d) their behavior can easily be observed on the surface of slides.

7. Why do you think Thomas uses the swimming behavior of microorganisms rather than that of a more obvious creature, such as a seal or a whale, for his example?
   because it is not obvious. Even the tiniest animal has its own way —

8. Label these sentences from the paragraph according to whether they represent details that are *major* (MA) or *minor* (MI) with respect to the main idea. *directly support the main idea*
   MA sentence 4   MI sentence 6   *examples*
   MI sentence 5   MI sentence 7
        examples

Selection 6   [1]It has sometimes been claimed that the United States could survive a nuclear attack by the Soviet Union, but the bare figures on the extent of the blast waves, the thermal pulses, and the accumulated local fallout dash this hope irrevocably. [2]They spell the doom of the United States. [3]And if one imagines the reverse attack on the Soviet Union, its doom is spelled out in similar figures. [4](The greater land mass of the Soviet Union and the lower megatonnage of the American forces might reduce the factor of overkill somewhat.) [5]Likewise, any country subjected to an attack of more than a few hundred megatons would be doomed. [6]Japan, China, and the countries of Europe, where population densities are high, are especially vulnerable to damage, even at "low" levels of attack. [7]There is no country in Europe in which survival of the population would be appreciable after the detonation of several hundred megatons; most European countries would be annihilated by tens of megatons. [8]And these conclusions emerge even before one takes into account the global ecological consequences of a holocaust, which would be superimposed on the local consequences. [9]As human life and the structure of human existence are seen in the light of each person's daily life and experience, they look impressively extensive and solid, but when human things are seen in the light of the universal power unleashed onto the earth by nuclear weapons they prove to be limited and fragile, as though they were nothing more than a mold or a lichen that appears in certain crevices of the landscape and can be burned off with relative ease by nuclear fire.

— Jonathan Schell,
The Fate of the Earth

A. Vocabulary

For each italicized word from the paragraph, choose the best definition according to the context in which it appears.

1. *irrevocably* [1]: (a) permanently; (b) insignificantly; (c) irreversibly; (d) undoubtedly.
2. *megaton* [5]: A unit of force equal to (a) one ton of TNT; (b) one hundred tons of TNT; (c) one thousand tons of TNT; (d) one million tons of TNT.
3. *vulnerable* [6]: (a) susceptible to injury; (b) insufficiently defended; (c) liable to criticism; (d) liable to succumb to persuasion or temptation.
4. *annihilated* [7]: (a) severely affected; (b) reduced to starvation; (c) destroyed; wiped out completely; (d) militarily defeated.
5. *ecological* [8]: Referring to the relationship between (a) countries; (b) citizens of nations and their governments; (c) organisms and their environments; (d) the defeated and their captors.
6. *holocaust* [8]: (a) a sacrificial offering that is consumed entirely by flames; (b) total destruction by fire; (c) breakdown in negotiations; (d) destruction of a race of people.
7. *superimposed on* [8]: (a) forced on; (b) placed on; (c) dependent on; (d) supported by.
8. *crevices* [9]: (a) narrow cracks; (b) distinctive features; (c) surface areas; (d) deep, wide holes.

B. Content and Structure

Choose the best answer.

1. The mode of discourse in this paragraph is (a) narration; (b) description; (c) exposition; (d) persuasion.
2. Which one sentence *best* reveals the author's purpose and serves to reinforce his main idea? Sentence _____ .
3. In your own words, state the main idea of the paragraph. _____
4. Look again at sentence 6. In the phrase "low levels of attack," Schell puts *low* in quotation marks (a) to show that he is providing us with a direct quotation; (b) to emphasize the word; (c) to show that he is being sarcastic and questioning the sense of using a word like "low" to describe a level of nuclear attack; (d) to show that he wants to keep the word separate from the rest of the text.

5. As used in sentence 5, *likewise* means (a) on the other hand; (b) in the same way; (c) for example; (d) in addition.

6. The last sentence contains an especially effective *simile* (an indirect imaginative comparison between two unlike things using "like" or "as"). First, decide what Schell is comparing to what. Then explain the meaning of the comparison in your own words.

   _Human life (things)_____ are being compared to ___mold or lichen___

   Explain. _Human being in daily life put up with a and is strong. But in time of nuclear war there is nothing_

(margin handwriting: in time of war they are equally insignificant - lot of stress He can do. He's weak -)

7. The author's *tone*—his attitude toward his subject—can best be described as (a) sharply critical; (b) ironic; wry and amusing; (c) neutral; showing little or no emotion; (d) cynical; distrusting human motives. *not motives*

8. The author apparently believes that (a) nuclear war is inevitable; (b) since an attack would destroy civilization, nuclear war should be prevented at all costs; (c) all countries possessing nuclear weapons should have a summit meeting; (d) developing nations should produce their own nuclear arms to counteract the threat from the Americans and the Soviets.

C. Inferences

On the basis of the evidence in the paragraph, mark these statements as follows: *A* for accurate inferences, *I* for inaccurate inferences, and *IE* for insufficient evidence.

___A___ 1. No country could survive a nuclear attack.

___A___ 2. Measured in megatonnage, the nuclear strength of the Soviet Union is superior to that of the United States.

___IE___ 3. The USSR and the U.S. have voluntarily agreed to stop producing nuclear weapons.

___IE___ 4. Most of the world's developed nations possess an arsenal of nuclear weapons.

___A___ 5. The chances of surviving a nuclear attack are particularly slim for nations with high population densities.

___I___ 6. A nuclear attack in one country would not have much effect on the environment of a neighboring country.

PRACTICE ESSAY

The following selection provides you with the opportunity to practice your new skills with a short essay. Read the passage carefully once. Look up any unfamiliar words in the dictionary. Next, answer the comprehension questions without looking back at the selection. Check your answers against the text. Then read the essay again, paying careful attention to paragraph structure and to any accurate inferences you can draw. As you work through the remaining questions, you should feel free to refer to the selection, if necessary.

Nonverbal Communication Patterns
Jane Goodall

Jane Goodall is an English biologist who, at the encouragement of the famous anthropologist and paleontologist, Louis B. Leakey, went to the Gombe Stream Game Reserve on the shores of Lake Tanganyika in 1960 to study chimpanzee behavior. Her book, *In the Shadow of Man,* describes her experience during her first years in Africa. Subsequent grants from the National Geographic Society have allowed her to expand her studies of primate life to include baboons, orangutans, and gorillas, which have become the subject of numerous television programs. The following short selection discusses the similarities between the ways humans and chimps communicate.

1   For me, one of the most striking behavioral similarities between man and chimpanzee lies in the nonverbal communication system—the repertoire of postures and gestures by which one chimpanzee communicates with his fellows. In many cases, it is not only the gesture which is so similar to that of a human (such as kissing, patting on the back, holding hands) but also the contexts in which such patterns are likely to occur.

2   When a chimpanzee is frightened he may reach to touch or embrace a companion, and he seems to derive comfort from such contact. When two chimpanzees are suddenly excited—if, for instance, they come across an unexpected supply of food—they are likely to indulge in much contact-seeking behavior of this sort, touching, embracing, kissing, patting until it seems they are calmed by the physical contact with each other. This apparent need for physical contact with another in times of stress is often vividly illustrated by a young chimpanzee who has been threatened or attacked by another. The victim may approach the aggressor, screaming and tense, and take up a submissive, crouching posture in front of him. In response to such behavior the aggressor typically reaches out to touch, pat or even embrace the screaming or whimpering subordinate. The effect of such a reassurance gesture on the victim is usually immediately apparent: his screams diminish, his whimpers gradually cease, and he slowly relaxes his tense posture. Sometimes he seems quite calm by the time he moves away.

3   When chimpanzees have been separated for a while they may, if they are close associates, show friendly behavior which we may call greeting. One individual may pat, embrace or kiss another, or they may reach out and hold hands.

4   Some of the patterns and contexts of chimpanzee aggression are also similar to some of our own. A chimpanzee who threatens another may make vigorous movements of upraised arm, he may run towards the other in an upright posture, sometimes waving both arms, he may throw rocks or other objects, often with good aim, or he may brandish a stick. During an actual attack he may bite, pull hair, scratch, punch, hit or kick.

5   Aggression may occur when two chimpanzees are competing for social status, for favored food in short supply or, very occasionally, for a female. A chimpanzee may become aggressive if a member of his immediate family is threatened or attacked. He may become irritable, and thus aggressive, if he

is in pain, or if subordinates make too much noise and commotion nearby. Very often, when one chimpanzee is threatened or attacked by a superior whom he dare not fight back, he redirects his aggressive feelings against a subordinate who happens to be nearby. In addition, the sight or sound of chimpanzees of a neighboring community may cause aggressive displays and, if a "stranger" is encountered, he or she may become the victim of a savage attack.

A. Comprehension

Choose the answer that best completes each statement. Do not refer to the selection.

1. The main idea of the essay is that (a) chimpanzees in confinement display the same behavior patterns as those in the wild; (b) observing chimpanzee behavior has yielded many new theories about the origin of human life; (c) there are many similarities between human and chimpanzee nonverbal communication systems; (d) chimpanzee and human aggression and the contexts in which it occurs are remarkably similar.

2. Chimpanzees show an apparent need for (a) variety in their diet; (b) physical contact in times of stress; (c) aggression to establish dominance within the group; (d) activities to release pent-up energy.

3. Which of the following reasons for aggression among chimpanzees was *not* included among the several that Goodall mentions? Aggression may occur when chimpanzees are competing (a) for attention from a parent; (b) for favored food in short supply; (c) for a female; (d) for social status within the group.

B. Inferences

On the basis of the evidence in the paragraph, mark these statements as follows: *A* for accurate inferences, *I* for inaccurate inferences, and *IE* for insufficient evidence. You may refer to the selection to answer the questions in this and in all the remaining exercises.

IE 1. The victim of an aggressive attack stays as far away from the aggressor as possible to avoid further attacks.

I 2. Chimpanzee aggression never results in any real physical injury.

IE 3. Chimpanzees are territorial and are intolerant of another chimpanzee group's presence in their space.

IE 4. Chimpanzees observed in captivity display the same system of gestures as those in the wild do.

A 5. Chimpanzees are sensitive to the same situations as humans are, such as fear, tension, and pain.

C. Structure

Choose the best answer.

1. Write the sentence that best expresses the main idea of the entire selection, then underline once the words that express the subject, and twice those that express the controlling idea.

One of the most striking behavioral similarities between man and chimpanzee lie in the nonverbal communication system —

2. Which two areas of chimpanzee communication does Goodall restrict herself to in the body of the essay? *When the chimpanzee is frightened* and *when he is aggressive*

3. The mode of discourse in the selection is (a) narration; (b) description; (c) exposition; (d) persuasion.

4. As used in paragraph 1, sentence 1, *striking* means (a) marvelous; amazing; (b) overwhelming; (c) interesting; (d) prominent.

5. To support her observations, Goodall relies mainly on (a) quotations from scientific articles; (b) examples and illustrations; (c) explanations to account for her observations; (d) opinions and subjective impressions.

6. Look again at paragraph 4. Which sentence represents the main idea? Sentence ___1___.

7. One can describe the *tone*—the author's attitude toward the subject—as (a) admiring, even laudatory; (b) objective; neutral; (c) amazed; filled with wonder and awe; (d) amused.

D. Vocabulary

For each of the following italicized words from the selection, choose the best definition according to the context in which it appears.

1. the *repertoire* of postures and gestures [paragraph 1]: (a) range or number of accomplishments of a particular group; (b) kinds of performances to be presented to an audience; (c) observable phenomena; (d) repetitious actions or behavior patterns.

2. they are likely to *indulge in* [2]: (a) participate in; (b) derive pleasure in; (c) allow themselves some special pleasure; (d) communicate with one another.

3. This apparent need . . . is *vividly* illustrated [2]: Describing something that is (a) realistic; (b) emphatic; (c) lifelike; immediate; (d) brilliant; distinct.

4. a *submissive,* crouching position [2]: (a) fearful; (b) threatening; (c) apologetic; (d) surrendering to another's will.

5. he may *brandish* a stick [4]: (a) display in an ostentatious or showy manner; (b) wave or flourish in a menacing way; (c) sharpen as if to make a weapon; (d) search for.

E. Variant Word Forms

From the list of inflected forms in parentheses, choose the form that grammatically fits into the space. Add endings (–s or –ed, for example) if necessary.

1. (similar, similarly, similarity): The repertoire of gestures and postures by which chimpanzees communicate with one another are strikingly ___similar___ to that of human beings.

2. (submission, submit, submissive, submissively): Ironically, when the victim of an aggressive attack approaches the aggressor and ___submits___ to his authority, the aggressor actually calms the victim.

3. (vigor, invigorate, vigorous, vigorously): During an aggressive attack, a chimpanzee may move his upraised arm _vigorously_

4. (aggression, aggressor, aggressive, aggressively): Chimpanzee _aggressor_ and their victims behave differently from human beings.

5. (irritation, irritate, irritable, irritably): A chimpanzee may become _irritable_ and therefore aggressive if he is in pain.

chapter 2 ‖ FOUR METHODS OF PARAGRAPH DEVELOPMENT

Now that you have developed some facility in picking out the topic sentence, making inferences, and determining the author's purpose, you can begin to analyze the structure of paragraphs. The next skill we will take up is determining the method the writer uses to develop or support the topic sentence. In this chapter we will be concerned with the first four of several methods of paragraph development: (1) examples and illustrations; (2) process; (3) comparison and contrast; and (4) definition. These four methods have to do with the particular *kinds of evidence* the author uses in the body of the paragraph. (The other three methods are more difficult and will be taken up in Chapter 3.) As you study the illustrative paragraphs, you will see that they are all examples of expository prose; indeed, some composition textbooks refer to these methods as *expository* methods of development.

A. EXAMPLES AND ILLUSTRATIONS

The method of paragraph development that uses *examples and illustrations* is the most common and the easiest to recognize. In this method, the writer supports a general statement by means of a series of specific, relevant examples, or sometimes by a single long illustration. The practice essay by Jane Goodall at the end of Chapter 1 makes extensive use of short examples to reinforce the main idea that humans and chimpanzees communicate in notably similar ways. And in his paragraph about the uniqueness of organisms, Lewis Thomas uses a single illustration of free-swimming bacteria to provide evidence for his main idea. Here are two more passages by Lewis Thomas. (You have probably already noticed that Thomas's paragraphs are little masterpieces.) In the first, Thomas provides the reader with a series of short examples to support his main idea which he states in the first sentence.

Almost anything that an animal can employ to make a sound is put to use. Drumming, created by beating the feet, is used by prairie hens, rabbits, and mice; the head is banged by woodpeckers and certain other birds; the males of deathwatch beetles make a rapid ticking sound by percussion of a protuberance on the abdomen against the ground; a faint but audible ticking is made by the tiny beetle *Lepinotus inquilinus*, which is less than two millimeters in length. Fish make sounds by clicking their teeth, blowing air, and drumming with special muscles against tuned inflated air bladders. Solid structures are set to vibrating by toothed bows

(handwritten margin notes:) see p 31 selection 3 · see p 35 · sel 5 · · Topic

in crustaceans and insects. The proboscis of the death's-head hawk moth is used as a kind of reed instrument, blown through to make high-pitched, reedy notes.

Gorillas beat their chests for certain kinds of discourse. Animals with loose skeletons rattle them, or, like rattlesnakes, get sounds from externally placed structures. Turtles, alligators, crocodiles, and even snakes make various more or less vocal sounds. Leeches have been heard to tap rhythmically on leaves, engaging the attention of other leeches, which tap back, in synchrony. Even earthworms make sounds, faint staccato notes in regular clusters. Toads sing to each other, and their friends sing back in antiphony.

Lewis Thomas,
"The Music of This Sphere," *Lives of a Cell*

In the following short passage, Thomas's main idea is that scientists who use animals for experiments always run the risk of being fooled by their subjects. It is supported by a single illustration about a German horse named Clever Hans.

Scientists who work on animal behavior are occupationally obliged to live chancier lives than most of their colleagues, always at risk of being fooled by the animals they are studying or, worse, fooling themselves. Whether their experiments involve domesticated laboratory animals or wild creatures in the field, there is no end to the surprises that an animal can think up in the presence of an investigator. Sometimes it seems as if animals are genetically programmed to puzzle human beings, especially psychologists.

The risks are especially high when the scientist is engaged in training the animal to do something or other and must bank his professional reputation on the integrity of his experimental subject. The most famous case in point is that of Clever Hans, the turn-of-the-century German horse now immortalized in the lexicon of behavioral science by the technical term, the "Clever Hans Error." The horse, owned and trained by Herr von Osten, could not only solve complex arithmetical problems, but even read the instructions on a blackboard and tap out infallibly, with one hoof, the right answer. What is more, he could perform the same computations when total strangers posed questions to him, with his trainer nowhere nearby. For several years Clever Hans was studied intensively by groups of puzzled scientists and taken seriously as a horse with something very like a human brain, quite possibly even better than human. But finally in 1911, it was discovered by Professor O. Pfungst that Hans was not really doing arithmetic at all; he was simply observing the behavior of the human experimenter. Subtle, unconscious gestures—nods of the head, the holding of breath, the cessation of nodding when the correct count was reached—were accurately read by the horse as cues to stop tapping.

Lewis Thomas,
"Clever Animals," *Late Night Thoughts on Listening to Mahler's Ninth Symphony*

B. PROCESS

step by step
procedure —

A second method of paragraph development is *process*. There are two kinds of process writing. In the first, called the *directive* kind, the author explains the steps, in chronological order, that one must follow to complete a project or to perform a task—such as how to study for final exams, how to develop a photograph, or how to lose ten pounds in a month. This use of process writing is found most often in laboratory or technical manuals, or in the thousands of "how-to" books that flood the book market each year. The following paragraph is reprinted from a standard reference book on home repairs and explains step by step how one goes about the task of cleaning paintbrushes.

Contrary to popular opinion, the job of cleaning a brush is actually a simple task which should take only a few minutes if attended to promptly. After wiping off excess paint, rub the bristles vigorously against sheets of old newspaper to remove as much paint as possible before washing. If a water-thinned paint was used, the brush should then be washed out in running water, taking care to flush all paint out of the center of the brush as well as off the outside. This is followed by a thorough shaking to remove excess water.

Brushes that have been used in a solvent-thinned paint should be washed out with several rinses of solvent (turpentine, benzine or mineral spirits) or with a commercially prepared liquid brush cleaner. If a solvent is used, the bristles should be worked vigorously underneath the surface of the liquid till the solvent has removed as much paint as possible. Two or three rinses will be needed to get bristles completely clean. If the brush is to be used again within a day or so, it can now be wrapped in heavy paper to preserve it. If the brush will be stored for a lengthy period of time, a final rinsing with detergent and warm water is advisable. Comb the bristles smooth and let them dry completely, then wrap in paper or foil to preserve the shape.

Bernard Gladstone,
The New York Times Complete Manual of Home Repair

The second kind of process writing, called the *informative* type, describes a phenomenon—how something works or how something developed or came into existence. The author uses chronological order, but the underlying purpose is different since the writer does not expect us to attempt to duplicate the process described. In this paragraph, naturalist Edward Abbey shows the process by which Snow Canyon in Arizona was formed. Notice that, in this case, the steps in the process are held together with time markers, phrases that show the transitions between stages ("about 1,000 years ago," "at the same time," and "in Triassic times").

Snow Canyon is dry, virtually waterless, containing but one remote year-round stream. The stream that largely formed the canyon through corrasion and erosion was blocked and diverted by recent volcanic activity.

About 1,000 years ago, molten magma found a weak point in the crustal structure and poured forth, cooling and solidifying as it moved into the head of what is now Snow Canyon. At the same time two cinder cones, each 800 to 900 feet high, formed above the volcanic vents. The cinder cones and the rough, jagged basaltic lava flows resemble those of Sunset Crater National Monument near Flagstaff, Arizona. In the background at both places stands a great volcanic mountain of a far more ancient period. At Sunset Crater this is the collapsed remnant (12,650 feet high) called the San Francisco Peaks; at Snow Canyon the old-timer that looms beyond is known as the Pine Valley Mountain, 10,360 feet high, a caldera of vast dimensions from which issued in Triassic times the many flows of lava that can now be seen in the Virgin River Valley between Saint George and Zion National Park.

Edward Abbey,
The Journey Home

C. COMPARISON AND CONTRAST

The *comparison and contrast* method is used to explain the similarities and differences between two things. The less common of the two, *comparison*, involves a discussion of *similarities* between two seemingly unlike or unrelated things. For example, a writer might explain what the seemingly unrelated situations of interviewing for a new job and meeting a new girlfriend's or boyfriend's parents have in common. *Contrast* properly refers to a discussion of the *differences* between two related or like things—for example, the Korean and the Vietnam wars, two science fiction movies, or two kinds of sports car. You may find comparison and contrast used together or singly, depending on the subject at hand. The following paragraph uses only *contrast*, since the author's purpose is to enumerate the essential differences between fairy tales and dreams.

There are, of course, very significant differences between fairy tales and dreams. For example, in dreams more often than not the wish fulfillment is disguised, while in fairy tales much of it is openly expressed. To a considerable degree, dreams are the result of inner pressures which have found no relief, of problems which beset a person to which he knows no solution and to which the dream finds none. The fairy tale does the opposite: it projects the relief of all pressures and not only offers ways to solve problems but promises that a "happy" solution will be found.

Bruno Bettelheim,
The Uses of Enchantment: The Meaning and Importance of Fairy Tales

Another kind of comparison/contrast paragraph reflects a "then–now" pattern. In the following paragraph, Marie Winn contrasts two concepts of childhood: the first from what she calls the "Golden Age of Childhood" (referring to the period before the 1960s) and the second from the current generation.

In the Golden Age of Childhood, parents rarely worried that their school-age children would get into any serious trouble in their hours away from home. The kids were pretty well in hand, parents believed, even the most stubborn and independent of the lot. A child might come to grief by breaking a window with a baseball or flunking a test in school or, at the worst, getting caught in a minor infraction such as sneaking into the movies or lifting a candy bar. Parents agonized over these problems, worrying that their son or daughter wouldn't get into college, wouldn't have the sort of moral fiber it takes to grow up to be President. But apart from the inevitable anxieties about sickness or accidents, mothers and fathers felt confident that nothing untoward was likely to happen in the course of their children's daily lives. Never in their worst fantasies did they imagine that their ten- or eleven-year-olds might smoke dope or get involved in serious sexual activity or run away from home and fall into the clutches of a child-prostitution ring. Parents then hardly knew that a drug called marijuana existed, much less feared that junior-high-school-age children might want to get high on it. As for child prostitution and the like—why, that sort of thing might go on in Tangier or the Casbah, but not around here!

Marie Winn,
Children Without Childhood

D. DEFINITION

Unlike the other methods described thus far, definition is most often used in conjunction with other methods of development. As a method, it is nearly self-explanatory. A writer defines a word, perhaps because it may be unfamiliar to the reader, or because it has an unusual etymology, or because the writer wants to ensure that the reader understands exactly how he or she is using a key term that might be open to varying interpretations, as is the case with abstractions like *honor* or *charisma*. The following illustration is a good example of a paragraph that accomplishes the first two purposes named above, defining and tracing the history of the term "white elephant."

That large portrait of your wealthy Aunt Jane, given by her and which you loathe but do not dare to take down from your wall; that large book-case, too costly to discard, but which you hope will be more in keeping with your future home; these, and a thousand other like items are "white elephants"—costly, but useless possessions. The allusion takes us to Siam. In that country it was the traditional custom for many centuries that a rare albino elephant was, upon capture, the property of the emperor—who even today bears the title, Lord of the White Elephant—and was thereafter sacred to him. He alone might ride or use such an animal, and none might be destroyed without his consent. Because of that latter royal prerogative, it is said that whenever it pleased his gracious majesty to bring about the ruin of a courtier who had displeased him, he would present the poor fellow with an elephant from his stables. The cost of feeding and caring for the huge animal that he might not use nor destroy—a veritable white elephant—gave the term its present meaning.

Charles Earle Funk,
A Hog on Ice

The next paragraph illustrates another use of the definition method. Sissela Bok, the author of a book called *Lying,* defines the term "white lie" in a particular way because she intends to use it in that way throughout the rest of her chapter. The purpose of this kind of definition is to clarify what might otherwise be open to individual interpretation, since each person clearly has his own idea of what actually constitutes a white lie.

White lies are at the other end of the spectrum of deception from lies in a serious crisis. They are the most common and the most trivial forms that duplicity can take. The fact that they are so common provides their protective coloring. And their very triviality, when compared to more threatening lies, makes it seem unnecessary or even absurd to condemn them. Some consider *all* well-intentioned lies, however momentous, to be white; in this book, I shall adhere to the narrower usage: a white lie, in this sense, is a falsehood not meant to injure anyone, and of little moral import. I want to ask whether there *are* such lies; and if there are, whether their cumulative consequences are still without harm; and, finally, whether many lies are not defended as "white" which are in fact harmful in their own right.

Sissela Bok,
Lying

Let us examine in more detail how these two writers actually constructed their definitions. The paragraph on "white elephants" uses three kinds of strategies: First, Funk lists some examples of typical white-elephant objects; next he provides us with a dictionary definition ("costly, but useless possessions"); and finally he ends with a short narrative explaining the origin of this term. Sissela Bok's paragraph on "white lies" offers a personal or subjective definition ("a falsehood not meant to injure anyone, and of little moral import"). Another way writers occasionally define words is to *define by negation*—meaning that the author might discuss what a particular word does *not* mean before arriving at what he or she considers to be an acceptable definition. Such is Peter Farb's method in this paragraph in which he attempts to arrive at a working definition of a pidgin language.

Considerable dispute exists about what a pidgin language is, for the simple reason that so many mistaken notions have been held for so long. Pidgin is not the corrupted form of a standard language—like the "broken" English spoken by an Italian tourist guide or that classic example of pseudo-pidgin, *Me Tarzan, you Jane.* Nor is it a kind of baby talk spoken by a plantation owner to his slaves, a master to his servants, or a merchant to his customers. And, finally, it is not a language that patronizingly makes concessions to the limited intelligence of "natives." A pidgin can best be described as a language which has been stripped of certain grammatical features. It is a new language that is not the mother tongue of any of its users, and it usually survives only so long as members of diverse speech communities are in contact.

Peter Farb,
Word Play: What Happens When People Talk

In the beginning of this section, it was suggested that definition is frequently used in combination with other methods of development. A good example of a paragraph that combines the definition method with, in this case, contrast, is the following passage by Ashley Montagu in which he attempts to distinguish between two related terms, parenthood and parentage:

It is apparently very necessary to distinguish between parenthood and parentage. Parenthood is an art; parentage is the consequence of a mere biological act. The biological ability to produce conception and to give birth to a child has nothing whatever to do with the ability to care for that child as it requires to be cared for. That ability, like every other, must be learned. It is highly desirable that parentage be not undertaken until the art of parenthood has been learned. Is this a counsel of perfection? As things stand now, perhaps it is, but it need not always be so. Parentage is often irresponsible. Parenthood is responsible. Parentage at best is irresponsibly responsible for the *birth* of a child. Parenthood is responsible for the *development* of a human being—not simply a child, but a human being. I do not think it is an overstatement to say that parenthood is the most important occupation in the world. There is no occupation for which the individual should be better prepared than this, for what can be more important to the individual, his family, his community, his society, his nation, and the world of humanity than the making of a good human being? And the making of a good human being is largely the work of good parents. And it *is* work—hard work—not to be irresponsibly undertaken or perfunctorily performed. Yet parenthood, perhaps like politics, is the only profession for which preparation is considered unnecessary.

Ashley Montagu,
The American Way of Life

What follows are six passages for you to work through to test your understanding of the first four methods of paragraph development.

EXERCISES

Selection 1   [1]The crop plants domesticated by the ancient Indian plant breeders of Middle and South America play a vital role in feeding the modern world. [2]Corn is a primary food in most countries that are not too cold and sunless for its cultivation. [3]It even competes with the native rice in parts of the Far East. [4]White potatoes developed by the highland Indians of Peru have become such a firmly established staple in lands with coolish climates that it is hard to imagine life there without them. [5]Sweet potatoes of the South American tropical forest are equally important in warm countries. [6]Kidney beans (Mexican) are the poor man's source of protein nearly everywhere except the Far East. [7]Peanuts (Peruvian) are not only an important industrial crop in many places but they are an essential part of the diet in large parts of Africa. [8]In addition, the long list of Indian contributions to the world's food includes lima beans, tomatoes, peppers, most kinds of squash and pumpkins, avocados, cocoa, pineapples and many lesser crops. [9]Nor were the Indians' contributions limited to edible plants. [10]Tobacco was widely cultivated in ancient America when the early explorers arrived, and they quickly introduced Europe to its pleasures.

Jonathan Norton Leonard,
Ancient America

Reinforce main idea - unifies paragraph

A. Vocabulary

For each italicized word from the paragraph, choose the best definition according to the context in which it appears.

1. *domesticated* [sentence 1]: (a) tamed; (b) accommodated to an environment; (c) introduced; (d) nurtured.

2. *staple* [4]: (a) tradition; (b) crop; (c) necessity for survival; (d) major commodity in steady demand.

B. Content and Structure

Choose the best answer.

1. Label the sentences in the paragraph according to whether they represent the main idea *(MAIN)*, a major supporting detail *(MA)*, or a minor supporting detail *(MI)*:

    sentence 1 MAIN   sentence 5 MA *different*
    sentence 2 MA   sentence 6 MA
    sentence 3 MI   sentence 7 MA
    sentence 4 MA

2. Consider again the sentence you labeled above as the main idea. Write the words that express the subject in the first space and those that represent the controlling idea in the second.
    Main idea *the crop plants domesticated of middle South Amer*
    Controlling idea *play a vital role in feeding to modern world*

3. The mode of discourse in the paragraph is (a) narration; (b) description; (c) exposition; (d) persuasion.

4. The method of paragraph development is (a) definition; (b) process; (c) example; (d) comparison and contrast.

5. What does the author want us to understand from this paragraph? (a) how the Indians developed the techniques that allowed them to domesticate so many different crops; (b) that the Indians made major contributions to today's food supply worldwide; (c) that Indian civilization was

remarkably advanced; (d) that all the food we eat today was first domesticated by the Indians.

6. Find a unifying phrase, that is, a phrase that repeats the main idea: in sentence _____ 8 ___.

Indian contribution to the world Food.

C. Inferences   On the basis of the evidence in the paragraph, mark these statements as follows: *A* for accurate inferences, *I* for inaccurate inferences, and *IE* for insufficient evidence.

___I___ 1. Food crops grown by ancient Indians have benefited mainly Third World, or undeveloped, countries.

___A___ 2. Many crops grown by the ancient Indians have become staple diets for diverse nations in the world.

___I___ 3. The primary staple diet in the Far East is corn.

___I___ 4. White potatoes can grow in any climate.

___IE___ 5. Peanuts are not an important part of the diet in South America.

___A___ 6. Tobacco was not originally grown in ancient Europe.

Selection 2   [1]The railroads brought new hordes of land-crazy people, and the new Americans moved like locusts across the continent until the western sea put a boundary to their movements. [2]Coal and copper and gold drew them on; they savaged the land, gold-dredged the rivers to skeletons of pebbles and debris. [3]An aroused and fearful government made laws for the distribution of public lands—a quarter section, one hundred and sixty acres, per person—and a claim had to be proved and improved; but there were ways of getting around this, and legally. [4]My own grandfather proved out a quarter section for himself, one for his wife, one for each of his children, and, I suspect, acreage for children he hoped and expected to have. [5]Marginal lands, of course, suitable only for grazing, went in larger pieces. [6]One of the largest land-holding families in California took its richest holdings by a trick: By law a man could take up all the swamp or water-covered land he wanted. [7]The founder of this great holding mounted a scow on wheels and drove his horses over thousands of acres of the best bottom land, then reported that he had explored it in a boat, which was true, and confirmed his title. [8]I need not mention his name: his descendants will remember.

John Steinbeck,
America and Americans

strong languages -
word appealing to emotions -
land-crazy -
locust -
savaged -

get on your point of view -

A. Vocabulary   For each italicized word from the paragraph, choose the best definition according to the context in which it appears.

massives

1. *hordes* [1]: (a) groups; (b) communities; (c) kinds; classes; (d) throngs; swarms.

2. *savaged* [2]: (a) attacked violently; (b) made angry or fierce; (c) trampled ferociously; (d) left untouched or wild.

3. *aroused* [3]: (a) unsympathetic; (b) stirred up; (c) angry; (d) civic-minded.

4. *marginal* [5]: Describing lands (a) that barely produce a sufficient amount; (b) around the perimeters of a piece of property; (c) adjacent to other pieces of property; (d) that grow basic crops.

B. Content and Structure

Choose the best answer.

1. The mode of discourse in sentences 1 and 2 is (a) narration; (b) description; (c) exposition; (d) persuasion.

2. Write the phrases from the first two sentences that helped you arrive at your answer for the first question. _mNe_ _____

_____

3. In sentence 1, Steinbeck refers to the new Americans as moving across the country like "locusts." What image does this metaphorical comparison convey about their behavior? _____

_____

4. The method of paragraph development in sentences 6 through 8 is (a) contrast; (b) comparison; (c) definition; (d) illustration.

5. In making laws governing the distribution of public lands, the government was attempting to (a) stop people from ruining the land, by regulating its use; (b) deny the new settlers the right to settle on public lands; (c) encourage farmers to raise crops for the new Western populations; (d) discourage other hopeful settlers from coming West and settling on public land.

6. The large landowner mentioned in sentences 6–8 obtained his land by (a) deliberately breaking the law because he knew he wouldn't get caught; (b) engaging in a deception which technically satisfied the laws' requirements; (c) pretending he was going to use the land for grazing; (d) cheating the government out of thousands of acres of land that he didn't deserve.

7. We can also infer that Steinbeck thinks the large landholder's scheme showed that he was actually (a) vicious; (b) far-sighted; (c) untrustworthy; (d) clever.

C. Inferences

On the basis of the evidence in the paragraph, mark these statements as follows: *A* for accurate inferences, *I* for inaccurate inferences, and *IE* for insufficient evidence.

_IE_ 1. This particular group of westward-bound settlers moved West after 1849.

_IE_ 2. The farmers took better care of the land they settled on than did the mineral prospectors.

_IE_ 3. "Proving" a quarter section of land required a year's residence and erecting some kind of structure.

_A_ 4. Bottom land is good farming land.

_I_ 5. The founder of the large holding was really Steinbeck's grandfather.

Selection 3   [1]Few people besides linguistics students and teachers of reading are aware of the complex mental manipulations involved in the reading process. [2]Shortly after learning to read, a person assimilates the process so completely that the words in books seem to acquire an existence almost equal to the objects or acts they represent. [3]It requires a fresh look at a printed page to recognize that those symbols that we call letters of the alphabet are completely abstract shapes bearing no inherent "meaning" of their own. [4]Look at an "o," for instance, or a "k." [5]The "o" is a curved figure; the "k" is an intersection of three straight lines. [6]Yet it is hard to divorce their familiar figures from their sounds, though there is nothing "o-ish" about an "o" or "k-ish" about a "k." [7]A reader unfamiliar with the Russian alphabet will find it easy to look at the symbol "Щ" and see it as an abstract shape; a Russian reader will find it harder to detach that symbol from its sound, *shch*. [8]And even when trying to consider "k" as an abstract symbol, we cannot see it without the feeling of a "k" sound somewhere between the throat and the ears, a silent pronunciation of "k" that occurs the instant we see the letter.

Marie Winn,
The Plug-In Drug

A. Vocabulary   For each italicized word from the paragraph, choose the best definition according to the context in which it appears.

1. *linguistics* [1]: The study of (a) mass media; (b) neurology; (c) literature; (d) language.

2. *assimilates* [2]: (a) absorbs and incorporates; (b) digests; (c) establishes; (d) modifies; makes certain changes.

3. *abstract* [3, 7, and 8]: (a) theoretical; not practical; (b) not easily understood; (c) apart from a concrete or specific instance; (d) meaningless; incomprehensible.

4. *inherent* [3]: (a) essential; intrinsic; (b) true; genuine; (c) intelligent; meaningful; (d) apparent; seeming.

B. Content and Structure   Choose the best answer.

1. The main idea of the whole paragraph is best expressed by sentence (a) 1; (b) 2; (c) 3; (d) 8.

2. The mode of discourse is (a) narration; (b) description; (c) exposition; (d) persuasion.

3. Mark the *two* methods of paragraph development the author uses: (a) example; (b) definition; (c) comparison; (d) contrast; (e) process.

4. What does Winn want us to understand about the reading process? That (a) no one understands exactly how one learns to read; (b) the process is so quickly assimilated that the reader can no longer separate the symbols and the sounds they represent; (c) linguistics students and teachers of reading are the only people aware of the complex process involved in

learning to read; (d) learning to read in English requires the same process as learning to read in Russian.

5. Winn mentions the Russian alphabet symbol "Щ" because (a) she wants to impress us with her knowledge of Russian; (b) that symbol is similar to the English *sh* sound; (c) a character from the alphabet of a language that is unfamiliar to most English readers better supports her idea that letters have no inherent meaning; (d) a Russian reader is able to see that symbol as an abstract shape, whereas an English reader is not.

C. Inferences

On the basis of the evidence in the paragraph, mark these statements as follows: *A* for accurate inferences, *I* for inaccurate inferences, and *IE* for insufficient evidence.

IE 1. Marie Winn is a teacher of reading.

A 2. The shape of the letter has no connection with the sound it makes.

IE 3. There is nothing "n-ish" about the letter "n."

Selection 4

[1]The history of the word "creole" itself dates back to the slave trade. [2]After slaves had been gathered from many parts of Africa, they were imprisoned in West African camps, euphemistically called "factories," for "processing" before being shipped out to "markets." [3]The managers of the factories took great care to separate slaves who spoke the same tribal language, thereby lessening the danger of revolt because the slaves were prevented from communicating with one another. [4]And further separation on the basis of language was made by the purchasers in the New World. [5]As a result, the only tongue the slaves had in common was a pidgin that originated in West Africa and developed in the colonies to which they were sent. [6]These pidgins became entrenched, and after a generation or two they began to expand to meet the needs of the slaves' way of life. [7]The slaves' new language became known as *créole*, a French word meaning "native" which in turn was derived from Portuguese.

[8]Nowadays "creole" refers to any language that developed from a pidgin by expansion of vocabulary and grammar and became the mother tongue for many speakers in a community. [9]The largest center of creole languages today is undoubtedly the Caribbean area, with more than six million speakers. [10]Several million additional people speak creoles in West Africa, South Africa, and Southeast Asia, and probably another three million people around the world use various pidgin languages. [11]Clearly, pidgin and creole are not rare or isolated phenomena; they number more speakers today than do such languages as Dutch, Swedish, or Greek.

Peter Farb,
Word Play

A. Vocabulary   For each italicized word from the paragraph, choose the best definition according to the context in which it appears.

1. *euphemistically* [2]: (a) realistically; (b) ironically; (c) less offensively; (d) profitably.

2. *thereby* [3]: (a) therefore; (b) by that means; (c) in this case; (d) afterward.

3. *entrenched* [6]: (a) widespread; exceedingly popular; (b) highly developed; complex; (c) firmly fixed; (d) open to attack.

4. *phenomena* (plural of *phenomenon*) [11]: (a) significant occurrences; (b) languages; (c) unexplainable or awe-inspiring events; (d) coincidences.

B. Content and Structure   Choose the best answer.

1. Mark the two choices that best describe Farb's purpose in this passage: to (a) trace the history of the word "creole"; (b) account for the variety in slave languages; (c) enumerate all the kinds of pidgin languages in the world; (d) define the word "creole" as it is currently used; (e) explain how the slaves were treated in the New World.

2. The mode of discourse is (a) narration; (b) description; (c) exposition; (d) persuasion.

3. The dominant method of paragraph development evident in both paragraphs is (a) process; (b) comparison; (c) contrast; (d) definition; (e) example.

4. The reason a pidgin language arose among New World slaves was that (a) slaveowners forced their slaves to abandon their native languages; (b) slaves refused to learn English, the language of their oppressors; (c) a pidgin was the only way slaves could surmount the variety of native languages represented in each group; (d) a pidgin language carried none of the stigma that the slaves' native languages did.

5. In sentence 8, the word *nowadays* is a transition that establishes (a) a shift or contrast; (b) a definition; (c) an example; (d) a conclusion.

C. Inferences   On the basis of the evidence in the paragraph, mark these statements as follows: *A* for accurate inferences, *I* for inaccurate inferences, and *IE* for insufficient evidence.

___ 1. Peter Farb speaks a creole language.

___ 2. The word "creole" is originally of Portuguese derivation.

___ 3. The author thinks the slaves' treatment was harsh.

___ 4. All slaves brought to the New World spoke creole.

___ 5. A pidgin language, if firmly enough established, can become a true creole language.

___ 6. A pidgin language is characterized by a simplified grammar and vocabulary.

___ 7. The Caribbean has more creole speakers today than the United States does.

___ 8. A creole language cannot be a speaker's mother tongue.

contradicts   *topic*

Selection 5   [1]There are not only essential similarities between myths and fairy tales; there are also inherent differences. [2]Although the same exemplary figures and situations are found in both and equally miraculous events occur in both, there is a crucial difference in the way these are communicated. [3]Put simply, the dominant feeling a myth conveys is: this is absolutely unique; it could not have happened to any other person, or in any other setting; such events are grandiose, awe-inspiring, and could not possibly happen to an ordinary mortal like you or me. [4]The reason is not so much that what takes place is miraculous, but that it is described as such. [5]By contrast, although the events which occur in fairy tales are often unusual and most improbable, they are always presented as ordinary, something that could happen to you or me or the person next door when out on a walk in the woods. [6]Even the most remarkable encounters are related in casual, everyday ways in fairy tales.

[7]An even more significant difference between these two kinds of story is the ending, which in myths is nearly always tragic, while always happy in fairy tales. [8]For this reason, some of the best-known stories found in collections of fairy tales don't really belong in this category. [9]For example, Hans Christian Andersen's "The Little Match Girl" and "The Steadfast Tin Soldier" are beautiful but extremely sad; they do not convey the feeling of consolation characteristic of fairy tales at the end. [10]Andersen's "The Snow Queen," on the other hand, comes quite close to being a true fairy tale.

Bruno Bettelheim,
The Uses of Enchantment:
The Meaning and Importance of Fairy Tales

A. Vocabulary   For each italicized word from the paragraph, choose the best definition according to the context in which it appears.

1. *inherent* [1]: (a) infinite; (b) essential; (c) implied; (d) significant.
2. *exemplary* [2]: (a) ordinary; (b) monotonous; (c) serving as a model; (d) serving to make a truth known.
3. *crucial* [2]: Extremely (a) difficult; (b) unusual; (c) dominant; (d) important.
4. *conveys* [3]: (a) communicates; (b) implies; (c) emphasizes; (d) inspires.
5. *grandiose* [3]: (a) greatness of scope; (b) of high moral value; (c) fantastic; impossible to imagine; (d) unrealistic.
6. *awe-inspiring* [3]: Arousing or inspiring (a) fright; terror; (b) a mixture of reverence, wonder, and dread; (c) love; charity; (d) a sense of miraculous events to come.
7. *steadfast* [9]: (a) silly; foolish; (b) clever; quick-witted; (c) stubborn; obstinate; (d) loyal; unswerving.
8. *consolation* [9]: (a) forgiveness; (b) revenge; (c) comfort; (d) sorrow.

B. Content and Structure   Choose the best answer.

1. The main idea of the two paragraphs is best stated in sentence ___1___.

2. The mode of discourse is (a) narration; (b) description; (c) exposition; (d) persuasion.

3. Bettelheim combines three methods of paragraph development in this passage. Write them in the spaces below. _Contrast_; _example_; _definition_. Which one predominates? _Contrast_

4. In sentences 2 and 5, *although* signifies that what follows is (a) an example; (b) a contrasting statement; (c) a statement admitting an error; an apology; (d) a statement admitting or conceding a truth.

5. In sentence 3, *put* in the expression "put simply," means (a) explained; (b) stated; (c) placed; (d) argued.

6. Which two *transitional expressions* — words or phrases linking ideas — signal a contrast?

   by contrast in sentence _5_.
   an even more significant difference in sentence _7_.

(margin note: not transitional expression — "sentence 10 "on the other hand")

7. According to the passage, the events in myths happen to (a) ordinary mortals like you and me; (b) unique and extraordinary figures; (c) improbable, unlikely characters; (d) kings, queens, and other royal figures.

8. One important characteristic of fairy tales is that they must (a) present extraordinary, even miraculous, events; (b) subtly suggest a moral truth; (c) end happily; (d) present ordinary events happening to ordinary characters.

C. Inferences

On the basis of the evidence in the selection, mark these statements as follows: *A* for accurate inferences, *I* for inaccurate inferences, and *IE* for insufficient evidence.

___A___ 1. One crucial difference between myths and fairy tales is the way events are related.

___I___ 2. A myth relates extraordinary events, whereas a fairy tale relates everyday occurrences.

___A___ 3. In both myths and fairy tales the characters are meant to be viewed as model figures.

___A___ 4. Hans Christian Andersen's fairy tale, "The Snow Queen," ends happily.

___A___ 5. Some of Hans Christian Andersen's stories resemble myths more than fairy tales.

(margin note: complaint)

Selection 6

[1]It's my impression that almost invariably the media stir up a fuss about the wrong movies. [2]If you take a child to Disney's "Dumbo," this is what the child sees: Dumbo's mother—a circus elephant—is so angry at kids who taunt Dumbo and pull his ears that she attacks them, and as a result she is beaten and locked in a cage for mad elephants. [3]Dumbo is left on his own, and the other elephants humiliate him constantly. [4]He's made into an elephant clown, and during a routine he's left at the top of a fireman's ladder in a burning house, crying elephant tears, because the human clowns fail to rescue him. [5]His only friend is another outcast—the

mouse Timothy. [6]Each sequence is brought up to its maximum psychological resonance, and when a child projects himself into this vat of bathos
and moroseness it's agony: the situations on the screen have immediate
correlations with his own terrors. [7]But what correlatives could there be
in "Indiana Jones and the Temple of Doom"? [8]It doesn't take advantage
of childhood traumas. [9]With its "Road to Morocco" sensibility, it constantly makes fun of itself, and it's as remote from children's real-life
fears as Sabu's escapades in "The Thief of Bagdad." [10]The emotional
mechanism of "Dumbo" is to make what happens to the cartoon animals
real to kids; the emotional mechanism in "Indiana Jones" is to make
what happens to the human characters unreal. [11]And the hero carries
you through—you know Indy won't die. [12]Grownups who are upset by the
menu at the banquet must be forgetting how cheerfully kids have traditionally sung such macabre ditties as "The worms crawl in, The worms
crawl out, The worms play pinochle on your snout, And one little worm,
Who's not too shy, Climbs into your ear, And out your eye" and "Great
green globs of greasy grimy gophers' guts, Mutilated monkey's meat,
Little birdies' dirty feet, Great green globs of greasy grimy gophers' guts,
And I forgot my spoon, Aw shucks."

Pauline Kael,
"The Current Cinema"

A. Vocabulary   For each italicized word from the paragraph, choose the best definition
according to the context in which it appears.

1. *taunt* [2]: (a) deceive; (b) jeer at; (c) humiliate; (d) mimic.

2. *mad* [2]: (a) deranged; insane; (b) angry; resentful; (c) wildly foolish;
   (d) sullen; sulky.

3. *resonance* [6]: (a) significance; (b) echoing; (c) enhancement; (d) intensity.

4. *bathos* [6]: (a) insincere or grossly sentimental feelings of sorrow or pity; (b)
   extreme triteness or dullness; (c) ridiculously abrupt transition from
   an elevated to a commonplace style; (d) inappropriate and insensitive
   depictions of reality.

5. *moroseness* [6]: (a) humiliation; (b) anxiety; (c) gloom; (d) ill fortune.

6. *correlations* [6] and *correlatives* [7]: (a) parallels; (b) consequences; (c) con-
   firmations; (d) characteristics.

7. *sensibility* [9]: (a) commonsense attitude; (b) keen intellectual perception;
   (c) ability to feel; sensitivity; (d) sense of appropriateness.

8. *macabre* [12]: (a) childish; (b) humorous; (c) legendary; (d) gruesome.

**B. Content
and Structure**   Choose the best answer.

see 7

1. The author's primary purpose is to (a) defend *Indiana Jones and the Temple of Doom* from media critics; (b) poke fun at contemporary children's
   movies; (c) criticize *Dumbo* for its emotional impact on children; (d) praise
   the media critics for alerting the movie audience to the harmful effects of
   Indiana Jones on young children.

2. The first sentence opens with the phrase, "It's my impression that. . . ." What does this phrase suggest that the author's mode of discourse will be? (a) narration; (b) description; (c) exposition; (d) persuasion.

3. The main idea of the paragraph is that (a) children should not see *Dumbo*; (b) *Indiana Jones* does not take advantage of childhood traumas; (c) media critics are wrong to criticize Steven Spielberg movies; (d) *Dumbo* scares children because its terrors are too real, while *Indiana Jones and the Temple of Doom* is perceived by children as pure fantasy.

4. Which *two* methods of paragraph development are evident? (a) comparison; (b) definition; (c) example; (d) contrast; (e) process.

5. According to Kael, *Dumbo* exploits children's fears of (a) being teased or humiliated; (b) being abandoned by their mother; (c) being caught in a burning building; (d) being an outcast; (e) only a and b; (f) all of the above.

6. In sentence 4, Kael metaphorically describes Dumbo's tears as "elephant tears," suggesting that the tears were (a) insincere; (b) enormous; (c) embarrassing; (d) improbable.

7. The purpose of sentence 10 is to (a) restate Kael's main judgment about the difference between the two movies; (b) act as a conclusion; (c) provide a concrete illustration; (d) define key terms according to the way the author wants us to understand them.

C. Inferences   On the basis of the evidence in the paragraph, mark these statements as follows: *A* for accurate inferences, *I* for inaccurate inferences, and *IE* for insufficient evidence.

___ 1. The media criticized *Indiana Jones* for being too frightening.

___ 2. The "bad guys" in the movie *Dumbo* are humans.

___ 3. *Dumbo* could upset impressionable or sensitive children.

___ 4. Children know that the scary scenes in *Indiana Jones* aren't real.

___ 5. The rating for *Dumbo* should be changed to PG–13 (parental guidance recommended for children under thirteen).

___ 6. *Road to Morocco* and *The Thief of Baghdad* are also frightening, potentially psychologically damaging, films for children.

___ 7. The main character of *Dumbo* is a victim, not a hero.

___ 8. Grownups are upset by the banquet shown in *Indiana Jones* because they think it is disgusting.

PRACTICE ESSAY

Degrees Brix
John McPhee

John McPhee (1931–   ) is an American nonfiction writer who has been a staff writer for *The New Yorker* magazine since 1965, and Ferris Professor of Journalism at Princeton University since 1975. A writer whose careful style is a model for writers and readers alike, McPhee has turned his attention to a wide array of subjects. Examples include a little-known area of New Jersey called the Pine Barrens (*The Pine Barrens,* 1968); canoeing (*The Survival of the Bark Canoe,* 1975); Alaska (*Coming into the Country,* 1977); geology (*Basin and Range,* 1981); and the Swiss army (*La Place de la Concorde Suisse,* 1984). The following short essay is reprinted from his book *Oranges.* For the benefit of those of us who thought frozen orange juice was merely juice concentrated and then frozen, McPhee explains the process by which it is made. (MacDowell, referred to in the beginning of the selection, is Dr. Louis Gardner MacDowell, known in Florida as the inventor of concentrate. He is also the Director of Research for the Florida Citrus Commission.)

1   The enormous factories that the frozen people have built as a result of MacDowell's idea more closely resemble oil refineries than auto plants. The evaporators are tall assemblages of looping pipes, quite similar to the cat-cracking towers that turn crude oil into gasoline. When oranges arrive, in semitrailers, they are poured into giant bins, so that a plant can have a kind of reservoir to draw upon. At Minute Maid's plant in Auburndale, for example, forty bins hold four million oranges, or enough to keep the plant going for half a day. From samples analyzed by technicians who are employed by the State of Florida, the plant manager knows what the juice, sugar, and acid content is of the fruit in each bin, and blends the oranges into the assembly line accordingly, always attempting to achieve as uniform a product as possible. An individual orange obviously means nothing in this process, and the rise of concentrate has brought about a basic change in the system by which oranges are sold.

2   Growers used to sell oranges as oranges. They now sell "pounds-solids," and modern citrus men seem to use the term in every other sentence they utter. The rise of concentrate has not only changed the landscape and the language; it has, in a sense, turned the orange inside out. Because the concentrate plants are making a product of which the preponderant ingredient is sugar, it is sugar that they buy as raw material. They pay for the number of pounds of solids that come dissolved in the juice in each truckload of oranges, and these solids are almost wholly sugars. Growers now worry more about the number of pounds of sugar they are producing per acre than the quality of the individual oranges on their trees. If the concentrate plants bought oranges by weight alone, growers could plant, say, Hamlins on Rough Lemon in light sand—a scion, rootstock, and soil combination that will produce extremely heavy yields of insipid and watery oranges.

3   As the fruit starts to move along a concentrate plant's assembly line, it is first culled. In what some citrus people remember as "the old fresh-fruit days," before the Second World War, about forty per cent of all oranges grown in Florida were eliminated at packinghouses and dumped in fields. Florida milk tasted like orangeade. Now, with the exception of the split and rotten fruit, all of Florida's orange crop is used. Moving up a conveyor belt, oranges are scrubbed with detergent before they roll on into juicing machines. There are several kinds of juicing machines, and they are something to see. One is called the Brown Seven Hundred. Seven hundred oranges a minute go into it and are split and reamed on the same kind of rosettes that are in the centers

of ordinary kitchen reamers. The rinds that come pelting out the bottom are integral halves, just like the rinds of oranges squeezed in a kitchen. Another machine is the Food Machinery Corporation's FMC In-line Extractor. It has a shining row of aluminum jaws, upper and lower, with shining aluminum teeth. When an orange tumbles in, the upper jaw comes crunching down on it while at the same time the orange is penetrated from below by a perforated steel tube. As the jaws crush the outside, the juice goes through the perforations in the tube and down into the plumbing of the concentrate plant. All in a second, the juice has been removed and the rind has been crushed and shredded beyond recognition.

4   From either machine, the juice flows on into a thing called the finisher, where seeds, rag, and pulp are removed. The finisher has a big stainless-steel screw that steadily drives the juice through a fine-mesh screen. From the finisher, it flows on into holding tanks. Orange juice squeezed at home should be consumed fairly soon after it is expressed, because air reacts with it and before long produces a bitter taste, and the juice has fatty constituents that can become rancid. In the extractors, the finishers, and the troughs of concentrate plants, a good bit of air gets into the juice. Bacilli and other organisms may have started growing in it. So the juice has to be pasteurized. In some plants, this occurs before it is concentrated. In others, pasteurization is part of the vacuum-evaporating process—for example, in the Minute Maid plant in Auburndale, which uses the Thermal Accelerated Short Time Evaporator (T.A.S.T.E.). A great, airy network of bright-red, looping tubes, the Short Time stands about fifty feet high. Old-style evaporators keep one load of juice within them for about an hour, gradually boiling the water out. In the Short Time, juice flows in at one end in a continuous stream and comes out the other end eight minutes later.

5   Specific gravity, figured according to a special scale for sugar solutions, is the measurement of concentrate. The special scale, worked out by a nineteenth-century German scientist named Adolf F. W. Brix, is read in "degrees Brix." Orange juice as it comes out of oranges is usually about twelve degrees Brix—that is, for every hundred pounds of water there are twelve pounds of sugar. In the Short Time, orange juice passes through seven stages. At each stage, there are sampling valves. The juice at the start is plain, straightforward orange juice but with a notable absence of pulp or juice vesicles. By the third stage, the juice is up to nineteen degrees Brix and has the viscosity and heat of fairly thick hot chocolate. The flavor is rich and the aftertaste is clean. At the fifth stage, the juice is up to forty-six degrees Brix—already thicker than the ultimate product that goes into the six-ounce can—and it has the consistency of cough syrup, with a biting aftertaste. After the seventh stage, the orange juice can be as high as seventy degrees Brix. It is a deep apricot-orange in color. It is thick enough to chew, and its taste actually suggests apricot-flavored gum. Stirred into enough water to take it back to twelve degrees Brix, it tastes like nothing much but sweetened water.

6   As a season progresses, the sugar-acid ratio of oranges improves. Pineapple Oranges, at their peak, are better in this respect than Hamlins at theirs; and Valencias are the best of all. So the concentrators keep big

drums of out-of-season concentrate in cold-storage rooms and blend them with in-season concentrates in order to achieve even more uniformity. Advertisements can be misleading, however, when they show four or five kinds of oranges and imply that each can of the advertiser's concentrate contains an exact blend of all of them. It would be all but impossible to achieve that. The blending phase of the process is at best only an educated stab at long-term uniformity, using whatever happens to be on hand in the cold rooms and the fresh-fruit bins. The blending is, moreover, merely a mixing of old and new concentrates, still at sixty degrees Brix and still all but tasteless if reconstituted with water.

7   The most important moment comes when the cutback is poured in, taking the super-concentrated juice down to forty-five degrees Brix, which MacDowell and his colleagues worked out as a suitable level, because three cans of tap water seemed to be enough to thaw the juice fairly quickly but not so much that the cooling effect of the cold concentrate would be lost in the reconstituted juice. Cutback is mainly fresh orange juice, but it contains additional flavor essences, peel oil, and pulp. Among the components that get boiled away in the evaporator are at least eight hydrocarbons, four esters, fifteen carbonyls, and sixteen kinds of alcohol. The chemistry of orange juice is so subtle and complicated that most identifications are tentative, and no one can guess which components form its taste, let alone in what proportion. Some of these essences are recovered in condensation chambers in the evaporators, and they are put back into the juice. The chief flavoring element in cutback is d-limonene, which is the main ingredient of peel oil. The oil cells in the skins of all citrus fruit are ninety per cent d-limonene. It is d-limonene that burns the lips of children sucking oranges. D-limonene reddened the lips of the ladies of the seventeenth-century French court, who bit into limes for the purpose. D-limonene is what makes the leaves of all orange and grapefruit trees smell like lemons when crushed in the hand. D-limonene is what the Martini drinker rubs on the rim of his glass and then drops into his drink in a twist of lemon. The modern Martini drinker has stouter taste buds than his predecessors of the seventeenth century, when people in Europe used to spray a little peel oil on the outside of their wineglasses, in the belief that it was so strong that it would penetrate the glass and impart a restrained flavor to the wine. In the same century, peel oil was widely used in Germany in the manufacture of "preservative plaguelozenges." In the fourteenth century in Ceylon, men who dived into lakes to search the bottom for precious stones first rubbed their bodies with orange-peel oil in order to repel crocodiles and poisonous snakes. Peel oil is flammable. Peel oil is the principal flavoring essence that frozen people put into concentrated orange juice in order to attempt to recover the flavor of fresh orange juice. "We have always had the flavor of fresh oranges to come up against," MacDowell told me. "People who make things like tomato juice and pineapple juice have not had this problem."

8   Because of freezes and other variables, concentrate has its good and bad years. In the past decade, for example, the '55s and '59s were outstanding. The '60s and '63s were quite poor. The '58s were even worse. But the '64s

were memorable. Concentrate plants lay down samples in a kind of frozen reference library—one six-ounce can from each half hour of each day's run. The relative excellence of any given concentrate year is established by taste panels of citrus scientists, who stand in black-walled booths that are lighted by red light bulbs and drink concentrate from brandy snifters. They decide, variously, whether the taste is stale, insipid, immature, or overmature; too sour, too sweet, too bitter, or too astringent; whether it seems to have been overheated or to contain too much peel oil; and whether it suggests buttermilk, cardboard, castor oil, or tallow.

A. Compre-
hension

Choose the answer that best completes each statement. Do not refer to the selection while doing this exercise.

1. The one factor that accounts for the basic change in the way oranges have been sold since World War II is (a) improved varieties of oranges; (b) a rise in the production of concentrate; (c) an increase in frozen orange-juice consumption in the U.S.; (d) an increase in the average sugar content of oranges grown today.

2. When concentrate plant producers buy oranges, they pay for "pounds-solids," meaning the number of pounds of (a) juice per pound of oranges; (b) sugar dissolved in the juice; (c) water per pound of oranges; (d) d-limonene in the orange rind.

3. The extracting machines, which are used to squeeze out the juice from the oranges, also remove (a) the pulp; (b) the "rag"—the stringy central portion and membranelike walls of the fruit; (c) the entire rind; (d) the seeds; (e) all of the above.

4. Commercial orange juice must be pasteurized to make it (a) free of bacilli and other organisms; (b) have a uniform consistency; (c) have a smooth texture when it is reconstituted by the consumer; (d) taste sweet, since unpasteurized concentrate tastes bitter.

5. The term "twelve degrees Brix" means that for every one hundred pounds of water there are (a) twelve different varieties of oranges used; (b) twelve separate steps to make the final product; (c) twelve pounds of sugar; (d) twelve pounds of orange solids and juice.

6. Orange-juice concentrate at twelve degrees Brix tastes like (a) regular reconstituted frozen orange juice; (b) cough syrup; (c) apricot-flavored gum; (d) sweetened water.

7. In the frozen orange-juice industry, the term "blending" means (a) mixing old-season and new-season concentrates; (b) mixing the products of four or five kinds of juice from oranges with the highest sugar content; (c) mixing juice, rind, and coloring agents to produce juice whose color is actually orange; (d) mixing the juice from Pineapple Oranges, Hamlins, and Valencias to produce an acceptable product.

8. In an attempt to recover the flavor of fresh orange juice, concentrate makers add (a) actual fresh orange juice; (b) orange-flavor water; (c) orange-peel oil; (d) concentrate from 1964, the best year in the industry.

B. Inferences   On the basis of the evidence in the selection, mark these statements as follows: *A* for accurate inferences, *I* for inaccurate inferences, and *IE* for insufficient evidence. You may refer to the selection to answer the questions for this and for all the remaining exercises.

1. The apparatus for making orange-juice concentrate looks similar to that used in refining oil to make gasoline.
2. The amount of sugar in each truckload of oranges is more important than the quality of juice the oranges produce.
3. Growers sell oranges according to their weight.
4. Before World War II, Florida cows ate the oranges that were unsuitable for making juice.
5. The by-products of making concentrate—seeds, rag, and pulp—are sold to make flavoring essences.
6. Pasteurization prevents tuberculosis bacteria from growing in the concentrate.
7. The oranges with the highest sugar–acid ratio are produced at the beginning of the growing season.
8. Concentrate producers normally use only juice from Valencia oranges because of their high quality.
9. The purpose of adding "cutback" is to put the flavor of orange juice back into the concentrate.
10. Peel oil was considered to have the ability to ward off the plague in seventeenth-century Germany.
11. Tomato-juice and pineapple-juice producers do not have to contend with the problem of flavor as do orange-juice producers.
12. The frozen-juice reference library contains technical manuals and scientific articles helpful in making concentrate.

C. Structure   Choose the best answer.

1. McPhee's main purpose is to (a) trace the history of the citrus industry in Florida; (b) explain how today's frozen orange-juice concentrate is made; (c) explain the importance of frozen concentrate to Florida's economy; (d) define the term "degrees Brix."
2. The primary mode of discourse used by the author is (a) narration; (b) description; (c) exposition; (d) persuasion.
3. The method of development most evident in the selection as a whole is (a) example; (b) illustration; (c) process; (d) comparison; (e) contrast; (f) definition.
4. Look again at paragraph 3. The purpose of this paragraph is to (a) describe two different juicing machines; (b) explain which fruit is used and which is discarded; (c) discuss modern technology used in the frozen-juice business; (d) show how quickly the oranges are shredded.
5. The *two* methods of paragraph development most evident in paragraph 5 are (a) example; (b) comparison; (c) contrast; (d) process; (e) definition.

6. In terms of the ingredients that go into making frozen concentrate, the one McPhee goes into the most detail about is (a) the oranges; (b) d-limonene; (c) the pulp; (d) the sugar.

7. From the evidence in the selection, what can you infer about McPhee's opinion of frozen orange juice? (a) He thinks today's orange juice is marvelous. (b) He thinks today's orange juice lacks flavor. (c) He thinks today's orange juice has been ruined by sophisticated technology. (d) His opinion of today's orange juice is not evident.

8. According to the selection, the orange-juice concentrate business is (a) confusing; (b) complex; (c) boring; (d) profitable.

D. Vocabulary   For each italicized word from the selection, choose the best definition according to the context in which it appears.

1. *insipid* and watery oranges [paragraph 2]: (a) unpalatable; (b) lacking flavor; (c) sugary; (d) foul-tasting.

2. the fruit is *culled* [3]: (a) gathered; (b) scrubbed; (c) sorted according to quality, with the inferior oranges rejected; (d) separated into groups according to size.

3. the oranges are split and *reamed* [3]: (a) removed; (b) formed into a particular shape; (c) shredded; (d) squeezed to release the juice.

4. the juice has fatty *constituents* [4]: (a) component parts; (b) tiny vessels; (c) potentially unhealthy elements; (d) chemical compounds.

5. that can become *rancid* [4]: (a) excessively sweet; (b) oily; greasy; (c) disagreeable; rank; (d) cancer-causing.

6. the *viscosity* of fairly thick hot chocolate [5]: (a) sweet flavor; (b) thickness; stickiness; (c) texture; (d) taste.

7. thicker than the *ultimate* product [5]: (a) fundamental; (b) final; (c) first; (d) refined.

8. the chemistry of orange juice is so *subtle* [7]: (a) difficult to analyze or detect; (b) not immediately obvious; (c) mathematically complex; (d) clever; tricky.

9. most identifications are *tentative* [7]: (a) inaccurate; (b) hazardous; (c) impossible; (d) uncertain.

10. the modern Martini drinker has *stouter* taste buds [7]: (a) more powerful; (b) stronger; sturdier; (c) weaker; less well-developed; (d) more peculiar.

11. his *predecessors* of the seventeenth century [7]: those who (a) drink excessively; (b) set fashion trends; (c) come before in time; (d) can predict the future.

12. *impart* a restrained flavor [7]: (a) reveal; disclose; (b) bestow; confer; (c) hint at; suggest; (d) limit; inhibit.

13. the *relative* excellence of any given concentrate year [8]: (a) considered in comparison to something else; (b) well-established; firm; (c) constantly varying; changeable; (d) undisputed; unarguable.

14. the taste is too bitter, or too *astringent* [8]: (a) sweet; (b) sour; (c) tangy; (d) harsh.

chapter 3

‖ **MORE METHODS OF PARAGRAPH DEVELOPMENT**

In this chapter we will be concerned with three additional methods of paragraph development: (1) analysis and classification; (2) cause and effect; and (3) analogy. These methods are a bit more difficult to recognize than those you learned about in the previous chapter.

A. ANALYSIS AND CLASSIFICATION

Analysis and classification traditionally are considered together, for even though they are actually separate methods, their underlying purpose is the same. Both methods involve the author's taking apart a larger subject and examining its separate parts to determine how each contributes to the whole. In *classification,* the writer divides a group of things into *classes* or *types* in order to describe the distinguishing characteristics of each. If you read a paragraph that begins "There are three types of blind dates," or one that has as its topic sentence "There are five subspecies of fish called darters," you can expect the writer to use classification to develop the subject. In Chapter 1, the paragraph by Mortimer Adler on page 22 was developed by classification; you may recall that Adler classified book owners into three types, according to how thoroughly they had read their books.

In contrast to classification, which always involves a number of things grouped into categories, *analysis* is a means by which a writer examines a *single* subject by looking at its separate elements or parts in order to see how each element contributes to the whole. A political writer, for example, might analyze a presidential speech by separating the whole (that one speech) into its component parts—the key points, the president's delivery, his ease in handling the television medium, the reaction of the public to the ideas set forth, and so on. A writer on international affairs might use analysis to discuss the economic problems facing underdeveloped nations. A student writer might use analysis to do a close study of a poem in which each line is examined in relation to the overall meaning of the poem. The analytical method is evident in scientific research, for example, when a chemist seeks to determine the chemical analysis of a substance.

In the following paragraph from her biography of the composer, Mozart, Marcia Davenport applies classification to the society of eighteenth-century Salzburg, home of the Mozart family from 1771 to 1777. In classifying the social hierarchy, notice that she indulges in some humorous exaggeration to make her point. (Incidentally, the parenthetical references "(K. 385)" and

"(K. 250)" simply refer to numbers from a system devised by the musical historian Köchel, by which he listed chronologically all the works in Mozart's large body of music.)

The alignment of social rank was rather rigid. The archbishop and a few nobles of importance kept very much aloof. Just below them there was a group of minor nobles and gentlemen, all attached to the court. With these the Mozarts sometimes associated, but their real friends were among an even lower class—good, substantial townspeople, like Lorenz Hagenauer, the landlord, and the Haffner family for whose private celebrations Wolfgang wrote the lovely "Haffner" symphony (K. 385), and the equally beautiful serenade (K. 250), both in D major. Below this Mozartian social level there was the typical lower class of the eighteenth century, poor and uneducated, concerned only with the price of salt and the cost of sausage. The town and its habits were summed up in an observation that "the country gentlemen hunt and go to church; those next below them go to church and hunt; the next lower rank eat, drink, and pray; and the lowest of all pray, drink, and eat. The two latter classes conduct their love-affairs in public, the two former in private; all alike live in sensual indulgence."

Marcia Davenport,
Mozart

The next paragraph by Irving Howe, who has written a detailed account of the experience of the eastern Europeans who emigrated to America, analyzes the origins of anti-Semitic prejudice in the United States. In addition, Howe explains how historians have roughly classified Jewish immigrants into two groups: the "old" immigrants, who were from northern Europe, and the "new" group, who were from southern and eastern Europe. For that reason, this example illustrates well how analysis and classification often work together.

In the 1860's and 1870's, when cheap labor was needed by the railroads and both western and southern states were eager to absorb white settlers, American business interests sent special agents to Europe in order to attract immigrants. Popular sentiment remained attached to the notion that America was uniquely the land of refuge from tyranny and a country where fixed class lines gradually softened. Jews, to be sure, were already encountering social discrimination in the 1870's, some of it due to a feeling that the recent immigrants from Germany, unlike their refined Sephardic cousins who had been here for a long time, were too "loud" and "pushy" in their social ascent. For the most part, however, there was not yet any large-scale articulation of anti-Semitic prejudice, if only because the Jews did not yet figure in the popular imagination as a major force in American life. Only during the last two decades of the century did the multiplication of aliens come to seem a national problem. Historians of immigration have distinguished, with rough usefulness, between "old" and "new" immigrants, the former mostly from northern and the latter from southern and eastern Europe. Close in cultural style to Protestant Americans, the "old" immigrants seemed more easily assimilable and thereby less threatening than the "new." By the eighties and nineties the mass influx consisted largely of "new" immigrants, ill-educated and often illiterate peasants whose manner could unnerve native Americans. And most immigrant Jews were regarded as among the "new."

Irving Howe,
World of Our Fathers

B. CAUSE AND EFFECT

You might think of the cause-and-effect method of paragraph development as a way of finding *reasons* to explain events, problems, or issues, along with their *results*. Cause and effect refers to a logical relationship between ideas as well as to a method of paragraph development. Let's say that a writer wants to discuss the phenomenon of international terrorism. To examine this situation, he or she has two choices: To describe the phenomenon—the increasing use of terrorism by extremist groups, particularly in the Middle East, to achieve certain demands (the *effects*). Then the writer can examine the reasons (the *causes*) to explain *why* this phenomenon is becoming more prevalent. Further, the writer might return to the effect part of the relationship and examine the long-range effects on the international community if terrorism is not stopped. The other choice is to reverse the pattern, beginning with the reasons and ending with the effects.

Whichever comes first—cause or effect—it is important for you to understand that this method always involves the questioning *why,* either stated or implied. If you encounter a paragraph that begins "America's continued dependence on foreign oil poses serious economic problems for the future," you can predict that the writer will examine the probable economic consequences (the *effects*) of our dependence on foreign oil (the *cause*) even though no question is explicitly stated. Some words that indicate causes are *because, for, for the reason that,* or the chiefly British *owing to*; words indicating effects include *the result, the consequences,* and *the outcome,* to cite some examples. The cause–effect pattern can also be indicated by transitional (linking) devices, such as *consequently, as a result,* or *as a consequence.*

Examine carefully the relationship between the sentences in the following paragraph:

[1]Parents today appear to have much uncertainty about their roles as moral guides. [2]Part of this uncertainty is a reaction against the fear techniques that were employed in moral teaching in former generations. [3]Since today's parent does not wish to teach his child moral attitudes through threats or exaggerated horror or fearful warnings he seems afraid to show any moral reactions to his child as if he might then create excessive guilt feelings in the child. [4]This means that many parents who have firm moral beliefs about lying, stealing, murder and destruction fail

to transmit them to their children in a profound and meaningful way.
[5]Parents tolerate the moral lapses or even the absence of moral principles in their children way beyond the period when we can expect a child
to have incorporated moral values in his own personality.

Selma Fraiberg,
The Magic Years

Sentence 1, the topic sentence, states a situation or a problem: parents
are uncertain about how to give their children moral guidance. In other
words, sentence 1 begins with the *effect*. Sentence 2 states the *cause* of this
uncertainty: parents are reacting against their own, presumably strict,
upbringings. However, the effect–cause pattern is only implied. There are no
signposts or transitions to guide you. The careful reader has to infer that
the phrase at the beginning of sentence 2 ("Part of this uncertainty is a reaction . . .") is meant to suggest a cause to explain the problem. (Can you
think of any other reasons to account for parents' uncertainty? Do you
accept this as a reasonable cause?) And sentences 3, 4, and 5 examine further *effects* that are the direct result of what was stated in sentence 2. The
pattern of this paragraph, then, is effect–cause–more effects. If you learn to
analyze the relationship between ideas in this way, you will soon become
skilled not only at predicting what will follow a topic sentence, but also at
seeing the direction of the ideas in paragraphs or longer passages.

Let us look at one more cause–effect example. Irving Howe, to whom you
were introduced in a previous selection, explains in this paragraph the reasons that anti-immigrant feelings intensified at the end of the nineteenth
century. Notice that the main idea (the *effect*) is stated in the last sentence
(the alien "hordes" represented a threat to the Americans' well-being). The
body of the paragraph cites the *causes* of their prejudice.

Remember to look up any words that are unfamiliar to you.

It would be an error to suppose that anti-immigrant feelings were confined to a single social class or political outlook. Brahmins and rednecks,
bourgeois and proletarians, reactionaries and populists—all joined the
outcry against the intruders. The one constant was that the outbreak of a
depression, something that occurred with distressing frequency during
the eighties and nineties, meant both a drop in the number of immigrants and a rise in sentiment against them. These were hard years in
American society: unsettled by the consequences of rapid industrializa-
tion and uncontrolled urbanization, tormented by incomprehensible economic collapses, haunted by the fear that the country, as it moved away
from the age of the independent farmer, might come to take on the social
bitterness of Europe. The "new" immigrants, helpless in urban slums,
seemed to many native Americans both symptom and cause of a spread-
ing social malaise. Could they be expected to honor the democratic outlook of the Founding Fathers? Would they not disdain the traditions of
individualism on which the nation had thrived? Were they not hopelessly
marred by ignorance, dependence, superstition? If so enlightened a public
figure as Henry George could write in 1883, "What in a few years more,

are we to do for a dumping-ground? Will it make our difficulty the less that our human garbage can vote?"—if so humane an intellectual could speak in this way, it need come as no surprise that mere editorialists and common folk began to look upon the alien "hordes" as a threat to their well-being.

Irving Howe,
World of Our Fathers

C. ANALOGY

Analogy, the last method of development, is perhaps the most difficult for readers to perceive. An analogy is an *extended metaphor,* that is, an imaginative comparison between two unlike things that helps to make clear the real subject at hand, or that provides a fresh way to look at a subject. A writer might, for instance, explain the workings of the human heart in terms of a more familiar object—a pump. The human eye is often compared, by means of analogy, to a camera. Another writer, wanting to describe someone's dissatisfaction with his or her job, might imaginatively compare that person's boss to a nagging spouse, thereby serving to heighten the impact of the real subject. The important point to remember is that an analogy is a *sustained* metaphor, since the comparison is extended throughout a paragraph or occasionally throughout a longer piece. (Analogies also can be misused; see *False Analogy* in the section on logical fallacies in Part 2, p. 186).

In the following paragraph, Christopher Rand uses an analogy—describing a city as if it were a machine—to explain the intricate workings of Los Angeles:

One way to view Los Angeles is as a machine. All modern cities are machines, but L.A. is more so than the others. It is a humming, smoking, ever-changing contraption, with mechanics incessantly working at it, trying to make improvements and to get the bugs out. Being a populous near-desert, it depends crucially on imported water. It is also under threat from floods, fires, and earthquakes, to which its technological daring makes it especially vulnerable. Because of its scatteredness, furthermore, it is concerned, day in and day out, with keeping a transport system moving at high speed. And finally it must deal with the waste products, the smog, and other obscenities, that its operations throw off.

Christopher Rand,
Los Angeles: The Ultimate City

In the next example, by playing with the analogy of language as a living thing, John Simon, a noted drama critic and writer on language who has an acerbic sense of humor, criticizes English speakers' insistence on saying *between you and I* instead of the correct *between you and me.* (How would you characterize Simon's tone—his emotional attitude toward the ordinary speaker of English—in this passage?)

Why does language keep changing? Because it is a living thing, people will tell you. Something that you cannot press forever, like a dead flower, between the pages of a dictionary. Rather, it is a living organism that, like a live plant, sprouts new leaves and flowers. Alas, this lovely albeit trite image is—as I have said before and wish now to say with even greater emphasis—largely nonsense. Language, for the most part, changes out of ignorance.

Certainly new words can become needed, and a happy invention or slang can sometimes supply useful, though usually perishable, synonyms. But by and large, linguistic changes are caused by the ignorance of speakers and writers, and in the last few centuries—given our schools, dictionaries, and books on grammar—such ignorance could have been, like the live nettle or poison ivy it is, uprooted. It is, or ought to be, possible to stop—or at least considerably delay—unnecessary change, of which one of the most preposterous and nefarious examples is the recently proliferating but still weedable *between you and I.*

To get back, however, to our initial botanical analogy: let us concede that language is indeed a living plant—a rhododendron, say. Well, a rhododendron can be depended on to sprout rhododendron leaves and rhododendron flowers as long as there is life in it. At no point will it start sprouting petunia blooms or *Ficus* leaves. Then why in the name of the living plant, or the living God, should we, after centuries of *between you and me,* switch to *between you and I?*

John Simon,
"Just Between Us," *Paradigms Lost*

The difficulty posed by the use of analogies is that it is easy to confuse the terms of the analogy. In the Rand paragraph, the subject is the city of Los Angeles, *not* machines. Simon's subject is language—or more specifically, a linguistic error he finds especially distressing—*not* gardening.

D. COMBINATION OF METHODS

Finally, you should recognize that, like life's problems for which there are seldom easy answers, the task of reading is a similarly complex one. Not all paragraphs can be as neatly categorized as the ones you have looked at so far. Although some writers use an easily recognizable method of paragraph development, not every one does. Within an essay or article, there are likely to be several different methods of development in evidence, as well as some paragraphs that use a combination of methods. The following paragraph is a good example of writing that employs a mix of the methods you have studied so far:

[1]The most common complicated sight a baby sees after birth is his mother's face, not as a still object in one plane, like a photograph, but as a dynamic and continually moving object with varied expressions and different associated contexts such as food and warmth. [2]How soon does a

baby come to distinguish his mother's face from others? [3]Genevieve Carpenter of the Behavior Development Research Unit at St. Mary's Hospital in London sat two-week-old babies in supportive chairs and, when they were alert, presented each with either his mother's face or the face of a woman the baby had never seen before in a framed opening in front of him. [4]She observed the babies' general behavior, where they looked, and for how long. [5]At two weeks the babies spent more time looking at their mothers' faces than they did at the strangers' faces. [6]In fact, when they were presented with the other women's faces, they frequently showed strong gaze aversion, looking right away, almost over their shoulders. [7]This kind of withdrawal suggests that the babies found the stimulus too intense or too novel.

Aidan MacFarlane,
"What a Baby Knows"

Though not really a topic sentence governing the information in the rest of the paragraph, sentence 1 states the subject—how a baby perceives its mother's face. Note that MacFarlane *defines* the baby's perception by using contrast ("not as a still object . . . but as . . ."). Sentence 2 poses a question, one that the author will presumably attempt to answer (using *analysis*). This question also appears to be the main idea of the paragraph. Sentences 3 through 6 answer the question by describing a *process:* a hospital experiment conducted to determine whether two-week-old babies could distinguish their mothers' faces from those of strangers. Sentence 6 also suggests an *effect*—the babies' reaction (gaze aversion) when they were confronted with strange faces. Sentence 7 presents a tentative *cause,* a reason for their reacting this way. In other words, MacFarlane relies on a combination of methods, rather than just one, to explore the main idea.

E. UNITY AND COHERENCE IN PARAGRAPHS

The methods of development we have studied thus far represent not only *kinds of evidence* that the writer uses to prove or support the main idea, but also *patterns of logical thinking.* When you read paragraphs, you probably do not have much difficulty following the direction of the ideas—unless, of course, the passage deals with very difficult subject matter or contains many unfamiliar words. Whether a writer uses one method of development or several, a good writer is careful to help the reader follow the main idea by ensuring that the paragraph has *unity*—that is, singleness of purpose. Every sentence in the paragraph should relate to the topic sentence. (In the same way, in an essay every paragraph should develop, support, and relate to the main idea or thesis statement.)

Besides having unity, well-constructed paragraphs and essays also have *coherence,* which literally means "sticking together." In prose writing, coherence means the logical relationship between each sentence in a paragraph (or between the paragraphs in an essay). At first glance, it may seem that studying the ways in which writers achieve coherence may be more appropriate in a composition course than in a reading course. However, seeing the methods by which writers link ideas logically is not only useful, it may be crucial to your accurate understanding of a passage. Sometimes your correct understanding of a passage may depend on a seemingly unimportant little word such as *but* or *yet.*

Repetition of Key Words and Phrases   Writers often repeat key words or phrases to achieve both unity and coherence, as well as to make it easier for the reader to follow the progression of ideas. To illustrate, read the following paragraph which has been printed twice, first as it was originally published, and second with key words and phrases italicized.

[1]Taste and smell are also affected by aging, but their changes are less understood and appreciated. [2]People who are in contact with the elderly will tell you that they have two major complaints—food and their children. [3]The complaint about food is easily explained when one considers how the taste buds work. [4]Distributed over the tongue, they last no longer than a few days each and then are replaced. [5]In keeping with the general slowing-down process, they are renewed more slowly than they are used up. [6]This means that the total number of effective taste buds declines, and, therefore, food tastes less savory. [7]Extensive dentures that cover a large portion of the oral cavity diminish the perception of taste even further. [8]In addition, there is the close interrelationship between smell and taste. [9]Anyone who has ever had a cold can testify to the fact that while the cold lasts, not only is the sense of smell reduced, but food loses its taste as well. [10]There is a similar deterioration in the sense of smell as a result of the process of aging.

Olga Knopf,
Successful Aging

[1]*Taste and smell* are also affected by *aging,* but *their* changes are less understood and appreciated. [2]People who are in contact with *the elderly* will tell you that they have two major *complaints—food* and their children. [3]The *complaint about food* is easily explained when one considers how *the taste buds* work. [4]Distributed over the tongue, *they* last no longer than a few days each and then are replaced. [5]In keeping with the general slowing-down process, *they* are renewed more slowly than *they* are used up. [6]This means that the total number of *effective taste buds declines,* and, therefore, *food tastes less savory.* [7]Extensive dentures that cover a large portion of the oral cavity *diminish the perception of taste* even further. *In addition,* there is the close interrelationship between *smell and taste.* [9]Anyone who has ever had a cold can testify to the fact that while the cold lasts, not only is *the sense of smell reduced,* but *food loses its taste* as well. [10]There is a *similar deterioration in the sense of smell* as a result of the *process of aging.*

Notice that the italicized words and phrases serve to keep you on track:

The key ideas (aging, diminished taste, loss of taste buds, and the relationship between taste and smell) are restated frequently enough to render the paragraph quite easy to read.

Transitions

Sclp 104 -

Clearly, repeating key words and phrases has the dual function of providing coherence and unity. But just as important to the reader are the signposts or markers called *transitions* that writers use to indicate either a logical progression or a shift in direction. In the Knopf paragraph above, *therefore* in the middle of sentence 6 signals that the clause at the end of the sentence is a conclusion drawn from the first part. And the transitional phrase *in addition* was italicized in sentence 8 because it has an important function—to alert the reader that the author is going to present another reason to explain the decline in the ability to taste among old people. Careful attention to transitional devices does a great deal to improve your reading comprehension.

To show you how crucial these devices are, here is a paragraph by George Orwell printed without the transitions:

After getting into the water the toad concentrates on building up his strength by eating small insects. He has swollen to his normal size again. He goes through a phase of intense sexiness. All he knows, at least if he is a male toad, is that he wants to get his arms round something. If you offer him a stick, or even your finger, he will cling to it with surprising strength and take a long time to discover that it is not a female toad. One comes upon shapeless masses of ten or twenty toads rolling over and over in the water, one clinging to another without distinction of sex. They sort themselves out into couples, with the male duly sitting on the female's back. You can distinguish males from females. The male is smaller, darker, and sits on top, with his arms tightly clasped round the female's neck. The spawn is laid in long strings which wind themselves in and out of the reeds and soon become invisible. The water is alive with masses of tiny tadpoles which rapidly grow larger, sprout hind legs, then forelegs, then shed their tails. The new generation of toads, smaller than one's thumbnail but perfect in every particular, crawl out of the water to begin the game anew.

Obviously, something is wrong here; reading this paragraph is like reading a novel with every tenth page missing, or like trying to put a bicycle together when the manufacturer has left out all the screws you need. It just does not hold together, and the sentences sound monotonous and choppy. Here is the actual version, this time printed with the transitions restored and italicized, making it much less tedious to read.

For a few days after getting into the water the toad concentrates on building up his strength by eating small insects. *Presently* he has swollen to his normal size again, *and then* he goes through a phase of intense sexiness. All he knows, at least if he is a male toad, is that he wants to get his arms round something, *and* if you offer him a stick, or even your finger, he will cling to it with surprising strength and take a long time to discover that it is not a female toad. *Frequently* one comes upon shapeless masses of ten or twenty toads rolling over and over in the water, one clinging to another without distinction of sex. *By degrees, however,* they sort themselves out into couples, with the male duly sitting on the female's back. You can *now* distinguish males from females, *because* the male is smaller, darker and sits on top, with his arms tightly clasped round the female's neck. *After a day or two* the spawn is laid in long strings which wind themselves in and out of the reeds and soon become invisible. *A few more weeks, and* the water is alive with masses of tiny tadpoles which rapidly grow larger, sprout hind legs, then forelegs, then shed their tails: *and finally, about the middle of the summer,* the new generation of toads, smaller than one's thumbnail but perfect in every particular, crawl out of the water to begin the game anew.

George Orwell,
"Some Thoughts on the Common Toad"

You will study transitions in greater detail in Chapter 4.

EXERCISES

Selection 1

¹The season of hibernating begins quite early for some of the creatures of outdoors. ²It is not alone the cold which causes it; there are a multiplicity of other factors—diminishing food supply; increased darkness as the fall days shorten; silence—frequently decisive. ³Any or all of these may be the signal for entrance into the Long Sleep, depending upon the habits and make-up of the particular creature. ⁴Among skunks, it is usually the coming of the cold that sends them, torpid, to their root-lined underground burrows; but many other mammals (for instance, ground squirrels) begin to grow drowsy when the fall sun is still warm on their furry backs and the food supply is not at all diminished. ⁵This ground-squirrel kind of hibernating, independent of the weather and the food supply, may be an old race habit, an instinctual behavior pattern like the unaccountable migrations of certain birds. ⁶Weather, food, inheritance, darkness—all of these obscurely play their parts in bringing on the annual subsidence into what one biologist has called "the little death." ⁷Investigation of the causes will need a good many years before they can be understood, for in captivity, where observation is more easy than in the wild, the hibernators often do not sleep at all.

Alan Devoe,
"The Animals Sleep," *Lives Around Us*

A. Vocabulary   For each italicized word from the paragraph, choose the best definition according to the context in which it appears.

1. *multiplicity* [sentence 2]: (a) a small number; (b) a large number; (c) an uncountable number; (d) an infinite number.

2. *torpid* [4]: (a) yawning; (b) lazy; (c) chilly; (d) inactive.

3. *unaccountable* [5]: (a) mysterious; (b) not responsible; (c) incomprehensible; (d) unable to be counted.

4. *subsidence* [6]: The process of (a) migrating; (b) making an appearance; (c) returning to normalcy; (d) becoming less active.

B. Content and Structure

Choose the best answer.

1. The mode of discourse in this paragraph is (a) narration; (b) description; (c) exposition; (d) persuasion.

2. Answer in your own words: What is the subject of this paragraph?

   The Hibernation because ____

   What does Devoe want us to understand about this subject?

   They are many factors that creates the process of Hibernation

3. Look at sentence 2. What is the relationship between the phrase "a multiplicity of other factors" and the phrases "diminishing food supply"; "increased darkness as the fall days shorten"; and "silence" which follow it? (a) definition of key terms; (b) cause–effect; (c) steps in a process; (d) examples of a general idea; (e) transitional devices.

4. Which *two* methods of paragraph development does Devoe use? (a) cause–effect; (b) analogy; (c) example; (d) definition; (e) process; (f) comparison.

5. With respect to the term "hibernation," the phrases "the little death" and "the Long Sleep" represent (a) technical or scientific terms; (b) dictionary definitions; (c) phrases that are synonyms; (d) phrases that are antonyms.

6. Look again at sentence 3. To what does the pronoun "these" refer, in the phrase "any or all of these"?

   (factors) that cause the Hibertation of the animals

7. Consider sentence 5. What is the connection between the reason groundsquirrels hibernate and the migration of certain birds? They are (a) similar; (b) different; (c) unusual; (d) bizarre; (e) incomprehensible.

8. In sentence 6, Devoe repeats the key terms "weather, food, inheritance, darkness," which were mentioned earlier in the paragraph. What does this repetition contribute to the paragraph as a whole? (a) paragraph development; (b) proof for the main idea; (c) paragraph unity; (d) transitions between ideas, signaling a shift in topic.

9. Consider again the word "obscurely" as it is used in sentence 6. Below are dictionary definitions for the adjectival forms of *obscure*. Which one best fits the context? (a) partially or altogether deficient in light; gloomy; (b) dingy; dull; (c) indistinctly heard; faint; (d) out of sight; hidden; (e) inconspicuous; unnoticed; (f) of undistinguished or humble descent, station, or reputation; (g) imperfectly known or understood.

10. As it is used in sentence 7, what does the transitional word "for" mean? (a) but; (b) for the purpose of; (c) for example; (d) because; (e) therefore.

C. Inferences   On the basis of the evidence in the paragraph, mark these statements as follows: *A* for accurate inferences, *I* for inaccurate inferences, and *IE* for insufficient evidence.

sentence 3

___I___ 1. All of the factors mentioned—diminishing food supply, increased darkness, silence—must be present for an animal to begin hibernation.

___I___ 2. All animals that hibernate follow a similar pattern, beginning in early fall and continuing until spring.

the are in the zoo don't

___I___ 3. All mammals hibernate in some way or other.

___A___ 4. Any one of several factors, or a combination of them, can trigger hibernation, depending on the species.

___IE___ 5. Humans are the only mammals that do not hibernate.

___A___ 6. The stimulus leading to hibernation may be an instinctive trait, independent of external factors.

___I___ 7. One cause of hibernation that remains constant for all species is the onset of cold weather.

___IE___ 8. The term "the Long Sleep" was what Native Americans called hibernation.

___A___ 9. Zoo animals often do not hibernate.

why not I?

_____ 10. The mysteries of why and how animals hibernate have now been solved.

Selection 2   [1]What has the telephone done to us, or for us, in the hundred years of its existence? [2]A few effects suggest themselves at once. [3]It has saved lives by getting rapid word of illness, injury, or famine from remote places. [4]By joining with the elevator to make possible the multistory residence or office bulding, it has made possible—for better or worse—the modern city. [5]By bringing about a quantum leap in the speed and ease with which information moves from place to place, it has greatly accelerated the rate of scientific and technological change and growth in industry. [6]Beyond doubt it has crippled if not killed the ancient art of letter writing. [7]It has made living alone possible for persons with normal social impulses; by so doing, it has played a role in one of the greatest social changes of this century, the breakup of the multigenerational household. [8]It has made the waging of war chillingly more efficient than formerly. [9]Perhaps (though not provably) it has prevented wars that might have arisen out of international misunderstanding caused by written communication. [10]Or perhaps—again not provably—by magnifying and extending irrational personal conflicts based on voice contact, it has caused wars. [11]Certainly it has extended the scope of human conflicts, since it impartially disseminates the useful knowledge of scientists and the babble of bores, the affection of the affectionate and the malice of the malicious.

John Brooks,
Telephone: The First Hundred Years

A. Vocabulary   For each italicized word from the paragraph, choose the best definition according to the context in which it appears.

1. *a quantum leap* [5]: (a) a slowly evolving change; (b) an abrupt change; (c) an application of a physical law; (d) an immeasurable calculation.

2. *impulses* [7]: (a) whims; sudden urges; (b) irrational notions; (c) tendencies; (d) events.

3. *impartially* [11]: (a) unjustly; (b) in the same way; (c) in an unbiased manner; (d) only partly.

4. *disseminates* [11]: (a) spreads; (b) gathers; (c) publishes; (d) transmits.

5. *malice* [11]: (a) kindness; (b) illegal act; (c) criticism; (d) ill will.

B. Content and Structure   Choose the best answer.

1. The mode of discourse in this paragraph is (a) narration; (b) description; (c) exposition; (d) persuasion.

2. The author's specific purpose is (a) to convince us of the telephone's usefulness; (b) to explain the effects the telephone has had on our society; (c) to examine the reasons the telephone has changed from being a luxury to an indispensable necessity; (d) to trace popular attitudes toward the telephone.

3. Which two sentences best express the main idea? Sentences ___1___ and ___2___.

4. The method of development used in the paragraph is (a) analogy; (b) process; (c) cause–effect; (d) analysis; (e) illustration.

5. In sentence 1, Brooks writes, "What has the telephone done *to us,* or *for us,* in the hundred years of its existence?" The italicized words reveal that the author will be concerned chiefly with (a) examples and illustrations; (b) interesting, engaging anecdotes; (c) specific as well as general statements; (d) advantages and disadvantages.

6. Look again at sentence 7. Which of the following is the best definition for the adjective "greatest" as Brooks uses it? (a) most remarkable or wonderful; (b) most significant or important; (c) most extensive in time or distance; (d) most superior in quality.

7. Label each sentence listed below as follows: *F* for a favorable result, *U* for an unfavorable result, and *B* for a result that is both favorable and unfavorable.

   sentence 3 __F__   sentence 8 ___U___
   sentence 4 __B__   sentence 9 ___F___
   sentence 5 __F__   sentence 10 __U__
   sentence 6 __U__   sentence 11 __B__
   sentence 7 __B__

8. Look again at the answer you wrote for sentence 7 in question 7 above.

What *judgment* can you make about the breakup of the multigenerational household? Is it a positive or a negative effect? What factors influenced your answer? *the judgments depends on the value on elderson multigenerational househdds, which depends on ones socio economics a ethnic group*

9. What is the relationship between sentences 9 and 10? (a) argument and supporting evidence; (b) cause–effect; (c) contrast; (d) two definitions of the same term.

why not c?

10. What is Brooks's attitude toward the telephone? It is (a) probably more favorable than unfavorable; (b) probably more unfavorable than favorable; (c) completely neutral, balanced between favorable and unfavorable; (d) not evident from the paragraph.

C. Inferences   On the basis of the evidence in the paragraph, mark these statements as follows: *A* for accurate inferences, *I* for inaccurate inferences, and *IE* for insufficient evidence.

_IE_ 1. The telephone is the most useful invention of the last one hundred years.

_A_ 2. The telephone has been only one influence that caused the breakup of the multigenerational home.

_A_ 3. The multistory residence or office building would have been impossible without the telephone.

look up sentence (4)

_IE_ 4. The telephone was invented before the elevator.

_I_ 5. No one writes letters any more.

_I_ 6. Misunderstandings about critical subjects, like war, are more likely to occur with the telephone than with written communication.

Selection 3   [1]The Gudgers' house, being young, only eight years old, smells a little dryer and cleaner, and more distinctly of its wood, than an average white tenant house, and it has also a certain odor I have never found in other such houses: aside from these sharp yet slight subtleties, it has the odor or odors which are classical in every thoroughly poor white southern country house, and by which such a house could be identified blindfold in any part of the world, among no matter what other odors. [2]It is compacted of many odors and made into one, which is very thin and light on the air, and more subtle than it can seem in analysis, yet very sharply and constantly noticeable. [3]These are its ingredients. [4]The odor of pine lumber, wide thin cords of it, heated in the sun, in no way doubled or insulated, in closed and darkened air. [5]The odor of woodsmoke, the fuel being again mainly pine, but in part also, hickory, oak, and cedar. [6]The odors of cooking. [7]Among these, most strongly, the odors of fried salt pork and of fried and boiled pork lard, and second, the odor of cooked corn. [8]The odors of sweat in many stages of age and freshness, this sweat being a distillation of pork, lard, corn, woodsmoke, pine, and ammonia.

mixture describe the odor

analysis of the odors

intricate analysis

[9]The odors of sleep, of bedding and of breathing, for the ventilation is poor. [10]The odors of all the dirt that in the course of time can accumulate in a quilt and mattress. [11]Odors of staleness from clothes hung or stored away, not washed. [12]I should further describe the odor of corn: in sweat, or on the teeth, and breath, when it is eaten as much as they eat it, it is of a particular sweet stuffy fetor,* to which the nearest parallel is the odor of the yellow excrement of a baby. [13]All these odors as I have said are so combined into one that they are all and always present in balance, not at all heavy, yet so searching that all fabrics of bedding and clothes are saturated with them, and so clinging that they stand softly out of the fibers of newly laundered clothes. [14]Some of their components are extremely 'pleasant,' some are 'unpleasant'; their sum total has great nostalgic power. [15]When they are in an old house, darkened, and moist, and sucked into all the wood, and stacked down on top of years of a moldering and old basis of themselves, as at the Ricketts', they are hard to get used to or even hard to bear. [16]At the Woods', they are blowsy and somewhat moist and dirty. [17]At the Gudgers', as I have mentioned, they are younger, lighter, and cleaner-smelling. [18]There too, there is another and special odor, very dry and edged: it is somewhere between the odor of very old newsprint and of a Victorian bedroom in which, after long illness, and many medicines, someone has died and the room has been fumigated, yet the odor of dark brown medicines, dry-bodied sickness, and staring death, still is strong in the stained wallpaper and in the mattress.

James Agee and Walker Evans,
Let Use Now Praise Famous Men

A. Vocabulary

For each italicized word from the paragraph, choose the best definition according to the context in which it appears.

1. *subtleties* [1]: (a) things so slight as to be difficult to detect; (b) contrasts; (c) unusual characteristics; (d) things that cannot be touched; intangibles.

2. *compacted* [2]: (a) solidly or firmly built; (b) designed to be small in size; (c) arranged within a small space; (d) closely and firmly united.

3. *distillation* [8]: (a) combination; (b) purified form; essence; (c) natural by-product; (d) chemical reaction.

4. *components* [14]: (a) devices; (b) odors; (c) constituent parts; (d) basic characteristics.

5. *nostalgic* [14]: (a) romantic; (b) referring to a longing for what is past; (c) describing something magic or unexplainable; (d) describing the unattainable; what one cannot have.

6. *moldering* [15]: (a) decaying; crumbling; (b) moldy; mildewed; (c) darkening; becoming obscured; (d) saturated; absorbing.

7. *fumigated* [18]: (a) sealed off; (b) thoroughly cleaned; (c) uninhabited; (d) disinfected.

---

*[Pronounced fē′tər] an exceptionally strong, offensive odor.

B. Content and Structure

Choose the best answer.

1. The mode of discourse in this paragraph is (a) narration; (b) description; (c) exposition; (d) persuasion.

2. Agee's specific purpose is to (a) describe the odors in one tenant farmer's house; (b) describe the way white tenant farmers live; (c) examine the economic situation of tenant-farmer families; (d) characterize his first impression upon entering a tenant farmer's house.

3. Agee combines two methods of development: (a) comparison and contrast; (b) example and illustration; (c) cause–effect and process; (d) analysis and classification.

4. Which sentence offers the best clue for the answer to question 3? Sentence ___3___.

5. The word *classical,* as it is used in sentence 1, means (a) ordinary; (b) subtle; (c) standard; (d) nostalgic.

6. The two sentences that unify the paragraph by restating the main idea are __13__ and __17__.

restate no 2

7. Agee characterizes the various odors at the Gudgers' house as (a) unpleasant; (b) pleasant; (c) capable of arousing a feeling of nostalgia; (d) sharp and distinct.

8. The word "blowsy," in sentence 16, is usually used to describe someone's appearance. What meaning do you think Agee intends the word to have in this context? _____

C. Inferences

On the basis of the evidence in the paragraph, mark these statements as follows: *A* for accurate inferences, *I* for inaccurate inferences, and *IE* for insufficient evidence.

__IE__ 1. The author stayed with the Gudgers for several weeks.

__IE__ 2. The author grew up in a house very much like the one the Gudgers lived in.

__A__ 3. The Gudgers, the Ricketts, and the Woods are all poor white southern families.

__A__ 4. The Gudgers' house is newer and cleaner than the average tenant farmer's house.   *the staple food is corn —*

__I__ 5. Potatoes are a staple food in the Gudgers' diet.

__A__ 6. The author found the odors in the Ricketts' house repugnant.

Selection 4

[1]Like silkworms munching mulberry leaves, we consumed, we little Shillingtonians, the school building, which had six classrooms on each of its two main floors. [2]Divided into the A and B classes, of about thirty each, we moved to the front of the building for the first grade, back to the middle for the second, and to the rear for the third, then straight upstairs to the fourth grade, forward to the fifth, and forward again to the sixth, the A section of which was taught by the immaculate, stern, gray-haired

elementary-school principal, Mr. Dickinson. [3]Afterthis grade, there was nothing left to do but fly through the windows onto Lancaster Avenue and east up the street toward Reading, past the five-sided corner, to the orange-brick high school, which held six grades, seventh through twelfth. [4]As a structure, it lacked the compactness and logic of the elementary school; the adamant distinction between the A's and the B's broke down into diversified "courses" (college prep, business), and long rows of lockers in the halls symbolized anarchic new stretches of possibility and freedom. [5]The A/B distinction, like the sheep/goats distinction anticipated in the Bible, was a hard one, and was especially hard on those on the borderline: a pair of male twins, as their marks fluctuated, were in and out of the A section via a kind of revolving door, now one and now the other and now neither. [6]And another boy, whom I got to know in high school, felt the old onus of being a B with such force that he eventually compensated by becoming a vice-president of the New York Stock Exchange. [7]The A's had the same side of the building as the girls' playground; the playground encircled the building like an asphalt moat, and the boys' and girls' sides were demarcated by the broad cement walks that led up to the front and back portals. [8]Even to chase a soccer ball into the girls' side was something of a sin, occasioning a flurry of shrieks. [9]So, male and female, A and B, we were divided up, and forbidden trespass; on the other hand, we all came from Shillington, a unique square mile of global surface, and thus we were united against the world: against Mohnton on the one side and Kenhorst on the other, against Wyomissing and Birdsboro, against the grade ahead of us (in which a number of our girls later found boyfriends) and the grade behind (which was to supply some of us boys with girlfriends), and, from the third grade on, against Japan and Germany. [10]Mountains of flattened tin cans and salvaged rubber in a corner of the boys' playground and a new hierarchy of prizes and mock-military rankings among the class leaders were easily assimilated into the preëxistent order of bells and birthdays and field days and of class photographs late in May, on the back school steps, which came to join the treasure of lost time in my mother's shoeboxes.

John Updike,
"A Soft Spring Night in Shillington"

A. Vocabulary For each italicized word from the paragraph, choose the best definition according to the context in which it appears.

1. *adamant* [4]: (a) traditional; (b) inflexible; (c) unintelligible; (d) capable of modification.

2. *anarchic* [4]: (a) unimaginable; (b) lacking control or order; (c) undemocratic; (d) privileged.

3. *fluctuated* [5]: (a) gradually improved; (b) deteriorated; (c) balanced out; (d) rose and fell.

4. *via* [5]: (a) on the road to; (b) by way of; (c) in the same fashion as; (d) because of.

5. *onus* [6]: (a) burden; stigma; (b) tradition; custom; (c) privilege; special advantage; (d) duty; responsibility.

6. *compensated* [6]: (a) substituted; (b) made up for; (c) became victorious; (d) retaliated; sought revenge.

7. *demarcated* [7]: (a) carefully laid out; (b) shown; represented; (c) clearly separated; (d) discriminated against.

8. *portals* [7]: (a) buildings; (b) playing fields; (c) doors; entrances; (d) lecture halls.

9. *hierarchy* [10]: (a) classification by rank; (b) treasure chest; (c) style; fashion; (d) era; period in time.

10. *assimilated* [10]: (a) transformed; altered; (b) incorporated; absorbed; (c) modeled; shaped; (d) valued more highly.

B. Content and Structure

Choose the best answer.

1. Mark any of the following that describe Updike's purpose in this paragraph: (a) to praise the Shillington educational system for its high standards; (b) to explain the organization of the elementary and high schools; (c) to describe a typical high-school student's social life during that era; (d) to explain the distinction between the A/B classes in elementary school; (e) to show how Shillingtonian youngsters viewed themselves in relation to the outside world.

2. Updike begins the paragraph with a metaphor by which he compares his elementary school classmates to "silkworms munching mulberry leaves." What does he mean by this metaphor? *Silworm will consume all the leave and classmates will take advantage of the chill the classes —*

3. In sentence 3, Updike uses the verb "fly" to describe the move from elementary to high school. What do you think he means to suggest? *That mean they couldn't wait to get into High school + upward movements.*

4. In explaining the division of students into A and B groups, Updike uses (a) definition; (b) classification; (c) comparison; (d) analogy; (e) cause–effect.

5. The basis for separating the lower-school grades into A and B groups was according to (a) parents' requests; (b) the teachers' and the principal's recommendations; (c) the students' grades; (d) pure whim on the part of the school's administration.

6. Updike uses the adjective "hard" in sentence 5 in two different ways. Consider the following definitions and match the one that seems appropriate to each context. (a) resistant to pressure; (b) rigorous; stringent; (c) stern; callous; (d) difficult to accomplish; (e) difficult to understand or endure; (f) cruel; oppressive; unjust.
   "The A/B distinction . . . was a *hard* one"
      definition ___d___
   ". . . and was especially *hard* on those on the borderline"
      definition ___f___

7. Which best describes the purpose of sentence 9? (a) to show the students' growing interest in members of the opposite sex; (b) to show the social divisions that operated in Shillington; (c) to show that, despite their separation by sex, Shillington students banded together and considered themselves unique; (d) to show the growing menace of a world war on a small American town.

8. The transitional phrase, "on the other hand," in sentence 9 suggests (a) an example; (b) a definition; (c) a conclusion; (d) a contrast.

9. Essentially, the greatest difference between the elementary school and the high school in Shillington was in the amount of (a) homework; (b) discipline; (c) freedom; (d) contact between the sexes.

10. What mood is suggested by the last phrase about the photographs that came "to join the treasure of lost time in my mother's shoeboxes"? (a) sadness; (b) joy; (c) enthusiasm; (d) nostalgia; (e) indifference.

C. Inferences   On the basis of the evidence in the paragraph, mark these statements as follows: *A* for accurate inferences, *I* for inaccurate inferences, and *IE* for insufficient evidence.

_____ 1. Being classified as a student in the B group had, at least for one student, long-term psychological effects.

_____ 2. The A class had a more rigorous academic program than the B class.

_____ 3. Updike was in the A class.

_____ 4. Like the playground, the classrooms were also segregated according to sex.

_____ 5. The A/B distinction was abandoned in high school.

_____ 6. Mohnton, Kenhorst, Wyomissing, and Birdsboro are the names of neighboring rival towns.

_____ 7. Elementary-school children in Shillington were expected to help the war effort.

_____ 8. Updike was a student in elementary school during World War II.

Selection 5   [1]A big, virgin forest defies the intellect because of the deep interconnectedness of life in it. [2]I sensed this in the twilit Siskiyou ridges on my first trip to the Klamath Mountains. [3]None of the books or museum exhibits I'd seen had quite prepared me for those ridges, and I didn't have much sense, at that point, of "reality." [4]It seemed possible that road work near Bluff Creek had been interrupted, as reports had it, by nocturnal visits from a being that left sixteen-inch, humanlike footprints in snow or dust, and that picked up pieces of heavy equipment and threw them in the creek. [5]This being—called "Omah" in Klamath Mountain Indian language, "Sasquatch" in the Pacific Northwest Indian language, and "Bigfoot" in English—is connected in Indian mythology with a variety of forest mysteries, from the calls of screech owls to spirits of the dead, "Omah" being a word applicable to many uncanny phenomena.

[6]There are hundreds of reports of eight-foot-tall, hairy giants in Klamath Mountain forests, seen in flashlight or headlight beams, or in daylight. [7]They have apelike or catlike faces, heavy jaws, and low foreheads. [8]They have short hair—black, red, brown, gray, or even white—sometimes long and stringy on the head, like a goat's. [9]They have massive muscles, including stout buttocks, and females have dangling breasts. [10]Hunters tell of aiming at shaggy beasts, which then turn around and display these breasts. [11]The giants walk like humans, but more gracefully, bending the knee as they put their weight on it. [12]Their stride has been estimated at half a car length, and they bound across midnight roads with demonic swiftness. [13]They make high-pitched whistling sounds. [14]Besides giant footprints, there are reports of giant feces containing remains of water plants and eggs of parasites known from humans in China and the Pacific Northwest and of clots of hair unattributable to any known animal. [15]An eight-millimeter film allegedly taken near Bluff Creek shows a barrel-chested, hairy female striding across a timber-strewn clearing.

[16]There is a consistency about most reports of giants. [17]Some are spectacular: giants lifting boulders for a meal of ground squirrels or hoisting automobiles by their back ends. [18]A few are preposterous: A man said a giant picked him up in his sleeping bag and carried him to a hidden valley, keeping him prisoner several days. [19]The giant lived with a mate and two children, a menage that lacked only a family dog in its middle-class domesticity. [20](The captive escaped by feeding a can of snuff to the giant, making him too sick for pursuit.) [21]But most giant stories are unassuming. [22]Someone in the woods sees a large, shaggy creature picking berries or pulling roots and realizes with a shock that the creature is shaped like a human being. [23]The creature looks up, sees that it is observed, and moves away. [24]It does not flee in panic as a bear often will. [25]It looks directly at the intruder, as a bear usually will not.

David Rains Wallace,
"Wonders of the Klamath"

A. Vocabulary   For each italicized word from the selection, choose the best definition according to the context in which it appears.

1. *defies* [1]: (a) confronts; (b) withstands; (c) challenges successfully; (d) rebels against.
2. *nocturnal* [4]: (a) secret; (b) unconfirmed; (c) nighttime; (d) bizarre.
3. *uncanny* [5]: (a) keen; perceptive; (b) unpopular; (c) inexplicable; mysterious; (d) unbelievable.
4. *stride* [12]: The length of (a) their arms; (b) their legs; (c) their body; (d) a single step.
5. *demonic* [12]: Suggesting something (a) unusual; (b) fiendish; (c) incredible; (d) amusing.
6. *unattributable* [14]: Describing something that (a) does not make sense; (b) cannot be visualized; (c) cannot be distinguished; (d) does not belong to a person or thing.

7. *allegedly* [15]: Describing something that is (a) scientific; technical; (b) probable; (c) asserted without proof; (d) done without permission.

8. *preposterous* [18]: (a) unreasonable; (b) believable; (c) weird; (d) absurd.

9. *menage* [19; pronunciation: mā-näzh′]: (a) an environment; (b) a household; (c) an arrangement; (d) a tall tale.

10. *unassuming* [21]: (a) ridiculous; ludicrous; (b) unproved; unsupported by evidence; (c) modest; not boastful; (d) frightening; inspiring terror.

B. Content and Structure

Choose the best answer.

1. According to the passage, the Klamath Mountains impressed the author for their (a) loneliness; (b) hostile environment; (c) sense of unreality; (d) fascinating geological formations.

2. For Wallace, the reports of a creature disturbing road work near Bluff Creek seemed (a) fanciful; (b) possible; (c) improbable; (d) true.

3. The names "Omah," "Sasquatch," and "Bigfoot" suggest that sightings of the beast to which they refer (a) are recent; (b) are unfounded; (c) have been occurring for a long time; (d) are common among the area's tourists.

4. With respect to the giants that supposedly inhabit the Klamath Mountain area, the author's purpose is to (a) substantiate the many sightings of these giants; (b) explore some of the stories about them; (c) discredit the stories concerning them; (d) describe his own experience confronting one of them.

5. The mode of discourse in the second paragraph is (a) narration; (b) description; (c) exposition; (d) persuasion.

6. To support the main idea, Wallace relies solely on (a) facts and verifiable scientific evidence; (b) unconfirmed reports, legends, and stories; (c) his own firsthand observations; (d) published articles in history books.

7. Sentence 14 suggests that the giant beasts may be (a) cannibalistic; (b) herbivorous, eating only plants; (c) carnivorous, eating only meat; (d) omnivorous, eating both plants and meat.

8. The method of development used in the third paragraph is (a) definition; (b) classification; (c) process; (d) analogy; (e) cause–effect; (f) comparison.

9. Label the following statements taken from the third paragraph using this system: *MAIN* (main idea); *MA* (major support); and *MI* (minor support):

   a. _MAIN_ There is a consistency about most reports of giants.

   b. _MA_ Some are spectacular.

   c. _MI_ Giants lifting boulders for a meal of ground squirrels or hoisting automobiles by their back ends.

   d. _MA_ A few are preposterous.

   e. _MI_ A man said a giant picked him up in his sleeping bag and carried him to a hidden valley, keeping him prisoner several days.

   f. _MA_ But most giant stories are unassuming.

g. _____ Someone in the woods sees a large, shaggy creature picking berries or pulling roots and realizes with a shock that the creature is shaped like a human being.

h. _____ The creature looks up, sees that it is observed, and moves away.

i. _____ It does not flee in panic as a bear often will.

j. _____ It looks directly at the intruder, as a bear usually will not.

10. In sum, from the evidence you are given, what judgment can you make about the existence of Bigfoot? Bigfoot (a) definitely doesn't exist; (b) probably doesn't exist; (c) might possibly exist; (d) probably does exist; (e) definitely does exist; (f) is only legendary, part of the great collective Indian imagination.

C. Inferences   On the basis of the evidence in the selection, mark these statements as follows: *A* for accurate inferences, *I* for inaccurate inferences, and *IE* for insufficient evidence.

1. Wallace went to the Klamath Mountains to go camping.

2. Bigfoot is strictly nocturnal, making his or her appearance only at night.

3. A hunter shot the eight-millimeter film of Bigfoot.

4. Bigfoot has human characteristics, notably the ability to walk erect.

5. Bigfoot is more curious about human beings than fearful.

6. Wallace believed all of the stories he heard about Bigfoot.

7. Large hairy giants have been found in other parts of the world, specifically in China and Europe.

8. Wallace was able to catch a glimpse of Bigfoot.

Selection 6   [1]Here at the age of thirty-nine I began to be old. [2]I felt stiff and weary in the evenings and reluctant to go out of camp; I developed proprietary claims to certain chairs and newspapers; I regularly drank three glasses of gin before dinner, never more or less, and went to bed immediately after the nine o'clock news. [3]I was always awake and fretful an hour before reveille.

[4]Here my last love died. [5]There was nothing remarkable in the manner of its death. [6]One day, not long before this last day in camp, as I lay awake before reveille, in the Nissen hut, gazing into the complete blackness, amid the deep breathing and muttering of the four other occupants, turning over in my mind what I had to do that day—had I put in the names of two corporals for the weapon-training course? [7]Should I again have the largest number of men overstaying their leave in the batch due back that day? [8]Could I trust Hooper to take the candidates class out map-reading?—[9]as I lay in that dark hour, I was aghast to realize that something within me, long sickening, had quietly died, and felt as a husband might feel, who, in the fourth year of his marriage, suddenly knew

that he had no longer any desire, or tenderness, or esteem, for a once-beloved wife; no pleasure in her company, no wish to please, no curiosity about anything she might ever do or say or think; no hope of setting things right, no self-reproach for the disaster. [10]I knew it all, the whole drab compass of marital disillusion; we had been through it together, the army and I, from the first importunate courtship until now, when nothing remained to us except the chill bonds of law and duty and custom. [11]I had played every scene in the domestic tragedy, had found the early tiffs become more frequent, the tears less affecting, the reconciliations less sweet, till they engendered a mood of aloofness and cool criticism, and the growing conviction that it was not myself but the loved one who was at fault. [12]I caught the false notes in her voice and learned to listen for them apprehensively; I recognized the blank, resentful stare of incomprehension in her eyes, and the selfish, hard set of the corners of her mouth. [13]I learned her, as one must learn a woman one has kept house with, day in, day out, for three and a half years; I learned her slatternly ways, the routine and mechanism of her charm, her jealousy and self-seeking, and her nervous trick with the fingers when she was lying. [14]She was stripped of all enchantment now and I knew her for an uncongenial stranger to whom I had bound myself indissolubly in a moment of folly.

Evelyn Waugh,
Brideshead Revisited

A. Vocabulary   For each italicized word from the paragraph, choose the best definition according to the context in which it appears.

1. *proprietary* [2]: A term that describes (a) a private owner; (b) one who desires to please; (c) one who is appointed; (d) what is customary.
2. *aghast* [9]: (a) disgusted; (b) saddened; (c) shocked; (d) surprised.
3. *esteem* [9]: (a) favorable regard; (b) love; (c) curiosity; (d) emotion.
4. self-*reproach* [9]: (a) deception; (b) blame; (c) defense; (d) realization.
5. *importunate* [10]: (a) impudent; (b) dreary; (c) intensely desirous; (d) stubbornly persistent.
6. *engendered* [11]: (a) produced; (b) engaged; (c) transformed; (d) recognized.
7. *aloofness* [11]: (a) alienation; (b) distance in human relationships; (c) acidity; bitterness; (d) snobbery.
8. *apprehensively* [12]: (a) cautiously; (b) consciously; (c) fearfully; (d) appreciatively.
9. *slatternly* [13]: (a) ungenerous; stingy; (b) untidy; slovenly; (c) stupid; meaningless; (d) improper; rude.
10. *indissolubly* [14]: Describing something that cannot be (a) distinguished; seen clearly; (b) broken; separated; (c) joined together; (d) discovered; revealed.

B. Variant Word Forms

From the list of inflected forms in parentheses, choose the form that grammatically fits into the sentence. Add endings (-s or -ed, for example) if necessary.

1. (fretfulness, fret, fretful, fretfully): Before reveille, I lay awake ___fretfully___.

2. (custom, customize, customary, customarily): Every evening I ___customarily___ drank three glasses of gin.

3. (reconciliation, reconcile, reconcilable, reconcilably): It was impossible for our differences to be ___reconciled___.

4. (resentment, resent, resentful, resentfully): I grew ___resentful___ of her falseness and jealousy.

5. (enchantment, enchanter, enchant): She was stripped of all her ___enchanting___ ways now.

6. (criticism, criticize, critical, critically): Each day I grew increasingly ___critical___ of her slatternly ways.

C. Content and Structure

Choose the best answer.

1. The dominant impression one gets of the narrator in the first paragraph is that he was (a) worn out and ill; (b) bored and set in his ways; (c) disillusioned; (d) nervous and tense.

2. The dominant impression one gets of the narrator from the second paragraph is that he has become (a) disillusioned; (b) apprehensive; (c) mistrustful; (d) aloof.

3. In the section comprising sentences 4–14, the method of paragraph development is (a) process; (b) illustration; (c) analogy; (d) analysis; (e) cause–effect.

4. In sentences 4–8, the narrator reveals his (a) unhappiness with army life; (b) concern with being promoted; (c) failure to follow the army's rules; (d) careful attention to detail and strict adherence to army rules.

5. The narrator compares his life in the army to (a) an unfaithful wife; (b) an unhappy marriage to a woman no longer loved; (c) an unhappy love affair; (d) a divorce from a woman he never loved.

6. Write the number of the sentence that first reveals this comparison. Sentence ___9___.

7. The narrator has discovered that the real cause of his unhappiness is (a) his inability to adjust to military life; (b) the boredom and routine of military life; (c) his approaching middle age and disillusionment with the army; (d) the faults inherent in the military system itself.

8. What keeps the narrator from leaving the army is (a) a sense of patriotic duty; (b) a feeling of optimism; (c) a sense of law and obligation; (d) a sense of honor.

9. Which of these dictionary definitions is appropriate for the word *compass* as it is used in sentence 10? (a) a device used to determine geographical direction; (b) a device for drawing circles or arcs; (c) an enclosing line

or boundary; (d) an enclosed space or area; (e) a range or scope; extent; (f) the range of a voice or an instrument.

10. We can accurately infer that the narrator (a) was once attracted to army life; (b) eventually asked for a discharge; (c) had been in the army for his entire adult life; (d) was so despondent that he needed psychiatric care.

PRACTICE ESSAY

The Perfect Killer
Jacques–Yves Cousteau

Jacques–Yves Cousteau (1910–   ) is a marine explorer, film producer, and writer, known primarily for the television series, "The Undersea World of Jacques Cousteau." He has received numerous awards for his work from the film festivals of Paris, Cannes, and Venice, and an Oscar for his documentary feature-film, "The Silent World." In addition to his research into ocean life aboard the *Calypso,* Cousteau's renown also derives from his contribution to the invention of the aqualung in 1943.

1   Putting men in cages to protect them from sharks is what we have been doing for the past twenty years, since we could not carry out such an operation in reverse, which would have been much more logical. These human zoos, cages of steel or aluminum, are hung beneath the *Calypso,* or even beneath one of the smaller boats, to provide our divers with a shelter in case of need. If all goes well, they do not use them. If relations between men and sharks become strained, the divers retreat toward a cage. If the situation becomes untenable, they enter the cage and give the signal to be brought up to the surface. It is because of these cages that we have been able to observe and film sharks during their most savage orgies of feeding.

2   The "perfect killer" is equipped with an enormous jaw set with incredibly sharp teeth, with a powerful and efficient means of propulsion, and with very sensitive devices of perception. However, this block of muscles is supported only by the relatively weak cartilaginous skeleton, the jaw is withdrawn beneath the head, the jawbone is lacking in rigidity, and the teeth do not really form a part of it. Can these contradictory characteristics be compatible?

3   It was not until fifteen years ago, when the *Calypso* became involved in a drama of the high seas, that I was able to observe closely the actual functioning of the killing machine that is a shark. One hundred miles north of the equator, in the middle of the Indian Ocean, the *Calypso* encountered a large number of sperm whales, dispersed in little groups of from three to seven each and moving quite slowly, probably because of the presence of numerous baby whales. We followed them all morning, sometimes very closely, so closely, in fact, that at a speed of only eight knots, we were unable to avoid a collision between the prow of the ship and a large female, probably weighing about twenty tons. Our precious underwater observation chamber was badly dented by the shock, and Louis Malle, who was in the chamber filming the

whales, got a rude jolt. We had just gotten under way again when a very young whale, about twelve feet in length and doubtless no more than a few weeks old, crashed into our port propeller. The sharp blades of the propeller sliced into the body of the unfortunate whale like a machine for slicing ham, and he began to bleed profusely. In spite of his wounds he swam off to rejoin his parents, and for some time the group of adults surrounded the little victim of the accident, trying to help and protect him. Then a very large male, probably the leader of the herd, lifted himself vertically out of the water, supporting himself on the violent lashing of his tail, and for several seconds held more than a third of his body above the level of the waves. In this position, he half-turned toward us and we were sure we could read fury in his glittering little eye. The *Calypso* had seriously wounded two of his charges and he seemed to be studying us carefully, weighing the possibility of revenge. But he apparently decided the danger was too great and plunged back into the ocean. The rest of the herd followed him almost at once, disappearing into the depths, leaving the mortally wounded baby behind. We cut short its suffering with a bullet in its head, and then secured it to the line from the crane on the quarterdeck.

4   It was not very long before the first shark was sighted, then there were two, ten, twenty. They were all *Carcharhinus longimanus*, the long-finned lords of the deep. They ranged in size from eight to twelve feet. They were joined very shortly by a superb blue shark, about fifteen feet in length, with a long, pointed snout, a slender silhouette, and enormous, expressionless eyes. He was a "blue whaler." Just behind their mouths, almost all the sharks carried a half dozen or so remoras, or sucking fish, oddly resembling decorations on the chest of a general, and they were all escorted by a cloud of pilot fish. While the protective cages and the diving and filming material were being prepared, I observed the behavior of the horde of sharks that now surrounded the bleeding whale. Where had these marauders come from, surging out of the immensity of the sea, a hundred and fifty miles from the nearest island, and with almost three miles of water beneath our keel? They had undoubtedly all been satellites of the school of sperm whales, remaining prudently in their wake, respectful of their power, but ready to take advantage of the slightest weakening, and living on the scraps of their meals.

5   The attitude of the sharks in their first approach was perfectly clear-cut. Carrying prudence to its extremes, they circled around the still-warm carcass of the baby whale, maintaining a constant, almost lazy, speed. But even so, they seemed very sure of themselves. They quite obviously had no fear of us. If we chased one of them away with boat hooks, he returned a moment later. Time was working for them, and they knew it. The prey could not escape them.

6   For an entire hour these maneuvers continued, and still not a single shark had ventured too close to the little whale. Then they began to touch him with their snouts, barely grazing him, one by one and hundreds of times, but making no attempt to bite. They behaved the same way with our protective cage.

7 Suddenly, the blue shark lunged and bit. With a single blow, as if from some giant razor, pounds of skin, of flesh, and of fat were sliced away. It was the signal; the orgy was about to begin.

8 With no apparent transition, the calm of the preliminary round gave way to the frenzy of sharing in the spoils. Each mouthful snatched by each passing shark dug a hole the size of a bucket in the body of the dead whale. I could not believe my eyes. Instinctively, and horrified, I thought of similar scenes which must have taken place after a shipwreck or the crash of a plane into the sea.

9 Because of the safety afforded by our cage—although it was constantly bumped and jostled by these ravenous beasts—we were able to film their saturnalia in close-up, at a distance of only a few feet. It was as a result of this experience that I learned the mechanism by which a shark bites into his prey.

10 The shark's jaw is located far back beneath his long snout, but this does not prevent him from biting directly into the flesh. When he opens the jaw, the lower jawbone is thrust forward while the snout is drawn back and up, until it makes almost a right angle with the axis of his body. At this moment, the mouth is located forward of the head and no longer beneath it. It resembles a large wolftrap, equipped with innumerable sharp and gleaming teeth. The shark plants this mechanism in the body of his victim and uses the weight of his own body in a series of frenzied convulsions, transforming the teeth of the jawbones into saws. The force of this sawing effect is such that it requires no more than an instant for a shark to tear off a splendid morsel of flesh. When the shark swims off, he has left a deep and perfectly outlined hole in the body of his victim. It is terrifying and nauseating to watch.

A. Comprehension

Choose the answer that best completes each statement. Do not refer to the selection while doing this exercise.

1. What enable Cousteau and his companions to film sharks and their behavior are (a) sophisticated underwater cameras; (b) radar devices that allow the boat to determine the sharks' precise location; (c) steel or aluminum cages; (d) trained divers who are willing to risk their lives for the sake of research.

2. Cousteau finds it odd or contradictory that the shark is equipped with (a) dull teeth; (b) remarkably good eyesight; (c) an underslung jaw that is lacking in rigidity; (d) a very poor sense of smell.

3. After the baby sperm whale was wounded by the propeller, the other whales first (a) rose up out of the water and threatened revenge; (b) surrounded the victim and tried to protect him; (c) swam away, abandoning the baby; (d) attacked the divers in the cages.

4. The school of long-finned sharks was accompanied by (a) sucking fish, pilot fish, and a blue shark; (b) several great white sharks; (c) tuna, bass, and other deep sea species; (d) a group of sand and leopard sharks.

5. Cousteau determined that the sharks following the *Calypso* (a) had traveled one hundred and fifty miles to find the wounded whale; (b) were more interested in the men than in the wounded whale; (c) were satellites of the sperm whale school; (d) had been following the boat all morning, waiting for one of the divers to slip up.

6. According to Cousteau, the sharks' initial behavior toward the wounded whale was (a) frenzied; (b) frightening to observe; (c) careful but self-assured; (d) respectful, unwilling to inflict any harm.

7. The sharks knew that time was on their side because (a) eventually the boat would go away; (b) the prey could not escape; (c) the baby whale would soon die; (d) the other whales were too timid to stay in the sharks' vicinity.

8. According to Cousteau's description, the shark is able to bite into the flesh of its victim because (a) the snout is extended while the jaw is retracted; (b) the jaw is extended while the snout draws back; (c) the teeth, which are normally retracted, protrude during the attack; (d) the mouth is located beneath the head.

B. Inferences   On the basis of the evidence in the selection, mark these statements as follows: *A* for accurate inferences, *I* for inaccurate inferences, and *IE* for insufficient evidence.

___I___ 1. Cousteau has designed special cages to trap sharks so they can be observed.

___I___ 2. The shark's cartilaginous skeleton is as hard and rigid as human bones.

___I___ 3. The *Calypso*'s mission in the Indian Ocean was to find a school of sperm whales for observation.

___A___ 4. The collision that occurred between the *Calypso* and the school of whales was the result of the boat's following them too closely.

___IE___ 5. The female whale that collided with the boat eventually died.

___A___ 6. Whales are protective of the group if they feel threatened or if a member is harmed.

___IE___ 7. The whales eventually swam away because they sensed the presence of sharks in the vicinity.

___A___ 8. Cousteau and the crew used the dead baby whale as bait to attract sharks.

___IE___ 9. Sharks possess a mechanism to detect blood that closely resembles radar.

___A___ 10. The blue shark acted as the leader of the group.

___IE___ 11. Sharks have poor eyesight.

___A___ 12. The relationship between the sharks and the school of whales was a symbiotic one.

C. Structure Choose the best answer.

1. In the space provided, write the sentence that *best* expresses the main idea of the entire selection.

   [handwritten: I was not, until fifteen years ago, when the Calypso became —]

   [handwritten margin: first sentence of par 3]

   _____ in paragraph ___3___.

2. Undoubtedly, one could argue that Cousteau uses all four modes of discourse in this selection, though one does seem to predominate. Which one? (a) narration; (b) description; (c) exposition; (d) persuasion.

3. The purpose of the selection is, specifically, (a) to establish scientific evidence for the often-made claim that the shark is a bloodthirsty killer; (b) to show in detail the mechanism that allows the shark to kill so efficiently; (c) to show the dangers in underwater research involving whales and sharks; (d) to explain the physical structure and social organization of one species of shark.

4. Cousteau emphasizes that the one feature of the shark that seems to be in the wrong place is its (a) teeth; (b) snout; (c) mouth; (d) dorsal fin.

5. The mode of discourse evident in paragraph 2 is (a) narration; (b) description; (c) exposition; (d) persuasion.

6. The word *anthropomorphism* means the attribution of human motivations or behavior to inanimate objects or to animals. Look again at paragraph 3 and find two instances of anthropomorphism in Cousteau's prose. *[handwritten: the whale surrounded the wounded baby, trying is to help and protect him; the male whale —]*

7. Look again at paragraph 4. Find and write down two metaphors (imaginative comparisons between unlike things): *[handwritten: Remoras to decoration of the chest of generals. sharks to satellites — pilot fish describe as travelling in the cloud]*

8. Note the phrases at the beginning of paragraphs 5 through 8 ("in their first approach," "for an entire hour," "suddenly," "with no apparent transition"). What method of paragraph development do these transitional phrases point to? (a) illustration; (b) definition; (c) classification; (d) analogy; (e) cause–effect; (f) process.

9. In describing the shark's teeth, Cousteau compares them to (a) needles; (b) knives; (c) saws; (d) a slicing machine.

10. Write the sentence that best sums up Cousteau's reaction to the incident he observed: *[handwritten: It is terrifying and nauseating to watch]*

D. Vocabulary For each italicized word from the selection, choose the best definition according to the context in which it appears.

1. if the situation becomes *untenable* [1]: (a) unendurable; (b) not defendable; (c) unpredictable; (d) unstable.

2. a powerful and efficient means of *propulsion* [2]: The process of (a) attacking; (b) perceiving with sense organs; (c) driving forward; (d) eating.

3. very *sensitive* devices of perception [2]: (a) touchy; quick to take offense; (b) easily irritated; (c) susceptible to others' feelings; (d) responsive to external conditions or stimulation.

4. Can these contradictory characteristics be *compatible*? [2]: Capable of (a) functioning; (b) efficient integration; (c) living together in a harmonious state; (d) being satisfactorily explained.

5. *dispersed* in little groups [3]: (a) scattered; (b) organized; (c) gathered closely together; (d) distributed.

6. he began to bleed *profusely* [3]: (a) minimally; (b) slowly; (c) abundantly; (d) continuously.

7. Where had these *marauders* come from? [4]: (a) vicious creatures; (b) raiders; plunderers; (c) savage killers; (d) predators.

8. remaining *prudently* in their wake [4]: (a) lazily; (b) wisely; (c) excitedly; (d) respectfully.

9. remaining prudently in their *wake* [4]: (a) vigil; watch; (b) sight; line of vision; (c) visible track left behind in the water; (d) the area to the front.

10. the frenzy of sharing in the *spoils* [8]: (a) objects of plunder or prey; (b) food that has rotted; (c) fun, entertainment, or games; (d) pleasurable experiences.

11. because of the safety *afforded* by our cages [9]: (a) performed; (b) offered; (c) provided; (d) encountered.

12. we were able to film their *saturnalia* [9]: An occasion of (a) bestial behavior; (b) unrestrained revelry; (c) insatiable hunger; (d) bloodthirsty attacks. [Note: see an unabridged dictionary for the etymology of this word.]

chapter 4 ‖ PATTERNS OF PARAGRAPH ORGANIZATION

We have thus far examined the fundamentals of reading paragraphs—picking out the subject and the controlling idea, determining the author's purpose, discerning major and minor supporting details, and methods of paragraph development. The various methods you have studied—illustration and example, process, analysis, cause–effect, and so forth—refer to the *content* or *subject*. These methods are the ways in which the writer develops and supports the main idea. Equally important in developing your ability to read analytically is the ability to follow the direction of a writer's ideas—that is, the *order* that a writer imposes on the sentences in a paragraph or on the paragraphs in an essay. Whereas the term *methods of development* refers to *what* the author is saying—the kinds of support used to defend the main idea—*patterns of organization* refers to *how* these ideas are arranged. Although the paragraph is remarkably flexible and subject to infinite variations, we can nevertheless isolate a few typical patterns of organization.

In this chapter we shall consider six basic patterns of organization: (1) chronological order, (2) spatial order, (3) deductive order, (4) a variation of deductive order, (5) inductive order, and (6) emphatic order. The first and second patterns are found most often in narrative and descriptive writing; the others are more likely to occur in expository or persuasive writing.

A. CHRONOLOGICAL ORDER

Chronological (or *time*) order, the easiest pattern to recognize, refers to the order in which events happen. It is used to tell a story (as you saw in the narrative paragraphs in Chapter 1), to relate an incident, to recount a historical event, to examine the life cycle of an animal, or to describe the steps in a process paragraph. In this paragraph, Eugene Kinkead uses chronological order to explain how snail darters reproduce.

During the spawning season, a female darter lays around six hundred eggs in the swift water of the gravel shoals in the shallowest parts of a river. The eggs, rolling along the bottom, have a sticky exterior, and will fasten onto a stone. There, for about two weeks, the embryos inside develop. Upon hatching, they drift downstream to a pool of deep water—if they are lucky, that is: infant mortality, as with most fish, is very high. Probably less than one or two per cent of the eggs laid produce adults. All kinds of darters, including snail darters, probably eat snail-darter eggs and larvae. The deepwater pools act as snail-darter nurseries. For some weeks, the larvae live on the unconsumed egg yolk they carry with them. They are strange, still embryonic-looking things, less than a quarter of an inch long. After the egg yolk is gone, they stay in the pool, feeding on microcrustaceans through the summer. By fall, the diet shifts to snails, and the fish make their way back upstream to the shallows.

Eugene Kinkead,
"Tennessee Small Fry"

Kinkead signals time order by means of transitional phrases ("during the spawning season," "for about two weeks," "upon hatching," "for some weeks," and "by fall").

B. SPATIAL ORDER

Spatial is derived from the word *space*. Thus, spatial refers to the arrangement of things in an environment. This pattern of organization is found most often in descriptive writing. A writer might use it to describe an object in its environment (such as a house in relation to the other houses on the block), or to describe an entire scene (such as the layout of a college campus or the view of a city from above). Spatial order makes it easy for the reader to picture what might otherwise be a jumble of impressions. Some typical ways writers arrange details spatially are from left to right or right to left, from near to far or far to near, from top to bottom or the reverse. Again, transitions help the reader visualize the scene. Examples of transitions in spatially ordered paragraphs might be "beyond the valley," "to the left of the door," "below his furrowed brow," or "farther down the highway." As you read this passage about cities of the Maya, underline any phrases that indicate spatial relationships.

A Maya city still untouched—and there are plenty of them—is a strange and somewhat frightening sight. From a high-flying airplane the jungle looks like an endless expanse of massed broccoli, the rounded treetops standing close together and giving no glimpse of the ground. If the airplane circles lower, a few crumbling walls of light-gray limestone appear above the green, like rocky islets poking out of a sea. Sometimes the eye catches a glimpse of a steep-sided pyramid rising from below.

Approached on foot the scene is strikingly different. The jungle floor is deeply shaded, with only occasional flecks of sunlight filtering through from the sky. There is little undergrowth; the ground is soft with rotting humus, and great trees stand solemnly with thick vines dripping down from their tops. Their buttressed trunks march up the sides of the pyramids, and exposed roots writhe like boa constrictors, prying the stones apart. Trees often sprout from the very apex of a pyramid and they cover lesser structures completely.

Jonathan Norton Leonard,
Ancient America

You should have marked "from a high-flying airplane," "if the airplane circles lower," and "approached on foot." These phrases show the contrast between the two views of the ancient city—one from the air and the other from ground level.

Let us look at one more example, a description by Berton Roueché of a southern Indiana town named Corydon, the scene of the one Civil War battle fought in Indiana. Roueché helps us visualize the town by means of spatial transitions. Using details arranged from far to near, he first shows us the view of the town from the heights surrounding it; by the end of the paragraph we have been brought to the center of town at the courthouse square. (John Hunt Morgan, mentioned in the third sentence, was a Confederate raider who swept through the town with a cavalry force of twenty-five hundred men and demanded a ransom of seven hundred dollars from each of the town's three flour mills.)

> Corydon sits deeply secluded in the bowl of its limestone valley. It is all but invisible from the wooded knobs and hilltop fields that surround it. One can come upon it only suddenly, and then (except by way of a riverine notch on the east) only from the very brink of its encircling heights. I saw the town first from the north, from the top of the mile-long slope that Morgan and his men had climbed in the aftermath of victory so many years ago—a dirt road then, a pot-holed highway now. But even from there the view was guarded. Halfway down the slope was a bridge across a tumbling stream (Big Indian Creek), with a yellow brick house in the early Greek Revival style (the McGrain House) in a broad, wooded lawn on the left and, off to the right, following a bend in the stream, the stacks and rooftops and lumberyards of the Keller (furniture) Manufacturing Company. Beyond the bridge, beyond the grounds of the McGrain House, the highway became a sidewalked street (North Capitol Avenue)—a tree-hung residential street of comfortable houses built close to the pavement, leading down and down and down to a faraway spread of space, an alteration of light: the courthouse square.

> Berton Roueché,
> "To Hear a Rooster Crow"

C. DEDUCTIVE ORDER

Deductive order is the most common pattern of organization in the English paragraph. It is the same pattern you saw in the section on placement of topic sentences in Chapter 1. Deductive order is sometimes called *general-to-specific order*, because the paragraph begins with a general statement (the topic sentence), which is then supported by a series of specific statements. The pattern of organization, then, is determined by the placement of the topic sentence. The first illustrative paragraph, a description of the sperm whale, uses the standard deductive pattern: topic sentence + supporting details. (Incidentally, here the author's use of punctuation is rather innovative, especially his colons, semicolons, and dashes. Do not let his unconventional punctuation get in the way of your comprehension.)

The sperm whale, for many, is the most awesome creature of the open seas. Imagine a forty-five-year-old male fifty feet long, a slim, shiny black animal with a white jaw and marbled belly cutting the surface of green ocean water at twenty knots. Its flat forehead protects a sealed chamber of exceedingly fine oil; sunlight sparkles in rivulets running off folds in its corrugated back. At fifty tons it is the largest carnivore on earth. Its massive head, a third of its body length, is scarred with the beak, sucker, and claw marks of giant squid, snatched out of subterranean canyons a mile below, in a region without light, and brought writhing to the surface. Imagine a 400-pound heart the size of a chest of drawers driving five gallons of blood at a stroke through its aorta; a meal of forty salmon moving slowly down 1,200 feet of intestine; the blinding, acrid fragrance of a 200-pound wad of gray ambergris lodged somewhere along the way; producing sounds more shrill than we can hear—like children shouting on a distant playground—and able to sort a cacophony of noise: electric crackling of shrimp, groaning of undersea quakes, roar of upwellings, whining of porpoise, hum of oceanic cables. With skin as sensitive as the inside of your wrist.

Barry Lopez,
"A Presentation of Whales"

The foregoing passage shows how deductive order is used in descriptive writing. The next passage shows deductive order used in exposition. In this case, Marie Winn's purpose is to show the difference in pace in reading and watching television. Each paragraph begins with a main idea, which is in turn followed by a series of supporting statements that explain further and prove the validity of the assertion.

When we read, clearly, we can control the pace. We may read as slowly or as rapidly as we can or wish to read. If we do not understand something, we may stop and reread it, or go in search of elucidation before continuing. If what we read is moving, we may put down the book for a few moments and cope with our emotions without fear of losing anything.

When we view, the pace of the television program cannot be controlled; only its beginning and end are within our control by clicking the knob on and off. We cannot slow down a delightful program or speed up a dreary one. We cannot "turn back" if a word or phrase is not understood. The program moves inexorably forward, and what is lost or misunderstood remains so.

Marie Winn,
The Plug-In Drug

Finally, as you may remember from Chapter 1, a writer may delay stating the main idea until after the opening sentences. Such an opening strategy is necessary if the writer wants to orient the reader to the subject or to contradict a commonly accepted idea. In this paragraph, Calvin

Trillin's purpose is to show the economic difficulties facing Midwestern farmers in the mid-1980s (a strange combination of boom and bust). He begins by citing the experts' view of what was wrong, in the first two sentences; in sentence 3, the topic sentence, he suggests that the farmers put the blame for their problems elsewhere.

[1]The experts said that some farmers—especially those sometimes called the Young Tigers, who bought up farmland almost as fast as the previous purchase could be appraised as collateral—had simply overextended themselves. [2]The experts said that some farmers had been shown to be poor managers. [3]That's not the way farmers saw it. [4]Farmers, of course, are accustomed to being buffeted by elements beyond their control—the weather, for instance, or some flip-flop in world grain prices. [5]This time, though, there was something particularly maddening about the combination of a boom—a boom celebrated by farm experts and bankers and government agricultural specialists as proof that expansion was the wave of the future—and a bust that cost some supposedly successful farmers the land that their more modest forebears had managed to hang on to for generations. [6] This time, also, it was more intense. [7]By some estimates, the farm foreclosures still going on in the Midwest represent the greatest dislocation of Americans since the Depression. [8]Some farmers blamed the bankers. [9]In Minnesota, a farmer and his son shot and killed two bankers they had lured to their farm. [10]Some farmers blamed the government or the grain embargo imposed in 1980, and organized tractor caravans to protest to the authorities. [11]A lot of farmers didn't know whom to blame. [12]They carried around a bitter, unfocussed anger that sometimes erupted into blockades at farm sales or shoving matches at courthouses. [13]In the last few years, it has become common for someone serving papers on a farmer to do so with a weapon handy.

Calvin Trillin,
"American Chronicles"

D. A VARIATION OF DEDUCTIVE ORDER

A variation of the typical deductive pattern involves a restatement of the main idea at the end of the paragraph. The restated main idea serves to underscore its importance, as you can see in this paragraph by Marie Winn:

A pervasive myth has taken hold of parents' imagination these days, contributing to their feeling of being powerless to control the fates of their children: the myth of the teenage werewolf. Its message is that no matter how pleasant and sweet and innocent their child might be at the moment, how amiable and docile and friendly, come the first hormonal surge of puberty and the child will turn into an uncontrollable monster. But unlike the lycanthrope who turns harmless at the next day's sunrise, the teenage werewolf, belief has it, remains monstrous for years and years. It is a terrible myth that darkens the years of parenthood.

Marie Winn,
Children Without Childhood

This variation of deductive order is also found in long paragraphs or in paragraphs dealing with complex ideas. The restatement helps the reader by reminding him or her of what the whole passage was about. Such use is nicely illustrated in the following paragraph reprinted from H. D. F. Kitto's classic study, *The Greeks*. Since the paragraph is rather long, restating the main idea—the great variety in the Greek landscape— keeps us on track.

Greece is a region of great variety. Mediterranean and subalpine conditions exist within a few miles of each other; fertile plains alternate with wild mountain country; many an enterprising community of seamen and traders had as neighbours an inland agricultural people that knew the sea and commerce hardly at all, traditional and conservative, even as wheat and cattle are traditional and conservative. Contrasts in Greece today can be startling. In Athens and the Piraeus you have at your disposal—or had, before the war—a large modern European city, with trams, buses and taxis, aeroplanes arriving every few hours, and a harbour crammed with ships going everywhere—to Aegina across the bay, up the east coast, up the west coast, through the Canal, to Alexandria, to the chief ports of Europe, to the Americas; but in a few hours you can make your way to parts of Central Greece or the Peloponnesus where for miles around the only roads are bridle-tracks and the only wheeled vehicle is the wheelbarrow. In Kalamata I was taken over a large, up-to-date flour-mill, into which the corn was brought directly, by suction, from the holds of the ships that had carried it; two days before, and not twenty miles away, I had seen threshing being done, in Old Testament style, by horses or mules careering around a circular threshing-floor in a corner of a field, and the winnowing done on the same spot with the never-failing help of the wind. In antiquity the contrasts are perhaps not so great, but they are still very striking. Variety meets us everywhere, and is a fact of great significance.

H. D. F. Kitto,
The Greeks

E. INDUCTIVE ORDER   *facts one at the time*

The opposite of deductive order is inductive order, or *specific-to-general order.* This pattern actually derives from a kind of thinking, called induction, which you will learn more about in the section on critical reading. For now, it is enough to know that the pattern involves a series of specific statements leading to a generalization (the topic sentence) that the reader can validly infer from those statements. Consider this series of statements: "In

1976, a pound of butter cost $.79, but in 1986 it cost $2.15; in 1976 a pound of hamburger cost $.99, but in 1986 it cost $2.89; in 1976 a loaf of wheat bread cost $.69, but in 1986 it cost $1.59." On the basis of these statements, a reasonable generalization (and topic sentence) would be: "The cost of basic food items increased dramatically in the ten-year period between 1976 and 1986." Furthermore, one can make an inductive argument from these figures: It is likely that food prices will continue to rise dramatically in the next decade. It is for this reason that inductive arguments are sometimes called *probability* arguments.

In the following paragraph, George Orwell uses inductive order to describe the neighborhood in Paris where he lived in the 1930s. Each sentence in the description points to the concluding sentence, "It was quite a representative Paris slum."

It was a very narrow street—a ravine of tall, leprous houses, lurching toward one another in queer attitudes, as though they had all been frozen in the act of collapse. All the houses were hotels and packed to the tiles with lodgers, mostly Poles, Arabs, and Italians. At the foot of the hotels were tiny *bistros,* where you could be drunk for the equivalent of a shilling. On Saturday nights about a third of the male population of the quarter was drunk. There was fighting over women, and the Arab navvies who lived in the cheapest hotels used to conduct mysterious feuds, and fight them out with chairs and occasionally revolvers. At night the policemen would only come through the street two together. It was a fairly rackety place. And yet amid the noise and dirt lived the usual respectable French shopkeepers, bakers and laundresses and the like, keeping themselves to themselves and quietly piling up small fortunes. It was quite a representative Paris slum.

George Orwell,
Down and Out in Paris and London

More typically, however, the inductive pattern is found in expository or persuasive writing. The following paragraph, from a book on language, illustrates the inductive pattern in exposition.

Healthy children, no matter where on the globe they live or the particular kind of language they speak, learn a native tongue. And they go through the same steps in acquiring their language at approximately the same speed, independently of whether they are deprived children or children brought up by doting parents who drill them in language skills. By about the age of three months, children use intonations similar to those changes in pitch heard in adult exclamations and questions. By about one year, they begin to speak recognizable words, and by the age of four or so they have mastered most of the exceedingly complex and abstract structures of their native tongues. In only a few more years children possess the entire linguistic system that allows them to utter and to understand sentences they have not previously heard. This remarkable accomplishment, most of it concentrated in only several years of development, is the birthright of every normal child. In contrast to this orderly development, which comes as a matter of course, many children have difficulty with reading, arithmetic, and swimming, even though they might receive considerable instruction. The child acquires his language merely by hearing it spoken in his native speech community. Yet his language is so complex that pages of diagrams, formulas, and explanatory notes are necessary to analyze even a brief statement made in it. . . . For the rest of his life the child will speak sentences he has never before heard, and when he thinks or reads, he will still literally talk to himself. He can never escape from speech.

Peter Farb,
Word Play: What Happens When People Talk

The next passage is an example of persuasive writing where the author supports her opinion that a new concept of "manhood" has developed over the last fifteen years. From the evidence cited—which consists solely of subjective opinions—she draws the conclusion that the new man has become more "feminized," though not necessarily "feminist."

In the 1970s, it had become an article of liberal faith that a new man would eventually rise up to match the new feminist woman, that he would be more androgynous than any "old" variety of man, and that the change, which was routinely expressed as an evolutionary leap from John Wayne to Alan Alda, would be an unambiguous improvement.

Today, a new man is at last emerging. Something has happened, however, both to our common expectations of what constitutes manhood and to the way many men are choosing to live.

I see the change in the popular images that define masculinity, and I see it in the men I know, mostly in their 30s, who are conscious of possessing a sensibility and even a way of life that is radically different from that of their fathers. These men have been, in a word, feminized, but without necessarily becoming more feminist.

Barbara Ehrenreich,
"The New Man"

F. EMPHATIC ORDER   → most important thing

Just as a good trial lawyer saves his best argument for last, the same principle governs the way many writers arrange their supporting statements (particularly in deductive paragraphs) so that they build in intensity, from the least important to the most important—hence the term *emphatic* order. Whether this actually deserves to be a separate category is open to question, since a paragraph arranged deductively may also use emphatic order for the arrangement of supporting details. In this short passage, for example, Bruno Bettelheim and Karen Zelan use emphatic order in their discussion of what influences a child's attitude toward reading. The key phrase, "the most important influence," clearly indicates the emphasis.

A child's attitude toward reading is of such importance that, more often than not, it determines his scholastic fate. Moreover, his experiences in learning to read may decide how he will feel about learning in general, and even about himself as a person.

Family life has a good deal to do with the development of a child's ability to understand, to use, and to enjoy language. It strongly influences his impression of the value of reading, and his confidence in his intelligence and academic abilities. But regardless of what the child brings from home to school, the most important influence on his ability to read once he is in class is how his teacher presents reading and literature. If the teacher can make reading interesting and enjoyable, then the exertions required to learn how will seem worthwhile.

Bruno Bettelheim and Karen Zelan,
"Why Children Don't Like to Read"

G. TRANSITIONS AND THEIR SPECIFIC FUNCTIONS

In Chapter 3, you were introduced to transitions—the words and phrases that writers use to link ideas logically and that help the reader follow the direction of the ideas. Not only does attention to transitions help you better understand what you read, in addition transitions may reveal the method of development used in the passage. For instance, at the beginning of this sentence, the phrase "for instance" signals that an example is coming; "in contrast" tells you that the writer is going to make a distinction; "as a result" indicates both a conclusion and the effect part of a cause–effect relationship.

Here is a list of types of transitions, arranged according to their specific function, meaning the relationship they reveal between the words preceding and the words following.

1. *Transitions signaling an additional statement (usually of equal importance):* and, in addition (to), additionally, as well as, besides, furthermore, moreover

Example: The house was badly neglected. The windows were broken *and* the paint blistered. *Moreover,* what had once been a well-tended lawn now was only a weed patch.

2. *Transitions signaling a contrast:* but, yet, however, nevertheless, nonetheless, while, whereas, on the other hand, in contrast (to), contrary to

Example: Mr. Clark saw Jimmy, his neighbor's son, break the living room window; *however,* the child refused to admit his guilt.

Example: Ann Smith was enthralled with the opera, *while* her husband, Bill, struggled to keep his eyes open.

3. *Transitions signaling an example or illustration:* for example, as an example, as an illustration, to illustrate, for instance, namely, specifically, that is to say, to wit [this last one is seldom used in modern prose]

Example: In response to protest groups, the television industry has changed the sort of violence portrayed in detective and police dramas. Violence now is more subdued, and when it does exist, it is depicted as a necessary and appropriate response to some evil. *To illustrate,* let us look at a typical episode of "Magnum P.I." . . .

4. *Transitions signaling a concession, or admitting a truth:* although, even though, in spite of, despite

Example: Although Jane undoubtedly was bright, her grades showed that she did not take her courses seriously.

5. *Transitions signaling emphasis:* indeed, in fact, certainly, without a doubt, undoubtedly, admittedly, unquestionably, truly

Example: Jason looked unhappy, *indeed* inconsolable.

6. *Transitions signaling steps in a process or chronological order:* first, second, third, next, the next step, further, then, before, after that, finally, last

Example: To make an omelet, *first* beat three eggs until fluffy. *Then* cook them slowly in a lightly buttered pan.

7. *Transitions signaling a conclusion:* to conclude, in conclusion, in summary, to summarize, thus, then, therefore, consequently, hence, as a result

Example: Marvin spent two hours a day in the reading laboratory, and he looked up every unfamiliar word he encountered in his reading. *As a result,* there was a dramatic improvement in his reading comprehension.

8. *Transitions signaling spatial order:* above, below, to the right (left), beyond, further on

Example: Beyond the valley, the San Gabriel Mountains rose, indistinct in the smoggy sunlight.

EXERCISES

Selection 1

[1]It happened one day about noon. [2]Going towards my boat, I was exceedingly surprised with the print of a man's naked foot on the shore, which was very plain to be seen in the sand. [3]I stood like one thunderstruck, or as if I had seen an apparition: I listened, I looked around me, but I could hear nothing, nor see anything. [4]I went up to a rising ground, to look further; I went up the shore and down the shore, but it was all one; I could see no other impression but that one. [5]I went to it again to see if there were any more and to observe if it might not be my fancy; but there was no room for that, for there was exactly the print of a foot, toes, heel, and every part of a foot. [6]How it came thither I knew not, nor could I in the least imagine; but, after innumerable fluttering thoughts, like a man perfectly confused and out of myself, I came home to my fortification, not feeling, as we say, the ground I went on, but terrified to the last degree, looking behind me at every two or three steps, mistaking every bush and tree, and fancying every stump at a distance to be a man. [7]Nor is it possible to describe how many various shapes my affrighted imagination represented things to me in, how many wild ideas were found every moment in my fancy, and what strange unaccountable whimsies came into my thoughts by the way.

Daniel Defoe,
Robinson Crusoe

A. Vocabulary   For each italicized word from the paragraph, choose the best definition according to the context in which it appears.

1. *apparition* [sentence 3]: (a) an unusual sight; (b) a ghostly figure; (c) a thunderbolt; (d) an evil spirit.

2. *fancy* [5]: (a) delusion; unfounded opinion; (b) fantastic invention; (c) whim; caprice; (d) imagination; play of the mind.

3. *thither* [6]: (a) from that place; (b) to that place; (c) without being seen; (d) without being heard.

4. *whimsies* [7]: (a) bizarre notions; (b) fantastic, impractical plans; (c) odd, capricious ideas; (d) quaint, obsolete notions.

Daniel Defoe published *Robinson Crusoe* in 1719, and certainly his sentence structure and word choice have an old-fashioned flavor. Aside from the vocabulary listed above, find one word in the paragraph that the dictionary labels "archaic." _affrightened_
What word would a modern writer use in its place? _frightened_ —

B. Content and Structure   Choose the best answer.

1. The mode of discourse in this paragraph is primarily (a) narration; (b) description; (c) exposition; (d) persuasion.

2. The pattern of organization is (a) spatial; (b) deductive; (c) variation of deductive; (d) inductive; (e) chronological.

3. The dominant impression the paragraph conveys is (a) anger; (b) confusion; (c) fear; (d) surprise.

4. Crusoe had believed the island to be uninhabited by humans. In addition to finding the footprint itself, what apparently disturbed him was the fact that (a) the print was very large; (b) the print was of a naked foot; (c) there was only one print; (d) he had not seen the print before.

Selection 2   [1]We were forever being organized into activities that, I suspect, looked good on paper and in school board reports. [2]New programs took over and disappeared as approaches to child education changed. [3]One year we would go without marks, on the theory that marks were a "poor motivating factor," "an unnatural pressure," and my laboriously researched science and social studies reports would come back with a check mark or a check plus inside the margin. [4]Another year every activity became a competition, with posters tacked up on the walls showing who was ahead that week, our failures and our glories bared to all the class. [5]Our days were filled with electrical gimmicks, film strips and movies and overhead projectors and tapes and supplementary TV shows, and in junior high, when we went audio-visual, a power failure would have been reason enough to close down the school.

Joyce Maynard,
Looking Back

A. Vocabulary For each italicized word from the paragraph, choose the best definition according to the context in which it appears.

1. *bared* [4]: (a) revealed; (b) made invisible; (c) exhibited; (d) praised.
2. *gimmicks* [5]: (a) inventions; (b) objects; (c) gadgets; (d) deceptive mechanisms.
3. *supplementary* [5]: (a) educational; (b) additional; (c) free; (d) extracurricular.

B. Content and Structure Choose the best answer.

1. The two sentences that best express the main idea are __1__ and __2__.
2. The pattern of organization is (a) chronological; (b) spatial; (c) deductive; (d) variation of deductive; (e) inductive.
3. The relationship between the two clauses in sentence 3 (separated by the conjunction "and") is (a) contrast; (b) cause–effect; (c) steps in a process; (d) general statement and an illustration.
4. Maynard uses quotation marks in sentence 3 around the phrases "poor motivating factor" and "an unnatural pressure" because they are (a) examples of educational jargon that she wants to poke fun at; (b) actual quotations from teachers; (c) trite or overused expressions; (d) phrases whose importance she wants to emphasize in the sentence.
5. The phrase that acts both as a contrasting and chronological transition is *another year* in sentence __4__.
6. *Hyperbole* (pronounced hī-pûr′bə-lē) refers to deliberate exaggeration for effect. Which sentence (or portion of a sentence) could be called an example of hyperbole? *a power failure would have been enough to close down the school*
7. How would you characterize the *tone,* or the emotional quality of Maynard's paragraph? (a) angry and resentful; (b) sarcastic and bitterly cynical; (c) neutral; impartial; (d) wryly humorous and amused.
8. We can accurately infer that, as a student, Maynard was (a) disrespectful to her teachers; (b) conscientious; (c) lazy and careless; (d) indifferent; bored.

Selection 3 [1]Like the animal life of this coast, the seaweeds tell a silent story of heavy surf. [2]Back from the headlands and in bays and coves the rockweeds may grow seven feet tall; here on this open coast a seven-inch plant is a large one. [3]In their sparse and stunted growth, the seaweed invaders of the upper rocks reveal the stringent conditions of life where waves beat heavily. [4]In the middle and lower zones some hardy weeds have been able to establish themselves in greater abundance and profusion. [5]These differ so greatly from the algae of quieter shores that they are almost a symbol of the wave-swept coast. [6]Here and there the rocks sloping to the sea glisten with sheets composed of many individual plants of a curious seaweed, the purple laver. [7]Its generic name, Porphyra, means "a purple dye." It belongs to the red algae, and although it has color variations on the Maine coast it is most often a purplish brown. [9]It resembles nothing so much as little pieces of brown transparent plastic cut out of someone's raincoat. [10]In the thinness of its fronds it is like the sea lettuce, but there is a double layer of tissue, suggesting a child's rubber balloon that has collapsed so that the opposite walls are in contact. [11]At the stem of the "balloon" Porphyra is attached strongly to the rocks by a cord of interwoven strands—hence its specific name, "umbilicalis." [12]Occasionally it is attached to barnacles and very rarely it grows on other algae instead of directly on hard surfaces. [13]When exposed at ebb tide under a hot sun, the laver may dry to brittle, papery layers, but the return of the sea restores the elastic nature of the plant, which, despite its seeming delicacy, allows it to yield unharmed to the push and pull of waves.

Rachel Carson,
The Rocky Coast

A. Vocabulary

For each italicized word from the paragraph, choose the best definition according to the context in which it appears.

1. *sparse* [3]: (a) sharp; prickly; (b) not densely crowded; (c) natural; (d) mature.

2. *stunted* [3]: (a) luxuriant; (b) struggling to survive; (c) dwarfed; (d) patchy; erratic.

3. *stringent* [3]: (a) vigorous; severe; (b) impossible to endure; (c) open; immediately apparent; (d) timeless; eternal.

4. *hardy* [4]: (a) expressing warmth; (b) brazenly daring; (c) courageous; stouthearted; (d) rugged; strong.

5. *profusion* [4]: (a) extravagance; (b) plentifulness; (c) density; (d) lavishness of display.

6. *generic* [7]: Referring to (a) a subspecies of plant; (b) a technical term; (c) a general term for a group or class; (d) a common, ordinary name.

7. *seeming* [13]: (a) apparent; (b) resembling; (c) suitable; proper; (d) amazing.

8. *yield* [13]: (a) furnish; give in return; (b) submit; give way to pressure or force; (c) live; survive; (d) stay fixed in one place.

B. Content and Structure

Choose the best answer.

1. In this paragraph, the author combines two modes of discourse: (a) narration and description; (b) description and exposition; (c) narration and exposition; (d) description and persuasion.

2. The author's purpose, specifically, is to (a) contrast species of seaweed found in various parts of the Atlantic coast; (b) demonstrate the strength of seaweed by describing one species, Porphyra; (c) explain how seaweed changes appearance according to the tides; (d) describe Porphyra so that the reader can visualize its unusual appearance.

3. The sentence that best expresses the main idea of the entire paragraph is sentence _____.

4. The pattern of organization in sentences 1–6 is (a) chronological; (b) inductive; (c) deductive; (d) spatial.

5. The pattern of organization used in the paragraph as a whole is (a) chronological; (b) inductive; (c) deductive; (d) spatial.

6. What makes the seaweed of the open coast so different from that found in bays and coves is (a) the presence of sharp rocks; (b) the cold sea temperatures; (c) the strong winds; (d) the heavy surf.

7. In sentence 11, *hence* means (a) in fact; (b) actually; (c) therefore; (d) in conclusion.

8. To describe the seaweed, Porphyra, Carson uses (a) similes; imaginative comparisons; (b) vague, generalized impressions; (c) factual, scientific language; (d) emotional language that appeals to the senses.

9. Carson compares Porphyra to a raincoat and a balloon to call attention chiefly to the plant's (a) color and texture; (b) practical use in industry; (c) durability and resemblance to other types of seaweed; (d) structure, appearance, and texture.

10. Apparently, what Carson finds most interesting about Porphyra is its (a) lavish range of colors; (b) ability to survive despite its fragile appearance; (c) complex structure and appearance; (d) adaptability to all types of climates and conditions.

C. Inferences   On the basis of the evidence in the paragraph, mark these statements as follows: *A* for accurate inferences, *I* for inaccurate inferences, and *IE* for insufficient evidence.

_____ 1. The difference between rockweeds that grow on the open coast and those that grow in bays is mainly their size.

_____ 2. In areas of the coast where the surf is heavy, seaweed rarely grows in abundance.

_____ 3. Porphyra has commercial uses, mainly as a source of purple dye.

_____ 4. The fronds of Porphyra are thin, fragile, and easily destroyed by waves.

_____ 5. The specific name of Porphyra, "umbilicalis," comes from the cord that attaches itself to rocks, much as the umbilical cord attaches a fetus to its mother.

Selection 4   [1]One of the most tenacious of the legends circulated with regard to sharks is the one which claims that he has poor eyesight. [2]Like all such information with no basis in truth, this legend is dangerous, since the unwarned diver may allow a shark to approach, in the hope of going unobserved. [3]Our experience on the *Calypso* has been considerably different. [4]One day, for example, when I went into the water on a shallow reef off the coast of Africa, near the Cape Verde Islands, I sighted a shark at a considerable distance from me. [5]I could scarcely make him out, and was only able to do so because his grayish color was silhouetted very clearly against the dazzling whiteness of the sand. [6]At that particular moment, I was floating at a very shallow depth, without making any movement, so that the sound of bubbles from my aqualung would be confused with the light splashing of the water. [7]I turned my eyes away for a few seconds, to study the symmetrical design of a giant ray just beneath me, which had half-covered itself with sand, as rays often do in an effort to make themselves invisible. [8]I am not sure now whether it was simple instinct or a perception of movement, but I turned back abruptly toward the location of the shark. [9]And immediately, every muscle of my body tensed. [10]He was no more than thirty feet away and was launched toward me as hard and swift as a missile. [11]My hands held no protective device and I was alone. [12]The sight of a shark coming at you head-on is very strange, and obviously it is from that angle that he seems most formidable. [13]The eyes are almost invisible, because of their lateral positioning, while the slit in the half-opened mouth, and the three regularly spaced fins give him the appearance of a malignant and terrifying symbol imagined by some Aztec sorcerer. [14]When he had approached to within two feet of the rubber fins I had hurled at him as a futile gesture of protection, the shark turned suddenly and swam back toward the depths.

Jacques–Yves Cousteau,
The Shark: Splendid Savage of the Sea

A. Vocabulary   For each italicized word from the paragraph, choose the best definition according to the context in which it appears.

1. *tenacious* [1]: (a) hazardous; dangerous; (b) stubborn; persistent; (c) ridiculous; absurd; (d) extensive; influential.

2. *silhouetted* [5]: (a) outlined; (b) superimposed; (c) painted; (d) contrasted.

3. *symmetrical* [7]: Describing an arrangement of parts that is (a) extraordinarily complex; (b) the same on either side of the median line; (c) out of proportion in relation to the whole; (d) designed for maximum efficiency and economy of movement.

4. *abruptly* [8]: (a) instinctively; (b) worriedly; (c) absent-mindedly; (d) suddenly.

5. *formidable* [12]: (a) awesome; arousing fear; (b) dangerous; (c) impressive in size and power; (d) difficult to defeat.

6. *lateral* [13]: Describing a position (a) on the bottom; (b) on the top; (c) on the sides; (d) toward the back.

7. *malignant* [13]: (a) cancerous; (b) evil; (c) awe-inspiring; (d) fearful.

8. *futile* [14]: (a) courageous; (b) threatening; (c) useless; (d) defensive.

B. Content and Structure

Choose the best answer.

1. What is the subject of this paragraph? _the shark having_
   a poor eyesight

   What does Cousteau want us to understand about this subject?
   that is eyesight is very good and it cant
   be dangerous to think it isn't

2. What is the purpose of sentence 1? (a) to state the main idea; **(b)** to state a common misconception that Cousteau wants to disprove; (c) to provide an electrifying anecdote that will entice the reader to continue reading; (d) to establish his authority with regard to the subject at hand.

3. The mode of discourse in sentences 4–14 is **(a)** narration; (b) description; (c) exposition; (d) persuasion.

4. Taken as a whole, the pattern of organization in the paragraph is **(a)** deductive; (b) inductive; (c) variation of deductive; (d) spatial; (e) emphatic.

5. The pattern of organization in sentences 4–14 is **(a)** chronological; (b) deductive; (c) inductive; (d) spatial.

6. Find three transitional phrases in the paragraph, write them in the spaces and indicate the specific function for each:

Transition	Sentence #	Function
at that particular moment	6	chronological
for example	4	illustration
and immediatly	9	chronological

7. In sentence 10, Cousteau compares the shark to a missile. What does he mean to suggest by this comparison? _both fast and destructive weapon_

8. The relationship between sentences 12 and 13 is (a) steps in a process; **(b)** statement and supporting details; (c) contrasting statements; (d) classification based on distinguishing characteristics.

9. In sentence 13, Cousteau describes the shark's appearance by saying that he resembled a symbol that might have been imagined by some Aztec sorcerer. This reference is meant to make us feel (a) pity; (b) sympathy; **(c)** terror; (d) admiration.

C. Inferences

On the basis of the evidence in the paragraph, mark these statements as follows: *A* for accurate inferences, *I* for inaccurate inferences, and *IE* for insufficient evidence.

_I_ 1. A shark's eyesight is not as keen as most people think.

_IE_ 2. The shark in this paragraph was a great white shark.

_IE_ 3. The *Calypso*'s mission on this trip was to investigate the legend that sharks have good vision.

_A_ 4. Until the event described here, Cousteau had believed that sharks' eyesight was poor.

[margin handwriting: transition change to some from one idea to another "and" by itself won't]

    5. The shark was merely curious about Cousteau and had no intention of harming him.

    6. Had Cousteau not thrown his rubber fins at the shark, it undoubtedly would have attacked him.

Selection 5

[1]As I approached the Gypsy camp for the first time, yellow, wild-looking, stiff-haired dogs howled and barked. [2]Fifteen covered wagons were spread out in a wide half circle, partly hiding the Gypsies from the road. [3]Around the campfires sat women draped in deep-colored dresses, their big, expressive eyes and strong, white teeth standing out against their beautiful dark matte skin. [4]The many gold pieces they wore as earrings, necklaces and bracelets sharpened their color even more. [5]Their shiny blue-black hair was long and braided, the skirts of their dresses were ankle-length, very full and worn in many layers, and their bodices loose and low-cut. [6]My first impression of them was one of health and vitality. [7]Hordes of small barefoot children ran all over the campsite, a few dressed in rags but most nearly naked, rollicking like young animals. [8]At the far end of the encampment a number of horses, tethered to long chains, were grazing; and of course there were the ever-present half-wild growling dogs. [9]Several men lay in the shade of an oak tree. [10]Thin corkscrews of bluish smoke rose skyward and the pungent, penetrating smell of burning wood permeated the air. [11]Even from a distance the loud, clear voices of these Gypsies resounded with an intensity I was not accustomed to. [12]Mingling with them, farther away, were the dull thuds of an ax, the snorting and neighing of horses, the occasional snapping of a whip and the high-pitched wail of an infant, contrasting with the whisper of the immediate surroundings of the camp itself.

Jan Yoors,
The Gypsies

A. Vocabulary

For each italicized word from the paragraph, choose the best definition according to the context in which it appears.

1. *bodices* [5]: (a) skirts; (b) sleeves; (c) top portions of dresses; (d) petticoats.
2. *vitality* [6]: (a) laziness; (b) enthusiasm; (c) curiosity; (d) energy.
3. *rollicking* [7]: (a) rolling; (b) prancing; (c) behaving; (d) romping.
4. *tethered* [8]: (a) restricted; (b) bound up; (c) draped in; (d) decorated.
5. *pungent* [10]: (a) sweetish; (b) biting; (c) sickening; (d) familiar.
6. *permeated* [10]: (a) perfumed; (b) polluted; (c) wafted through; (d) pervaded.

B. Content and Structure

Choose the best answer.

1. The mode of discourse in this paragraph is (a) narration; (b) description; (c) exposition; (d) persuasion.

2. A good title for this paragraph would be (a) A Study of Gypsy Life; (b) Will Gypsies Survive? (c) I Decide to Become a Gypsy; (d) First Impressions of a Gypsy Camp.

3. What two nouns does Yoors use to characterize the Gypsies? ____Health____ and ____vitality____ in sentence __6__.

4. The pattern of organization is (a) deductive; (b) spatial; (c) chronological; (d) inductive; (e) emphatic.

5. Yoors uses many words that appeal to our senses in this passage. Which does he *not* emphasize? Words pertaining to (a) sight; (b) smell; (c) sound; (d) touch; (e) colors.

6. Which best represents Yoors's opinion of these Gypsies? He thinks they are (a) lazy and dirty; (b) fascinating; (c) weird; (d) untrustworthy.

C. Inferences   On the basis of the evidence in the paragraph, mark these statements as follows: *A* for accurate inferences, *I* for inaccurate inferences, and *IE* for insufficient evidence.

_IE_ 1. The Gypsy camp the author observed was in America.

_IE_ 2. The author had expected the Gypsy camp to be entirely different.

_IE_ 3. Gypsies are persecuted in most countries.

_A_ 4. Gypsy culture, at least the culture represented by this group, is essentially nomadic.

_IE_ 5. In Gypsy culture, the women do all the work, while the men lie around and enjoy themselves.

Selection 6   [1]More and more cable subscribers have been buying videocassette recorders, with which they can record shows off their cable systems or off the networks and watch them at times of their own choosing—a practice known in the business as "time-shifting." [2]Although time-shifting may increase the accessibility of certain cable programs to many subscribers, the cable-industry people nonetheless appear to be worried—as the commercial broadcasters certainly are—about the effects of VCRs on revenues from advertiser-supported program services. [3]They fear that if time-shifting spreads sufficiently it may play havoc with the prevailing audience-ratings system upon which advertising agencies rely so heavily. [4]And the advertising people complain that the use of VCRs by cable subscribers is throwing into confusion the measurement of which parts of the cable audiences are watching which programs, and when. [5]Furthermore, the advertising people appear to be disturbed by what they consider another hateful practice, known on Madison Avenue as "zapping": when a VCR-owning cable subscriber eventually plays an advertiser-supported progam that he has previously recorded, he has the ability, when a commercial starts, to quickly skip over it by pressing the fast-forward button—zapping it—and thereby frustrating the purpose of the advertising people who put their money into the show. [6]And so the great recent increase in

VCR ownership, accompanied by the increase in time-shifting and in zapping commercials, appears to have underlined whatever uncertainties many advertising people already may have been having about the desirability of using cable as a major advertising medium.

Thomas Whiteside,
"Cable Television"

A. Vocabulary

For each italicized word from the paragraph, choose the best definition according to the context in which it appears.

1. *accessibility* [2]: (a) entertainment value; (b) popularity; (c) profitability; (d) ability to be used or obtained.

2. *nonetheless* [2]: (a) also; in addition; (b) nevertheless; even so; (c) clearly; obviously; (d) as a result; consequently.

3. *play havoc with* [3]: (a) ruin; (b) expand; (c) confuse; (d) make major changes in.

4. *prevailing* [3]: (a) popular; (b) predominant; (c) effective; (d) current.

5. *underlined* [6]: (a) drawn a line under; (b) weakened; (c) preyed on; (d) emphasized.

B. Content and Structure

Choose the best answer.

1. Whiteside's purpose is to (a) persuade us that VCR ownership is ruining the advertising industry; (b) present the concerns of the advertising and cable television people about increased ownership of VCRs; (c) present his own opinions about the effects of VCR ownership; (d) explain how "time-shifting" and "zapping" work with a VCR.

2. The mode of discourse is (a) narration; (b) description; (c) exposition; (d) persuasion.

3. Mark any of these methods of paragraph development that Whiteside uses: (a) illustration; (b) analogy; (c) process; (d) cause–effect; (e) definition; (f) analysis.

4. Which of the following *best* states the main idea of this paragraph? (a) The VCR is the most important invention to the entertainment industry since the invention of television itself. (b) Broadcasters and advertisers are concerned about the increased use of VCRs in American homes. (c) More and more cable subscribers have been buying VCRs. (d) The increased use of VCRs has caused advertising agencies to question the desirability of using cable television as a major advertising medium.

5. Mark the *two* patterns of organization evident in the paragraph: (a) deductive; (b) variation of deductive; (c) chronological; (d) spatial; (e) inductive; (f) emphatic.

6. Look again at sentence 2. What is the relationship between the first clause ("although time-shifting may increase the accessibility of certain cable programs to many subscribers") and the rest of the sentence? The first clause represents (a) an example; (b) a definition; (c) an admission of truth; (d) a cause preceding an effect.

7. Apparently, advertisers rely heavily on (a) cable television for the major source of advertising revenue; (b) word-of-mouth recommendations for their products; (c) audience-rating systems that measure which part of an audience is watching what programs; (d) business analyses and predictions of the number of households subscribing to cable and purchasing VCRs.

8. The transitional word *furthermore* in sentence 5 signals (a) a contrasting statement; (b) a definition; (c) a conclusion; (d) an additional statement of equal importance; (e) another stage in the chronology.

9. According to the paragraph, "zapping" means the practice of (a) shifting the times when one watches programs; (b) fast-forwarding the tape to eliminate commercials; (c) erasing old tapes and recording over them; (d) illegally copying rented movies and selling them for a profit.

10. Judging from the evidence in the paragraph, what is Whiteside's opinion about VCRs? (a) He thinks VCRs are merely a clever gimmick. (b) He thinks VCRs lend themselves to all sorts of hateful practices. (c) He thinks VCRs have thrown the cable and advertising industries into chaos, threatening to cause their imminent ruin. (d) His own opinion of VCRs is not evident.

C. Inferences   On the basis of the evidence in the paragraph, mark these statements as follows: *A* for accurate inferences, *I* for inaccurate inferences, and *IE* for insufficient evidence.

____ 1. Commercial and cable broadcasters alike are concerned about the effects of VCR ownership on their industries.

____ 2. Television programs are financed by revenue from advertising sponsors.

____ 3. If the practice of "time-shifting" becomes more widespread among VCR owners, the audience-rating business will be hurt.

____ 4. The term "Madison Avenue" refers to the place where most of the cable television networks are located.

____ 5. The advertising industry was initially enthusiastic about committing large amounts of money to sponsoring cable television programs.

PRACTICE ESSAY

Everybody's Sport
John Knowles

American writer John Knowles is best known for his novel, *A Separate Peace,* which has become a classic work for American high school and college students.

1   In many ways a pool is the best place to do real swimming. Free water tends to be too tempestuous, while in a pool it is tamed and imprisoned; the challenge has been filtered out of it along with the bacteria.

2   I did my first swimming in a pool, and have tried pools in many places since then. The most glittering was the Eden Roc pool of the Hotel du Cap d'Antibes, and the most enjoyable was at a kind of oasis in Texas where I was stationed with the Air Force. Here, a swimming pool was a real blessing, for this part of Texas lacked water to drink, let alone to swim in. Many days a cloud of dust—"Oklahoma!" the Texans called it—blew over and settled down upon us, our cots, and everything else. Finally we learned that water had been struck nearby and that two crude swimming pools had been built.

3   One of the pools was very cold, and the other was colder. To us in Texas in July, they had the power to exhilarate, to free us from the sunlight which fell like metal from the blank sky. They offered all you could ask of water, all you could wish for in swimming. No indoor pool could rival them.

4   Nevertheless, indoor pools excel in one way—in the use of artifice to enhance the pleasure of swimming. The best artificial effects I have seen are in the Exhibition Pool at Yale University.

5   It is surrounded by a large, dark green amphitheater which slopes steeply upward. Shining in the center of this somber oval is the pool, its white tile deck and pastel blue water glittering frivolously away. If you stand beside it alone, with no one in the water or the seats, you become aware of an august silence, as though you were in a mechanized cathedral.

6   I was there alone one day when someone began throwing control switches. Banks of lights overhead and along the sides went out and only the pool remained lighted, from below the surface, glowing like a luminous, smoky, green-blue cloud suspended in a black cavern. I dived in. The light seemed amazingly to increase my buoyancy; the water bore me up as though I were made of cork and could float forever.

7   In fierce contrast to such peace and glamour is the surf, which is charged with challenge. Surf swimming is much better managed now, of course; in the old days people who had come near drowning were revived by being hanged from the heels, or bled, or rolled over a barrel, or, as sometimes happened, pushed back into the water lest God consider it impious for men to bring back someone so close to eternity. We know better now, but even so, the surf's disturbing undercurrent is there for every swimmer to feel, and on rough days the warnings go up and swimmers are restricted to a particular area or kept out of the water altogether.

8   The surf at such moments is not to be trifled with. In fact you never trifle with the surf; when it is in a playful mood, the surf trifles with you. That's the joy of swimming in it. Along comes a large but playful wave. It rises up and smacks you, shoves you along, knocks you off your feet like a big clumsy dog trying to ingratiate itself with a child. You are the child. It doesn't matter if you hold an Olympic gold medal; in the surf you wallow and are knocked around like any dog-paddler.

9   Another wave swells up, growing more intimidating by the moment. As it nears you, the great crest breaks, an immense amount of rushing water is

about to crash over your head. You are just a morsel of flotsam, but you happen to be human and you have the ingenuity which raised your ancestors out of the water in the first place. You put your arms in front of you, your head between them, and dive through the wave. Despite its tremendous force, it hurtles harmlessly over you and smashes its energy ineffectually against the shore.

10   A new swell approaches, and you decide to ride it in. This is a much trickier feat. You turn your body toward shore and glance coolly over your shoulder to note how big the wave is, how fast it is coming and, most crucially of all, when it will break. Your judgment, let's say, is just right. You are already planing toward the beach when the wave reaches you. It bears you surgingly up and forward, and just then the threatening tracery along its crest breaks, not over you but under you. You can feel its chaotic turbulence beating all along your body. It goes on and on, like some rolling hydraulic engine beneath you, shooting you wildly toward shore. At last it beaches you, with a certain grudging gentleness. Victory.

11   More usually, you are too far from shore and begin to plane too soon, so that the wave lifts you up briefly, like King Kong balancing a match box, then contemptuously lets you fall and sweeps on. Or worse, you are too close to shore, and as you watch the approach of the wave with that cool glance over your shoulder, you notice that the foam is thickening too soon along its crest. The wave suddenly transforms itself into a top-heavy, rushing wall; it's too late to turn and dive into it, too late to run, too late to duck. The wave breaks on top of you. Now you're helpless; the breaker embroils you, grinds you in its vortex, somersaults you six or eight times and then tosses you up on the shore like a piece of spent seaweed. Surf swimming is perhaps the most elemental of all athletic experiences; you give over your being to the action of waves, currents, tides—things titanic and even cosmic.

12   These are some of the joys of swimming. In all its forms, even in competitive swimming, the source of our pleasure is facing and conquering the challenge of water. Watch any child, after he has been alarmed by a ducking or two, gingerly find his way to a delighted confidence when he learns that water will actually support him. As he learns to deal with it, the water will become the best playground he ever had, with just enough echo of the challenge left in it to keep him always stimulated.

13   Swimming is essentially a simple and even a humble sport. It inspires none of the mass adulation of baseball, or the protocol of tennis or the folklore of fishing or the *esprit de corps* of skiing. Most sports require equipment ranging from a ball to a bull, but swimming is independent even of the fins and goggles and other innovations that have brought so much new fun in the water. This is the sport of commoners. All you need to enjoy it is a certain amount of water—the most abundant substance on earth.

A. Comprehension   Choose the answer that best completes each statement. Do not refer to the selection while doing this exercise.

1. Knowles states that a pool is the best place for real swimming because free water is too (a) unpredictable; (b) scary; (c) tempestuous; (d) exhilarating.

2. One way in which pools are superior to free water is (a) their use of artificial devices, especially lighting; (b) their controlled temperatures; (c) the fact that they can be built anywhere; (d) the fact that they can be enjoyed throughout the year.

3. The lighting system at the Yale University Exhibition Pool enhanced Knowles's enjoyment of swimming by seeming to increase his (a) stamina; (b) buoyancy; (c) sense of frivolity; (d) energy.

4. The central point Knowles makes about the ocean is that (a) it is dangerous to all but the best swimmers; (b) it requires tremendous stamina and skill to outwit its undercurrent and power; (c) it treats all swimmers alike regardless of their swimming abilities; (d) it never allows swimmers a victory.

5. Knowles characterizes swimming as "a simple and even a humble sport" and "the sport of commoners" because (a) it is generally enjoyed in public places; (b) it requires no fancy or expensive equipment; (c) it does not require much skill; (d) it has little status in comparison to other sports.

B. Inferences   On the basis of the evidence in the selection, mark these statements as follows: *A* for accurate inferences, *I* for inaccurate inferences, and *IE* for insufficient evidence. You may refer to the selection to answer the questions in this and in all the remaining exercise sections.

_____ 1. Ironically, Texas ground water is cold, at least in one part of the state, despite the hot air temperature.

_____ 2. Knowles won an Olympic gold medal for swimming.

_____ 3. In the old days, lifesaving techniques were both crude and inhumane.

_____ 4. Diving under a wave is risky, since the tremendous force can overpower even the strongest swimmer.

_____ 5. The key element to riding a wave successfully is careful timing.

C. Structure   Choose the best answer.

1. Which of the following choices best expresses the thesis statement (the main idea) of the entire essay? (a) "In many ways a pool is the best place to do real swimming"; (b) "The surf is not to be trifled with"; (c) "Swimming is essentially a simple and even a humble sport"; (d) "These are some of the joys of swimming. In all its forms, even in competitive swimming, the source of our pleasure is facing and conquering the challenge of water."

2. In relation to paragraph 3, the word *nevertheless* in paragraph 4 signals (a) an example; (b) a conclusion; (c) an additional statement of equal importance; (d) a contrast.

3. In paragraph 3, Knowles describes the Texas sky as "blank," by which he means that it was (a) cloudless; (b) gray; (c) heavy; (d) white.

4. What mode of discourse does Knowles use in paragraphs 5 and 6? (a) narration; (b) description; (c) exposition; (d) persuasion.

5. In paragraphs 8–11, which method of paragraph development is most evident? (a) contrast; (b) illustration; (c) cause–effect; (d) process.

6. Write the sentence, and the number of the paragraph in which it occurs, that marks the transition between the two parts of the essay:

   In fierce contrast to such peace and glamour is the surf ,

   in paragraph _7_ .

7. Examine the following paragraphs and determine whether the pattern of organization is deductive, a variation of deductive, inductive, chronological, spatial, or emphatic.

   paragraph 5 _spatial_   paragraph 10 _chronological_
   paragraph 8 _deduc_   paragraph 11 ~~inductive~~ _chronological._
   paragraph 9 _chronolog_   paragraph 12 _deductive_ .

   emphatic?

8. In paragraph 8, Knowles refers to Olympic gold medal swimmers and dog paddlers. On what basis is he classifying swimmers? According to their (a) age; (b) size; (c) skill and experience; (d) level of stamina and energy.

9. Throughout the essay, Knowles uses several figures of speech—imaginative comparisons to heighten the effect of his ideas—three of which follow. The terms of the comparison are given for you. In your own words, state the characteristic or quality that the author has in mind for each metaphor.

   Paragraph 8: "Along comes a large but playful wave. It rises up and smacks you, shoves you along, knocks you off your feet like a big clumsy dog trying to ingratiate itself with a child."
   A wave is being compared to a dog.
   Which characteristic of a dog is Knowles referring to? _playfull_

   Paragraph 9: "You are just a morsel of flotsam. . . ." You, the swimmer, are being compared to a morsel of flotsam.
   What quality of flotsam is Knowles referring to? (See a dictionary, if necessary.) _its float_

   Paragraph 11: ". . . the wave lifts you up briefly, like King Kong balancing a match box."
   The wave is being compared to King Kong, and the swimmer is compared to a match box.
   What characteristic of King Kong is Knowles referring to? _his strength and size_

   What characteristic of a match box is Knowles referring to? _lightness — it can be easely lift and thrown in the air_

10. Read the last sentence of paragraph 11 again. What is the relationship between the two parts of the sentence (separated by a semicolon)? (a) cause–effect; (b) steps in a process; (c) general and specific attributes; (d) contrast.

D. Fact and Opinion   Mark the following statements from the selection, using this key: *F* if it represents a *fact* (a true statement that is verifiable) and *O* if it represents an *opinion* (a statement that reflects the author's own feelings or subjective point of view).

_____ 1. "A pool is the best place to do real swimming."

_____ 2. "This part of Texas lacked water to drink, let alone to swim in."

_____ 3. "Indoor pools excel in one way—in the use of artifice to enhance the pleasure of swimming."

_____ 4. "That's the joy of swimming in it. . . . It knocks you off your feet like a big clumsy dog."

_____ 5. "Water—the most abundant substance on earth."

E. Vocabulary   For each italicized word from the selection, choose the best definition according to the context in which it appears.

1. Free water tends to be too *tempestuous* [paragraph 1]: (a) challenging; (b) turbulent; (c) relaxing; (d) wind-driven.

2. the use of *artifice* [4]: (a) something contrived to achieve a desired effect; (b) deliberate deception; (c) object produced by human workmanship; (d) a carefully planned environment.

3. an *august* silence [5]: (a) ominous; (b) breathtaking; (c) inspiring awe and admiration; (d) inspiring fear and respect.

4. glowing like a *luminous* cloud [6]: Full of (a) color; (b) shadows; (c) glitter; (d) light.

5. lest God consider it *impious* [7; pronounced im′ pē-əs]: (a) selfish; (b) lacking reverence; (c) improper; (d) foolish.

6. a dog trying to *ingratiate* itself [8]: (a) be ungrateful; (b) play with; (c) win favor; (d) make an extra effort.

7. in the surf you *wallow* [8]: (a) strike with a hard blow; (b) roll around clumsily; (c) are abundantly supplied; (d) billow; surge forth.

8. a wave grows more *intimidating* [9]: (a) threatening; (b) intense; (c) enormous; (d) terrifying.

9. you have the *ingenuity* [9]: (a) physical strength; (b) intelligence; (c) inventive skill; imagination; (d) will or drive to succeed.

10. This is a much trickier *feat* [10]: (a) act of skill; exploit; (b) risk; (c) decision; (d) strategy.

11. the wave *contemptuously* lets you fall [11]: (a) lightly; (b) aggressively; (c) clumsily; (d) scornfully.

12. the breaker *embroils* you [11]: (a) involves in an argument; (b) entangles; throws into confusion; (c) covers completely; (d) threatens to harm.

13. the waves are things *titanic* [11]: (a) terrifying; (b) fundamental; (c) having enormous strength; (d) incomprehensible.

14. the waves are even *cosmic* [14]: (a) sophisticated; worldly; (b) harmonious; (c) pertaining to the divine realm; (d) pertaining to the universe.

15. It inspires none of the mass *adulation* of baseball [13]: (a) excessive praise; (b) appeal; (c) hysteria; (d) pleasure; satisfaction.

Other words you should know the meaning of:
vortex [11]
esprit de corps [13]

F. Variant Word Forms   From the list of inflected forms in parentheses, choose the form that fits grammatically into the space. Add endings (-s or -ed, for example) if necessary.

1. (exhilaration, exhilarate, exhilarating): Knowles found the contrast between the hot Texas air and the cold temperature of the pool *exhilarating*.

2. (enhancement, enhance, enhanced, enhancing): The use of artificial devices *enhanced* the joys of swimming in an indoor pool.

3. (buoyancy, buoy, buoyant, buoyantly): A lighted pool gives the illusion of *buoying* up the swimmer.

4. (fierceness, fierce, fiercely): In contrast to swimming in a pool, ocean swimming is much more *fierce*.

5. (chaos, chaotic, chaotically): Even the strongest swimmer cannot withstand the *chaotic* turbulence of a large ocean wave.

chapter 5 ‖ LANGUAGE

In this chapter, we will be concerned with language in prose—with words and the effect they have on the reader. Specifically, we will examine denotation and connotation of words, slanted language, the way words can be misused and abused, and figurative language. It is crucial to your understanding of tone, the subject of the next chapter, that you understand the way words work.

Let us start with an analogy. Imagine that a person knows nothing about cars. This person looks under the hood and sees only a jumble of rods, cylinders, and other unidentifiable objects, all of which he or she vaguely knows have something to do with the car's functioning. With some training, however, such a person—previously thought to be hopeless mechanically—can learn not only to name the parts but also understand how each works to make the car run. In the same way, an inexperienced reader may look at a piece of prose and see only a tangle of words. By now, however, you have made substantial progress toward understanding how a writer communicates the main idea, organizes the supporting ideas, and develops them in a coherent way. It remains only to examine the power of words in their context, the way a writer's carefully chosen language affects us, the way words arouse our feelings. Authors write not only because they have something to communicate, but because they want to reach our emotions, to make us feel and respond to their ideas. It is for this reason that these difficult aspects of analytical reading are saved for these last chapters. A thorough grounding in the ways writers express themselves will go a long way both to improve your understanding of what you read and to enhance your enjoyment and appreciation of written prose.

A. DENOTATION AND CONNOTATION

First, it is necessary to evaluate the writer's choice of words, particularly for the specific effect they create for the reader. Some words are used to arouse positive feelings, some are meant to be neutral, and others are meant to convey a negative response. *Denotation* refers to a word's explicit, or literal, meaning; it is for this reason that denotation is sometimes referred to as the dictionary definition of a word. The word *desk,* for example, denotes or points to the piece of furniture made of wood or metal where one sits to study or work, and therefore does not conjure up any particular emotional feeling. Similarly, the word *lemon* usually points to a kind of fruit that belongs to the citrus family. *Connotation,* on the other hand, refers to the cluster of suggestions, emotional responses, or implications—positive or negative—that a word carries with it in addition to its literal or explicit meaning (its denotation).

The word *lemon,* for example, was cited as an example of denotation in the previous paragraph, but it might also have a negative connotation in a different context if, for example, one describes a car as a "lemon." In the same way, *dog* is generally neutral (and denotative), since it refers literally to the four-legged house pet. But "she worked like a dog" suggests an uncomplaining diligence, and therefore has a positive connotation; "he looks like a dog" is, however, decidedly uncomplimentary. On the other hand, *purebred* has a positive connotation, while *cur* carries negative overtones. *Nude* has a positive connotation (coming from its association with art), whereas *naked* can have a negative connotation, as in the phrase "naked women." *Childlike* sounds positive (suggesting sweetness, innocence, and the other endearing traits children have), whereas *childish* has a negative connotation, whether it is used to describe children or adults. One last example: The dictionary lists several words as synonyms for *secret,* including *stealthy, covert, clandestine, furtive, surreptitious,* and *underhand.* The notes after the definitions clarify their meanings and suggest both their denotative and connotative meanings. All apply to something purposely concealed from view or knowledge, but *secret* is the most general and, therefore, the weakest (or least judgmental) in suggesting anything beyond its basic meaning. The rest all carry varying degrees of negative connotative associations. As you already know from the introductory section on vocabulary, these explanations from the dictionary are invaluable in determining exactly what emotional response a writer has in mind and what impact a word is meant to have on the reader.

B. LANGUAGE MISUSED AND ABUSED

Slanted Language   Language can be used unscrupulously by writers to manipulate the reader, to incite or inflame passions, or to soften the impact of ideas that might otherwise be more realistically or harshly interpreted. As a critical reader, you should be particularly alert to language that attempts to manipulate you—not through careful, reasoned thought, but through appeals to your emotions. We call this kind of verbal manipulation *slanted language.* In this section, we will look briefly at three kinds of slanted language: weasel words, euphemisms, and sneer words.

(1) Weasel Words.   In a clever book on the advertising industry, Carl Wrighter defines weasel words like this:

A weasel word is "a word used in order to evade or retreat from a direct or forthright statement or position" (Webster). In other words, if we can't say it, we'll weasel it. And, in fact, a weasel word has become more than just an evasion or retreat. We've trained our weasels. They can do anything. They can make you hear things that aren't being said, accept as truths things that have only been implied, and believe things that have only been suggested. Come to think of it, not only do we have our weasels trained, but they, in turn, have got you trained. When *you* hear a weasel word, you automatically hear the implication. Not the real meaning, but the meaning *it* wants *you* to hear.

Carl Wrighter,
"Weasel Words," *I Can Sell You Anything*

Wrighter goes on to enumerate examples of weasel words, such as:

helps
"helps you stay dry," "helps stop bad breath," "helps keep your floor shiny"—none of these phrases suggests that the product *actually does* what it claims to do;

virtually
"virtually frostfree," "virtually new," "since 1949, boys and girls in our kindergarten virtually finish 10 or more books before grade 1"—since "virtually" means "in essence or effect," but not "in fact," the claim is absurd

the look of or *the feel of*
"has the look of real leather" (describing vinyl), "has the feel of real wool" (describing polyester)

Look for your own examples of clever weasel words in television or magazine advertisements.

(2) Euphemisms. A *euphemism* is a supposedly inoffensive word or phrase substituted for an offensive one. Writers often resort to euphemisms to soften our perception of events, to change our beliefs, or to cover up what the real situation is.

During World War II, Japanese-Americans living on the West Coast were forced to move to what the government called "relocation centers." However, the places where the Nazis and the Soviets imprisoned Jews and other captives were referred to disparagingly by the Allies as "concentration camps." During the Vietnam War, euphemisms were widely used in government reports about the American presence in Southeast Asia. For example, the 1970 American invasion of Cambodia was described by the government as an "incursion," thereby making it sound less serious than the more negative "invasion." Bombs were known as "anti-personnel weapons"; herbicides became known as "defoliants"; the war itself (which, in fact, was never declared by Congress) was continually referred to as a "conflict"; and the U.S. didn't withdraw; the American presence was "de-escalated." Some euphemisms are ridiculous. A savings-and-loan in Los Angeles calls its tellers "money hostesses." An elevator operator calls himself a "vertical transportation operator." A botched surgery is "a therapeutic misadventure."

At their very worst, euphemisms amount to language pollution, something George Orwell warned about in his famous 1946 essay, "Politics in the English Language." Some of the earlier examples cited were merely humorous, others ridiculous, but some can be dangerous, constituting what is called "doublespeak," a deliberate misuse of words by government officials, advertisers, and even teachers.

In business, euphemisms can be used to cover up crimes. It was discovered that the president of a major Hollywood film studio had embezzled more than $60,000 by forging other people's signatures on checks and had cheated on his expense account by more than $300,000. Because he was well-respected by the company's board, the company issued press releases describing the forgery euphemistically as "unauthorized use of another person's signature" and the phony expense-account transactions as "unauthorized use of the company's funds." It wasn't until the story leaked to the newspapers and several reporters began doing their own investigating that the true nature of the crimes was made public.

In an article called "Down with Doublespeak," Fred Hechinger discusses the Committee on Doublespeak, part of the National Council of Teachers of English, whose magazine, *Quarterly Review of Doublespeak,* publishes examples of particularly awful misused language. For example: The State Department recently decided to stop using the word "killing" in official reports on human rights in other countries. The new doublespeak term: "unlawful or arbitrary deprivation of life." A school principal, whose proposal for a swimming pool was turned down, resubmitted the proposal with a new title, "Aquatic Therapy Department." Companies who intend to lay off people say their plan is to "resize our operations to the level of profitable market opportunities."

Hechinger concludes his article with this paragraph:

> At the heart of the English teachers' battle against doublespeak is more than a concern with the quality of speech and writing, with good or poor performance in English. The deliberate misuse of words amounts to dishonesty. In the hands of government, it is a weapon to mislead the public. In business affairs, it is designed to hoodwink customers or stockholders. In the long run, as has been illustrated by every totalitarian government, it kills the people's sensitivity to violations of human rights. On the surface, doublespeak sounds amusing; its point, however, is that words are serious business.
>
> Fred H. Hechinger,
> "Down with Doublespeak"

(3) Sneer Words.   As we saw in the case of euphemisms, a writer can shape our perception of events—softening reality by using euphemisms, or intensifying an already difficult situation by using *sneer words*. The term *sneer word* is apt, since it conveys scorn, derision, and contempt. During the 1979–1980 occupation of the American Embassy in Iran, journalists and reporters began using sneer words to describe the Iranian occupiers, reflecting the public's (and presumably the press's) growing frustration over the hostage crisis. In this passage, William Safire describes what happened:

> As the crisis began, those who took over the American Embassy in Tehran were described as Iranian students. After a while, the word

"students" began to appear in quotation marks, as if reporters were uncomfortable with the designation. Finally, former diplomat Henry E. Catto Jr. demanded: "What schools do these people attend? . . . What course are they taking, American Humiliation 101? The fact is that these young Iranians are political terrorists, blackmailers and kidnappers, and they should be so labeled. . . . They are 'students' to the gullible."

Since "students" is a word connoting youth and idealism, many reporters and commentators—to avoid the appearance of being manipulated by propagandists—took to placing quotation marks around the term, or to adding sneer words.

Sneer words are those adjectives that put some distance between the speaker and the subject by saying, "I'm using this next word under protest." Examples of sneer words are "self-proclaimed," "self-styled," "would-be," "purported" and that Soviet favorite, "so-called." Thus, the terrorists at the embassy were referred to as "the so-called students"; if the commentator was on television, the listener could almost hear the quotation marks added: "The so-called 'students' . . ." Reporters who were unhappy with quotation marks, but did not want to go so far as calling the occupiers "terrorists," chose the neutral "militants."

William Safire,
"Sneer Words in the News"

Jargon

Jargon is the specialized language used by members of a particular trade, group, or profession. In and of itself, jargon is not necessarily bad, and it is certainly natural for specialists to employ terms that outsiders might not understand. For example, while most of us associate the word *holiday* with a day at the beach, a hiking trip, or simply a day when we can sleep late, to a house painter the word means a spot on the wall that his brush missed. This is an inoffensive use of jargon, one that the reader could probably figure out from the context. The computer revolution has introduced many terms into the language that are properly part of computer jargon, such as *interface* which is often used to describe what two people do when they talk to each other. *Input* is commonly used to describe a suggestion. A professor at Rutgers University, Ross Baker, has written a parody of the first line of the Declaration of Independence, using computerese: "When at a given point in time in the human-events cycle, the phase-out of political relationships is mandated, a clear signal needs to be communicated to the world as to why we are putting independence on-line." (Quoted in Donald Hall's article, "A Fear of Metaphors," *New York Times Magazine*, July 14, 1985.)

At its best, jargon is useful, providing a verbal shorthand between two people, both of whom are fluent in the terminology and subject. At its worst, jargon is infuriating because the reader knows that the writer is unable to communicate even the simplest idea in clear prose. A good way to grasp the misuse and abuse of modern language is to read the following piece by Russell Baker, the political writer whose column is syndicated widely in American newspapers. Baker has rewritten the fairy tale, "Little Red Riding Hood," in order to poke fun at the worst aspects of modern English—

pompous language, the inflated diction of bureaucrats and politicians, and academic jargon.

In an effort to make the classics accessible to contemporary readers, I am translating them into the modern American language. Here is the translation of "Little Red Riding Hood":

Once upon a point in time, a small person named Little Red Riding Hood initiated plans for the preparation, delivery and transportation of foodstuffs to her grandmother, a senior citizen residing at a place of residence in a forest of indeterminate dimension.

In the process of implementing this program, her incursion into the forest was in mid-transportation process when it attained interface with an alleged perpetrator. This individual, a wolf, made inquiry as to the whereabouts of Little Red Riding Hood's goal as well as inferring that he was desirous of ascertaining the contents of Little Red Riding Hood's foodstuffs basket, and all that.

"It would be inappropriate to lie to me," the wolf said, displaying his huge jaw capability. Sensing that he was a mass of repressed hostility intertwined with acute alienation, she indicated.

"I see you indicating," the wolf said, "but what I don't see is whatever it is you're indicating at, you dig?"

Little Red Riding Hood indicated more fully, making one thing perfectly clear—to wit, that it was to her grandmother's residence and with a consignment of foodstuffs that her mission consisted of taking her to and with.

At this point in time the wolf moderated his rhetoric and proceeded to grandmother's residence. The elderly person was then subjected to the disadvantages of total consumption and transferred to residence in the perpetrator's stomach.

"That will raise the old woman's consciousness," the wolf said to himself. He was not a bad wolf, but only a victim of an oppressive society, a society that not only denied wolves' rights, but actually boasted of its capacity for keeping the wolf from the door. An interior malaise made itself manifest inside the wolf.

"Is that the national malaise I sense within my digestive tract?" wondered the wolf. "Or is it the old person seeking to retaliate for her consumption by telling wolf jokes to my duodenum?" It was time to make a judgment. The time was now, the hour had struck, the body lupine cried out for decision. The wolf was up to the challenge. He took two stomach powders right away and got into bed.

The wolf had adopted the abdominal-distress recovery posture when Little Red Riding Hood achieved his presence.

"Grandmother," she said, "your ocular implements are of an extraordinary order of magnitude."

"The purpose of this enlarged viewing capability," said the wolf, "is to enable your image to register a more precise impression upon my sight systems."

"In reference to your ears," said Little Red Riding Hood, "it is noted with the deepest respect that far from being underprivileged, their elongation and enlargement appear to qualify you for unparalleled distinction."

"I hear you loud and clear, kid," said the wolf, "but what about these new choppers?"

"If it is not inappropriate," said Little Red Riding Hood, "it might be observed that with your new miracle masticating products you may even be able to chew taffy again."

This observation was followed by the adoption of an aggressive posture on the part of the wolf and the assertion that it was also possible for him, due to the high efficiency ratio of his jaw, to consume little persons, plus, as he stated, his firm determination to do so at once without delay and with all due process and propriety, notwithstanding the fact that the ingestion of one entire grandmother had already provided twice his daily recommended cholesterol intake.

There ensued flight by Little Red Riding Hood accompanied by pursuit in respect to the wolf and a subsequent intervention on the part of a third party, heretofore unnoted in the record.

Due to the firmness of the intervention, the wolf's stomach underwent ax-assisted aperture with the result that Red Riding Hood's grandmother was enabled to be removed with only minor discomfort.

The wolf's indigestion was immediately alleviated with such effectiveness that he signed a contract with the intervening third party to perform with grandmother in a television commercial demonstrating the swiftness of this dramatic relief for stomach discontent.

Russell Baker,
"Little Red Riding Hood Revisited"

Clichés

Finally, there are clichés, the fossilized, stale expressions that tell the careful reader that a lazy writer is at work. Here are a few examples: "She is as pretty as a picture"; "He is as happy as a clam with his new job"; "The new proposal for a sewage-treatment plant has received a groundswell of support from the community"; "My boss always has an ax to grind"; "His novel was a labor of love"; "The accident victim lay at death's door." To end this section on a humorous note, here is a spoof on clichés. Not only does the writer poke fun at the "tough-guy" form of detective fiction, but the story itself is "chock-full" of trite expressions.

Eric Elfman is just a shade over 18. He has a ready smile, a way with words, and he knows a good thing when he sees one.

Recently he won the "Great American Cliché Contest," which entitles him to a week of fun in the sun for two at the fabulous Fontainebleau Hotel in Miami Beach.

"I couldn't believe it when I heard the news," Elfman recalled last week in a rare, exclusive interview. "It was like a dream come true."

The tension had been mounting for months. Elfman had seen an ad for the contest at a bookstore. It was a promotion for a book called "The Great American Cliché" by Lawrence Paros.

"I didn't want good fortune to pass me by," Elfman said.

"I guess you could say I was ready when opportunity knocked."

Elfman didn't waste any time getting started. He hopped a bus back to his apartment in Westchester, just a stone's throw from the Los Angeles airport.

As he bent over his typewriter, his mind teeming with clichés, he could see the giant silver birds lifting slowly off the tarmac. But Elfman barely noticed. He was buried in his work.

This is what he wrote, the fruit of his labors, a brief but poignant detective story that helped make Elfman what he is today:

"It was a dark and lonely night when she walked into my office.

" 'I'm in trouble,' she said.

"Suddenly the phone rang.

" 'This time we mean business,' the voice on the other end barked. 'Lay off or I'll send over a couple of my boys.'

"The line in my hand went dead.

"When I looked up, she had disappeared. But that's the way it goes in this business. Win a few, lose a few. The case was closed.

"Somewhere outside, a dog was barking."

Looking back on it all, Elfman said the idea for his winning entry came to him out of the blue. He didn't think he had a Chinaman's chance of winning. Clichés from all corners of the country were flooding the offices of the Workman Publishing Co. in New York.

"I was a mere lad, just a face in the crowd," Elfman said. "But I hoped against hope. I gave it my best shot. That's really all any man can do."

For Elfman, it was "the thrill of a lifetime" when he heard the voice on the phone announcing his triumph. His beaming parents were proud as peacocks, but Elfman himself took it all in stride.

"Fame is fleeting," Elfman said. "I'm not going to rest on my laurels. I'm going to keep my shoulder to the wheel and my nose to the grindstone."

Elfman's ultimate goal is a career as a filmmaker. He and a friend produced one movie when Elfman was attending Westchester High School. It was called "Attack of the Killer Peanuts."

"We lost $30 on it," Elfman said. "But there are many pitfalls on the road to success. It's a long, hard journey to the top, and it's lonely when you get there. But I guess there's something inside me that just keeps driving me on."

Elfman's busy as a beaver these days, preparing for his trip to Miami Beach, pursuing his studies in cinema at UCLA and working weekends as a stock clerk at a discount store.

"I've always said a little hard work never hurt anybody," he said. "If a job's worth doing, it's worth doing right."

Nonetheless, his heart is set on "getting away from it all" once he has his bags packed and is actually on his way to Miami Beach. Not only will he be lounging in luxury on the beach, he'll also be wined and dined at such fabled nightspots as the Club Gigi and the Boom Boom Room.

"I haven't decided who to take with me yet," Elfman said. "All my friends have been acting real friendly since I won. You know what they say: With friends like that, who needs enemies?"

Outside Elfman's apartment, gray clouds scuttled across the sky. Occasionally, the din of the rush-hour traffic wafted up through the open windows.

The atmosphere inside was warm and friendly. There was a temptation to linger, but my nose for news told me it was time to go. "Miami Beach is a nice place to visit, but I wouldn't want to live there," Elfman said as I headed for the door.

"Yeah," I mumbled.

The door shut behind me. But that's the way it goes in this business. Win a few, lose a few. The interview was over.

Somewhere outside, a dog was barking.

William Overend,
"Local Boy Makes Good"

C. FIGURATIVE LANGUAGE

Finally, we come to the most difficult, yet the most inventive and interesting, use of language—figures of speech, or figurative language. This term refers to the use of words, not in their literal sense, but in a metaphorical or imaginative way. Although you may associate figurative language primarily with poetry, prose writers also use it to give great immediacy, greater drama, or stronger impact to an otherwise commonplace idea. The two most common figures of speech are metaphor and simile. Both are characterized by imaginative comparisons between two essentially unlike things.

A *metaphor* refers to a *direct* comparison in which the dominant quality or characteristic of one thing is transferred to another. Literally, such transference of meaning does not make sense, but the reader knows to interpret it as a comparison. In the phrase, "a will of granite," we are meant to see that the characteristics of granite—hardness, durability, and inflexibility—are being likened to the person's steadfastness and unwillingness to change. My dog, admittedly old, fat, and lazy, was once humorously described as "a barrel perched on four toothpicks." In the practice essay at the end of Chapter 4, John Knowles metaphorically described the ocean swimmer as "flotsam" to emphasize the swimmer's powerlessness against the turbulent force of the ocean.

The second figure of speech is the *simile*—an imaginative comparison stated explicitly, usually with the words "like," "as though," "as if," "as . . . as." Here are some examples:

1. The light seemed amazingly to increase my buoyancy; the water bore me up *as though* I were made of cork and could float forever. (John Knowles)

2. There are only three months of rain in the whole year, and these begin in December, ending the hottest season when the air is *as* tight and dry *as* a drum skin. (Elizabeth Marshall Thomas)

3. The bark is thin and smooth and rather pink and sags in folds toward the base of the tree *like* the skin on an elephant's leg. (Elizabeth Marshall Thomas describing the baobab tree, which grows in the Kalahari Desert)

Notice that in each simile above, the terms of the comparison are stated explicitly so that there is no need to puzzle over what the writer intended.

How does one go about analyzing figures of speech? Taking the last example, we can ask these questions:

What is being compared to what?
The bark of the tree is being compared to the skin on an elephant's leg.

What quality of an elephant's leg does the writer have in mind?
An elephant's skin is dry, almost brittle-looking. It is dusty gray in color, its surface creased, seamed, and cracked. The skin looks ten sizes too big for the flesh underneath. Which of these is right? The phrase "sags in folds" tells us that Thomas intends us to visualize the last quality mentioned, since bark is normally tightly bound to the tree. The comparison, then, is most apt, giving us a much clearer picture than would a literal description.

To analyze figures of speech, always remember that the *literal* subject is being compared to something *metaphorical,* not the other way around. In this same example, tree bark is being compared to elephant skin, rather than the skin being compared to tree bark.

EXERCISES—PART I

Analyzing Figurative Language   Following are some short passages containing figurative language for you to analyze. Using separate paper, first decide if the figure of speech is a metaphor or a simile, then decide what is being compared to what. Finally, briefly explain the meaning of the comparison.

1. As we smoked we watched some of the little brown forest skinks hunting among the roots of the trees around us. These little lizards always looked neat and shining, as though they had been cast in chocolate and had just that second stepped out of the mould, gleaming and immaculate. (Gerald Durrell, *A Zoo in My Luggage*)

2. They [the two Civil War generals, Grant and Lee] were two strong men, these oddly different generals, and they represented the strengths of two conflicting currents that through them, had come into final collision. (Bruce Catton, "Grant and Lee")

3. Quite a few years ago when I was living in my little town on the coast of California a stranger came in and bought a small valley where the Sempervirens redwoods grew, some of them three hundred feet high. We

used to walk among those trees, and the light colored as though the great glass of the Cathedral at Chartres had strained and sanctified the sunlight. (John Steinbeck, *America and Americans*)

4. In truth, Snow Canyon is not a spectacular place. Small in area (65,000 acres), it contains no waterfalls or geysers, no tremendous cliffs such as those of Zion, no deep and narrow canyons. However, like any portion of the earth's surface that has not been engulfed by industry, there is much of great interest and beauty if you take the time and make the effort to see it. (Edward Abbey, *The Journey Home*)

5. The realization that anger had driven them both out of the house, that their passionate detestation of one another had blinded them to their commitment to the house and to him traveled crookedly up through his heart like a fissure made by an earthquake in a wall, leaving on one side innocence and trust and on the other, the lingering ruefulness and gloom of an orphaned spirit. (Susan Cheever, *Home Before Dark*)

6. And then, abruptly, she woke up beside him in her own bed one early spring morning and knew she loathed him and couldn't wait to get him out of the house. She felt guilty, but guilty in the way one feels guilty when about to discommode some clinging slug that has managed to attach itself to one's arm or leg. (Gail Godwin, "Amanuensis," *Mr. Bedford and the Muses*)

7. He [the North Carolina tobacco farmer] looks for a gentle slope that will allow good drainage, and scratches out a rectangle in the skin of the black earth—long and narrow and typically equal to about twenty yards of narrow rural highway. He doses the wound liberally with chemicals to kill the weeds and fungus and covers the whole thing carefully with a clear plastic bandage; then he leaves, hoping that he has selected a good spot, that the chemicals will do their work, and that the elements will cooperate with him or, at the very least, do him no harm. (Dwayne Walls, "The Golden Token," *The Chickenbone Special*)

8. Let us go then, you and I,
When the evening is spread out against the sky
Like a patient etherised upon a table
(T. S. Eliot, "The Love Song of J. Alfred Prufrock")

9. "Death, it seems," Garp wrote, "does not like to wait until we are prepared for it. Death is indulgent and enjoys, when it can, a flair for the dramatic." (John Irving, *The World According to Garp*)

10. Prose consists less and less of *words* chosen for the sake of their meaning, and more and more of phrases tacked together like the sections of a prefabricated henhouse. . . . (George Orwell, "Politics and the English Language")

EXERCISES—PART II

Selection 1
[1]I watch them every year, the six-year-olds, buying lunch boxes and snap-on bow ties and jeweled barrettes, swinging on their mothers' arms as they approach the school on registration day or walking ahead a little,

stiff in new clothes. [2]Putting their feet on the shoe salesman's metal foot measure, eying the patent leather and ending up with sturdy brown tie oxfords, sitting rigid in the barber's chair, heads balanced on white-sheeted bodies like cherries on cupcakes, as the barber snips away the kindergarten hair for the new grown-up cut, striding past the five-year-olds with looks of knowing pity (ah, youth) they enter elementary school, feigning reluctance—with scuffing heels and dying TV cowboy groans shared in the cloakroom, but filled with hope and anticipation of all the mysteries waiting in the cafeteria and the water fountain and the paper closet, and in the pages of the textbooks on the teachers' desks. [3]With pink erasers and a sheath of sharpened pencils, they file in so really bravely, as if to tame lions, or at least subdue the alphabet. [4]And instead, I long to warn them, watching this green young crop pass by each year, seeing them enter a red-brick, smelly-staircase world of bathroom passes and penmanship drills, gongs and red x's, and an unexpected snap to the teacher's slingshot voice (so slack and giving, when she met the mothers). [5]I want to tell them about the back pages in the teacher's record book, of going to the principal's office or staying behind an extra year. [6]Quickly they learn how little use they'll have for lion-taming apparatus. [7]They are, themselves, about to meet the tamer.

Joyce Maynard,
Looking Back

A. Vocabulary

For each italicized word from the paragraph, choose the best definition according to the context in which it appears.

1. *striding* [sentence 2]: Walking in a way that is (a) hurried; (b) nervous; (c) vigorous; (d) slow.
2. *feigning* [2]: (a) assuming; (b) hoping; (c) thinking; (d) pretending.
3. *subdue* [3]: (a) quiet down; (b) master; (c) conquer; (d) learn to write.

B. Content and Structure

Choose the best answer.

1. Maynard's purpose is, specifically, (a) to tell a story about what happens to most first graders; (b) to describe a scene—first graders' enthusiastic preparations for school and the reality they will encounter; (c) to explain an increasing problem in the American educational system; (d) to persuade the reader that the educational system in this country must be revamped.
2. Maynard's paragraph is composed almost entirely of specific, concrete details. The underlying method of development governing them is (a) cause–effect; (b) steps in a process; (c) analysis; (d) contrast.
3. Find a transitional phrase in the paragraph that relates to the method of development you marked in question 2 above.
   _____ and instead _____ in sentence __4__.
4. The pattern of organization is (a) deductive; (b) variation of deductive; (c) inductive; (d) chronological.

5. In sentence 2, Maynard describes the shoes the children eye ("patent leather") and the shoes they end up buying ("sturdy brown tie oxfords"). Both descriptive phrases are denotative, but they also have connotative meanings. What associations do these two types of shoes have to a first grader? *They are symbolic to them. As if they were showing success.*

6. Find and write down two phrases that specifically (and humorously) illustrate the reference to "feigning reluctance" mentioned in sentence 2. *Look of knowing pity -sent 2 -*

7. In sentence 4, Maynard refers to the first graders as "this green young crop." What does this metaphor mean? *that they are not mature. He compares them to vegetables -*

8. In sentence 4, to what does Maynard compare the teacher's voice? *to a slingshot -* Explain the metaphor. *The teacher's voice varies. When she is with the mothers it as nice and with students more tighten -*

9. One metaphor is central to your understanding of this paragraph. First, fill in these blanks.
   The children are being compared to *Lions*.
   The teacher is being compared to *Tamers -*.
   Explain the metaphor, in your own words, in terms of what the metaphor says about the children's experiences in the school system.

10. Maynard writes from the point of view of (a) a first grader; (b) a parent; (c) a teacher; (d) a student who has already experienced first grade.

11. Which words best describe the tone of Maynard's paragraph? (a) bitter and hostile; (b) scornful yet sympathetic; (c) respectful yet critical; (d) objective and detached.

12. This paragraph comes from a longer essay. Which portion of the essay do you think it comes from? (a) the introduction; (b) the body—supporting paragraphs; (c) the conclusion; (d) there is no way to tell which part it comes from.

Selection 2

[1] . . . it was so hot that I went down to the creek instead, to cool my feet in one of its stagnant sumps, a poor substitute for my Red Cross swims, which had just ended, but at least water.

[2]The heat was always more intense in the creek, more dusty and dry and piercing than anywhere else. [3]Crackling and powdery, it stung the nostrils and eyes, prickled in little hives all over the body. [4]Beds of gravel glared; dragonflies glittered in tall, chalky weeds; cicadas droned, broke off, droned again. [5]Sweat rolled down my ribs as I walked, patching my shirt and gathering damply in the band of my shorts. [6]When I saw a

swarm of gnats, I plodded over to it and with the toe of my tennis shoe splashed aside the scum of a sunken pool. [7]Then, after pulling off my shoes, I stepped in and stood immersed to the ankles. [8]The water was sun-filled, warm, the clear golden brown of cider. [9]I scratched my prickling body, rubbed my stinging eyes until little stars revolved, then slowly took off my shorts and shirt, and then my undershirt, and stretched out full length in the shallow water, rolling with lazy greed until I was wet all over. [10]After getting up again, I stood looking down my glistening body for a while, then, picking up my clothes and shoes, walked on in my underpants. [11]I felt sun-dazed, reckless, like an African animal, sleepy, yet somehow intent and ready for anything, a hot, loose-limbed beast prowling.

Ella Leffland,
Rumors of Peace

A. Vocabulary

For each italicized word from the selection, choose the best definition according to the context in which it appears.

1. *stagnant* [1]: (a) polluted; poisoned; (b) lacking liveliness; (c) not moving or flowing; (d) muddy; sticky.

2. *piercing* [2]: (a) scorching; (b) penetrating; (c) stinging; (d) burning.

B. Content and Structure

Choose the best answer.

1. The mode of discourse in this selection is primarily (a) narration; (b) description; (c) exposition; (d) persuasion.

2. The dominant impression of the creek is that it is (a) open and spacious; (b) clear and cool; (c) hot and dusty; (d) lonely and isolated.

3. Which *two* patterns of organization are evident in the paragraph? (a) spatial; (b) chronological; (c) deductive; (d) variation of deductive; (e) inductive; (f) emphatic.

4. The narrator of the passage is probably (a) a little girl of about six or seven; (b) a girl of about twelve or thirteen; (c) a young woman of nineteen or twenty; (d) an adult woman.

5. Look at sentence 8. Is the figure of speech a metaphor or simile? What is compared to what? What quality is emphasized? Metaphor —
   lit = water   fig = cider.   Color Brown —

6. Look at sentence 11. Is the figure of speech a metaphor or simile? What is compared to what? What quality is emphasized?
   lit: Her to fig = African animal —   prowling —

C. Language Analysis

Answer the following questions.

1. How would you characterize the word *sump* as it is used in sentence 1 to describe the creek? (a) denotative; (b) connotative with positive overtones; (c) connotative with negative overtones; (d) figurative.

2. In sentence 3, which of the five senses is Leffland appealing to? (a) touch; (b) sight; (c) hearing; (d) smell; (e) taste.

3. How would you characterize the word *glared* as it is used in sentence 4? (a) denotative; (b) connotative with positive overtones; (c) connotative with negative overtones; (d) figurative.

4. Would you characterize the sensation described in sentence 8 as pleasant or unpleasant? _____ pleasant _____

5. In sentence 9, Leffland writes that she rubbed her stinging eyes until "little stars revolved." Is the quoted phrase literal or figurative? _____fig_____

6. An oxymoron (pronounced ŏk sē-môr′ŏn′) is a figure of speech which joins incongruous or contradictory terms, for example, "a mournful optimist." Look through the paragraph and find an example of an oxymoron.

_____

7. As used in sentence 11, is the adjective *reckless* (a) denotative; (b) connotative with positive overtones; (c) connotative with negative overtones; (d) figurative?

8. Also in sentence 11, the adjective *hot* seems to be used ambiguously because it suggests two different meanings. What are they? _____

_____

Selection 3   ¹The character of this world only a few miles above our heads can hardly be appreciated from the pressurised, heated and oxygen-enriched cabin of a passenger aircraft. ²Float up to it instead in an open basket suspended beneath a balloon. ³For the first few hundred metres, noises from below, of car engines, snatches of chatter, a striking clock, sound distantly in a curiously unreal way. ⁴But soon all is silence, broken only by the creak of the basket and the sporadic roar of the burner that produces a blast of hot air and gives the balloon its lift. ⁵The atmosphere gets steadily colder. ⁶You are travelling with the wind, like many another creature swept up here by rising hot air, and therefore all seems still, even though you may be moving very swiftly indeed in relation to the earth beneath. ⁷But that may already be hidden from you beneath a bank of cloud. ⁸The air you breathe is rapidly becoming thinner and therefore each breath you take contains less oxygen. ⁹Since you are standing still in the cramped basket, this is not likely to trouble you. ¹⁰Indeed, you may be largely unaware that there is any change in the physical character of the air. ¹¹This is what makes it so dangerous, for as your brain receives less oxygen, so it becomes less efficient and your faculties begin to dull. ¹²Long before you are aware of any physical impairment, you may have lost the ability to make competent judgements. ¹³So by the time your altimeter shows that you have reached a height of 5000 metres, you will be wise to start breathing oxygen through a mask.

¹⁴The world you have entered is one of extraordinary beauty. ¹⁵Far below, a gauzy sheet of cloud may veil the surface of the land. ¹⁶Hills project through it, like islands in a white sea. ¹⁷All around sail great

clouds, their lower margins flat and horizontal, but their upper surfaces billowing and surging in rapidly-changing plumes. [18]As you approach their level, the extraordinary speed of the currents within them becomes vividly and frighteningly apparent. [19]To be caught by one of the thermals that feed them and be carried up into them would almost certainly be lethal. [20]Within them, air currents are sweeping up and down with such force that they would rip apart the balloon. [21]Above these clouds, there may be wisps of others at very high altitudes indeed and, beyond them, the clear dark blue of space.

David Attenborough,
The Living Planet

A. Vocabulary   For each italicized word from the selection, choose the best definition according to the context in which it appears.

1. *sporadic* [4]: (a) deafening; (b) isolated; (c) widely scattered; (d) irregularly occurring.

2. *faculties* [11]: (a) inherent powers; abilities; (b) eyes; (c) sensory perceptions; (d) brain cells.

3. *impairment* [12]: (a) change; (b) diminishment in strength; (c) improvement; (d) capacity.

4. *lethal* [19]: (a) serious; (b) dangerous; (c) foolish; (d) deadly.

B. Content and Structure   Choose the best answer.

1. The author's purpose in both paragraphs is to (a) provide instructions for using a hot air balloon; (b) criticize people who insist on traveling by airplane; (c) describe the character of the world a few miles above the ground; (d) explain the dangers of riding in a hot air balloon.

2. In the first paragraph, Attenborough discusses a process. Is this an *informative* process or a *directive* process? _informative_____

3. The details in sentences 3 and 4 appeal to our sense of (a) sight; (b) hearing; (c) touch; (d) taste; (e) smell.

4. In sentence 6, the phrase "like many another creature swept up here by rising hot air" is (a) literal; (b) figurative; (c) connotative with positive overtones; (d) connotative with negative overtones.

5. The transitional word *indeed* in sentence 10 indicates (a) an example; (b) emphasis; (c) a contrast; (d) a conclusion; (e) a figure of speech.

6. Apparently, the risky part of riding in a hot air balloon is (a) lack of experience; (b) lack of oxygen; (c) loss of hot air inside the balloon; (d) lack of air pressure.

7. Which *two* patterns of organization are used in the second paragraph? (a) chronological; (b) spatial; (c) deductive; (d) variation of deductive; (e) emphatic.

8. The relationship between the two parts of sentence 17 (separated by the word *horizontal*) is (a) term and its definition; (b) statement and supporting detail; (c) statement and conclusion; (d) contrasting statements.

9. In sentence 17, the descriptive words *sail, billowing,* and *surging* convey (a) a feeling of loneliness; (b) an impression of immense size; (c) a feeling of wonder; (d) a sense of motion.

10. Find one example of a figure of speech in the second paragraph and analyze it in the space below. What is being compared to what?
    Clouds is/are compared to _ocean waves_.
    Metaphor or simile? _Metaphor_
    Explain the figure of speech. _sweep up and down_

11. According to the second paragraph, what impresses the author most? (a) the blue color of space; (b) the appearance of the land below; (c) the speed of the currents, especially the thermals; (d) the size of the clouds.

12. We can accurately infer that *thermals,* mentioned in sentence 19, are (a) hot air currents; (b) cold air currents; (c) giant, fast-moving clouds; (d) wisps of clouds.

Alliteration • "D" sound -

Selection 4

Sublime: when it so bad, we see the poetic or beauty in it. (but not here!)

[1]During the whole of a dull, dark, and soundless day in the autumn of the year, when the clouds hung oppressively low in the heavens, I had been passing alone, on horseback, through a singularly dreary tract of country, and at length found myself, as the shades of the evening drew on, within view of the melancholy House of Usher. [2]I know not how it was—but, with the first glimpse of the building, a sense of insufferable gloom pervaded my spirit. [3]I say insufferable; for the feeling was unrelieved by any of that half-pleasurable, because poetic, sentiment with which the mind usually receives even the sternest natural images of the desolate or terrible. [4]I looked upon the scene before me—upon the mere house, and the simple landscape features of the domain—upon the bleak walls—upon the vacant eye-like windows—upon a few rank sedges—and upon a few white trunks of decayed trees—with an utter depression of soul which I can compare to no earthly sensation more properly than to the after-dream of the reveller upon opium—the bitter lapse into everyday life—the hideous dropping off of the veil. [5]There was an iciness, a sinking, a sickening of the heart—an unredeemed dreariness of thought which no goading of the imagination could torture into aught of the sublime. [6]What was it—I paused to think—what was it that so unnerved me in the contemplation of the House of Usher? [7]It was a mystery all insoluble; nor could I grapple with the shadowy fancies that crowded upon me as I pondered.

Edgar Allan Poe,
"The Fall of the House of Usher"

A. Vocabulary

For each italicized word from the paragraph, choose the best definition according to the context in which it appears.

1. *oppressively* [1]: (a) lightly; (b) gloomily; (c) heavily; (d) powerfully.

2. *singularly* [1]: (a) lonely; (b) unusually; (c) strangely; (d) particularly.

3. *melancholy* [1]: (a) stern; forbidding; (b) pensive; thoughtful; (c) terrifying; menacing; (d) sad; gloomy.

4. *pervaded* [2]: (a) spread through; (b) prevented; (c) invaded; (d) rushed into.

5. *desolate* [3]: (Note that "desolate" here is used as a noun, though it is properly an adjective.) (a) burdensome; (b) dreary; (c) intimidating; (d) empty.

6. *domain* [4]: (a) field of study; (b) kingdom; (c) territory; realm; (d) panorama.

7. *reveller* [4]: One who (a) rebels; (b) seeks pleasure; (c) is addicted; (d) celebrates.

8. *lapse* [4]: (a) slipping into a lower state; (b) fall from grace; (c) transformation; (d) awareness of reality.

9. *goading* [5]: (a) irritating; (b) touching; (c) tickling; (d) prodding.

10. *sublime* [5]: (a) submission; (b) nobility; loftiness; (c) the unconscious; (d) high moral purpose.

11. *grapple with* [7]: (a) attempt to cope with; (b) struggle over; (c) seize and hold tightly; (d) understand clearly.

12. *pondered* [7]: (a) rode; (b) dismounted; (c) labored; (d) considered carefully.

Other words you should know:

1. *Sedges* [4] are a kind of plant resembling grasses except for their solid stems. What does the word *rank* connote as a descriptive word for these plants? __unpleasant , disgusting new__

2. What is the modern equivalent of the archaic word *aught* in sentence 5? __anything__

B. Content and Structure

Choose the best answer.

1. Poe's purpose in this paragraph is to describe both the House of Usher and (a) its occupants; (b) the surrounding countryside; (c) the narrator's reactions to the house; (d) the origin of his inspiration to write about the house.

2. What dominant impression of the House of Usher does the narrator suggest? __Mystery , gloom .__

3. The narrator implies that (a) the occupants of the house were dead; (b) he had visited the house many times before; (c) the weather and time of year added to his feeling of gloom; (d) he had been in a bad temper before he arrived at the house.

4. The narrator also implies that the house and grounds were (a) badly neglected and seemingly uninhabited; (b) inhabited by ghosts or evil spirits; (c) once splendid examples of the way aristocrats lived; (d) remote enough not to attract curious passersby.

5. In sentence 3, the phrase "because poetic" might be worded differently in modern English by the addition of two words. Rewrite the phrase in modern English. __because it is poetic —__

6. Find two metaphors in the paragraph and analyze them as follows:
   (a) What is being compared to what?
   depression is/are being compared to _after dream of opium eater_
   Metaphor or simile? _No longer simile_
   Explain the figure of speech. _The depression the man fell to compared to the after dream of opium eater when he comes back to reality._
   (b) What is being compared to what?
   windows is/are being compared to _eyes (vacant of ...)_.
   Metaphor or simile? _Simile_
   Explain the figure of speech. _____

7. In sentence 5, the word *torture* is used for its connotative effect. What is it meant to suggest? _Unpleasant sensation. Turst was torture —

8. In sentence 7, what specifically does the pronoun *it* refer to? _to what unnerved him —

9. The pattern of organization that governs the descriptive details and the narrator's own reactions is (a) chronological; (b) deductive; (c) inductive; (d) spatial; (e) emphatic.

10. What emotional feeling does Poe convey in this paragraph? (a) terror and fear; (b) dread and suspense; (c) curiosity and anxiety; (d) boredom and lack of interest.

PRACTICE ESSAY

I Know Why the Caged Bird Sings
Maya Angelou

Maya Angelou (1928–   ) is a well-known writer who grew up in the South. The titles of her autobiographical works are *I Know Why the Caged Bird Sings* (1970), from which this selection comes; *Just Give Me a Cool Drink of Water 'Fore I Die* (1971); *Gather Together in My Name* (1974); and *The Heart of a Woman* (1981). In addition to her prose writing, Angelou has written and produced a ten-part television series on African traditions in American life. During the 1960s, she worked for Martin Luther King, Jr.'s Southern Christian Leadership Conference.

1   When I was three and Bailey four, we had arrived in the musty little town, wearing tags on our wrists which instructed—"To Whom It May Concern"—that we were Marguerite and Bailey Johnson Jr., from Long Beach, California, en route to Stamps, Arkansas, c/o Mrs. Annie Henderson.

2   Our parents had decided to put an end to their calamitous marriage, and Father shipped us home to his mother. A porter had been charged with our welfare—he got off the train the next day in Arizona—and our tickets were pinned to my brother's inside coat pocket.

3   I don't remember much of the trip, but after we reached the segregated southern part of the journey, things must have looked up. Negro passengers,

who always traveled with loaded lunch boxes, felt sorry for "the poor little motherless darlings" and plied us with cold fried chicken and potato salad.

4   Years later I discovered that the United States had been crossed thousands of times by frightened Black children traveling alone to their newly affluent parents in Northern cities, or back to grandmothers in Southern towns when the urban North reneged on its economic promises.

5   The town reacted to us as its inhabitants had reacted to all things new before our coming. It regarded us a while without curiosity but with caution, and after we were seen to be harmless (and children) it closed in around us, as a real mother embraces a stranger's child. Warmly, but not too familiarly.

6   We lived with our grandmother and uncle in the rear of the Store (it was always spoken of with a capital s), which she had owned some twenty-five years.

7   Early in the century, Momma (we soon stopped calling her Grandmother) sold lunches to the sawmen in the lumberyard (east Stamps) and the seedmen at the cotton gin (west Stamps). Her crisp meat pies and cool lemonade, when joined to her miraculous ability to be in two places at the same time, assured her business success. From being a mobile lunch counter, she set up a stand between the two points of fiscal interest and supplied the workers' needs for a few years. Then she had the Store built in the heart of the Negro area. Over the years it became the lay center of activities in town. On Saturdays, barbers sat their customers in the shade on the porch of the Store, and troubadours on their ceaseless crawlings through the South leaned across its benches and sang their sad songs of The Brazos while they played juice harps and cigar-box guitars.

8   The formal name of the Store was the Wm. Johnson General Merchandise Store. Customers could find food staples, a good variety of colored thread, mash for hogs, corn for chickens, coal oil for lamps, light bulbs for the wealthy, shoestrings, hair dressing, balloons, and flower seeds. Anything not visible had only to be ordered.

9   Until we became familiar enough to belong to the Store and it to us, we were locked up in a Fun House of Things where the attendant had gone home for life.

10   Each year I watched the field across from the Store turn caterpillar green, then gradually frosty white. I knew exactly how long it would be before the big wagons would pull into the front yard and load on the cotton pickers at daybreak to carry them to the remains of slavery's plantations.

11   During the picking season my grandmother would get out of bed at four o'clock (she never used an alarm clock) and creak down to her knees and chant in a sleep-filled voice, "Our Father, thank you for letting me see this New Day. Thank you that you didn't allow the bed I lay on last night to be my cooling board, nor my blanket my winding sheet. Guide my feet this day along the straight and narrow, and help me to put a bridle on my tongue. Bless this house, and everybody in it. Thank you, in the name of your Son, Jesus Christ, Amen."

¹²   Before she had quite arisen, she called our names and issued orders, and pushed her large feet into homemade slippers and across the bare lye-washed wooden floor to light the coal-oil lamp.

¹³   The lamplight in the Store gave a soft make-believe feeling to our world which made me want to whisper and walk about on tiptoe. The odors of onions and oranges and kerosene had been mixing all night and wouldn't be disturbed until the wooded slat was removed from the door and the early morning air forced its way in with the bodies of people who had walked miles to reach the pickup place.

¹⁴   "Sister, I'll have two cans of sardines."

¹⁵   "I'm gonna work so fast today I'm gonna make you look like you standing still."

¹⁶   "Lemme have a hunk uh cheese and some sody crackers."

¹⁷   "Just gimmie a coupla them fat peanut paddies." That would be from a picker who was taking his lunch. The greasy brown paper sack was stuck behind the bib of his overalls. He'd use the candy as a snack before the noon sun called the workers to rest.

¹⁸   In those tender mornings the Store was full of laughing, joking, boasting and bragging. One man was going to pick two hundred pounds of cotton, and another three hundred. Even the children were promising to bring home fo' bits and six bits.

¹⁹   The champion picker of the day before was the hero of the dawn. If he prophesied that the cotton in today's field was going to be sparse and stick to the bolls like glue, every listener would grunt a hearty agreement.

²⁰   The sound of the empty cotton sacks dragging over the floor and the murmurs of waking people were sliced by the cash register as we rang up the five-cent sales.

²¹   If the morning sounds and smells were touched with the supernatural, the late afternoon had all the features of the normal Arkansas life. In the dying sunlight the people dragged, rather than their empty cotton sacks.

²²   Brought back to the Store, the pickers would step out of the backs of trucks and fold down, dirt-disappointed, to the ground. No matter how much they had picked, it wasn't enough. Their wages wouldn't even get them out of debt to my grandmother, not to mention the staggering bill that waited on them at the white commissary downtown.

²³   The sounds of the new morning had been replaced with grumbles about cheating houses, weighted scales, snakes, skimpy cotton and dusty rows. In later years I was to confront the stereotyped picture of gay song-singing cotton pickers with such inordinate rage that I was told even by fellow Blacks that my paranoia was embarrassing. But I had seen the fingers cut by the mean little cotton bolls, and I had witnessed the backs and shoulders and arms and legs resisting any further demands.

²⁴   Some of the workers would leave their sacks at the Store to be picked up the following morning, but a few had to take them home for repairs. I winced to picture them sewing the coarse material under a coal-oil lamp with fingers stiffening from the day's work. In too few hours they would have to walk back to Sister Henderson's Store, get vittles and load, again, onto

the trucks. Then they would face another day of trying to earn enough for the whole year with the heavy knowledge that they were going to end the season as they started it. Without the money or credit necessary to sustain a family for three months. In cotton-picking time the late afternoons revealed the harshness of Black Southern life, which in the early morning had been softened by nature's blessing of grogginess, forgetfulness and the soft lamplight.

A. Comprehension

Choose the answer that best completes each statement. Do not refer to the selection while doing this exercise.

1. The author and her older brother, Bailey, were sent from California to their grandmother who lived in (a) Arizona; (b) Mississippi; (c) Arkansas; (d) Georgia.

2. The town reacted to the children first with caution, then with (a) curiosity; (b) hostility; (c) familiarity; (d) warmth.

3. Momma, the author's grandmother, built her general store (a) at the crossroads between the black and white centers of town; (b) in the center of the black area; (c) in the center of the white area; (d) in the country, near the plantation.

4. In the early morning, the cotton pickers displayed (a) pessimism; (b) weariness; (c) optimism; (d) resignation.

5. The worst problem the plantation workers faced was that (a) their wages would not cover their debts or sustain them through the year; (b) they were unskilled and unable to go to Northern industrial cities for better jobs; (c) the plantation owners deliberately underpaid them; (d) the cotton fields were badly eroded and, as a result, the crop became smaller each year.

B. Inferences

You may refer to the selection to answer the questions in this section and in all the remaining sections.

1. What can you infer about why Angelou and her brother could not remain with their parents in California? *working → They were divorcing and trying to pull their life back together.*

2. Read paragraphs 7 and 8 again. What can you infer about Momma's business abilities? *She was a good business woman. She knew how to attract her clientele.*

3. Look at paragraphs 8 and 9. Why might merchandise like chicken feed and shoestrings represent a "Fun House of Things" for the children? *because the store was full of little things that children could play with.*

4. Read paragraph 11 again. What can you infer about the grandmother's character? *She was very religious*

5. Read paragraph 23 again. What can you infer about the stereotype of "gay song-singing cotton pickers"?

C. Structure Choose the best answer.

1. The primary mode of discourse is (a) narration; (b) description; (c) exposition; (d) persuasion.

2. The paragraph that acts like a transition or pivot between the two parts of the essay is number __21__.

3. The relationship between the two parts of the essay is contrast. What is being contrasted? _mornings optimism_ and _afternoons pessimism_

4. Write the sentence and the number of the paragraph that best states the main idea or thesis of the essay: _In cotton picking the late afternoons revealed the harshness of black southern life_ in paragraph __24__.

5. Explain the function of the last sentence in the essay. _It shows the contrast between mornings and afternoons likes._

6. How would you characterize the author's attitude toward the black cotton pickers? It is (a) harsh and bitter; (b) gentle and reserved; (c) philosophical and reflective; (d) compassionate and sympathetic.

D. Language Analysis Answer the following questions.

1. As used in sentence 1, the adjective *musty* is (a) literal; (b) denotative; (c) connotative with negative overtones; (d) connotative with positive overtones; (e) figurative.

2. Analyze the figure of speech in paragraph 5.
What is being compared to what?
resident is/are compared to _a mother_.
Metaphor or simile? _simile_
Explain the figure of speech. _resident of the town welcome children as if they were a stranger's child can have forever._

3. In paragraph 10, the descriptive phrases "caterpillar green" and "frosty white" are examples of (a) metaphors; (b) similes; (c) denotation; (d) euphemisms.

4. In paragraph 13, Angelou emphasizes details about the lamplight in the early morning to show that (a) electric lights were expensive; (b) the light softened the harsh reality of the pickers' day; (c) her grandmother was stingy and refused to use electric light bulbs; (d) the town was primitive and lacked electricity.

5. Analyze the figure of speech in paragraph 19.
What is being compared to what?
cotton is/are compared to _glue_.
Metaphor or simile? _simile_
Explain the figure of speech. _cotton is sticky like glue_

6. In paragraph 23, what is the meaning of the word *mean* in the phrase "the mean little cotton bolls"? _cruel._

E. Vocabulary   For each italicized word from the selection, choose the best definition according to the context in which it appears.

1. the North *reneged on* its promise [paragraph 1]: (a) failed to carry out; (b) disowned; renounced; (c) made good on; (d) modified.

2. two points of *fiscal* interest [7]: (a) social; (b) racial; (c) scenic; (d) economic.

3. the *lay* center of activities [7]: pertaining to the (a) church; (b) common man; (c) most lively; (d) most popular.

4. the cotton was going to be *sparse* [19]: (a) plentiful; (b) skimpy; not growing densely; (c) of poor quality; (d) difficult to pick.

5. a *hearty* agreement [19]: expressing (a) courage; (b) fear and anxiety; (c) exuberance and warmth; (d) insincerity.

6. with *inordinate* rage [23]: (a) blind; irrational; (b) impossible to control; (c) emotional; heartfelt; (d) excessive; immoderate.

7. my *paranoia* was embarrassing [23]: the feeling that one is being (a) exploited; (b) ridiculed; (c) persecuted; (d) pursued.

8. I *winced* to picture them [24]: (a) worried; (b) flinched; (c) was accustomed; (d) longed.

Other words you should know:
winding sheet [11]
vittles [24; usual spelling: *victuals*]

chapter 6 ‖ TONE

In this last chapter of Part I, we will put everything together. Specifically, we will look at how a writer's words—the choice of denotative or connotative words and the use of figurative language—contribute to the tone of a piece of writing. In addition to tone, we will examine the subtleties involved in irony, and the ways in which irony can be used (wit and humor, satire, and deadpan humor, etc.).

A. AN EXPLANATION OF TONE

Some of the exercises in the preceding chapters have asked you to identify the tone of a passage, so the term should not be completely unfamiliar. *Tone* refers to the emotional feeling, mood, or quality of a piece of writing. In technical and scientific prose the author's tone is usually objective and impartial as befits the purpose of conveying information, not arousing emotions. Newspaper articles, except for editorials, generally are also written (or are supposed to be written) in an objective manner, since their purpose is to convey factual information, not to provide subjective views. But in all other kinds of writing, the writer's tone can reflect any of the emotional stances one can think of. The writer may be sympathetic, bitter, hostile, angry, serious, self-serving, humorous, befuddled, caustic, ironic, earnest, witty, or nasty—to cite just a few examples. In conversation, a speaker's emotional attitude is indicated by gesture, tone of voice, and facial expression, in addition to the actual words spoken. But in writing, tone can be conveyed only by the words on the page (although, as you will see later, punctuation can occasionally indicate tone). The reader's task, then, is to re-create for himself or herself the feelings the printed words are meant to arouse. Let us examine some of the elements that contribute to the tone of a passage: (1) the choice of details; (2) the diction (choice of words); and (3) the arrangement of those words (the writer's manner of expression).

First, read the following paragraph, a description of the Mayan civilization which flourished in southern Mexico and Central America around 1000 AD.

While the Valley of Mexico was still reaching for its first period of dominance around the dawn of the Christian era the brilliant and isolated civilization of the Maya was taking shape far to the south. The Maya were a special breed with a distinctive language and the peculiar profile—sloping forehead, prominent curving nose and full lips—that is endlessly depicted on their ancient monuments and is still common among their descendants in modern Yucatán. The Maya have been called the Greeks of the New World, but the appellation is not accurate. The Maya were the Maya; they were like no other people, and their civilization was like no other.

Jonathan Norton Leonard,
Ancient America

At first glance, this paragraph appears to be impartial. But note that the diction, the use of such phrases as "the brilliant and isolated civilization," "a special breed," "a distinctive language," and "their civilization was like no other," in addition to the favorable comparison to the ancient Greeks, all reveal an underlying tone of admiration. Clearly, the writer is sympathetic, and he wishes us to be equally admiring.

The next example reveals a completely different emotional attitude. Caskie Stinnett, a resident of an island off the coast of Maine, describes the changes (for the worse, according to him) that are occurring in Maine —the result, he complains, of progress, of "Maine's trying to become like everyplace else." In this paragraph, which comes in the middle of his article, he cites one casualty of this misguided progress: his barber shop.

My dog can't go in the barber shop with me anymore, but I don't know why because she curled up by the door and minded her own business until I got out of the chair, when she would gaze at me in astonishment, wondering how I had changed so much in just a few minutes. The sign now says, Sorry, No Dogs. The word *sorry* is pure hypocrisy and I resent it; it gives off a hollow ring like a spurious coin when tapped on the counter. My barber, whom I have called Nick for the past twelve years, has informed me that he is now a stylist, not a barber, and that he would appreciate it if I would call him Mr. Nicholas in the future. I'm looking for a new barber.

Caskie Stinnett,
"A Room with a View," *Down East*

How would you describe the tone of this paragraph? Even though the content represents a valid complaint, he seems more amused than angry, at least from the details he provides about the barber shop. The tone can probably best be described as wry, reflecting mild amusement.

The last example comes from the opening paragraph of a short story by Cynthia Ozick in which she introduces us to Rosa Lublin, the main character:

Rosa Lublin, a madwoman and a scavenger, gave up her store—she smashed it up herself—and moved to Miami. It was a mad thing to do. In Florida she became a dependent. Her niece in New York sent her money and she lived among the elderly, in a dark hole, a single room in a "hotel." There was an ancient dresser-top refrigerator and a one-burner stove. Over in a corner a round oak table brooded on its heavy pedestal, but it was only for drinking tea. Her meals she had elsewhere, in bed or standing at the sink—sometimes toast with a bit of sour cream and half a sardine, or a small can of peas heated in a Pyrex mug. Instead of maid service there was a dumbwaiter on a shrieking pulley. On Tuesdays and Fridays it swallowed her meager bags of garbage. Squads of dying flies blackened the rope. The sheets on her bed were just as black—it was a five-block walk to the laundromat. The streets were a furnace, the sun an executioner. Every day without fail it blazed and blazed, so she stayed in her room and ate two bites of a hard-boiled egg in bed, with a writing board on her knees; she had lately taken to composing letters.

Cynthia Ozick,
"Rosa"

What is the tone here? Pretty grim, I would say. First, there is the description of Rosa as a "madwoman" and a "scavenger" and later as a "dependent." She lives in "a dark hole" in a "hotel" (the quotation marks suggest that the place is not a typical hotel). Actually, as you read on, you discover that it is a shabby and run-down hotel. The place is filthy. She doesn't have enough to eat. The outside environment is even more hostile than her mean little room ("The streets were a furnace, the sun an executioner"). Notice that the writer does not comment directly on Rosa's plight; she lets the details and her choice of words set the tone. We are made to feel at once repelled by, and sympathetic to, this character.

Earlier in this section it was suggested that punctuation can occasionally indicate tone. In the previous selection, the quotation marks around "hotel" call its label into question, for example. Here is another example, this time from a newspaper headline. In the spring of 1985, President Reagan presented an extensive tax-reform bill to Congress. The front-page headline in the next day's *San Francisco Chronicle* said: "Reagan Reveals His Plan for 'Radical' Tax Reform." The quotation marks around the word "radical" suggest that the writer thought the plan was not at all radical, as Reagan and his supporters claimed. ("Radical" here means fundamental or basic, going to the source of a problem.) The tone of the headline, then, can be described as critical. If the writer had omitted the quotation marks ("Reagan Reveals His Plan for Radical Tax Reform"), the tone would have been more positive and complimentary.

B. THE IRONIC STANCE

Perceiving irony causes more difficulty for readers than any other stance assumed by writers. The best way to grasp it is to look at many examples. An *ironic tone* is the result of the writer's deliberately saying the opposite of what he or she really means. The writer assumes that the reader will see through the pretense and recognize that the words express something different from their literal meaning. The dictionary defines irony in many ways, but for our purposes, here are the three most relevant ones: (1) the use of words to convey the opposite of their literal meaning; (2) an expression or utterance marked by a deliberate contrast between the apparent and intended meaning; (3) the incongruity between what might be expected and what actually occurs. In real life, it is the last sense of the word that governs an ironic situation, one that occurs because of a twist of fate, a chance encounter, a reversal of what one might normally expect. One would describe as ironic, for example, the marriage of two former high school sweethearts after twenty years spent apart, because it represents a reversal of the usual pattern. Most high school sweethearts at their twentieth reunion wonder what they ever saw in each other. It is ironic when a rich man wins a state lottery or when a firehouse burns down.

But detecting irony in writing is tricky because it is a general term with many shades of meaning, as the first two definitions presented earlier suggest—from simple amusement and a keen appreciation of life's absurdities to scathing sarcasm. Let us look first at two passages, both nonfiction, whose authors attempt to explain what irony is.

> The essence of irony is the implied contrast between what is and what, in a more nearly perfect world, might be; and the effect of irony, similarly, lies in the striking disparity between the writer's apparent attitude—that is, his seeming seriousness, or his pretended lack of seriousness—and what he really means. When an author adopts an ironical manner, he is commenting upon the shortcomings of life, the weaknesses of mankind, or, sometimes, the frailties of individual beings. The ironist often is said to be a disappointed idealist, who laughs only to keep from crying or committing suicide. His disillusionment may be only temporary and may spring from a trivial cause; it may, on the other hand, be almost cosmic in its scope and represent a sweeping rejection of the whole of life and all of mankind. Thus irony has a wide variety of tones and shadings, running the gamut from unmitigated, pathological bitterness to mere gay amusement.
>
> Richard Altick,
> *Preface to Critical Reading*

The second explanation of irony stems from its writer's experience fighting against the Germans in the Second World War, and it confirms the feeling of profound disillusionment that the paragraph by Altick above referred to.

> Irony describes the emotion, whatever it is, occasioned by perceiving some great gulf, half-comic, half-tragic, between what one expects and what one finds. It's not quite "disillusion," but it's adjacent to it. My experience in the war was ironic because my previous innocence had prepared me to encounter in it something like the same reasonableness that governed prewar life. This, after all, was the tone dominating the American relation to the war: talk of "the future," allotments and bond purchases carefully sent home, hopeful fantasies of the "postwar world." I assumed, in short, that everyone would behave according to the clear advantages offered by reason. I had assumed that in war, like chess, when you were beaten you "resigned"; that when outnumbered and outgunned

you retreated; that when you were surrounded you surrendered. I found out differently, and with a vengeance. What I found was people obeying fatuous and murderous "orders" for no reason I could understand, killing themselves because someone "told them to," prolonging the war when it was hopelessly lost because—because it was unreasonable to do so. It was my introduction to the shakiness of civilization. It was my first experience of the profoundly irrational element, and it made ridiculous all talk of plans and preparations for the future and goodwill and intelligent arrangements. Why did the red-haired young German machine-gunner firing at us in the woods not go on living—marrying, going to university, going to the beach, laughing, smiling—but keep firing long after he had made his point, and so require us to kill him with a grenade?

Paul Fussell,
"My War"

Armed with these definitions of irony, we can next examine the many shades of meaning that encompass this term. The shades of meaning might be clearer if you can imagine a continuum, a horizontal line on which to plot them. Moving from left to right along the continuum, we move from the most gentle forms of irony to the nastiest.

➡ ───

WIT / IRONY / SATIRE / CYNICISM / SARCASM / SARDONICISM

The dictionary once again provides us with useful working definitions, although you will note that there is much overlapping, and that irony does not necessarily have to be a characteristic element in every instance.

Wit *humorist*
have to think about
it —

This term implies mental keenness, the ability to discern those elements of a situation or condition that relate to what is cosmic, and the talent for making an effective comment on them.
Example: Oscar Wilde, the Irish dramatist, once defined eternity as two people and a ham.

Irony

This term was defined at the beginning of this section.
Example: George Bernard Shaw, the English playwright, loathed the music of Brahms, the nineteenth-century German composer, once saying that listening to Brahms was "like listening to paint dry." Apparently, Shaw also considered uninvited guests a nuisance, so he posted this notice on his door:

RULES FOR VISITORS

1. If you don't see what you want, don't be too shy to ask. Probably we don't have it anyway.

2. If the service is not up to snuff, just holler. Nobody will pay you any mind, but your tonsils can use the exercise.

3. We will gladly cash your check if you leave your watch, fur coat, or car as collateral. No wives or in-laws accepted.

4. If you are displeased in any way by the attentions of the resident Doberman pinscher, just remember—things could be worse. You could be at a Brahms concert.

Quoted in Veronica Geng's
"Settling an Old Score"

Irony, along with a tinge of sarcasm, abounds in this notice, but a double irony ensued when the visitors, instead of being offended by Shaw's rules, missed the point, copied his notice, and put it up on the walls in their own houses.

Satire

satise – mechanceté.

An expression or literary work that seeks to expose folly and wickedness, often by means of irony and sarcasm, is satirical.

Example: In Jonathan Swift's classic satirical essay, "A Modest Proposal" (published in 1729), he proposes a solution for a serious problem in Ireland. Thousands of beggars were wandering the countryside, their plight ignored by their landlords who were rich landowners of English descent. His satiric solution was that a certain number of Irish children be served for dinner at the tables of these landlords. Swift writes: "I grant this food will be somewhat dear, and therefore very proper for landlords, who, as they have already devoured most of the parents, seem to have the best title to the children." Unsuspecting students are horrified when they first encounter this essay, primarily because they think the written word must always be taken literally.

Cynicism

mankind – criticism selfish

Cynicism is characterized by scorn for the motives and virtues of others; the belief that people are motivated by selfishness. The cynical tone is mocking and sneering, often bitter; it may or may not involve irony.

Example 1: When a rich man donates money to a charity, cynics say that his motive is to get a charitable deduction on his tax return.

Example 2: In 1985, CocaCola announced that the company was "reformulating" Coke, in an apparent effort to keep up with the increasing popularity of Pepsi Cola. After "New Coke" made its appearance, so many die-hard Coke drinkers objected that four months later the company brought back the original formula. It decided, however, to market both Cokes; "New Coke" would be available along with the original formula, now called "CocaCola Classic." The company maintained that its fans had spoken and that it had listened; but cynics jokingly suggested that the company might have orchestrated the whole thing, that it never really intended to eliminate the original formula forever, and that it simply wanted to call attention to itself and to regain its leading position in the soft-drink market.

Sarcasm

Bitterness

This refers to an expression or attitude that is sharply mocking or contemptuous, typically utilizing statements or implications pointedly opposite or irrelevant to the underlying purport. Sarcasm suggests open taunting *Raillerie* and ridicule; though it uses irony, its effect is considerably harsher, revealing an intention to hurt.

Example: In an essay called "The Corruption of English," John Simon recounts the case of a woman who was denied tenure as an instructor of freshman composition at a Florida college. Simon quotes extensively from a poorly written memo by the teacher's division director, poking fun throughout at its writer's mistakes. One of the division director's objections to the teacher was the teacher's statement in her syllabus that her students "should not use one word when there is a better (more precise) word to say what they mean." Simon quotes from the director's memo, adding his own remarks in brackets: "Denotative definitions of English words can vary from one to ten or more definitions. Very few English words, usually nouns, have less [correctly: *fewer*] than two meanings. [Actually, quite a few leap to mind; for example, nincompoop, numskull, ignoramus, cretin, division director.]"

Sardonicism

This term can describe both content and manner of expression and is associated with scorn, derision, mockery, and cynicism. It is closely associated with sarcasm.

Example: In *The Dragons of Eden,* astrophysicist Carl Sagan recounts a quotation from John Locke, the seventeenth-century English philosopher: "Beasts abstract not," meaning that animals can't think. Bishop Berkeley, an eighteenth-century philosopher, commented: "If the fact that brutes abstract not be made the distinguishing property of that sort of animal, I fear a great many of those that pass for men must be reckoned in their number." Can you figure out why this remark is sardonic?

As a way of summarizing this section on irony, read the following humorous article which effectively combines irony, satire, sarcasm, and sardonicism. It is a comment on an ad for the Park Lane Hotel that appeared in several national magazines. The Park Lane Hotel is owned by Leona Helmsley, who has a reputation for running a tight ship. (An ad for the Palace, one of her other hotels, shows Helmsley wearing a full-length evening gown standing in a courtyard in front of the hotel; she is giving orders to a tree-trimmer perched on a ladder. The copy beneath her picture says, "It's the only Palace in the world where the Queen stands guard." Pretentious ads like this are perfect targets for satirical comment.) Apparently, no detail concerning a hotel's operation is too insignificant for Helmsley. Even the quality of the cream served at high tea, or a guest's complaint about the cream, requires her attention.

Show of hands: How many of you out there read, even on an occasional basis, the *New Yorker*? Good. And how many of you have followed with morbid interest the advertisements placed therein by Leona M. Helmsley, President of the Park Lane Hotel, an establishment of putative elegance at 36 Central Park South, New York City? Yes.

Did you perhaps see the ad about a month ago that featured Leona herself—hair by Ann Miller, clothes by Adolfo of Buffalo, sitting at her Louis Quatorze desk with Central Park arranged behind her like a shroud—contemplating a sheet of paper? Just over her right shoulder, in reverse type, is the discreet headline: "When a hotel is letter perfect, guests keep coming back."

Underneath this alarming photograph is a facsimile of a letter allegedly written by Leona M. Helmsley to one Olaf Johansen of Stevens Point, Wisconsin. The letter goes like this:

"Dear Mr. Johansen:

"Being from America's dairy heartland, you were probably surprised when you requested cream during our High Tea at the Park Lane Hotel and were asked which kind you prefer.

"Our clotted cream, which is flown to us fresh all the way from Devonshire, England, is hardly what you'd expect to pour from a pitcher, as the true test of this English tradition is whether or not it can stand a spoon upright.

"The next time you're with us, try the cream with one of our Scottish scones, and I'm sure it will all start to make sense!"

An odd, I'm sure you will agree, missive. Let us together try to reconstruct the events that might have led up to this document. Olaf Johansen (and, quite possibly, Mrs. Johansen), visiting New York as guests of the Sharp Cheddar Association, decide, after a feverish day of shopping along Fifth Avenue, to stop by the Park Lane to partake of its famous High Tea.

Johansen, as it happens, having spent some years in England as a young man, likes his tea with plenty of cream and lots of sugar. Being a person of Scandinavian temperament, he is not tempted by the sticky little pastries or the crumbly little scones; what he wants is his sweet tea and plenty of it.

Comes the tea; comes the cream. He tries to pour B into A. No go. He calls the waitress over.

Johansen: "This cream won't go into my tea. I require a cream that will go into my tea. This cream is almost . . . clotted."

Waitress: "This cream comes all the way from Devonshire, England, where they like cream so ripe you can build end tables out of it. Important people the world over prefer their cream in large chunks."

Johansen: "But I need cream for my tea."

Waitress: "Put it on your scones, as thousands of prestigious people do."

Johansen: "This is an outrage. I shall write your president.

Waitress: "Oh, do. She loves to answer mail."

A week later, the ever-vigilant Helmsley, fresh from yet another photo session during which she destroys an entire truckload of unacceptably tacky crystal goblets, gets a brisk note from Olaf Johansen, safely ensconced in his Wisconsin home.

Johansen writes: "I tried your High Tea cream the other day and found it more suitable for bricklaying than drinking. It was, not to put too fine a point on it, spoiled. I was outraged, and said so. Please explain. Sincerely yours, etc."

Helmsley then pens the letter we have already read. She places it in an envelope and seals it with cunning red wax.

"There," she says to herself. "That'll keep Johansen coming back for more."

Jon Carroll,
"Innkeeper to the Seriously Disgruntled"

Deadpan Humor   Specific words or phrases, or the choice of details, are not the only ways of arriving at irony in writing. It may also result from the use of a sort of deadpan humor—so called because it refers to the brand of humor characteristic of comedians who deliver their lines without registering facial expression. (Jack Benny was and Jackie Gleason is particularly adept at this.) It is a subtle sort of humor, so muted that we are required to regard the situation itself as humorous or ironic, even though the words themselves are not particularly funny.

In a famous article called "The Yellow Bus," Lillian Ross describes a 1960 trip to New York City by several graduating seniors from the Bean Blossom Township High School in Bean Blossom, Indiana. Throughout the article, Ross shows two cultures in contact—and in conflict. In short, the students are from an isolated rural area, and the fast-paced, sophisticated New York they encounter is thoroughly alien to them. The following passage, from the middle of the article, illustrates well the problems both of perceiving a writer's ironic intentions and of knowing the precise attitude toward the subject that the writer herself held.

At 5 P.M. of this second day in the city of New York, the members of the Bean Blossom senior class returned to their hotel and stood in the lobby for a while, looking from some distance at a souvenir-and-gift stand across from the registration desk. The stand was stocked with thermometers in the form of the Statue of Liberty, in two sizes, priced at seventy-nine cents and ninety-eight cents; with silver-plated charm bracelets; with pins and compacts carrying representations of the Empire State Building; with scarves showing the R.C.A. Building and the U.N. Building; and with ashtrays showing the New York City skyline. Mike Richardson edged over to the stand and picked up a wooden plaque, costing ninety-eight cents, with the Statue of Liberty shown at the top, American flags at the sides, and, in the middle, a poem, inscribed "Mother," which read:

> To one who bears the sweetest name
> And adds a luster to the same
> Who shares my joys
> Who cheers when sad
> The greatest friend I ever had
> Long life to her, for there's no other
> Can take the place of my dear mother.

After reading the poem, Mike smiled.
"Where ya from?" the man behind the stand asked him.

"Indiana," Mike said, looking as though he were warming up. "We've been on this tour? The whole day?"

"Ya see everything?" the man asked.

"Everything except the Empire State Building," said Mike.

"Yeah," said the man, and looked away.

Mike was still holding the plaque. Carefully, he replaced it on the stand. "I'll come back for this later," he said.

Without looking at Mike, the man nodded.

Lillian Ross,
"The Yellow Bus"

My experience with this piece is that students tend to interpret the writer's tone according to their own background. Students who have lived in rural areas perceive the New Yorkers, represented here by the man behind the souvenir stand, as jaded and unfriendly; city dwellers find the Bean Blossomites hopelessly naïve. But what attitude do Ross's words really convey? In fact, both interpretations—if tempered a bit—are right; we are not meant to choose sides. Like Cynthia Ozick, in her description of Rosa Lublin, Ross implies her judgment through her choice of details (the cheap souvenirs for sale; the saccharine poem, "Mother," that makes Mike smile; and the short, unsatisfactory conversation we overhear between Mike and the counter attendant). The tone is not so much sarcastic as it is gently unsympathetic to both parties. But, as in making inferences, an accurate determination of a writer's tone sometimes depends on one's own experiences.

One last comment on irony. A writer can be critical—whether mildly or sharply so—and not be ironic. Turn for a moment to pp. 36–37. The tone of Jonathan Schell's paragraph about the likely effects of a nuclear war is decidedly critical, but not ironic. Remember that irony always involves a contradiction between the apparent and the intended use of the words, something different from what the words really mean.

EXERCISES—PART I

Determining Tone   Here are some short passages for you to practice with. Read each carefully, consider the continuum printed earlier, and decide what the tone is for each.

(1)   [In this first passage from her novel, *Mrs. Dalloway,* Virginia Woolf describes the character of Richard Dalloway, Clarissa Dalloway's husband, from the point of view of Peter Walsh who was once in love with Clarissa and, in fact, wanted to marry her himself.]

He was a thorough good sort; a bit limited; a bit thick in the head; yes; but a thorough good sort. Whatever he took up he did in the same matter-of-fact sensible way; without a touch of imagination, without a spark of brilliancy, but with the inexplicable niceness of his type. He ought to have been a country gentleman—he was wasted on politics. He was at his best out of doors, with horses and dogs—how good he was, for instance, when that great shaggy dog of Clarissa's got caught in a trap and had its paw half torn off, and Clarissa turned faint and Dalloway did the whole thing; bandaged, made splints; told Clarissa not to be a fool. That was what she liked him for perhaps—that was what she needed. "Now, my dear, don't be a fool. Hold this—fetch that," all the time talking to the dog as if it were a human being.

But how could she swallow all that stuff about poetry? How could she let him hold forth about Shakespeare? Seriously and solemnly Richard Dalloway got on his hind legs and said that no decent man ought to read Shakespeare's sonnets because it was like listening at keyholes (besides the relationship was not one that he approved). No decent man ought to let his wife visit a deceased wife's sister. Incredible! The only thing to do was to pelt him with sugared almonds—it was at dinner. But Clarissa sucked it all in; thought it so honest of him; so independent of him; Heaven knows if she didn't think him the most original mind she'd ever met!

Virginia Woolf,
Mrs. Dalloway

(2)   But Sir William Bradshaw stopped at the door to look at a picture. He looked in the corner for the engraver's name. His wife looked too. Sir William Bradshaw was so interested in art.

Virginia Woolf,
Mrs. Dalloway

(3)   Sunlight in Beverly Hills has an autumnal quality, both harsh and introspective, that is jarringly at odds with the hot-pink, awning-green, terra-cotta, and gold colored houses that offer themselves for inspection brazenly and nakedly on Sunset Boulevard. If you have grown up among grimy tenements and shuttered and reserved brownstones, there is no way you can understand the smugness and stridency of public architecture on Sunset Boulevard. All houses on Sunset Boulevard are public. They all look as if they had been designed for a giant Monopoly board and set down on their parcels of land for permanent exhibition. There is something chilling in their apparent expansiveness, an air of duplicity prevails: these are houses that are meant to be seen from cars or tourist buses; shelter is the least of their functions. Their blank, supercilious windows, which look out on gravel paths and Mercedes and imported palm trees, seem almost to refute any notion that real people live and move behind them. In this harsh light, objects are clearly defined, and one feels one's own outlines blur in comparison.

Barbara Grizzuti Harrison,
"Hotel California"

(4)   My county police officer told me the shed at the end of my dock on the mainland should be kept locked, and I asked why in view of the fact that the shed contained only ½ pint of two-cycle outboard oil, an ancient sponge that I used two years ago when I last washed my car, a red chair with only three legs, and a June 8, 1976, issue of *Time* Magazine. He shrugged his shoulders, a way of saying take all the risks you want but don't call me after you've been robbed. Nonetheless, I got a lock but I expect any day to find it forced; the lock seems to imply there is something inside worth locking up. A few days ago I unlocked the door and looked inside; the oil, sponge, chair, and *Time* were okay. I breathed easier, but in my heart I longed for the old days when the shed not only was unlocked but the door frequently flapped open, especially when the wind came from the east.

Caskie Stinnett,
"Room with a View"

(5)   The idea behind the MX missile system is sound enough. Place bomb-bearing missiles on wheels and keep them moving constantly through thousands of miles of desert so enemy bombers will not have a fixed target. To confuse things further, move decoy missiles over the same routes so the enemy cannot distinguish between false missiles and the real thing.

As my strategic thinkers immediately pointed out, however, the MX missile system makes very little sense unless matched by an MX Pentagon system. What is the point, they asked, of installing a highly mobile missile system if its command center, the Pentagon, remains anchored like a moose with four broken legs on the bank of the Potomac River?

This is why we propose building 250 moveable structures so precisely like the Pentagon that no one can tell our fake Pentagons from the real thing and to keep all of them, plus the real Pentagon, in constant motion through the country.

Our first plan was to move only the real Pentagon, which would be placed on a large flat-bottom truck bed and driven about the countryside on the existing highway system. We immediately realized, however, that this would not provide sufficient protection against nuclear attack. The Pentagon is very big and easily noticeable. When it is driven along at 55 miles per hour, people can see it coming from miles away. It attracts attention. In short, it is a fat, easily detected target.

With 250 fake Pentagons constantly cruising the roads, the problem is solved. Now, trying to distinguish the real Pentagon from the fake Pentagons, enemy attackers will face the maddening problem of finding a needle in a haystack. With 251 Pentagons in circulation, the sight of a Pentagon on the highway will attract no more attention than a politician's indictment. Thus we foil the enemy's spies.

Still, to add another margin of security we will confuse matters further by building 1,500 Pentagon-shaped fast-food restaurants along the nation's highways.

Each will be an exact replica of the real Pentagon, at least as seen from the outside. Inside, of course, they will be equipped to provide all the necessities for producing acute indigestion, thus providing the wherewithal of highway travel and, in the process, earning the Government a little return on its investment.

Occasionally, when generals and admirals tire of touring and yearn for a little stability, the real Pentagon will be parked alongside the road to masquerade as a fast-food Pentagon. The danger of highway travelers wandering in for a quick hot dog and making trouble while the authentic Pentagon is in the "parked" or "fast-food" mode has also been considered.

These interlopers will simply be told by receptionists that hot dogs are in the back of the building and directed to walk the long route around the Pentagon's outer ring. As they drop from exhaustion they will be removed by military police, carried to their cars, given free hot dogs and advised that next time they should enter their Pentagon fast-food dispensary through the rear door.

There are problems to be ironed out in the MX Pentagon, but we are too busy at the moment perfecting our MX Congress system to trifle with details. With 850 United States Capitols on the highway, we have an extremely touchy problem in deciding whether a Capitol or a Pentagon should have the right of way when they meet at an intersection.

Russell Baker,
"Universal Military Motion"

EXERCISES—PART II

Selection 1

[1]We continue to share with our remotest ancestors the most tangled and evasive attitudes about death, despite the great distance we have come in understanding some of the profound aspects of biology. [2]We have as much distaste for talking about personal death as for thinking about it; it is an indelicacy, like talking in mixed company about venereal disease or abortion in the old days. [3]Death on a grand scale does not bother us in the same special way: we can sit around a dinner table and discuss war, involving 60 million volatilized* human deaths, as though we were talking about bad weather; we can watch abrupt bloody death every day, in color, on films and television, without blinking back a tear. [4]It is when the numbers of dead are very small, and very close, that we begin to think in scurrying circles. [5]At the very center of the problem is the naked cold deadness of one's own self, the only reality in nature of which we can have absolute certainty, and it is unmentionable, unthinkable. [6]We may be even less willing to face the issue at first hand than our predecessors because of a secret new hope that maybe it will go away. [7]We like to think, hiding the thought, that with all the marvelous ways in which we

*Literally, evaporated.

seem now to lead nature around by the nose, perhaps we can avoid the central problem if we just become, next year, say, a bit smarter.

[8]"The long habit of living," said Thomas Browne, "indisposeth us to dying." [9]These days, the habit has become an addiction: we are hooked on living; the tenacity of its grip on us, and ours on it, grows in intensity. [10]We cannot think of giving it up, even when living loses its zest—even when we have lost the zest for zest.

Lewis Thomas,
"The Long Habit"

A. Vocabulary   For each italicized word from the selection, choose the best definition according to the context in which it appears.

1. *evasive* [sentence 1]: Characterized by (a) uncertainty and anxiety; (b) avoidance and ambiguity; (c) naïveté; innocence; (d) fear and confusion.

2. *indelicacy* [2]: Something that is (a) crude; offensive to good taste; (b) incapable of being understood; (c) unpleasant; a cause of discomfort; (d) inappropriate; unsuitable.

3. *predecessors* [6]: (a) scientists; (b) offspring; future generations; (c) ancestors; earlier generations; (d) fortune tellers; prophets.

4. *tenacity* [9]: (a) occupancy; (b) force; power; (c) stubbornness; (d) the act of holding or clinging tightly to.

5. *zest* [10]: (a) wholehearted interest; enjoyment; (b) purpose; ultimate goal; (c) creativity; imagination; (d) will to survive.

B. Content and Structure   Choose the best answer.

1. The main idea of the passage is that (a) medical science will someday find the secret of immortality; (b) war and other calamities have hardened us to death on a mass scale; (c) human beings are characterized by an irrational fear of death, an unwillingness to face the inevitable; (d) despite scientific advancements and a better understanding of life's processes, our attitude toward death has changed little from primitive times.

2. Which phrase in the passage expresses the controlling idea? ___tangled and evasive___ in sentence __1__.

3. Thomas's specific purpose is to (a) tell a story; (b) describe a scene; (c) explain an aspect of human behavior; (d) persuade the reader to accept his opinion.

4. The relationship between sentences 2, 3, and 4 is (a) contrast; (b) terms and their definitions; (c) statement, evidence, and conclusion; (d) cause–effect.

5. What is the relationship between paragraph 1 (sentences 1–7) and paragraph 2 (sentences 8–10)? (a) general statement and illustration; (b) cause–effect; (c) comparison and contrast; (d) explanation and conclusion redefining the main idea.

6. In sentence 4, Thomas writes, "we begin to think in scurrying circles," by which he compares our thoughts to circles that (a) are confused and tangled, as in a maze; (b) continue forever, into infinity; (c) gradually become smaller and smaller, leading ultimately to the center–ourselves; (d) whirl around quickly, creating a dizzying effect.

7. In sentence 5, Thomas writes, "At the very center of the problem is the naked, cold deadness of one's own self." His choice of words is meant to (a) make us feel pity for our eventual fate; (b) shock us into reality; (c) soften what might otherwise be harshly interpreted; (d) make us feel helpless, at the mercy of a higher power.

8. The "secret new hope" Thomas mentions in sentence 6, and the phrase "becoming smarter" in sentence 7, actually refer to (a) our faith in religious miracles; (b) our ease in accepting our mortality; (c) our hope of a scientific breakthrough that would prevent our dying; (d) achieving new levels of intellectual knowledge that would make the prospect of dying less devastating.

9. Sentence 7 contains an implied metaphor. In the phrase "to lead nature around by the nose," nature is being compared to _an animal_.

10. The tone of this passage can best be described as (a) gentle and sympathetic; (b) cynical; distrustful of human motives; (c) nasty and sarcastic; (d) witty and lightly humorous.

C. Inferences   On the basis of the evidence in the selection, mark these statements as follows: *A* for accurate inferences, *I* for inaccurate inferences, and *IE* for insufficient evidence.

I   1. Modern man is unable to accept death as easily as his predecessors did.

IE   2. To primitive man, death was simply part of the inevitable process of life, a final stage in the natural cycle of birth, life, and death.

IE   3. Science will eventually control nature and will find a way to make human beings immortal.

IE   4. Bloody scenes from wars should be prohibited from being shown on television.

A   5. The concept of death means little until it affects us or someone close to us.

Selection 2   [1]A species is a group that can produce fertile offspring by crosses within but not outside itself. [2]The mating of different breeds of dogs yields puppies which, when grown, will be reproductively competent dogs. [3]But crosses between species–even species as similar as donkeys and horses–produce infertile offspring (in this case, mules). [4]Donkeys and horses are therefore categorized as separate species. [5]Viable but infertile matings of more widely separated species–for example, lions and tigers–sometimes occur, and if, rarely, the offspring are fertile, this indicates

ironic
human

only that the definition of species is a little fuzzy. [6]All human beings are members of the same species, *Homo sapiens,* which means, in optimistic Latin, "Man, the wise." [7]Our probable ancestors, *Homo erectus* and *Homo habilis*—now extinct—are classified as of the same genus (*Homo*) but of different species, although no one (at least lately) has attempted the appropriate experiments to see if crosses of them with us would produce fertile offspring.

Carl Sagan,
The Dragons of Eden

A. Vocabulary   For each italicized word from the paragraph, choose the best definition according to the context in which it appears.

1. *competent* [2]: (a) permissible; (b) well-qualified; (c) well-developed; (d) capable.

2. *infertile* [3 and 5]: Incapable of (a) reproducing; (b) having sexual relations; (c) maturing; (d) developing normally.

3. *viable* [5]: Capable of (a) reproducing; (b) breathing; (c) living; (d) mating.

B. Content and Structure   Choose the best answer.

1. Which sentence represents the main idea of the paragraph? ___1___

2. With respect to the rest of the paragraph, the topic sentence represents (a) a statement of cause and effect; (b) an example; (c) an analogy; (d) a definition; (e) a process to be explained step-by-step.

3. Which method of development does Sagan use? (a) comparison; (b) contrast; (c) example; (d) cause–effect; (e) classification.

4. Sagan's purpose is (a) to tell a story; (b) to describe a scene; (c) to explain the meaning of a term; (d) to present an argument about a controversial subject.

5. The pattern of organization is (a) deductive; (b) variation of deductive; (c) inductive; (d) chronological; (e) emphatic.

6. The relationship between sentences 1 and 2 is (a) cause–effect; (b) contrast; (c) example and general principle; (d) general principle and example.

7. According to the paragraph, a species is defined according to whether or not a member produces (a) offspring that resemble it exactly; (b) infertile offspring; (c) fertile offspring; (d) offspring capable of mating with members of other species.

8. The product of a donkey and a horse is (a) rare; (b) called a donkey; (c) called a mule; (d) fertile.

9. The tone of sentences 1–5 can best be described as (a) sarcastic; sardonic; (b) ironic; witty; (c) humorous; amused; (d) objective; neutral.

10. The tone of sentences 6 and 7 can best be described as (a) sarcastic; sardonic; (b) ironic; witty; (c) humorous; amused; (d) objective; neutral.

C. Inferences   On the basis of the evidence in the paragraph, mark these statements as follows: *A* for accurate inferences, *I* for inaccurate inferences, and *IE* for insufficient evidence.

_A__   1. Dogs represent one species of animal.

_I__   2. Donkeys and horses are unable to mate.

_IE__   3. Few scientists agree on the meaning of the term *species*.

_I__   4. In the term *Homo sapiens*, the word *Homo* refers to the species to which man belongs.

A   _IE__   5. A species is a category of a genus.

_I__   6. Science will someday find a definite answer to the question of modern man's ability to mate successfully with *Homo erectus* and *Homo habilis*.

Selection 3   (Note: The chimpanzee who is the subject of this passage, Cholmondeley— or Chumley as he was known to his friends—was being donated to the London Zoo. The author had promised the owner to take the chimp back to England on his way home from Africa.)

[1]He arrived in the back of a small van, seated sedately in a huge crate. [2]When the doors of his crate were opened and Chumley stepped out with all the ease and self-confidence of a film star, I was considerably shaken; standing on his bow legs in a normal slouching chimp position, he came up to my waist, and if he had straightened up his head would have been on a level with my chest. [3]He had huge arms and must have measured at least twice my size round his hairy chest. [4]Owing to bad tooth growth, both sides of his face were swollen out of all proportion, and this gave him a weird pugilistic look. [5]His eyes were small, deep-set, and intelligent; the top of his head was nearly bald, owing, I discovered later, to his habit of sitting and rubbing the palms of his hands backward across his head, an exercise which seemed to afford him much pleasure and which he persisted in until the top of his skull was quite devoid of hair. [6]This was no young chimp such as I had expected, but a veteran about eight or nine years old, fully mature, strong as a powerful man, and, to judge by his expression, with considerable experience of life. [7]Although he was not exactly a nice chimp to look at (I had seen handsomer), he certainly had a terrific personality; it hit you as soon as you set eyes on him. [8]His little eyes looked at you with great intelligence, and there seemed to be a glitter of ironic laughter in their depths that made one feel uncomfortable.

[9]He stood on the ground and surveyed his surroundings with a shrewd glance, and then he turned to me and held out one of his soft, pink-palmed hands to be shaken, with exactly that bored expression that one sees on the faces of professional hand-shakers. [10]Round his neck was a thick chain, and its length drooped over the tailboard of the lorry and disappeared into the depths of his crate. [11]With an animal of less personality

than Chumley, this would have been a sign of his subjugation, of his captivity. [12]But Chumley wore the chain with the superb air of a Lord Mayor; after shaking my hand so professionally, he turned and proceeded to pull the chain, which measured some fifteen feet, out of his crate. [13]He gathered it up carefully into loops, hung it over one hand, and proceeded to walk into the hut as if he owned it. [14]Thus, in the first few minutes of arrival, Chumley had made us feel inferior; he had moved in, not, we felt, because we wanted him to, but because he did. [15]I almost felt I ought to apologize for the mess on the table.

Gerald Durrell,
"The Life and Death of Cholmondeley"

A. Vocabulary

For each italicized word from the selection, choose the best definition according to the context in which it appears.

1. *sedately* [1]: (a) calmly; in a dignified manner; (b) nervously; apprehensively; (c) arrogantly; haughtily; (d) uncomfortably; awkwardly.
2. *pugilistic* [4]: having the appearance of (a) a military officer; (b) a movie star; (c) a fighter; (d) a vicious animal.
3. *ironic* [8]: (a) cynical; distrustful; (b) satirical; ridiculing; (c) sarcastic; suggesting a superior attitude; (d) nasty; cruel.
4. *shrewd* [9]: (a) bored; (b) impartial; (c) deliberately deceptive; (d) keenly perceptive.
5. *subjugation* [11]: (a) boredom; indifference; (b) defeat; enslavement; (c) cooperative spirit; (d) subjectivity; introspective nature.

B. Content and Structure

Choose the best answer.

1. This passage combines two modes of discourse: (a) description and persuasion; (b) description and exposition; (c) narration and persuasion; (d) narration and description.
2. The dominant impression of Chumley that Durrell wants to convey is his (a) wisdom and experience; (b) large size; (c) maturity; (d) superior attitude.
3. The sentence that *best* describes Chumley's character as it is revealed throughout the passage is (a) sentence 6; (b) sentence 7; (c) sentence 8; (d) sentence 12; (e) sentence 14.
4. With respect to the end of paragraph 1, the second paragraph serves as (a) an explanation; (b) a contrasting example; (c) an illustration; (d) a conclusion.
5. The relationship between sentences 11 and 12 is (a) cause–effect; (b) general statement and illustration; (c) contrast; (d) two steps in a process.
6. The passage contains three figures of speech to describe Chumley's character. Find them and, in the spaces provided, write what Chumley is compared to:

_____a film star_____ in sentence __2__
___professional hand shaker___ in sentence __9__
_____a Lord mayor_____ in sentence __12__

7. Study the figures of speech for question 6 and, in your own words, state the image of Chumley they are meant to convey. _____

8. The tone of the passage can best be described as (a) ironic, wry, and amused; (b) sarcastic; ridiculing; (c) serious; earnest; (d) complaining; aggrieved.

C. Inferences   On the basis of the evidence in the selection, mark these statements as follows: *A* for accurate inferences, *I* for inaccurate inferences, and *IE* for insufficient evidence.

_I_ 1. Durrell had never seen a chimp before.

_A_ 2. Chumley was not an especially attractive chimp.

_I_ 3. Chumley was embarrassed by the chains used to tether him to his crate.

_IE_ 4. Chumley liked his surroundings to be clean and orderly.

_A_ 5. Chumley was accustomed to being the center of attention.

Selection 4   [1]Dagwood Bumstead represents an important archetype in the American psyche—the irrelevant male. [2]He is still in the strip, but he is only there as an object of ridicule and a symbol of inadequacy and stupidity. [3]His job was breeding, and now that that is done with, and Alexander and Cookie produced, he remains on as a fool, and the butt of many jokes.

[4]His name is absurd, the name of an irrelevant person, a clown. [5]"Bumstead" is silly: Perhaps it is close to "bump" and to "lump," which suggests, perhaps, *lumpenproletariat.** [6]"Bum" also means tramp and rear end, neither of which is flattering. [7](Strange to think that the offspring of this nothing would be named Alexander, the name of a world conqueror.) [8]His face, with those two dots for eyes and the hair standing out in two tufts, as if they were horns and he were cuckolded, is ludicrous, and even more so since Blondie is relatively realistically drawn, often with a good bit of leg showing. [9]Actually Dagwood's face has changed from the first strips; when he was a rich young man he was portrayed more realistically. [10]Now, with the cuckold hairdo, he represents an ancient tradition in comedy: the man whose wife has been unfaithful to him but who is unaware of it. [11]This humor is based on exposure and ignorance—we know something Dagwood doesn't. [12]And Dagwood's general inadequacy at the job and around the house fits in well with the notion that he is probably inadequate in the bedroom.

Asa Arthur Berger,
"Blondie: The Irrelevance of the American Husband"

*German; literally, the ragged, shabby working classes.

A. Vocabulary   For each italicized word from the selection, choose the best definition according to the context in which it appears.

1. *archetype* [1]: (a) character; (b) kind of drawing; (c) original model; (d) hero.
2. *psyche* [1]: (a) culture; (b) fantasy; (c) temperament; (d) soul.
3. *irrelevant* [1]: having no (a) effect; (b) meaning; (c) future; (d) feelings.
4. *cuckolded* [8]: refers to a husband whose wife (a) ignores him; (b) commits adultery; (c) nags him; (d) laughs at his weaknesses.
5. *ludicrous* [8]: (a) absurd; (b) unrealistic; (c) incomplete; (d) peculiar.

B. Content and Structure   Choose the best answer.

1. Which sentence best expresses the main idea of the passage? sentence ____1____
2. Write the phrase from the sentence that you chose for question #1 that expresses the controlling idea. __the irrelevant male -__
3. The mode of discourse in this passage is (a) narration; (b) description; (c) exposition; (d) persuasion.
4. Berger's purpose, specifically, is to (a) trace the development of Bumstead's role; (b) describe Bumstead's original significance; (c) show how Bumstead's name and appearance reveal his character; (d) examine the humorous aspects of Blondie and Bumstead.
5. The relationship between sentences 1 and 2 is (a) a term and its definition; (b) cause–effect; (c) contrast; (d) general statement and a specific illustration.
6. The method of development used in sentences 4–7 is (a) cause–effect; (b) process; (c) analogy; (d) analysis; (e) comparison.
7. In sentence 7, Berger is (a) using figurative language; (b) using sneer words; (c) using denotative language; (d) being ironic.
8. The relationship between sentences 9 and 10 is contrast. What is being contrasted? ____original face____ and ____after the strips____
9. As it is used in sentence 9, *actually* means (a) really; (b) generally; (c) formerly; (d) in fact.
10. The relationship between the two parts of sentence 10 is (a) steps in a process; (b) concept and a supporting analogy; (c) contrast; (d) statement and an explanation.
11. Berger suggests that the way Bumstead is drawn makes him look (a) inadequate; (b) foolish; (c) handsome; (d) repulsive.
12. Berger's choice of words, for example, "fool," "bum," "bump," "lump," "*lumpenproletariat*," "clown," "cuckold," are examples of (a) sneer words; (b) euphemisms; (c) denotative language; (d) figurative language; (e) jargon.
13. For evidence to support his ideas, Berger relies chiefly on (a) illustrations from several Blondie comic strips; (b) his own subjective opinions and interpretations; (c) factual information; (d) research from scholarly works on the history of comedy.

Inadequate in the bedroom to —

14. What evidence does Berger cite as support for the last sentence?

Since Bumstead is inadequate in the house and in his job he probably

15. The tone of the passage can best be described as (a) cynical; distrustful of human motives; (b) humorous; witty; (c) objective; impartial; (d) sarcastic; mocking.

C. Inferences On the basis of the evidence in the passage, mark these statements as follows: *A* for accurate inferences, *I* for inaccurate inferences, and *IE* for insufficient evidence.

_I_ 1. The stereotype of American husbands is that they are irrelevant—objects of ridicule and symbols of inadequacy and stupidity.

_IE_ 2. In the strip, Blondie, Alexander, and Cookie constantly make Bumstead the object of their jokes.

_A_ 3. Bumstead is drawn less realistically than Blondie.

_A_ 4. The characterization and manner of drawing Bumstead's picture has changed since the cartoon was first published.

_IE_ 5. Blondie is frequently depicted as being unfaithful to Bumstead.

_I_ 6. Berger finds the cartoon strip insulting and offensive to men.

PRACTICE ESSAY

"Notes and Comment," *The New Yorker,* May 27, 1985

The following letter from an unidentified correspondent appeared in *The New Yorker.* The letter alludes to two much-discussed controversies of the spring of 1985. First, President Reagan visited the Bitburg cemetery during a state visit to Germany but, because the cemetery was the burial site of several SS Nazi soldiers, his visit was intensely criticized by many people, particularly American Jewish groups, who felt that the visit symbolized an American acceptance of Nazi atrocities. The second controversy concerned South Africa's apartheid (separatist) policy. That spring, for example, students at many American universities conducted marches, rallies, and sit-ins—reminiscent of the 1960s—aimed at coercing their administrations to divest all stock holdings in American corporations conducting business in South Africa. The anti-apartheid movement gained even more adherents when, in the summer of 1985, South African blacks rioted against the white-supremacist government's policies, resulting in the government's imposing a state of emergency and in the deaths of hundreds of blacks. In the United States, the South African movie, *The Gods Must Be Crazy,* was the target of many boycotts, as this letter mentions.

1 Mother's Day, I have to admit, is one of those so-called holidays that make me want to go underground and crack the greeting-card lobby that I'm sure is at the bottom of it all. But my folks and I live in the same city, so it's never been hard for them to reach out and pin me, and when they suggested celebrating Mother's Day with lunch at their favorite Hungarian café on the upper East Side and a movie—the much publicized foreign-film hit "The

Gods Must Be Crazy"—I was there on time in shirt and tie and three-piece suit. My mother had had a few tough weeks: because she was born in Berlin and survived the Nazi regime, the whole Bitburg incident and the recent Holocaust remembrances wiped out, at least for the moment, the forty years of relative calm and security she had known as a New Yorker. Retreating for a few hours into a familiar environment (the café) and then a hermetic one (the movies) seemed like a good plan—especially for someone who happened to know more than the news media could ever know about the horrors of the Holocaust, and was eager to somehow get past it. Lunch was pleasant, as was the leisurely stroll down to the East Sixty-eighth Street movie theatre, where we stood in the ticket holders' line for about fifteen minutes before the film. Though the film has been running here for almost a year to sold-out houses, I knew little about it except that it had something to do with African primitives facing the modern world, and that it was a comedy. Apparently, someone felt that it wasn't, for there was a young white man representing Brooklynites Against Apartheid handing out leaflets to all of us in the line and imploring us to ask for refunds instead of going in, because the film was produced by a white South African. Since the movie had been running for almost a year without any reported trouble, I wondered what could be so bad, and I adopted a let-me-see-for-myself attitude, and so did everyone else in the line.

2   After we were seated and the lights dimmed and the Twentieth Century-Fox logo passed, two young women seated toward the front stood up and began protesting the showing of the film, on the ground that the film did not truly portray the plight of black South Africans; and they succeeded in stopping the film temporarily. The lights came on, and the women continued their speech, only to be drowned out by irate patrons demanding their removal. Shouts went up, and there was a crossfire of feelings. "This is America, and if you want to protest you can do it outside!" a woman yelled from the balcony. A young man called out, "We paid our five dollars! Let us decide for ourselves!" A little voice from the back rang out, saying, "Why not just let them speak?" "Out! Out! Out! Out!" the majority of the audience began chanting. I looked at my mother, sitting next to me, and I could see that she was upset. "If these people"—she meant the two women—"are so committed that they are willing to spend ten dollars to come into a hostile place and get thrown out, there must be some reason," she said. A theatre employee appeared, to the applause of the majority, and he was a little physical in dealing with the two women. Several people shouted at him to take it easy, but most of the audience continued to shout angrily at the women. A few minutes later, things settled down, the theatre darkened again, and the movie began. Just after the opening credits, a young man in the front row stood up and said, in a British accent, "I would like to point out that this is a racist film that supports—" and he was drowned out by an infuriated crowd, which now wanted the police to intervene. The young man was undaunted. "I will not leave here until I have a chance to say what I have to say," he said. The atmosphere in the theatre—on the upper East Side, on Mother's Day afternoon—grew increasingly tense as demands for the young

man's removal became more vehement, and as one or two people in the audience ventured to tell the rest that maybe there was a point worth listening to. "Leave with him! Out! Out! Out!" the chant rose. Finally, two cops arrived, smiling and slightly bewildered by the cheers that met their entrance. The young man left peaceably, and order was almost restored when a bearded fellow in his early twenties stood up in the back and said, "Look, I'm *not* part of this group, I paid for the movie just like everyone else here, but maybe it's important that we think about taking a moral stand on issues that affect people's lives, instead of just wanting to be entertained. If people had felt as strongly as this about protecting the Jews in Germany, my grandfather might be alive today instead of having been gassed in Dachau." Then I heard a familiar voice saying, "He's right, and you better not tell me to shut up." There was my sixty-four-year-old mother facing down the entire theatre, and she was trembling.

A. Comprehension

Choose the answer that best completes each statement. Do not refer to the selection while doing this exercise.

1. The occasion for the correspondent's invitation to his parents was (a) Yom Kippur; (b) Memorial Day; (c) his mother's birthday; (d) Mother's Day.
2. The movie that the correspondent took his parents to see was (a) *Out of Africa*; (b) *The Gods Must Be Crazy*; (c) *Yentl*; (d) *A Passage to India*.
3. During World War II, the correspondent's mother (a) was imprisoned in Dachau; (b) escaped to France; (c) lived in Berlin; (d) lived in the United States.
4. The protesters, both outside and inside the theater, objected to the movie because (a) it depicted Africans in an uncomplimentary way; (b) it glorified apartheid policies in South Africa; (c) it painted a favorable picture of Nazi activities during the Second World War; (d) it was made by a white South African.
5. As the various protesters continued their harangues, the theater patrons (a) rioted, attacking the protesters and innocent bystanders; (b) became increasingly angry and tense; (c) became mildly annoyed, but continued to watch the movie uncomplainingly; (d) were sympathetic and immediately joined forces with the throng of protesters.
6. The message that both the young man who spoke at the end and the correspondent's mother were trying to get across is that (a) we must not forget the lessons of World War II; (b) sometimes we must take a moral stand at our own expense when other people's lives are affected; (c) the patrons should all boycott the movie and leave the theater at once; (d) we should be tolerant and forgive nations for wrongs they have committed in the past.

B. Inferences

On the basis of the evidence in the selection, mark these statements as follows: *A* for accurate inferences, *I* for inaccurate inferences, and *IE* for insufficient evidence. You may refer to the selection to answer the questions in this and in all the remaining sections.

1. The correspondent thinks that Mother's Day is a plot by the greeting card industry to make money.
2. The correspondent's mother was imprisoned in a German concentration camp during World War II.
3. The correspondent and his family are Jewish.
4. Initially, the protesters who disrupted the movie's showing were not greeted with sympathy by the audience.
5. The film's producer, a white South African, supports his government's apartheid policy.
6. When the two women protesters first disrupted the beginning of the movie, the correspondent's mother was angry at the interruption.
7. The correspondent's mother opposed President Reagan's visit to Germany's Bitburg cemetery.
8. The correspondent's mother is probably unaccustomed to speaking before a large audience.
9. The correspondent was impressed with his mother's willingness to speak out.
10. Because of the protests, the movie was cancelled.

C. Structure

Choose the best answer.

1. The mode of discourse in this letter is primarily (a) narration; (b) description; (c) exposition; (d) persuasion.
2. The writer's purpose, essentially, is to (a) relate a highly emotional incident; (b) persuade the reader to boycott *The Gods Must Be Crazy*; (c) condemn the apartheid policies of the South African government; (d) criticize the movie crowd for its unwillingness to take a stand on a controversial issue.
3. Look again at the end of paragraph 1. The attitude of the correspondent and the theater audience before the protests began was one of (a) irritation; (b) curiosity; (c) hostility; (d) sympathy.
4. The beginning of paragraph 2 contains a metaphor. To what does the writer compare the audience's feelings? ___creative___
5. Consider this sentence from paragraph 2: "The atmosphere in the theatre—on the upper East Side, on Mother's Day afternoon—grew increasingly tense as demands for the young man's removal became more vehement. . . ." Implied in this sentence is (a) sarcasm; (b) satire; (c) irony; (d) deadpan humor; (e) wit and amusement.
6. What the correspondent wants us to understand about his mother was her (a) inability to grasp what was happening in the theater; (b) extraordinary sensitivity to issues where human rights are at stake; (c) bitterness and refusal to forgive the wrongs committed against her during the war; (d) keen perceptions about current events, particularly the political situation in South Africa.

7. The tone of this letter is complex. In your own words, try to explain your emotional reactions to it.

deeper humor + ironic

D. Vocabulary   For each italicized word from the selection, choose the best definition according to the context in which it appears.

1. a *hermetic* environment [1]: (a) entertaining; (b) idyllic; (c) impervious to outside influences; (d) highly charged emotionally.

2. *imploring* us to ask for refunds [1]: (a) appealing; (b) encouraging; (c) requiring; (d) asking.

3. the *plight* of black South Africans [2]: (a) political situation; (b) economic status; (c) difficult situation; (d) racial situation.

4. drowned out by *irate* patrons [2]: (a) irrational; (b) angry; (c) mildly annoyed; (d) violence-prone.

5. the young man was *undaunted* [2]: (a) not discouraged; resolute; (b) fearful; intimidated; (c) hostile; ready to attack; (d) embarrassed; humiliated.

6. demands became more *vehement* [2]: (a) loud; noisy; (b) widespread; pervasive; (c) insistent; (d) forceful; intense.

7. slightly *bewildered* by the cheers [2]: (a) amused; (b) confused; (c) frightened; (d) pleased.

part 2 | READING CRITICALLY: EVALUATING WHAT YOU READ

From the exercises you worked through in Part I, it should have become apparent that analytical reading requires thoroughness and careful attention to words and their connotations. Beyond possessing the fundamental abilities of accurate comprehension, retention, and inference drawing, however, an excellent reader must also develop a critical sense, a means of judging the worth of what you read. While you should not unquestioningly accept everything you read just because it is in print, neither should you reject a writer's attempts to communicate simply because you dislike or disagree with what he or she says or with the way in which it is said. A middle ground might be termed a healthy skepticism, a willingness to read what the author has to say carefully, and to question its validity or soundness, to determine if it contains unstated or unproved assumptions, opinions masquerading as facts, claims unsupported by evidence, or any of a number of logical fallacies. Your ability to detect distortions, generalizations, appeals to your emotions or sympathy not accompanied by appeals to reason, and your skill in seeing the deliberate or blatant use of slanted language will serve you well and lead to a keener critical stance. By "reading critically," then, we do not mean "critical" in the negative sense of tearing down, but a method of reading characterized by careful evaluation and judgment.

Some of what is published is very good, some is mediocre, and some is terrible. How do you tell the difference? What criteria should you use to judge prose, to determine whether a piece of writing is "good" or "bad"? Here are some fundamental standards for judging prose: First, the main idea or thesis (or argument, in persuasive writing) should be clearly stated. Second, the writer should have defined key words—especially abstract words open to multiple interpretations—to indicate the way he or she intends to use them, thereby avoiding ambiguity or misinterpretation. Third—especially in persuasive writing—the writer should present logically arranged evidence relevant to the thesis. Finally, the evidence should be convincing, logically sound, and of a sufficient amount to support the point under discussion.

What can go wrong? How do writers—intentionally or not—err? What we will be concerned with in this section is reasoning, the rules of simple logic that should govern the writing process and the ways that you, as a critical reader, can detect weaknesses when those rules are broken.

A. UNCOVERING ARGUMENTS

To evaluate a writer's argument, you first need to determine what that argument actually is. As used here, *argument* refers to the specific proposition that the writer is putting forth, the subject for discussion or analysis about which there may be a difference of opinion. In the statement, "We must support the school bond issue so that Spring Valley High School can build a new gymnasium," the writer has stated the proposition clearly and unequivocally; and even if we do not agree with it, we know exactly what is being proposed. But detecting arguments is not always as easy as in this example. Consider these advertising slogans. What is the argument underlying each?

- "Come to Marlboro Country"
  (Argument: Smoke Marlboro cigarettes)
- "Value Without Compromise—Century 25's Cigarettes"
  (Argument: Smoke Century 25 cigarettes)
- "AT&T: The Right Choice"
  (Argument: Subscribe to AT&T's phone service)
- "Why give the common, when you can give the preferred? Tanqueray Gin. A singular experience."
  (Argument: Give Tanqueray gin)
- "Audi. The art of engineering."
  (Argument: Drive an Audi)
- "Tide. America's Favorite"
  (Argument: Use Tide)
- "Easily the Most Magnificent Resort Built in America in the Past Century and a Half—The Sagamore"
  (Argument: Stay at The Sagamore)

What is striking about these slogans is the lack of any meaningful evidence that warrants our acceptance of the product. Either the evidence is nonexistent ("Marlboro Country"), or the claims made for them are ridiculously vague ("a singular experience"), pretentious ("the art of engineering"), or inflated ("the most magnificent resort . . .").

But more to the point, the argument is hidden, although it is obvious that the purpose of the ad is to sell the product. Before you can evaluate the worth of what you read (including advertisements), you must be able to decide exactly what the writer is proposing, what is being argued for or against. Even newspaper articles from the news section (as opposed to editorials) contain arguments. Though we tend to believe that newspapers present factual information, in fact, many newspapers present arguments, for and against, in articles on controversial issues. For example, the subject of the following newspaper article is the controversy surrounding the federal government's plan to erect a nativity scene on the public expanse of lawn in Washington, D.C., known as the Ellipse. Read the article carefully, then note the arguments implicit in the article, both for and against the display, in separate columns on a sheet of paper.

Washington

The American Civil Liberties Union yesterday assailed a plan for a nativity scene as part of the federal government's official Christmas display, calling it unconstitutional.

"It looks like it's the government favoring one religion," ACLU attorney Elizabeth Symonds said. "The Constitution says that's not allowed."

However, a National Park Service official said a Supreme Court ruling in a Rhode Island case apparently legalized government sponsorship of the nativity scene in the annual Pageant of Peace on the Ellipse, just south of the White House.

"It was decided that if we could obtain a nativity scene, it would be legal," said the official, Sandra Alley.

The park service does not have funds for a nativity scene, but Alley said a man from Vienna, Va., has volunteered to donate one, and officials will decide whether to include the scene "in the next 10 days or so."

The display included a nativity scene until 1973, when a federal appellate court ruled that it was illegal. Since then, private religious groups have been allowed to display a nativity scene on the Ellipse, but Alley said that was not considered part of the governmental display.

In March, the high court ruled that a depiction of Christ's birth is a cultural symbol, like Santa Claus, and does not constitute government sponsorship of religion.

Symonds of the ACLU said: "We're not anti-religion in the least. What we're talking about is the entanglement between the government and religion."

"ACLU Challenges Plan for D.C. Nativity Scene"

Throughout this part of the book, you will have more opportunities to find the arguments in a variety of reading passages.

B. UNSTATED ASSUMPTIONS

In addition to determining the central argument, you also need to develop skill in uncovering the underlying assumptions, which lay the foundation upon which the argument rests. Every kind of writing has a whole complex of hidden or unstated assumptions, or premises, beneath the surface; these are presumed true and the writer also presumes that the reader shares them. The first of these premises is that writers have a stake in your accepting their ideas; even the most altruistic writers hope that their works will sell. Cynicism aside, let us look at some ordinary arguments to see if we can detect the hidden, or unstated, arguments upon which they rest. This step is crucial, for the question of whether we can accept the argument in great part depends on whether we can accept the hidden assumptions that underlie it.

• Cigarette smoking should be banned in public places.

The writer's assumption is easy to detect in this example: Smoke from cigarettes, so-called secondary smoke, harms nonsmokers. Yet this assumption, though probably true to some extent, is neither stated nor proved true. On the surface, one would need much more information before accepting this argument.

• Criminals who use guns to commit crimes should receive mandatory jail sentences.

Again, before you can properly evaluate this argument, you must first decide if you can accept the premise underlying it. The argument—stated clearly enough—rests on one unstated assumption: that the inevitability of a jail sentence deters criminals from using guns. Without evidence to support this, we have a right to be skeptical. Evidence is needed here, perhaps in the form of comparative statistics on crime rates in states that have "use-a-gun, go-to-jail" laws versus those that do not, for us to accept the second assumption. To repeat, if you cannot accept the underlying premises, then you probably cannot accept the argument that relies on their acceptance.

One last example. A politician addresses a Chamber of Commerce meeting and says:

• "America's first priority is to maintain a strong defense, no matter how great the cost."

The statement, first of all, represents an opinion, not a fact. Embedded in it are the unstated assumptions, first, that a strong defense is good and, second, that a strong defense is more important than all other programs for which the government spends money (education, welfare, national parks, Social Security, and so forth).

Here is a portion of a speech to examine for unstated assumptions. In 1984, the Reagan administration proposed sending money to the Nicaraguan rebels (the so-called "Contras") who were fighting the Sandinistas, arguing that if America didn't provide this aid, it would be responsible for causing a takeover similar to what occurred in Southeast Asia in 1975. (The Sandinistas had overthrown the American-supported Somoza regime and had declared themselves sympathetic to communism.) The Senate turned down the administration's request for $14 million in military aid, citing its fear that such a commitment would result in increased American participation in Nicaragua's affairs, reminiscent of our presence in Vietnam. (Note that both sides in this controversy cited the Vietnam experience, but each meant something entirely different by it.) During 1985 and 1986, the administration intensified its requests that Congress appropriate money for the Contras. What follows is a portion of a speech made on April 25, 1985, by Secretary of State George Schultz, in which he pleaded for aid for the anti-Sandinista rebels:

[1]Those who assure us that these dire consequences are not in prospect are some of those who assured us of the same in Indochina before 1975. [2]The litany of apology for communists, and condemnation for America and our friends, is beginning again. [3]Can we afford to be naïve again about the consequences when we pull back, about the special ruthlessness of communist rule? [4]Do the American people really accept the notion that we, and our friends, are the representatives of evil?

[5]The American people believe in their country and in its role as a force for good. [6]They want to see an effective foreign policy that blocks

aggression and advances the cause of freedom and democracy. [7]They are tired of setbacks, especially those that result from restraints imposed on ourselves."

On a sheet of paper, list the unstated assumptions that Schultz's argument rests on.

C. KINDS OF REASONING

After you have decided what the argument actually is and on what assumptions it rests, it remains to evaluate the evidence the writer has used to support the proposition. This involves determining if the evidence leads to a valid conclusion, that is, if the conclusion derives logically from the support. In Chapters 2 and 3 of Part I, you studied several methods of paragraph development. Essentially, these methods are derived from the kinds of evidence—examples, analogy, cause–effect, and the like—that a writer brings to bear upon the main idea; but these are primarily expository methods. In this section, we are concerned more with evidence used in argumentative or persuasive writing. In addition, in Chapter 4 you learned the difference between deductive and inductive paragraph order. In terms of logic, however, the two kinds of reasoning we will examine here—*deduction* and *induction*—mean something different. They refer to patterns of reasoning, or more simply, to the way in which a writer constructs and supports an argument. Since we are constantly bombarded with arguments ("buy this," "vote for that," "accept this proposal," "don't associate with that person"), as critical thinkers and readers we need to recognize the difference between deductive and inductive reasoning and to recognize whether a particular argument is valid or invalid.

Deductive Reasoning   Deduction moves from a general statement to a specific application or conclusion. (Hence, you can see the reason for calling a paragraph using general–specific order a deductively ordered paragraph.) A deductive argument is traditionally expressed as a syllogism, an argument that takes two premises which are assumed to be true, and produces a conclusion or new truth from them. Here is a classic example. (Note the syllogism form and the labeling of each statement.)

> *Major premise:* All men are mortal.
> *Minor premise:* John is a man.
> *Conclusion:* John is mortal.

The syllogism is valid because the premises already contain or imply the conclusion, so if one accepts the premises, then one must also accept the conclusion.

Let us look at another example.

Major premise: All Frenchmen are good lovers.
Minor premise: Pierre is a Frenchman.
Conclusion: Pierre is a good lover.

This syllogism is logically valid because Pierre has been placed in a class in which all the members are said to share the same characteristic. Therefore, we can deduce (arrive at the conclusion) that Pierre also shares it. Yet the premise that all Frenchmen are good lovers is obviously untrue, since it is a generalization that can be invalidated by the existence of even one less-than-good French lover. So, while the syllogism is logically *valid* because it follows the correct form, it is nevertheless not *true* because we cannot accept the generalization contained in the major premise. You can easily see that this business of *truth* is a bit tricky. For the purposes of this section, D. L. McDonald's definition seems workable: "It is only when terms are defined and mutually accepted that one can begin marshaling evidence to prove the truth of a statement." McDonald goes on to explain the statement that truth is statistically derived:

> A man can insist that fire engines are red because he is expressing a general opinion. Though a "Napoleon" might call them a mass hallucination, he is sure that fire engines exist. Though the color-blind might cavil, he knows they are colored red. And though foreigners or semanticists might do otherwise, he uses the word "red." The reason he speaks the truth and the dissenters do not is that he is in the majority. If the majority did not perceive the engines, or saw them as green, or described them as "rouge," he would be locked up as a babbling, color-blind visionary. "Truth" is what people agree to call true.

> D. L. McDonald,
> *The Language of Argument*

Deductive arguments can also be fallacious or *invalid*.

Major premise: All students who didn't attend class failed.
Minor premise: Paul failed the class.
Conclusion: Paul didn't attend class.

The conclusion does not follow logically from the two premises because Paul has not been placed in the group of students who did not attend class. His failure could have been the result of something else—failure to do the assignments or to pass the tests or his sleeping in class. Therefore, the conclusion cannot be deduced from the two premises.

Here is another kind of invalid syllogism.

Major premise: If John doesn't stop smoking, he will get cancer.
Minor premise: John will stop smoking.
Conclusion: John won't get cancer.

In this syllogism the conclusion can be valid only if John *doesn't* stop smoking. Because the general condition ("not stopping smoking") is not contained in the minor premise, the argument is invalid. In other words, one can't introduce a new term in the second premise. It is also possible that John may stop smoking and get cancer anyway.

Here are two more syllogisms, one valid and the other invalid:

Major premise: The Catholic Church is opposed to abortion.
Minor premise: John is Catholic.
Conclusion: John is opposed to abortion.

Major premise: The Catholic Church is opposed to abortion.
Minor premise: John is opposed to abortion.
Conclusion: John is Catholic.

In the first example, a valid deductive argument, John has been put in the class of those who are against abortion; therefore, the conclusion is valid. Notice, however, that the argument, though logically valid, may not necessarily be *true,* since not all members of the Catholic Church adhere firmly to its teachings. But in the second example, the conclusion cannot be validly drawn, since one does not have to be a Catholic to be opposed to abortion. As we have seen, a deductive argument can be valid logically (because it follows the correct form), but invalid because the premises are either untrue or absurd. To illustrate:

Major premise: All Democrats are wild-eyed radicals.
Minor premise: John Smith is a Democrat.
Conclusion: John Smith is a wild-eyed radical.

Major premise: All lemons are yellow.
Minor premise: My car is a lemon.
Conclusion: My car must be yellow.

The first syllogism is incorrect because, as we have seen before, the major premise is both an untrue statement and a generalization. In the second example, the syllogism is invalid because the term "lemon" means something different in the major and minor premises. Consider this syllogism:

Major premise: All dogs have tails.
Minor premise: This airplane has a tail.
Conclusion: This airplane is a dog.

In this example, the major premise is about dogs, not airplanes, so the premise cannot lead to a conclusion about airplanes.

In the real world, however, deductive arguments do not present themselves in neat syllogisms like these. Usually, the argument has been abbreviated with one of the premises, or perhaps even the conclusion, omitted. For example, consider this argument: "This man should not be allowed to vote because he doesn't speak English." Recast into a valid syllogism, the argument would be written like this:

Major premise: Only English speakers can vote.
Minor premise: This man is unable to speak English.
Conclusion: This man cannot vote.

Here are more examples of everyday deductive arguments, along with their missing or implied parts:

• If you don't vote, then you can hardly criticize the government. (Missing major premise: Only voters can criticize the government.)

• Blondes have more fun, so it is easy to see why Muffie Ferguson has a lot of fun. (Missing minor premise: Muffie Ferguson has blonde hair.)

• To pass that class, you have to attend, but Paul never attended. (Missing conclusion: Paul did not pass the class.)

All the above are *valid* deductive arguments, but following are two *invalid* ones.

• Everyone knows that Henry Jones is a communist because he doesn't believe in the free enterprise system.

Here is the same argument, rewritten as a syllogism.

Major premise: Communists do not believe in the free enterprise system.
Minor premise: Henry Jones does not believe in the free enterprise system.
Conclusion: Henry Jones is a communist.

The argument is invalid because Henry Jones has not been placed in the group of people called communists. This is a common form of invalid deductive reasoning: condemning a person because he or she shares an attribute with a group held in contempt.

Here is an example of an invalid deductive argument that rests on an untrue major premise:

• A teenage girl's father says: "My daughter's boyfriend must be a punk because he wears an earring." Again, in syllogism form:

Major premise: Only punks wear earrings.
Minor premise: My daughter's boyfriend wears an earring.
Conclusion: My daughter's boyfriend is a punk.

Inductive Reasoning The opposite of deductive reasoning is *induction,* the process of arriving at a conclusion or a prediction on the basis of incomplete information. An inductive argument involves a *likely* conclusion of what will *probably* occur, and it is for this reason that inductive arguments are sometimes called probability arguments. In fact, just about everything we know, or claim to know, we learned through the process of induction. We know, for example, that fire engines are red. We learned this by noting that the fire engines we have seen are red. (Notice that we are basing this conclusion on incomplete information, since we could never possibly see all the fire engines there are in the world. And, in fact, some fire engines are *not* red; some are bright yellow; others are white.) So our conclusion should really be a tentative one, and we can more safely say, "Most fire engines are red," or "All the fire engines I have ever seen have been red."

Here is another example:

English 101 required six papers.
English 210 required four papers.
English 440 required eight papers.
Conclusion: It is likely that English 550 will require a lot of writing.

In this case, the conclusion rests on specific evidence about three English classes, from which the conclusion may be safely assumed. (Notice, however, that the conclusion may not be *true,* since English 550 could be a grammar class, requiring no writing at all.) This illustrates why inductive arguments are less certain than are deductive ones, which, if they are valid, must always produce the conclusion suggested in the premises.
    Following is another example:

• Every American president since Richard Nixon has failed in his attempt to present Congress with a balanced budget. It is probable that President Reagan will not be able to keep the promise he made during his reelection campaign to balance the budget.

The argument in this example rests on information that is implied: Since the three presidents after Nixon (Gerald Ford, Jimmy Carter, and Ronald Reagan in his first term) were unable to balance the budget, the likelihood of Reagan's balancing the budget in his second term is slim.
    Inductive arguments are often used with *sampling.*

• Sixty percent of the Americans we interviewed think that prison sentences for violent crimes are too lenient.

On the basis of the sample, we can conclude that 60 percent of the population as a whole probably shares this concern. But it should be noted here that the method of sampling is crucial: The number of people interviewed should be large; and they should be representative, drawn from a cross section of the general population in terms of geographic area, income, and educational level. If six of the first ten people on the morning's bus run expressed concern over prison sentences, we could say that the conclusion was invalid because it was based on too small a sample.
    As you saw in the above sample, inductive arguments are invalid if they are derived from skimpy statistics. Here are some other kinds of invalid inductive arguments.
    Sweeping Generalization. Sometimes called "glittering generalities," these generalizations sound good because they offer instant appeal, but logically they are indefensible.

• Most Americans fear death. Most Brazilians fear death. Most Norwegians fear death. It is human nature to fear death.

Here, the writer has used a leap: On the basis of unsubstantiated views of people in only three countries, the writer concludes that all people share a fear of death.

- Don't ever buy a German shepherd. They're too skittish.

Implied here is a generalization that all German shepherds are skittish; even one serene German shepherd invalidates the generalization.

Hasty Generalization. This example of faulty reasoning is just what it sounds like: a generalization drawn in haste from insufficient evidence.

- The former "boat people" have certainly adjusted well to American life. The Cambodian-owned grocery store in my neighborhood is well-run and profitable, and it's remarkable how easily the family has assimilated American middle-class values.

After sampling only one family, the writer has jumped to the unwarranted conclusion that this particular family represents the entire class of Indo-chinese refugees who have settled in America. In this case, then, the sample is simply not *representative*. We should expect the writer to summon up many more examples than one to prove a point. If a writer can point to only an example or two, we can assume those examples to be isolated; in this case, the claim should be treated as an opinion, rather than as a fact, which would need substantially more verification. (There is a saying in Yiddish: " 'For example' is no proof.")

Generalizing from Insufficient, Unreliable, or Unavailable Evidence. Arguments proceeding from this kind of generalization are common, particularly in cases which can't be verified. Those who believe in UFOs, for example, may point to unconfirmed incidents from an unidentified farmer who happened to see a strange object with flashing lights circling over his cornfield. The argument goes like this: Extraterrestrial beings must be visiting us because a farmer saw a spaceship circling over his land. (While surely there have been a number of unexplained sightings, evidence for them frequently seems far-fetched. It seems a bit strange that such sightings are not reported in towns or cities where a number of people would have observed them.) A similar invalid argument occurs when evidence is cited which may be true, but which is unavailable, such as the argument that it is possible for an eight-year-old girl to become pregnant. The evidence? A case of an eight-year-old girl in a little village in a remote part of the Andes mountains who conceived a child. To confirm this would be nearly impossible.

EXERCISES

Evaluate the following arguments by first trying to determine if the argument is deductive or inductive. Then decide if it is valid or invalid. (For the purposes of this exercise, leave aside the stickier matter of whether the argument is true.)

1. The only good Indian is a dead Indian.

2. If the OPEC nations reduce the price of oil, there will soon be a world-wide glut of oil. In 1986, the OPEC nations reduced the price of oil, and a glut ensued.

3. The whole food-stamp program is riddled with fraud. Why, just yesterday the girl in front of me in line at the supermarket paid for her T-bone steak with food stamps!

4. Heinrich must be a good car mechanic because he is German.

5. It's certain that the school bond issue on this ballot will fail. Seventy-five percent of the residents we interviewed at Golden Years Retirement Home plan to vote against it.

6. You can't expect the police commission to investigate charges of police brutality.

7. Adlai Stevenson lost the presidential election in 1956 primarily because he was divorced.

8. All roses are red. This flower is red. It must be a rose.

9. If John loses his job, his wife will divorce him, but since John will not lose his job, his wife will not leave him.

10. Seven out of ten dentists surveyed recommend Trident gum for their patients who chew gum.

11. That man must be rich if he drives a Mercedes.

12. Ten-year-old daughter to her mother: "May I get my ears pierced? Everyone at school has pierced ears." Mother: "Who have pierced their ears?" Daughter: "Sally and Ilana."

13. If abortions are not granted to women on demand, there will be an increase in the number of unwanted children, and if that happens, we can expect to see an increase in the incidence of child abuse.

14. Vermont, Maine, Connecticut, Massachusetts, and New York have been successful in eliminating roadside litter by implementing deposit laws on beverage cans. California would do well to follow these states' example if it wants to solve its litter problem.

15. All dogs have four legs.
That cat has four legs.
That cat is a dog.

16. All A are B; all C are A; therefore, all C are B.

17. All Americans love freedom. All the people in Happy Valley are Americans. Therefore, all the people in Happy Valley love freedom.

18. The divorce rate went up 50 percent last year. Two of the four couples in our bridge group got divorced.

19. Of course prehistoric creatures like the Loch Ness monster exist. I've seen a newspaper photo of a large black shape in Loch Ness that is larger than any fish would be.

20. All kids just love peanut butter and jelly sandwiches. Every day Charlotte, Claire, Stephanie, and Sarah take peanut butter and jelly sandwiches in their lunch boxes.

D. APPEALS IN ARGUMENTS

In Chapter 5, you were introduced to some tactics writers use in persuasive writing—whether their aim was simply to convince you to accept their point of view or to buy a product, or their motives were less savory—to manipulate your thinking. You saw how writers use slanted language (euphemisms, sneer words, weasel words) to color the argument and to sway us for or against something. Writers of persuasive prose often attempt to influence our thinking by appealing to various instincts. The careful persuasive writer uses evidence that is sound, convincing, and appropriate, thereby appealing to our intellect. We can accept the argument because the evidence, whether in the form of examples, statistics, or reasoned discourse, persuades us to accept the writer's way of thinking. But there are other sorts of appeals that you should be aware of as critical readers; and you should be able to recognize when a writer is using one of these appeals, especially if it replaces reasoned discourse for evidence. Briefly, the main ones are:

Appeal to the Emotions

- "Lower your taxes!"
- "Stop the land grab!"
- "A vote for the school bond issue is a vote for our children."
- "Let's get those criminals off the street and into jail, where they belong."

Appeal to Patriotism

- "How can you be against aid to Nicaragua? America has always risen to the defense of nations trying to fight their oppressors."
- Bumper sticker: "Keep an auto worker employed. Buy American."
- "Better dead than Red."

Appeal to Prejudice

- "Mexican farm-workers take jobs away from Americans who are out of work."
- "Men shouldn't be nurses. After all, women are traditionally the ones who care for others."
- "Once one house is sold to a (fill in the minority group of your choice), the whole neighborhood will become _____."

Appeal to Fear   During a strike by pilots of a national airline in 1985, the newspapers were full of letters on both sides of the issue. Here is a representative one, written by a striking pilot:

"I am proud to be a member of the striking pilot's association, and I just hope that all those people who have written attacking us for our stand are not caught on some dark and stormy night, strapped in the seat of an aircraft piloted by a scab hired at the last minute who probably hasn't had adequate training."

Appeal to Authority

- "My English teacher says that "bureau" should be pronounced bur'ee-oh, and she ought to know what's right."
- "I'm going to buy a Silver Edition Bullet car. All the best people in town own them."
- "A recent medical journal said that eating eggs causes heart disease, so I'm not going to eat eggs any more."
- "Annette Funicello says that Skippy peanut butter contains less sugar than all the other leading brands."

The following letter appeared in the *Los Angeles Times*. It illustrates the effectiveness of combining appeals to reason and to the emotions in persuasive writing:

> One year ago I wrote about the lack of safety of television ads depicting unsafe driving. Today, with great sadness, I write in horror of the danger of the drunk driver. My 16-year-old niece lives no more. Her heart does beat, however, in the chest of a 52-year-old man, and a kidney does function in a 3-year-old girl. Sara was killed April 26 by a drunk driver in Solana Beach.
>
> What can we learn? What can we do besides mourn her tragic and useless passing? Must we continue to accept 25,000 slaughtered Americans annually due to drunk driving? I asked a judge. He said that we are a unique society of drivers, millions and millions of them, and drinkers and drug users, millions and millions of them. Even with stiffer penalties, he stated, we'd never get all the drunk drivers processed, never get juries to concur on long prison terms. "It's somewhat hopeless," he stated.
>
> I say that it is not hopeless. Take the weapon of death away from those clearly out of self-control. Sure, take the license, but also take the car away on the first offense of drunk driving. Force the driver into treatment and make him prove that he is fit to drive again.
>
> Sara had a greater right to life than does the drinking or drug-using driver have a right to drive. Sure, he needs to get to work, etc. Sara needed to live. I urge all people who want to stay alive, and want their loved ones to stay alive, to seriously consider this unsolved and continuing problem on our highways. We must change the laws; we must stop slapping the wrists of the intoxicated killers; the carnage can and must be stopped.
>
> Richard B. Levin, M.D.,
> "What Can We Learn from Great Tragedies?" *Los Angeles Times*

E. THE QUESTION OF AUTHORITY

If you recall, the last example in the section on appeals to authority referred to a TV advertisement that shows Annette Funicello endorsing

Skippy peanut butter. This example leads us to another important matter in evaluating arguments. Exactly who is making the claim? What criteria should we use to judge whether the writer is actually an authority? First, the writer should be qualified to speak on the subject. Advertisers frequently use famous people to add an air of authority to their sales pitch, and so we see O. J. Simpson touting a national car-rental agency, Loretta Lynn selling shortening, and John Madden selling everything from beer to trucks. That these celebrities are actually knowledgeable authorities about the quality of the goods they are advertising is questionable. We could say that, since Annette Funicello is a mother, she is therefore interested in the amount of sugar in the peanut butter her children eat, and that Loretta Lynn appears to bake constantly when she is not singing. But their roles as real authorities are open to question. You should also be skeptical of claims for "recent medical research," or of "a leading medical expert" who endorses various remedies. Failure to name the actual study or the expert's name lends the argument less credence compared with, for example, a statement from the head of cancer research at Sloan–Kettering Institute urging Americans to increase the amount of fiber in their diets as a way of preventing certain types of cancer.

Besides being knowledgeable, an authority must be reliable—that is, we must be able to believe that he or she is telling the truth—and unbiased. You would not expect a heroin pusher to be a reliable or disinterested authority for an argument proposing a methadone treatment center, nor would you expect a vegetarian to give you an unbiased account of the nutritional value of meat. You should always ask yourself, What does this person stand to gain or lose by my accepting (or rejecting) the argument? After all, the car salesman is trying to sell you a car, not to objectively debate the merits of competing brands. In the same way, the authorities a writer cites should be subjected to the same scrutiny. Knowing the background of a writer is also helpful in anticipating (or in detecting) *bias*—any personal preference, inclination, or prejudice that might inhibit an impartial or objective viewpoint. For example, it is likely that a vegetarian, who has made a deliberate choice to avoid or to abstain entirely from eating meat, will be influenced by that personal preference; therefore, while it is not absolutely assured that he or she cannot write objectively about meat and nutrition, one should nonetheless be alert to the possibility of one-sided evidence. Knowing a writer's political bent, or his or her particular prejudices, will help you weigh the argument. The recommendation at the beginning of this section still pertains here—maintain a healthy skepticism when you encounter persuasive tactics.

F. LOGICAL FALLACIES

We have already examined some ways in which arguments can be invalid —an incorrect syllogism in the case of deductive reasoning, or insufficient evidence, small sampling, hasty generalization, and so forth in the case of inductive reasoning. What remains are *logical fallacies,* examples of incorrect reasoning which also render an argument false or invalid. Here, in alphabetical order, are some common fallacies and illustrations of arguments employing them.

Ad Hominem Argument   In Latin, *ad hominem* means "against the man." Otherwise known as character assassination, an *ad hominem* argument attacks one's character or deeds and ignores the issues.

- "Senator Snortum is a notorious womanizer, and last year he was caught using his stationery allowance to buy a mink coat for his girlfriend. No responsible senator should vote for the mass transit bill he is sponsoring."

Bandwagon Appeal   This logical fallacy asks the reader to believe something by appealing to his desire to "get on the bandwagon," that is, to be on the winning side.

- "Don't vote for Proposition 9. The polls show it is losing 65 to 35."

A not very subtle variation is "Everyone else is doing it; why can't I?," which parents hear from small children (and from teenagers, who ought to know better). The bandwagon fallacy is also evident in claims of what "everyone" supposedly believes, as in this argument:

- "Everyone knows that pornography causes violent crimes."

Begging the Question   In this fallacy, the writer *assumes* to be true that which is his or her responsibility to prove. In other words, the argument rests on an argument which is presumed true, but which has not, in fact, been demonstrated. Here are two examples of arguments that beg the question:

- "When did you stop beating your wife?"
- "Vitamins promote good health, so if you want to be healthy, you should take vitamins."

In the first example, it is assumed, but not proved, that the husband used to beat his wife. In the second example, the claim that vitamins promote good health is similarly assumed to be true. Notice, too, that the argument and the conclusion are nearly identical.

Either–Or Fallacy   Sometimes called *false dilemma,* this fallacy occurs when the writer presents the reader with only two choices, thereby ignoring other possibilities or alternatives.

- "A woman should stay home and tend her house and children. If she wants a career, she should forget about having children."

Here, the argument rests on two choices, and the writer ignores the fact that many women can successfully combine a career—whether full-time or part-time—with having children. Exhortations for one to choose sides use this fallacy, as well:

- "When the final war between the races comes, which side will you be on—black or white?"

False Analogy   Properly used, an analogy can be an effective persuasive tactic by showing that the characteristics of one thing are similar to something unrelated. (Refer to Chapter 3 if you have forgotten what an analogy is.) But if the dissimilarities outweigh the similarities, or if the analogy breaks down because the terms have only one feature in common, then the analogy must be judged false.

- "America is like one big, happy family."

Clearly, a country as vast and complex and problem-ridden as America has more dissimilarities than similarities when compared with a family, happy or otherwise.

   In the following argument, a politician seeking reelection claims that a second term is necessary to accomplish the goals he or she didn't accomplish in the first term:

- "You wouldn't change horses in the middle of a stream, would you?"

What is the connection between keeping one's office and changing horses in the middle of a stream? While it might conceivably be dangerous to change horses in the middle of a raging torrent, there might also be cases where it would be desirable—if the horse is exhausted, for example. Therefore, the argument rests on an analogy that doesn't hold up, since it implies that there is some sort of danger involved in electing a new official.

False Cause   This fallacy presents a false cause–effect relationship. The supposed cause may be only a coincidence, or it may be so remote that it is doubtful as a credible cause.

- "John read so many books when he was studying for his PhD, that he eventually had to wear glasses. It's obvious that reading too much weakens your eyes."

The cause here is false (or at least questionable), since John's deteriorating vision was merely coincidental with his increased reading load. One's vision normally deteriorates as a natural consequence of aging.

   An argument employing a *remote* false cause might be something like this:

- "I knew I should have cancelled the tennis match today. My astrological forecast in the paper warned me not to engage in any competitive activities. That's why I lost."

Post hoc, ergo propter hoc   This fallacy—its name being derived from the Latin phrase meaning "after this, therefore because of this"—suggests that, because event B occurred after event A, event A caused event B. As in the preceding fallacy, the cause–effect relationship is faulty. If you walk under a ladder and are hit by a bus ten minutes later, it is fallacious to argue that misfortune occurred because you were foolish enough to defy the superstition of walking under a ladder. A broken mirror does not mean that seven years of bad luck will ensue. The wart on your hand was not caused by touching someone's pet frog. One can easily see that the *post hoc* fallacy is at the root of superstitious practices. But the *post hoc* fallacy can be used in other ways as well, for example:

- A company president says, "Agreeing to labor's demand for increased salaries was a costly mistake. Just look at how low the production figures were for last month!"

It is fallacious for the president to argue that because the pay raise occurred first, it necessarily caused the decline in output. Perhaps orders were down, or perhaps a high number of workers were ill or on vacation.

Slippery Slope   The metaphoric name of this fallacy will help you remember it. This fallacy suggests that one step in the wrong direction will lead to more and more undesirable occurrences, ending up at the bottom of a slippery, muddy slope (in other words, doom). For example, in 1964, when Lyndon Johnson proposed a national health insurance plan for people over 65 (what eventually became Medicare) as part of his "Great Society" program, opponents often attacked the plan by using the "slippery slope" fallacy:

- "If Congress approves Johnson's proposal for a national health insurance program for old people, who knows where it will end? The next step will be health insurance for all Americans, and if that happens, then all the doctors in the country will be working for the federal government, and you won't be able to go to a private doctor any more. And if we have socialized medicine, what's to stop the government from nationalizing all the railroads and other important industries? Pretty soon no one will have any incentive to work any more. America will be socialistic."

Two Wrongs Make a Right   This last fallacy is commonly used to make wrongdoing legitimate because others engage in it. For example, during the Watergate crisis in 1973, Richard Nixon's supporters frequently asserted that Nixon had not done anything different from any other president; he just got caught. In other words, the argument assumes that a precedent exists for bribery, dirty tricks, and cover-ups of crimes, thereby making other misdeeds acceptable.

EXERCISES

To give you some practice evaluating arguments, try to determine what particular fallacy each of the following represents. If the writer seems to be making an appeal to your sympathy, to fear, or to some other emotion, indicate that as well.

1. Taxpayer grumbling before April 15: "I don't see what's wrong with under-reporting a little here and a little there on my declared income. Everybody else does."

2. It's no wonder Joe Johnson became a convicted ax-murderer. According to an interview, he was subjected to a rigid toilet training regimen when he was a toddler.

3. Every student of American history knows that if it weren't for Herbert Hoover, there would have been no Depression.

4. Life is just like a deck of cards. You take the hand you are dealt.

5. George Washington warned the nation about excessive entanglements in the affairs of other countries. If we had followed his advice, we wouldn't have gotten involved in Southeast Asia or Central America.

6. A student wrote a placement essay to determine in which college English class she was eligible to enroll, but, on the basis of her essay, she placed in a lower-level class than she expected. She went to the coordinator and asked if she could write a second essay to be evaluated. The coordinator refused, saying, "If a chest x-ray indicated that your lungs were tubercular, you wouldn't ask for a second x-ray to be taken."

7. A magazine advertisement for E. F. Hutton, the brokerage firm, depicts a construction engineer holding a blueprint in front of a large uncompleted building. The text says: "Builders around the world listen to me. I listen to E. F. Hutton."

8. Isn't it true that blondes have more fun?

9. First it was cigarettes that were supposed to cause cancer. Then it was coffee, saccharine, and bacon. Now I hear charcoal-broiled hamburgers cause cancer. It's getting so that you can't eat anything anymore without worrying about getting cancer.

10. A national brokerage firm was found guilty of defrauding banks out of millions of dollars by illegally floating checks (writing checks on non-existent funds). When a stockbroker working for the company was asked if the bad publicity had affected her business, she answered, "Oh no. Everyone knows that every other brokerage firm in the country has always done the same thing. It's a common business practice."

11. Wife to husband: "I washed your car for you last week. Now it's your turn to wash mine."
Smart-aleck husband: "Yes, and you had a baby, too. Now I suppose you'll want me to have the next one."

12. Detergent ad: "If you want miraculously white clothes, use Soapy Detergent. It's a washday miracle."

13. "Everybody knows that giving people a handout just makes them lazy and unwilling to work."

14. In 1985 the Pentagon was investigating charges of criminal fraud within General Dynamics. Specifically, the company was accused of billing the government for country-club memberships for executives; in addition, the government was billed for an executive's dog kennel bill. One editorial questioned the government's investigation, saying that if the Pentagon spends time policing company expense accounts, it will never have time to worry about what the Russians are up to.

15. An ad for Ayer's Sarsaparilla juice around 1935: "Mary C. Amesbury, 80 years of age, well known in Rockport, Maine, says: 'For forty years I was troubled with a humor in the blood, which manifested itself in painful eruptions on my skin. At times I was a great sufferer, and tried all kinds of remedies, but found no relief for my complaint until I commenced using Ayer's Sarsaparilla. Ten bottles of this excellent medicine completely cured me.' "

16. A dog breeder refused to reimburse a customer who unknowingly purchased a pedigreed dog with a serious defect that later required surgery. The breeder argued, "You wouldn't expect your doctor to reimburse you if your child needed surgery."

17. Ad for an insurance company: "Fifty thousand satisfied customers can't be wrong!"

18. Ad for a personal computer: "Johnny's parents bought him a personal computer, and his grades went from Cs to As. Why deny your child the opportunity to get a good education?"

19. "Legalizing marijuana is a dangerous idea. Once marijuana is legalized, users will graduate to progressively more dangerous addictive drugs and, eventually, we'll be no more than a nation of freaked-out zombies."

20. A Republican says, "After all, Teddy Kennedy was once involved in a car accident in which a young woman was killed. Why should I vote for him for president?"

21. From a newspaper editorial: "All the members of the present city council have a reputation for wheeling and dealing. If those who make up the council are elected, we can be sure that the council will do nothing but wheel and deal."

22. "Yesterday I forgot to take my vitamins, and now I have a cold. It's clear that vitamins prevent colds."

23. The slogan on New Hampshire license plates: "Live free or die."

24. Over a period of fifteen years, three children (ages three months to twelve years) who live in a small Northern California town were diagnosed as having various types of cancer. (Happily, all were successfully treated.) A neighboring town, which is twice as large, has had no incidence of childhood cancer during the same period. A writer for the local paper wrote an article about the situation, and arrived at the conclusion that the town's water was responsible for the disease, since that was the one factor that all the children had in common. She suggested that worried parents might buy bottled water as an alternative to using the town's water supply.

A. THE READER'S RESPONSIBILITY

So far, we have examined the writer's responsibility to present fair evidence and the various irresponsible or manipulative devices a writer may use to sway you. But what is the reader's responsibility? Why do students frequently misinterpret what they read, then offer lame excuses such as, "Well, that's what I got out of it." One cause of misinterpretation is not knowing what a key word means. Consider, for example, this sentence: "The defense attorney used a *meretricious* argument to get his client acquitted." One might read this sentence and think: Meretricious sounds similar to merit, so a meretricious argument must be something good. Unhappily, the reader is way off base, since "meretricious" means, in this context, "attracting attention in a vulgar manner." (Applied to a person, incidentally, "meretricious" means "resembling or pertaining to a prostitute.")

A second cause of misinterpretation is the practice of making false assumptions, of allowing your expectations, or your own personal prejudices, to interfere with what the writer is really saying, or of drawing inferences where none can validly be drawn. For example, at the beginning of this section, you read a newspaper article about the American Civil Liberties Union's challenge to the National Park Service's plan to erect a Christmas nativity scene in a public park in Washington, D.C. The careless reader might insert his or her own prejudices or jump to an unwarranted conclusion like this: "Nativity scenes are part of the holiday season, and everyone enjoys them, so why are these people against them? The reason they are against them must be that ACLU members are anti-Christian. And, if they are anti-Christian, they must be Jewish or maybe even atheist. Otherwise, why would they be against such a plan?" In fact, the article says in a quite straightforward manner that the ACLU's only objection was that erecting a symbolic Christian scene on government property defies the principle of separation of church and state and suggests that the government is favoring one religion over another. The ACLU would object to a Chanukah display or a statue of Buddha for the same reason.

The lesson is, do not read more into what you read than is actually there, and don't allow your expectations, biases, or prejudices to interfere with your understanding of what you read.

EXERCISES

The exercises for this section consist of several examples of persuasive writing to give you practice in implementing your critical reading skills. These passages represent editorials from the op-ed pages of newspapers, from nationally syndicated columns, and by magazine- and newspaper-editorial writers. For each passage, follow these steps:

1. Determine the writer's main argument or proposition.
2. Decide what kind of evidence the writer has provided to support the argument.
3. Evaluate the evidence according to the criteria discussed in this section. Is it fair? Does it appear to be reliable? Is there enough evidence to make the argument convincing?

4. Are there any blatant attempts to manipulate you by appealing to your emotions, your prejudices, or the like?

5. Does the writer appear to be biased or unbiased? Would the writer gain or lose anything by your accepting the main argument?

6. Are there any logical fallacies present?

7. Are there any examples of manipulative language—sneer words, euphemisms, slanted language—that are intended to influence your thinking?

8. Do you accept the writer's argument? Why, or why not? If you need more information before you can accept it, what would you need to know?

Selection 1

The US House should be embarrassed by its irresponsibility in approving an amendment by Rep. Chalmers P. Wylie (R–Ohio) to cut off federal funds for a Braille edition of Playboy magazine. Pieties and morality aside, the House action is nothing more than censorship.

Wylie's claim that his primary object is to prevent the use of federal funds for the translation and distribution of Playboy is hogwash. He is trying to impose his own morality on others—in this case blind readers who depend on material from the Library of Congress.

The evidence that Wylie is more concerned with morality than taxpayer dollars came from one of his spokesmen, who said that the use of federal funds to provide "to any blind person copies of a magazine, the essence of which is to promote sexual promiscuity as a value judgment, is inappropriate activity."

A few sentences later, the spokesman referred to the magazine as "an example of promiscuity, since they have a different nude person featured every month."

Wylie, and his spokesman, did not mention that the Braille edition of Playboy features only interviews, articles and editorials. The nude centerfolds and other pictures are not translated for the shocking titillation of blind readers.

Perhaps if Wylie spent more time reading the articles and less time worrying about the photos he would understand why, after a nationwide poll, Playboy was selected for Braille production.

Wylie has the freedom not to read Playboy if he believes that it is a depraved publication; the same is true for the congressmen who helped him to subvert the First Amendment to the Constitution. They cannot, however, determine what others can read.

The House trampled on the rights of blind citizens by voting against a $103,000 appropriation for the Braille Playboy. The Senate Appropriations Committee, before which the amendment is pending, should treat this flagrant attempt at censorship with the contempt it deserves.

"Censorship in Braille,"
Boston Globe

Selection 2

Every decade or so, a disgruntled group or some influential citizen concludes that "The Star-Spangled Banner" is no longer fit to be the national anthem. The most commonly adduced arguments are that it is too difficult to sing and that its lyrics are too bellicose for this uneasy nuclear age.

It is true that "The Star-Spangled Banner's" vertiginous octaval range makes it a melodic obstacle course for the average American singer, but history and tradition require that it be the national anthem—as it has been officially for 54 years and unofficially for more than a century.

The latest assault comes from US Rep. Andrew Jacobs (D–Ind.), the sponsor of a bill to supplant "The Star-Spangled Banner" with "America the Beautiful," the choice of most opponents of the anthem. Jacobs says that "apart from the fact that martial considerations do not measure the length and breadth of our society, I believe we should have a national anthem that someone besides an opera star can sing."

The "martial considerations" seem strained. Anyone whose fears of nuclear annihilation are inflamed by hearing the lyrics "the bombs bursting in air" is either very silly or in need of psychiatric assistance.

It is worth noting that in 1966 Irving Berlin's "God Bless America" was played in a pregame ritual at the Chicago White Sox' Comiskey Park. When it was suggested to Berlin that his song become the national anthem, he said he was delighted that it had been played, but then stated—unequivocally:

"There is only one national anthem, and I certainly don't want anything else to take the place of it."

Flawed as it may be musically, and outdated lyrically, Francis Scott Key's "Star-Spangled Banner" should continue to wave.

"A Grand Old Anthem,"
Boston Globe

Selection 3

(Richard A. Viguerie is editor of the *Conservative Digest*)

Between 10,000 and 50,000 children in this country are being taught at home. In some places, the Constitutional right of parents to teach their children is recognized by state authorities. In others, parents keep their children out of the public schools by registering them in private schools (and then keeping them home) or simply by not telling authorities about their children.

There are many reasons parents want to teach their children at home. For example, Seventh Day Adventists do not believe in sending their children to school before age eight. Many parents do not like the subtle (and not-so-subtle) anti-religious indoctrination that occurs at many schools. In some cases, it is only at home that a gifted child or a child with a learning disability can get the special treatment he or she needs.

With few exceptions, children taught at home are better educated than children educated in the public schools. They get along better with adults and many are able to enter college at age fifteen or sixteen.

Home schooling was the rule rather than the exception for most of this nation's history. Abraham Lincoln, Franklin Roosevelt, Robert Frost, and Margaret Mead are among the presidents, poets, and scientists who received much of their education at home.

The education establishment opposes home schooling as a threat to some of its most cherished notions. Like the growth of private schools, the recent increase in the number of children taught at home is a direct challenge to the bizarre idea that only "professional" educators can teach. Once it becomes clear that children are generally better off if they stay away from public schools, the education establishment—including the National Education Association and the U.S. Department of Education—will have a lot of explaining to do.

Across this country, many truly qualified teachers are mortified at what the education establishment has done to their profession. Today it is generally the less qualified students who are attracted to education courses in college. To get a good job as a teacher, it is more important to learn how to teach than it is to learn the subject matter; as a result, we have math teachers without much training in science.

In 1979–80, students planning to become teachers scored an average of 339 on the verbal portion of the SAT test—80 points below the national average.

Because most members of Congress refuse to support vouchers or tuition tax credits, private schools are available only to those who can afford to pay public school taxes and private school tuition. If we prohibit home schooling, or regulate it so strictly that only a few families are eligible, we are denying many parents the only alternative they have to the public schools. And we are making law-breakers out of decent, God-loving citizens who want to provide the best education possible for their children.

Parents willing to take the time and trouble to educate their children should have the opportunity to do so without breaking the law.

Richard A. Viguerie,
"Thunder on the Right: A Plea for Home Schooling," *San Francisco Chronicle*

Selection 4   (Doug Wilhide is associate creative director at Colle & McVoy Advertising in Minneapolis and lectures on copywriting at the University of Minnesota.)

I lost a battle last spring. Not a big one; most people will never notice. Not especially hard fought, either. But I feel bad about it. For the first time in my attempt to teach writing to college students, I was persuaded to change a grade.

It happened like this: Two marginal students complained about receiving a C. They wrote letters, added numbers, divided things, came up with averages and percentages, and claimed that the numbers showed they wrote at a B level, not a C level. It went before a committee. The vote was 5 to 1. I yielded.

But first, I put up some token resistance. I explained that the point was being missed, that the course was in writing, not arithmetic, and that judgments about writing are more complex than playing with numbers. I also argued that part of the course dealt with the problem of learning to trust subjective, qualitative decision making when it comes to learning how to write well.

To become a good self-editor, for instance, a student needs to trust judgments that have nothing to do with things quantitative and objective: It's not the number of pages turned in, it's what's on them.

I even argued, forcing things a bit perhaps, that the ability to think beyond numbers and trust subjectivity was part of the difference between "meets requirements" (C) and "exceeds requirements" (B). I failed to convince the committee and I failed to convince those two students.

My battle was a minor one and I lost it, but it's not the first time and it's no big deal. As I get older, compromise gets easier. But I feel bad because I think others shared in the defeat.

The department where I teach writing now has two students who are represented to be (at least in the numbers) something they are not. The department has also implicitly agreed that writing, and the evaluation of it, is a simple enough matter to be quantifiable, perhaps no more complex than running an elevator—as long as you know the numbers you can get where you're going.

The liberal-arts college where this department exists has also lost something. There is now one more case, among thousands, where higher grades were given than were earned.

Already nearly everyone in a major program in this college has a B+ average. The scale has changed from failing/excelling to better/best. Failing and excelling still go on, of course, but the grading system is no longer capable of recognizing which is which.

And the students lost, although they think they won. Somewhere we failed each other. I failed to convince them that they should put aside the world of numbers, perfect corners, and formulas when it comes to writing. They failed to grasp what I tried to help them learn about valuing the work more than the symbol for it; about improving an essential skill rather than working for an easy reward; about thinking and judging for themselves rather than depending on an arbitrary and ultimately unimportant grading system.

I feel bad about losing this battle, not because it was lost: There are many battles that are won in the losing and this one probably could not have been won anyway.

I feel bad because I didn't fight harder. I argued to myself that I was paid to teach writing, not to defend some Maginot Line against grade inflation for the noble cause of upholding standards in the liberal arts.

But maybe that is part of the job. There are hundreds of little battles like this every academic year. Some are won and some are not and in both cases there are heroes. I should have tried harder. I feel bad about that.

Doug Wilhide,
"In the Battle Against Grade Inflation, the Winners Are Often the Losers,"
Chronicle of Higher Education

Selection 5   (Tom Wicker is a nationally syndicated newspaper columnist.)

For U.S. military forces, an invasion of Nicaragua would be "like falling off a log," says an intelligence officer. And an official of the Army's Southern Command estimates that it would take only two weeks to gain control of 60 percent of the Nicaraguan population.

No sweat, a "U.S. political-military officer in the region" told Joel Brinkley and Bill Keller of The New York Times:

"The U.S. would come in heavily for a month or so, mostly with air strikes against major facilities. Then a new government would be put into place, and it would come with its own army" to clean up whatever resistance might remain.

If that sounds familiar, it is. Sanitary air power with its "surgical strikes" was supposed to make short work of the primitive Vietcong and the North Vietnamese, too, with few American casualties from a dirty ground war. For a long decade of death and destruction, the United States searched for a popular and effective government to "put into place" in Saigon—never grasping that a government hand-picked in Washington could have little legitimacy in Vietnamese eyes.

Does that reflect the much-derided "Vietnam syndrome" or "fear of the use of power"? No, it reflects the hard but essential lessons—taught not just in Vietnam but in Afghanistan—that political problems don't necessarily have military solutions, and that military and technological might can't always overcome a politically or patriotically motivated populace.

But Nicaragua would be different, Brinkley and Keller were told, while compiling two articles about the possibility of a U.S. invasion. For one thing, the population would "rise up" to support the invaders—a proposition that ignores the history of gringo military intervention in Central America and assumes that Nicaraguans so hate the Sandinista government that they'd welcome another intervention and a new U.S. occupation.

If that's the case, would the Sandinistas have armed Nicaraguans so extensively and given military training to so many? Why doesn't this armed people rise now and join the "Contras"? Isn't it as likely that a U.S. invasion would generate patriotic support for the Sandinistas that they couldn't win for themselves?

And if the government the United States would "put into place" were derived, as is probable, from the same Contras, elements of the Somoza regime that Nicaraguans really did rise against would be restored to power. Would such a government be likely to gain sufficient popular support to win a quick war over the Marxist but nationalist guerrillas the Sandinistas would send to the jungles? American experience in Vietnam and Soviet experience in Afghanistan argue against it.

Suppose it didn't turn out to be a "splendid little war"? As one cautious colonel warned: "I've been in the army 24 years and I've never seen anything neat."

Tom Wicker,
"Ready for Another 'Splendid Little War'?" *The New York Times*

Selection 6 (Merle Ellis is a San Francisco Bay Area butcher who writes a newspaper column for consumers on such topics as buying cuts of meat, suggestions for cutting one's own meat, and ways of saving money at the butcher counter.)

Enough is too much already! I mean, come on, gimme a break! Just how much anti-meat polyunsaturated vocal vegetarian drivel is a relatively intelligent carnivore expected to take before becoming defensively vicious, even to the point of a protective snarl? This column, in case you should miss the point, is a snarl.

If you choose a vegetarian diet for religious, philosophical, perceived (factual or fantasized) "health benefits" or for whatever reason—fine— go for it! But please, don't preach to me about it.

I have never said anything against a vegetarian diet in this column. However, I would urge you to learn as much as you can about nutrition before you embark on one. That's just common sense. Maintaining good health on a strict vegetarian diet requires more sound nutritional information than generally is found on the side of a cereal box.

Don't accept as fact everything you are told by the clerk at your local health food store or what some famous spokesperson for some low-saturated something tells you on television. Those people are trying to sell you something—that's what they're paid to do. Their knowledge of and concern for your nutritional needs are, to say the least, very limited, if not, indeed, a little more than somewhat suspect.

No intelligent person in this country is apt to argue with the fact that we probably would be wise to reduce the amount of fat in our diets. I resent, however, the idea that "fat" and "meat" are one and the same.

The commercial for Puritan oil (currently on the tube), for example, drives me up the wall. John Housman is, without question, a fine actor. Anyone who has watched even one episode of "The Paper Chase" will agree, I'm sure. When he says Puritan oil has less saturated FAT-T (when Housman says fat it's a four-letter word) than safflower oil, I believe him. What really bothers me is that every time he says "fat" the commercial cuts to a tight shot of a chef in the background coming down with a cleaver on a big piece of beef, "trimming the fat." In comparing one vegetable oil with another, beef gets the bad rap.

But that somewhat soft-sell subliminal negativism isn't nearly as offensive to this carnivore as the rantings of some vocal vegetarians. Ann Seranne, in her book "Good Food Without Meat," makes the following statements in her introduction:

"What we eat is a matter of custom and habit. . . . In prehistoric times the eating of human flesh was taken as much for granted as the eating of animal flesh. . . .

"Have we really evolved very far from these primitive customs? The offering of Grace before the host carves the blood-rare roast beef, the suckling pig with the rosy apple in its mouth or the plump-breasted turkey is very reminiscent of the prayer that primitive man offered up to his god during the ceremony of sacrifice.

"For many years now I have found myself questioning and criticizing the meat eating society in which we live. . . . Perhaps in a few hundred years we will have evolved to a higher state of consciousness and, with the help of science, can and will become a race of vegetarians who recognize that every living animal cherishes the gift of life.

"The youth of today are not willing to remain within the emotional or intellectual confines of the past. They are seeking the truth and they are discovering the universal law of love, which works whenever it is applied. Their God did not create creatures with the capacity to feel pain, fear, friendship and affection to be used for food."

WOW! By the time I had finished reading that I was ready to hang up the tools of my trade and turn vegetarian. Maybe take a guilt trip to some serene section of the society we live in and open up a health food store; do something to make amends for misguiding so many for so long.

I turned to the back jacket of her book to learn more about this gourmet guru. There, along with a brief biography, was a picture of the lady smiling a seemingly sincere and pleasant smile, with a cute little Yorkshire terrier doggy under her arm, and wearing a fur coat. A WHAT? Yeah! A fur coat—looked like mink.

Merle Ellis,
"A Beef Against Vegetarians," *San Francisco Chronicle*

PRACTICE ESSAY

The Penalty of Death
H. L. Mencken

H. L. Mencken (1880–1956) was born in Baltimore, Maryland. As a reporter, columnist, and essay writer, he was distinguished by his iconoclastic ideas and his sharp wit. (As an example, he once proposed that one member of the U.S. Senate be chosen by lottery each year to die by hanging—he thought this might keep our public officials honest.) His first articles appeared in *The Smart Set,* and later in *The American Mercury,* a newspaper which he founded and edited. Though first published in 1926, "The Penalty of Death" is still both highly readable and timely. The piece appeared originally in a collection of his writings, *Prejudices: Fifth Series* (1926), and Mencken later revised it for reprinting in *A Mencken Chrestomathy* (1949), an anthology of his best writings.

1   Of the arguments against capital punishment that issue from uplifters, two are commonly heard most often, to wit:

1. That hanging a man (or frying him or gassing him) is a dreadful business, degrading to those who have to do it and revolting to those who have to witness it.
2. That it is useless, for it does not deter others from the same crime.

2   The first of these arguments, it seems to me, is plainly too weak to need serious refutation. All it says, in brief, is that the work of the hangman is

unpleasant. Granted. But suppose it is? It may be quite necessary to society
for all that. There are, indeed, many other jobs that are unpleasant, and yet
no one thinks of abolishing them—that of the plumber, that of the soldier,
that of the garbage-man, that of the priest hearing confessions, that of the
sand-hog, and so on. Moreover, what evidence is there that any actual hangman complains of his work? I have heard none. On the contrary, I have
known many who delighted in their ancient art, and practised it proudly.

3   In the second argument of the abolitionists there is rather more force,
but even here, I believe, the ground under them is shaky. Their fundamental
error consists in assuming that the whole aim of punishing criminals is to
deter other (potential) criminals—that we hang or electrocute A simply in
order to so alarm B that he will not kill C. This, I believe, is an assumption
which confuses a part with the whole. Deterrence, obviously, is *one* of the
aims of punishment, but it is surely not the only one. On the contrary, there
are at least half a dozen, and some are probably quite as important. At least
one of them, practically considered, is *more* important. Commonly, it is
described as revenge, but revenge is really not the word for it. I borrow a
better term from the late Aristotle: *katharsis. Katharsis,* so used, means a
salubrious discharge of emotions, a healthy letting off of steam. A school-
boy, disliking his teacher, deposits a tack upon the pedagogical chair; the
teacher jumps and the boy laughs. This is *katharsis.* What I contend is that
one of the prime objects of all judicial punishments is to afford the same
grateful relief (*a*) to the immediate victims of the criminal punished, and
(*b*) to the general body of moral and timorous men.

4   These persons, and particularly the first group, are concerned only indirectly with deterring other criminals. The thing they crave primarily is
the satisfaction of seeing the criminal actually before them suffer as he
made them suffer. What they want is the peace of mind that goes with the
feeling that accounts are squared. Until they get that satisfaction they are
in a state of emotional tension, and hence unhappy. The instant they get it
they are comfortable. I do not argue that this yearning is noble; I simply
argue that it is almost universal among human beings. In the face of injuries
that are unimportant and can be borne without damage it may yield to
higher impulses; that is to say, it may yield to what is called Christian charity. But when the injury is serious Christianity is adjourned, and even
saints reach for their sidearms. It is plainly asking too much of human
nature to expect it to conquer so natural an impulse. A keeps a store and
has a bookkeeper, B. B steals $700, employs it in playing at dice or bingo,
and is cleaned out. What is A to do? Let B go? If he does so he will be unable
to sleep at night. The sense of injury, of injustice, of frustration will haunt
him like pruritus. So he turns B over to the police, and they hustle B to
prison. Thereafter A can sleep. More, he has pleasant dreams. He pictures B
chained to the wall of a dungeon a hundred feet underground, devoured by
rats and scorpions. It is so agreeable that it makes him forget his $700. He
has got his *katharsis.*

5   The same thing precisely takes place on a larger scale when there
is a crime which destroys a whole community's sense of security. Every

law-abiding citizen feels menaced and frustrated until the criminals have been struck down—until the communal capacity to get even with them, and more than even, has been dramatically demonstrated. Here, manifestly, the business of deterring others is no more than an afterthought. The main thing is to destroy the concrete scoundrels whose act has alarmed everyone, and thus made everyone unhappy. Until they are brought to book that unhappiness continues; when the law has been executed upon them there is a sigh of relief. In other words, there is *katharsis.*

6   I know of no public demand for the death penalty for ordinary crimes, even for ordinary homicides. Its infliction would shock all men of normal decency of feeling. But for crimes involving the deliberate and inexcusable taking of human life, by men openly defiant of all civilized order—for such crimes it seems, to nine men out of ten, a just and proper punishment. Any lesser penalty leaves them feeling that the criminal has got the better of society—that he is free to add insult to injury by laughing. That feeling can be dissipated only by a recourse to *katharsis,* the invention of the aforesaid Aristotle. It is more effectively and economically achieved, as human nature now is, by wafting the criminal to realms of bliss.

7   The real objection to capital punishment doesn't lie against the actual extermination of the condemned, but against our brutal American habit of putting it off so long. After all, every one of us must die soon or late, and a murderer, it must be assumed, is one who makes that sad fact the cornerstone of his metaphysic. But it is one thing to die, and quite another thing to lie for long months and even years under the shadow of death. No sane man would choose such a finish. All of us, despite the Prayer Book, long for a swift and unexpected end. Unhappily, a murderer, under the irrational American system, is tortured for what, to him, must seem a whole series of eternities. For months on end he sits in prison while his lawyers carry on their idiotic buffoonery with writs, injunctions, mandamuses, and appeals. In order to get his money (or that of his friends) they have to feed him with hope. Now and then, by the imbecility of a judge or some trick of juridic science, they actually justify it. But let us say that, his money all gone, they finally throw up their hands. Their client is now ready for the rope or the chair. But he must still wait for months before it fetches him.

8   That wait, I believe, is horribly cruel. I have seen more than one man sitting in the death-house, and I don't want to see any more. Worse, it is wholly useless. Why should he wait at all? Why not hang him the day after the last court dissipates his last hope? Why torture him as not even cannibals would torture their victims? The common answer is that he must have time to make his peace with God. But how long does that take? It may be accomplished, I believe, in two hours quite as comfortably as in two years. There are, indeed, no temporal limitations upon God. He could forgive a whole herd of murderers in a millionth of a second. More, it has been done.

**A. Compre-
hension**

Choose the answer that best completes each statement. Do not refer to the selection while doing this exercise.

1. Mencken's primary reason for supporting the death penalty is (a) that it deters other criminals from committing similar crimes; (b) that it provides a healthy emotional outlet for the criminal's victims and for society at large; (c) that it is preferable to a long and indeterminate prison sentence; (d) that it guarantees the protection of innocent members of society.

2. Mencken defines *katharsis* (also spelled *catharsis*) as (a) a means of relieving tension and anxiety; (b) a salubrious discharge of emotions; (c) a noble yearning; (d) Christian charity.

3. According to Mencken, the victim of a crime wants to see (a) new laws passed guaranteeing capital punishment for every serious crime; (b) the criminal assured of a speedy trial and execution; (c) the criminal suffer as he made the victim suffer; (d) the criminal pay restitution to his victim.

4. Mencken advocates the death penalty for (a) crimes involving the deliberate and inexcusable taking of human life; (b) every homicide, no matter what the circumstances; (c) all serious crimes that threaten the well-being and security of the larger community; (d) any murderer who, having served a prison sentence, commits a second murder.

5. One aspect of the death penalty that disturbs Mencken is (a) the legal wrangling over technicalities, which often results in a guilty person being released from prison; (b) the interference from anti-death-penalty advocates who prevent the execution from being carried out; (c) the overly complicated legal maneuvering lawyers engage in, especially for the benefit of clients with money; (d) the interminable waiting for execution that the guilty person must endure while the lawyers go through the appeals process.

B. Inferences   On the basis of the evidence in the selection, mark these statements as follows: *A* for accurate inferences, *I* for inaccurate inferences, and *IE* for insufficient evidence. You may refer to the selection to answer the questions in this section, and all the remaining sections.

_____ 1. The death penalty has been proved to deter other criminals from engaging in the same crime.

_____ 2. The yearning for revenge is central to Christian doctrine.

_____ 3. *Katharsis* is a term invented by Mencken to describe revenge or getting even.

_____ 4. The most efficient form of execution is hanging.

_____ 5. Once decided upon, the death penalty should be administered quickly, without recourse to long delays and appeals.

_____ 6. Mencken has witnessed several executions.

_____ 7. Mencken thinks some criminal lawyers are greedy.

_____ 8. The criminal justice system in the U.S. should be overhauled.

C. Structure   Choose the best answer.

1. The mode of discourse in this selection is (a) narration; (b) description; (c) exposition; (d) persuasion.

2. In your own words, state the central thesis or main idea of "The Penalty of Death."

_____

_____

3. In paragraph 1, Mencken mentions two arguments frequently put forth by "uplifters." What does the author mean by this term?

_____

In terms of language, "uplifters," as used here, is an example of (a) an analogy; (b) a sneer word; (c) a figure of speech; (d) jargon; (e) a euphemism.

4. In the first sentence of paragraph 1, the transitional expression "to wit" means (a) for example; (b) thus; (c) to be witty; (d) namely.

5. When Mencken argues that the hangman's job may be unpleasant, but other occupations, like the plumber's and the garbageman's, are equally unpleasant, his argument is fallacious. Which fallacy does he commit? (a) *post hoc, ergo propter hoc*; (b) false or questionable cause; (c) *ad hominem*; (d) false analogy; (e) two wrongs make a right.
Explain your choice.

6. Mencken uses the term *katharsis* rather than revenge because (a) *katharsis* is not really the same thing as revenge; (b) he wants to impress us with his fancy vocabulary; (c) he thinks Aristotle's term, coming as it does from the classical Greek era, is more precise; (d) he wants to use a euphemism for a term that might be offensive to Christian readers.

7. In paragraph 4, when Mencken writes that people really want to see that "accounts are squared," he means that (a) society should be able to even the score with the criminal for his misdeeds; (b) the embezzler should pay back the money he embezzled; (c) America should conform to the criminal justice systems of other countries; (d) the victims feel grateful relief when a dangerous criminal is caught.

8. In paragraph 4, Mencken writes, "In the face of injuries that are unimportant and can be borne without damage it may yield to higher impulses; that is to say, it may yield to what is called Christian charity." This is a roundabout way of saying that, with lesser crimes, one can (a) still impose harsh penalties; (b) forgive the criminal for his crime; (c) take the law into one's own hands and retaliate; (d) offer the criminal hope for rehabilitation.

9. The method of paragraph development in the second half of paragraph 4 is (a) cause–effect; (b) illustration; (c) contrast; (d) definition; (e) analysis–classification.

10. Look again at the first two sentences of paragraph 6. Their purpose is to (a) qualify the argument and anticipate opposing arguments; (b) offer more evidence to support the main argument; (c) help Mencken establish himself as a humane, concerned citizen; (d) offer an emotional plea to the reader for his main argument.

11. In paragraph 7, the author suggests that the execution can take place only when the condemned man's money for legal appeals is exhausted. His tone here can best be described as (a) sarcastic; (b) witty and amusing; (c) gently and wryly ironic; (d) sharply critical.

12. Look again at paragraph 8. The main argument for delaying a murderer's execution is to give him time to make his peace with God. Mencken thinks this idea is (a) ridiculously cruel; (b) valid and appropriate; (c) overly lenient; (d) legally indefensible.

D. Vocabulary   For each italicized word from the selection, choose the best definition according to the context in which it appears.

1. hanging a man is *degrading* [paragraph 1]: (a) exposing them to contempt or dishonor; (b) debasing and corrupting; (c) lowering in rank or status; (d) disgusting; repulsive.

2. it does not *deter* others from the same crime [1]: (a) allow; (b) discourage; (c) terrify; (d) exclude.

3. the first argument is too weak to need serious *refutation* [2]: (a) proving false or erroneous; (b) proving valid or sound; (c) proving popular with society at large; (d) proving impossible to verify one way or another.

4. a *salubrious* discharge of emotions [3]: (a) unpredictable; irrational; (b) unwarranted; uncalled-for; (c) impulsive; without premeditated thought; (d) healthy; wholesome.

5. the general body of moral and *timorous* men [3]: (a) lacking in courage; (b) timid; fearful; (c) law-abiding; (d) patriotic.

6. injuries that can be *borne* without damage [4]: (a) endured; (b) punished; (c) maintained; (d) overlooked.

7. Christianity is *adjourned* [4]: (a) ridiculed; (b) cancelled; (c) suspended until a later date; (d) considered irrelevant.

8. here, *manifestly,* the business of deterring others is no more than an afterthought [5]: (a) arguably; (b) contradictorily; (c) surely; (d) plainly.

9. this feeling can be *dissipated* [6]: (a) explained; (b) tolerated; (c) made to disappear; (d) made corrupt.

10. by *wafting* the criminal to realms of bliss [6]: (a) gently conveyed; (b) dragging in chains; (c) sending with no remorse; (d) punishing.

11. by wafting the criminal to realms of *bliss* [6]: (a) eternal damnation; (b) serene happiness; joy; (c) purgatory; a place of atonement; (d) a heavenly abode.

12. lawyers carry on with their idiotic *buffoonery* [7]: (a) posturing; foolishness; (b) arguments over trivial matters; (c) courtroom theatrics; (d) delays; procrastinating.

13. by the *imbecility* of a judge [7]: (a) carelessness; (b) honest error; (c) attention to legal details; (d) mental deficiency.

14. there are no *temporal* limitations upon God [8]: pertaining to (a) moral choices; (b) punishment; (c) time; (d) reason.

Other words you should know the meanings of:

sand-hog [1]
pedagogical [3]
sidearms [4]
pruritus [4]
metaphysic [7]
writs, injunctions, and mandamuses [7]
juridic [7]

E. Variant Word Forms

From the list of inflected forms in parentheses, choose the form that fits grammatically into the space. Add endings (-s or -ed, for example) if necessary.

1. (abolish, abolition, abolitionist): There are two central arguments for the _____ of the death penalty.
2. (menace, menacing): The presence of an unapprehended criminal _____ the entire community.
3. (exterminate, extermination): No one, according to Mencken, argues against _____ the condemned prisoner.
4. (justify, justification): Delaying a condemned man's execution cannot be _____ on any grounds.
5. (limit, limitation): God's forgiveness is not _____ by time.

F. Questions for Analysis

1. What evidence in the essay suggests that Mencken likes playing with words?
2. Look again at paragraph 1. When Mencken says that he has known many executioners who "delighted in their ancient art," what are we to make of this?
3. In supporting his argument for *katharsis,* in paragraph 3, Mencken mentions a school-boy prank directed at an unpopular teacher. Is this example on the same level as the subject of the essay? Does it seem too trivial for the subject, or can you defend its inclusion?
4. How would you describe the argument Mencken puts forth in paragraph 4? Is it convincing or not? What led you to your answer?
5. What motive, or motives, does Mencken ascribe to those who seek to delay carrying out an execution?
6. What was your attitude toward the death penalty for the "deliberate and inexcusable taking of a human life" before you read this selection? Have your ideas changed in any way as a result of reading this essay?

part 3 | READING AND STUDYING TEXTBOOK MATERIAL

Reading textbooks requires a different approach from the intensive, analytical work you have been doing in Parts 1 and 2 of this book. When you read a textbook, your primary purpose is to extract information. Therefore, intensive analysis of rhetorical patterns and recognition of subtleties in tone and word choice are not as important as they are when you read other kinds of material such as articles, essays, and short stories.

This is not to say, however, that you should ignore the structure of textbook chapters. Textbook writers use methods of paragraph development and patterns of organization to present their ideas for the same reason that other writers do—to organize the material in a way that enables the reader to grasp it easily and to follow the direction of ideas without difficulty. And, since you have gained some skill in recognizing these techniques, your comprehension and ability to remember what you have read, whether in textbooks or elsewhere, should improve.

In fact, textbook material should normally present less of a problem for you than will other kinds of nonfiction prose, simply because textbook authors typically try to present their material in the most straightforward manner possible and to organize their ideas clearly enough that the reader can grasp them readily. Also, textbook writers usually try to avoid the kinds of subtleties and rhetorical flourishes with which other writers strive so hard to endow their writing. The organization of chapters in textbooks is deliberately mechanistic as a result. Generally they begin with a brief outline or overview of what is in the chapter and they end with a quiz or some other device to help you measure what you have learned. In the body of the chapter, the relative importance of the topics discussed is shown graphically by the use of varying typefaces and type sizes: Large letters and boldface type indicate major heads; smaller letters and italicized type denote subheads, and so forth. Look at the layout of the chapter in any standard textbook to see how this system works. Finally, modern textbooks are filled with charts, graphs, tables, and illustrations which help to explain and interpret the points made in the text. All these devices are there to make the reading/study process easier.

Mastering the content is the most important objective when you read textbook material, but you should not ignore the writer's purpose and tone. Although the purpose of most textbook writers is to inform and explain (exposition), personal biases are inevitable, and you should be alert for them. The author may have a secondary purpose—to persuade you to agree with his or her beliefs or particular approach to the subject. You should try to determine, then, what that particular belief or approach is, while also trying to identify which beliefs and approaches the writer does not agree with. One way to uncover this information, if it is relevant, is to read the preface.

For example, Conrad Phillip Kottak's excellent textbook, *Cultural Anthropology,* reflects the particular branch of that discipline in which Kottak has specialized—sociocultural anthropology. This fact colors the way Kottak presents information. The sociocultural approach stresses that human behaviors such as aggression and waging war are the result of adaptation to specific cultures and environments and are not inborn in human beings. Thus, in Kottak's book, the sociobiologists—those who believe that human behavior is genetically or biologically determined—do not fare very well, particularly the "popular" sociobiologists like Robert Ardrey. Here is a case where knowing the author's bias is useful, for it helps you to evaluate what you read in that particular textbook, and it provides a useful starting place for the investigation of other approaches. In other words, if you read books by Ardrey (*African Genesis* or *The Territorial Imperative*), you will be in a better position to evaluate their approaches because you will know the arguments against them.

To repeat, the purpose of reading textbooks is to extract information, preferably with a minimal expenditure of time. But students often waste their study time by making two mistakes. First, some students begin reading the assigned chapter at the first page and when they have finished the assignment, they may not remember very much of what they read. A student closes the book and says, "Well, that's over with. I've finished the assignment." A week or so later, he may remember almost nothing because, as he says, "I haven't actually studied it yet." The problem here is obvious, and it is no wonder that during midterm and final-exam periods one sees so many wan faces and baggy eyes. This method of study means that the student must not only read all the required chapters again before the test, but he must study everything for the first time as well.

The second mistake is the habit of smearing textbook pages with a colored-ink marker. If done wisely, underlining is helpful, but often using the marker actually delays or postpones real learning. It suggests to the student that what is underlined is something that will eventually have to be learned. The way to correct these two inefficient study systems is simple. Make the most of your study time by learning the material *as you go along,* resist the temptation to underline everything in the chapter, and put into practice a *system* for reading textbooks and studying from them.

A. THE SQ3R STUDY SKILLS METHOD

There are various study skills methods taught in high school and college courses—PQ3R, PQ4R, SQ4R, SQ3R. All derive from a system developed by Francis P. Robinson, and all involve the basic principles that students often omit from their study time: preview and review. The method I teach my students is SQ3R, which stands for:

S   **SURVEY**
Q   **QUESTION**
R   **READ**
R   **RECITE**
R   **REVIEW**

The SQ4R and PQ4R methods add an extra "R" step—"Rite" (Write), meaning that one can take notes after the Read step. If you prefer, you can substitute note taking for the Recite step. (See the next section on note taking for suggestions.)

Here is how the SQ3R system works. Before you start to read an assigned textbook chapter, **SURVEY** its contents by quickly reading and thinking about as many of the following parts of the chapter as the author provides:

• the chapter title
• the chapter outline
• the chapter introduction
• the main heads and subordinate heads (note the difference in typefaces)
• the chapter summary
• review questions or questions for discussion

The purpose of surveying is to give you a framework, an overview of what the chapter will discuss before you spend any time reading it. In this way, you can fit the various parts into a coherent whole while you are reading it, and there will not be any unfamiliar material, since the major points will already be familiar to you. This survey step should take no more than ten minutes.

Next, for the **QUESTION** step, go back to the beginning of the chapter and turn the chapter title and the main and subordinate heads into questions which you expect will be answered in each section. For example, consider this subhead from a chapter on marketing (from an introduction-to-business textbook):

CHANGING AGE PATTERNS: THEIR IMPACT ON MARKETS

You might turn that into a question by asking, What is the impact of changing age patterns on business markets? What are the differences in buying habits among age groups?

Or consider this head from the animal behavior section of a biology textbook:

Communication by Chemicals

You might ask, How do animals communicate by chemicals? What kinds of chemicals are involved? What animals communicate in this way? Be sure, however, that your questions are not the kind which can be answered by yes or no. Asking yourself if animals do in fact communicate by chemicals is not a particularly helpful question.

During these two stages, you should also ask yourself what you already know about the material, in order to avoid spending time studying what is familiar to you (or what is obvious or a matter of common sense). In this way, the S–Q steps not only give you a framework for your reading, but they also show what parts of the chapter you will need to emphasize in your study time.

The next step, **READ**, will be both easier and more purposeful as a result of your having surveyed the whole chapter. As you read each section and subsection, keep in mind the questions you asked during the Q step and read to find the answers to them. After you have read a section or subsection, stop for a moment and **RECITE** the important points. Then go on to the next section, reading and reciting in the same way. As noted earlier, you might want to substitute note taking for the **RECITE** stage.

Once you have finished reading the entire chapter, you should **REVIEW** –immediately! If you do this right after you finish each chapter, the need to review before a test will be substantially reduced, since the material will be completely familiar to you. To review, look over the chapter once more, restudying the main points in each section, reading the summary, and taking advantage of any discussion questions or review quizzes the author may have provided. Another effective technique is to review all the accumulated chapters you have already studied at the end of every week. This works especially well in preparing for a midterm exam, which could conceivably cover the material in eight or ten chapters, or roughly half the text.

B. TAKING NOTES

You will recall that the fourth step of the SQ3R method is to recite the key points in each section. This method works well for students who learn well *aurally* ("through the ears"). Other students learn better *visually:* they can assimilate material more easily if they read it in print, or perhaps if they write it down themselves. (To test which way you learn, ask a friend to say aloud a difficult surname, one with an uncommon spelling and pronunciation. Then ask to have it spelled aloud. If you can learn to spell it by merely hearing it spelled, it is probable that you are an aural learner. If you need to write it down or see it on paper, then you are more likely to be a visual learner. Many colleges have learning centers where you can take a battery of tests to determine your specific learning requirements and abilities in much greater detail and with much greater accuracy.)

For visual learners, merely studying the original pages during the review step may be sufficient. However, some students profit from writing information themselves, much as young children are often taught to study spelling words by writing each one ten times. If you want to substitute note taking for the **RECITE** step, here are some suggestions for developing good note-taking skills:

• Keep your notes brief. Most students make the mistake of taking overly copious notes which include far too much information. On a chapter quiz, or even on a midterm exam covering several chapters, a teacher can ask only so much information and the questions will very likely cover main concepts and principles, not trivial or incidental information. You should be able to confine your notes for a standard-length textbook chapter to one or two pages.

- Duplicate the author's classification of material into main and subordinate heads. You can devise your own system or use this traditional outline form:

    I. **(Main Heads)**
        A. **(Subordinate Heads)**
            1. **(Sub-subheads)**
            2.
        B. **(Subordinate Heads)**
            1. **(Sub-subheads)**
            2.
    II. and so forth

- Be sure to underline key terms and provide a clear and concise definition of each one. This is especially necessary if you are preparing for a test in which you have to define and/or illustrate important terms.

- Use the author's terms rather than your own for important principles (e.g., *photosynthesis* or *iambic pentameter*). It is all right to paraphrase general material, but take care not to introduce distortions.

- To save space and time, use standard abbreviations (or develop your own system):

    info – information
    rdg – reading
    inst – institution
    govt – government
    intl – international
    w/ or w. – with
    c. – century
    @ – around
    e.g. – for example [Latin – *exempli gratia*]
    n.b. – important [Latin – *nota bene*, meaning "note well"]   and so forth

- Most important, write legibly. It is very frustrating to be unable to decipher notes you have written several weeks earlier. Note the chapter number and the page numbers at the beginning in case you need to refer to the text while you are studying.

C. TAKING TESTS

Ask your instructor to announce the sort of test you will be given so that you can direct your energy toward the appropriate method of preparation. Objective tests (multiple choice, matching, true/false, identification, and so forth) require more attention to details than do subjective tests (essay or short essay questions), which typically emphasize one's mastery of basic concepts or the ability to apply basic concepts to new situations.

For whichever kind of test you are preparing, start early—several days before the test, rather than the night before. Organize your study time efficiently, taking advantage of hour breaks between classes or time waiting for the bus, and setting aside specific hours each week for each course. From my teaching experience, students get into difficulty in two ways: first, by procrastinating, waiting until the night before to start studying for a big test or to write a paper; and second, by trying to cram too many courses (and often too many work hours) into a term. At the beginning of the term, make a realistic appraisal of what each of your courses will require, and set up a workable study/work schedule, one that does not demand that you be Superman or Wonder Woman. A good night's sleep before exams is eminently desirable, and if you allot your study time over several days rather than over an hour or two, this is also entirely feasible.

Taking Objective Tests.   Arrive early. Bring a couple of extra pencils or pens and any other required materials like a dictionary (if allowed) or blue books. A small bottle of white-out is indispensable when you are taking exams that involve writing your own answers. Avoid listening to or engaging in the sort of panicky conversations often heard just prior to a test. They are counterproductive and can undermine your confidence.

Once you receive the test, read each set of directions before you start marking answers. Students often lose valuable points by ignoring the instructions. For example, on a multiple-choice vocabulary question, do not assume that you are being asked to choose the best definition for each word. You might have been asked for the closest *antonym*.

Next, go through the test from start to finish, answering those questions which you know readily and positively. Then go through the items again, this time choosing your best answer for the items you were doubtful about the first time through. If a question still puzzles you, leave it, or put a faint check mark next to it. Do not dwell too long on any single item on an objective test, since you can better devote that time to answering questions for which you are reasonably sure of the answers. If you have no idea of what an answer should be, make a guess only if you are sure that you will not lose points by guessing. If you are not penalized, it is better to put down your best guess than to leave an answer blank. Finally, go through the test again—one item at a time—to doublecheck your answers. *Never* turn in an answer sheet that you have not doublechecked.

Taking Essay Tests.   The general advice from the previous section also applies to taking essay exams, but you have to tackle the actual test-taking part differently. The most critical part in doing well on an essay test is to know what you are being asked to do. Read the question(s) carefully, paying particular attention to the instructions and the key terms. Decide what the question is directing you to do. Here are some common instructions used in essay questions with an explanation of what each requires:

List: This instruction requires only simple enumeration of items.

Define: Provide a clear definition, not merely a synonymous word, for each term.

List and define: a combination of the two instructions above. Be sure to do both.

Explain/discuss/examine/analyze/describe: These instructions are often used interchangeably. They indicate that your instructor wants you to separate the issue under discussion into its component parts and to explain each part in detail as it relates to the whole; perhaps to provide reasons why the situation exists or how it relates to background or historical information (if appropriate); perhaps to suggest the effects of a situation, or to offer an explanation of the diversity of opinions that prevail upon the subject. These words are thus used as general catchall instructions where you are required to explore a subject in some depth. In a question which begins "Examine the causes and effects of . . ." restrict yourself to the cause–effect pattern.

Trace: Using chronological order, list and explain the successive stages leading to an event or a particular situation. This is frequently encountered in history or political science exams.

Compare: Examine the similarities between two things.

Contrast: Examine the differences between two things.

Compare and contrast: Be sure to do both.

Illustrate: Explain a principle by citing an example or illustration of it.

Agree or disagree: This set of instructions asks you to take a side and to explain your reasons for choosing it.

Some sample essay questions from various disciplines follow. Read each carefully, underline the key word or words in the instructions, and determine what it is you are being asked to do.

1. Define the theory of *proactive* interference in learning and provide an illustration from your own experience. (psychology)

2. Contrast the Shakespearean, Spencerian, and Petrarchan sonnet forms and give an example of each from the sonnets you have studied. (literature)

3. Analyze the political effects of the German–Soviet nonaggression pact of 1936 on both countries. Which country received more benefits from the pact's implementation? Explain. (history)

4. Explain Ebbinghaus's curve of forgetting. How was the experiment set up? What did the experiment show? What conclusion did he draw from it? (psychology)

5. Which kind of test provides a better measurement of one's learning—objective or subjective? Why? (impromptu essay topic in English)

6. Trace the economic role played by the Roman Catholic Church in Europe from 1000 to 1600. (history)

7. Compare the theme of illusion in any two of Ibsen's plays you have read. (literature)

8. What are the two methods of depreciating items on a federal income tax form? (accounting)

9. List and explain three systems of kinship terminology used to describe the same generation of relatives. (anthropology)

10. Explain the ways in which the Federal Reserve Board can control the money supply. (economics)

11. Contrast the political and social ideas of Hamilton and Jefferson. (history)

12. Agree or disagree: The American presidency should be limited to one six-year term. (political science)

Suppose you have an essay question to answer in an hour's time. If you have a choice of questions, settle on one quickly, obviously the one you know most about or are most confident of. Spend a few minutes (five or ten at most) thinking about your answer and jotting down notes or making a brief outline). Formulate your opening statement, which should be the main idea, by turning the question into a declarative statement. For example, if you are asked "What are the differences between the Petrarchan and the Shakespearean sonnet forms?" you might open your essay with this sentence: "Although the Petrarchan and Shakespearean forms are both classified as sonnets, there are significant differences in rhyme scheme, division of verse lines, and subject matter." Note that this sentence demonstrates to the instructor that you know what you are being asked to do, as evidenced by the repetition of the key terms (the two kinds of sonnet) and the key operating word, "the difference." It also lets the instructor know that you have a firm grasp of the subject and that you are going to get right to it. You can then proceed to support the main idea. As you are writing your answer, make note of the time so that you can judge just how much information you will be able to include in the body of your essay. If time is short, give only the main principles; if you have a more leisurely time period, add as much relevant illustrative or supporting material as you can without becoming tedious. Even if you are not finished with your answer, spend the last five or ten minutes proofreading and revising. It seems more sensible to turn in a polished piece of writing, one where spelling, grammar, and punctuation errors have been corrected, than to turn in a messy, careless piece of writing that covers all the material. And yes, neatness *does* count. A messy or illegible presentation is not only hard to read, but does not show off your knowledge in its best light. A little bottle of white-out is indispensable for covering over errors.

Two sections from standard college textbooks follow; one is from an introduction to psychology, and the other was taken from an introductory business text. Unless your instructor has other assignments for you, practice the SQ3R study skills method and note taking with these passages. Each one ends with a brief review quiz which lets you test how well you absorbed the material. The first excerpt, Memory, comprises the first half of its source's Chapter 7, Memory and Thought.

Textbook Selection	**Memory** Sandra Scarr and James Vander Zanden

MEMORY

Sensory Storage
Short-Term Memory
Long-Term Memory
Improving Memory

What components of existence make your life a uniquely human kind of experience? You may answer this question in a great many ways. Nonetheless, to answer it, you must call on both memory and thought. You must recollect certain of your previous experiences and then order these experiences in some meaningful fashion. In sum, you must mentally draw on remembered elements of your past and find relevant relationships or linkages among these elements. Indeed, the very fact that you must employ memory and thought to answer the question (or, for that matter, any question) suggests that both components are central aspects of the human experience. Without memory, you would not have any sense of yourself as a being who changes and grows through time. And without conscious thought, you would exist in a mental vacuum.

MEMORY

In the previous chapter, we considered learning. We stressed that learning involves the acquisition of skills and knowledge that allow individuals to adapt to their environment by building on previous experience. However, these new potentials for behavior must be retained. You must be able to store this potential over time and then activate it when you need it. Memory serves this function. **Memory** is the ability to recall, recognize, or relearn previously practiced behaviors more rapidly than new behaviors. You might think of memory as your mental "savings." Learning and memory are closely related processes. By virtue of learning, to-be-remembered material enters storage so that it can be retrieved later. Psychologists distinguish among three kinds of memory, each of which has a different purpose and time span. **Sensory storage** holds information for only an instant; **short-term memory** keeps it in mind for about twenty seconds; **long-term memory** stores it indefinitely.

Sensory Storage

When you see or hear something, you are able to hold the input for a fraction of a second in sensory storage. Unless it goes into short-term memory, the impression is then lost. For example, when you watch a movie, you do not notice the gaps between frames. The actions seem smooth because each frame is held in sensory storage until the next frame arrives. One frame, however, could strike your retina and disappear without your being aware of it or able to store it in memory.

The psychologist George Sperling (1960) demonstrated this phenomenon in an ingenious experiment. He used a tachistoscope (a device that presents a picture for a very brief time) to present a group of letters to people for one-twentieth of a second. Previous studies had shown that if you present a stimulus such as:

$$
\begin{array}{ccc}
\text{T} & \text{D} & \text{R} \\
\text{S} & \text{R} & \text{N} \\
\text{F} & \text{Z} & \text{K}
\end{array}
$$

people will usually be able to remember four or five of the letters after the array has disappeared. Sperling believed that people took a mental photograph of the letters, and were able to read back only a few before the picture faded. He told the people in his experiment that after he had flashed the letters on the tachistoscope screen, he would immediately present a tone. On hearing a high tone, the subjects were to tell him the top row, a medium tone the middle row, and a low tone the bottom row. Once people learned this system, they were indeed able to remember any row of letters. Thus he proved that subjects retain a brief image of the whole picture so that they can still read off the items in the correct row *just after* the picture has left the screen.

The information held momentarily by the senses has not yet been narrowed down or analyzed. It is like a short-lived but highly detailed photograph or tape recording. You can demonstrate sensory storage for yourself:

- Move a pencil back and forth before your eyes as you stare immediately ahead. Note that a shadowy image trails behind the moving pencil.
- Tap a pencil on your desk. Note how the distinctiveness of the sound in your mind has a very brief tapering-off period.
- Tap a pencil against your arm. At first you feel the immediate sensation. But then the feeling fades away and later you simply recall that you tapped yourself with a pencil.

Sensory storage maintains a rather complete reproduction of the world as it is received by your sensory system. It has a tremendous capacity. Indeed, there is virtually no limit to the amount of information that can be very temporarily recorded there.

Short-Term Memory

The things you have in your conscious mind at any one moment are being held in short-term memory. The short-term store is your working memory. However, as you go about your daily activities you are not required to pay close attention to it. You have probably had the experience of listening to someone only partially and then having that person accuse you of not paying attention. You deny it, and in order to prove your innocence, you repeat to him, word for word, the last words he said. You can do this because you are holding the words in short-term memory. Usually, however, the sense of what he was saying does not register on you until you repeat the words out loud. Repeating the words makes you pay attention to them. This response is what psychologists mean by *rehearsal*.

Rehearsal   To keep information in short-term memory for more than a few seconds, you have to repeat it to yourself, in your mind or out loud. When you look up a telephone number, for example, you can remember the seven-digits long enough to dial them *if* you repeat them several times. If you are distracted or make a mistake in dialing, the chances are you will have to look up the number again. It has been lost from short-term memory. Hence each memory trace is "regenerated" or "reset" by rehearsal, at which point it begins decaying again.

Psychologists have measured short-term memory by seeing how long a subject can retain a piece of information without rehearsal. The experimenter shows the subject a card with three letters on it, such as CPQ. However, at the same time the experimenter makes the subject perform a task in order to prevent her from rehearsing the letters. For example, the researcher might ask the subject to start counting backward by threes from 798 as soon as the card is flashed. If the subject performs the task for only a short time, she will usually remember the letters. But if she is kept from rehearsing for more than eighteen seconds, the information will be forgotten (Brown, 1958; Peterson and Peterson, 1959). Thus short-term memory seems to last for less than twenty seconds without rehearsal.

Capacity   Short-term memory is quite limited in capacity. It can hold only about seven unrelated items. Consider, for example, what happens when someone quickly reels off a series of digits to you. You are able to keep only about seven or eight of them in your immediate memory. Beyond that number, you begin to confuse the digits. The same would be true if the unrelated items were a random set of words. You typically do not notice this limit to your capacity because you usually do not have to store so many unrelated items in your immediate memory. Either the items are linked together (as when you listen to the words in a sentence) or they are rehearsed and placed in long-term memory.

The most interesting aspect of this limit, discovered by George Miller (1956), is that it involves about seven items of *any* kind. Each item may consist of a collection of many other items, but if the items are all packaged into one "chunk," then there is still only one item. Thus you can remember about seven unrelated sets of initials, such as COMSAT, DDT, SST, or the initials of your favorite radio stations, even though you cannot remember all the letters separately. This capability occurs because you have connected, or "chunked," them together previously, so that DDT is one item, not three.

One of the tricks of memorizing a good deal of information quickly is to chunk together the items as you receive them. If you connect items in groups, you have fewer to remember. For example, you may find that you remember new phone numbers in two or three chunks (555–6794 or 555–67–94) rather than as a string of seven digits (5–5–5–6–7–9–4). As Figure 7.1 illustrates, you use chunking to remember visual as well as verbal inputs.

Forgetting   You store countless amounts of information in memory, but you also forget a great deal. This fact undoubtedly troubles you—for example, when you

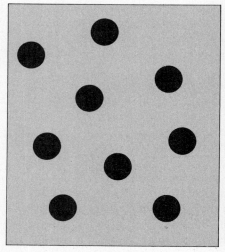 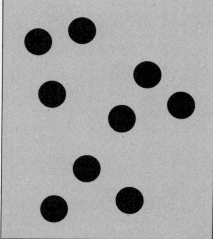

Glance quickly at the left figure in this pair, then look away. How many dots did you see? Now do the same with the right figure. You were probably more sure and more accurate in your answer for the right figure because the organization of the dots into a small number of chunks makes it easier to process the information. *(Doug Armstrong)*

find that you cannot remember the name of a person to whom you were introduced only moments ago. Admittedly, forgetting results in the loss of many potential skills and valuable information. But if you did not forget, your mind would be cluttered with so many unrelated items that you would have great difficulty retrieving and selecting the information that you need. Memory is best for information that people find useful and relevant to their present interests.

Psychologists find that a number of factors contribute to forgetting (Adams, 1976). According to *decay theory*, the memory traces containing stored information deteriorate (Broadbent, 1963; Reitman, 1971, 1974). Unless the information is periodically used and hence rehearsed, it weakens and eventually is erased. The process is like the fading of a photograph over time or the progressive erosion of the inscription on a tombstone (Hulse, Deese, and Egeth, 1975).

Another factor in forgetting is highlighted by *displacement theory* (Waugh and Norman, 1965; Ellis and Hunt, 1977). As noted earlier, there are approximately seven slots available in short-term memory for information. As items enter short-term memory, they are placed in the next available slot. When all the slots are in use, incoming information takes priority.

It displaces or "bumps out" an old item from one of the slots. Hence the old item is "forgotten."

Long-Term Memory

Long-term memory is where you store information for future use (see Figure 7.2). It can be thought of as a kind of filing cabinet or storage bin for names, dates, words, faces, and countless other items (see the boxed insert). When you say that someone has a good memory, you usually mean that the person can recall a good deal of this type of information. But long-term memory also contains representations of a great many experiences and sensations. You may not have thought about your childhood home for years, but you can probably still visualize it.

Encoding

Encoding is the process by which information is put into the memory system. It involves perceiving information, abstracting from it one or more features, and creating corresponding memory traces for these features. Since the encoding process takes place during the presentation of to-be-remembered information, the distinction between learning and memory is becoming increasingly blurred by much current psychological research (Ellis and Hunt, 1977). Indeed, the psychologist Endel Tulving (1968) says that learning is simply an improvement in retention. Thus, as viewed by Tulving, to investigate learning is to investigate memory.

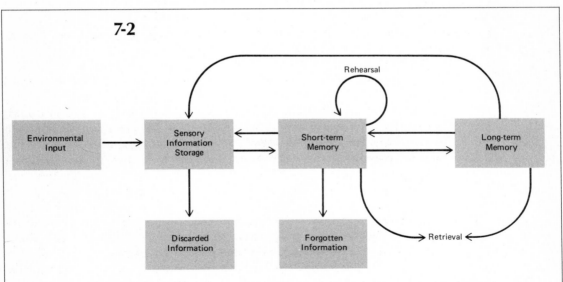

7-2

The flow of information processing. Input to the senses is stored temporarily, and some of it is passed on into short-term memory. Information may be kept in short-term memory by rehearsal or it may be passed on to long-term memory. Material stored in both short- and long-term memory is used in making decisions. The decision process results in outputs such as talking, writing, or moving. *(Adapted from Vander Zanden and Pace, 1984)*

Information processing is sometimes likened to an office filing system. Suppose that you work in the office of the college dean. One of your responsibilities is to file letters in the appropriate folders. You have a letter from the dean of another college suggesting that your school modify its form for transferring course credit from one institution to another. Under what category are you going to file the letter? Will you file it under the sender's name, under "Course Transfer Forms," under "Suggestions," or under some other category (perhaps creating a new category with a new folder)? The procedure you employ must be consistent. You cannot file this letter under the sender's name and the next similar letter under "Course Transfer Forms." How you file the item will have major implications for your ability to retrieve the letter at a later time. As with the filing system, how you encode information in memory has a profound impact on your subsequent ability to recognize or recall an item.

A number of experiments have suggested that the information organized in a long-term memory is *semantic*—that is, based on its meaning (Loftus and Loftus, 1976). Psychologists have investigated these matters by undertaking studies employing recognition items. Subjects are provided with a list of words that they are asked to study—termed *learning items*. After a lapse of time, they are provided with a second list of words. Some words were on the first list while other words—termed *distractor items*—were not. The researcher then asks the subjects to check those words that were on the earlier list.

In recognition tests, the similarity between the learning words and the distractor words produces a striking effect. If subjects are shown the word "car" on the first list, they are much more likely later to think, erroneously, that they saw the word "auto," "vehicle," "Ford," or "Honda" than to think they saw "tar" or "cap." Hence, individuals are more likely to mistake new words for old words if the new words are related to the old words in meaning than if the new words look or sound like the old word (are phonemically related). In sum, research suggests that the dominant mode of representation in long-term storage is semantic (Anisfeld and Knapp, 1968; Grossman and Eagle, 1970).

Meaning is but one attribute that you use for encoding in memory. You may also encode items in terms of their physical appearance, sound, odor, taste, and feel. *Episodic memory* is remembrance of whole events and places. Recall, for instance, the gymnasium in your high school or college. Recall the location of the doors, windows, and basketball hoops. Recall its pungent odor. And recall the drone of voices and the staccato of bouncing basketballs. Psychologists find that episodes and places that become a part of memory are as resistant to forgetting as are semantic features (Kintsch, 1977).

In the process of encoding, you typically select a number of features from some stimulus item and store this material as a unit in memory. The richer the sample of features, the better your retention will be. In your everyday life, you often encode material in terms of both meaning and physical attributes. For instance, the psychologist Paul A. Kolers (1976) had subjects read textual material upside down (after 160 pages of practice, they read it almost as rapidly as they read normally oriented text). A year later, he had the subjects read this same material and some new material, all of which was again inverted. He found that the subjects were faster on pages that they had previously read than on new pages. Kolers argues that because reading in this strange fashion requires considerable effort to decode—to abstract meaning from the upside-down print—the information is strongly represented in memory.

The more categories an item is filed under, the more easily it can be retrieved. (It is somewhat like placing a copy of the dean's letter in each of a number of folders with different headings.) For instance, you probably can recognize the sound of a particular musical instrument (say, the piano) no matter what tune is being played on it. You can also recognize a particular tune no matter what instrument is playing it. This pattern of recognition suggests that a single item of information may be "indexed" under several "headings," so that it can be reached in a number of ways. Hence "the attractive teller at the First Street Bank" might be indexed under "First Street Bank," "bank tellers," "potential friends," "blondes," and possibly several other categories as well.

Finally, the order in which you receive information affects your retention of it. You tend to remember the information you first receive—a tendency called the *primacy effect*—and material that you last receive before recall—a tendency called the *recency effect*. You typically forget the material in the middle. The first items in a list of to-be-remembered words get your attention; the last ones are still in short-term memory when you attempt to recall them. The words in the middle of the list enjoy neither advantage, and so you are more likely to forget them.

Remembering

Memory is not simply a matter of encoding and storage. It also requires that you retrieve appropriate information when you need it. When you wish to recall information, you must employ a cue that will allow you to narrow the domain in your memory in which you conduct the search.

Consider again the analogy of the office filing system. Let us say that you filed the letter to the dean in the folder labeled "Suggestions." Some four months later, the dean asks you to find the letter, since he or she is now ready to act on the matter. The dean's files contain thousands of folders. Whenever you are asked to retrieve a letter, you do not undertake your task by beginning with "A" and working your way alphabetically through all the folders until you locate the item. Instead, you employ a cue to narrow the search. Thus you are likely to look under the letter-sender's name, under "Course Transfer Forms," and so on. And usually you will find the letter. However, if you filed it under "Suggestions" and you have neglected to search this folder, the letter will be technically available but inaccessible because of a retrieval breakdown. Likewise, an item may be contained in your memory store but be unavailable because you do not have the relevant cue. For practical purposes the item is forgotten. In sum, retrieval is *cue-dependent* (Tulving and Psotka, 1971; Tulving, 1974).

In general, the better the cues that you employ in memory search, the better will be your retrieval of information from long-term memory. For this reason, recognition is usually easier than recall. In **recognition**, your task is simply one of picking out certain information from a group of items as the remembered material. In contrast, **recall** requires that you supply for yourself all the information on a subject. For instance, in recognition questions you are asked: "Which of the following individuals was the fourth president of the United States? (a) John Adams; (b) Abraham Lincoln; (c) Thomas Jefferson; (d) James Madison" or "If you multiply 7 by 6 the answer is: (a) 12; (b) 34; (c) 42; (d) 63." Recall questions ask: "Name the fourth president of the United States" or "Recite the multiplication tables by seven."

In recognition tasks, you have both the cue and the item, and your job is to figure out which of the items is correct. In recall tasks, you must provide the cues for yourself. Hence recognition and recall share one process in common (decision on what item is correct) but differ in that recall requires an additional process (generation of the correct item) (Anderson and Bower, 1972). In the example, if you are asked to name the fourth president of the United States, you must search your long-term store for the names of presidents and *then* decide which person was the fourth president. But if you are provided with a recognition task (for instance, a multiple-choice question), you are not required to retrieve the names of the presidents. You need only decide which of the listed individuals is the president in question. Recognition permits you to by-pass the generation phase and move directly to the decision phase.

In sum, you typically can recognize a good deal more than you can recall. That is why you sometimes find yourself admitting to an acquaintance, "Your face looks familiar, but I just can't remember your name." Remembering a person's name is a recall task, while remembering the face is a recognition task because the face is there as a cue.

We have pointed out that retrieval failures account for much of your forgetting from long-term memory. Part of the difficulty stems from *interference* (McGeoch, 1942). This problem arises because you often index or classify a number of items under the same cue. When you use the cue to get at one of the items in storage, the other ones are also recalled, preventing you from remembering the desired item (Lewis and Anderson, 1976).

One source of interference is termed *retroactive interference*—the learning of new material interferes with the recall of old material. Most commonly, interference of this sort is going on in the following type of situation. Someone asks you, "Who beat the Green Bay Packers three weeks ago?" If the Green Bay Packers have lost their last four games to four different teams, you may have difficulty recalling the information. Although you may have encoded the information three Sundays ago, you now have difficulty retrieving the material because you have since encoded information regarding the Packers' subsequent losses.

Another source of interference is termed *proactive interference*—material learned earlier interferes with the learning of new material. When children are trying to learn their multiplication tables, they commonly encounter this sort of interference problem. They do not find it difficult to remember a single multiplication item such as $5 \times 7 = 35$. But as soon as you begin teaching them $5 \times 9 = 45$ and $6 \times 7 = 42$, you are establishing for them competing associations to each of the elements in the original problem. The 5×7 and 35 that is already in storage interferes with their remembering something new: 5×9 and 45, and 6×7 and 42.

Interference leads to an interesting paradox. If facts about some topic (for instance, neurotransmitters) interfere with one another, then the more facts you know about the topic, the slower you should be at retrieving information about the topic. In other words, the more expert or knowledgeable you are on a matter, the worse you should be at answering questions about it. But this prediction contradicts your intuition that the more you know about something, the better you are at answering questions about the topic.

Fortunately, organizing the facts on a topic can offset the effects of interference (Smith, Adams, and Schorr, 1978; Reder and Ross, 1983). Organization involves dividing material into small units and placing these units within appropriate categories. In this manner, each piece of information fits logically with the others. Improved recall is thought to result from this procedure, since you use category labels as retrieval cues and hence reduce memory load in recall (Tulving and Pearlstone, 1966). The principle is similar to that discussed earlier in the chapter, namely, if information can be chunked or hooked into some meaningful category, you can retain it better.

Reconstruction   If you try to remember something that happened in the past, you will find it hard to be entirely accurate. Probably you will recall a few facts and then use these facts to construct the "other facts." The process of bridging the gaps in memory with inferences about things that may have been true is termed **reconstruction**. For instance, the psychologist Donald Norman (Lindsay and Norman, 1977:372) has asked people such questions as, "What were you doing on Monday afternoon in the third week of September two years ago?" The types of responses he gets typically go something like this:

1. Come on. How should I know? (*Experimenter:* Just try it, anyhow.)
2. OK. Let's see: Two years ago . . .
3. I would be in high school in Pittsburgh . . .
4. That would be my senior year.
5. Third week in September—that's just after summer—that would be the fall term.
6. Let me see. I think I had chemistry lab on Mondays.
7. I don't know. I was probably in the chemistry lab.
8. Wait a minute—that would be the second week of school. I remember he started off with the atomic table—a big, fancy chart. I thought he was crazy, trying to make us memorize that thing.
9. You know, I think I can remember sitting . . .

This response protocol illustrates how your memory system operates with this type of retrieval problem. First you try to rephrase the question in the form of a specific date, then you attempt to determine what you were doing about that time. You organize your search around temporal "landmarks" (line 4: "my senior year"). The protocol reveals that the recall process is hardly easy. Note the fragmentary recall of what has in fact been experienced (line 8: "a big, fancy chart") with reconstructions of what "must" have been experienced (line 9: "I think I can remember sitting . . ."). The process appears as a looping, questioning activity, with the larger problem broken up into a series of subproblems. Hence the search is active and constructive.

Some of the implications of reconstruction in memory are highlighted by cases of eyewitness testimony (see the boxed insert). The process has also been demonstrated in other experimental settings. For instance, Rand J. Spiro (1976) had subjects read one of two stories about an engaged couple, Margie and Bob. In both of the stories, Bob tells Margie that he is strongly opposed to having children. In one version, Margie feels the same way as does Bob. In the other version, she is shocked and dismayed by Bob's feelings because she strongly desires children.

EYEWITNESS TESTIMONY

One of the most dramatic tests of recognition memory involves the account of eyewitnesses to a crime. Few bits of evidence are more impressive than the eyewitness who tells a jury, "He's the one. I saw him do it." Indeed, the psychologist Elizabeth Loftus (1974) has shown that even after a witness has been discredited (in this study, the defense attorney had proved that the witness's eyesight was too poor to see the face of a robber from where he stood), jurors were still far more likely to convict the defendant.

Lawyers can cite many cases of people who were falsely accused by the eyewitnesses to a crime. For example, in 1979, Father Bernard Pagano, a Roman Catholic priest from Wilmington, Delaware, went on trial for a series of armed robberies of small shops in the Wilmington area. The trial captured national attention. Newspapers had labeled the gunman the "gentleman bandit" because he was always well dressed and well groomed and displayed impeccable manners. Seven witnesses positively identified Father Pagano as the robber. Yet literally at the eleventh hour, another man, Ronald Clouser, confessed to the robberies. Clouser knew details of the crimes that only the real bandit could have known (details that had not come out in court or been carried by the press). The state then dropped the charges against the priest.

Psychologists, too, have provided many demonstrations of eyewitness fallibility. In one study at Brooklyn College, forensic psychologist Roger Buckhout (1974) staged a purse snatching in one of his classes. When fifty-two students who had seen the incident looked at two videotaped lineups, all but ten said they recognized the culprit. But thirty-five of these forty-two eyewitnesses picked the wrong man! Interestingly enough, the witnesses who were most sure of themselves were somewhat more likely to accuse an innocent man.

Loftus (1974) has done a fascinating series of experiments showing that when people are asked to recall the details of auto accidents, they, too, are likely to distort the facts. After groups of college students had seen a filmed accident, she asked some of them, "About how fast were the cars going when they hit each other?" The average estimate was 34 miles per hour. When she substituted the word "smashed" for "hit" in the above question, another group of students remembered the cars as having gone significantly faster—an average estimate of 41 miles per hour.

Lawyers have long been aware of the effects of leading questions, but the courts continue to act as if human memory were a videotape that enabled the witness to conjure up an instant replay of a crime. In reality, memory involves an active process of filling in the gaps on the basis of a person's attitudes and expectations. Buckhout, who has testified in over seventy trials, notes:

> Uncritical acceptance of eyewitness testimony seems to be based on the fallacious notion that the human observer is a perfect recording device—that everything that passes before his or her eyes is recorded and can be pulled out by sharp questioning or refreshing one's memory. . . . This is impossible —human perception and memory function effectively by being selective. A human being has no particular need for perfect recall; perception and memory are decision-making processes affected by the totality of a person's abilities, background, environment, attitudes, motives, and beliefs, and by the methods used in testing recollection of people and events. [Quoted by Rodgers, 1982a:33–34]

Complicating matters, the eyewitness to a crime or an accident frequently observes a confusing situation under stressful conditions. It is no surprise to psychologists, then, that eyewitnesses are so frequently wrong.

Three sketches from contradictory descriptions of the "Son of Sam" killer, an assailant in another famous case, show that eyewitnesses have different memories of his appearance. *(Jim Anderson/ Woodfin Camp & Assoc.)*

Sam: the latest sketches
Cops' update alters description

The first drawing of Son of Sam made on July 29, 1976 after the Bronx killing of Donna Lauria, 18.

On Nov. 27 the .44-caliber killer struck for the third time. Victim Donna DeMasi, 17, saw him like this.

In the same Nov. 27 shooting, Joanne Lomino, 18—paralyzed for life—supplied the details for this sketch.

After reading the stories, Spiro had the subjects engage in an unrelated task (such as filling out consent forms for the experiment). While they were performing this task, he casually mentioned either that Bob and Margie eventually got married or that they broke up and never got married. Subjects returned anywhere from two days to six weeks later for a recall test. The results showed that subjects consistently reconciled their memories of the stories with the comments made by the experimenter. For example, in the condition where Margie is shocked and the experimenter says the couple got married, subjects "recalled" such things as "They underwent counseling" or "They decided to compromise and adopt children." But in the condition where Margie is shocked and the couple break up, the subjects did not introduce these "facts." Clearly, recall is often much more than the passive reproduction of stored memories.

Improving Memory   Many techniques for improving memory are based on efficient organization of the things you learn and on chunking information into easily handled packages (matters discussed earlier in the chapter). Hence techniques that assist you in organizing and chunking otherwise unrelated items are likely to improve your memory. One of the advantages of note taking derives from this fact. Indeed, some research suggests that the probability of recalling an item that occurs in your notes is about seven times that of items not in your notes (Howe, 1970).

Memory Strategies   Other factors also influence your ability to retrieve material from memory. These factors include meaningfulness, association, lack of interference, and rehearsal. The more meaningful something is, the easier it will be to remember. For example, you would be more likely to remember the six letters "dfirne" if they were arranged to form the word "friend." Not surprisingly, teachers can increase their instructional effectiveness by relating new elements of information to children's existing knowledge (White and Gagné, 1976).

You also remember things more vividly if you associate them with things already stored in memory or with a strong emotional experience. As pointed out earlier, the more categories under which you index a memory, the more accessible it is. If an input is analyzed and indexed under many categories, each association can serve as a trigger for the memory. If you associate the new information with strong sounds, smells, tastes, textures, and so on, any of these stimuli could trigger the memory. The more senses you use when trying to memorize something, the more likely it is that you will be able to retrieve it.

Similarly, it helps in learning something if you protect your memory from interference. For instance, when studying new material you would be well advised to avoid studying quite similar material with it. Instead of studying history right after political science, study biology in between. Another method is to space out your learning. Trying to absorb large amounts of information at one extended sitting results in a good deal of interference. It is more effective to study manageable units, each at its own time. Still another method to protect your memory from interference is to *overlearn* material—to keep on rehearsing it even after you think you know it well. As stressed earlier in the chapter, rehearsal—the cycling of information through the memory store—contributes a great deal to the retention process.

Mnemonic Devices

Mnemonic devices are techniques that people employ for remembering things better. The ancient Greeks memorized speeches by mentally walking around their homes or neighborhoods and "placing" each line of a speech in a different spot, *the method of loci*. Once they had made the associations, they would recall the speech by mentally retracing their steps and "picking up" each line. Another device is the *pegword method* ("One is a bun, two is a shoe," and so on). (See the boxed insert.) A mnemonic device with which you may be more familiar is the rhyme used to recall the number of days in each month ("Thirty days hath September . . .").

Mnemonic devices are not magical. Indeed, they involve extra work—making up words, stories, and so on. But the very effort of trying to do this may help you to remember things.

The Mind of a Mnemonist

One of the best-documented cases of a man with an astounding memory is presented in A. R. Luria's delightful book *The Mind of a Mnemonist* (1968). In the 1920s, a newspaper reporter came to Luria's laboratory to participate in a memory experiment. The Russian psychologist was amazed to learn that S. (as he called the reporter) could easily repeat lists of thirty, fifty, or seventy numbers after he had heard them once. He could repeat them backward and forward with equal ease. And when Luria asked him for some of the same lists more than fifteen years later, S. still remembered them.

Perhaps as a result of Luria's tests, S. began another career, this one as a professional mnemonist: he would repeat complicated lists that were supplied by people sitting in the audience. How did he manage to perform this feat? Every word or number would conjure up rich visual images, which S. easily remembered. For example, in one performance the audience provided him with the following nonsensical formula:

$$N \cdot \sqrt{d^2 \, x \, \frac{85}{vx}} \cdot \sqrt[3]{\frac{276^2 \cdot 86x}{n^2v \cdot 264} \, n^2b}$$

$$= sv \, \frac{1,624}{32^2} \cdot r^2s$$

S. was able to repeat the information perfectly after studying it for a few minutes. He later told Luria a story he had made up to help remember the formula: "Neiman *(N)* came out and jabbed at the ground with his cane (.). He looked up at a tall tree which resembled the square root sign ($\sqrt{\ }$), and thought to himself: 'No wonder the tree has withered and begun to expose its roots. After all, it was here when I built these two houses' (d^2)" (1968:49). And so on.

But being a professional mnemonist is not all roses. One of S.'s biggest problems was learning to forget. His brain was cluttered with old lists of words, numbers, and letters. Even when he tried to relax, his mind would be flooded with vivid images from the past. S. also had trouble reading: every word brought a sea of images, and he had trouble focusing on the underlying meaning of a passage. Partly because of these problems, Luria wrote, "S. struck one as a disorganized and rather dull-witted person" (1968:65).

MNEMONIC TECHNIQUES

Human beings have long been concerned with the practical art of memory. Various stage entertainers have capitalized on this interest and have advertised themselves as possessing unusual memory powers. Until recently, psychologists ignored the techniques employed by memory performers, since they were thought to practice trickery and deception. Only in the past decade or so have psychologists come to appreciate the value of various memory procedures in simplifying certain memory tasks. Further, such techniques afford many insights into the organization and operation of memory (Norman, 1972). Two of the more useful techniques are the method of loci and the pegword system.

METHOD OF LOCI

The method of loci, or the method of places, was employed by orators in classical Greece and Rome to perform what we today would consider prodigious feats of memory (Yates, 1966). It consists of two steps. First, learn in their naturally occurring sequential order some geographical locations with which you are intimately familiar, for instance, the layout of your living quarters, the paths you take between classes, or the floor plans of a building. Second, associate a visual image of the to-be-remembered item with a location in the series; place the items in the order you wish to remember them as you progress along your imaginary walk. In other words, deposit at each location a mental image constructed from the material you wish to memorize. Upon recall, revisit in your mind each place in the house (path or building) in their proper order, retrieving from each the image that you have left there.

By way of illustration, visualize a walk through your home or apartment. You enter the front door, move next through the entryway, then to the living room, to the dining room, to the kitchen, and so on. Use these loci for memorizing a shopping list, for instance, eggs, lettuce, coffee, soap, and milk. Imagine Humpty Dumpty blocking the doorway, heads of lettuce rolling down the hallway, a gigantic coffee pot hanging from the ceiling of the living room, soap suds overflowing in the dining room, and a cow sitting at your kitchen table (do not worry if the images are logical; it may actually help if they are absurd).

7-3

The method of loci. Mentally imagine items from a grocery list placed in sequential locations in your home. Then undertake an imaginary walk in which you retrieve each item in turn from its location as you pass from one room to the next. *(From Vander Zanden and Pace, 1984)*

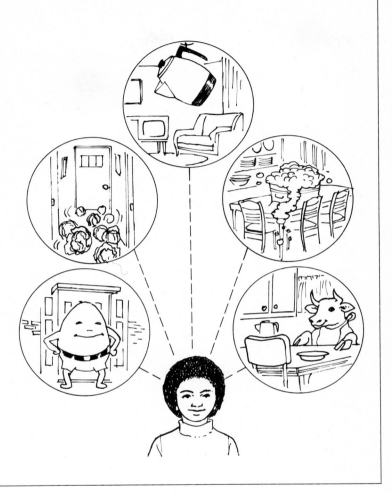

(See Figure 7.3.) Later, attempt to recall the items, in order, by taking an imaginary walk in which you again activate each visual image as you go from one room to the next.

PEGWORD SYSTEM

The pegword system was introduced in England in 1879 by John Sambrook. It consists of memorizing a jingle that has the pegs on which you hang the to-be-remembered items by means of imagery. As with the method of loci, the pegword system can be used to remember shopping lists, errands, sets of facts in educational psychology, historical events, and the like.

First, learn the following jingle:

ONE is a BUN
TWO is a SHOE
THREE is a TREE
FOUR is a DOOR
FIVE is a HIVE
SIX is STICKS
SEVEN is HEAVEN
EIGHT is a GATE
NINE is a LINE
TEN is a HEN

Next, visually associate each item in your shopping list with one of the peg-words as in Table 7.1. To recall the items, you recite the jingle and retrieve the item associated with each pegword.

The method of loci and the pegword system improve memory by a factor of two or three times over normal free recall. They allow you to place the information into storage in an organized and meaningful fashion and then to recall it with explicit retrieval cues. Further, the techniques employ visual imagery. As such, both methods maximize memory by combining a number of potent mnemonic strategies.

Table 7.1 The Pegword System

Pegword	List Word	Mnemonic Image
one-bun	eggs	a bun eating Humpty Dumpty
two-shoe	lettuce	a head of lettuce growing out of a shoe
three-tree	coffee	coffee pots growing out of tree branches
four-door	soap	soap suds flowing through a doorway
five-hive	milk	milk running from a milk beehive

Source: Vander Zanden and Pace (1984).

Questions for Review

1. What is the psychological definition of *memory*?
   recall - recognise, relearn -

2. List and explain the differences between the three kinds of memory.
   Sensory storage - only last an instant
   the short term memory - last 20 seconds
   Long term mem - lost forever

3. Why do we forget? _If we don't recite or retell or use periodically_

4. Look again at Figure 7.2. Explain the chart in your own words.
   Environmental input goes to sensory information storage -
   then goes to short term memory, and can be kept there if
   we recite information or can go to long term memory, retrieval
   is the material stored in both short term and long term memory and
   help in making decisions -

5. What is *encoding*? _process by witch information is put into the system . (stage is ...)_

6. In what ways are encoding and memory storage similar to an office filing system? _they both have to be filed under category. the most appropriate catergory, the easier it will be to find it_

7. Two problems with one's long-term memory are failure in retrieval and the two kinds of interference. Explain these problems. _____

8. What term is used to describe the process of bridging the gaps in one's memory? _____

9. Why should a jury not accept the testimony of an eyewitness to a crime uncritically? _____

10. As aids to improving your memory, how do the *method of loci* and the *pegword system* work? _____

The second selection is an entire chapter from a standard introductory business text. The review quiz at the end is included in the original chapter as well.

Textbook Selection

An Introduction to Marketing
David J. Rachman and Michael H. Mescon

During the 1970s, businesspeople, worried about inflation, tried to increase productivity and cut costs. During the early 1980s, they worried about recession and used every possible strategy simply to stay in business. Now they're worried about keeping up with a changing business environment characterized by changing consumer values, deregulation, and fierce competition. As a result, they're knocking themselves out to win over the customer. By means of polls, interviews, and questionnaires, they are trying to say and do all that they can to elicit the magic "yes." They even use marketing consultants to complete the perfect match, saying, in effect, "Win the consumer for me and name your own price." Even such conservative industries as railroads and utilities are courting consumers, for as one marketing vice-president pointed out, "The customer is the most important product . . . because if he doesn't like what we have, he can go elsewhere."

What is the function known as marketing, and why has it become business's number one competitive weapon? In this chapter we'll find out.

CHAPTER FOCUS

After reading the material in this chapter, you will be able to:

• define marketing, and indicate its importance in our economy

- cite the eight major functions of marketing
- name the three stages in the evolution of marketing over the last century
- point out the population statistics and trends that are most important to marketers today
- describe several rational and emotional motives that affect people's buying habits
- name the characteristics that distinguish the industrial market from the consumer market
- specify the four basic components of the marketing mix and how they should vary with the product and customer

When quarterly losses at Atari Inc., the high-tech manufacturer of video games, began to exceed $50 million, its board of directors searched for a new chief executive. The man they hired wasn't an engineer or a computer specialist, but rather James J. Morgan, Philip Morris's crack marketer. Morgan is generally credited with keeping Marlboro, Merit, and Virginia Slims among the nation's best-selling cigarettes, and so he is partially responsible for Philip Morris's top-ranking $11.7 billion annual income.

In a similar vein, the electronics division of Mattel, Inc., recently lured a marketing executive away from a beauty-aids company to serve as its president, and the new head of the burgeoning Apple Computer Inc. is John Sculley, who cut his teeth in marketing while he was president of Pepsi-Cola. Why have so many young firms hired marketing specialists as chief executive officers? Many companies, especially new high-tech firms, are learning that quality products do not sell automatically on their own merits. If customers don't want what a firm sells, don't know a product exists, or can't afford something, they won't buy. Nor will they be able to buy if the product isn't distributed so that they can get it. It is up to marketers to come up with the products consumers want, put them into homes and businesses, and keep customers coming back for more.

WHAT IS MARKETING? Much of the nation's cheese is made in Wisconsin and much of its lettuce is grown in California, yet these foods are sold in most states, thanks to marketing. Folger's coffee and Charmin bathroom tissue, two standards on today's supermarket shelves, were lowly regional products before clever marketers got hold of them. Whether or not you have Wisconsin cheese or Folger's coffee in your kitchen, as a consumer you benefit from marketing, just as business does, because it gives you an option to use products and services you might not have access to otherwise.

Marketing, basically, is *finding out what buyers want or need and then getting it to them, to the profit or benefit of everyone involved in the transaction.* Marketing encompasses a wide range of functions, including *buying, selling, storing, financing, risk bearing, transporting, standardization and grading,* and *securing information.* Table 1 briefly describes each of these essential marketing functions.

Table 1   Essential Marketing Functions

- **Buying:** Wholesale and retail operations must buy what they want to sell. Manufacturers must buy materials. All businesses buy the services of employees.

- **Selling:** Businesses sell products and services to other businesses and to individuals, using personal selling, advertising, sales promotion, and publicity to enhance sales prospects.

- **Transporting:** Shipping goods from their place of manufacture to their place of sale is a major expense for many businesses, but it increases their usefulness. For example, who in New Hampshire would buy gasoline if it were necessary to go to Houston to get it?

- **Storing:** Businesses store goods until customers are ready to buy them. Bookstores, for example, keep dictionaries and atlases in stock, rather than waiting for customers to request them before ordering them.

- **Financing:** Most businesses borrow against future sales to buy, promote, transport, and store their products.

- **Risk bearing:** Marketing carries the risk that people will not buy enough of a product to make it profitable to produce it.

- **Standardization and grading:** Quality and quantity control standards, many of which are set by the federal government, free buyers from having to check each unit. For example, eggs are graded so that if you buy a dozen grade A, large eggs you know you're getting high-quality eggs of uniform size.

- **Securing information:** Businesses gather information about their markets by using market research.

Marketing is crucial for retail businesses, but it is equally important for other types of businesses too. Makers of materials, such as steel, must market their products to potential customers—auto makers, appliance manufacturers, builders, and others. Makers of high-tech products, including the most advanced robots, also must market to companies and individuals who can use them. Services, such as the Century 21 real estate company, have turned to marketing to increase the number of their customers. And marketing techniques have even been embraced by lawyers, who, in the face of an increasingly crowded field, have resorted to advertising and competitive pricing to capture new clients. Ideas, too, can be marketed by applying the same approaches that sell detergent.

In this chapter and the three that follow, we will examine marketing activities in some depth. We begin by asking, "What is a market?"

The Market Itself   Christmas 1983 is likely to be remembered as the year of the Cabbage Patch Kids. It was a crazy time. Children all over America practically threatened to turn against Santa Claus if they did not receive one of the homely, soft dolls that were all the rage. Parents, in turn, assaulted salespeople and each other so their kids would not be disappointed on Christmas morning. One man reportedly flew to London from the Midwest to buy a $20 doll for $100. Why?

The story of the Cabbage Patch Kids is a marketing dream come true. At Coleco Industries, market research analysts found that adults and kids alike reacted enthusiastically to the prospect of being able to "adopt" a plain, one-of-a-kind "baby" doll. Based on the results of observation sessions, follow-up interviews, and psychological studies, Coleco began marketing the dolls in the summer of 1983. Their popularity skyrocketed, especially after the media picked up the story and reported that stores were unable to keep enough in stock to meet the demand. By the end of the year almost 3 million white and black Kids had been adopted, and Coleco geared up to add Asian and Hispanic Cabbage Patch Kids to the growing roster of adoptees.

Cabbage Patch fever notwithstanding, dolls have long been a popular gift for children. Parents and grandparents the world over can always be counted on to buy dolls of one kind of another. These doll buyers constitute a **market**, that is, *a group of people who need or desire a specific product or service and have the money to buy it.*

The total market for goods and services consists of two large segments: the *consumer market* and the *business market.* The consumer market consists of individuals or households that purchase goods and services for personal use. The business market is made up of business enterprises that buy goods and services for resale or in order to continue their own operation. Often businesses try to distinguish certain groups from the overall market by age, sex, geographic location, income and spending patterns, population size, and mobility in order to market their product more successfully. Using these factors alone or in combination, they attempt to **segment the market**, that is, *to target marketing efforts toward a specific fraction of the total market.* The market for bubble gum, for example, is made up largely of kids, whereas adults comprise the market for breath-freshening chewing gum.

CHANGES IN MARKETING CONCEPTS

Marketing has changed dramatically in the last half-century, as rapid technological advances and increased competition for customers have forced many firms to be aggressive simply to stay in business. These days it takes more than the proverbial better mousetrap to get ahead of the competition and stay there.

Commercial goods: products, such as office supplies and equipment, used by business and industry in adminstering their affairs. *Examples:* word processor, duplicating machine.

Industrial goods: products used in manufacturing other products for either the consumer or the business market. *Examples:* sheet metal, earth mover.

TYPES OF BUSINESS GOODS

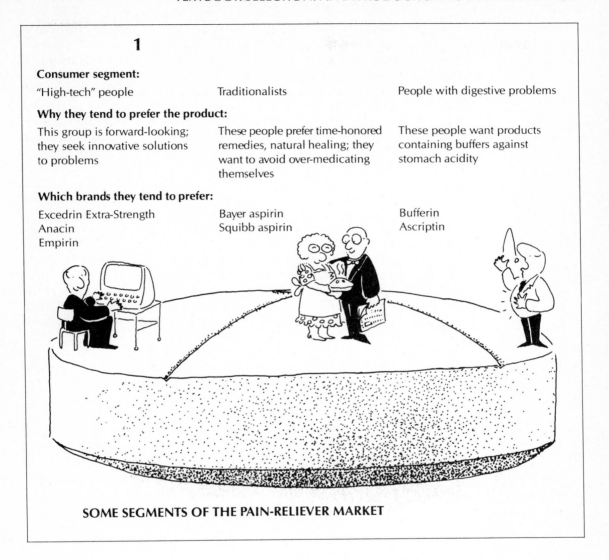

1

Consumer segment:

| "High-tech" people | Traditionalists | People with digestive problems |

Why they tend to prefer the product:

This group is forward-looking; they seek innovative solutions to problems

These people prefer time-honored remedies, natural healing; they want to avoid over-medicating themselves

These people want products containing buffers against stomach acidity

Which brands they tend to prefer:

Excedrin Extra-Strength
Anacin
Empirin

Bayer aspirin
Squibb aspirin

Bufferin
Ascriptin

SOME SEGMENTS OF THE PAIN-RELIEVER MARKET

Production-Oriented Marketing

Until the 1930s, many business executives viewed marketing simply as an offshoot of production. They concentrated on manufacturing and limited their marketing efforts to taking orders and shipping goods. Henry Ford, for example, focused on ways to produce his cars more quickly and cheaply, knowing that people would buy as many cars as he could manufacture.

Some modern companies still use production-oriented marketing, but it may be too limited for many of today's products. At least one highly successful Japanese company has learned this lesson the hard way. Sony, one of the most respected names in consumer electronics, began coasting in 1982.

After opening up the video-recorder market with its Betamax, Sony did not improve or refine its product. Furthermore the company kept its prices high, believing Sony's name and reputation for quality would keep sales up despite competition. Competitors developed better video recorders, which they sold for less than Sony's. In the second quarter of 1983, Sony paid for its arrogance: profits crashed by a stunning 57 percent.

Sales-Oriented Marketing

As production capacity increased in the United States in the late 1920s, business leaders began to realize that they would have to persuade people to buy all the goods they could make, and so they expanded their marketing activities. To stimulate demand for their products they spent more on advertising. They also began to develop trained sales forces that could seek out and sell to the thousands of potential customers across the country.

The rapid growth of radio in the late 1920s and the 1930s boosted the shift in emphasis from production to sales. For the first time a manufacturer was able to get a sales message to millions of people at one time. The power of radio advertising transformed scores of brand names, such as Jell-O and Lipton Tea, into household words. Of course, the advent of television in the late 1940s provided the most potent advertising medium of all. TV made it possible—and, by now, commonplace—for a company to introduce a new product to the entire nation overnight.

The Total Marketing Concept

Since World War II, it has become important to serve the consumer, and marketing has come to be equated with an approach known as **total marketing**. Total marketing added to the traditional definition of marketing the concept of *giving the buyer a say in what goods or services the firm sells*. In other words, the efforts of all the firm's departments should be coordinated to produce what the consumer wants. Today this approach may be necessary for survival in many consumer markets, where the capacity to produce goods often outstrips consumer demand and an increasing number of businesses are vying for a limited number of customers.

As part of the growing trend toward total marketing, there has been an increasing emphasis on the marketing function of getting information through market research. Essentially, **market research** attempts to find out:

1. *what products or services the consumer wants;*
2. *what forms, colors, packaging, price ranges, and retail outlets the consumer prefers;* and
3. *what types of advertising, public relations, and selling practices are most likely to appeal to the consumer.*

This information helps manufacturers decide what to make and how to sell it.

PROFILING THE CONSUMER

Efficient total marketing begins, of course, with getting an accurate picture of the consumers who are being targeted. For example, many of the people who grew up eating frozen TV dinners now wouldn't go near what

Convenience goods: products that are readily available, low-priced, and heavily advertised, and that consumers buy quickly and often. *Examples:* bread, razor blades, soft drinks.

Shopping goods: products for which a consumer spends a lot of time shopping, comparing prices, quality, and style. *Examples:* furniture, jewelry, appliances.

Specialty goods: products, usually brand items, that a consumer will make a particular effort to locate. *Examples:* perfume, high-fashion clothing.

TYPES OF CONSUMER GOODS

they consider junk food. They crave low-calorie gourmet fare instead, if sales volume is any indication. Stouffer's Lean Cuisine is so "hot" that factories churn out these 300-calorie-or-less delectables six days a week, but supermarkets can't stock them fast enough. The same goes for Campbell's Soup's Le Menu line of "Continental" classics, including chicken parmigiana with fettuccini Alfredo and green beans (500 calories).

Many of the consumers who want to dine on higher-quality prepared food are women in the work force (52 percent of adult females are employed outside the home). But according to a study of more than 13,000 supermarket consumers in Baltimore, Houston, Los Angeles and Minneapolis, nearly half of all shoppers today are men. And there's a swelling tide of singles who have more to spend on time-saving foods than their married counterparts and who want the convenience of cooking a single portion, plus a vast population of persons in the twenty-five–forty-five age range who earn $25,000 or more per year and have a special interest in low-calorie foods. Even allowing for some overlap among these groups, the market for gourmet-style convenience foods is considerable.

The success of the new lines of frozen dinners might not have come about had the frozen-food packagers not asked some important questions about the changing needs of American consumers. The questions they asked were

THE HIGH-TECH HORIZON

HIGH TECH AND TOTAL MARKETING

Few markets illustrate the importance of total marketing as clearly as the markets for high technology do. Bankruptcy has taught many high-tech companies this lesson the hard way. In the early days of computers, for example, most manufacturers followed a simple marketing scheme: they would produce a computer, put it on a shelf, and wait for it to sell—a classic example of production-oriented marketing. Before long most young firms realized they would have to teach their customers about the product, using sales-oriented marketing to inform customers why they should have the product. But recently, growing demand and technological advances have forced a shift to total marketing. More and more manufacturers now try to find out what customers' needs and specifications are, and respond to them directly. Computer firms that brought their marketing efforts to this stage quickly and efficiently are still in the business. The others are learning the details of bankruptcy law.

Robotics is a high-technology area that is only now making the transition from sales-oriented marketing to total marketing. U.S. robotics firms are still fighting an uphill battle in the sales-oriented marketing stage: many in both management and labor fear that robots will displace human labor, so the robotics firms are having to educate their customers about the potential of robots.

Meanwhile, as the benefits customers can reap from installing robots in their factories become more obvious, and as more capital-strong companies enter the market, robotics firms are starting to pay greater attention to customer preferences. General Electric, for example, assures customers that its intricate nationwide service system is equipped to cope with robotic ills. Cincinnati Milacron, another giant company that is entering robotics, is drawing customers by pointing to its longstanding reputation in the machine-tool industry. Smaller robotics firms, which are desperately trying to elbow their way into the market, offer even more satisfying advantages. Prab Robots has acquired new plants that will allow it to manufacture robots with a wide range of skills. Prab's approach is to assure buyers that they are getting a robot that does as much as needed—and no more. International Robomation/Intelligence, meanwhile, has managed to cut the typical $30,000–$50,000 price to less than $10,000. It may be the first robotics company to apply the ultimate concept of total marketing: selling a discount version.

Source: Philip Maher, "Coming to Grips with the Robot Market," *Industrial Marketing*, January 1982, pp. 93–98.

the same ones all marketers ask when they are trying to get their target consumers into sharp focus. First they want to know the facts about a given market. How many people might use a certain product? Where do they live? How old are they? How well educated are they? How much do they earn, and how do they spend their money? Such facts are the subject of **demography**—

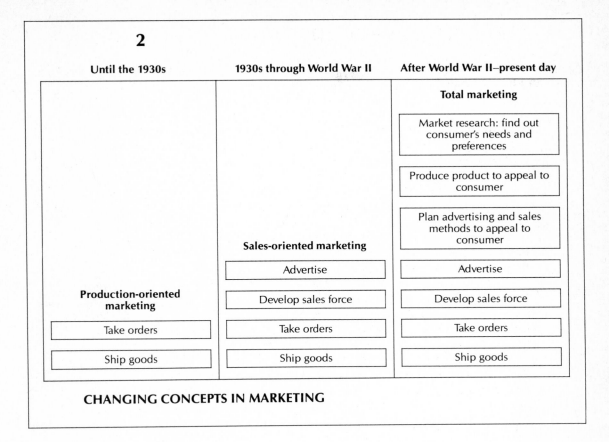

2

Until the 1930s	1930s through World War II	After World War II–present day
		Total marketing
		Market research: find out consumer's needs and preferences
		Produce product to appeal to consumer
		Plan advertising and sales methods to appeal to consumer
	Sales-oriented marketing	
		Advertise
Production-oriented marketing	Advertise	Develop sales force
	Develop sales force	Take orders
Take orders	Take orders	Ship goods
Ship goods	Ship goods	

CHANGING CONCEPTS IN MARKETING

the study of population—an area of research that is one of the marketing manager's basic sources of information.

The second kind of marketing information tells something about why consumers in a particular market behave the way they do. For example, why would a college professor and a crane operator who both make $25,000, live in the same city, and have the same size families tend to buy different kinds of motorcycles, cars, or types of food? To answer questions of this sort, marketing managers turn to **psychology**—*the study of individual behavior*—and **sociology**—*the study of group behavior.* From sociological research, marketing people acquire general information about ethnic, religious, cultural, social, and economic groups and the influences of these groups on people's behavior.

Who Are the Big Spenders?

Eighteen to Thirty-Four: The New Breed

At present, the "hottest" consumer category is the eighteen- to thirty-four age group, the TV generation with money to spend. They are the young marrieds who buy houses, cars, appliances—all the goods needed to run a

3

By comparing the proportion of each age group in the population in 1960 with the 1970, 1978, and 1982 proportions, you can trace the growth and decline of several important market segments.

In 1960, for instance, there were 20,415,823 young children and babies in the country. Twenty-two years later, there were only 17,404,275. What would this decline have meant for the baby-food, infant-toy, and disposable diaper industries?

On the other hand, the number of young adults swelled from 39,024,936 to 63,881,895, as the generation that started with the post-World War II baby boom came of age. What industries would benefit from this increase?

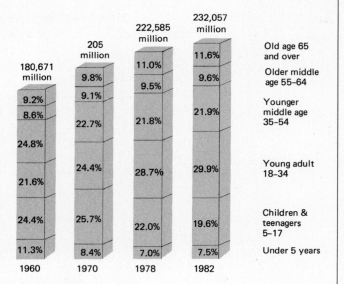

**THE CHANGING AGE MIX OF AMERICANS:
POPULATION CHANGES MEAN CHANGES IN MARKETS**

household and raise a family. They are also the young unmarrieds, a group that has grown steadily as an economic and social force.

Marketers view this generation, particularly the twenty-five- to thirty-four-year-olds, as a new breed of consumer, the most educated buying group in American history. Almost half have been to college, and one-quarter possess degrees. With one-third of the purchasing power of all U.S. consumers and a combined annual income of $335 billion, they dominate the American economy. The fact that many of the women in this group are in the work force contributes to their clout, creating new segments for products and services. Since young adults are enthusiastic TV viewers, they're particularly susceptible to automobile commercials. They are heavy consumers of time-saving devices, such as food processors, and items their parents viewed as luxuries, such as second cars, microwave ovens, color TVs and vacation packages. Sports figure importantly in their lives, as does physical fitness, a trend reflected in the emergence of such publications as *Jogging* magazine. Because they often buy on credit, their spending habits account for a 20 percent decline in the national savings rate and a rise in the total consumer debt. Yet the materialism of this group is balanced by what some marketers refer to as "earth values" (simple, inexpensive, and durable) and "feather values" (self-indulgent, showy, sensual, and expensive)—values that may be a combination of the anti-Establishment outlook of this group's teen years and a more Establishment-oriented way of thinking that developed as they matured.

Over Sixty-Five: The Fastest- Growing Age Group

In the early 1970s, marketers noticed that the over-sixty-five population was growing faster than other groups. Between 1970 and 1980, the membership of this group rose by 31.4 percent—from 20 million to 26.3 million people. Furthermore, the number of persons over the age of eighty-five increased 9.1 percent between 1980 and 1982, to 2.4 million. The American woman now has a life expectancy of eighty-four, the highest in human history.

Another significant characteristic of this group is their rising income. Increasing numbers of Americans are choosing to continue working past the conventional retirement age of sixty-five, and there is some pressure on Congress to provide higher Social Security payments to people who work longer. If employer-mandated retirement at a fixed age were to be prohibited by law, as Senator Claude Pepper of Florida has advocated, many more people might continue working full time well beyond age sixty-five. These people no longer have children living at home, many have paid off their home mortgages, and Medicare pays a large part of their medical bills. Therefore, even though their income after retirement may be limited to Social Security and a pension, a greater portion of it is available for travel, and for health- and personal-care products.

Where Do Consumers Live?

A company must consider geography when evaluating the sales potential of its goods and services, because climate and lifestyle have an impact upon what people buy. A clothing manufacturer, for example, needs to know if the market for heavy winter clothes is shrinking because people are moving to warmer areas. Similarly, a restaurant franchisor would want to sell more franchises in the flourishing states of Texas and the Southwest than in the depressed North Central states, whose population has declined in recent years. And an appliance manufacturer would be more likely to establish a new production facility in a region where the population is increasing, assuming other conditions (such as costs) are favorable.

Americans are among the most mobile people in the world. In 1980, according to the U.S. Census Bureau, about 17 percent of the population changed residence. This is down from 19 percent in 1970, and 21 percent in 1960, but it is still a significant number. Where are Americans moving? They are migrating to the Sunbelt—the area of the United States that stretches from Virginia south to Florida and west to California (one out of every ten Americans now lives in California). And they are leaving the farms and large cities for small metropolitan areas.

Growth of the Sunbelt

The population of the Sunbelt states has increased by 20 percent for the past decade, a growth rate that is down from a peak of 25 percent for the 1970s. Nevertheless, this region is now growing about 2 percent a year—twice the national average.

Many of the new Sunbelt residents are from the North Central states. Minnesota, for example, lost 900,000 people to the Sunbelt between 1980 and 1982, as a record number of businesses decided to take advantage of lower taxes and better access to markets. Northeastern states have been somewhat more stable, having lost only 108,000 between 1980 and 1982, mostly from Pennsylvania and New York.

Growth of Small Cities and Towns

Industrialized societies such as ours characteristically experience population growth in large urban centers and a decline in the number of people living in rural areas. Yet, according to the 1980 census, the rural population of the United States grew as fast as urban areas between 1970 and 1980, despite the fact that fewer people still live on farms. In fact, many areas that were once considered to be rural are now classified as urban.

What has happened is that people have forsaken the large metropolitan centers and gone to live in small towns and cities and in unincorporated areas near urban centers. The population of towns and unincorporated areas rose about 11 percent between 1970 and 1980, and cities having between 10,000 and 50,000 residents grew more than 30 percent.

New Urban Patterns

One result of the migration to less crowded population centers has been the development of sprawling metropolitan areas without a clearly defined center. As neighboring towns and small cities have expanded and people have taken up residence in between them, many of them have physically merged, and their combined population and density are great enough to warrant the area's designation as a metropolitan area. Houma-Thibodaux, Louisiana, is one such area. In 1983, Thibodaux had just 15,810 residents and Houma had 32,602, but the Census Bureau has classified the Houma-Thibodaux area, which includes people living in the area surrounding and between the two cities, as a metropolitan area because 176,876 people make their homes there.

In some cases, small cities have simply been overwhelmed by their suburbs as people, industry, and other institutions moved away from the center city. For example, Benton Harbor, Michigan (1983 population: 14,707), has been designated the center city of a new metropolitan area with a population of 171,276.

What do these changes mean? For one thing, we probably will not see the development of any more center cities surrounded by suburbs whose residents depend on the city for jobs, entertainment, services, and the like. In addition, there is no longer a sharp distinction, statistically speaking, between what is rural and what is urban: we are becoming a more urban people living in a less urban environment.

Other Consumer Characteristics: Education, Income, Buying Habits

Marketers are also interested in consumers' education levels: educated people tend to make more money, and they have a taste for certain types of goods such as foreign travel and hardcover books. Likewise, the incomes consumers earn are crucial to marketers' planning. Of particular interest is **disposable personal income,** the *personal income that a family is free to spend after taxes.* All families must spend a certain percentage of their disposable personal income on necessities such as food, clothing, and shelter.

But the higher a family's income, the more **discretionary income** it has—*income that can be spent on nonessentials,* such as entertainment, vacation travel, weekend homes, and restaurant dining.

Studying Consumer Behavior

Think for a minute about some of the products you've seen advertised or come across in stores and supermarkets—Perrier water, Campbell's alphabet soup, mink vests, down parkas, and so on. Who were these items created for? What would make someone buy a mink vest? The answers to these questions are the concern of consumer-behavior researchers. They want to know how people decide to spend money, credit, and time; what products, services, and ideas attract people and why; when, where, and how consumers purchase and use goods; and who or what influences decisions. Companies that invest substantial sums of money to develop and market new products use this kind of information to reduce the risks involved and increase the chances of success. Market researchers classify the buying public into two groups. The first group consists of *ultimate consumers* (everybody), whose purchases fall into three categories: personal use—say, buying yourself a tennis racket; family use—for example, buying toothpaste the whole family will like; and someone else's use—buying men's cologne for Father's Day. The second category of buyers is collectively referred to as *organizational consumers:* businesses, professional offices, nonprofit institutions, schools, and government. Psychological and sociological factors affect the buying habits of both groups, as we shall see.

The Psychology of Buying

There are many theories about what induces people to buy products. This section will focus on the ones most widely used by marketers.

CONSUMER DECISIONS One way to look at the psychology of buying is in terms of how consumers make decisions. A simple formula sums up the decision-making process nearly everyone goes through when making a purchase:

$$\text{Need} + \text{Ability to buy} + \begin{array}{l}\text{Attitudes toward brand names} \\ \text{under which product is sold}\end{array}$$
$$= \text{Choice}$$

Let's say you need a new car. Though a Chevrolet Malibu will satisfy the need, you opt for a costlier, more prestigious Mercedes-Benz, knowing that you can afford it, its quality will serve you well, and that the car will impress people because it's a widely accepted status symbol. Thus, your needs for quality and status as well as function have entered into your decision.

RATIONAL VS. EMOTIONAL MOTIVES Imagine that you are standing at a store counter buying a wool scarf. If someone approached and asked why you were buying it, you might say you want to keep your neck warm in cold weather. This would be a **rational motive**, *prompted by reason.* Rational motives relate to cost, dependability, and usefulness, elements marketers appeal to when selling goods.

- *Cost* invariably determines what consumers buy—if all other considerations, such as the quality of different brands and the consumer's ability to pay for any of these brands, are equal.
- *Dependability* is important to upper-middle-class consumers who will pay more for products that work better and last longer.
- *Usefulness* is important to consumers who buy products for functional purposes—the wool scarf, for example. By finding more uses for products, marketers can increase sales.

Emotional motives, on the other hand, *arise from feelings rather than reason.*

- *Sensory satisfaction*—pleasure for the sense of taste, touch, sight, and hearing—is a basic emotional drive. The food and beverage industries, for example, rely upon taste appeal to sell products.
- *Fear,* rooted in the instinct for self-preservation, motivates people to take care of themselves and to avoid unnecessary risks. Life, health, fire and theft insurance, health foods, and safety devices for cars are sold on the basis of fear.
- *Pride* in one's position, home, family, or appearance sells products that enhance the consumer's image.
- *Sociability,* the desire to be with other people, helps market soft drinks, restaurants, and resorts.
- *Emulation*—the desire to imitate others—is another motive marketers rely on. People like to identify with movie stars, athletes, and other celebrities, such as the ones featured in many of the TV ads for the American Express Card.

Rational and emotional motives usually overlap because consumers have multiple motives for buying something. A wool scarf, for example, will keep you warm, but it might also appeal to your senses of sight and touch.

Psychographics: The Lifestyle Profile

Psychographics is a relatively new specialty that *characterizes consumers in terms of their behavior and attitudes.* A psychographic profile might draw hundreds of responses to statements about activities, interests, opinions, and social roles that help peg an individual's lifestyle. For example, a person who agrees with statements such as "I shop a lot for discounts," "I usually watch the advertisements for sales," and "A person can save a lot of money shopping around for bargains," would fall into the category of Price-Conscious Consumer. Heavy users of margarine and other forms of shortening might like housekeeping, be child-oriented, and fit into a Homebody category. Psychographic profiles identify market segments, target new products and reposition existing ones, develop media guidelines, and aid marketers in packaging design and product formulation.

Business Buyers: A Different Breed

Most of this chapter has been devoted to individual consumers because of their diverse characteristics and wide range of buying motives. But business buyers and markets are equally important to the economy. *Marketing to business,* or **industrial marketing**, has some unique characteristics. Look at the number of buyers, for example: whereas Procter & Gamble and Colgate-Palmolive compete to sell their products to millions of individual consumers, the most profitable market for the computers produced by IBM and Apple Computer Inc. is made up of a much smaller number of large businesses. Therefore industrial marketers will use somewhat different approaches from the ones used to market consumer goods.

Assume that Citibank, a major banking institution with branches throughout the New York metropolitan area, announced that it was going to overhaul its entire computer system. IBM and Apple both want to sell their systems to Citibank. What marketing methods will they use? What approaches will they take? In industrial marketing, products or services are generally sold for functional reasons rather than by brand name or attractiveness, because of their considerable cost and the need to tailor them to fit the customer's needs. The motivation for acquiring technical business equipment or services is usually rational, based on its usefulness to the buyer. Businesses try to avoid investing in unnecessary services or products, especially when costs may total many thousands, or even millions, of dollars. Emotional motives do not heavily influence business buyers.

The salesperson of a business service or product requires a technical background; he or she must be prepared to sell on the basis of cost and reliability. The customer is an employee of a business firm, government agency, or nonprofit institution, who is likely to be knowledgeable about the products or services being considered. The purchasing agent at Citibank, for example, will be capable of weighing the comparative advantages of one computer system over another. Moreover, the business buyer possesses negotiating skills that ordinary consumers lack. Because huge investments are involved, the business buyer will require assurance that the marketer understands the company's rational and technical needs. The marketer must provide this assurance. For instance, at Citibank, the marketer must guarantee the buyer that a computer system will be installed on schedule at the agreed price, and that service will be prompt and competent if anything goes wrong.

Impulse buying rarely occurs in business marketing, because the purchase time generally takes months, allowing for approvals, necessary modifications to the product, and delivery. Yet, even though buying services or equipment for business is a rational process, the personal relationship between buyer and seller can influence sales as surely as it influences the sale of consumer products. Creating and maintaining such relationships is part of the marketing person's job.

THE MARKETING MIX: THE FOUR Ps

The variety of smaller market segments within the consumer and business market is enormous, and targeting the correct one is half the marketing battle. In any total marketing program the other half of the battle is determining the **marketing mix**, *the blend of product, price, promotion, and place (or distribution) that satisfies the demands of the chosen market segment.* The strategies that succeed generally blend *the four Ps*—as the marketing mix is commonly called—to develop the most lucrative market. Let's look at each of the four Ps in turn.

Product   A businessperson's first marketing decision concerns the products or services that will attract customers in the target market. The key is to determine consumers' needs and wants and translate them into desirable products and services. Rising crime rates, for example, have created a target market among small businesses for a growing number of security services. Similarly, the rapid increase in the number of working women has inspired clothing manufacturers to include more high-priced women's suits in their overall product mix: many women have discovered they need to "dress for success" just as men do.

Changing conditions require the continuous re-evaluation of product lines. Procter & Gamble, for example, is the largest consumer packaged-goods company in America. It sells Ivory soap, Tide detergent, Pampers disposable diapers, and Charmin toilet tissue, to name only a few of its successful products. But success can be dangerous. Many of the markets in which P&G products dominate are no longer growing, and some of their products are losing their market share in increasingly crowded markets. To ensure continued profit growth, P&G has expanded into new territories—soft drinks, fruit juices, and drugs.

Price   Having made the basic decisions about the product line, the marketing manager must decide how the company should price its products. Sometimes low prices will maximize profits. Supermarkets have used this tactic successfully on two levels. Most offer unbranded, so-called *generic* products at the lowest price and offer their own brand, usually at a slightly higher price, in addition to the still-higher-price commercial brands. On the other hand, the desirability of some products depends on a high-quality image, which a high price helps to confer. The factors that enter into decisions about both product line and pricing will be discussed in Chapter 10.

Promotion   Very often the most important decision a marketing manager makes is how the manufacturer should inform prospective customers about its products. This involves promotion, which includes the sales approach. Some marketing strategists, like those at Avon Products, may decide to emphasize direct selling and spend most of their promotion dollars to train and pay salespeople. Others, like producers of soap and headache remedies, promote their products through advertising, primarily on television. Department stores also spend heavily on advertising, but they choose newspapers as the most effective medium. The alternatives are many and the choice may determine the success of a marketing effort. We'll discuss promotion in Chapter 11.

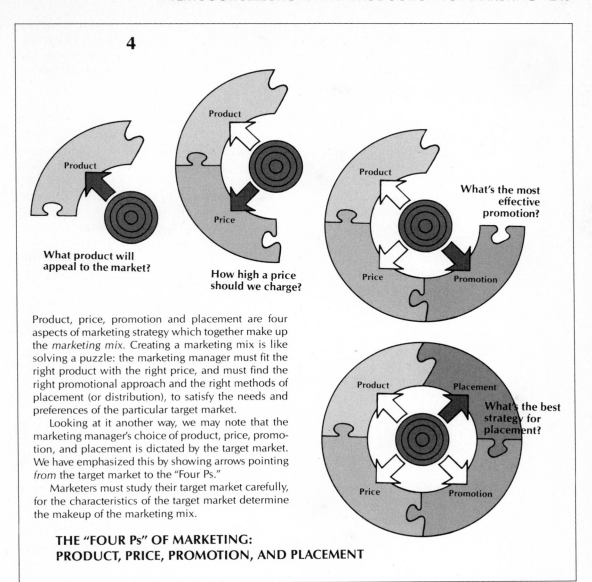

4

What product will
appeal to the market?

How high a price
should we charge?

What's the most
effective
promotion?

What's the best
strategy for
placement?

Product, price, promotion and placement are four
aspects of marketing strategy which together make up
the *marketing mix*. Creating a marketing mix is like
solving a puzzle: the marketing manager must fit the
right product with the right price, and must find the
right promotional approach and the right methods of
placement (or distribution), to satisfy the needs and
preferences of the particular target market.

Looking at it another way, we may note that the
marketing manager's choice of product, price, promotion, and placement is dictated by the target market.
We have emphasized this by showing arrows pointing
from the target market to the "Four Ps."

Marketers must study their target market carefully,
for the characteristics of the target market determine
the makeup of the marketing mix.

**THE "FOUR Ps" OF MARKETING:
PRODUCT, PRICE, PROMOTION, AND PLACEMENT**

Place   The fourth element in the marketing mix is place (or distribution): how
the manufacturer gets its products to the customers. Transportation is the
major factor here, but place also entails decisions about distribution outlets.
Tupperware, for example, distributes directly to the consumer through its
party approach. Most clothing companies, on the other hand, sell to retailers,
who resell to consumers. Some manufacturers employ multiple placement
systems. Thus Whirlpool Corporation sells the Whirlpool brand of appliances to distributors for sale to dealers, and it also makes the Kenmore
brand, which it ships directly to Sears Roebuck and Company. Sears itself

sells through its stores and by catalogue. HARTMARX makes suits and sportswear for independent retailers, but also makes them available to consumers through its own retail stores, including Wallach's and Baskin. In short, there are many ways of distributing goods. We'll discuss them further in Chapter 12.

Putting It All Together

The trick in marketing is to figure out a clever way to combine the four Ps in such a manner as to increase profits—and gain a larger share of the market. The right marketing mix is largely responsible for Noxell Corporation's stunning growth in the recession-ravaged cosmetics field in recent years. While Revlon and other luxury cosmetic firms gasped for air in the late 1970s and early 1980s, Noxell's sales soared and so did its profits. Its secret was keen manipulation of the four Ps. Noxell was quick to notice that demand for inexpensive, no-nonsense cosmetics rose as more women entered the work force. It had been successfully selling Noxzema face creams to that market for years and had developed a line of low-priced cosmetics in the 1960s, so the decision was made to gear up promotion. Advertising now consumes some 20 percent of Noxell's sales, but who hasn't heard of its Cover Girl line? But no matter how heavily cosmetics are advertised, they, like other frequently purchased items, must be widely available. Knowing this, Noxell managed to place Cover Girl not only in drugstores but in supermarkets as well. The combination of good placement, low price, high recognition, and good product allowed Noxell to grow during a difficult period when many firms were merely seeking creative ways to cut losses.

CHAPTER REVIEW

Many companies are learning that they need not only good products but also marketing skills in order to succeed. They must be able to identify consumer needs and to satisfy them in a mutually beneficial manner. Those people who want a given product and can buy it constitute its market.

The process of marketing includes all the activities by which goods and services move from the producer to the consumer. There are eight basic marketing functions: buying, selling, transporting, storing, financing, risk bearing, standardization and grading, and securing information.

Marketing has changed radically over the past half-century. At one time most firms were production oriented and restricted marketing activities primarily to taking orders and shipping goods. Then came sales-oriented marketing, which emphasized selling. Since World War II, however, most large firms have shifted to a consumer-oriented approach known as the total marketing concept, which has relied increasingly on market research. This approach is now also being used in industry.

Population statistics are a basic marketing tool. They can indicate with reasonable accuracy how many people there are, how old they are, what they earn, how they spend their money, and where they live.

The psychology of buying looks at consumer decision making in terms of rational and emotional motives. Rational factors include cost, dependability, and usefulness. Emotional factors are satisfaction of the senses, fear, pride, sociability, and emulation. Both types of motive often enter into the decision to buy a product or service.

Marketers use psychographics to uncover characteristics that demographic and sociological surveys can't isolate—to draw profiles of individual consumers and decide whether they're likely to want to use particular products.

Industrial buyers form a different market from individual consumers with respect to motivation, product, sales personnel, customer, and purchase time. Technical and rational considerations predominate with industrial buyers, but they need assurances from the marketer that the company will do the job it promises.

The marketing manager tries to develop a marketing mix that will have the greatest appeal to the target market. The marketing mix consists of four elements, the so-called four Ps: product, promotion, price, and placement.

KEY WORDS

marketing
market
market segment
total marketing
market research
demography
psychology
sociology

disposable personal income
discretionary income
rational motive
emotional motive
psychographics
industrial marketing
marketing mix

REVIEW QUESTIONS

1. Define marketing and explain why it is important to the American economy.
2. How does the total marketing concept differ from the approaches that it replaces: product-oriented and sales-oriented marketing?
3. Why is it important for businesses to identify target markets for their products?
4. What is the fastest-growing age group in the nation today? Describe their overall consumer behavior.
5. What is the difference between disposable personal income and discretionary income?
6. List several rational motives and emotional motives for buying.
7. What have been the major geographic shifts of the past decade and what are their implications for marketing?
8. How does industrial buying differ from consumer buying?
9. What are the four Ps of marketing, which make up the marketing mix?

part 4 ‖ READING ESSAYS AND ARTICLES

INTRODUCTION: HOW TO READ AN ESSAY

In the first two parts to this textbook, the practice essays at the end of each chapter provided the opportunity to apply analytical skills to works longer than a single paragraph or two. However, perhaps a few words need to be devoted to establishing the worth of reading long works in the first place. Why is the essay the staple of reading assignments in composition and reading courses? Before the invention of the copying machine, anthologies of nonfiction prose were rare. Students in freshman English normally were assigned entire texts to read; these served as the basis for both reading and writing assignments. The copying machine, on the other hand, made possible the proliferation of anthologies—collections of essays, articles, and short stories. The result has been that students can be introduced to a much wider variety of subjects and a more diverse assortment of styles and forms than was possible before. The essay, after all, can be read in one sitting. Its relatively short length means that a class can discuss it thoroughly in one or two sessions. And, for the purposes of this book, analytical questions concerning a selection of only three or four pages are less taxing than would be the case if students were assigned an entire book to read. Although the anthology has been criticized for offering the "snippet," or "cut-and-paste," approach to reading, the anthology does have the advantage of giving its readers suggestions for further reading, thereby enabling a student who has enjoyed a short passage or essay by a particular writer to read the work from which it was extracted in its entirety.

For most students, the first questions are: Why should I read this essay? What am I going to get out of it? Aside from the fact that the essay is required reading, the answer is that you will get plenty out of it if you give it the proper attention and time to ensure that you understand its component parts as thoroughly as possible. The truism that practice makes perfect applies here: The more practice you get in careful, attentive reading, the more competent you will become. There is no advantage to *not* reading, and students who seldom read on their own, or who try to zip through their assigned readings (hoping that the instructor will not call on them during class discussion), are missing an important part of the intellectual experience. When you begin to read an essay, you might think of yourself as a detective who is searching for clues into its meaning, looking closely at its difficult parts as though through a magnifying glass, putting the pieces of the puzzle together until they all fit and you have a thorough understanding and appreciation of the whole.

Before we look at the specific questions you should bear in mind as you read, let us examine the characteristics of the essay. If you consider the paragraph to be an essay in miniature—as it has often been described—then the essay must exemplify the techniques and characteristics which you have already studied in Part 1. The word *essay* derives from the French—the noun *essai,* and the verb *essayer* meaning "to attempt"—and the essay form reflects this etymology. An *essay* is a sustained piece of prose in which the author attempts to set down significant ideas, describe experiences, convey information, analyze issues, or set forth a proposition. Like the paragraph, a well-written essay has a main idea called a *thesis,* it has a direction, and it has adequate development, unity, and coherence. Unlike the paragraph, however, which is limited in scope due to its brevity, the essay is more flexible and therefore subject to greater variation in length, organization, language, and methods of development. Furthermore, except in student writing assignments or textbooks like this one, paragraphs seldom occur alone, since one paragraph usually is not sufficient to explain a complex idea. In an essay, the paragraph serves to move the author's ideas forward, and each paragraph relates logically to the others.

The forms an essay may take are numerous. It may be a personal narrative recounting an incident, a description of a scene or of a feeling or emotion, a presentation of scientific information, a personal confession of past errors, an emotional plea to resolve a controversy, or an examination of a problem and its repercussions. The essay form is eminently adaptable. An essay may represent any of the four modes of discourse—narration, description, exposition, or persuasion—whether singly or in combination, although usually one mode predominates. And an essay may be any length. It may be a 300-word theme that you write for your composition class, or it may be 100 pages or more. Essays written by professional writers typically run between 500 and 5,000 words in length, but its length clearly is unimportant in terms of defining its form. If you think back to the practice essays in Parts 1 and 2, you can easily see that the essay is a remarkably diverse instrument for communicating ideas.

Like the paragraph, the essay typically is divided into three parts: the beginning (the introduction), the middle (the body or supporting paragraphs), and the end (the conclusion). The main idea—comparable to the topic sentence of a paragraph—is expressed in a *thesis statement,* which may appear anywhere in the essay, though it is most often found in the beginning paragraphs. The thesis is the author's central proposition, the idea he or she wants to convey. Just as you learned to do for paragraphs, ask yourself these two questions: What is the subject? What does the writer want me to understand about this subject? The answer to the second question represents the controlling idea.

The most important skill needed for reading anything, whether a paragraph or an essay, is to find the main idea. Given its diversity of forms, the essay poses greater problems for students. Where should you look? Some writers announce the main idea in the first sentence. Others save it for the end, making the supporting paragraphs lead up to a combined thesis and conclusion. Still other writers do not state the thesis at all, preferring to let the supporting paragraphs reveal the main idea. This method is called the *implied thesis*. Most often, however, essays follow this classic pattern: The writer introduces the general subject in the opening paragraphs (typically the first two or three), thereby orienting the reader to the topic at hand. Following this introductory portion, the writer presents the thesis statement. Some textbooks call this approach the "funnel" pattern. But don't expect bells and whistles to alert you to the thesis statement. Few writers announce that a particular sentence is meant to represent the main idea. Those two useful questions presented in the introduction to this text can be dusted off and tried again: What is the subject? And, what does the writer want me to understand about that subject?

Once you have established what the thesis statement is, you can proceed to separate the essay into its component parts, determining where the introduction ends and the body begins, and where the body gives way to the conclusion. Sometimes, making a brief outline of the tripartite division helps you see the overall structure more clearly, just as an aerial view of a city reveals its layout more clearly than does a ground-level view.

The body portion of the essay develops and supports the thesis by whatever methods of development the writer thinks are appropriate. A good essay is characterized by adequate development. Not only should the writer fully explore the implications of the proposition, but he or she should also anticipate and answer questions or opposing arguments if the purpose of the essay is to convince or to defend a controversial idea. Finally, a well-constructed essay exhibits the same principles of unity and coherence that you studied in Chapters 3 and 4. Principal methods used by writers to ensure singleness of purpose and clarity of organization are: transitions, both within as well as between paragraphs; parallel phrases, clauses, or sentences; and repetitions of key words and phrases. The careful writer also orders the paragraphs logically, typically using emphatic (least important to most important) order. The conclusion may be a summary, a restatement of main ideas, a logical deduction to be drawn from the evidence cited, a recommendation, a warning for the future, or a challenge. Again, the specific form depends on the writer's purpose, audience, and subject.

Armed with this overview of the essay form, you now can turn to the problem of how to tackle assigned readings. For each essay assignment, plan to spend at least an hour or two preparing (more if the piece is long or complex). Read the essay through once without stopping. Use a pencil to quickly mark any sentences or paragraphs that you could not grasp readily during this first cursory reading, or any words that were not part of your active reading vocabulary. (These are words which, although you may have seen them in print or perhaps heard them before, you cannot provide good definitions in your own words.) After the first reading, read the essay again —slowly and carefully—and perhaps even a third time to put the pieces together. Of course, you should look up those troublesome words on the later readings. While you are reading, keep the questions at the end of this section in mind, and when you have completed your final reading, review the questions once more, making sure that you can provide answers to them. If something eludes you, make a note of it so you can raise the point in class discussion. In this way, you will ensure your success in answering the questions which accompany each selection. Eventually, the process will become automatic to you, and you won't have to refer to the questions each time you have an assignment.

1. Who is the author? In most anthologies, as in this text, a brief headnote identifies the writer and provides some biographical information. Knowing about the author is useful for determining the writer's audience and his or her purpose in writing.

2. The second question follows from the first. Who is the writer writing for? Is the audience the general reading public or does the level of vocabulary or the inclusion of special terms suggest that the writer is appealing to a narrower group, one which may have specialized knowledge? If the latter is the case, is it possible, nevertheless, to understand the main ideas, even if some of the information is too technical?

3. What seems to be the writer's *purpose*? Here, a quick review of the *modes of discourse* in Chapter 1 might help. Besides the main purpose, does the writer appear to have secondary purposes in mind as well? If so, what are they?

4. Most crucial, what is the *thesis*? Where is it located? If its placement is unusual (say, at the end of the essay), is there a reason? Once you have located the thesis, can you paraphrase it?

5. What are the main parts of the selection? At what point does the writer stop introducing and begin the body or supporting paragraphs? Where does the body end and the conclusion begin? Can you outline the essay's main parts? An overview of the essay will help you see the progression of ideas more clearly.

6. Since we read to learn new information, what are we meant to learn? What are the main ideas of the essay? What specifically does the writer want us to understand about the subject at hand? Once you have located the thesis, you can isolate the supporting ideas that bolster the thesis or main argument. For all of the essays in Part 4, the first exercise tests your comprehension, these questions having been derived from the body of the essay. To test how well you understood the main ideas, follow the directions and do not refer to the selection as you answer them.

7. What *inferences* are we meant to draw from the main ideas? What conclusions? What has the piece done to educate you about the world? How does the information accord with what you already know? How are you better off for having read it?

8. Aside from unfamiliar words which you should add to your vocabulary notebook, are there any unusual words? Any metaphors or similes? Any evocative words? How does the author's choice of words suit the purpose, the audience, and the content?

Before you go off on your own and jump into the readings in this section, you may find it useful to examine a classic essay according to the preceding discussion of the essay form. "The Spider and the Wasp" by Alexander Petrunkevitch is a much-reprinted essay which presents a fascinating look at one little part of the insect world: the deadly confrontation between the tarantula and its enemy, the digger wasp. After you finish reading it, we will return to the eight questions posed above and attempt to arrive at some answers.

SAMPLE ESSAY

The Spider and the Wasp
Alexander Petrunkevitch

Alexander Petrunkevitch was born in Russia in 1875, and was educated in Moscow and later at the University of Freiberg, Germany. An authority on American spiders, he taught at Harvard, Yale, and Indiana universities, in addition to being active as a translator and author on Russian subjects.

1   In the feeding and safeguarding of their progeny the insects and spiders exhibit some interesting analogies to reasoning and some crass examples of blind instinct. The case I propose to describe here is that of the tarantula spiders and their arch-enemy, the digger wasps of the genus Pepsis. It is a classic example of what looks like intelligence pitted against instinct—a strange situation in which the victim, though fully able to defend itself, submits unwittingly to its destruction.

2   Most tarantulas live in the tropics, but several species occur in the temperate zone and a few are common in the southern U.S. Some varieties are large and have powerful fangs with which they can inflict a deep wound. These formidable looking spiders do not, however, attack man; you can hold one in your hand, if you are gentle, without being bitten. Their bite is dangerous only to insects and small mammals such as mice; for a man it is no worse than a hornet's sting.

3   Tarantulas customarily live in deep cylindrical burrows, from which they emerge at dusk and into which they retire at dawn. Mature males wander about after dark in search of females and occasionally stray into houses. After mating, the male dies in a few weeks, but a female lives much longer and can mate several years in succession. In a Paris museum is a tropical specimen which is said to have been living in captivity for 25 years.

4   A fertilized female tarantula lays from 200 to 400 eggs at a time; thus it is possible for a single tarantula to produce several thousand young. She takes no care of them beyond weaving a cocoon of silk to enclose the eggs. After they hatch, the young walk away, find convenient places in which to dig their burrows and spend the rest of their lives in solitude. Tarantulas feed mostly on insects and millepedes. Once their appetite is appeased, they digest the food for several days before eating again. Their sight is poor, being

limited to sensing a change in the intensity of light and to the perception of moving objects. They apparently have little or no sense of hearing, for a hungry tarantula will pay no attention to a loudly chirping cricket placed in its cage unless the insect happens to touch one of its legs.

5   But all spiders, and especially hairy ones, have an extremely delicate sense of touch. Laboratory experiments prove that tarantulas can distinguish three types of touch: pressure against the body wall, stroking of the body hair and riffling of certain very fine hairs on the legs called trichobothria. Pressure against the body, by a finger or the end of a pencil, causes the tarantula to move off slowly for a short distance. The touch excites no defensive response unless the approach is from above where the spider can see the motion, in which case it rises on its hind legs, lifts its front legs, opens its fangs and holds this threatening posture as long as the object continues to move. When the motion stops, the spider drops back to the ground, remains quiet for a few seconds and then moves slowly away.

6   The entire body of a tarantula, especially its legs, is thickly clothed with hair. Some of it is short and woolly, some long and stiff. Touching this body hair produces one of two distinct reactions. When the spider is hungry, it responds with an immediate and swift attack. At the touch of a cricket's antennae the tarantula seizes the insect so swiftly that a motion picture taken at the rate of 64 frames per second shows only the result and not the process of capture. But when the spider is not hungry, the stimulation of its hairs merely causes it to shake the touched limb. An insect can walk under its hairy belly unharmed.

7   The trichobothria, very fine hairs growing from disklike membranes on the legs, were once thought to be the spider's hearing organs, but we now know that they have nothing to do with sound. They are sensitive only to air movement. A light breeze makes them vibrate slowly without disturbing the common hair. When one blows gently on the trichobothria, the tarantula reacts with a quick jerk of its four front legs. If the front and hind legs are stimulated at the same time, the spider makes a sudden jump. This reaction is quite independent of the state of its appetite.

8   These three tactile responses—to pressure on the body wall, to moving of the common hair and to flexing of the trichobothria—are so different from one another that there is no possibility of confusing them. They serve the tarantula adequately for most of its needs and enable it to avoid most annoyances and dangers. But they fail the spider completely when it meets its deadly enemy, the digger wasp Pepsis.

9   These solitary wasps are beautiful and formidable creatures. Most species are either a deep shiny blue all over, or deep blue with rusty wings. The largest have a wing span of about four inches. They live on nectar. When excited, they give off a pungent odor—a warning that they are ready to attack. The sting is much worse than that of a bee or common wasp, and the pain and swelling last longer. In the adult stage the wasp lives only a few months. The female produces but a few eggs, one at a time at intervals of two or three days. For each egg the mother must provide one adult tarantula, alive but paralyzed. The tarantula must be of the correct species to

nourish the larva. The mother wasp attaches the egg to the paralyzed spider's abdomen. Upon hatching from the egg, the larva is many hundreds of times smaller than its living but helpless victim. It eats no other food and drinks no water. By the time it has finished its single gargantuan meal and become ready for wasphood, nothing remains of the tarantula but its indigestible chitinous skeleton.

10 The mother wasp goes tarantula-hunting when the egg in her ovary is almost ready to be laid. Flying low over the ground late on a sunny afternoon, the wasp looks for its victim or for the mouth of a tarantula burrow, a round hole edged by a bit of silk. The sex of the spider makes no difference, but the mother is highly discriminating as to species. Each species of Pepsis requires a certain species of tarantula, and the wasp will not attack the wrong species. In a cage with a tarantula which is not its normal prey the wasp avoids the spider, and is usually killed by it in the night.

11 Yet when a wasp finds the correct species, it is the other way about. To identify the species the wasp apparently must explore the spider with her antennae. The tarantula shows an amazing tolerance to this exploration. The wasp crawls under it and walks over it without evoking any hostile response. The molestation is so great and so persistent that the tarantula often rises on all eight legs, as if it were on stilts. It may stand this way for several minutes. Meanwhile the wasp, having satisfied itself that the victim is of the right species, moves off a few inches to dig the spider's grave. Working vigorously with legs and jaws, it excavates a hole 8 to 10 inches deep with a diameter slightly larger than the spider's girth. Now and again the wasp pops out of the hole to make sure that the spider is still there.

12 When the grave is finished, the wasp returns to the tarantula to complete her ghastly enterprise. First she feels it all over once more with her antennae. Then her behavior becomes more aggressive. She bends her abdomen, protruding her sting, and searches for the soft membrane at the point where the spider's leg joins its body—the only spot where she can penetrate the horny skeleton. From time to time, as the exasperated spider slowly shifts ground, the wasp turns on her back and slides along with the aid of her wings, trying to get under the tarantula for a shot at the vital spot. During all this maneuvering, which can last for several minutes, the tarantula makes no move to save itself. Finally the wasp corners it against some obstruction and grasps one of its legs in her powerful jaws. Now at last the harassed spider tries a desperate but vain defense. The two contestants roll over and over on the ground. It is a terrifying sight and the outcome is always the same. The wasp finally manages to thrust her sting into the soft spot and holds it there for a few seconds while she pumps in the poison. Almost immediately the tarantula falls paralyzed on its back. Its legs stop twitching; its heart stops beating. Yet it is not dead, as is shown by the fact that if taken from the wasp it can be restored to some sensitivity by being kept in a moist chamber for several months.

13 After paralyzing the tarantula, the wasp cleans herself by dragging her body along the ground and rubbing her feet, sucks the drop of blood oozing from the wound in the spider's abdomen, then grabs a leg of the flabby,

helpless animal in her jaws and drags it down to the bottom of the grave. She stays there for many minutes, sometimes for several hours, and what she does all that time in the dark we do not know. Eventually she lays her egg and attaches it to the side of the spider's abdomen with a sticky secretion. Then she emerges, fills the grave with soil carried bit by bit in her jaws, and finally tramples the ground all around to hide any trace of the grave from prowlers. Then she flies away, leaving her descendant safely started in life.

14   In all this the behavior of the wasp evidently is qualitatively different from that of the spider. The wasp acts like an intelligent animal. This is not to say that instinct plays no part or that she reasons as man does. But her actions are to the point; they are not automatic and can be modified to fit the situation. We do not know for certain how she identifies the tarantula—probably it is by some olfactory or chemo-tactile sense—but she does it purposefully and does not blindly tackle a wrong species.

15   On the other hand, the tarantula's behavior shows only confusion. Evidently the wasp's pawing gives it no pleasure, for it tries to move away. That the wasp is not simulating sexual stimulation is certain, because male and female tarantulas react in the same way to its advances. That the spider is not anesthetized by some odorless secretion is easily shown by blowing lightly at the tarantula and making it jump suddenly. What, then, makes the tarantula behave as stupidly as it does?

16   No clear, simple answer is available. Possibly the stimulation by the wasp's antennae is masked by a heavier pressure on the spider's body, so that it reacts as when prodded by a pencil. But the explanation may be much more complex. Initiative in attack is not in the nature of tarantulas; most species fight only when cornered so that escape is impossible. Their inherited patterns of behavior apparently prompt them to avoid problems rather than attack them. For example, spiders always weave their webs in three dimensions, and when a spider finds that there is insufficient space to attach certain threads in the third dimension, it leaves the place and seeks another, instead of finishing the web in a single plane. This urge to escape seems to arise under all circumstances, in all phases of life and to take the place of reasoning. For a spider to change the pattern of its web is as impossible as for an inexperienced man to build a bridge across a chasm obstructing his way.

17   In a way the instinctive urge to escape is not only easier but often more efficient than reasoning. The tarantula does exactly what is most efficient in all cases except in an encounter with a ruthless and determined attacker dependent for the existence of her own species on killing as many tarantulas as she can lay eggs. Perhaps in this case the spider follows its usual pattern of trying to escape, instead of seizing and killing the wasp, because it is not aware of its danger. In any case, the survival of the tarantula species as a whole is protected by the fact that the spider is much more fertile than the wasp.

1. Petrunkevitch is identified in the biographical headnote as an expert on spiders (an arachnologist). Even though he is a scientist, his style is sufficiently clear that even the technical terms are understandable. We

can also assume, for the time being, that his report will be a scientific account, one that is objective and impartial in the presentation of ideas.

2. His audience appears to be the general reader, not other scientists. The information about the spider and the digger wasp is described in specific terms but the language is not formidable. For example, in paragraph 7 Petrunkevitch uses a technical term, trichobothria, to describe the very fine hairs on the tarantula's legs, yet he is careful to define this term immediately ("very fine hairs growing from disklike membranes on the legs"). Since this is a term that a fellow spider expert would probably know, the inclusion of the contextual definition suggests that Petrunkevitch has a wider audience in mind. Furthermore, the process described in the body of the essay, the digger wasp's victimization of the tarantula, would be common knowledge to an expert.

3. Petrunkevitch appears to have two purposes. The primary one is to show the way in which the behavior of these two species presents a classic confrontation between reasoning and instinct. His secondary purpose (essential if we are to understand the main ideas in the essay) is to explain the reproductive habits of both species. Both purposes are expository, though there are strong descriptive elements included, especially in paragraphs 6 and 7.

4. Paragraph 1 nicely demonstrates the "funnel" pattern mentioned earlier. Look again at the progression of the three sentences that comprise this paragraph. Sentence 1 orients us to the general subject—the contrast between intelligence and instinct in the insect world. In addition, he includes the specific activities that will demonstrate this conflict—the feeding and safeguarding of their progeny (offspring). Sentence 2 introduces the two species he will present as his "case," and the third sentence states his point of view, that their confrontation is a strange one. Sentence 3 also reiterates that the conflict is between reasoning and instinct. Since the thesis is embodied by all three sentences, we might suggest something like this as a paraphrase:

> The strange confrontation between the tarantula and its enemy, the digger wasp, is a classic example of intelligence versus blind instinct.

Thus, the introduction accomplishes three things: It succinctly orients us to the subject, it reveals the purpose, and it includes the subject and the controlling idea.

5. Here is a schematic outline of the essay's main parts:

> Introduction [paragraph 1]
> Body [2–15]
> Conclusion [16–17]

The middle portion can be subdivided further, as follows:

> Explanation and description of tarantulas [2–8]
> Explanation and description of the digger wasp [9–10]

More detailed explanation of the process mentioned in paragraph 9 [11–13]

Analysis of the reasons and significance of these two species' behavior [14–15]

On our first reading, we might think that the whole discussion about the spider's sense of touch, the hair that covers its body, and the three kinds of tactile responses is only an irrelevant or trivial detail. But the explanation of the process by which the digger wasp nourishes her larva depends on this crucial information, the main point being that the tarantula behaves uncharacteristically ("stupidly," Petrunkevitch says), doing nothing to defend itself against the wasp's molestation. In emphasizing the tarantula's sensitive hairs and tactile responses, Petrunkevitch makes the wasp's pawing all the more gruesome.

6. The answer to these questions should be obvious at this point. Petrunkevitch dramatically supports the thesis by his precise description of the digger wasp's search for food, her method of determining the appropriateness of the particular species of tarantula, and so forth. We also learn something else significant—that the breeding habits and numbers of offspring are vastly different for these two species. The large number of eggs produced by the female tarantula contrasted with the digger wasp's relatively small output suggests that the tarantula is a suitable victim (and food source) for the digger wasp—suitable because this provides a way in which the numbers of tarantulas are kept in check. Finally, and more important, Petrunkevitch's explanation about why the tarantula behaves so stupidly (at least from the human point of view) suggests an implicit definition of intelligence. The digger wasp acts "intelligently" because her actions are purposeful; she can also modify her actions (i.e., abandon her molestation of an intended victim if she has chosen the wrong species of tarantula). The tarantula behaves "stupidly" because it is not in the nature of spiders to attack and because the species operates solely from instinct (as evidenced by its inability to change the pattern of its web). Therefore, it cannot adapt its behavior to suit the circumstances. It is the ability to adapt and to resist attacks which seems to be Petrunkevitch's implicit working definition for intelligence or reasoning.

7. Possible conclusions: Nature has provided a mechanism for keeping the tarantula population stable since the tarantula lays several hundred eggs, while the digger wasp lays only a handful. The conventional wisdom about the severity of tarantula bites is disproved in the selection. The rest of the questions depend on one's knowledge and experience.

8. Petrunkevitch's word choice is the best clue for determining that he is writing for a general audience. Throughout his description of the digger wasp's search for, and preparation of, the tarantula as food for her larva, he relies on *anthropomorphic* words—those which suggest that the female digger wasp has human motivations. (Another way to interpret the language is to say that Petrunkevitch imposes his own interpretation of motives and feelings on the insects' behavior. Whichever way you

describe the language, the effect is to make the selection much more readable (but less "scientific," since technical writing is typically impersonal and objective, with little in the way of authorial intrusions). For example, consider these sentences:

> [paragraph 11]: The tarantula shows an amazing tolerance to this exploration. . . . The molestation is so great and so persistent that the tarantula often rises on all eight legs, as if it were on stilts.

> [11]:   Meanwhile the wasp, having satisfied itself that the victim is of the right species, moves off a few inches to dig the spider's grave. . . . Now and again the wasp pops out of the hole to make sure that the spider is still there.

> [12]:   When the grave is finished, the wasp returns to the tarantula to complete her ghastly enterprise. First she feels it all over once more with her antennae. Then her behavior becomes more aggressive. . . . From time to time, as the exasperated spider slowly shifts ground, the wasp turns on her back and slides along with the aid of her wings, trying to get under the tarantula for a shot at the vital spot. . . .

> [12]: Now at last the harassed spider tries a desperate but vain defense.

> [13]: Then she emerges, fills the grave with soil carried bit by bit in her jaws, and finally tramples the ground all around to hide any trace of the grave from prowlers. Then she flies away, leaving her descendant safely started in life.

Petrunkevitch also uses an anthropomorphic metaphor to emphasize the tarantula's inability to adapt its behavior to the circumstances. In paragraph 16, he states that spiders always weave their webs in three dimensions. "For a spider to change the pattern of its web is as impossible as for an inexperienced man to build a bridge across a chasm obstructing his way."

Is Petrunkevitch's personal commentary—his intrusion of nonscientific adjectives and adverbs to describe the insects' behavior—justified? If you review questions two and three, the answer which follows is yes. Petrunkevitch is writing for an audience of laymen, not an audience of spider experts. The language is clear, precise, and evocative. As a result, his description of the spider's struggle against its enemy is made more immediate.

Part 4 consists of twenty essays and articles on a variety of subjects. They are divided into four groups, according to their relative levels of difficulty. It is recommended that you read all of the selections, even if your instructor does not assign the entire lot. Any practice you get in addition to your regular assignments will serve you well in improving your analytical skills.

Selection 1 **The Desert**
Elizabeth Marshall Thomas

Elizabeth Marshall Thomas (1931–   ) was born in Boston, Massachusetts, and was graduated from Radcliffe. A professional writer who has published several books and numerous articles on anthropology, she has traveled extensively in Africa to gather material. Her first book, *The Harmless People,* published in 1959, is an account of the Bushmen, the people who live in the subject of this selection— the Kalahari Desert.

1   There is a vast sweep of dry bush desert lying in South-West Africa and western Bechuanaland,* bordered in the north by Lake Ngami and the Okovango River, in the south by the Orange River, and in the west by the Damera Hills. It is the Kalahari Desert, part of a great inland table of southern Africa that slopes west toward the sea, all low sand dunes and great plains, flat, dry, and rolling one upon the other for thousands of miles, a hostile country of thirst and heat and thorns where the grass is harsh and often barbed and the stones hide scorpions.

2   From March to December, in the long drought of the year, the sun bakes the desert to powdery dry leaves and dust. There are no surface waters at all, no clouds for coolness, no tall trees for shade, but only low bushes and grass tufts; and among the grass tufts grow brown thistles, briers, the dry stalks of spiny weeds, all tangled into knots during the rains, now dry, tumbled, and dead.

3   The Kalahari wuld be very barren, very devoid of landmarks, if it were not for the baobab trees, and even these grow far from each other, some areas having none. But where there is one it is the biggest thing in all the landscape, dominating all the veld, more impressive than any mountain. It can be as much as two hundred feet high and thirty feet in diameter. It has great, thick branches that sprout haphazardly from the sides of the trunk and reach like stretching arms into the sky. The bark is thin and smooth and rather pink, and sags in folds toward the base of the tree like the skin on an elephant's leg, which is why a baobab is sometimes called an elephant tree. Its trunk is soft and pulpy, like a carrot instead of wooden, and if you lean against it you find that it is warm from the sun and you expect to hear a great heart beating inside. In the spring, encouraged by moisture, these giants put out huge white flowers resembling gardenias, white as moons and fragrant, that face down toward the earth; during the summer they bear alum-like dry fruits, shaped like pears, which can be eaten. In the Kalahari there is no need of hills. The great baobabs standing in the plains, the wind, and the seasons are enough.

4   Usually in the hot months only small winds blow, leaving a whisper of dry leaves and a ripple of grass as though a snake has gone by, but occasionally there is a windy day when all the low trees of the veld are in motion, swinging and dipping, and the grass blows forward and back. When there is

---

*Bechuanaland is now named Botswana.

no wind, heat accumulates in the air and rises in thick, shuddering waves that distort everything you see, the temperature rises to 120° Fahrenheit and more, and the air feels heavy pressing against you, hard to breathe.

5   June and July are the months of winter. Then water left standing freezes at night, and with the first light of morning all the trees and grass leaves are brittle with frost. The days warm slowly to perhaps 80° at noon, but by night when the sun sets yellow and far, far away over the flat veld the cold creeps back, freezing the moisture from the dark air so that the black sky blazes with stars. In winter the icy wind, pouring steadily across the continent from the Antarctic, blows all night long.

6   There are only three months of rain in the whole year, and these begin in December, ending the hottest season when the air is as tight and dry as a drum skin. Under the rain—which is sometimes torrential, drenching the earth, making rivers down the sides of trees, sometimes an easy land rain that blows into the long grass like a mist—the heat and drought melt away and the grass turns green at the roots. Soon the trees flower, and in the low places the dry dust becomes sucking mud. Towering clouds, miles away, widen the horizon and all the bushes which stretch in an unchanging expanse over dune after dune now blossom and bear white or red or violet flowers. But the season is short, and the plants bud, flower, and fruit very quickly; in March the drought creeps in, just as the veld fruits ripen and scatter their seeds.

7   When the rains stop, the open water is the first to dry, making slippery mud and then caked white earth. By June only little soaks of waterholes remain, hidden deep in the earth, covered with long grass. These, which are miles apart, dry up by August, and then travel in the veld is nearly impossible. Because of this, large areas of the Kalahari remain unexplored.

A. Comprehension   Choose the answer that best completes each statement. Do not refer to the selection while doing this exercise.

1. The Kalahari Desert is located in (a) Egypt and Morocco; (b) South-West Africa and Botswana; (c) the Union of South Africa; (d) Zambia and Zaire.

2. Exploring and traveling in the Kalahari region are difficult because of the absence of (a) shelters; (b) adequate roads; (c) surface waters; (d) a food supply.

3. The baobab tree is sometimes called an elephant tree because (a) its bark sags in folds like an elephant's skin; (b) its bark is grey and creased like an elephant's skin; (c) its trunk resembles an elephant's trunk; (d) its trunk is thick like an elephant's legs.

4. The baobab tree is particularly characterized by its (a) poisonous fruit; (b) hard, brittle trunk; (c) ability to grow in the absence of water; (d) enormous size.

5. In the Kalahari, the winter months are (a) December to March; (b) June to July; (c) March to June; (d) August to September.

B. Inferences   On the basis of the evidence in the paragraph, mark these statements as follows: *A* for accurate inferences, *I* for inaccurate inferences, and *IE* for insufficient evidence. You may refer to the selection to answer the questions in this section, and all the remaining sections.

_____ 1. In the Kalahari, the long months of drought cause vegetation to be harsh and stunted.

_____ 2. Baobab trees are numerous throughout the Kalahari region.

_____ 3. The Kalahari desert is so inhospitable that it is uninhabited by people or animals.

_____ 4. Drought characterizes the weather in the Kalahari for three-quarters of the year.

_____ 5. The winter months are marked by extremes of temperature.

_____ 6. The author disliked traveling in the Kalahari.

C. Structure   1. This essay combines two modes of discourse: (a) narration and description; (b) description and exposition; (c) exposition and persuasion; (d) narration and exposition.

2. Write the sentence that best expresses the thesis of the essay.

_____

_____

Underline the words that express the controlling idea.

3. For the following paragraphs, decide which of these patterns of organization Thomas uses. Some paragraphs may have more than one answer.

deductive   spatial
inductive   chronological
variation of deductive   emphatic

paragraph 1 _____
paragraph 3 _____
paragraph 5 _____
paragraph 6 _____
paragraph 7 _____

4. Judging from the way Thomas describes the baobab tree in paragraph 3, which quality does she mean to emphasize above all others? (a) its bizarre, ugly appearance; (b) its usefulness as a food source for the region's inhabitants; (c) the fact that it resembles a giant animal more than a tree; (d) its amazing ability to withstand a harsh environment.

5. In the last sentence of paragraph 3, Thomas says, "The great baobabs standing in the plains, the wind, and the seasons are enough," by which she means that (a) the region is truly inhospitable; (b) these features can sustain human life; (c) these features are sufficient to make the region both unique and fascinating; (d) these features make the region difficult to endure.

6. In paragraph 4, these phrases, "a whisper of dry leaves," "the grass blows forward and back," and "thick shuddering waves," all convey a feeling of (a) motion; (b) harshness; (c) great noise; (d) anxiety.

7. Write the main idea of paragraph 5:

_____

8. Find a simile in paragraph 6:

_____

D. Fact and Opinion

For each of the following statements from the selection, mark *F* if it represents a fact—a statement that can be verified or proved true—or *O* if it represents an opinion—a statement reflecting the author's subjective point of view.

_____ 1. The Kalahari Desert is in southern Africa.

_____ 2. The drought in the Kalahari Desert normally lasts from March to December each year.

_____ 3. The baobab trees are remarkable in appearance.

_____ 4. In southern Africa, the winter months are in June and July, the reverse of winter in the northern hemisphere.

_____ 5. The Kalahari is a hostile, barren environment.

E. Vocabulary

For each italicized word from the selection, choose the best definition according to the context in which it appears.

1. the grass is harsh and often *barbed* [paragraph 1]: having (a) short stalks; (b) sharp, pointed ends; (c) a reddish-yellow color; (d) soft, hair-like projections.

2. the Kalahari would be *barren* [3]: (a) inhospitable; (b) uninhabitable; (c) lacking vegetation; (d) dry; lacking water.

3. the Kalahari would be *devoid* of landmarks [3]: (a) possessing; (b) sharing; (c) without a need for; (d) completely lacking.

4. dominating all the *veld* [3]: (a) open areas; (b) hilly areas; (c) swampy areas; (d) forested areas.

5. the leaves are *brittle* with frost [5]: (a) heavy; (b) white; (c) sharp; (d) easy to break.

6. the rain is *torrential* [6]: (a) wild; raging; (b) hardly noticeable; (c) impossible to escape; (d) unpredictable.

F. Vocabulary Fill-Ins

Before you begin this exercise, be sure that you know the meaning of all the words below. From the list, choose a word that fits both grammatically and contextually in each blank. Use each word in the list only once, and add noun or verb endings (such as *-s* or *-ed*) if necessary. (Note that there are more words than blanks.)

vast	border	drought	drench
brittle	encourage	accumulate	usually
hostile	torrential	resemble	devoid
dominate	distort	haphazardly	barren

1. The Kalahari Desert is described as a _____ sweep of land _____ in the north and south by rivers.
2. The climate of the Kalahari is _____; the landscape is nearly _____ of landmarks, except for the giant baobab trees, which rise up, _____ all the veld.
3. The thick branches of the baobab tree sprout _____ from the trunk, and the bark _____ the sagging skin of an elephant.
4. The heat during the dry months is intense, and on a windless day, it _____ in the air and rises in waves that make everything look _____.
5. The long months of _____ end in December, when the _____ rains come, _____ the earth and turning the grass green again.

G. Questions for Analysis

1. What is the dominant impression Thomas conveys of the Kalahari Desert? What specific words and phrases convey this impression?
2. What are some reasons that the baobab tree is significant for the area? Why is it unique?
3. How would you describe the climate of the Kalahari in the summer and winter?

Selection 2

My First Meeting With Miss Sullivan
Helen Keller

Helen Keller (1880–1968) devoted her life to working for the handicapped. Born in Tuscumbia, Alabama, she was deaf and blind from the age of nineteen months as the result of an illness. After graduating from Radcliffe in 1904, she devoted nearly all of her life to helping the blind and the deaf. Anne Sullivan Macy was her teacher and companion from 1887 to 1936. The story of her early years with Miss Sullivan was made into a play and later a film, *The Miracle Worker*. This account of her meeting with Miss Sullivan is from her autobiography, *The Story of My Life*, published in 1954.

1   The most important day I remember in all my life is the one on which my teacher, Anne Mansfield Sullivan, came to me. I am filled with wonder when I consider the immeasurable contrast between the two lives which it connects. It was the third of March, 1887, three months before I was seven years old.
2   On the afternoon of that eventful day, I stood on the porch, dumb, expectant. I guessed vaguely from my mother's signs and from the hurrying to and fro in the house that something unusual was about to happen, so I went to the door and waited on the steps. The afternoon sun penetrated the mass of honeysuckle that covered the porch, and fell on my upturned face. My fingers lingered almost unconsciously on the familiar leaves and blossoms which had just come forth to greet the sweet southern spring. I did not know what the future held of marvel or surprise for me. Anger and bitterness had

preyed upon me continually for weeks and a deep languor had succeeded this passionate struggle.

3   Have you ever been at sea in a dense fog, when it seemed as if a tangible white darkness shut you in, and the great ship, tense and anxious, groped her way toward the shore with plummet and sounding-line, and you waited with beating heart for something to happen? I was like that ship before my education began, only I was without compass or sounding-line, and had no way of knowing how near the harbour was. "Light! give me light!" was the wordless cry of my soul, and the light of love shone on me in that very hour.

4   I felt approaching footsteps. I stretched out my hand as I supposed to my mother. Some one took it, and I was caught up and held close in the arms of her who had come to reveal all things to me, and, more than all things else, to love me.

5   The morning after my teacher came she led me into her room and gave me a doll. The little blind children at the Perkins Institution had sent it and Laura Bridgman had dressed it; but I did not know this until afterward. When I had played with it a little while, Miss Sullivan slowly spelled into my hand the word "d-o-l-l." I was at once interested in this finger play and tried to imitate it. When I finally succeeded in making the letters correctly I was flushed with childish pleasure and pride. Running downstairs to my mother I held up my hand and made the letters for doll. I did not know that I was spelling a word or even that words existed; I was simply making my fingers go in monkey-like imitation. In the days that followed I learned to spell in this uncomprehending way a great many words, among them *pin, hat, cup* and a few verbs like *sit, stand* and *walk*. But my teacher had been with me several weeks before I understood that everything has a name.

6   One day, while I was playing with my new doll, Miss Sullivan put my big rag doll into my lap also, spelled "d-o-l-l" and tried to make me understand that "d-o-l-l" applied to both. Earlier in the day we had had a tussle over the words "m-u-g" and "w-a-t-e-r." Miss Sullivan had tried to impress it upon me that "m-u-g" is *mug* and that "w-a-t-e-r" is *water,* but I persisted in confounding the two. In despair she had dropped the subject for the time, only to renew it at the first opportunity. I became impatient at her repeated attempts and, seizing the new doll, I dashed it upon the floor. I was keenly delighted when I felt the fragments of the broken doll at my feet. Neither sorrow nor regret followed my passionate outburst. I had not loved the doll. In the still, dark world in which I lived there was no strong sentiment or tenderness. I felt my teacher sweep the fragments to one side of the hearth, and I had a sense of satisfaction that the cause of my discomfort was removed. She brought me my hat, and I knew I was going out into the warm sunshine. This thought, if a wordless sensation may be called a thought, made me hop and skip with pleasure.

7   We walked down the path to the well-house, attracted by the fragrance of the honeysuckle with which it was covered. Some one was drawing water and my teacher placed my hand under the spout. As the cool stream gushed over one hand she spelled into the other the word *water,* first slowly, then

rapidly. I stood still, my whole attention fixed upon the motions of her fingers. Suddenly I felt a misty consciousness as of something forgotten—a thrill of returning thought; and somehow the mystery of language was revealed to me. I knew then that "w-a-t-er" meant the wonderful cool something that was flowing over my hand. That living word awakened my soul, gave it light, hope, joy, set it free! There were barriers still, it is true, but barriers that could in time be swept away.

8   I left the well-house eager to learn. Everything had a name, and each name gave birth to a new thought. As we returned to the house every object which I touched seemed to quiver with life. That was because I saw everything with the strange, new sight that had come to me. On entering the door I remembered the doll I had broken. I felt my way to the hearth and picked up the pieces. I tried vainly to put them together. Then my eyes filled with tears; for I realized what I had done, and for the first time I felt repentance and sorrow.

9   I learned a great many new words that day. I do not remember what they all were; but I do know that *mother, father, sister, teacher* were among them— words that were to make the world blossom for me, "like Aaron's rod, with flowers." It would have been difficult to find a happier child than I was as I lay in my crib at the close of that eventful day and lived over the joys it had brought me, and for the first time longed for a new day to come.

A. Comprehension   Choose the answer that best completes each statement. Do not refer to the selection while doing this exercise.

1. Anne Sullivan arrived at Helen Keller's house three months before Helen's (a) third; (b) fourth; (c) sixth; (d) seventh birthday.

2. For weeks before Miss Sullivan arrived, Helen's life was characterized by (a) marvel and surprise; (b) darkness and anger; (c) blissful ignorance; (d) confusion and bewilderment.

3. Miss Sullivan began Helen's education by trying to teach her an important lesson: (a) that she should take good care of her possessions; (b) that words were spelled with letters; (c) that everything has a name; (d) that she should learn to control her violent emotions.

4. After Helen broke the doll, she felt no sorrow or regret because (a) she had felt no affection or tenderness for the doll; (b) she was jealous of Miss Sullivan's achievements; (c) she resented Miss Sullivan's presence in the house; (d) she was angry at Miss Sullivan for being so patient.

5. The course of Helen's life changed when she learned that (a) guilt is the natural result of wrongdoing; (b) education can break down emotional or psychological barriers; (c) a knowledge of words could awaken her mind and set her free; (d) thoughts and emotions can be felt without having the knowledge of the words we normally use to describe them.

B. Inferences   On the basis of the evidence in the selection, mark the statements below as follows: *A* for accurate inferences, *I* for inaccurate inferences, and *IE* for insufficient evidence. You may refer to the selection to answer the questions in this section, and all the remaining sections.

_IF_ 1. Before Miss Sullivan's arrival, Helen was a difficult child.

_IF_ 2. Before Miss Sullivan arrived, Helen's mother had tried to teach her words and their spelling.

_F_ 3. Miss Sullivan had no experience teaching blind children prior to her coming to the Keller house.

_A_ 4. According to Keller, a thought cannot properly be called a thought until it can be expressed in words.

_F_ 5. It took Helen several weeks to grasp the connection between objects or actions and the words used to represent them.

C. Structure

1. The predominant mode of discourse in this selection is (a) narration; (b) description; (c) exposition; (d) persuasion.

2. Write the sentence that expresses the thesis of the essay. _the most important day_ _____ in paragraph _1_.

3. In the second sentence of paragraph 1, when Keller refers to the "contrast between two lives," to which two lives is she referring? _Her live before Miss Sullivan came and after_

4. In the same sentence, the pronoun "it" refers to (a) "contrast"; (b) "two lives"; (c) "wonder"; (d) "the most important day."

5. In paragraph 2, what does the word "dumb" mean? _saying nothing_

6. Paragraph 3 contains an analogy. What two things is Keller comparing? _her life is compared to the life of someone on a ship at night in the complete darkness_

7. An _oxymoron_ (pronounced ŏk′-sē-mōr′ŏn) is a figure of speech or a type of figurative language in which a writer combines two contradictory or incongruous terms, such as "a mournful optimist" or "a living death." Look through paragraph 3 again and find two examples of oxymorons: _white darkness_ _____ and _wordless cry_ .

8. Though Miss Sullivan plays a crucial role in Keller's life, we only see her indirectly. According to Keller's version of events, what seem to be Miss Sullivan's most distinctive attributes? _her patience_

9. Look again at paragraph 8. What specifically is Keller referring to in the phrase "the strange, new sight" that had come to her? _Miss Sullivan_

10. Throughout the selection, both before and after Miss Sullivan's arrival, which sense did Helen rely on most? _Touch_

D. Vocabulary

For each italicized word from the selection, choose the best definition according to the context in which it appears.

1. I stood on the porch, *dumb,* expectant [paragraph 2]: (a) hesitant; (b) stupid; (c) speechless; (d) anxious.

2. my fingers *lingered* on the familiar leaves [2]: (a) stayed on the surface of; (b) touched the surface of; (c) stroked the surface of; (d) shredded into little pieces.

3. a deep *languor* had succeeded this passionate struggle [2]: (a) oppressive quiet; (b) lassitude; sluggishness; (c) nervous anxiety; tension; (d) bitterness, nastiness.

4. as if a *tangible* white darkness shut you in [3]: capable of being (a) understood; (b) penetrated; (c) erased; (d) touched.

5. I was *flushed* with childish pleasure and pride [5]: (a) pale; (b) white; (c) red; (c) yellow.

6. I persisted in *confounding* the two [6]: (a) not understanding; (b) distinguishing between; (c) confusing; (d) refusing to learn.

E. Vocabulary Fill-Ins

Before you begin this exercise, be sure that you know the meaning of all the words below. From the list, choose a word that fits in each blank both grammatically and contextually. Use each word only once, and add noun or verb endings (such as *-s* or *-ed*) if necessary. (Note that there are more words than blanks.)

contrast	tangible	keenly	persist
vainly	imitation	consciousness	fragment
languor	succeed	immeasurable	repentance
prey	sensation	penetrate	vaguely

1. Keller writes that the _____ between her life before Miss Sullivan arrived and after her education began was _____.

2. On the day of Miss Sullivan's arrival, Helen felt _____ from her mother's activity that something unusual was going to happen, something that might relieve the anger and deep sense of _____ that had _____ upon her.

3. Keller describes the _____ she felt but could not put into words; she writes that she felt like a ship lost in a fog so dense that it was like a _____ white darkness.

4. Helen quickly _____ in making the letters for "doll," but she did so only in monkey-like _____.

5. When Helen tried _____ to put the _____ of the broken doll together, she felt for the first time a feeling of _____.

F. Questions for Analysis

1. From what she implies, what sort of child do you think Helen was before she began her education?

2. In paragraph 3, Keller describes the "light" that she could not find in the "dense fog" of her early life. In literal terms, what does she mean by these words?

3. Why was Helen initially unable to feel repentance and sorrow for her destruction of the doll? What is Keller suggesting about the nature of emotions in her recounting of this incident?

Selection 3   # Growing Up
Russell Baker

Russell Baker (1925–   ) is one of this country's foremost humorists and political writers. Born in Virginia, he was a staff reporter for *The Baltimore Sun* from 1947–1953. Since 1962, he has written a column called "Observer" for the *New York Times,* which is syndicated in many other American newspapers. He has published several collections of his columns, including *Poor Russell's Almanac* (1972) and *The Rescue of Miss Yaskell and Other Pipe Dreams* (1983). [Baker's parody of "Little Red Riding Hood" is found in Chapter 5, and another satiric piece appears in Part 2, Reading Critically.] He was awarded the Pulitzer Prize for distinguished commentary in 1979, and another Pulitzer Prize for literature in 1982 for his autobiography, *Growing Up.* The selection reprinted here is Chapter 2 of that book. As is evident, Baker's mother is the dominant character, a young impoverished widow who worked hard protecting her meager resources and pushing and prodding her children so they would "make something" of themselves.

1   I began working in journalism when I was eight years old. It was my mother's idea. She wanted me to "make something" of myself and, after a levelheaded appraisal of my strengths, decided I had better start young if I was to have any chance of keeping up with the competition.

2 The flaw in my character which she had already spotted was lack of "gumption." My idea of a perfect afternoon was lying in front of the radio rereading my favorite Big Little Book, *Dick Tracy Meets Stooge Viller.* My mother despised inactivity. Seeing me having a good time in repose, she was powerless to hide her disgust. "You've got no more gumption than a bump on a log," she said. "Get out in the kitchen and help Doris do those dirty dishes."

3 My sister Doris, though two years younger than I, had enough gumption for a dozen people. She positively enjoyed washing dishes, making beds, and cleaning the house. When she was only seven she could carry a piece of short-weighted cheese back to the A&P, threaten the manager with legal action, and come back triumphantly with the full quarter-pound we'd paid for and a few ounces extra thrown in for forgiveness. Doris could have made something of herself if she hadn't been a girl. Because of this defect, however, the best she could hope for was a career as a nurse or schoolteacher, the only work that capable females were considered up to in those days.

4   This must have saddened my mother, this twist of fate that had allocated all the gumption to the daughter and left her with a son who was content with Dick Tracy and Stooge Viller. If disappointed, though, she wasted no energy on self-pity. She would make me make something of myself whether I wanted to or not. "The Lord helps those who help themselves," she said. That was the way her mind worked.

5   She was realistic about the difficulty. Having sized up the material the

Lord had given her to mold, she didn't overestimate what she could do with it. She didn't insist that I grow up to be President of the United States.

6   Fifty years ago parents still asked boys if they wanted to grow up to be President, and asked it not jokingly but seriously. Many parents who were hardly more than paupers still believed their sons could do it. Abraham Lincoln had done it. We were only sixty-five years from Lincoln. Many a grandfather who walked among us could remember Lincoln's time. Men of grandfatherly age were the worst for asking if you wanted to grow up to be President. A surprising number of little boys said yes and meant it.

7   I was asked many times myself. No, I would say, I didn't want to grow up to be President. My mother was present during one of these interrogations. An elderly uncle, having posed the usual question and exposed my lack of interest in the Presidency, asked, "Well, what *do* you want to be when you grow up?"

8   I loved to pick through trash piles and collect empty bottles, tin cans with pretty labels, and discarded magazines. The most desirable job on earth sprang instantly to mind. "I want to be a garbage man," I said.

9   My uncle smiled, but my mother had seen the first distressing evidence of a bump budding on a log. "Have a little gumption, Russell," she said. Her calling me Russell was a signal of unhappiness. When she approved of me I was always "Buddy."

10   When I turned eight years old she decided that the job of starting me on the road toward making something of myself could no longer be safely delayed. "Buddy," she said one day, "I want you to come home right after school this afternoon. Somebody's coming and I want you to meet him."

11   When I burst in that afternoon she was in conference in the parlor with an executive of the Curtis Publishing Company. She introduced me. He bent low from the waist and shook my hand. Was it true as my mother had told him, he asked, that I longed for the opportunity to conquer the world of business?

12   My mother replied that I was blessed with a rare determination to make something of myself.

13   "That's right," I whispered.

14   "But have you got the grit, the character, the never-say-quit spirit it takes to succeed in business?"

15   My mother said I certainly did.

16   "That's right," I said.

17   He eyed me silently for a long pause, as though weighing whether I could be trusted to keep his confidence, then spoke man-to-man. Before taking a crucial step, he said, he wanted to advise me that working for the Curtis Publishing Company placed enormous responsibility on a young man. It was one of the great companies of America. Perhaps the greatest publishing house in the world. I had heard, no doubt, of the *Saturday Evening Post*?

18   Heard of it? My mother said that everyone in our house had heard of the *Saturday Post* and that I, in fact, read it with religious devotion.

19   Then doubtless, he said, we were also familiar with those two monthly

pillars of the magazine world, the *Ladies Home Journal* and the *Country Gentleman.*

20 Indeed we were familiar with them, said my mother.

21 Representing the *Saturday Evening Post* was one of the weightiest honors that could be bestowed in the world of business, he said. He was personally proud of being a part of that great corporation.

22 My mother said he had every right to be.

23 Again he studied me as though debating whether I was worthy of a knighthood. Finally: "Are you trustworthy?"

24 My mother said I was the soul of honesty.

25 "That's right," I said.

26 The caller smiled for the first time. He told me I was a lucky young man. He admired my spunk. Too many young men thought life was all play. Those young men would not go far in this world. Only a young man willing to work and save and keep his face washed and his hair neatly combed could hope to come out on top in a world such as ours. Did I truly and sincerely believe that I was such a young man?

27 "He certainly does," said my mother.

28 "That's right," I said.

29 He said he had been so impressed by what he had seen of me that he was going to make me a representative of the Curtis Publishing Company. On the following Tuesday, he said, thirty freshly printed copies of the *Saturday Evening Post* would be delivered at our door. I would place these magazines, still damp with the ink of the presses, in a handsome canvas bag, sling it over my shoulder, and set forth through the streets to bring the best in journalism, fiction, and cartoons to the American public.

30 He had brought the canvas bag with him. He presented it with reverence fit for a chasuble. He showed me how to drape the sling over my left shoulder and across the chest so that the pouch lay easily accessible to my right hand, allowing the best in journalism, fiction, and cartoons to be swiftly extracted and sold to a citizenry whose happiness and security depended upon us soldiers of the free press.

31 The following Tuesday I raced home from school, put the canvas bag over my shoulder, dumped the magazines in, and, tilting to the left to balance their weight on my right hip, embarked on the highway of journalism.

32 We lived in Belleville, New Jersey, a commuter town at the northern fringe of Newark. It was 1932, the bleakest year of the Depression. My father had died two years before, leaving us with a few pieces of Sears, Roebuck furniture and not much else, and my mother had taken Doris and me to live with one of her younger brothers. This was my Uncle Allen. Uncle Allen had made something of himself by 1932. As salesman for a soft-drink bottler in Newark, he had an income of $30 a week; wore pearl-gray spats, detachable collars, and a three-piece suit; was happily married; and took in threadbare relatives.

33 With my load of magazines I headed toward Belleville Avenue. That's where the people were. There were two filling stations at the intersection with Union Avenue, as well as an A&P, a fruit stand, a bakery, a barber

shop, Zuccarelli's drugstore, and a diner shaped like a railroad car. For several hours I made myself highly visible, shifting position now and then from corner to corner, from shop window to shop window, to make sure everyone could see the heavy black lettering on the canvas bag that said THE SATURDAY EVENING POST. When the angle of the light indicated it was suppertime, I walked back to the house.

34   "How many did you sell, Buddy?" my mother asked.

35   "None."

36   "Where did you go?"

37   "The corner of Belleville and Union Avenues."

38   "What did you do?"

39   "Stood on the corner waiting for somebody to buy a *Saturday Evening Post*."

40   "You just stood there?"

41   "Didn't sell a single one."

42   "For God's sake, Russell!"

43   Uncle Allen intervened. "I've been thinking about it for some time," he said, "and I've about decided to take the *Post* regularly. Put me down as a regular customer." I handed him a magazine and he paid me a nickel. It was the first nickel I earned.

44   Afterwards my mother instructed me in salesmanship. I would have to ring doorbells, address adults with charming self-confidence, and break down resistance with a sales talk pointing out that no one, no matter how poor, could afford to be without the *Saturday Evening Post* in the home.

45   I told my mother I'd changed my mind about wanting to succeed in the magazine business.

46   "If you think I'm going to raise a good-for-nothing," she replied, "you've got another thing coming." She told me to hit the streets with the canvas bag and start ringing doorbells the instant school was out next day. When I objected that I didn't feel any aptitude for salesmanship, she asked how I'd like to lend her my leather belt so she could whack some sense into me. I bowed to superior will and entered journalism with a heavy heart.

47   My mother and I had fought this battle almost as long as I could remember. It probably started even before memory began, when I was a country child in northern Virginia and my mother, dissatisfied with my father's plain workman's life, determined that I would not grow up like him and his people, with calluses on their hands, overalls on their backs, and fourth-grade educations in their heads. She had fancier ideas of life's possibilities. Introducing me to the *Saturday Evening Post,* she was trying to wean me as early as possible from my father's world where men left with their lunch pails at sunup, worked with their hands until the grime ate into the pores, and died with a few sticks of mail-order furniture as their legacy. In my mother's vision of the better life there were desks and white collars, well-pressed suits, evenings of reading and lively talk, and perhaps—if a man were very, very lucky and hit the jackpot, really made something important of himself—perhaps there might be a fantastic salary of $5,000 a year to support a big house and a Buick with a rumble seat and a vacation in Atlantic City.

48 And so I set forth with my sack of magazines. I was afraid of the dogs that snarled behind the doors of potential buyers. I was timid about ringing the doorbells of strangers, relieved when no one came to the door, and scared when someone did. Despite my mother's instructions, I could not deliver an engaging sales pitch. When a door opened I simply asked, "Want to buy a *Saturday Evening Post*?" In Belleville few persons did. It was a town of 30,000 people, and most weeks I rang a fair majority of its doorbells. But I rarely sold my thirty copies. Some weeks I canvassed the entire town for six days and still had four or five unsold magazines on Monday evening; then I dreaded the coming of Tuesday morning, when a batch of thirty fresh *Saturday Evening Post*s was due at the front door.

49 "Better get out there and sell the rest of those magazines tonight," my mother would say.

50 I usually posted myself then at a busy intersection where a traffic light controlled commuter flow from Newark. When the light turned red I stood on the curb and shouted my sales pitch at the motorists.

51 "Want to buy a *Saturday Evening Post*?"

52 One rainy night when car windows were sealed against me I came back soaked and with not a single sale to report. My mother beckoned to Doris.

53 "Go back down there with Buddy and show him how to sell these magazines," she said.

54 Brimming with zest, Doris, who was then seven years old, returned with me to the corner. She took a magazine from the bag, and when the light turned red she strode to the nearest car and banged her small fist against the closed window. The driver, probably startled at what he took to be a midget assaulting his car, lowered the window to stare, and Doris thrust a *Saturday Evening Post* at him.

55 "You need this magazine," she piped, "and it only costs a nickel."

56 Her salesmanship was irresistible. Before the light changed half a dozen times she disposed of the entire batch. I didn't feel humiliated. To the contrary. I was so happy I decided to give her a treat. Leading her to the vegetable store on Belleville Avenue, I bought three apples, which cost a nickel, and gave her one.

57 "You shouldn't waste money," she said.

58 "Eat your apple." I bit into mine.

59 "You shouldn't eat before supper," she said. "It'll spoil your appetite."

60 Back at the house that evening, she dutifully reported me for wasting a nickel. Instead of a scolding, I was rewarded with a pat on the back for having the good sense to buy fruit instead of candy. My mother reached into her bottomless supply of maxims and told Doris, "An apple a day keeps the doctor away."

61 By the time I was ten I had learned all my mother's maxims by heart. Asking to stay up past normal bedtime, I knew that a refusal would be explained with, "Early to bed and early to rise, makes a man healthy, wealthy, and wise." If I whimpered about having to get up early in the morning, I could depend on her to say, "The early bird gets the worm."

62 The one I most despised was, "If at first you don't succeed, try, try again."

This was the battle cry with which she constantly sent me back into the hopeless struggle whenever I moaned that I had rung every doorbell in town and knew there wasn't a single potential buyer left in Belleville that week. After listening to my explanation, she handed me the canvas bag and said, "If at first you don't succeed . . ."

63 Three years in that job, which I would gladly have quit after the first day except for her insistence, produced at least one valuable result. My mother finally concluded that I would never make something of myself by pursuing a life in business and started considering careers that demanded less competitive zeal.

64 One evening when I was eleven I brought home a short "composition" on my summer vacation which the teacher had graded with an A. Reading it with her own schoolteacher's eye, my mother agreed that it was top-drawer seventh grade prose and complimented me. Nothing more was said about it immediately, but a new idea had taken life in her mind. Halfway through supper she suddenly interrupted the conversation.

65 "Buddy," she said, "maybe you could be a writer."

66 I clasped the idea to my heart. I had never met a writer, had shown no previous urge to write, and hadn't a notion how to become a writer, but I loved stories and thought that making up stories must surely be almost as much fun as reading them. Best of all, though, and what really gladdened my heart, was the ease of the writer's life. Writers did not have to trudge through the town peddling from canvas bags, defending themselves against angry dogs, being rejected by surly strangers. Writers did not have to ring doorbells. So far as I could make out, what writers did couldn't even be classified as work.

67 I was enchanted. Writers didn't have to have any gumption at all. I did not dare tell anybody for fear of being laughed at in the schoolyard, but secretly I decided that what I'd like to be when I grew up was a writer.

A. Comprehension

Choose the answer that best completes each statement. Do not refer to the selection while doing this exercise.

1. When Baker writes that he began working in journalism at the age of eight, he is referring to (a) his favorite pastime of reading Big Little Books like *Dick Tracy Meets Stooge Viller*; (b) his writing humorous columns for his school newspaper; (c) his paper route delivering the evening newspaper in his neighborhood; (d) selling the *Saturday Evening Post* door to door.

2. According to Baker, his mother thought the main flaw in his character was lack of "gumption," by which she meant (a) lack of intelligence; (b) lack of foresight; (c) lack of initiative; (d) lack of perseverance.

3. Doris, Baker's sister, was (a) two years older; (b) two years younger; (c) his twin; (d) four years older; (e) four years younger.

4. Belleville, the commuter town where Baker lived as a child, is located in (a) Connecticut; (b) Virginia; (c) New York; (d) New Jersey.

5. When Baker's uncle asked him what he wanted to be when he grew up, he replied that he wanted to be (a) a garbageman; (b) a newspaper writer; (c) President of the United States; (d) a salesman.

6. The real reason Baker had so much difficulty selling magazines was that (a) it was 1932, the worst year of the Depression, and people had no money to spend on luxuries like magazines; (b) the *Saturday Evening Post* was not a popular magazine; (c) Baker was too timid to ask people to subscribe to the magazine; (d) Baker's sales pitch was not convincing, despite his mother's coaching.

7. When Doris proved better at selling magazines than Baker, he felt (a) proud; (b) relieved; (c) humiliated; (d) angry.

8. After three years trying to sell magazines, Baker's mother suggested that he might become a writer. The idea appealed to him because (a) he knew it would please his mother; (b) he had always been good at making up stories; (c) writers didn't have to have gumption; (d) he knew his friends at school would be impressed with his new ambition.

B. Inferences   On the basis of the evidence in the selection, answer these inference questions. You may refer to the selection to answer the questions in this section, and all the remaining sections.

1. Read paragraph 1 again. What can you infer about his mother's assessment of her son's strengths? _____

   _____

2. Judging from paragraph 2, what did Baker's mother think of reading for pleasure? _____

3. Reread paragraph 3. How would you assess Doris's character from the account of the short-weighted cheese incident? _____

4. According to paragraphs 29 and 30, toward what audience was the *Saturday Evening Post* directed? _____

5. What can you infer about Uncle Allen's financial situation from paragraph 32? _____

6. Read paragraph 43 again. Why did Uncle Allen subscribe to the magazine? _____

7. Reread paragraph 47. What can you infer about his mother's own social background? _____

8. Judging from paragraphs 59 and 60, why did Doris report Baker's wasting of a nickel to buy three apples? _____

9. According to his mother (see paragraph 63), for what reason had Baker failed as a magazine salesman? _____

10. Read paragraph 67 again. What would Baker's schoolmates have thought of his wanting to become a writer? _____

C. Structure   1. The mode of discourse used in this selection is (a) narration; (b) description; (c) exposition; (d) persuasion.

2. Which of the following excerpts *best* describes the character of Baker's mother as it is revealed in the selection? (a) " 'If at first you don't succeed, try, try again.' This was the battle cry with which she constantly sent me back into the hopeless struggle whenever I moaned that I had rung every doorbell in town and knew there wasn't a single potential buyer left in Belleville that week." (b) " . . . a new idea had taken life in her mind. Halfway through supper she suddenly interrupted the conversation. 'Buddy,' she said, 'maybe you could become a writer.' " (c) "If disappointed, though, she wasted no energy on self-pity. She would make me make something of myself whether I wanted to or not." (d) ". . . my mother, dissatisfied with my father's plain workman's life, determined that I would not grow up like him and his people, with calluses on their hands, overalls on their backs, and fourth-grade educations in their heads. She had fancier ideas of life's possibilities."
Defend your answer. _____

3. Which of the following best describes the tone of the selection as a whole? (a) sarcastic; sardonic; (b) witty and amusing; (c) hostile; belligerent; (d) sharply critical; resentful.

4. In your own words, how would you describe the character of Baker's mother? _____

5. How would you describe Baker's attitude toward his mother?

_____

6. How would you characterize the dialogue between the Curtis Publishing Company executive, Baker's mother, and Baker himself in paragraphs 12–29? _____
Explain your answer. _____

7. In paragraph 2 and again in paragraph 9, Baker refers to himself as being, in his mother's eyes, a "bump budding on a log." What does this expression mean? _____

8. In paragraph 32, Baker says that his Uncle Allen took in "threadbare" relatives. What does he mean? _____

_____

9. Look at paragraph 47 again. Which method of paragraph development is represented there? (a) example; (b) definition; (c) analogy; (d) comparison; (e) contrast; (f) process.

10. Which adjectives best describe Baker's brand of humor? (a) wry and self-deprecating; (b) sarcastic and sardonic; (c) nasty and bitter; (d) preposterous and absurd.

D. Vocabulary   For each italicized word from the selection, choose the best definition according to the context in which it appears.

1. a levelheaded *appraisal* of my strengths [paragraph 1]: (a) summary; (b) evaluation; (c) criticism; (d) calculation.

2. this twist of fate had *allocated* all the gumption to the daughter [4]: (a) limited; confined; (b) reserved; saved; (c) designated for a special purpose; (d) distributed; allotted.

3. one of the weightiest honors that could be *bestowed* in the world of business [21]: (a) considered; (b) imagined; (c) used; (d) conferred.

4. allowing the best in journalism to be *extracted* [30]: (a) removed for publication; (b) pulled out; (c) obtained by pressure; (d) determined; calculated.

5. I *embarked* on the highway of journalism [31]: (a) resisted the temptation of; (b) set out on; (c) made a firm resolution about; (d) enthusiastically anticipated.

6. 1932, the *bleakest* year of the Depression [32]: (a) most unsheltered or barren; (b) coldest; harshest; (c) most discouraging or depressing; (d) most sickly; palest.

7. Uncle Allen *intervened* [43]: (a) interfered with force; (b) entered as a third party; (c) interrupted rudely; (d) came to the rescue.

8. she was trying to *wean* me from my father's life [47]: (a) detach; (b) isolate; (c) discourage; (d) protect.

9. a few sticks of furniture as their *legacy* [47]: (a) inheritance from previous generations; (b) something handed down to future generations; (c) sole possessions; (d) reward for a job well done.

10. I *canvassed* the entire town [48]: (a) examined carefully; (b) conducted a survey; (c) went through soliciting orders; (d) penetrated; spread throughout.

11. brimming with *zest* [54]: (a) ecstasy; (b) self-confidence; (c) physical energy; (d) wholehearted interest.

12. my mother reached into her bottomless supply of *maxims* [60 and 61]: (a) sayings expressing moral truths; (b) popular sentiments; (c) old-fashioned, obsolete notions; (d) ridiculous superstitions.

13. being rejected by *surly* strangers [66]: (a) arrogant; domineering; (b) sullenly rude; ill-humored; (c) indifferent; impartial; (d) impoverished.

E. Questions for Analysis

1. How would you characterize the relationship between Baker and his mother according to the information we are given in the essay?

2. What evidence is there to suggest that Baker is indulging in hyperbole (deliberate exaggeration) in his recounting of his stint as a magazine salesman?

3. Look again at paragraph 4. Is his implication that the only suitable careers for girls in the 1930s were nursing and teaching historically accurate?

Selection 4 **The Wolf**
Barry Holstun Lopez

Barry Holstun Lopez (1945–   ) is a writer whose subjects have ranged from American Indian legends to wolves. He has a degree from the University of Notre Dame, and has done graduate work at the University of Oregon. The book from which this selection is drawn, *Of Wolves and Men,* is a fascinating account of the place wolves have occupied throughout civilization, our attitudes toward them, and most important, what our attitudes toward wolves reveal about human nature.

1   Imagine a wolf moving through the northern woods. The movement, over a trail he has traversed many times before, is distinctive, unlike that of a cougar or a bear, yet he appears, if you are watching, sometimes catlike or bearlike. It is purposeful, deliberate movement. Occasionally the rhythm is broken by the wolf's pause to inspect a scent mark, or move off the trail to paw among stones where a year before he had cached meat.

2   The movement down the trail would seem relentless if it did not appear so effortless. The wolf's body, from neck to hips, appears to float over the long, almost spindly legs and the flicker of wrists, a bicycling drift through the trees, reminiscent of the movement of water or of shadows.

3   The wolf is three years old. A male. He is of the subspecies *occidentalis,* and the trees he is moving among are spruce and subalpine fir on the eastern slope of the Rockies in northern Canada. He is light gray; that is, there are more blond and white hairs mixed with gray in the saddle of fur that covers his shoulders and extends down his spine than there are black and brown. But there are silver and even red hairs mixed in, too.

4   It is early September, an easy time of year, and he has not seen the other wolves in his pack for three or four days. He has heard no howls, but he knows the others are about, in ones and twos like himself. It is not a time of year for much howling. It is an easy time. The weather is pleasant. Moose are fat. Suddenly the wolf stops in mid-stride. A moment, then his feet slowly come alongside each other. He is staring into the grass. His ears are rammed forward, stiff. His back arches and he rears up and pounces like a cat. A deer mouse is pinned between his forepaws. Eaten. The wolf drifts on. He approaches a trail crossing, an undistinguished crossroads. His movement is now slower and he sniffs the air as though aware of a possibility for scents. He sniffs a scent post, a scrawny blueberry bush in use for years, and goes on.

5   The wolf weighs ninety-four pounds and stands thirty inches at the shoulder. His feet are enormous, leaving prints in the mud along a creek (where he pauses to hunt crayfish but not with much interest) more than five inches long by just over four wide. He has two fractured ribs, broken by a moose a year before. They are healed now, but a sharp eye would notice the irregularity. The skin on his right hip is scarred, from a fight with another wolf in a neighboring pack when he was a yearling. He has not had anything but a few mice and a piece of arctic char in three days, but he is not hungry. He is traveling. The char was a day old, left on rocks along the river by bears.

6   ᵃThe wolf is tied by subtle threads to the woods he moves through. ᵇHis fur carries seeds that will fall off, effectively dispersed, along the trail some miles from where they first caught in his fur. ᶜAnd miles distant is a raven perched on the ribs of a caribou the wolf helped kill ten days ago, pecking like a chicken at the decaying scraps of meat. ᵈA smart snowshoe hare that

eluded the wolf and left him exhausted when he was a pup has been dead a year now, food for an owl. ᵉThe den in which he was born one April evening was home to porcupines last winter.

7   It is now late in the afternoon. The wolf has stopped traveling, has lain down to sleep on cool earth beneath a rock outcropping. Mosquitoes rest on his ears. His ears flicker. He begins to waken. He rolls on his back and lies motionless with his front legs pointed toward the sky but folded like wilted flowers, his back legs splayed, and his nose and tail curved toward each other on one side of his body. After a few moments he flops on his side, rises, stretches, and moves a few feet to inspect—minutely, delicately—a crevice in the rock outcropping and finds or doesn't find what draws him there. And then he ascends the rock face, bounding and balancing momentarily before bounding again, appearing slightly unsure of the process—but committed. A few minutes later he bolts suddenly into the woods, achieving full speed, almost thirty miles per hour, for forty or fifty yards before he begins to skid, to lunge at a lodgepole pine cone. He trots away with it, his head erect, tail erect, his hips slightly to one side and out of line with his shoulders, as though hindquarters were impatient with forequarters, the cone inert in his mouth. He carries it for a hundred feet before dropping it by the trail. He sniffs it. He goes on.

8   The underfur next to his skin has begun to thicken with the coming of fall. In the months to follow it will become so dense between his shoulders it will be almost impossible to work a finger down to his skin. In seven months he will weigh less: eighty-nine pounds. He will have tried unsuccessfully to mate with another wolf in the pack. He will have helped kill four moose and thirteen caribou. He will have fallen through ice into a creek at twenty-two below zero but not frozen. He will have fought with other wolves.

9   He moves along now at the edge of a clearing. The wind coming down-valley surrounds him with a river of odors, as if he were a migrating salmon. He can smell ptarmigan and deer droppings. He can smell willow and spruce and the fading sweetness of fireweed. Above, he sees a hawk circling, and farther south, lower on the horizon, a flock of sharp-tailed sparrows going east. He senses through his pads with each step the dryness of the moss beneath his feet, and the ridges of old tracks, some his own. He hears the sound his feet make. He hears the occasional movement of deer mice and voles. Summer food.

10   Toward dusk he is standing by a creek, lapping the cool water, when a wolf howls—a long wail that quickly reaches pitch and then tapers, with several harmonics, long moments to a tremolo. He recognizes his sister. He waits a few moments, then, throwing his head back and closing his eyes, he howls. The howl is shorter and it changes pitch twice in the beginning, very quickly. There is no answer.

11   The female is a mile away and she trots off obliquely through the trees. The other wolf stands listening, laps water again, then he too departs, moving quickly, quietly through the trees, away from the trail he had been on. In a few minutes the two wolves meet. They approach each other briskly, almost formally, tails erect and moving somewhat as deer move. When they

come together they make high squeaking noises and encircle each other, rubbing and pushing, poking their noses into each other's neck fur, backing away to stretch, chasing each other for a few steps, then standing quietly together, one putting a head over the other's back. And then they are gone, down a vague trail, the female first. After a few hundred yards they begin, simultaneously, to wag their tails.

12   In the days to follow, they will meet another wolf from the pack, a second female, younger by a year, and the three of them will kill a caribou. They will travel together ten or twenty miles a day, through the country where they live, eating and sleeping, birthing, playing with sticks, chasing ravens, growing old, barking at bears, scent-marking trails, killing moose, and staring at the way water in a creek breaks around their legs and flows on.

**A. Compre-
hension**

Choose the answer that best completes each statement. Do not refer to the selection while doing this exercise.

1. The wolf described in the selection lives in (a) Alaska; (b) Canada; (c) Minnesota; (d) Colorado.

2. September is considered to be an easy time for wolves because (a) tourists and hunters have left the area; (b) the wolf pack has been reunited; (c) scents are particularly strong in the fall; (d) the moose are fat and food is plentiful.

3. The wolf who is the subject of the essay is (a) scarred from rifle shots; (b) scarred from fights with other animals; (c) afflicted with parasites and rabies; (d) in perfect health and in the prime of his life.

4. Which *two* changes does the wolf undergo in the winter? (a) weight gain; (b) weight loss; (c) increase in sexual desire; (d) decrease in sexual desire; (e) change in outer fur color to white; (f) thickened underfur; (g) lowered body temperature.

5. In the relationship between the wolf and the woods he inhabits, the wolf is (a) a valuable contributor to its ecology; (b) a destructive scavenger whose numbers should be reduced; (c) its undisputed leader; (d) a predator of the harmless animals who inhabit it.

B. Inferences

On the basis of the evidence in the selection, answer these inference questions. You may refer to the selection to answer the questions in this section, and all the remaining sections.

1. What can you infer from paragraph 2 about the way a wolf moves? _He moves gracefully_

2. Read paragraph 4 again. For the wolf, what purpose is served by a scent post, in this case a blueberry bush? _Marks the wolf territory –_

3. Judging from paragraph 6, how does the wolf contribute to other animals' survival in the woods? _balance of nature – natural cycle –_

4. Reread paragraph 7. Why doesn't Lopez know what the wolf finds when he inspects a rock outcropping? _____

5. From paragraph 8, what can you infer about the way wolves hunt animals—singly or in groups? _____ *in groups* _____

6. What can you infer from paragraph 9 about a wolf's sense of smell, hearing, and touch? _____ *Very keen* — _____

7. How do wolves communicate, according to paragraphs 10 and 11? _____ *with Howls and Squeaks* — _____

8. From his account, what can you infer about the author's attitude toward wolves? _____ *Sympathetic — conservationist* _____

C. Structure

1. Which mode of discourse does this selection represent? _____ Defend your answer.

2. Lopez emphasizes the wolf's (a) ruthless nature and fearlessness; (b) indifference to danger and lack of caution; (c) instinctive accommodation to the environment; (d) instincts to procreate and kill for its survival.

3. The pattern of organization most evident throughout the selection as a whole is (a) spatial; (b) inductive; (c) chronological; (d) emphatic.

4. Look again at paragraph 6. Label its sentences using the following key: *MAIN* (main idea); *MA* (major support); *MI* (minor support).

   sentence a _____   sentence d _____
   sentence b _____   sentence e _____
   sentence c _____

5. The method of paragraph development in paragraph 6 is (a) analogy; (b) process; (c) definition; (d) example.

6. In that same paragraph, which pattern of organization does Lopez use? (a) spatial; (b) chronological; (c) emphatic; (d) deductive; (e) inductive.

7. In paragraphs 4, 7, and 11, Lopez describes various poses and actions he observed in the wolf which are similar to those of (a) a moose; (b) a dog; (c) a cat; (d) a monkey.

8. Lopez uses the present tense of verbs throughout the selection to show that (a) he wrote the piece at the same time he made his observations; (b) the wolf who is the subject of this selection is still alive; (c) the wolf who is the subject of this selection is representative of other male wolves living in the same area of the same subspecies; (d) the wolf will not be exterminated, no matter how strong the campaign against them is.

D. Vocabulary

For each italicized word from the selection, choose the best definition according to the context in which it appears.

1. over a trail he has *traversed* many times [paragraph 1]: (a) wandered over; (b) crossed; (c) investigated; (d) hunted in.

2. he had *cached* meat [1—pronounced like "cashed"]: (a) hidden; (b) hunted; (c) killed; (d) eaten.

3. the movement would seem *relentless* [2]: (a) lacking caution; (b) lacking purpose; (c) steady; persistent; (d) graceful.

4. the wolf is tied by *subtle* threads [6]: (a) strong; (b) barely noticeable; (c) clear; (d) unseen.

5. the seeds will fall off, effectively *dispersed* [6]: (a) lost; (b) scattered; (c) planted; (d) dropped.

6. a snowshoe hare that *eluded* the wolf [6]: (a) attacked; (b) chased; (c) outran; (d) escaped from.

7. the cone *inert* in his mouth [7]: (a) motionless; (b) wet; (c) suspended; (d) forgotten.

8. a long wail that reaches pitch and then *tapers* [10]: (a) gets louder; (b) diminishes; (c) stops; (d) trembles.

9. she trots off *obliquely* [11]: (a) at an angle; (b) straight ahead; (c) purposefully; (d) coquettishly.

10. down a *vague* trail [11]: (a) hidden; (b) not easily described; (c) not clearly visible; (d) impassable; unapproachable.

E. Questions for Analysis

1. In paragraph 4, Lopez describes the wolf's behavior during September, remarking that "It is not a time of year for much howling." What might be some reasons that wolves would howl during other months of the year?

2. Read paragraph 7 again. What makes Lopez's sentence structure in this paragraph effective?

3. What is unusual about the author's style and the order of details in the last sentence of paragraph 12?

4. What was your attitude toward wolves before you read this essay? What was the basis for that attitude? Has this selection altered your views in any way, or has it reinforced them? Explain specifically.

Selection 5

It's Just Too Late
Calvin Trillin

Born in 1935 in Kansas City, Missouri, Calvin Trillin was educated at Yale, after which he became a reporter for *Time*. Since 1963, he has been a staff writer for *The New Yorker*, for which he regularly contributes articles for a column called "U.S. Journal." In addition to books about the pleasures of eating—*American Fried: Adventures of a Happy Eater* (1974) and *Alice, Let's Eat* (1978)—Trillin has published a collection of essays called *Killings*, his attempt at understanding American culture by way of exploring several cases involving the deaths of ordinary people. The death of sixteen-year-old FaNee Cooper is described in "It's Just Too Late."

Knoxville, Tennessee
March 1979

1   Until she was sixteen, FaNee Cooper was what her parents sometimes called an ideal child. "You'd never have to correct her," FaNee's mother has said. In sixth grade, FaNee won a spelling contest. She played the piano and the flute. She seemed to believe what she heard every Sunday at the

Beaver Dam Baptist Church about good and evil and the hereafter. FaNee was not an outgoing child. Even as a baby, she was uncomfortable when she was held and cuddled. She found it easy to tell her parents that she loved them but difficult to confide in them. Particularly compared to her sister, Kristy, a cheerful, open little girl two and a half years younger, she was reserved and introspective. The thoughts she kept to herself, though, were apparently happy thoughts. Her eighth-grade essay on Christmas—written in a remarkably neat hand—talked of the joys of helping put together toys for her little brother, Leo, Jr., and the importance of her parents' reminder that Christmas is the birthday of Jesus. Her parents were the sort of people who might have been expected to have an ideal child. As a boy, Leo Cooper had been called "one of the greatest high-school basketball players ever developed in Knox County." He went on to play basketball at East Tennessee State, and he married the homecoming queen, JoAnn Henson. After college, Cooper became a high-school basketball coach and teacher and, eventually, an administrator. By the time FaNee turned thirteen, in 1973, he was in his third year as the principal of Gresham Junior High School, in Fountain City —a small Knox County town that had been swallowed up by Knoxville when the suburbs began to move north. A tall man, with curly black hair going on gray, Leo Cooper has an elaborate way of talking ("Unless I'm very badly mistaken, he has never related to me totally the content of his conversation") and a manner that may come from years of trying to leave errant junior-high-school students with the impression that a responsible adult is magnanimous, even humble, about invariably being in the right. His wife, a high-school art teacher, paints and does batik, and created the name FaNee because she liked the way it looked and sounded—it sounds like "Fawn-*ee*" when the Coopers say it—but the impression she gives is not of artiness but of soft-spoken small-town gentility. When she found, in the course of cleaning up FaNee's room, that her ideal thirteen-year-old had been smoking cigarettes, she was, in her words, crushed. "FaNee was such a perfect child before that," JoAnn Cooper said some time later. "She was angry that we found out. She knew we knew that she had done something we didn't approve of, and then the rebellion started. I was hurt. I was very hurt. I guess it came through as disappointment."

2   Several months later, FaNee's grandmother died. FaNee had been devoted to her grandmother. She wrote a poem in her memory—an almost joyous poem, filled with Christian faith in the afterlife ("Please don't grieve over my happiness/Rejoice with me in the presence of the Angels of Heaven"). She also took some keepsakes from her grandmother's house, and was apparently mortified when her parents found them and explained that they would have to be returned. By then, the Coopers were aware that FaNee was going to have a difficult time as a teenager. They thought she might be self-conscious about the double affliction of glasses and braces. They thought she might be uncomfortable in the role of the principal's daughter at Gresham. In ninth grade, she entered Halls High School, where JoAnn Cooper was teaching art. FaNee was a loner at first. Then she fell in with what could only be considered a bad crowd.

3   Halls, a few miles to the north of Fountain City, used to be known as Halls Crossroads. It is what Knoxville people call "over the ridge"—on the side of Black Oak Ridge that has always been thought of as rural. When FaNee entered Halls High, the Coopers were already in the process of building a house on several acres of land they had bought in Halls, in a sparsely settled area along Brown Gap Road. Like two or three other houses along the road, it was to be constructed basically of huge logs taken from old buildings —a house that Leo Cooper describes as being, like the name FaNee, "just a little bit different." Ten years ago, Halls Crossroads was literally a crossroads. Then some of the Knoxville expansion that had swollen Fountain City spilled over the ridge, planting subdivisions here and there on roads that still went for long stretches with nothing but an occasional house with a cow or two next to it. The increase in population did not create a town. Halls has no center. Its commercial area is a series of two or three shopping centers strung together on the Maynardville Highway, the four-lane that leads north into Union County—a place almost synonymous in east Tennessee with mountain poverty. Its restaurant is the Halls Freezo Drive-In. The gathering place for the group FaNee Cooper eventually found herself in was the Maynardville Highway Exxon station.

4   At Halls High School, the social poles were represented by the Jocks and the Freaks. FaNee found her friends among the Freaks. "I am truly enlighted upon irregular trains of thought aimed at strange depots of mental wards," she wrote when she was fifteen. "Yes! Crazed farms for the mental off—Oh! I walked through the halls screams & loud laughter fill my ears—Orderlys try to reason with me—but I am unreasonable! The joys of being a FREAK in a circus of imagination." The little crowd of eight or ten young people that FaNee joined has been referred to by her mother as "the Union County group." A couple of the girls were from backgrounds similar to FaNee's, but all the boys had the characteristics, if not the precise addresses, that Knoxville people associate with the poor whites of Union County. They were the sort of boys who didn't bother to finish high school, or finished it in a special program for slow learners, or got ejected from it for taking a swing at the principal.

5   "I guess you can say they more or less dragged us down to their level with the drugs," a girl who was in the group—a girl who can be called Marcia—said recently. "And somehow we settled for it. It seems like we had to get ourselves in the pit before we could look out." People in the group used marijuana and Valium and LSD. They sneered at the Jocks and the "prim and proper little ladies" who went with the Jocks. "We set ourselves aside," Marcia now says. "We put ourselves above everyone. How we did that I don't know." In a Knox County high school, teenagers who want to get themselves in the pit need not mainline heroin. The Jocks they mean to be compared to do not merely show up regularly for classes and practice football and wear clean clothes; they watch their language and preach temperance and go to prayer meetings on Wednesday nights and talk about having a real good Christian witness. Around Knoxville, people who speak of well-behaved high-school kids often seem to use words like "perfect," or even

"angels." For FaNee's group, the opposite was not difficult to figure out. "We were into wicked things, strange things," Marcia says. "It was like we were on some kind of devil trip." FaNee wrote about demons and vultures and rats. "Slithering serpents eat my sanity and bite my ass," she wrote in an essay called "The Lovely Road of Life," just after she turned sixteen, "while tornadoes derail and ever so swiftly destroy every car in my train of thought." She wrote a lot about death.

6   FaNee's girl friends spoke of her as "super-intelligent." Her English teacher found some of her writing profound—and disturbing. She was thought to be not just super-intelligent but super-mysterious, and even, at times, super-weird—an introverted girl who stared straight ahead with deep-brown, nearly black eyes and seemed to have thoughts she couldn't share. Nobody really knew why she had chosen to run with the Freaks—whether it was loneliness or rebellion or simple boredom. Marcia thought it might have had something to do with a feeling that her parents had settled on Kristy as their perfect child. "I guess she figured she couldn't be the best," Marcia said recently. "So she decided she might as well be the worst."

7   Toward the spring of FaNee's junior year at Halls, her problems seemed to deepen. Despite her intelligence, her grades were sliding. She was what her mother called "a mental dropout." Leo Cooper had to visit Halls twice because of minor suspensions. Once, FaNee had been caught smoking. Once, having ducked out of a required assembly, she was spotted by a favorite teacher, who turned her in. At home, she exchanged little more than short, strained formalities with Kristy, who shared their parents' opinion of FaNee's choice of friends. The Coopers had finished their house—a large house, its size accentuated by the huge old logs and a great stone fireplace and outsize "Paul Bunyan"-style furniture—but FaNee spent most of her time there in her own room, sleeping or listening to rock music through ear-phones. One night, there was a terrible scene when FaNee returned from a concert in a condition that Leo Cooper knew had to be the result of mari-juana. JoAnn Cooper, who ordinarily strikes people as too gentle to raise her voice, found herself losing her temper regularly. Finally, Leo Cooper asked a counsellor he knew, Jim Griffin, to stop in at Halls High School and have a talk with FaNee—unofficially.

8   Griffin—a young man with a warm, informal manner—worked for the Juvenile Court of Knox County. He had a reputation for being able to reach teenagers who wouldn't talk to their parents or to school administrators. One Friday in March of 1977, he spent an hour and a half talking to FaNee Cooper. As Griffin recalls the interview, FaNee didn't seem alarmed by his presence. She seemed to him calm and controlled—Griffin thought it was something like talking to another adult—and, unlike most of the teenagers he dealt with, she looked him in the eye the entire time. Griffin, like some of FaNee's friends, found her eyes unsettling—"the coldest, most distant, but, at the same time, the most knowing eyes I'd ever seen." She expressed affec-tion for her parents, but she didn't seem interested in exploring ways of get-ting along better with them. The impression she gave Griffin was that they

were who they were, and she was who she was, and there didn't happen to be any connection. Several times, she made the same response to Griffin's suggestions: "It's too late."

9   That weekend, neither FaNee nor her parents brought up the subject of Griffin's visit. Leo Cooper has spoken of the weekend as being particularly happy; a friend of FaNee's who stayed over remembers it as particularly strained. FaNee stayed home from school on Monday because of a bad headache—she often had bad headaches—but felt well enough on Monday evening to drive to the library. She was to be home at nine. When she wasn't, Mrs. Cooper began to phone her friends. Finally, around ten, Leo Cooper got into his other car and took a swing around Halls—past the teenager hangouts like the Exxon station and the Pizza Hut and the Smoky Mountain Market. Then he took a second swing. At eleven, FaNee was still not home.

10   She hadn't gone to the library. She had picked up two girl friends and driven to the home of a third, where everyone took five Valium tablets. Then the four girls drove over to the Exxon station, where they met four boys from their crowd. After a while, the group bought some beer and some marijuana and reassembled at Charlie Stevens's trailer. Charlie Stevens was five or six years older than everyone else in the group—a skinny, slow-thinking young man with long black hair and a sparse beard. He was married and had a child, but he and his wife had separated; she was back in Union County with the baby. Stevens had remained in their trailer—parked in the yard near his mother's house, in a back-road area of Knox County dominated by decrepit, unpainted sheds and run-down trailers and rusted-out automobiles. Stevens had picked up FaNee at home once or twice—apparently, more as a driver for the group than as a date—and the Coopers, having learned that his unsuitability extended to being married, had asked her not to see him.

11   In Charlie's trailer, which had no heat or electricity, the group drank beer and passed around joints, keeping warm with blankets. By eleven or so, FaNee was what one of her friends has called "super-messed-up." Her speech was slurred. She was having trouble keeping her balance. She had decided not to go home. She had apparently persuaded herself that her parents intended to send her away to some sort of home for incorrigibles. "It's too late," she said to one of her friends. "It's just too late." It was decided that one of the boys, David Munsey, who was more or less the leader of the group, would drive the Coopers' car to FaNee's house, where FaNee and Charlie Stevens would pick him up in Stevens's car—a worn Pinto with four bald tires, one light, and a dragging muffler. FaNee wrote a note to her parents, and then, perhaps because her handwriting was suffering the effects of beer and marijuana and Valium, asked Stevens to rewrite it on a large piece of paper, which would be left on the seat of the Coopers' car. The Stevens version was just about the same as FaNee's, except that Stevens left out a couple of sentences about trying to work things out ("I'm willing to try") and, not having won any spelling championships himself, he misspelled a few words, like "tomorrow." The note said, "Dear Mom and Dad. Sorry I'm late. Very late. I left your car because I thought you might need it tomorrow. I love you all, but this is something I just had to do. The man talked to me

privately for one and a half hours and I was really scared, so this is something I just had to do, but don't worry, I'm with a very good friend. Love you all. FaNee. P. S. Please try to understand I love you all very much, really I do. Love me if you have a chance."

12   At eleven-thirty or so, Leo Cooper was sitting in his living room, looking out the window at his driveway—a long gravel road that runs almost four hundred feet from the house to Brown Gap Road. He saw the car that FaNee had been driving pull into the driveway. "She's home," he called to his wife, who had just left the room. Cooper walked out on the deck over the garage. The car had stopped at the end of the driveway, and the lights had gone out. He got into his other car and drove to the end of the driveway. David Munsey had already joined Charlie Stevens and FaNee, and the Pinto was just leaving, travelling at a normal rate of speed. Leo Cooper pulled out on the road behind them.

13   Stevens turned left on Crippen Road, a road that has a field on one side and two or three small houses on the other, and there Cooper pulled his car in front of the Pinto and stopped, blocking the way. He got out and walked toward the Pinto. Suddenly, Stevens put the car in reverse, backed into a driveway a hundred yards behind him, and sped off. Cooper jumped in his car and gave chase. Stevens raced back to Brown Gap Road, ran a stop sign there, ran another stop sign at Maynardville Highway, turned north, veered off onto the old Andersonville Pike, a nearly abandoned road that runs parallel to the highway, and then crossed back over the highway to the narrow, dark country roads on the other side. Stevens sometimes drove with his lights out. He took some of the corners by suddenly applying his hand brake to make the car swerve around in a ninety-degree turn. He was in familiar territory—he actually passed his trailer—and Cooper had difficulty keeping up. Past the trailer, Stevens swept down a hill into a sharp left turn that took him onto Foust Hollow Road, a winding, hilly road not much wider than one car.

14   At a fork, Cooper thought he had lost the Pinto. He started to go right, and then saw what seemed to be a spark from Stevens's dragging muffler off to the left, in the darkness. Cooper took the left fork, down Salem Church Road. He went down a hill, and then up a long, curving hill to a crest, where he saw the Stevens car ahead. "I saw the car airborne. Up in the air," he later testified. "It was up in the air. And then it completely rolled over one more time. It started to make another flip forward, and just as it started to flip to the other side it flipped back this way, and my daughter's body came out."

15   Cooper slammed on his brakes and skidded to a stop up against the Pinto. "Book!" Stevens shouted—the group's equivalent of "Scram!" Stevens and Munsey disappeared into the darkness. "It was dark, no one around, and so I started yelling for FaNee," Cooper has testified. "I thought it was an eternity before I could find her body, wedged under the back end of that car. . . . I tried everything I could, and saw that I couldn't get her loose. So I ran to a trailer back up to the top of the hill back up there to try to get that lady to call to get me some help, and then apparently she didn't think that I

was serious. . . . I took the jack out of my car and got under, and it was dark, still couldn't see too much what was going on . . . and started prying and got her loose, and I don't know how. And then I dragged her over to the side, and, of course, at the time I felt reasonably assured that she was gone, because her head was completely—on one side just as if you had taken a sledgehammer and just hit it and bashed it in. And I did have the pleasure of one thing. I had the pleasure of listening to her breathe about the last three times she ever breathed in her life."

16   David Munsey did not return to the wreck that night, but Charlie Stevens did. Leo Cooper was kneeling next to his daughter's body. Cooper insisted that Stevens come close enough to see FaNee. "He was kneeling down next to her," Stevens later testified. "And he said, 'Do you know what you've done? Do you really know what you've done?' Like that. And I just looked at her, and I said, 'Yes,' and just stood there. Because I couldn't say nothing." There was, of course, a legal decision to be made about who was responsible for FaNee Cooper's death. In a deposition, Stevens said he had been fleeing for his life. He testified that when Leo Cooper blocked Crippen Road, FaNee had said that her father had a gun and intended to hurt them. Stevens was bound over and eventually indicted for involuntary manslaughter. Leo Cooper testified that when he approached the Pinto on Crippen Road, FaNee had a strange expression that he had never seen before. "It wasn't like FaNee, and I knew something was wrong," he said. "My concern was to get FaNee out of the car." The district attorney's office asked that Cooper be bound over for reckless driving, but the judge declined to do so. "Any father would have done what he did," the judge said. "I can see no criminal act on the part of Mr. Cooper."

17   Almost two years passed before Charlie Stevens was brought to trial. Part of the problem was assuring the presence of David Munsey, who had joined the Navy but seemed inclined to assign his own leaves. In the meantime, the Coopers went to court with a civil suit—they had "uninsured-motorist coverage," which requires their insurance company to cover any defendant who has no insurance of his own—and they won a judgment. There were ways of assigning responsibility, of course, which had nothing to do with the law, civil or criminal. A lot of people in Knoxville thought that Leo Cooper had, in the words of his lawyer, "done what any daddy worth his salt would have done." There were others who believed that FaNee Cooper had lost her life because Leo Cooper had lost his temper. Leo Cooper was not among those who expressed any doubts about his actions. Unlike his wife, whose eyes filled with tears at almost any mention of FaNee, Cooper seemed able, even eager to go over the details of the accident again and again. With the help of a school-board security man, he conducted his own investigation. He drove over the route dozens of times. "I've thought about it every day, and I guess I will the rest of my life," he said as he and his lawyer and the prosecuting attorney went over the route again the day before Charlie Stevens's trial finally began. "But I can't tell any alternative for a father.

I simply wanted her out of that car. I'd have done the same thing again, even at the risk of losing her."

18   Tennessee law permits the family of a victim to hire a special prosecutor to assist the district attorney. The lawyer who acted for the Coopers in the civil case helped prosecute Charlie Stevens. Both he and the district attorney assured the jurors that the presence of a special prosecutor was not to be construed to mean that the Coopers were vindictive. Outside the courtroom, Leo Cooper said that the verdict was of no importance to him—that he felt sorry, in a way, for Charlie Stevens. But there were people in Knoxville who thought Cooper had a lot riding on the prosecution of Charlie Stevens. If Stevens was not guilty of FaNee Cooper's death—found so by twelve of his peers—who was?

19   At the trial, Cooper testified emotionally and remarkably graphically about pulling FaNee out from under the car and watching her die in his arms. Charlie Stevens had shaved his beard and cut his hair, but the effort did not transform him into an impressive witness. His lawyer—trying to argue that it would have been impossible for Stevens to concoct the story about FaNee's having mentioned a gun, as the prosecution strongly implied —said, "His mind is such that if you ask him a question you can hear his mind go around, like an old mill creaking." Stevens did not deny the recklessness of his driving or the sorry condition of his car. It happened to be the only car he had available to flee in, he said, and he had fled in fear for his life.

20   The prosecution said that Stevens could have let FaNee out of the car when her father stopped them, or could have gone to the commercial strip on the Maynardville Highway for protection. The prosecution said that Leo Cooper had done what he might have been expected to do under the circumstances—alone, late at night, his daughter in danger. The defense said precisely the same about Stevens: he had done what he might have been expected to do when being pursued by a man he had reason to be afraid of. "I don't fault Mr. Cooper for what he did, but I'm sorry he did it," the defense attorney said. "I'm sorry the girl said what she said." The jury deliberated for eighteen minutes. Charlie Stevens was found guilty. The jury recommended a sentence of from two to five years in the state penitentiary. At the announcement, Leo Cooper broke down and cried. JoAnn Cooper's eyes filled with tears; she blinked them back and continued to stare straight ahead.

21   In a way, the Coopers might still strike a casual visitor as an ideal family—handsome parents, a bright and bubbly teenage daughter, a little boy learning the hook shot from his father, a warm house with some land around it. FaNee's presence is there, of course. A picture of her, with a small bouquet of flowers over it, hangs in the living room. One of her poems is displayed in a frame on a table. Even if Leo Cooper continues to think about that night for the rest of his life, there are questions he can never answer. Was there a way that Leo and JoAnn Cooper could have prevented FaNee from choosing the path she chose? Would she still be alive if Leo Cooper had

not jumped into his car and driven to the end of the driveway to investigate? Did she in fact tell Charlie Stevens that her father would hurt them—or even that her father had a gun? Did she want to get away from her family even at the risk of tearing around dark country roads in Charlie Stevens's dismal Pinto? Or did she welcome the risk? The poem of FaNee's that the Coopers have displayed is one she wrote a week before her death:

> I think I'm going to die
> And I really don't know why.
> But look in my eye
> When I tell you good-bye.
> I think I'm going to die.

A. Comprehension

Choose the answer that best completes each statement. Do not refer to the selection while doing this exercise.

1. Even as a young child, FaNee Cooper was (a) outgoing and happy; (b) moody and sullen; (c) reserved and introspective; (d) alienated and withdrawn.

2. The Cooper family lived near (a) Des Moines, Iowa; (b) Springfield, Illinois; (c) Knoxville, Tennessee; (d) Louisville, Kentucky.

3. JoAnn Cooper, FaNee's mother, learned that her daughter was not a perfect child when she discovered that FaNee had been (a) using marijuana; (b) using alcohol; (c) cutting school; (d) smoking cigarettes.

4. The gathering place for FaNee and her group of friends was (a) the intersection at the center of Halls Crossroads; (b) the Maynardville Highway Exxon gas station; (c) the Halls Freezo Drive-In; (d) the local Pizza Hut.

5. The two social extremes at Halls High School were represented by (a) the jocks and the freaks; (b) the college-bound and the dropouts; (c) the drug users and the abstainers; (d) the Christians and the atheists.

6. The main subject of FaNee's writings was (a) suicide; (b) the devil; (c) drugs; (d) death.

7. Jim Griffin, the counselor who tried to talk to FaNee about her problems, was unsettled by her (a) incoherent speech; (b) distrust of her parents' motives; (c) cold, yet knowing, eyes; (d) inability to separate reality and fantasy.

8. Aside from the fact that he was five or six years older than FaNee and her friends, another reason that her parents found Charlie Stevens unsuitable was that he (a) had been in prison; (b) had dropped out of high school; (c) was continually stoned on drugs; (d) was married.

9. According to Charlie Stevens's testimony, he was fleeing in the Pinto because FaNee had told him that (a) her father had a gun and intended to hurt them; (b) she wanted to run away from her parents forever; (c) she loved him and wanted to marry him; (d) she was going to be sent to a school for wayward girls.

10. Concerning the death of FaNee Cooper, the jury (a) could not reach a verdict; (b) acquitted Charlie Stevens; (c) found Charlie Stevens guilty; (d) found FaNee's father guilty of contributory negligence.

B. Inferences   On the basis of the evidence in the selection, answer these inference questions. You may refer to the selection to answer the questions in this section, and all the remaining sections.

1. Read paragraph 1 again. What can you infer about FaNee Cooper's religious upbringing? _____

2. Also from paragraph 1, what can you infer about the kind of principal Leo Cooper is? _____

3. Reread paragraphs 3 and 4. What can you infer about the socio-economic status of the "Union County group" with whom FaNee was friends? _____

4. Also from paragraph 4, how would you describe the Jocks' religious beliefs? _____

5. What do FaNee's writings, as discussed in paragraph 5, suggest about her? _____

6. What do you think FaNee meant by her response to Jim Griffin (in paragraph 8), "It's too late"? _____

7. What can you infer from paragraph 17 about David Munsey's navy career? _____

8. Read paragraph 19 again. Why did the prosecutor in the case say that it would have been impossible for Stevens to invent the story about FaNee's reference to a gun? _____

C. Structure   1. The mode of discourse in this selection is primarily (a) narration; (b) description; (c) exposition; (d) persuasion.

2. Trillin's specific purpose in writing is to (a) warn young people about the dangers of drugs and of getting involved with the wrong group of friends; (b) warn parents about the temptations teenagers are confronted with today; (c) assign the blame for FaNee Cooper's death; (d) examine the circumstances surrounding FaNee Cooper's death.

3. In paragraph 1, Trillin describes Leo Cooper's manner by saying that he gives the impression of "a responsible adult [who] is magnanimous, even humble, about invariably being in the right." First, paraphrase this characterization. _____

Does this characterization confirm or contradict Cooper's subsequent actions? _____
Explain. _____
_____

4. Which statement from the selection best explains the reason for FaNee's rebellion? _____
_____

5. In what way is it important to understand the nature of the differences between the Jocks and the Freaks? _____
_____

6. In paragraph 18, Trillin writes that "the presence of a special prosecutor was not to be construed to mean that the Coopers were vindictive." Does Trillin mean for us to believe this? What did Leo Cooper stand to gain by Charlie Stevens's conviction for his daughter's death? Explain.
_____
_____

7. The question at the heart of "It's Just Too Late" is mentioned in paragraph 18. Who was guilty of FaNee's death? According to his account of the incident, which of the following *seems* to be Trillin's answer to the question? FaNee's death was probably caused by (a) her own mistakes and the harmful influence of the Freaks she associated with; (b) Charlie Stevens's reckless driving; (c) Leo Cooper's pursuit of Stevens's car; (d) a tragic combination of circumstances and mistakes on the part of everyone involved in the tragedy.

8. The overall tone of the selection can best be described as (a) hostile; judgmental; (b) impartial; objective; (c) sarcastic; cynical; (d) accusatory; vindictive; (e) sympathetic; compassionate.
Defend your answer by pointing to specific passages.

D. Vocabulary

For each italicized word from the selection, choose the best definition according to the context in which it appears.

1. she was reserved and *introspective* [paragraph 1]: (a) given to private thought; (b) shy; timid; (c) self-critical; (d) moody; sullen.

2. *errant* junior-high-school students [1]: (a) roving, especially in search of adventure; (b) straying from the proper course or standards; (c) lacking consistency or regularity; (d) those who commit serious sins or offenses.

3. a responsible adult is *magnanimous* [1]: (a) serious; (b) arrogant; (c) noble of mind and heart; (d) greatly concerned; caring.

4. soft-spoken small-town *gentility* [1]: condition of being (a) narrow-minded; having parochial values; (b) politically and socially conservative; (c) snobbish; haughty; (d) refined; well-bred.

5. she was apparently *mortified* [2]: (a) near death; (b) mortally wounded; (c) humiliated; having wounded pride; (d) angry; resentful.

6. the double *affliction* of glasses and braces [2]: a condition causing (a) discomfort; (b) physical pain; (c) intense suffering; (d) emotional distress.

7. in a *sparsely* settled area [3; also see *sparse* in paragraph 10]: (a) densely; in a crowded manner; (b) recently; (c) thinly; not densely; (d) conspicuously deficient.

8. Halls Crossroads was *literally* a crossroads [3]: referring to a term that is used (a) in its strict sense or meaning; (b) imaginatively; figuratively; (c) in an exaggerated or hyperbolic way; (d) carefully; precisely.

9. a place almost *synonymous with* mountain poverty [3]: (a) implicated; guilty of; (b) full of; replete; (c) equivalent in meaning; (d) having the same characteristics as.

10. the social *poles* were represented [4]: (a) groups with opposite tendencies; (b) powerful or exclusive groups; cliques; (c) ideal or perfect groups; (d) groups symmetrically or equally arranged.

11. got *ejected* from it [4]: (a) discouraged; (b) expelled; (c) educated; (d) compelled.

12. *prim* and proper little ladies [5]: proper to the point of (a) being repulsive; (b) being ridiculous; (c) affectation; (d) being envied.

13. they preach *temperance* [5]: (a) rejuvenation; (b) repentance; (c) salvation; (d) moderation.

14. its size *accentuated* by the huge old logs [7]: (a) emphasized; (b) diminished; (c) accented; (d) complemented.

15. *decrepit,* unpainted sheds [10]: (a) uninhabited; (b) austere; (c) broken-down; (d) poorly made.

16. some sort of home for *incorrigibles* [11]: people who cannot be (a) trusted; (b) reformed; (c) accepted; (d) imprisoned.

17. *veered* off onto the old Andersonville Pike [13]: (a) skidded; (b) capsized; (c) flipped; (d) turned.

18. in a *deposition* [16—pronounced dĕp′ə-zĭsh′ən]: (a) diary entry; (b) published letter; (c) testimony made under oath; (d) courtroom appearance.

19. *indicted* for involuntary manslaughter [16—pronounced ĭn-dīt′əd]: (a) formally accused of a crime; (b) found guilty; (c) sentenced to a prison term; (d) acquitted; found innocent.

20. not to be *construed* to mean [18]: (a) discussed; debated; (b) explained; interpreted; (c) concluded; summarized; (d) criticized; attacked.

21. the Coopers were *vindictive* [18]: (a) cleared of blame or suspicion; (b) revengeful; unforgiving; (c) soft-hearted; sympathetic; (d) justified; excused.

22. Cooper testified *graphically* [19]: (a) convincingly; compellingly; (b) dramatically; emotionally; (c) vividly; clearly; (d) using pictures and charts.

23. impossible for Stevens to *concoct* the story [19]: (a) conclude; (b) invent; (c) elaborate on; (d) remember.

24. the *sorry* condition of his car [19]: (a) regrettable; (b) causing sorrow; (c) inferior; poor; (d) unsafe.

E. Questions for Analysis

1. In what way is Trillin's description of Leo Cooper's character central to understanding the tragedy of FaNee Cooper's death?

2. In paragraph 17, Trillin cites the two extremes of opinion about Leo Cooper's actions the night of FaNee's death. ["A lot of people in Knoxville thought that Leo Cooper had, in the words of his lawyer, 'done what any daddy worth his salt would have done.' There were others who believed that FaNee Cooper had lost her life because Leo Cooper had lost his temper."] How do you interpret his action? What other clues in the essay suggest that Leo Cooper was the primary cause of his daughter's death?

3. If you had been Leo Cooper, what would you have done?

4. Trillin mentions very little about the relationship among the members of the Cooper family, but from the information we are given, what would you say was the chief problem in the relationship between FaNee and her parents?

Selection 6

The Voices of Time
Edward T. Hall

Born in Webster Groves, Missouri, Edward Hall (1914–   ) received his Ph.D. from Columbia University. Since 1967, he has been a professor of anthropology at Northwestern University, and he has conducted anthropological research in Micronesia, the southwestern part of the United States, and Europe. In addition, he has published numerous books, both scholarly and popular, on anthropology. "The Voices of Time" comes from *The Silent Language,* Hall's investigation into the way people communicate by their behavior and gesture.

1   Time talks. It speaks more plainly than words. The message it conveys comes through loud and clear. Because it is manipulated less consciously, it is subject to less distortion than the spoken language. It can shout the truth where words lie.

2   I was once a member of a mayor's committee on human relations in a large city. My assignment was to estimate what the chances were of non-discriminatory practices being adopted by the different city departments. The first step in this project was to interview the department heads, two of whom were themselves members of minority groups. If one were to believe the words of these officials, it seemed that all of them were more than willing to adopt non-discriminatory labor practices. Yet I felt that, despite what they said, in only one case was there much chance for a change. Why? The answer lay in how they used the silent language of time and space.

3   Special attention had been given to arranging each interview. Department heads were asked to be prepared to spend an hour or more discussing their thoughts with me. Nevertheless, appointments were forgotten; long waits in outer offices (fifteen to forty-five minutes) were common, and the length of the interview was often cut down to ten or fifteen minutes. I was usually kept at an impersonal distance during the interview. In only one case did the department head come from behind his desk. These men had a position and they were literally and figuratively sticking to it!

4   The implication of this experience (one which public-opinion pollsters might well heed) is quite obvious. What people do is frequently more important than what they say. In this case the way these municipal potentates handled time was eloquent testimony to what they inwardly believed, for the structure and meaning of time systems, as well as the time intervals, are easy to identify. In regard to being late there are: "mumble something" periods, slight apology periods, mildly insulting periods requiring full apology, rude periods, and downright insulting periods. The psychoanalyst has long been aware of the significance of communication on this level. He can point to the way his patients handle time as evidence of "resistances" and "transference."

5   Different parts of the day, for example, are highly significant in certain contexts. Time may indicate the importance of the occasion as well as on what level an interaction between persons is to take place. In the United States if you telephone someone very early in the morning, while he is shaving or having breakfast, the time of the call usually signals a matter of utmost importance and extreme urgency. The same applies for calls after 11:00 P.M. A call received during sleeping hours is apt to be taken as a matter of life and death, hence the rude joke value of these calls among the young. Our realization that time talks is even reflected in such common expressions as, "What time does the clock *say?*"

6   An example of how thoroughly these things are taken for granted was reported to me by John Useem, an American social anthropologist, in an illuminating case from the South Pacific. The natives of one of the islands had been having a difficult time getting their white supervisors to hire them in a way consistent with their traditional status system. Through ignorance the supervisors had hired too many of one group and by so doing had disrupted the existing balance of power among the natives. The entire population of the island was seething because of this error. Since the Americans continued in their ignorance and refused to hire according to local practice, the head men of the two factions met one night to discuss an acceptable reallocation of jobs. When they finally arrived at a solution, they went en masse to see the plant manager and woke him up to tell him what had been decided. Unfortunately, it was then between two and three o'clock in the morning. They did not know that it is a sign of extreme urgency to wake up Americans at this hour. As one might expect, the American plant manager, who understood neither the local language nor the culture nor what the hullabaloo was all about, thought he had a riot on his hands and called out the Marines. It simply never occurred to him that the parts of the day have a different meaning for these people than they have for us.

7   On the other hand, plant managers in the United States are fully aware of the significance of a communication made during the middle of the morning or afternoon that takes everyone away from his work. Whenever they want to make an important announcement they will ask: "When shall we let them know?" In the social world a girl feels insulted when she is asked for a date at the last minute by someone whom she doesn't know very well, and the person who extends an invitation to a dinner party with only three

or four days' notice has to apologize. How different from the people of the Middle East with whom it is pointless to make an appointment too far in advance, because the informal structure of their time system places everything beyond a week into a single category of "future," in which plans tend to "slip off their minds."

8   Advance notice is often referred to in America as "lead time," an expression which is significant in a culture where schedules are important. While it is learned informally, most of us are familiar with how it works in our own culture, even though we cannot state the rules technically. The rules for lead time in other cultures, however, have rarely been analyzed. At the most they are known by experience to those who lived abroad for some time. Yet think how important it is to know how much time is required to prepare people, or for them to prepare themselves, for things to come. Sometimes lead time would seem to be very extended. At other times, in the Middle East, any period longer than a week may be too long.

9   How troublesome differing ways of handling time can be is well illustrated by the case of an American agriculturalist assigned to duty as an attaché of our embassy in a Latin country. After what seemed to him a suitable period he let it be known that he would like to call on the minister who was his counterpart. For various reasons, the suggested time was not suitable; all sorts of cues came back to the effect that the time was not yet ripe to visit the minister. Our friend, however, persisted and forced an appointment which was reluctantly granted. Arriving a little before the hour (the American respect pattern), he waited. The hour came and passed; five minutes—ten minutes—fifteen minutes. At this point he suggested to the secretary that perhaps the minister did not know he was waiting in the outer office. This gave him the feeling he had done something concrete and also helped to overcome the great anxiety that was stirring inside him. Twenty minutes—twenty-five minutes—thirty minutes—forty-five minutes (the insult period)!

10   He jumped up and told the secretary that he had been "cooling his heels" in an outer office for forty-five minutes and he was "damned sick and tired" of this type of treatment. This message was relayed to the minister, who said, in effect, "Let him cool his heels." The attaché's stay in the country was not a happy one.

11   The principal source of misunderstanding lay in the fact that in the country in question the five-minute-delay interval was not significant. Forty-five minutes, on the other hand, instead of being at the tail end of the waiting scale, was just barely at the beginning. To suggest to an American's secretary that perhaps her boss didn't know you were there after waiting sixty seconds would seem absurd, as would raising a storm about "cooling your heels" for five minutes. Yet this is precisely the way the minister registered the protestations of the American in his outer office! He felt, as usual, that Americans were being totally unreasonable.

12   Throughout this unfortunate episode the attaché was acting according to the way he had been brought up. At home in the United States his responses would have been normal ones and his behavior legitimate. Yet

even if he had been told before he left home that this sort of thing would happen, he would have had difficulty not *feeling* insulted after he had been kept waiting forty-five minutes. If, on the other hand he had been taught the details of the local time system just as he should have been taught the local spoken language, it would have been possible for him to adjust himself accordingly.

13 What bothers people in situations of this sort is that they don't realize they are being subjected to another form of communication, one that works part of the time with language and part of the time independently of it. The fact that the message conveyed is couched in no formal vocabulary makes things doubly difficult, because neither party can get very explicit about what is actually taking place. Each can only say what he thinks is happening and how he feels about it. The thought of what is being communicated is what hurts.

AMERICAN TIME

14 People of the Western world, particularly Americans, tend to think of time as something fixed in nature, something around us and from which we cannot escape; an ever-present part of the environment, just like the air we breathe. That it might be experienced in any other way seems unnatural and strange, a feeling which is rarely modified even when we begin to discover how really differently it is handled by some other people. Within the West itself certain cultures rank time much lower in overall importance than we do. In Latin America, for example, where time is treated rather cavalierly, one commonly hears the expression, "Our time or your time?" *"Hora americana, hora mejicana?"*

15 As a rule, Americans think of time as a road or a ribbon stretching into the future, along which one progresses. The road has segments or compartments which are to be kept discrete ("one thing at a time"). People who cannot schedule time are looked down upon as impractical. In at least some parts of Latin America, the North American (their term for us) finds himself annoyed when he has made an appointment with somebody, only to find a lot of other things going on at the same time. An old friend of mine of Spanish cultural heritage used to run his business according to the "Latino" system. This meant that up to fifteen people were in his office at one time. Business which might have been finished in a quarter of an hour sometimes took a whole day. He realized, of course, that the Anglo-Americans were disturbed by this and used to make some allowance for them, a dispensation which meant that they spent only an hour or so in his office when they planned on a few minutes. The American concept of the discreteness of time and the necessity for scheduling was at variance with this amiable and seemingly confusing Latin system. However, if my friend had adhered to the American system he would have destroyed a vital part of his prosperity. People who came to do business with him also came to find out things and to visit each other. The ten to fifteen Spanish-Americans and Indians who used to sit around the office (among whom I later found myself after I had learned to relax a little) played their own part in a particular type of communications network.

16   Not only do we Americans segment and schedule time, but we look ahead and are oriented almost entirely toward the future. We like new things and are preoccupied with change. We want to know how to overcome resistance to change. In fact, scientific theories and even some pseudo-scientific ones, which incorporate a striking theory of change, are often given special attention.

17   Time with us is handled much like a material; we earn it, spend it, save it, waste it. To us it is somewhat immoral to have two things going on at the same time. In Latin America it is not uncommon for one man to have a number of simultaneous jobs which he either carries on from one desk or which he moves between, spending a small amount of time on each.

18   While we look to the future, our view of it is limited. The future to us is the foreseeable future, not the future of the South Asian that may involve centuries. Indeed, our perspective is so short as to inhibit the operation of a good many practical projects, such as sixty- and one-hundred-year conservation works requiring public support and public funds. Anyone who has worked in industry or in the government of the United States has heard the following: "Gentlemen, this is for the long term! Five or ten years."

19   For us a "long time" can be almost anything—ten or twenty years, two or three months, a few weeks, or even a couple of days. The South Asian, however, feels that it is perfectly realistic to think of a "long time" in terms of thousands of years or even an endless period. A colleague once described their conceptualization of time as follows: "Time is like a museum with endless corridors and alcoves. You, the viewer, are walking through the museum in the dark, holding a light to each scene as you pass it. God is the curator of the museum, and only He knows all that is in it. One lifetime represents one alcove."

20   The American's view of the future is linked to a view of the past, for tradition plays an equally limited part in American culture. As a whole, we push it aside or leave it to a few souls who are interested in the past for very special reasons. There are, of course, a few pockets, such as New England and the South, where tradition is emphasized. But in the realm of business, which is the dominant model of United States life, tradition is equated with *experience*, and experience is thought of as being very close to if not synonymous with know-how. Know-how is one of our prized possessions, so that when we look backward it is rarely to take pleasure in the past itself but usually to calculate the know-how, to assess the prognosis for success in the future.

21   Promptness is also valued highly in American life. If people are not prompt, it is often taken either as an insult or as an indication that they are not quite responsible. There are those, of a psychological bent, who would say that we are obsessed with time. They can point to individuals in American culture who are literally time-ridden. And even the rest of us feel very strongly about time because we have been taught to take it so seriously. We have stressed this aspect of culture and developed it to a point unequaled anywhere in the world, except, perhaps, in Switzerland and north Germany. Many people criticize our obsessional handling of time. They attribute

ulcers and hypertension to the pressure engendered by such a system. Perhaps they are right.

A. Comprehension
Choose the answer that best completes each statement. Do not refer to the selection while doing this exercise.

1. The main idea of the selection is (a) government agencies should study the way different groups view time as a way of solving interracial tensions; (b) Americans are more conscious of time and schedules than are other cultural groups; (c) the way people handle time is often a better indication of their thinking than the words they use; (d) Americans should be sensitive to the ways other cultures view time and space.

2. The importance of the occasion is determined primarily by (a) the status of the people who are interacting; (b) the observance of common courtesies such as shaking hands; (c) the prompt adherence to schedules; (d) the time of day that the occasion takes place.

3. For Americans, being awakened in the middle of the night is (a) a sign of extreme urgency; (b) an example of extreme rudeness; (c) an unforgivable insult; (d) a sign that a momentous decision has been made.

4. In America, the term "lead time" means (a) how long one can politely be kept waiting for an appointment; (b) the time of day when one should break bad news; (c) advance notice for appointments or social functions; (d) an indefinite time in the future.

5. If an American wants to show respect, he or she arrives at an appointment (a) five minutes early; (b) half an hour early; (c) exactly on time; (d) five minutes late.

6. For a Latin American, a wait of forty-five minutes indicates (a) an insult; (b) only a slight delay; the beginning of the waiting period; (c) the outer limits of the waiting period; (d) the normal time people with appointments are kept waiting.

7. Americans view time as (a) a circle; (b) a space with infinite dimensions; (c) a road or ribbon stretching into the future; (d) a chart with blocks neatly marking the days, weeks, and months.

8. In the realm of business, Americans regard tradition as being synonymous with (a) cultural heritage; (b) experience and know-how; (c) historical events of great importance; (d) a museum with valuable artifacts from the past.

B. Inferences
On the basis of the evidence in the selection, mark these statements as follows: *A* for accurate inferences, *I* for inaccurate inferences, and *IE* for insufficient evidence. You may refer to the selection to answer the questions in this section, and all the remaining sections.

_____ 1. The department heads whom Hall interviewed about ways to end discriminatory labor practices were not really interested in ending them.

_____ 2. The way a person handles time often reveals his personality more than what he says or does.

_____ 3. The natives of the South Pacific island who went to see the plant manager in the middle of the night were being deliberately rude.

_____ 4. For the natives of the South Pacific island, waking someone up in the middle of the night indicates a matter of life and death.

_____ 5. Making an appointment with a Middle Easterner more than a week in advance shows extreme rudeness.

_____ 6. The American was kept waiting by the Latin minister partly because the American had forced an appointment.

_____ 7. Diplomats should not only learn the language of the place where they are stationed, but also its local time system.

_____ 8. The meaning of time for a particular culture is usually understood unconsciously and cannot be explained explicitly to an outsider.

_____ 9. Most cultures are as strict about adhering to schedules as Americans are.

_____ 10. To an American, the way Latin Americans conduct business is inefficient, time-consuming, and confusing.

_____ 11. In relation to the South Asian conception of time, our view of the future is more limited.

_____ 12. The Swiss and North Germans are more concerned with traditions—the accomplishments of the past—than other Western Europeans.

_____ 13. It is nearly impossible for a member of one cultural group to adopt the time system of another culture.

_____ 14. Latin Americans have a lower incidence of ulcers and hypertension than North Americans.

C. Structure

1. Write the sentence that best states the main idea of the entire selection.

_____

_____

2. The primary mode of discourse in this selection is (a) narration; (b) description; (c) exposition; (d) persuasion.

3. To support the ideas, which _two_ methods of paragraph development does Hall rely on most? (a) definition; (b) analogy; (c) examples; (d) illustrations; (e) process; (f) comparison; (g) contrast.

4. Look again at paragraph 4. What method of development is used in the fourth sentence (beginning "In regard to being late . . .")? (a) example; (b) comparison; (c) cause–effect; (d) definition; (e) process; (f) classification.

5. The psychiatrist's terms for the way patients handle time, mentioned at the end of paragraph 4, are examples of (a) jargon; (b) euphemisms; (c) sneer words; (d) metaphors; (e) connotative words.

6. What *two* patterns of organization are used in paragraph 6? (a) deductive; (b) variation of deductive; (c) inductive; (d) chronological; (e) spatial; (f) emphatic.

7. Paragraphs 9–12 recount the experience of an American attaché who was kept waiting for an appointment in a Latin country. What idea does this story support? _____

8. In paragraph 10, what does the phrase "cooling his heels" mean?

_____

9. In the first sentence of paragraph 15, the transitional phrase, "as a rule," means (a) it is always the rule; (b) it is generally true; (c) it is commonly believed; (d) it is a fact.

10. Hall says, in paragraph 17, that Americans handle time like a material. He specifically suggests, with this analogy, that Americans handle time as if it were _____.

11. In paragraph 19, Hall describes the South Asian conception of time by using another analogy. Use your own words to explain what South Asians perceive a lifetime to be. _____

_____

12. With respect to his discussion of time and the difference in the ways Americans and other cultures perceive it, the author's tone is best described as (a) neutral; objective; (b) impassioned; eager; (c) angry; resentful; (d) informative; lightly humorous; (e) judgmental; biased; (f) preachy; tediously didactic.

D. Vocabulary   For each italicized word from the selection, choose the best definition according to the context in which it appears.

1. it is *manipulated* less consciously [paragraph 1]: (a) tampered with falsely; (b) controlled; handled; (c) considered; thought of; (d) comprehended; understood.

2. the *implication* of this experience [4]: that which is (a) learned; (b) indirectly suggested; (c) considered; (d) enjoyed.

3. these municipal *potentates* [4]: those who have (a) power and position; (b) money and fame; (c) unlimited time; (d) a strong sense of morality.

4. *eloquent* testimony [4]: (a) rational; sound; (b) persuasive; expressive; (c) emotionally moving; (d) subtle; not obvious.

5. a matter of *utmost* importance [5]: (a) trivial; insignificant; (b) moderate; (c) critical; (d) great.

6. an *illuminating* case [6]: (a) interesting; (b) relevant; (c) enlightening; (d) famous.

7. the entire population was *seething* [6]: (a) enraged; (b) violently agitated; (c) perplexed; (d) irritated.

8. the head men of two *factions* [6]: (a) religious groups; (b) political parties; (c) tribal groups; (d) groups in conflict.

9. an acceptable *reallocation* of jobs [6]: the act of (a) distributing again according to a plan; (b) retaliating against; (c) organizing again; (d) classifying again.

10. they went *en masse* [6—pronounced ĕn măs′]: (a) in a fit of rage; (b) in twos and threes; (c) in one group; (d) in a show of force.

11. what the *hullabaloo* was all about [6]: (a) worry; (b) conflict; (c) protest; (d) uproar.

12. the minister who was his *counterpart* [9]: (a) one who is superior to another; (b) one who supervises another; (c) one who closely duplicates another's functions; (d) one who is an enemy of another.

13. the message is *couched* in no formal vocabulary [13]: (a) expressed; (b) described; (c) said aloud; (d) made intelligible.

14. neither party can get very *explicit* [13]: (a) emotional; (b) enthusiastic; (c) disturbed; (d) precise.

15. time is treated rather *cavalierly* [14]: (a) arrogantly; haughtily; (b) with an ill-considered sureness; offhandedly; (c) with a militaristic regularity; (d) with a sense of cheerful abandon.

16. compartments which are to be kept *discrete* [15]: (a) separate; distinct; (b) respectful; modest; (c) empty; unfilled; (d) available; free.

17. some allowance, a *dispensation* for them [15]: (a) help; comfort; (b) forgiveness; (c) a specific arrangement; (d) an order; a command.

18. the necessity for scheduling was *at variance* [15]: (a) impossible to do; (b) under discussion; (c) scheduled for revision; (d) in conflict with.

19. this *amiable* Latin system [15]: (a) congenial; showing a friendly disposition; (b) bewildering; complex; (c) erratic; unpredictable; (d) inefficient; time-wasting.

20. scientific theories and some *pseudo*-scientific ones [16]: the prefix *pseudo-* means (a) named; (b) nearly; (c) false; (d) opposite.

21. to *inhibit* the operation of many projects [18]: (a) inherit; (b) prevent; (c) cease; (d) encourage.

22. to assess the *prognosis* for success [20]: (a) recipe; formula; (b) possibility; feasibility; (c) forecast; probable outcome; (d) secret; hidden plan.

23. those of a psychological *bent* [21]: (a) the state of being crooked; (b) an individual tendency or inclination; (c) the limit of endurance; (d) a structural member.

24. the pressure *engendered* by the system [21]: (a) produced; (b) prepared; (c) perpetuated; (d) increased.

E. Questions for Analysis

1. For the next day, observe people around you in social situations, paying particular attention to how they handle time and space. For example, what do people say when they are late? Does what they say depend on how late they are? Consider, too, the distance between people when they speak. Do your observations accord with Hall's? What additional

conclusions can you draw about American behavior patterns according to how they use time?

2. If you are familiar with the people and customs of another culture, how do its inhabitants use time and space in ways that are different from Americans? Does their behavior indicate anything about their system of values?

Selection 7   **Girlfriends**
Susan Allen Toth

Susan Allen Toth (1940–   ) graduated from Smith College, did graduate work at the University of California at Berkeley, and received her Ph.D. from the University of Minnesota. She lives in St. Paul, Minnesota with her daughter, and teaches English at Macalester College. The author of numerous magazine articles, she has also published two books: *Blooming,* an account of growing up in Ames, Iowa, from which "Girlfriends" comes, and *Ivy Days,* the story of her college years at Smith.

1   Girlfriends were as essential as mothers. I could survive weeks, even months, without a boyfriend, although I did need to be able to produce one in those endless circular conversations of "Who do you like best?" "Do you think he likes me or Celia better" "Don't you agree with us that Herb is a nerd?" "Would you ever sit next to Jim if you didn't have to?" But I always had to have a best friend.

2   A set of girlfriends provided a sense of security, as belonging to any group does. But having a best friend was more complicated: using a friend as a mirror or as a model, expanding your own knowledge through someone else's, painfully acquiring social skills. What little we learned about living with another person in an equal relationship, outside our own families, we learned from our girlfriends. It certainly wasn't a full preparation for marriage, but it was the only one some of us ever got.

3   My earliest memory of a best friend is a humiliating one. After spending a year in California in third grade, I returned to Ames to skip a grade and suddenly enter fifth. We had just moved to a new house in a different neighborhood, so I also had to switch to the other elementary school on the campus side of town. Both schools joined at Welch Junior High, where we children remained together, a relatively unchanging group, until we moved downtown to merge with Central Junior High in Ames High School. By then our social alliances had been firmly forged.

4   My year away had erased a lot, and I was a new kid in fifth grade, suspiciously smart and a year too young. I felt lost and lonely, and the only girl who would consent to spend any time with me on the playground or after school was Margie Dwyer. Margie, though rather pretty, was shy and awkward. Her dark hair was twisted in old-fashioned braids on top of her head, emphasizing her sallow skin. I seem to remember she wore one dark plaid jumper all the time. Her father was a janitor somewhere at the college, and they lived in a basement apartment in an old building not far from our

house. I don't remember visiting there, or her parents, but I do remember how grateful I was to hold hands with Margie, who smiled at me as we skipped in unison down the sidewalk. But I clearly knew then and remembered with shame later that Margie, like me, was a social pariah. She had no set of friends, no status. After we stopped being best friends the next year, she became best friends with "Sappy" Strickland, the dumbest girl in class. Years later Margie dropped out of high school and married an older man, an auto mechanic. No one noticed.

5   What humiliates me about my memory of Margie is how quickly I dropped her when, in sixth grade, I was suddenly adopted into an acceptable set of friends. There weren't, in fact, many sets to choose from. With two sections of each grade, about thirty students in each, we had a "pool" of sixty; roughly half of those were boys; so thirty girls had to divide themselves into appropriate groups. Six formed the elite, a group so tight, so deliberately exclusive, that they earned themselves the name of "the Society Six." They were the prettiest, most sophisticated, and stylish girls and naturally included all the ninth-grade cheerleaders. They chose the boyfriends they wanted from the homeroom presidents, athletes, and other "neat" boys.

6   Needless to say, with my plumpness, brains, wicked tongue and awkward uncertainties, I did not belong to the "Society Six." Years later, so many years I had not heard of or seen any of the "Society Six" for two decades, I was talking at dinner to a psychiatrist about our junior-high social groups. I had never been a cheerleader, I told him self-effacingly, but then I added, "You know, they didn't end up all that well. One of them, Delaney Deere, lost all her popularity when she got to high school. She started going with an older man from Des Moines, quit school, and left town. I wonder what ever happened to her." He smiled with that knowing look a psychiatrist acquires, and said quietly, "Still hurts, doesn't it?" "What?" I said. "I mean, your not getting to be a cheerleader. Not being one of that High Society, or whatever-you-call-it. Why do you still take such satisfaction in what happened to that Delaney girl?" He smiled again and went to find another rumaki, while I stared speechless at my plate.

7   But if I couldn't be a member of the Society Six, I was delighted to be accepted into the next group on the social scale, a larger and more fluid one, ten or fifteen girls, democratic enough at least to be nameless. One of its leaders was Kristy Harbinger, whose parents were good friends of my mother's. On the day Kristy asked me to come over to her house after school to play "Sorry," I knew I had made it. Kristy and the other girls in this group were from various backgrounds, some with faculty parents, others with fathers who included an insurance salesman, a banker, a plumber, an oil-company representative who toured the state for Mobil. What your father did wasn't important, though you needed to have a house where you could bring friends home without embarrassment.

8   Most of us attended the nearby Presbyterian, Methodist or Baptist churches, but by ninth grade, when parochial schools ended, we had two Catholic friends as well. I'm not sure on what grounds we admitted others as friends, how we made up the guest lists for our slumber parties or Valentines

or birthdays, how we knew whom to call to go to the movies. Most of us went on to college, but we certainly didn't base our friendship on intellectual merit. Most of us were moderately attractive, but one or two of us didn't date at all for years. Most of us were "popular," but I don't know exactly why. Perhaps we merely defined ourselves in relation to the Society Six and to all the other girls below us, the loners, the stupid ones, the fat ones. We had absorbed already by sixth grade a set of careful and cruel distinctions.

9   Whatever the sociology of our group, it was large enough to absorb newcomers and to permit trading best friends. When Kristy Harbinger asked me to her house to play "Sorry," I was already involved with Joyce Schwartz. For almost a year Kristy, Joyce and I uneasily maneuvered to see who would be whose best friend. I liked Joyce because she was more mature than I. Her body already rounded nicely, and when she wore a sweater, it had real bumps. When she turned a corner, Joyce flounced, her skirt swirling in a flutter of pleats. Even her hair seemed bouncier than mine, a neat cap of natural waves, while mine hung relentlessly straight in a long ponytail. Though I knew a little about teasing boys, Joyce actually flirted, her eyes flashing and her sparkly teeth dazzling the bewildered boy who would lean his bike awkwardly on the sidewalk while he tried to keep up with her jokes and jibes. To me Joyce represented self-confidence; my mother, who didn't like her much, said she thought Joyce was "tough" and "a little mean." We were probably talking about the same thing.

10   Although Joyce hadn't started to date then in sixth grade—no really nice girl did till seventh or eighth—she seemed to me to know more about boys, about life, than I did. For one thing, her parents fought. Since my mother had been widowed when I was just seven, I couldn't remember much about my parents' marriage, though my mother said they had been very happy and she still wept when she spoke of my father. None of my other friends' parents ever argued in front of me, except in brief, unthreatening exchanges of mild displeasure: "Oh, George, I *told* you to pick that up!" "How can we be out of beer *again?*" "No, I do *not* want to go out to dinner." But the Schwartzes really fought, yelling loudly and banging doors. At least Mr. Schwartz did. He was a large, flabby man with quick, shifty eyes—like Joyce's, only hers were set in a pretty face—and he had a quick, loud temper. When he came home, he always had a few pleasant words for us—Joyce openly flirted with him, as she did with the boys on the streets—but then he would ask us to leave, go outside, play upstairs, and soon we would hear his booming voice as he argued with his wife. Joyce's mother was pale, brown-haired, washed-out, with so little personality that I wondered if Mr. Schwartz shouted at her just to get some response. I never heard her answers from behind the closed doors. Sometimes, Joyce said matter-of-factly, her father hit her mother. "Not real hard," she added. I was shocked, not only by this disclosure of violence but by my knowledge that Mr. Schwartz was a leading deacon in his church. I was sure my own Collegiate Presbyterian wouldn't have stood for it.

11   Visiting the Harbingers' after school with Kristy was a complete change. Mrs. Harbinger, who was warm, friendly, and still poignantly beautiful,

presided over a house filled with comforting sounds and smells: chocolate-chip cookies fresh from the oven, a ringing phone, the padding of active feet, shouts and laughter from Kristy's older brother and his friends. Doors slammed, but the sound was a happy one of activity, not the warning prelude it was at the Schwartzes'. Joyce Schwartz liked to come to the Harbingers' too, but she preferred to be asked by herself, not with me. Kristy Harbinger, understandably flattered by our jealous attentions, played us against each other. I remember dragging home heartsick, running to my room to cry, because Kristy and Joyce, whispering and giggling together at recess, had hurried off after school before I could catch up with them. Once I asked Joyce if she wanted to go to a Saturday-afternoon movie, only to be told, snippily, that she was already going with Kristy. "But if you want," she said, with a wide smile that made me seethe, "I'll find out if you can go with us." Whenever Joyce had something particularly nasty to say, she smiled. Her self-control always enraged me. Speechless, I turned away. We both knew that the three of us couldn't go together. Who would sit next to whom in the theatre? Who would get the prized middle seat? Whose house would we go to afterward? If we went to Schwartzes', would Joyce ignore me? If we went to Harbingers', though, couldn't Kristy join with Joyce in playing Ping-Pong while I waited disconsolately on the sidelines? If we played "Sorry" and I lost, wouldn't Joyce smile widely? And if we went to my house, didn't I know for sure that Joyce would complain there was nothing to do and leave early, probably with Kristy, so I couldn't follow?

12   Exactly how this triangle of tension sagged and lost one side I cannot now recall. But by the end of sixth grade, with subtle shifts in the social quicksands, I had risen and Joyce had fallen. Her flirtatiousness had come to seem brazen, her stylishness a bit cheap. She had begun to date, a sluggish, heavy football player who had almost flunked fifth grade; despite his athletic skills, he wasn't a boyfriend many of us wanted. Joyce's choice seemed to confirm a growing sense that she wasn't, in fact, quite the right sort. Meanwhile I had been elected homeroom secretary and probably shown other signs of promise. When Kristy showed me her latest list of friends, I had moved to the top. I quickly put her at the top of my list, too, and we were finally best friends.

13   Most memories of girlfriends lose their bitterness after sixth grade. Though Kristy and I did not remain best friends, I settled comfortably for the next six years into her gang. When I remember my desperate scrabbling in fifth-grade darkness, clinging to Margie Dwyer, and contrast it to my sailing with relative ease through junior high and high school in a convoy of friends, I am frightened for my own daughter. What will be her source of support? If she has to hang onto the edges of a group longer than I did, can I help her? Should I? What can I do about the other little girls, the ones *she* rejects, won't ask to her birthday parties, doesn't want to play with? Would life at the edges develop qualities I missed? If she doesn't have the girlfriends I did, will she be content? Will I?

14   Once the relentless search for a "best friend" merged into group acceptance, the tenor of my life depended not so much on family or on boyfriends

as it did on girlfriends. My mother was always there in the background, of course, a quiet support. Boyfriends drifted across my skies, dreamy clouds, fierce thunder, dramatic lightning: they passed, and the weather changed. But my girlfriends filled my days with the steady pulse of constant companionship. When I remember what I actually *did,* outside of school and evenings at home, I always see myself with one or more girlfriends.

15   What did we do? Mostly, I think, we talked. We talked on the buses, in the halls, at our lockers, in the classrooms, between classes in the toilets, after school at the bus stop. Once home, we called each other up almost instantly and talked on the phone until some parent couldn't stand it any longer. Then we hung up for a while with promises to call back later. What on earth, our parents asked us, did we find to talk about? But it wasn't so much the topics we found engrossing, I think, the boys, teachers, clothes, gossip. All that talking built up a steady confidence that the trivia of our lives were worth discussion, that our *lives* were worth discussing, that we as individuals were worth someone's attention. "Do you think I ought to get my hair cut?" was a question that asked not only "How would I look with my hair shorter?" but "Do you *care* how I look?" Teachers snapped and lectured; parents discussed and argued; boys teased and muttered; but the steady hum of girlfriends, punctuated by laughter and whispers, was a reassuring continuo.

16   Besides talking, girlfriends went places with each other. No self-respecting boy would ever be seen shopping with a girl. We girls usually shopped in twos or threes, after school or on Saturday afternoons, not only to approve new purchases, but for the sheer fun of trying on new clothes. We were all known in Younkers, and although Mrs. Corter, the no-nonsense saleswoman, would tell us firmly to leave if someone else wanted the dressing room, until she did we could use the store as though it were a costume shop and we were actresses trying on different roles. Some afternoons we slipped into formals, very carefully, while Mrs. Corter hovered disapprovingly nearby, eagle-eyed for any rip or tear. We floated before the mirrors in layers of pink tulle or swooshes of yellow satin, admiring how much older we looked with bare shoulders and boned-in strapless bodices. We tried on the new cotton spring dresses as soon as they arrived in midwinter, assuring Mrs. Corter that we were already "looking for an Easter dress." She wasn't fooled and whipped the dresses back to the racks as fast as we slipped them off. We giggled to each other, crowded into the tiny dressing room together, knowing her irritation.

17   Drifting up and down Main Street, we had regular rounds. We'd browse quickly through Penney's and Ward's, if we were really killing time, and maybe pause at Marty's, a collegiate sportswear shop. We didn't feel right yet in the Shetland sweaters and matching pleated skirts that Marty's sold to Iowa State girls. But we stroked the cashmeres, sorted through cocktail dresses, and tried to imagine ourselves older and shapelier. We would only "look in" at Carole's, not daring to stay too long under the snooty, hard stares of the two saleswomen with pouffed lacquered hair, bright lipstick and shiny nails. Then we'd wander toward the library, or stop at Edith's Gift

Shoppe to see whose new wedding patterns of silver and china were on display, maybe drink a Coke at the Rainbow Café before catching the bus home. And all the time we talked, talked, talked.

18 On weekends we went to the movies. By high school many of us dated, and sometimes we'd go with our boyfriends. But, with the bolstering company of two other girls—one wasn't enough—we'd go in a gang together, not caring whether we had dates or not. Sometimes the boys would come in their gangs, too, and we carefully arranged to sit so there'd be an empty row behind us for them. Couples migrated toward the back or the balcony, detached from our noisy, laughing, poking crowd, and we pretended not to notice them as we streamed down the aisles.

19 Since I was easily embarrassed on movie dates, fidgeting when a boy and I had to stare at a love scene side-by-side, I was happiest going to the movies with the girls. Then I could whisper whatever I wanted, unafraid of sounding foolish, surrounded by friendly elbows and nudging knees. Engulfed in the comforting blackness of the theatre, we could sometimes ask each other questions that would have been impossible elsewhere. One Sunday afternoon at the movies I briefly glimpsed the limits of my knowledge about sex. We girls had gone to see *The Barefoot Contessa,* a murky but dramatic love story in which Ava Gardner, a sexpot who verges on nymphomania, eventually marries mysterious but handsome Rossano Brazzi. On their wedding night, however, he appears at their bedroom door and announces that he cannot sleep with her. The words escape me after all these years, but not their doom-laden import. I vaguely remember Rossano telling Ava, who lay there visibly panting, that he was "wounded in the war." What I acutely remember is the dialogue that then took place in the New Ames Theater. Seated next to me was Leslie Gerard, a girl who was, everyone agreed, thoroughly nice. Her pleasant personality had led her to the presidency of Y-Teens, leadership in her church youth group, membership on Student Council. Sturdy and forthright, she would have been our captain if we'd had any girls' athletic teams. But Leslie did not date yet, and her mother did not let her stay overnight at slumber parties. So perhaps I shouldn't have been surprised when Leslie leaned over to me, puzzled, and said, "What does that mean, he was wounded in the war?" While I paused, one of the boys in the row behind us guffawed loudly. He had heard Leslie's question too. Leaning forward, he stuck his face between our heads and stage-whispered so that both rows could hear, "He had his balls shot off!" The boys collapsed in laughter, while a few of the bolder girls giggled and the rest blushed and looked straight ahead. Under cover of the laughter, Leslie, still undaunted, leaned toward me again and, barely audible, whispered in my ear, "What are balls?" "Tell you later," I hissed back quickly. But the fact was I didn't know. Someone else came to Leslie's and my rescue after the show was over.

20 Besides shopping and going to movies together, we girls herded together to attend dances and parties, those where you didn't need dates, as well as football and basketball games and track meets. Small towns in Iowa had girls' basketball, but Ames was too sophisticated for such pastimes. Girls who liked sports could swim or play tennis. But otherwise we watched the

boys, cheering and caring so intensely whether they won or lost that we regularly wept or shouted ourselves hoarse. When the Ames High football team swept down the field, or a center dunked a difficult jump shot, we shared the boys' triumph; it was one of the few times we thought of us all belonging together and working for a common goal. Since I was a clumsy athlete, I was perfectly happy to sit in my black skirt and orange jacket, blending into the cheering section, a small but vital part of the whole. Even Leslie Gerard, whose skill at basketball amazed our gym teacher, and who regularly pleaded, usually vainly, for one of us girls to "shoot a few baskets after school," never murmured the wish that we could have a girls' team. She sat in the front of the section, captain of the Pep Squad, and cheered more loudly than all of us.

21   Even when we had boyfriends in high school, we spent our spare after-noons and weekend daytimes with girls. Boys had jobs, cars, athletics. Mostly we saw them at night under artificial lights. Boys were dates; girls were friends. We girls went sledding or skating together in the winter; swam, roller-skated and rode bikes in the summer. With other girls we took danc-ing, swimming, tennis lessons; we accompanied each other on family picnics and even vacations. A girlfriend was as close as the nearest telephone.

22   A girlfriend wasn't someone for whom you had to plan activities. My closest friend in high school, Peggy O'Reilly, and I always knew what the other felt like or wanted to do, and we usually wanted to do the same thing. Sometime during our Saturday mornings downtown, one of us would always ask the other, "What about going into Eschbach's?" In the late fifties, few of us could afford the expensive new long-playing records. Eschbach's Music Store, with two small glass-enclosed listening booths, tolerantly allowed us to take one l.p. at a time into a booth, sit on the floor, and lose ourselves in the music. Plugging one ear and holding the other close to the speaker, you could almost get the sensation of hi-fi. We never had any doubt about what records to listen to, since Peggy and I shared a terrible crush on Frank Sinatra. Those were his revival years, when his lean face, slouched hat, and hunched shoulders proclaimed on album after album, "How I need someone to watch over me!" Peggy and I felt he was singing to us, discerning our inarticulate fears of being lonely and rejected. Frank Sinatra knew that we weren't always sure life was going to be wonderful. We didn't know whether anyone would ever love us. He understood, and he told us how we felt. So we mooned and dreamed in Eschbach's glass booth, until, like Mrs. Corter in Younkers, an impatient clerk tapped at the window and motioned us out. Sighing, we left our melancholy in the stuffy little room and wandered out into the sunshine. "You know" I said to Peggy, "when I'm twenty-one he'll only be forty-six. Don't you think that would be all right?" Peggy smiled, nodded reassuringly, and linked her arm with mine. She was sure it would be all right. She was, after all, my best friend.

23   The spring we graduated from high school, we girls began to feel the first twinges of separation. Though some of us were planning to go to Iowa State, many of us were scattering east and west, to New York, Pennsylvania, Massachusetts, California. We couldn't believe that we wouldn't still keep in

touch, stay close and spend our vacations together; but we also knew that something was ending. More deliberately than usual, we organized "girl parties," after-school and weekend get-togethers where we tried to pretend that nothing had changed. During the summer, while we sewed and shopped for college, we even practiced giving "luncheons," baking casseroles from our mother's cookbooks and entertaining each other with tunafish and noodles, deviled eggs in white sauce, and almost anything based on cream-of-mushroom soup. We "dressed up" and came at twelve-thirty for grape juice and ginger ale. Our mothers looked on tolerantly, helping in the kitchen, tactfully disappearing when "guests" arrived. Perhaps they could see what was happening. They may have remembered their own graduations and losses, old friends who had married and disappeared forever under other names in other towns.

24   We didn't hear anyone tell us about the process of sorting out, about how, over the years, friendships wax, wane, and disappear. After all, I sadly admitted years later, when I had to face the fact that a once-close friend and I had so completely lost touch that I no longer knew her job, address, or phone number, if I kept truly close to all the friends I've valued in the places I've lived, I would not be able to do anything else. Keeping up a friendship does take conversation, letters, phone calls. There is never enough time.

25   As we sat around a crowded luncheon table that summer of graduation, comfortably gossiping, ostentatiously drinking coffee like grown-ups, many of us had known each other for as long as we could remember. We would not have believed that we would never sit together like this again, that in two or three years some of us would have seen each other for the last time, that twenty years later only one or two of a whole table of ten would still have news of any of the others. Our mothers didn't warn us. What good would it have done? They joined us for dessert and laughed when Leslie Gerard tried, unsuccessfully, to smoke a cigarette all the way through.

26   By September the splintering was impossible to ignore. The first girls left for "rush" at Iowa State while those of us going later to our colleges hung around, took hurried phone calls that announced "I'm pledging Gamma Phi" or "Tri Delt wants me!" and pretended knowledgeable interest. One by one we waved each other off as the family car, loaded with suitcases, turned toward Lincoln Way and the road out of town. I was one of the last to leave. Late in September, a few days before I was to take the train east, I decided to attend the opening Ames High football game. No one else was free that night, and I went alone. I was a little late. When I walked onto the cinder path that led to the lighted bleachers, I knew I had made a mistake. Another Pep Squad sat in the stands, wearing the same trim orange-and-black jackets senior girls got from the Kiwanis Club every year. Though most of the faces in the crowd were familiar, they weren't my friends. A few waved. One girl called out curiously, "Hey, Sue! Haven't you gone yet?" When I stood for the school song, I felt for the first time as though it didn't sound quite right on my tongue. At the half I left, telling some of the new seniors who brushed by me that I had to go home to pack. They looked polite but uninterested. Moving in a huddle toward the refreshment stand, a blur of orange under the

pole lights, they chattered excitedly to each other. Hurrying past them, I almost ran to my car.

27   That particular kind of belonging was over. My close friends in college didn't cling together the way we girls had in Ames. After I was married, my women friends had even less in common: one was single and gay, another married to someone my husband didn't like, a third didn't like my husband. We certainly never got together in a group. After my divorce, I had to learn how to do things alone, to stand in a movie line on Saturday night, to swim happily by myself in a public pool, to drive to a strange town and stay alone in a strange hotel. It wasn't easy, and there are times when I'm still not as good at it as I'd like to be.

28   But the joy of girlfriends wasn't over. Growing up with girls who talked, laughed, and shared together gave me a precious resource I have never lost. When I sprawl in a friend's sunny kitchen, drinking coffee and comparing notes about when and where we'll plant our sugar snow peas; when, paring carrots, I cradle a receiver to one ear and ask urgently, "But what did you say to your mother *then?*"; when I'm invited to a friend's for Sunday-night pizza because, she says, "We haven't seen you for a while" but I know she really means, "You're sounding blue"; when my college roommate from twenty years ago calls from Vancouver, anxious over the tone of my last letter; when another friend, even busier than I am, yells over the shouts and screams of four children, "I'm just calling to check in"; I feel a link that goes back to Margie Dwyer. The hand that reached out to me in fifth grade is still there.

A. Compre-hension

Choose the answer that best completes each statement. Do not refer to the selection while doing this exercise.

1. The city in Iowa where Toth grew up is (a) Iowa City; (b) Ames; (c) Davenport; (d) Des Moines.

2. Toth states that her memory of being best friends with Margie Dwyer is humiliating because (a) she was ashamed of Margie's father's occupation; (b) she stole Margie's former best friend away; (c) she quickly dropped Margie when she was adopted into an acceptable group of friends; (d) Toth spread an untrue rumor at school about Margie.

3. The members of the "Society Six" all had in common (a) good grades and a keen interest in intellectual matters; (b) rich parents and memberships in the town's best clubs; (c) expensive clothes and cars; (d) looks, sophistication, and style.

4. Compared to the "Society Six," the group that Toth was associated with was considerably more (a) popular, especially with boys; (b) intelligent; (c) civic-minded and sports-minded; (d) fluid and democratic.

5. Toth describes her relationship wtih Joyce Schwartz and Kristy Harbinger, and the trio's constant jockeying for the favored position, as a triangle of (a) tension; (b) deceit; (c) selfishness; (d) worry.

6. What Toth did with her girlfriends chiefly was (a) study; (b) play sports; (c) talk and go shopping; (d) have slumber parties.

7. For Toth and her friends, the first indication of any interest in boy-girl relationships occurred at (a) dances and parties; (b) the movies; (c) athletic events; (d) church-sponsored social activities.

8. After graduation from high school, Toth and her circle of friends for the first time experienced (a) anxiety; (b) competitiveness; (c) separation; (d) loneliness.

B. Inferences   On the basis of the evidence in the selection, answer these inference questions. You may refer to the selection to answer the questions in this section, and all the remaining sections.

1. Read paragraph 2 again. Of all the qualities a best friend provided, which does Toth think is the most important? _Preparation for marriage_

2. According to paragraph 4, how was intelligence valued among fifth graders in Ames? _suspeciously_

3. Judging from paragraph 6, was the psychiatrist right about Toth's still being hurt by not being a cheerleader and a member of the "Society Six"? _yes_

4. Why was Joyce Schwartz eventually dropped from the triangle (see paragraph 12)? _She got the wrong boyfriend_

5. Reread paragraph 15. In what important way were girlfriends more important than boyfriends, or even than parents? _they were reassuring way of confirming the importance of their life_

6. What did the empty row behind the girls in the theater, mentioned in paragraph 18, represent? _a interest in the opposite sex_

7. How would you characterize Toth's knowledge of the world, as evidenced by paragraph 19? _naive_

8. Read paragraph 20 again. Aside from the fact that Ames was "too sophisticated" to have a girls' basketball team, as did the smaller towns in Iowa, what might be another reason that only the boys had athletic teams? _____

9. Judging from paragraph 22, what did Peggy O'Reilly and Frank Sinatra have in common? _____

10. In paragraph 28, what is Toth emphasizing about the role of girlfriends, no matter what one's age? _their sense of helping sharing + feeling of solidarity_

C. Structure   1. Which of the following sentences from the selection best states the main idea? (a) "Needless to say, with my plumpness, brains, wicked tongue, and awkward uncertainties, I did not belong to the 'Society Six.'" (b) "A set of girlfriends provided a sense of security, as belonging to any group does." (c) "What little we learned about living with another person in an equal relationship, outside our own families, we learned from our girlfriends. It certainly wasn't a full preparation for marriage, but it was the only one some of us ever got." (d) "But the joy of girlfriends wasn't over. Growing

up with girls who talked, laughed, and shared together gave me a precious resource I have never lost."
Defend your choice.

2. In your own words, explain Toth's purpose in writing. _show what important girlfriends were for her_

3. Of the four modes of discourse—narration, description, exposition, and persuasion—which two seem to prevail? _exposit + Narative_

4. Which sentence is the topic sentence in paragraph 8? _last sentence_ _We had absorbed already by sixth grade a set of cruel distinction careful_
Which pattern of organization is used in that paragraph? (a) deductive; (b) variation of deductive; (c) inductive; (d) spatial; (e) chronological.

5. The method of paragraph development that is most evident in the section comprised by paragraphs 10 and 11 is (a) definition; (b) classification; (c) comparison; (d) contrast; (e) analogy.

6. How would you characterize the questions Toth poses at the end of paragraph 13? _____

What image of Toth do they convey? _____

7. In paragraph 14, Toth uses a metaphor. What is being compared to what? _____ is/are compared to _____.
Explain the metaphor. _____

8. Which of the following best characterizes the tone of this selection, especially of paragraphs 23 to 28? (a) mawkish; overly sentimental; (b) nostalgic; bittersweet; (c) cynical; pessimistic; (d) unbiased; impartial.

D. Vocabulary   For each italicized word from the selection, choose the best definition according to the context in which it appears.

1. our social *alliances* [paragraph 3]: (a) aspirations; (b) ambitions; (c) relationships; (d) concerns.

2. had been firmly *forged* [3]: (a) advanced gradually; (b) formed; shaped; (c) decided upon; (d) reproduced fraudulently.

3. Margie, like me, was a social *pariah* [4]: (a) outcast; (b) butterfly; (c) success; (d) climber.

4. six formed the *elite* [5]: the group with (a) the most money; (b) the best education; (c) the most prestige and power; (d) the highest social ambitions.

5. I told him *self-effacingly* [6]: (a) self-mockingly; (b) not drawing attention to oneself; modestly; (c) critical of one's own abilities; (d) confident of one's own abilities.

6. still *poignantly* beautiful [11]: (a) physically painful; (b) keenly distressing to the mind; (c) affectingly; touching to the emotions; (d) neatly; skillfully.

7. the warning *prelude* [11]: (a) introduction; (b) conclusion; (c) punishment; (d) argument.

8. her flirtatiousness had come to seem *brazen* [12]: (a) affected; artificial; (b) bold; shameless; (c) risky; dangerous; (d) wicked; spiteful.

9. once the *relentless* search [14]: (a) fruitless; (b) long; arduous; (c) steady; persistent; (d) pitiless; merciless.

10. the *tenor* of my life [14]: (a) progress; general sense; (b) tendency; inclination; (c) boundaries; limits; (d) emotional characteristics.

11. the *trivia* of our lives [15]: (a) important events; (b) inessential, insignificant matters; (c) games; contests; (d) diversions; distractions.

12. the *bolstering* company of two other girls [18]: (a) supporting; (b) entertaining; (c) appreciative; (d) continuing.

13. a *murky* but dramatic love story [19]: (a) daring; bold; (b) stirring; gripping; (c) overly sentimental; maudlin; (d) dark; gloomy.

14. their doom-*laden* import [19]: doom- (a) struck; (b) burdened; (c) threatening; (d) conscious.

15. one of the boys *guffawed* [19]: (a) giggled; (b) snickered; (c) laughed explosively; (d) laughed derisively.

16. Leslie, still *undaunted* [19]: (a) uncomprehending; (b) not discouraged; (c) not concerned; (d) not embarrassed.

17. *discerning* our inarticulate fears [22]: (a) exposing; (b) discharging; (c) quelling; (d) perceiving.

18. our *inarticulate* fears [22]: (a) unexpressed; (b) indescribable; (c) unimaginable; (d) intact; unimpaired.

19. we left our *melancholy* [22]: (a) sadness; depression of the spirits; (b) pensive reflection; contemplation; (c) emotional state characterized by sullenness and outbreaks of violent anger; (d) intense feelings of dejection.

20. *tactfully* disappearing when guests arrived [23]: (a) obligingly; (b) unwillingly; (c) discreetly; (d) silently.

21. friendships *wax, wane,* and disappear [24]: Wax and wane are opposites, meaning (a) appear and disappear; (b) gradually increase and gradually decrease; (c) slowly gain speed and slowly lose speed; (d) quickly flare up and then burn out.

22. *ostentatiously* drinking coffee [25]: (a) guiltily; (b) idly; (c) purposefully; (d) in a showy manner.

E. Variant Word Forms

For each italicized word in parentheses, write the required form in the space provided. Add endings for plural nouns and verb tenses if necessary. You might need to consult an unabridged dictionary.

1. (*acquire*—use the noun form): The _____ of social skills, even with the help of a best friend, is a painful process.

2. (*humiliating*—use the noun form): Toth still remembers, with a feeling of _____, her first best friend.

3. (*exclusive*—use the verb form): The elite group, the "Society Six," _____ other girls on the basis of looks, style, and sophistication.

4. (*disclosure*—use the verb form): When Joyce Schwartz _____ her father's abuse of her mother, Toth was understandably shocked.

5. (*flattered*—use the noun form): Joyce Schwartz and Toth competed for Kristy Harbinger's attention by using _____.

6. (*enraged*—use the noun form): Toth felt _____ when Joyce deliberately excluded her from activities.

7. (*disconsolately*—use the adjective form): When she was excluded from her two best friends' activities, Toth often felt _____.

8. (*triumph*—use the adverb form): When the Ames High football team swept _____ down the field, the girls were just as enthusiastic as the boys.

F. Questions for Analysis

1. From this chapter, what inference can you make about the sort of community Ames, Iowa, was in the 1950s?

2. If you are a woman, do you agree with Toth that having a best friend is often the only education one gets before marriage about living with another person in an equal relationship? In the years since Toth grew up, how might this observation have become no longer relevant?

3. Toth clearly finds girlfriends important, not only during her formative adolescent and teenage years, but even as an adult. If you are a woman, how does your own experience conform to what Toth describes? If you are a man, what are the characteristics of friendships between young males? How do relationships between males differ from those between girls?

Selection 8

Danger Aloft
William M. Carley

William M. Carley is a staff reporter for the *Wall Street Journal*. He writes mainly on the transportation industry, especially the airline sector. The year 1985 was the worst in aviation history for airplane crashes, most of which were caused by mechanical problems or defects of one sort or another. The grim statistics of deaths from airplane crashes during that year have made Carley's statement in paragraph 4, that flying is now safer than taking your car, inaccurate. Nonetheless, the collision in 1977 between a KLM Royal Dutch jet and a Pan Am jet on the Canary Island of Tenerife, which killed 587 people and injured 57, still remains the worst aviation disaster in history.

1   Thinking he had clearance to take off, the captain of a KLM Royal Dutch Airlines jumbo jet roared down the fog-shrouded runway at Tenerife in the Canary Islands. A few seconds later, a taxiing Pan American World Airways jumbo loomed up in the fog. Desperately, the KLM captain yanked his control column back in an attempt to take off and fly over the Pan Am plane. But it was too late. The collision claimed 583 lives, the worst disaster in aviation history.

2   The elements of "human error" involved in the 1977 Tenerife holocaust, unfortunately, haven't been limited to that accident. In fact, human errors are being repeated with frightening frequency at airports all around the world. In several cases that have received little or no publicity, major crashes have been avoided by only the narrowest of margins. In a case where the margin wasn't there—the Pacific Southwest Airlines collision with a Cessna over San Diego last year—144 died.

3   James King, chairman of the National Transportation Safety Board, is one of the many worried federal officials. "We're in danger of having our own Tenerife right here in the U.S.," he says.

4   Airline travel in general, it should be noted, is relatively safe. The fatal accident rate has been dropping more or less steadily for years, and now flying is much safer than, for example, taking your own car. But the air-transport system is still subject to fatal flaws, and the most common flaw, the safety board says, is human error.

5   Perhaps the most serious problem of human error is the potential for communications breakdowns, which can easily lead to collisions. Good communications between pilots and the controllers who direct aircraft are vital. But in case after case, miscalculations, misunderstandings or simply missed messages because of garbled radio transmissions have broken the chain of communication.

6   The possibility of human error, and perhaps a breakdown in communications, may have been illustrated in the Western Airlines crash in Mexico City Wednesday. The DC10 came in for a landing, not on the right-hand runway, which was open, but on a nearby runway on the left, which was closed for repairs. The plane hit a truck and then careened into a building, killing 75 persons.

7   Recognizing the human-error problem—and particularly the potential for communications breakdowns—the Federal Aviation Administration, which operates the air traffic control system in the U.S., is experimenting with a new communications procedure in the eastern U.S. The National Transportation Safety Board, which investigates accidents and makes recommendations to the FAA, has studied the problem, with the focus on a near-collision at LaGuardia Airport in New York. And the National Aeronautics and Space Administration has conducted another study, based on reports from pilots and air traffic controllers around the U.S.

8   That near-misses are frequent, especially around airports, is indisputable. The NASA study, for example, found, over a two-year period ended June 30, 1978, no fewer than 135 potential conflicts of planes taxiing, taking off or landing. Of these, 37 involved near-collisions, and in some cases speeding planes missed each other by just 10 feet. NASA adds that the search of its files for such incidents wasn't complete—indicating probably even more close calls.

9   A brief listing of a few recent incidents suggests the gravity of the problem:

10   —O'Hare International Airport, Chicago, May 15, 1978. A United Airlines DC8 jet is cleared into takeoff position. As the pilot pulls onto the

runway, he glances left. He sees a United 747 jumbo coming in for a landing and heading right for him. Instead of turning down the runway, the DC8 pilot jams the throttles forward, rolling straight across and off the runway seconds before the 747 swooshes by and lands.

11   –Miami International Airport, Sept. 29, 1977. An Eastern Airlines 727 has begun its takeoff roll. Just then a tow truck pulling another 727 begins creeping across the runway ahead. The Eastern pilot slams on the brakes and stops less than 100 yards short of the towed plane.

12   –Philadelphia International Airport, Jan. 25, 1978. An American Airlines 707 is approaching a runway for landing, just as a commuter-airline plane moves onto the same runway for takeoff. The American pilot aborts his landing and pulls up and away from the airport.

13   –O'Hare International, Chicago, Feb. 15, 1979. A Flying Tiger Line 747 jumbo cargo jet touches down for landing, just as a Delta Air Lines 727 begins to taxi across the same runway from the left. The Flying Tiger jumbo hurtles toward the Delta plane at more than 100 miles an hour. At the last moment, the Tiger pilot steers off the runway to the right, smashes into snowbanks and rips off the landing gear.

14   The main way that safety experts try to avoid such hazards in the future is to conduct detailed painstaking investigations of accidents and near-accidents. One such investigation, by the safety board, involved a near-miss at LaGuardia on June 21, 1978.

15   Thunderstorms surrounded New York City that day and closed many of the air corridors that planes use to leave the city's airports. Departing flights at LaGuardia were delayed nearly four hours. As a result, taxiways were badly congested; nearly 70 planes were waiting to take off between 6 P.M. and 10 P.M.

16   "It was a dark night," one pilot recalls. "Runway lights were up bright, there were aircraft all over the airport with their taxi lights rotating, beacons on. It was a mess."

17   Up in the LaGuardia tower, three men were trying to handle the crush of planes. One was the ground controller, instructing planes where to taxi. The second was the local controller, in charge of the runways and instructing planes to take off and land. (Because the two men were communicating with pilots on separate radio frequencies–the normal procedure–a pilot taking off wouldn't hear instructions to another pilot taxiing.) The third key man in the tower was the crew coordinator, responsible for coordinating actions by ground, local and other controllers.

18   The three were trying to juggle planes as rapidly as possible; in one 17-minute period, there were 227 transmissions over the ground controller's radio alone. But some pilots, frustrated at waiting for hours, were snapping at the controllers over the radio.

19   Then about 9:45 P.M., an air corridor to the northwest opened up that would permit a DC9 belonging to North Central Airlines (recently merged into Republic Airlines) to take off for Milwaukee. But LaGuardia was so jammed with planes that the North Central aircraft couldn't use taxiways to get to the end of the runway. So the ground controller told the North

Central pilot to move onto the runway itself at its midpoint, then taxi to its end so he could turn around for takeoff.

20 In the tower, the ground controller asked the local controller's permission to use the runway for taxiing, and says he got an affirmative answer from someone, either the local controller or the coordinator. The local controller doesn't recall it. (Tape recordings in the tower cover radio transmissions, but not conversations within the tower.) The coordinator was on a hot line to another air-control center; he doesn't think he used on the phone any words that the ground controller might have misunderstood as a clearance. In any event, acoustics in the LaGuardia tower were poor at the time; the tower interior was being renovated, and it lacked the carpeting normally used on floors and walls to cut noise from nearby jet engines.

21 Cleared by the ground controller, the North Central plane began moving onto runway 13. But on a separate radio frequency, the local controller had cleared an executive jet to take off on runway 13, and that jet already was accelerating down the airstrip.

22 Edward Erickson, the North Central pilot, saw the executive jet's lights coming in the darkness, and at a safety-board hearing he testified that at first he thought it was a motor vehicle. "But then . . . we could see the rotating beacons" on an aircraft. The North Central plane, halfway onto the runway, couldn't get off in time. "There was nothing we could do," Capt. Erickson said. "We were taxiing on one engine—it didn't taxi fast on one engine, no power." The captain halted the North Central plane and flashed on his landing lights in hopes the executive jet would see them. "I turned on all the lights I could," he said.

23 The copilot of an Eastern Airlines plane then waiting on the ground looked out of his cockpit toward the runway. "The first thing I realized was an airplane was rolling down runway 13, and . . . I said, 'Oh my God, look what is happening.' "

24 In the final seconds, however, the pilot of the executive jet saw the lights on the North Central plane. Though the executive jet was rolling at 100 miles an hour, its pilot managed to cut engine thrust and slam on the brakes, and his craft veered off the runway, just missing the motionless North Central airliner.

25 Analysis of this incident shows several factors at work, safety experts say. Weather was bad. LaGuardia was severly congested. Pilots and controllers, under heavy workloads and suffering long delays, were showing signs of losing patience. The stage was set for a close call. In this case, the safety board blamed the controllers for failing to coordinate properly the movement of the executive jet with the North Central plane. The pilots were praised for averting a collision.

26 The analysis also indicates how communications between controllers and pilots might be improved. As a result of the incident, the FAA is experimenting with a new procedure in some Eastern states. Now, an airplane cannot taxi onto a runway with permission of the ground controller; he must get permission directly from the local controller, the one who also clears aircraft for takeoff and landing on the runway.

27   But even if the controllers get it right, pilots may err. Tenerife is the most dramatic example, and safety experts increasingly believe that subtle psychological factors contributed to that calamity. An overanxious pilot, along with bad weather and a freak radio squeal, led to disaster.

28   It all began when a chartered Pan Am jet left Los Angeles for the Canary Islands with 373 passengers, many of them vacationers from California. About the same time, a KLM jet left Schiphol Airport near Amsterdam with 234 passengers. While both planes were en route to Las Palmas, also in the Canary Islands, a bomb exploded in that terminal, and several planes, including the Pan Am and KLM jets, were diverted to nearby Tenerife. The KLM and Pan Am planes arrived early in the afternoon of May 27, 1977.

29   KLM's captain was 50-year-old Jacob Veldhuyzen van Zanten. He was the airline's chief of pilot training, a prestigious post although he spent more time on training duties than on regular flights. "He was like a general with a lot of medals," one safety expert says. With his prestige, the captain wouldn't be likely to yield if questioned by a junior crew member.

30   The KLM pilot was affable while on the ground at Tenerife, but he also was under pressure. He had been on duty for more than nine hours. If he stayed at Tenerife much longer, crew members would reach the limit on their flying time before they got back to Amsterdam. Hence, the 747 would have to remain overnight in the Canary Islands, and KLM flight schedules and passengers' plans would be disrupted.

31   But if they hurried to leave, and there weren't any weather or air traffic delays en route, the KLM crew might make it back to Amsterdam in time. If they were late in arriving at Amsterdam, they faced tough Dutch disciplinary measures, including possible fines and prison terms. As they awaited permission to depart, cockpit conversation went like this:

32   KLM engineer: "What are the repercussions (of exceeding flight limits)?"

33   KLM crew members: "You'll face the judge. . . ."

34   KLM engineer: "Then you are hanged from the highest tree."

35   KLM captain: "Suppose you get a flat tire and you hit a couple of runway lights—then you are really hanging."

36   While the KLM and Pan Am planes were waiting, the weather at Tenerife deteriorated. "When we landed, the weather was beautifully clear and sunny; we could clearly see the surrounding mountains," Pan Am stewardess Joan Jackson recalled later. But, "as we sat there, we watched the fog roll in. It was amazing how fast the mountains were obliterated."

37   When it came time to leave, the KLM plane couldn't use taxiways to get to the end of the runway at Tenerife; most taxiways were jammed with other planes diverted from Las Palmas. So the KLM plane was cleared to taxi down the airport's only runway. The Pan Am plane was cleared to taxi down the runway behind the KLM jet. As the Pan Am plane began to move after a two-hour wait, happy passengers broke into applause.

38   The Tenerife controller had ordered the Pan Am plane to taxi part way down the runway to a turnoff and then exit to a taxiway that was clear. But the fog had become so thick the Pan Am crew could barely see; they missed their assigned turnoff and continued taxiing on down the runway.

39 Meanwhile, the KLM craft had reached the end of the runway and turned around. The captain still needed two separate clearances, for air-traffic control (ATC) and for takeoff, but the captain began to advance the throttles anyway.

40 KLM copilot: "Wait a minute, we don't have an ATC clearance."

41 KLM captain, retarding the throttles: "I know that, go ahead ask."

42 KLM copilot reads ATC clearance back to the tower, but even before he finishes, the pilot advances throttles again. The copilot tells the tower hurriedly: "We are now at takeoff." (That commonly means, "takeoff position.")

43 Tower: "Okay—stand by for takeoff. I will call you."

44 But only the word "okay" was clear. The Pan Am crew, to inform everyone that their plane still was on the runway, radioed the tower. That transmission caused a squeal that partly blocked the rest of the tower's order to the KLM crew to stand by. Saying, "We go!" the KLM captain gunned the 747 down the runway. The next two transmissions were heard in the KLM cockpit.

45 Tower: "Roger Papa Alpha (Pan Am) . . . report the runway clear."

46 Pan Am: "Okay, we'll report when we're clear."

47 KLM engineer, in the KLM cockpit: "Is he not clear, that Pan American?"

48 KLM pilot: "Oh, yes."

49 In the dense fog, the Pan Am crew couldn't see the KLM jet roaring down the runway toward them, but the radio transmissions alarmed them.

50 Pan Am pilot: "Let's get the hell out right here. . . ."

51 Pan Am copilot: "Yeh, he's anxious, isn't he?"

52 Pan Am pilot: "There he is—look at him—goddamn—that—that son of a bitch is coming."

53 Pan Am copilot: "Get off, get off, get off."

54 For about five agonizing seconds, the Pan Am pilot tried to steer his jumbo jet off the runway. The KLM jumbo, as it struck the Pan Am plane, was going about 130 miles an hour. Most of the 583 who died were killed on impact or in the subsequent searing fires.

55 Following an investigation, Spanish authorities said the primary cause of the accident was the fact that the KLM captain, apparently worrying about crew flight limits, took off without clearance. Important contributing factors were bad weather, congestion and the radio squeal that partly blocked the tower's instruction to KLM to stand by. In addition, the Spanish authorities listed as a contributing factor the fact that the Pan Am plane missed its turnoff, but they termed that mistake not very relevant because the Pan Am plane had radioed that it was still on the runway.

A. Comprehension

Choose the answer that best completes each statement. Do not refer to the selection while doing this exercise.

1. When James King, chairman of the National Transportation Safety Board, says, "We're in danger of having our own Tenerife right here in the U.S.," he means that (a) flight controllers are overworked and often suffer

from fatigue; (b) our airports are dangerously overcrowded as more people fly; (c) airplanes are often poorly designed and mechanically unsafe; (d) human error accounts for a growing number of disasters.

2. For years prior to 1977, when the KLM and Pan American jets collided, the fatal accident rate had (a) steadily increased; (b) steadily decreased; (c) stayed the same; (d) moved up and down erratically, depending on the number of serious accidents each year.

3. The typical cause of human errors Carley describes is (a) pilots falling asleep in the cockpit; (b) hijackings; (c) communications breakdowns; (d) pilots' incompetence.

4. In the near-collision of an executive jet with a North Central plane at LaGuardia Airport in 1978, the investigators placed the primary blame on (a) bad weather; (b) faulty transmission of messages from the control tower; (c) the executive jet pilot's inattentiveness; (d) the controllers' failure to coordinate the two planes' takeoffs.

5. In the Tenerife air crash, the Dutch pilot of the KLM plane was anxious to take off because (a) the crew would reach the limit on their flying time, causing serious repercussions; (b) he could see that the weather was quickly deteriorating; (c) he was tired and tense from being on duty too long; (d) he thought he understood takeoff and landing procedures better than the controllers did.

B. Inferences   On the basis of the evidence in the selection, mark these statements as follows: *A* for accurate inferences, *I* for inaccurate inferences, and *IE* for insufficient evidence. You may refer to the selection to answer the questions in this section, and all the remaining sections.

_____ 1. Of the incidents cited, mechanical failure accounted for half the collisions or near-misses.

_____ 2. The FAA (Federal Aviation Administration) is not bound to accept recommendations from the National Transportation Safety Board.

_____ 3. Most collisions or near-misses occur when planes are landing or taking off.

_____ 4. One factor the LaGuardia and Tenerife incidents had in common was a breakdown in communications between controllers and pilots.

_____ 5. It is common practice for controllers to use separate radio frequencies to instruct pilots.

_____ 6. Flight controllers are overworked.

_____ 7. Most aircraft incidents involving human error occur in the United States.

_____ 8. The KLM captain in the Tenerife incident was overly confident of his judgment.

C. Structure

1. Read the first three paragraphs again. Then write the sentence that best expresses the thesis of the article.

   _____

   _____

2. In support of the main idea, Carley relies primarily on (a) analysis; (b) examples and illustrations; (c) explanations of steps in a process; (d) emotional arguments.

3. In the section comprised by paragraphs 14–24, the main pattern of organization is (a) deductive; (b) inductive; (c) chronological; (d) spatial.

4. The method of development used to support the topic sentence in paragraph 25 is (a) cause–effect; (b) process; (c) classification; (d) definition; (e) comparison.

5. The function of paragraph 27, with respect to the body of the article, is to serve as (a) another argument; (b) an illustration; (c) a transition between main sections of the body; (d) a summary of preceding body paragraphs.

6. The mode of discourse used in the section comprised by paragraphs 28–54 is (a) narration; (b) description; (c) exposition; (d) persuasion.

7. Look again at the last two sentences of paragraph 29. What is the relationship between them? (a) contrast; (b) steps in a process; (c) cause–effect; (d) key term and its definition.

8. The author's description of the events before the Tenerife crash is meant to convey (a) amazement; (b) suspense; (c) disgust; (d) irony.

9. Carley reprints the conversations that took place in the cockpits of both the KLM and the Pan Am jets because he wants the reader to feel (a) the pilots' frustration at having to wait; (b) the pilots' concern for their passengers' safety; (c) the rivalry between the two crews; (d) tension and a sense of immediacy.

10. The method of development used in the last paragraph is (a) definition; (b) cause; (c) effect; (d) comparison; (e) analogy; (f) example.

D. Vocabulary

For each italicized word from the selection, choose the best definition according to the context in which it appears.

1. the fog-_shrouded_ runway [paragraph 1]: (a) sheltered; (b) protected; (c) enveloped; (d) disguised.

2. the 1977 Tenerife _holocaust_ [2]: (a) great destruction by fire; (b) accident; (c) incident; (d) misfortune.

3. _garbled_ radio transmissions [5]: (a) unclear; (b) selected; (c) unintelligible; (d) intercepted.

4. the _gravity_ of the problem [9]: (a) origin; (b) force; (c) consequence; (d) seriousness.

5. _averting_ a collision [25]: (a) declaring; (b) preventing; (c) causing; (d) avoiding.

6. pilots may *err* [27]: (a) become forgetful; (b) become impatient; (c) make a mistake; (d) violate a rule.

7. several planes were *diverted* [28]: (a) distracted; (b) turned aside from a course; (c) misdirected; (d) rerouted to other areas.

8. the KLM pilot was *affable* [30]: (a) amiable; (b) sociable; (c) tense; (d) well-mannered.

9. the *repercussions* of exceeding flight limits [32]: (a) arguments against; (b) indirect effects of; (c) rules for; (d) statements concerning.

10. the mountains were *obliterated* [36]: (a) completely destroyed; (b) ruined; (c) obscured; (d) erased.

E. Questions for Analysis

1. Is Carley's purpose to narrate, explain, or persuade, or is it perhaps a combination? Explain.

2. Is James King, mentioned in paragraph 3, a reliable authority to quote on the role of human error in plane crashes? Why or why not?

3. What are some solutions that might at least decrease the possibility of human error as one cause of air crashes?

4. Can you think of other instances of tragedies that have resulted from subordinates' unwillingness to question their superiors' orders?

5. Is this article effective as a piece of journalism or not? Explain.

Selection 9   # Shooting an Elephant
George Orwell

George Orwell (1903–1950) was the pen name of Eric Blair, one of England's most outstanding twentieth-century writers. Orwell's writing encompasses many genres —essays, novels, and journalism. Best known of his works are *Down and Out in Paris and London, Animal Farm,* and *Nineteen Eighty-Four,* as well as his classic essays, "Politics and the English Language," "A Hanging," and "Shooting an Elephant."

1   In Moulmein, in lower Burma, I was hated by large numbers of people— the only time in my life that I have been important enough for this to happen to me. I was sub-divisional police officer of the town, and in an aimless, petty kind of way anti-European feeling was very bitter. No one had the guts to raise a riot, but if a European woman went through the bazaars alone somebody would probably spit betel juice over her dress. As a police officer I was an obvious target and was baited whenever it seemed safe to do so. When a nimble Burman tripped me up on the football field and the referee (another Burman) looked the other way, the crowd yelled with hideous laughter. This happened more than once. In the end the sneering yellow faces of young men that met me everywhere, the insults hooted after me when I was at a safe distance, got badly on my nerves. The young Buddhist priests were the worst of all. There were several thousands of them in the town and none of them seemed to have anything to do except stand on street corners and jeer at Europeans.

2   All this was perplexing and upsetting. For at that time I had already made up my mind that imperialism was an evil thing and the sooner I chucked up my job and got out of it the better. Theoretically—and secretly, of course—I was all for the Burmese and all against their oppressors, the British. As for the job I was doing, I hated it more bitterly than I can perhaps make clear. In a job like that you see the dirty work of Empire at close quarters. The wretched prisoners huddling in the stinking cages of the lock-ups, the gray, cowed faces of the long-term convicts, the scarred buttocks of the men who had been flogged with bamboos—all these oppressed me with an intolerable sense of guilt. But I could get nothing into perspective. I was young and ill educated and I had had to think out my problems in the utter silence that is imposed on every Englishman in the East. I did not even know that the British Empire is dying, still less did I know that it is a great deal better than the younger empires that are going to supplant it. All I knew was that I was stuck between my hatred of the empire I served and my rage against the evil-spirited little beasts who tried to make my job impossible. With one part of my mind I thought of the British Raj as an unbreakable tyranny, as something clamped down, in *saecula saeculorum,** upon the will of prostrate peoples; with another part I thought that the greatest joy in the world would be to drive a bayonet into a Buddhist priest's guts. Feelings like these are the normal by-products of imperialism; ask any Anglo-Indian official, if you can catch him off duty.

3   One day something happened which in a roundabout way was enlightening. It was a tiny incident in itself, but it gave me a better glimpse than I had had before of the real nature of imperialism—the real motives for which despotic governments act. Early one morning the sub-inspector at a police station the other end of the town rang me up on the 'phone and said that an elephant was ravaging the bazaar. Would I please come and do something about it? I did not know what I could do, but I wanted to see what was happening and I got on to a pony and started out. I took my rifle, an old .44 Winchester and much too small to kill an elephant, but I thought the noise might be useful *in terrorem*. Various Burmans stopped me on the way and told me about the elephant's doings. It was not, of course, a wild elephant, but a tame one which had gone "must." It had been chained up, as tame elephants always are when their attack of "must" is due, but on the previous night it had broken its chain and escaped. Its mahout, the only person who could manage it when it was in that state, had set out in pursuit, but had taken the wrong direction and was now twelve hours' journey away, and in the morning the elephant had suddenly reappeared in the town. The Burmese population had no weapons and were quite helpless against it. It had already destroyed somebody's bamboo hut, killed a cow and raided some fruit-stalls and devoured the stock; also it had met the municipal rubbish van and, when the driver jumped out and took to his heels, had turned the van over and inflicted violences upon it.

---

*Literally, "in the all time of all times"; idiomatically, for all eternity.

4   The Burmese sub-inspector and some Indian constables were waiting for me in the quarter where the elephant had been seen. It was a very poor quarter, a labyrinth of squalid bamboo huts, thatched with palm-leaf, winding all over a steep hillside. I remember that it was a cloudy, stuffy morning at the beginning of the rains. We began questioning the people as to where the elephant had gone and, as usual, failed to get any definite information. That is invariably the case in the East; a story always sounds clear enough at a distance, but the nearer you get to the scene of events the vaguer it becomes. Some of the people said that the elephant had gone in one direction, some said that he had gone in another, some professed not even to have heard of any elephant. I had almost made up my mind that the whole story was a pack of lies, when we heard yells a little distance away. There was a loud, scandalized cry of "Go away, child! Go away this instant!" and an old woman with a switch in her hand came round the corner of a hut, violently shooing away a crowd of naked children. Some more women followed, clicking their tongues and exclaiming; evidently there was something that the children ought not to have seen. I rounded the hut and saw a man's dead body sprawling in the mud. He was an Indian, a black Dravidian coolie, almost naked, and he could not have been dead many minutes. The people said that the elephant had come suddenly upon him round the corner of the hut, caught him with its trunk, put its foot on his back and ground him into the earth. This was the rainy season and the ground was soft, and his face had scored a trench a foot deep and a couple of yards long. He was lying on his belly with arms crucified and head sharply twisted to one side. His face was coated with mud, the eyes wide open, the teeth bared and grinning with an expression of unendurable agony. (Never tell me, by the way, that the dead look peaceful. Most of the corpses I have seen looked devilish.) The friction of the beast's foot had stripped the skin from his back as neatly as one skins a rabbit. As soon as I saw the dead man I sent an orderly to a friend's house nearby to borrow an elephant rifle. I had already sent back the pony, not wanting it to go mad with fright and throw me if it smelt the elephant.

5   The orderly came back in a few minutes with a rifle and five cartridges, and meanwhile some Burmans had arrived and told us that the elephant was in the paddy fields below, only a few hundred yards away. As I started forward practically the whole population of the quarter flocked out of the houses and followed me. They had seen the rifle and were all shouting excitedly that I was going to shoot the elephant. They had not shown much interest in the elephant when he was merely ravaging their homes, but it was different now that he was going to be shot. It was a bit of fun to them, as it would be to an English crowd; besides they wanted the meat. It made me vaguely uneasy. I had no intention of shooting the elephant—I had merely sent for the rifle to defend myself if necessary—and it is always unnerving to have a crowd following you. I marched down the hill, looking and feeling a fool, with the rifle over my shoulder and an ever-growing army of people jostling at my heels. At the bottom, when you got away from the huts, there was a metalled road and beyond that a miry waste of paddy fields a thousand yards across, not yet ploughed but soggy from the first rains and dotted

with coarse grass. The elephant was standing eight yards from the road, his left side toward us. He took not the slightest notice of the crowd's approach. He was tearing up bunches of grass, beating them against his knees to clean them, and stuffing them into his mouth.

6   I had halted on the road. As soon as I saw the elephant I knew with perfect certainty that I ought not to shoot him. It is a serious matter to shoot a working elephant—it is comparable to destroying a huge and costly piece of machinery—and obviously one ought not to do it if it can possibly be avoided. And at that distance, peacefully eating, the elephant looked no more dangerous than a cow. I thought then and I think now that his attack of "must" was already passing off; in which case he would merely wander harmlessly about until the mahout came back and caught him. Moreover, I did not in the least want to shoot him. I decided that I would watch him for a little while to make sure that he did not turn savage again, and then go home.

7   But at that moment I glanced round at the crowd that had followed me. It was an immense crowd, two thousand at the least and growing every minute. It blocked the road for a long distance on either side. I looked at the sea of yellow faces above the garish clothes—faces all happy and excited over this bit of fun, all certain that the elephant was going to be shot. They were watching me as they would watch a conjurer about to perform a trick. They did not like me, but with the magical rifle in my hands I was momentarily worth watching. And suddenly I realized that I should have to shoot the elephant after all. The people expected it of me and I had got to do it; I could feel their two thousand wills pressing me forward, irresistibly. And it was at this moment, as I stood there with the rifle in my hands, that I first grasped the hollowness, the futility of the white man's dominion in the East. Here was I, the white man with his gun, standing in front of the unarmed native crowd—seemingly the leading actor of the piece; but in reality I was only an absurd puppet pushed to and fro by the will of those yellow faces behind. I perceived in this moment that when the white man turns tyrant it is his own freedom that he destroys. He becomes a sort of hollow, posing dummy, the conventionalized figure of a sahib. For it is the condition of his rule that he shall spend his life in trying to impress the "natives," and so in every crisis he has got to do what the "natives" expect of him. He wears a mask, and his face grows to fit it. I had got to shoot the elephant. I had committed myself to doing it when I sent for the rifle. A sahib has got to act like a sahib; he has got to appear resolute, to know his own mind and do definite things. To come all that way, rifle in hand, with two thousand people marching at my heels, and then to trail feebly away, having done nothing—no, that was impossible. The crowd would laugh at me. And my whole life, every white man's life in the East, was one long struggle not to be laughed at.

8   But I did not want to shoot the elephant. I watched him beating his bunch of grass against his knees with that preoccupied grandmotherly air that elephants have. It seemed to me that it would be murder to shoot him. At that age I was not squeamish about killing animals, but I had never shot an elephant and never wanted to. (Somehow it always seems worse to kill a *large* animal.) Besides, there was the beast's owner to be considered. Alive,

the elephant was worth at least a hundred pounds; dead, he would only be worth the value of his tusks, five pounds, possibly. But I had got to act quickly. I turned to some experienced-looking Burmans who had been there when we arrived, and asked them how the elephant had been behaving. They all said the same thing: he took no notice of you if you left him alone, but he might charge if you went too close to him.

9 It was perfectly clear to me what I ought to do. I ought to walk up to within, say, twenty-five yards of the elephant and test his behavior. If he charged, I could shoot; if he took no notice of me, it would be safe to leave him until the mahout came back. But also I knew that I was going to do no such thing. I was a poor shot with a rifle and the ground was soft mud into which one would sink at every step. If the elephant charged and I missed him, I should have about as much chance as a toad under a steam-roller. But even then I was not thinking particularly of my own skin, only of the watchful yellow faces behind. For at that moment, with the crowd watching me, I was not afraid in the ordinary sense, as I would have been if I had been alone. A white man mustn't be frightened in front of "natives"; and so, in general, he isn't frightened. The sole thought in my mind was that if anything went wrong those two thousand Burmans would see me pursued, caught, trampled on, and reduced to a grinning corpse like that Indian up the hill. And if that happened it was quite probable that some of them would laugh. That would never do. There was only one alternative. I shoved the cartridges into the magazine and lay down on the road to get a better aim.

10 The crowd grew very still, and a deep, low, happy sigh, as of people who see the theater curtain go up at last, breathed from innumerable throats. They were going to have their bit of fun after all. The rifle was a beautiful German thing with cross-hair sights. I did not then know that in shooting an elephant one would shoot to cut an imaginary bar running from ear-hole to ear-hole. I ought, therefore, as the elephant was sideways on, to have aimed straight at his ear-hole; actually I aimed several inches in front of this, thinking the brain would be further forward.

11 When I pulled the trigger I did not hear the bang or feel the kick—one never does when a shot goes home—but I heard the devilish roar of glee that went up from the crowd. In that instant, in too short a time, one would have thought, even for the bullet to get there, a mysterious, terrible change had come over the elephant. He neither stirred nor fell, but every line of his body had altered. He looked suddenly stricken, shrunken, immensely old, as though the frightful impact of the bullet had paralyzed him without knocking him down. At last, after what seemed a long time—it might have been five seconds, I dare say—he sagged flabbily to his knees. His mouth slobbered. An enormous senility seemed to have settled upon him. One could have imagined him thousands of years old. I fired again into the same spot. At the second shot he did not collapse but climbed with desperate slowness to his feet and stood weakly upright, with legs sagging and head drooping. I fired a third time. That was the shot that did for him. You could see the agony of it jolt his whole body and knock the last remnant of strength from his legs. But in falling he seemed for a moment to rise, for as his hind legs

collapsed beneath him he seemed to tower upward like a huge rock toppling, his trunk reaching skyward like a tree. He trumpeted, for the first and only time. And then down he came, his belly toward me, with a crash that seemed to shake the ground even where I lay.

12 I got up. The Burmans were already racing past me across the mud. It was obvious that the elephant would never rise again, but he was not dead. He was breathing very rhythmically with long rattling gasps, his great mound of a side painfully rising and falling. His mouth was wide open—I could see far down into caverns of pale pink throat. I waited a long time for him to die, but his breathing did not weaken. Finally I fired my two remaining shots into the spot where I thought his heart must be. The thick blood welled out of him like red velvet, but still he did not die. His body did not even jerk when the shots hit him, the tortured breathing continued without a pause. He was dying, very slowly and in great agony, but in some world remote from me where not even a bullet could damage him further. I felt that I had got to put an end to that dreadful noise. It seemed dreadful to see the great beast lying there, powerless to move and yet powerless to die, and not even to be able to finish him. I sent back for my small rifle and poured shot after shot into his heart and down his throat. They seemed to make no impression. The tortured gasps continued as steadily as the ticking of a clock.

13 In the end I could not stand it any longer and went away. I heard later that it took him half an hour to die. Burmans were bringing dahs and baskets even before I left, and was told they had stripped his body almost to the bones by the afternoon.

14 Afterward, of course, there were endless discussions about the shooting of the elephant. The owner was furious, but he was only an Indian and could do nothing. Besides, legally I had done the right thing, for a mad elephant has to be killed, like a mad dog, if its owner fails to control it. Among the Europeans opinion was divided. The older men said I was right, the younger men said it was a damn shame to shoot an elephant for killing a coolie, because an elephant was worth more than any damn Coringhee coolie. And afterward I was very glad that the coolie had been killed; it put me legally in the right and it gave me a sufficient pretext for shooting the elephant. I often wondered whether any of the others grasped that I had done it solely to avoid looking a fool.

A. Comprehension

Choose the answer that best completes each statement. Do not refer to the selection while doing this exercise.

1. In this essay, Orwell describes an experience he had while working as a colonial police officer in (a) India; (b) Ceylon; (c) Burma; (d) Pakistan.
2. The natives treated Orwell with (a) respect; (b) indifference; (c) curiosity; (d) hatred.
3. Orwell states, "I had . . . to think out my problems in the utter silence that is imposed on every Englishman in the East." Who or what imposed

this silence? (a) his own ethical standards and conscience; (b) his immediate superior; (c) an unwritten code governing colonial officials of the British Empire; (d) his native counterparts.

4. The natives were unable to kill the rampaging elephant because (a) it was illegal; (b) they had no weapons; (c) they were afraid; (d) elephants were regarded as sacred.

5. The crowd followed Orwell primarily because (a) they secretly hoped he would not be able to shoot the elephant; (b) they were angry at his decision; (c) they were curious about how the conflict would end; (d) they wanted to have some fun at the expense of a colonial officer.

6. The real reason Orwell shot the elephant was that (a) he did not want to look foolish in front of the crowd; (b) the elephant had killed one man and therefore had to be shot; (c) his superiors had commanded him to shoot it; (d) he was afraid the elephant would attack more innocent people.

B. Inferences   On the basis of the evidence in the selection, mark these statements as follows: *A* for accurate inferences, *I* for inaccurate inferences, and *IE* for insufficient evidence. You may refer to the selection to answer the questions in this section, and all the remaining sections.

_____   1. The Burmese had often rioted against British colonial rule.

_____   2. The Burmese were contemptuous of the British imperialist system of government.

_____   3. Orwell had mixed feelings about both the imperialist system and the Burmese he was supposed to supervise.

_____   4. Orwell especially resented the attitude of the Buddhist priests.

_____   5. The attack of "must" that an elephant periodically undergoes refers to a temporary state of frenzy.

_____   6. Tame elephants in the East are used primarily as circus animals.

_____   7. Orwell was powerless to act against the will of the crowd watching him.

_____   8. Orwell knew exactly where to fire his shot.

_____   9. It was illegal for the people to strip the meat from the elephant's carcass.

_____   10. As an Indian, the elephant's owner had no legal case or means of recourse against Orwell for shooting his elephant.

C. Structure   1. The primary mode of discourse in this essay is (a) narration; (b) description; (c) exposition; (d) persuasion.

2. The incident Orwell writes about at the heart of the essay is intended to reveal (a) the threat large crowds pose to the safety of the individual; (b) the horror of death; (c) the fundamental weakness of the imperialist system and its agents; (d) the racial tensions between the Burmese and the British.

3. The purpose of paragraph 2 is to explain Orwell's (a) feelings of inadequacy; (b) feelings of hostility; (c) confusion; (d) ambivalence.

4. Find and write five metaphors from paragraph 7 that relate to performing or acting in front of an audience.

   a. _____
   b. _____
   c. _____
   d. _____
   e. _____

   Next, carefully study these metaphors and the order Orwell imposes on them. What contrast do they reveal? What is the fundamental irony of imperialism that Orwell intends us to see? _____
   _____

5. In paragraph 9, what is the metaphor Orwell uses to describe his predicament? _____ is compared to _____ .
   Explain this metaphor. _____
   _____

6. Read Orwell's description of the elephant's death in paragraphs 11 and 12 again. How would you describe his word choice? _____
   What might be some reasons that Orwell describes the elephant's prolonged agony in such detail? _____
   _____

7. In Orwell's description of the elephant's death, he writes that one could imagine the elephant "thousands of years old," and later that "he was dying, very slowly and in great agony, but in some world remote from me where not even a bullet could damage him further." What does Orwell mean by these phrases? _____
   _____

8. Which of the following sentences from the selection best represents Orwell's thesis? (a) "In Moulmein, in lower Burma, I was hated by large numbers of people—the only time in my life that I have been important enough for this to happen to me." (b) "All I knew was that I was stuck between my hatred of the empire I served and my rage against the evil-spirited little beasts who tried to make my job impossible." (c) "And it was at this moment, as I stood there with the rifle in my hands, that I first grasped the hollowness, the futility of the white man's dominion in the East." (d) "The crowd would laugh at me. And my whole life, every white man's life in the East, was one long struggle not to be laughed at."

D. Vocabulary   For each italicized word from the selection, choose the best definition according to the context in which it appears.

1. a *petty* kind of anti-European feeling [paragraph 1]: (a) spiteful; (b) small; unimportant; (c) easily observed; (d) irritable.

2. *jeer* at Europeans [1]: (a) laugh at; (b) shout at mockingly; (c) complain about; (d) poke fun at.

3. the younger empires that are going to *supplant* it [2]: (a) serve as a model for; (b) support; (c) compensate; (d) replace.

4. an unbreakable *tyranny* [2]: (a) absolute power; (b) merciless slave driver; (c) perfect deity; (d) impenetrable mystery.

5. the will of the *prostrate* peoples [2]: something that is lying down because of (a) weakness; (b) illness; (c) humility; (d) exhaustion.

6. the real motives for which *despotic* governments act [3]: (a) popularly elected; (b) democratic; (c) absolute; tyrannical; (d) imperialistic.

7. an elephant was *ravaging* the bazaar [3]: (a) visiting; (b) causing damage to; (c) wandering around aimlessly in; (d) disrupting.

8. a *labyrinth* of squalid bamboo huts [4]: (a) collection; (b) sparse settlement; (c) neatly laid out plan; (d) maze.

9. a labyrinth of *squalid* bamboo huts [4]: (a) wretched; (b) morally repulsive; (c) crudely built; (d) humble.

10. an army of people *jostling* at my heels [5]: (a) following; (b) pushing and shoving; (c) surging; (d) increasing rapidly.

11. a *miry* waste of paddy fields [5]: (a) tangled; (b) enormous; (c) muddy; (d) barren.

12. the *garish* clothes [7]: (a) dazzling; (b) gaudy; loud in color; (c) ragged; (d) somber; subdued in color.

13. a *conjurer* about to perform a trick [7]: (a) acrobat; (b) elephant rider; (c) circus ringmaster; (d) magician.

14. the *futility* of the white man's dominion [7]: (a) ineffectiveness; (b) stupidity; (c) cruelty; (d) idleness.

15. he has got to appear *resolute* [7]: (a) inflexible; (b) courageous; (c) unwavering; (d) faithful.

16. I was not *squeamish* about killing animals [8]: (a) excited; (b) confident; (c) easily sickened; (d) prudish.

17. the last *remnant* of strength [11]: (a) surviving trace; (b) indication; (c) pretense; (d) something left over.

18. a sufficient *pretext* for shooting the elephant [14]: (a) piece of legal evidence; (b) excuse; (c) authority; (d) rationalization.

E. Variant Word Forms

For each italicized word in parentheses, write the required form in the space provided. Add endings for plural nouns and verb tenses if necessary. You might need to consult an unabridged dictionary.

1. (*imperialism*—use an adjective): The incident with the elephant and the crowd of Burmese natives taught Orwell the fundamental weakness of the British _____ system.

2. (*theoretically*—use a noun): In _____, Orwell was in favor of the Burmese natives.

3. (*oppressed*—use another adjective): The _____ conditions in the jails were especially distressing to Orwell.

4. (*tyranny*—use an adjective): The British Raj in Burma represented a despotic, _____ government.

5. (*immense*—use a noun): The _____ of the crowd surprised Orwell.

6. (*futility*—use an adjective): Orwell knew that all the white man's efforts in the East were essentially _____.

7. (*glee*—use an adjective): The crowd grew bigger by the minute and increasingly _____ about the anticipated show.

8. (*rhythm*—use an adverb): After the elephant was shot, he breathed _____ but in long, rattling gasps.

F. Questions for Analysis

1. This essay implies many conflicts, for example, that between the individual and the force of a large hostile crowd. What are some other conflicts that Orwell either states or implies?

2. "Shooting an Elephant" reveals certain cultural traits that are radically different from those of Westerners. Look through the essay and find a few examples. How do these illustrations help explain (or perhaps justify) Orwell's contempt for the natives? Do you think that, for their part, the natives' actions are justified?

3. Where in the essay does Orwell reveal the heartless attitude toward people that the Burmese so openly display? Is this brutalizing effect of the incident justifiable or not?

Selection 10

The Jollity Building: Indians, Heels, and Tenants
A. J. Liebling

A. J. Liebling (1904–1963) was one of America's most literate and witty journalists. He began his career as a sports writer for the *New York Times,* and later wrote for the *New York World* and the *New York World–Telegram and Journal.* As a staff writer for *The New Yorker,* from 1935 until his death, he wrote a column on American newspapers called "The Wayward Press." Numerous collections of his columns have been published, among them *The Jollity Building* (1962), from which this selection is taken, and *The Most of A. J. Liebling* (1963). Some of Liebling's best writing has to do with the characters who inhabited the Broadway area of New York during the 1930s and early 1940s. Buildings like the Jollity Building, and the characters who occupied them, no longer exist, but we still have Liebling's description of the area and one group of hangers-on he called "The Telephone Booth Indians."

The Telephone Booth Indians range over a territory approximately half a mile square, bounded longitudinally by Sixth and Eighth Avenues in New York, and in latitude by the south side of Forty-second and the north side of Fifty-second Streets. This in part coincides with what is called humorously Broadway, the Heart of the World, and is in fact a sort of famine area, within which the Indians seek their scanty livelihood. Scattered about the district are a few large structures like the Jollity Building, but less imaginary, which are favorite camping grounds of the Indians because they contain large numbers of telephone booths necessary to the tribe's survival. The Telephone Booth Indians are nomads who have not attained the stage of culture in which they carry their own shelter. Like the hermit crab, the Telephone Booth Indian, before beginning operations, must find a habitation abandoned by some other creature, and in his case this is always a telephone booth.

1   In the Jollity Building, which stands six stories high and covers half of a Broadway block in the high Forties, the term "promoter" means a man who mulcts another man of a dollar, or any fraction or multiple thereof. The verb "to promote" always takes a personal object, and the highest praise you can accord someone in the Jollity Building is to say, "He has promoted some very smart people." The Jollity Building—it actually has a somewhat different name, and the names of its inhabitants are not the ones which will appear below—is representative of perhaps a dozen or so buildings in the upper stories of which the small-scale amusement industry nests like a tramp pigeon. All of them draw a major part of their income from the rental of their stores at street level, and most of them contain on their lower floors a dance hall or a billiard parlor, or both. The Jollity Building has both. The dance hall, known as Jollity Danceland, occupies the second floor. The pool-room is in the basement. It is difficult in such a building to rent office space to any business house that wants to be taken very seriously, so the upper floors fill up with the petty nomads of Broadway—chiefly orchestra leaders, theatrical agents, bookmakers, and miscellaneous promoters.
2   Eight coin-box telephone booths in the lobby of the Jollity Building serve as offices for promoters and others who cannot raise the price of desk space on an upper floor. The phones are used mostly for incoming calls. It is a matter of perpetual regret to Morty, the renting agent of the building, that he cannot collect rent from the occupants of the booths. He always refers to them as the Telephone Booth Indians, because in their lives the telephone booth furnishes sustenance as well as shelter, as the buffalo did for the Arapahoe and Sioux. A Telephone Booth Indian on the hunt often tells a prospective investor to call him at a certain hour in the afternoon, giving the victim the number of the phone in one of the booths. The Indian implies, of course, that it is a private line. Then the Indian has to hang in the booth until the fellow calls. To hang, in Indian language, means to loiter. "I used to hang in Forty-sixth Street, front of *Variety,*" a small bookmaker may say, referring to a previous business location. Seeing the Indians hanging in the telephone booths is painful to Morty, but there is nothing he can do about it. The regular occupants of the booths recognize one another's rights. It may be understood among them, for instance, that a certain orchestra leader receives calls in a particular booth between three and four in the afternoon and that a competitor has the same booth from four to five. In these circum-stances, ethical Indians take telephone messages for each other. There are always fewer vacancies in the telephone booths than in any other part of the Jollity Building.
3   While awaiting a call, an Indian may occasionally emerge for air, unless the lobby is so crowded that there is a chance he might lose his place to a

transient who does not understand the house rules. Usually, however, the Indian hangs in the booth with the door open, leaning against the wall and reading a scratch sheet in order to conserve time. Then, if somebody rings up and agrees to lend him two dollars, he will already have picked a horse on which to lose that amount. When an impatient stranger shows signs of wanting to use a telephone, the man in the booth closes the door, takes the receiver off the hook, and makes motions with his lips, as if talking. To add verisimilitude to a long performance, he occasionally hangs up, takes the receiver down again, drops a nickel in the slot, whirls the dial three or four times, and hangs up again, after which the nickel comes back. Eventually the stranger goes away, and the man in the booth returns to the study of his scratch sheet. At mealtimes, the Telephone Booth Indians sometimes descend singly to the Jollity Building's lunch counter, which is at one end of the poolroom in the basement. The busiest lunch periods are the most favorable for a stunt the boys have worked out to get free nourishment. An Indian seats himself at the counter and eats two or three *pastrami* sandwiches. As he is finishing his lunch, one of his comrades appears at the head of the stairs and shouts that he is wanted on the telephone. The Indian rushes upstairs, absent-mindedly omitting to pay for his meal. Barney, the lunch-counter proprietor, is too busy to go after him when he fails to return after a reasonable time. An Indian can rarely fool Barney more than once or twice. The maneuver requires nice timing and unlimited faith in one's accomplice. Should the accomplice fail to make his entrance, the Indian at the counter might be compelled to eat *pastrami* sandwiches indefinitely, acquiring frightful indigestion and piling up an appalling debt.

4   Morty, the renting agent, is a thin, sallow man of forty whose expression has been compared, a little unfairly, to that of a dead robin. He is not, however, a man without feeling; he takes a personal interest in the people who spend much of their lives in the Jollity Building. It is about the same sort of interest that Curator Raymond Ditmars takes in the Bronx Zoo's vampire bats. "I know more heels than any other man in the world," Morty sometimes says, not without pride. "Everywhere I go around Broadway, I get 'Hello, how are you?' Heels that haven't been with me for years, some of them." Morty usually reserves the appellation "heel" for the people who rent the forty-eight cubicles, each furnished with a desk and two chairs, on the third floor of the Jollity Building. These cubicles are formed by partitions of wood and frosted glass which do not quite reach the ceiling. Sufficient air to maintain human life is supposed to circulate over the partitions. The offices rent for $10 and $12.50 a month, payable in advance. "Twelve and a half dollars with air, ten dollars without air," Morty says facetiously. "Very often the heels who rent them take the air without telling me." Sometimes a Telephone Booth Indian acquires enough capital to rent a cubicle. He thus rises in the social scale and becomes a heel. A cubicle has three advantages over a telephone booth. One is that you cannot get a desk into a telephone booth. Another is that you can play pinochle in a cubicle. Another is that a heel gets his name on the directory in the lobby, and the white letters have a bold, legitimate look.

5   The vertical social structure of the Jollity Building is subject to continual shifts. Not only do Indians become heels, but a heel occasionally accumulates $40 or $50 with which to pay a month's rent on one of the larger offices, all of them unfurnished, on the fourth, fifth, or sixth floor. He then becomes a tenant. Morty always views such progress with suspicion, because it involves signing a lease, and once a heel has signed a lease, you cannot put him out without serving a dispossess notice and waiting ten days. A tenant, in Morty's opinion, is just a heel who is planning to get ten days' free rent. "Any time a heel acts prosperous enough to rent an office," Morty says, "you know he's getting ready to take you." A dispossessed tenant often reappears in the Jollity Building as an Indian. It is a life cycle. Morty has people in the building who have been Telephone Booth Indians, heels, and tenants several times each. He likes them best when they are in the heel stage. "You can't collect rent from a guy who hangs in the lobby," he says in explanation, "and with a regular tenant of an unfurnished office, you got too many headaches." He sometimes breaks off a conversation with a friendly heel by saying "Excuse me, I got to go upstairs and insult a tenant."

6   As if to show his predilection for the heels, Morty has his own office on the third floor. It is a large corner room with windows on two sides. There is a flattering picture of the Jollity Building on one of the walls, and six framed plans, one of each floor, on another wall. Also in the office are an unattractive, respectable-looking secretary and, on Morty's desk, a rather depressing photograph of his wife. The conventionality of this *décor* makes Morty unhappy, and he spends as little time as possible in his office. Between nine o'clock in the morning, when he arrives and dejectedly looks through his mail for rent checks he does not expect to find, and six-thirty in the evening, when he goes home to Rockaway, he lives mostly amid the pulsating activity outside his office door.

7   The furnished cubicles on the third floor yield an income of about $500 a month, which, as Morty says, is not hay. Until a few years ago, the Jollity Building used to feel it should provide switchboard service for these offices. The outgoing telephone calls of the heels were supposed to be paid for at the end of every business day. This system necessitated the use of a cordon of elevator boys to prevent tenants from escaping. "Any heel who made several telephone calls toward the end of the month, you could kiss him good-by," Morty says. "As soon as he made up his mind to go out of business he started thinking of people to telephone. It was cheaper for him to go out of business than settle for the calls, anyhow. The only way you can tell if a heel is still in business, most of the time, anyway, is to look in his office for his hat. If his hat is gone, he is out of business." A minor annoyance of the switchboard system was the tendency of heels to call the operator and ask for the time. "None of them were going anywhere, but they all wanted to know the time," Morty says resentfully. "None of them had watches. Nobody would be in this building unless he had already hocked his watch." There are lady heels, too, but if they are young Morty calls them "heads." (Morty meticulously refers to all youngish women as "heads," which has the same meaning as "broads" or "dolls" but is newer; he does not want his conversation to sound archaic.)

Heads also abused the switchboard system. "One head that used to claim to sell stockings," says Morty, "called the board one day, and when the operator said, 'Five o'clock,' this head said, 'My God, I didn't eat yet!' If there had been no switchboard, she would never have known she was hungry. She would have saved a lot of money."

8   As a consequence of these abuses, the switchboard was abolished, and practically all the heels now make their telephone calls from three open coin-box telephones against the wall in a corridor that bisects the third floor. The wall for several feet on each side of the telephones is covered with numbers the heels have jotted down. The Jollity Building pays a young man named Angelo to sit at a table in a small niche near the telephones and answer incoming calls. He screams "Who?" into the mouthpiece and then shuffles off to find whatever heel is wanted. On days when Angelo is particularly weary, he just says, "He ain't in," and hangs up. He also receives and distributes the mail for the heels. Angelo is a pallid chap who has been at various periods a chorus boy, a taxi driver, and a drummer in one of the bands which maintain headquarters in the Jollity Building. "Every time a heel comes in," Angelo says, "he wants to know 'Are you sure there isn't a letter for me that feels like it had a check in it? . . . That's funny, the fellow swore he mailed it last night.' Then he tries to borrow a nickel from me so he can telephone."

9   Not having a nickel is a universal trait of people who rent the cubicles, and they spend a considerable portion of the business day hanging by the third-floor telephones, waiting for the arrival of somebody to borrow a nickel from. While waiting, they talk to Angelo, who makes it a rule not to believe anything they say. There are no booths in the corridor because Morty does not want any Telephone Booth Indians to develop on the third floor.

10   Morty himself often goes to visit with Angelo and terrifies the heels with his bilious stare. "They all say they got something big for next week," he tells Angelo in a loud, carrying voice, "but the rent is 'I'll see you tomorrow.'" Morty's friends sometimes drop in there to visit him. He likes to sit on Angelo's table with them and tell about the current collection of furnished-office inhabitants. "Who is that phony-looking heel who just passed, you want to know?" he may say during such a recapitulation. "Hey, this is funny. He happens to be legitimate—autos to hire. The heel in the next office publishes a horse magazine. If he gets a winner, he eats. Then there's one of them heels that hires girls to sell permanent waves for fifty cents down, door to door. The girl takes the fifty cents and gives the dame a ticket, but when the dame goes to look for the beauty parlor it says on the ticket, there is no such beauty parlor at that address.

11   "We got two heels writing plays. They figure they got nothing to do, so they might as well write a play, and if it clicks, they might also eat. Then we got a lady heel who represents Brazilian music publishers and also does a bit of booking; also a head who is running a school for hat-check girls, as it seems the hat-check profession is very complicated for some of the type of minds they got in it. Those heads who walk through the hall are going no place. They just stick their potato in every office and say, 'Anything for me

today?' They do not even look to see if it is a theatrical office. If they expected
to find anything, they would not be over here. What would anybody here
have to offer? Once in a while a sap from the suburbs walks into one of the
offices on this floor thinking he can get some talent cheap. 'Sure,' some heel
says, 'I got just the thing you want.' They run down in the lobby looking for
somebody. They ask some head they meet in the lobby, 'Are you a performer?' They try the other little agents that they know. The whole date is
worth probably four dollars, and the forty cents' commission they split sometimes four ways."

12   Morty's favorite heel of the current lot is a tall Chesterfieldian old man
named Dr. Titus Heatherington, who is the president of the Anti-Hitlerian
League of the Western Hemisphere. Dr. Heatherington for many years lectured in vacant stores on sex topics and sold a manual of facts every young
man should know. "The line became, in a manner of speaking, exhausted,"
Dr. Heatherington says, "because of the increasing sophistication of the contemporary adolescent, so I interested myself in this great crusade, in which I
distribute at a nominal price a very fascinating book by Cornelius Vanderbilt, Jr., and everything in it must be exactly as stated, because otherwise
Hitler could have sued Mr. Vanderbilt for libel. Incidentally, I sell a lot more
books than I have for years. I do particularly well at Coney Island."

13   Heels are often, paradoxically, more affluent than the official lessees of
larger offices. Many fellows who rent the big units take in subtenants, and if
there are enough of them, each man's share of the rent may be less than the
$10 a month minimum rent a heel has to pay. One two-desk office on the
fourth, fifth, or sixth floor may serve as headquarters for four theatrical
agents, a band leader, a music arranger, a manager of prize fighters, and a
dealer in pawn tickets. They agree on a schedule by which each man has the
exclusive use of a desk for a few hours every day, to impress people who call
by appointment, and the office is used collectively, when no outsiders are
present, for games of rummy. All the fellows in the office receive their telephone calls on a single coin-box machine affixed to the wall. Subtenants
often make bets among themselves, the amount of the wager corresponding
to each bettor's share of the rent. The loser is supposed to pay double rent,
the winner nothing. This causes difficulties for Morty when he comes to
collect the rent. The official lessee always protests that he would like to pay
on the dot but the other boys haven't paid him. Subtenants who have won
bets consider themselves absolved of any responsibility, and the fellows who
are supposed to pay double are invariably broke. Morty makes an average of
fifteen calls to collect a month's rent on an office, and thus acquires a much
greater intimacy with the tenants than the agents of a place like Rocke-
feller Center or River House.

14   Desk room in a large office has the advantage of being much more dignified than a cubicle on the third floor, but there is one drawback: Morty's rule
that not more than two firm names may be listed on the directory in the
lobby for any one office. Callers therefore have to ask the elevator boys
where to find some of the subtenants. If the elevator boys do not like the
subtenant in question, they say they never heard of him. Nor will the

implacable Morty permit more than two names to be painted on any office door. Junior subtenants get around the rule by having a sign painter put their names on strips of cardboard which they insert between the glass and the wooden frame of the door or affix to the glass by strips of tape. "You cannot let a tenant creep on you," Morty says in justification of his severity. "You let them get away with eight names on the door, and the next thing they will be asking you for eight keys to the men's room."

15 Morty's parents were named Goldberg, and he was born in the Bensonhurst region of Brooklyn. He almost finished a commercial course in high school before he got his first job, being an order clerk for a chain of dairy-and-herring stores. In the morning he would drive to each of these stores and find out from the store managers what supplies they needed from the company's warehouse. Since he had little to do in the afternoons, he began after a while to deliver packages for a bootlegger who had been a high-school classmate and by chance had an office in the Jollity Building. The name on the door of the office was the Music Writers Mutual Publishing Company. About a quarter of the firms in the building at that time were fronts for bootleggers, Morty recalls. "Repeal was a terrible blow to property values in this district," he says. "Bootleggers were always the best pay." Seeing a greater future in bootlegging than in dairy goods and herring, Morty soon went to work for his old classmate on a full-time basis. The moment Morty decided that his future lay on Broadway, he translated his name from Goldberg into Ormont. " '*Or*' is French for gold," he sometimes explains, "and '*mont*' is the same as 'berg.' But the point is it's got more class than Goldberg."

16 By diligent application, Morty worked his way up to a partnership in the Music Writers Mutual Publishing Company. The partners made good use of their company's name. They advertised in pulp magazines, offering to write music for lyrics or lyrics for music, to guarantee publication, and to send back to the aspiring song writer a hundred free copies of his work, all for one hundred dollars. The Music Writers Mutual agreed to pay him the customary royalties on all copies sold. There never were any royalties, because Morty and his partner had only the author's hundred copies printed. They kept a piano in their office and hired a professional musician for thirty-five dollars a week to set music to lyrics. Morty himself occasionally wrote lyrics to the tunes clients sent in, and had a lot of fun doing it. At times the music business went so well that the partners were tempted to give up bootlegging. There were so many similar publishing firms, however, that there was not a steady living in it. "But you would be surprised," Morty says now, "how near it came to paying our overhead." The volume of mail made it look bona fide. They built up a prosperous semi-wholesale liquor business, specializing in furnishing whisky to firms in the Garment Center, which used it for presents to out-of-town buyers. "The idea on that stuff was that it should be as reasonable as possible without killing anybody," Morty says. "It was a good, legitimate dollar." The depression in the garment industry ruined the Music Writers Mutual Publishing Company's business even before repeal and left Morty broke.

17   The Jollity Building belongs to the estate of an old New York family, and in the twenties the trustees had installed as manager one of the least promising members of the family, a middle-aged, alcoholic Harvard man whom they wanted to keep out of harm's way. Morty had been such a good tenant and seemed so knowing a fellow that the Harvard man offered him a job at twenty-five dollars a week as his assistant. When the manager ran off with eleven thousand dollars in rents and a head he had met in the lobby, Morty took over his job. He has held it ever since. The trustees feel, as one of them has expressed it, that "Mr. Ormont understands the milieu." He now gets fifty dollars a week and two per cent of the total rents, which adds about two thousand a year to his income.

18   The nostalgia Morty often feels for the opportunities of prohibition days is shared by the senior tenant in the building, the proprietor of the Quick Art Theatrical Sign Painting Company, on the sixth floor. The sign painter, a Mr. Hy Sky—a name made up of the first syllable of his first name, Hyman, and the last syllable of a surname which no one can remember—is a bulky, red-faced man who has rented space in the Jollity Building for twenty-five years. With his brother, a lean, sardonic man known as Si Sky, he paints signs and lobby displays for burlesque and movie houses and does odd jobs of lettering for people in all sorts of trades. He is an extremely fast letterer and he handles a large volume of steady business, but it lacks the exhilaration of prohibition years. Then he was sometimes put to work at two o'clock in the morning redecorating a clip joint, so that it could not be identified by a man who had just been robbed of a bank roll and might return with cops the next day. "Was that fun!" Hy howls reminiscently. "And always cash in advance! If the joint had green walls, we would make them pink. We would move the bar opposite to where it was, and if there was booths in the place, we would paint them a different color and change them around. Then the next day, when the cops came in with the sap, they would say, 'Is this the place? Try to remember the side of the door the bar was on as you come in.' The sap would hesitate, and the cops would say, 'I guess he can't identify the premises,' and they would shove him along. It was a nice, comfortable dollar for me."

19   Hy has a clinical appreciation of meretricious types which he tries unsuccessfully to arouse in Morty. Sometimes, when Hy has a particularly preposterous liar in his place, he will telephone the renting agent's office and shout, "Morty, pop up and see the character I got here! He is the most phoniest character I seen in several years." The person referred to seldom resents such a description. People in the Jollity Building neighborhood like to be thought of as characters. "He is a real character," they say, with respect, of any fascinatingly repulsive acquaintance. Most promoters are characters. Hy Sky attributes the stability of his own business to the fact that he is willing to "earn a hard dollar." "The trouble with the character," he says, "is they are always looking for a soft dollar. The result is they knock theirselves out trying too hard to have it easy. So what do they get after all? Only the miss-meal cramps." Nevertheless, it always gives Hy a genteel pleasure to collaborate, in a strictly legitimate way, with any of the promoters he knows.

The promoter may engage him to paint a sign saying, "A new night club will open soon on these premises. Concessionaires interested telephone So-and-So at such-and-such a number." The name is the promoter's own, and the telephone given is, as Hy knows, in a booth in the Jollity lobby. The promoter, Hy also knows, will place this sign in front of a vacant night club with which he has absolutely no connection, in the hope that some small hat-check concessionaire with money to invest in a new club will read the sign before someone gets around to removing it and take it seriously. If the concessionaire telephones, the promoter will make an appointment to receive him in a Jollity cubicle borrowed from some other promoter for the occasion and will try to get a couple of hundred dollars as a deposit on the concession. If successful, he will lose the money on a horse in the sixth race at an obscure track in California. The chances of getting any money out of this promotional scheme are exceedingly slight, but the pleasure of the promoter when the device succeeds is comparable to that of a sportsman who catches a big fish on a light line. Contemplation of the ineffectual larceny in the promoter's heart causes Hy to laugh constantly while lettering such a sign. A contributory cause of his laughter is the knowledge that he will receive the only dollar that is likely to change hands in the transaction—the dollar he gets for painting the sign.

20 Musicians are not characters, in Hy's estimation, but merely a mild variety of phony. As such, they afford him a tempered amusement. When two impressive band leaders in large, fluffy overcoats call upon him for a communal cardboard door sign, toward the cost of which each contributes twenty-five cents, he innocently inquires, "How many of you are there in that office?" One of the band leaders will reply grandiosely, "Oh, we all have separate offices; the sign is for the door to quite a huge suite." Hy laughs so hard he bends double to relieve the strain on his diaphragm. His brother, Si, who lives in continual fear that Hy will die of apoplexy, abandons his work and slaps Hy's back until the crowing abates. "A suite," Hy repeats weakly at intervals for a half-hour afterward, "a huge suite they got, like on the subway at six o'clock you could get." Hy also paints, at an average price of twenty-five cents, cardboard backs for music racks. These pieces of cardboard, whose only function is to identify the band, bear in bright letters its name, which is usually something like Everett Winterbottom's Rhumba Raiders. When a Jollity Building band leader has acquired a sign for his door and a set of these lettered cardboards, he is equipped for business. If, by some unlikely chance, he gets an engagement, usually to play a week end in a cabaret in Queens or the Bronx, he hurries out to the curb on Seventh Avenue in front of Charlie's Bar & Grill where there are always plenty of musicians, and picks up the number of fellows he requires, generally four. The men tapped go over to Eighth Avenue and get their instruments out of pawn. A musician who owns several instruments usually leaves them all in a pawnshop, ransoming one when he needs it to play a date and putting it back the next day. If, when he has a chance to work, he lacks the money to redeem an instrument, he borrows the money from a Jollity Building six-for-fiver, a fellow who will lend you five dollars if you promise to pay him six

dollars within twenty-four hours. Meanwhile, the band leader looks up a fellow who rents out orchestra arrangements guaranteed to be exact, illegal copies of those one or another of the big bandsmen has exclusive use of. The band leader puts the arrangements and his cardboards under his arm and goes down to Charlie's to wait for the other musicians to come back from the hock shop. That night Everett Winterbottom's Rhumba Raiders ride again. The only worry in the world the Raiders have, at least for the moment, is that they will have to finish their engagement before a union delegate discovers them and takes away their cards. Each man is going to receive three dollars a night, which is seven dollars below union scale.

A. Comprehension

Choose the answer that best completes each statement. Do not refer to the selection while doing this exercise.

1. The inhabitants of the Jollity Building are small-scale members of (a) the garment industry; (b) a gambling fraternity; (c) the amusement and entertainment industry; (d) a bootlegging business.

2. Morty, the renting agent for the building, calls its first-floor occupants Telephone Booth Indians because (a) most of them are of Indian descent; (b) the telephone booth is the main source of survival for them, just as the buffalo was for the Indians; (c) their faces are stern and impassive, like those of some Indians; (d) their customs and system of values resemble those of Indians.

3. Morty calls the occupants of the forty-eight cubicles on the third floor of the Jollity Building (a) Broadway Indians; (b) heels; (c) tenants; (d) deadbeats.

4. The switchboard service for the third floor offices at the Jollity Building was eventually abolished because (a) the operators kept running off with the Indians or tenants from the building; (b) the building's occupants often neglected to pay their telephone bill; (c) the continual flux of occupants in the building made the system unworkable; (d) the system was abused by the building's occupants.

5. The young man who answers incoming calls on the building's third floor is named (a) Dr. Heatherington; (b) Angelo; (c) Ormont; (d) Hyman.

6. The reason heels are often more affluent than the official tenants of larger offices is that (a) they take in subtenants, thus reducing their share of the rent; (b) they often win big at the racetrack; (c) they succeed in arranging lucrative engagements for the performers they represent; (d) they are only pretending to be poor to avoid paying rent.

7. According to both Morty and Hyman, the best days for making money were during (a) World War I; (b) World War II; (c) the Depression; (d) Prohibition.

8. One way to compliment an acquaintance in the Jollity Building is to call him (a) a promoter; (b) a tenant; (c) a character; (d) an Indian.

9. Money raised in a phony night club deal is usually spent on (a) pastrami sandwiches; (b) repainting the night club to make it look legitimate; (c) hiring concessionaires; (d) bets at the horse races.

10. The musicians who can be found in front of Charlie's Bar & Grill on Seventh Avenue keep their instruments (a) in pawnshops; (b) in the Jollity Building; (c) in the night clubs where they play on weekends; (d) in special rehearsal rooms.

B. Inferences   On the basis of the evidence in the selection, mark these statements as follows: *A* for accurate inferences, *I* for inaccurate inferences, and *IE* for insufficient evidence. You may refer to the selection to answer the questions in this section, and all the remaining sections.

_____ 1. The Jollity Building is located in New York City.

_____ 2. In Jollity Building slang, the verb "to promote" means to advertise another person's talents.

_____ 3. Legitimate and respectable businesses also rent space in the Jollity Building.

_____ 4. All of the Jollity Building's Telephone Booth Indians are ethical about taking messages for one another.

_____ 5. The money Telephone Booth Indians raise is usually spent on rent, clothing, and food.

_____ 6. Few vacancies occur in the telephone booths because the first floor is the most desirable and most impressive part of the Jollity Building.

_____ 7. The hierarchy or status system in the Jollity Building is rigid, not allowing for any movement up or down on the social scale.

_____ 8. Morty is cynical about the Jollity Building's inhabitants and their stories.

_____ 9. Morty prefers the heels to the other kinds of occupants because they have more interesting backgrounds.

_____ 10. A telephone call in the Jollity Building costs a dime.

_____ 11. Changing his name from Goldberg to Ormont greatly boosted Morty's career in the music business.

_____ 12. When the building's trustees say that "Mr. Ormont understands the milieu," they are insulting him.

_____ 13. In the Jollity Building, when Hyman calls someone "the most phoniest character," he is referring to the character's preposterous lies.

_____ 14. The schemes the promoters at the Jollity Building hatch are big-time, complicated deals involving large sums of money.

_____ 15. The musicians who can be hired on the street in front of Charlie's Bar & Grill on Seventh Avenue are not members of the musicians' union because the union dues are exorbitantly high.

C. Structure   1. Which mode of discourse predominates in this selection? (a) narration; (b) description; (c) exposition; (d) persuasion. Explain your choice. _____

2. Which of the following best explains Liebling's purpose in writing? (a) to explain the economic effects of the Depression and the end of Prohibition on the entertainment industry in New York City; (b) to describe the Jollity Building and the surrounding area of Broadway; (c) to explain the vertical social structure of the Jollity Building and its occupants' means of survival; (d) to criticize the entertainment industry in New York City for neglecting talented entertainers who are thus forced to turn to petty larceny to survive.

3. What is the dominant method of development in this essay? (a) analogy; (b) classification; (c) cause–effect; (d) process; (e) definition. Specifically, how is this method of development put to use in the essay?

_____

4. The method of development in paragraph 3 is (a) process; (b) definition; (c) example; (d) analogy; (e) cause–effect; (f) analysis.

5. In paragraph 4, Liebling says that Morty's expression has been compared, a little unfairly, to that of a dead robin. What exactly does this figure of speech mean? _____

6. The tone of this selection—Liebling's emotional attitude toward the Jollity Building and its occupants—can best be described as (a) critical; judgmental; (b) caustic; sardonic; (c) admiring; laudatory; (d) neutral; impartial; (e) witty; amused.

D. Vocabulary   For each italicized word from the selection, choose the best definition according to the context in which it appears.

1. a man who *mulcts* another man [paragraph 1]: (a) penalizes; (b) obtains by fraud or deception; (c) insures; guarantees; (d) steals; robs.

2. the petty *nomads* of Broadway [1]: small-time (a) thieves; (b) promoters; (c) people with no fixed business address; (d) derelicts.

3. a matter of *perpetual* regret [2]: (a) indefinite; (b) deep; profound; (c) insincere; (d) unceasing; continual.

4. the telephone booth furnishes *sustenance* [2]: (a) food and shelter; (b) security; insurance; (c) a refuge; safe haven; (d) a means of livelihood.

5. he might lose his place to a *transient* [3]: one who (a) is a guest; (b) moves around from place to place; (c) is a newcomer; (d) takes over another's property or territory.

6. to add *verisimilitude* to a long performance [3]: (a) the appearance of being real; (b) drama; emotion; (c) polish; practice; (d) a sense of importance.

7. unlimited faith in one's *accomplice* [3]: (a) partner in crime; (b) boldness; brashness; (c) best friend; (d) accomplishment.

8. piling up an *appalling* debt [3]: (a) uncollectable; (b) frightful; horrifying; (c) incredible; unbelievable; (d) unacceptable.

9. a thin, *sallow* man [4]: describing a complexion that is (a) reddish; (b) purple; (c) whitish; (d) yellowish.

10. Morty usually reserves the *appellation* "heel" [4]: (a) insulting term; epithet; (b) nickname; (c) name; (d) affectionate term.

11. Morty says *facetiously* [4]: describing a sense of humor that is (a) bitter; (b) sarcastic; (c) ridiculous; (d) playfully jocular.

12. to show his *predilection* for the heels [6]: (a) suspicion; (b) distrust; (c) personal dislike; (d) personal preference.

13. the conventionality of the *décor* [6]: (a) style; decoration; (b) physical environment; (c) space; (d) physical layout.

14. amid the *pulsating* activity [6]: (a) frenzied; excited; (b) throbbing; vigorous; (c) calming; tranquil; (d) physically rejuvenating.

15. Morty *meticulously* refers [7]: (a) dejectedly; (b) insultingly; (c) carefully; (d) invariably.

16. he does not want to sound *archaic* [7]: (a) sexist; discriminatory; (b) antiquated; outdated; (c) uninformed; ignorant; (d) up-to-date; current.

17. Angelo is a *pallid* chap [8]: (a) sullen; glum; (b) ambitious; motivated; (c) thin; gaunt; (d) abnormally pale.

18. terrifies the heels with his *bilious* stare [10]: (a) sour-tempered; (b) evil; (c) frightful; (d) rude.

19. during such a *recapitulation* [10]: (a) conversation; dialogue; (b) summary; restatement; (c) description; discussion; (d) question-and-answer session.

20. I distribute at a *nominal* price [12]: (a) exorbitant; (b) average; (c) acceptable; (d) minimal.

21. heels are often, *paradoxically,* more affluent [13]: describing (a) a bizarre situation; (b) an apparent contradiction; (c) an unhappy truth; (d) a matter of circumstances.

22. subtenants consider themselves *absolved* [13]: (a) relieved of an obligation; (b) forgiven for their wrongs; (c) destined by fate; (d) wronged; deceived.

23. the *implacable* Morty [14]: (a) incapable of being pleased; (b) incapable of being upset; (c) impracticable; (d) inflexible.

24. made it look *bona fide* [16]: (a) authentic; (b) impressive; (c) deceptive; (d) prosperous.

25. Mr. Ormont understands the *milieu* [17—French: pronounced mǐl-yŏo′]: (a) situation; (b) environment; (c) customs; (d) protocol.

26. a lean, *sardonic* man [18]: (a) stingy; greedy; (b) humorously pleasant; (c) scornful; cynical; (d) nasty; bitter.

27. a clinical appreciation of *meretricious* types [19]: those who (a) attract attention in a vulgar manner; (b) behave pompously; (c) are representative of a certain group; (d) are criminally inclined.

28. it always gives Hy a *genteel* pleasure [19]: (a) affectedly polite or sincere; (b) hypocritical; (c) genuine; real; (d) legitimate.

29. one of the band leaders will reply *grandiosely* [20]: (a) generously; (b) affectedly impressive; (c) sincerely; (d) disinterestedly.

30. until the crowing *abates* [20]: (a) vanishes; (b) weakens; (c) intensifies; (d) subsides.

Part of the charm of Liebling's piece lies in the use of 1930s slang, which affirms the class and occupation of the people who inhabited the Jollity Building. Pay attention to the context, or consult an unabridged dictionary, and write the meaning of these slang expressions:

1. A Telephone Booth Indian *on the hunt* [paragraph 2]

   _____

2. the Indian has *to hang* in the booth [2]

   _____

3. reading *a scratch sheet* [3] _____

4. "Any time a heel acts prosperous enough to rent an office," Morty says, "you know he's getting ready *to take you*." [5]

   _____

5. an income of about $500 a month, which, as Morty says, is *not hay* [7]

   _____

6. they just stick *their potato* in their office [11]

   _____

7. "You cannot let a tenant *creep* on you," Morty says. [14]

   _____

8. redecorating *a clip joint* [15] _____
9. a *hard dollar*/a *soft dollar* [19]_____

   _____

10. "So what do they get after all? Only the *miss-meal cramps*." [19]

    _____

E. Questions for Analysis

1. From Liebling's characterization, how would you describe Morty, the rental agent for the Jollity Building?
2. A. J. Liebling was regarded as one of the great journalists in America. On the basis of this selection, what can you infer contributed to his reputation?
3. Liebling never directly reveals his attitude toward the denizens of the Jollity Building or toward their attempts at petty larceny. Do you think he finds them pathetic, is he glorifying them, or is his attitude something altogether different?

Selection 11

The Moment of Being
John N. Bleibtreu

John Bleibtreu (1926–   ) studied with the Bolivian philosopher and mystic Osca Ichazo in Arica, Chile, and later worked at the Arica Institute, a sensitivity training center in New York. A frequent contributor to magazines, Bleibtreu has studied the research done in ethology (the study of animal behavior) extensively, and published the results of this research in *The Parable of the Beast,* from which this selection is taken.

1   The cattle tick is a small, flat-bodied, blood-sucking insect with a curious life history. It emerges from the egg not yet fully developed, lacking a pair of legs, and sex organs. In this state it is still capable of attacking cold-blooded animals such as frogs and lizards, which it does. After shedding its skin several times, it acquires its missing organs, mates, and is then prepared to attack warm-blooded animals.

2   The eyeless female is directed to the tip of a twig on a bush by her photosensitive skin, and there she stays through darkness and light, through fair weather and foul, waiting for the moment that will fulfill her existence. In the Zoological Institute, at Rostock, prior to World War I ticks were kept on the ends of twigs, waiting for this moment for a period of eighteen years. The metabolism of the insect is sluggish to the point of being suspended entirely. The sperm she received in the act of mating remains bundled into capsules where it, too, waits in suspension until mammalian blood reaches the stomach of the tick, at which time the capsules break, the sperm are released and they fertilize the eggs which have been reposing in the ovary, also waiting in a kind of time suspension.

3   The signal for which the tick waits is the scent of butyric acid, a substance present in the sweat of all mammals. This is the only experience that will trigger time into existence for the tick.

4   The tick represents, in the conduct of its life, a kind of apotheosis of subjective time perception. For a period as long as eighteen years nothing happens. The period passes as a single moment; but at any moment within this span of literally senseless existence, when the animal becomes aware of the scent of butyric acid it is thrust into a perception of time, and other signals are suddenly perceived.

5   The animal then hurls itself in the direction of the scent. The object on which the tick lands at the end of this leap must be warm; a delicate sense of temperature is suddenly mobilized and so informs the insect. If the object is not warm, the tick will drop off and reclimb its perch. If it is warm, the tick burrows its head deeply into the skin and slowly pumps itself full of blood. Experiments made at Rostock with membranes filled with fluids other than blood proved that the tick lacks all sense of taste, and once the membrane is perforated the animal will drink any fluid, provided it is of the right temperature.

6   [a]The extraordinary preparedness of this creature for that moment of time during which it will re-enact the purpose of its life contrasts strikingly with the probability that this moment will ever occur. [b]There are doubtless many bushes on which ticks perch, which are never by-passed by a mammal within range of the tick's leap. [c]As do most animals, the tick lives in an absurdly unfavorable world—at least so it would appear to the compassionate human observer. [d]But this world is merely the environment of the animal. [e]The world it perceives—which experimenters at Rostock called its *umwelt,*

its perceptual world—is not at all unfavorable. [f]A period of eighteen years, as measured objectively by the circuit of the earth around the sun, is meaningless to the tick. [g]During this period, it is apparently unaware of temperature changes. [h]Being blind, it does not see the leaves shrivel and fall and then renew themselves on the bush where it is affixed. [i]Unaware of time it is also unaware of space, and the multitudes of forms and colors which appear in space. [j]It waits, suspended in duration for its particular moment of time, a moment distinguished by being filled with a single, unique experience; the scent of butyric acid.

7   Though we consider ourselves far removed as humans from such a lowly insect form as this, we too are both aware and unaware of elements which comprise our environment. We are more aware than the tick of the passage of time. We are subjectively aware of the aging process; we know that we grow older, that time is shortened by each passing moment. For the tick, however, this moment that precedes its burst of volitional activity, the moment when it scents butyric acid and is thrust into purposeful movement, is close to the end of time for the tick. When it fills itself with blood, it drops from its host, lays its eggs, and dies.

8   For us humans, death seems to come in a more random fashion. Civilized as we pretend to be, we know very little about time and the transformations of living things that occur within it. We know little about growth and aging, which, it would seem, are stimulated by the passage of time which streams around us carrying us with it; and about death, or the termination of biological time.

A. Comprehension

Choose the answer that best completes each statement. Do not refer to the selection while doing this exercise.

1. The subject of this selection is (a) experiments with insects at the Rostock Zoological Institute; (b) the life history of the cattle tick; (c) the difference between human and animal perceptions of time; (d) the difference in the manner of death for humans and animals.

2. The adult cattle tick's metabolism cannot be activated until it becomes aware of the scent of butyric acid, a substance present (a) only in cattle; (b) in the blood of all mammals; (c) in the sweat of all mammals; (d) in all bushes and trees.

3. Ironically, the adult cattle tick has no (a) sense of taste; (b) sense of smell; (c) sense of direction; (d) sex organs.

4. According to Bleibtreu, the suspended existence the cattle tick must undergo illustrates (a) a senseless existence; (b) a hostile environment; (c) objective time perception; (d) subjective time perception.

5. Bleibtreu emphasizes that, like the cattle tick, humans (a) live in a state of suspension; (b) know little about growth, aging, and death; (c) are keenly aware of the passage of time; (d) undergo the same reproductive cycle.

B. Inferences   On the basis of the evidence in the selection, mark these statements as follows: *A* for accurate inferences, *I* for inaccurate inferences, and *IE* for insufficient evidence. You may refer to the selection to answer the questions in this section, and all the remaining sections.

_____ 1. The cattle tick is unable to detect light.

_____ 2. For the cattle tick, reproduction, which occurs when the tick lays its eggs, signifies that death is near.

_____ 3. A cattle tick who never comes into contact with a mammal eventually dies.

_____ 4. After its metabolism is activated by the scent of butyric acid, the cattle tick lives a long life.

_____ 5. The cattle tick can detect temperature changes both in the environment and on an animal's skin.

_____ 6. It is probable that many cattle ticks never complete their life cycle.

_____ 7. The Zoological Institute at Rostock is the only scientific institution where the cattle tick has been studied.

_____ 8. Unlocking the mysteries of the cattle tick will advance human understanding of life and death.

C. Structure   1. Which sentence from the essay best represents both the thesis statement and the author's underlying purpose? (a) "The cattle tick is a small, flat-bodied, blood-sucking insect with a curious life history." (b) "This [the scent of butyric acid] is the only experience that will trigger time into existence for the tick." (c) "The tick represents, in the conduct of its life, a kind of apotheosis of subjective time perception." (d) "The extraordinary preparedness of this creature for that moment of time during which it will re-enact the purpose of its life contrasts strikingly with the probability that this moment will ever occur." (e) "We know little about growth and aging, which, it would seem, are stimulated by the passage of time which streams around us carrying us with it; and about death, or the termination of biological time."

2. The mode of discourse in the essay is (a) narration; (b) description; (c) exposition; (d) persuasion.

3. The method of paragraph development in paragraphs 2 and 5 is (a) analysis; (b) definition; (c) contrast; (d) process; (e) illustration.

4. The method of paragraph development in paragraph 4 is (a) definition; (b) process; (c) classification; (d) contrast; (e) analogy.

5. The topic sentence of paragraph 6 is sentence _____.

6. The method of paragraph development in paragraph 6 is (a) example; (b) classification; (c) definition; (d) analysis; (e) analogy.

7. Which two methods of development are represented in the essay as a whole? _____ and _____.

8. When Bleibtreu states that the cattle tick's existence depends solely on the presence of butyric acid, this emphasizes from the human viewpoint

the tick's (a) uselessness in the animal kingdom; (b) slim chances for fulfillment; (c) impossibility of fulfillment; (d) meaningless, senseless existence.

9. Bleibtreu's purpose in paragraphs 7 and 8 is to (a) summarize the tick's biological cycle; (b) relate the tick's life cycle to human knowledge of life processes and perception of time; (c) warn us that life is short and too easily taken up with trivial matters; (d) contrast the lowly cattle tick with human ideals and lofty aspirations; (e) compare the human life cycle with that of the cattle tick.

10. Which group of readers do you think Bleibtreu has in mind as his audience? (a) scientific researchers; (b) the general reading public; (c) a group of readers with a higher level of education and sophistication than the general reading public; (d) philosophers.

D. Vocabulary   For each italicized word from the selection, choose the best definition according to the context in which it appears.

1. her *photosensitive* skin [paragraph 2]: sensitive to (a) heat; (b) sights; (c) smells; (d) light.

2. the metabolism is *suspended* [2]: (a) hung up; (b) held in abeyance or in an undecided state; (c) barred from a privilege or position; (d) supported or kept from falling without attachment.

3. the eggs have been *reposing* in the ovary [3]: (a) stored; (b) lying at rest; (c) placing trust in; (d) waiting.

4. an *apotheosis* of subjective time perception [4]: (a) legend passed from generation to generation; (b) rule to be emulated; (c) ideal; primary example; (d) apocalypse.

5. *subjective* time perception [4]: (a) existing within the mind; (b) neutral; (c) fixed; limited; (d) imaginative.

6. sense of temperature is suddenly *mobilized* [6]: (a) moved to a new location; (b) put into operation; (c) put into battle; (d) responded to.

7. once the membrane is *perforated* [5]: (a) touched; (b) sensitized; (c) broken; (d) pierced.

8. a *lowly* insect form [7]: (a) simple; humble; (b) unaware; (c) complicated; (d) pitiable.

9. burst of *volitional* activity [7]: describing the act of (a) requiring; (b) willing; (c) maturing; (d) dying.

10. death seems to come in a more *random* fashion [8]: (a) certain; (b) conscious; (c) predictable; (d) unsystematic.

E. Variant Word Forms   From the list of inflected forms in parentheses, choose the form that fits grammatically into the space. Add endings (-s or -ed, for example) if necessary.

1. (curiosity, curious, curiously): The subject of this essay, the cattle tick, has a _____ life history.

2. (metabolism, metabolize, metabolic, metabolically): The cattle tick is _____ sluggish.

3. (experiment, experimental, experimentally): Researchers have _____ with the cattle tick to determine what sense organs it possesses.

4. (absurdity, absurd, absurdly): The cattle tick's environment can only be described as unfavorable and _____.

5. (termination, terminate, terminal, terminally): The cattle tick is undoubtedly not aware when its biological time is _____.

F. Questions for Analysis

1. Surely other animals possess the same characteristics that Bleibtreu assigns to the cattle tick, namely the lack of awareness of time and space (see paragraph 6). Why, then, has Bleibtreu chosen this lowly insect as the subject of his essay?

2. What is ironic (and perhaps tragic, from our viewpont) about the cattle tick's life cycle after it has been activated by the scent of butyric acid?

3. Read paragraphs 7 and 8 again. How are we like the cattle tick? How are we different?

4. The title of the book from which this selection was taken is *The Parable of the Beast*. What is a parable? In what way does this essay represent a parable? (If you are unsure of the meaning of parable, look it up in the dictionary.)

Selection 12 **Mayakovsky Billboard**

Andrea Lee

Andrea Lee, one of the most talented young American writers, was born in Philadelphia in 1943. After receiving both her BA and MA in English from Harvard, she and her husband Tom went to the USSR in 1978, where they studied at state universities in both Moscow and Leningrad. *Russian Journal,* the book from which "Mayakovsky Billboard" is reprinted, is a highly readable account of her experiences in the Soviet Union. She is also a frequent contributor of short stories to *The New Yorker.*

1   In Mayakovsky Square, not far from the Tchaikovsky Concert Hall, a big computerized electric sign sends various messages flashing out into the night. An outline of a taxi in green dots is accompanied by the words: "Take Taxis—All Streets Are Near." This is replaced by multicolored human figures and a sentence urging Soviet citizens to save in State banks. The bright patterns and messages come and go, making this one of the most sophisticated examples of advertising in Moscow. Even on chilly nights when I pass through the square, there is often a little group of Russians standing in front of the sign, watching in fascination for five and ten minutes as the colored dots go through their magical changes. The first few times I saw this, I chuckled and recalled an old joke about an American town so boring that people went out on weekends to watch the Esso

sign. With each month I live here, however, I'm more and more tempted to join the spectators in Mayakovsky Square.

2   Tourists I've met here invariably refer to Moscow as a "gray" city: this impression, when I examine it, does not come entirely from the weather—I've lived through grayer Novembers in Paris—or from the color of the buildings, a surprising number of which are painted in charming pastels. It springs more from the unbeautiful aspect of the crowds (Russian bodies and faces are heavy; Russian clothes, when not actually hideous, are monotone and forgettable), and most of all, from the lack of Western-style advertising. Advertising, of course, is the glamorous offspring of capitalism and art: why advertise in a country where there is only one brand, the State brand, of anything, and often not enough even of that? There is nothing here comparable to the glittering overlay of commercialism that Americans, at least, take for granted as part of our cities; nothing like the myriad small seductions of the marketplace, which have led us to expect to be enticed. The Soviet political propaganda posters that fill up a small part of the Moscow landscape with their uniformly cold red color schemes and monumental robot-faced figures are so unappealing that they are dismissable. (It's interesting to try to figure out exactly whom these posters are aimed at. Every Russian I know, even the most conservative, finds them dreadful; perhaps they're intended for a future race of titans.)

3   I realize now, looking back, that for at least my first month in Moscow, I was filled with an unconscious and devastating disappointment. Hardly realizing it, as I walked around the city, I was looking for the constant sensory distractions I was accustomed to in America. Like many others my age, I grew up reading billboards and singing advertising jingles; my idea of beauty was shaped—perniciously, I think—by the models with painted eyes and pounds of shining hair whose beauty was accessible on every television set and street corner. In Moscow, I found none of this easy stimulation—only the rarer, more demanding pleasures of nature and architecture: rain on the gold domes inside the Kremlin walls; yellow leaves stuck to a wet pavement; a decayed stone grotesque on the peeling front of a mansion in the Arbat; a face in a subway crowd.

4   Living in these comparatively simple surroundings has made my inner life more intense. Tom and I have found that our dreams have gained color and our memories have become sharper; we are both more attentive to beauty. I finally understand in part the Russian phenomenon of staring: now, when I see a well-cut dress (terribly rare), a handsomely bound book (still rarer), or an attractive face, I stare with amazing persistence, until my ravenous eyes are satisfied. Tom and I have found that we can sit for an hour looking—just looking—with lingering pleasure at the most banal American magazine—*Good Housekeeping,* for example—stunned by the attractiveness of its layout and photographs. Last week I received a tiresome dunning letter from the alumni office of my university; I was about to throw it away when my Russian friend Olga snatched it, stared at the elaborate graphics of the letterhead, and said, "It's so beautiful . . . may I have it?" Later I found she'd pinned it up beside her bed.

⁵   Everywhere we go in Moscow, we find a frantic enthusiasm for any kind of natural or man-made beauty. At parties, pretty girls are feted with an innocent, extravagant adulation from men and women alike; ordinary people show a passion for art and literature which might be suspect as a pose in America. The deepest roots of this quality of Russian life are hard to discern, and I am setting aside the ugly fact of government censorship of the arts, which obviously plays its own perverse role in intensifyng enthusiasm for beauty. I mean to observe here only that a more austere environment seems to favor sensitivity. This isn't a new idea at all, of course. People on islands, in prisons, in monasteries have all discovered the same thing. But it's a remarkable feeling to have my mind clearing up week by week, like a lens that was filmed and dim, until, just as the year goes dark with winter, I've started to see the subtle points of light in this gray city.

A. Comprehension

Choose the answer that best completes each statement. Do not refer to the selection while doing this exercise.

1. The Mayakovsky billboard attracts spectators because (a) Russians are interested in the political messages it displays; (b) such colorful advertising displays are rare in the USSR; (c) it is the only form of advertising in the entire nation; (d) the billboard displays useful suggestions about where to buy scarce commodities.

2. When tourists describe Moscow as a "gray" city, they are referring to (a) the gloomy weather; (b) the color the buildings are painted; (c) the gloomy and oppressive political and social climate; (d) the dull Russian clothes and lack of Western-style advertising.

3. Initially, upon her arrival in Moscow, the author missed (a) sensory distractions; (b) Western goods such as fashions and magazines; (c) a wide assortment of competing brands for consumer items; (d) the presence of physically attractive people.

4. To Lee's surprise, her friend Olga was fascinated by (a) the graphics of her university's letterhead; (b) Lee's Western clothes; (c) the diversity of products available in the U.S.; (d) a copy of *Good Housekeeping* magazine.

5. According to Lee, the reason Russians stare is that (a) staring is a compliment in the USSR, unlike the United States, where it is considered bad manners; (b) beautiful things to stare at are not common; (c) they find the colorful attire of foreigners irresistible; (d) they are suspicious of foreigners who are so different from themselves.

B. Inferences

On the basis of the evidence in the selection, mark these statements as follows: *A* for accurate inferences, *I* for inaccurate inferences, and *IE* for insufficient evidence. You may refer to the selection to answer the questions in this section, and all the remaining sections.

_____ 1. The Mayakovsky billboard broadcasts only political propaganda messages.

_____ 2. There is little choice in consumer goods in the USSR.

_____ 3. Soviet citizens ignore political propaganda posters for the most part.

_____ 4. Russian books are not as attractively bound as American books.

_____ 5. The Russians' fascination with beauty does not go beyond physical things.

_____ 6. Americans' perception and appreciation of beauty is considerably different from that of the Russians.

C. Structure 1. Which of the following sentences taken from the selection best represents the thesis? (a) "In Mayakovsky Square, not far from the Tchaikovsky Concert Hall, a big computerized electric sign sends various messages flashing out into the night." (b) "With each month I live here, however, I'm more and more tempted to join the spectators in Mayakovsky Square." (c) "Everywhere we go in Moscow, we find a frantic enthusiasm for any kind of natural or man-made beauty." (d) "I mean to observe here only that a more austere environment seems to favor sensitivity."

2. The dominant mode of discourse in this selection is (a) narration; (b) description; (c) exposition; (d) persuasion.

3. Look again at the last sentence of paragraph 3. Which mode of discourse does it represent? (a) narration; (b) description; (c) exposition; (d) persuasion.

4. In that same sentence, what does the phrase "easy stimulation" specifically refer to? _____

5. Which of these methods of development is implicit in the selection as a whole? (a) process; (b) analogy; (c) example; (d) contrast; (e) comparison; (f) definition.

6. The last sentence of the essay contains a simile. What is being compared to what? _____ is/are compared to _____ .
Explain the simile in your own words. _____

D. Vocabulary   For each italicized word from the selection, choose the best definition according to the context in which it appears.

1. one of the most _sophisticated_ examples of advertising [paragraph 1]: (a) complicated; refined; (b) unusual; rare; (c) perverse; corrupted; (d) self-serving.

2. tourists _invariably_ refer to Moscow [2]: (a) seldom; (b) constantly; (c) complainingly; (d) understandably.

3. the _myriad_ small seductions of the marketplace [2]: (a) entertaining; (b) colorful; (c) trivial; (d) large, indefinite number.

4. the myriad small _seductions_ of the marketplace [2]: (a) temptations; (b) messages; (c) corruptions; (d) unfulfilled desires.

5. expect to be _enticed_ [2]: (a) trapped; (b) lured; (c) overwhelmed; (d) transformed.

6. a future race of *titans* [2]: (a) dull, colorless people; (b) people of colossal size and strength; (c) people who can be easily subjugated; (d) politically active citizens.

7. I was filled with *devastating* disappointment [3]: (a) unexpected; (b) unwelcome; (c) overwhelming; (d) long overdue.

8. my idea of beauty was shaped *perniciously* [3]: (a) destructively; (b) prematurely; (c) severely; (d) immorally.

9. I stare until my *ravenous* eyes are satisfied [4]: (a) curious; (b) unbelieving; (c) greedy for gratification; (d) predatory.

10. the most *banal* American magazine [4]: lacking (a) color; vividness; (b) style; pizazz; (c) good taste; propriety; (d) freshness; imagination.

11. a tiresome *dunning* letter [4]: a letter (a) requesting biographical information; (b) requesting donations; (c) demanding payment; (d) announcing a contest.

12. pretty girls are *feted* [5]: (a) honored; (b) surrounded; (c) bothered; (d) praised.

13. with an innocent, extravagant *adulation* [5]: (a) adoration; (b) excessive praise; (c) lack of sophistication; (d) enthusiasm.

14. censorship plays its own *perverse* role [5]: (a) wrongly stubborn; (b) persistent in what is wrong; (c) contradictory; (d) cranky; peevish.

15. a more *austere* environment [5]: (a) corrupt; evil; (b) severe or stern in appearance; (c) colorful; gaudy; (d) without ornamentation; simple.

E. Questions for Analysis

1. Lee says that American commercialism has "myriad small seductions of the marketplace" (paragraph 2). Assuming that she is correct, what does this phrase suggest about the essential difference between American and Soviet culture?

2. In paragraph 3, Lee says that her idea of beauty was shaped by advertising. To what extent does her statement hold true for you?

Selection 13   **The Three Little Pigs**
Bruno Bettelheim

Bruno Bettelheim (1903–   ) was born in Vienna and came to the United States in 1929. As a psychologist and educator, he was associated for many years with the University of Chicago, where he directed the Orthogenic School for the treatment of disturbed children. A prolific writer, he has published several books on children, including several books on the identification and treatment of emotionally disturbed children. In addition, he has published many books for a more general audience, among them, *Children of the Dream* (1962), an account of children raised on Israeli kibbutzes; *The Uses of Enchantment*, a Freudian analysis of children's fairy tales (1976), from which this selection comes; and, with Karen Zelan, *On Learning to Read: The Child's Fascination with Meaning* (1982). [Note: The original version of "The Three Little Pigs," which Bettelheim uses as the basis of his analysis, is reprinted at the end of the exercises. If you are unfamiliar with it, be sure to read it before you read Bettelheim's selection.]

1   The myth of Hercules deals with the choice between following the pleasure principle or the reality principle in life. So, likewise, does the fairy story of "The Three Little Pigs."

2   Stories like "The Three Little Pigs" are much favored by children over all "realistic" tales, particularly if they are presented with feeling by the storyteller. Children are enraptured when the huffing and puffing of the wolf at the pig's door is acted out for them. "The Three Little Pigs" teaches the nursery-age child in a most enjoyable and dramatic form that we must not be lazy and take things easy, for if we do, we may perish. Intelligent planning and foresight combined with hard labor will make us victorious over even our most ferocious enemy—the wolf! The story also shows the advantages of growing up, since the third and wisest pig is usually depicted as the biggest and oldest.

3   The houses the three pigs build are symbolic of man's progress in history: from a lean-to shack to a wooden house, finally to a house of solid brick. Internally, the pigs' actions show progress from the id-dominated personality to the superego-influenced but essentially ego-controlled personality.

4   The littlest pig builds his house with the least care out of straw; the second uses sticks; both throw their shelters together as quickly and effortlessly as they can, so they can play for the rest of the day. Living in accordance with the pleasure principle, the younger pigs seek immediate gratification, without a thought for the future and the dangers of reality, although the middle pig shows some growth in trying to build a somewhat more substantial house than the youngest.

5   Only the third and oldest pig has learned to behave in accordance with the reality principle: he is able to postpone his desire to play, and instead acts in line with his ability to foresee what may happen in the future. He is even able to predict correctly the behavior of the wolf—the enemy, or stranger within, which tries to seduce and trap us; and therefore the third pig is able to defeat powers both stronger and more ferocious than he is. The wild and destructive wolf stands for all asocial, unconscious, devouring powers against which one must learn to protect oneself, and which one can defeat through the strength of one's ego.

6   "The Three Little Pigs" makes a much greater impression on children than Aesop's parallel but overtly moralistic fable of "The Ant and the Grasshopper." In this fable a grasshopper, starving in winter, begs an ant to give it some of the food which the ant had busily collected all summer. The ant asks what the grasshopper was doing during the summer. Learning that the grasshopper sang and did not work, the ant rejects his plea by saying, "Since you could sing all summer, you may dance all winter."

7   This ending is typical for fables, which are also folk tales handed down from generation to generation. "A fable seems to be, in its genuine state, a narrative in which beings irrational, and sometimes inanimate, are, for the purpose of moral instruction, feigned to act and speak with human interests and passions" (Samuel Johnson). Often sanctimonious, sometimes amusing, the fable always explicitly states a moral truth; there is no hidden meaning, nothing is left to our imagination.

8   The fairy tale, in contrast, leaves all decisions up to us, including whether we wish to make any at all. It is up to us whether we wish to make any application to our life from a fairy tale, or simply enjoy the fantastic events it tells about. Our enjoyment is what induces us to respond in our own good time to the hidden meanings, as they may relate to our life experience and present state of personal development.

9   A comparison of "The Three Little Pigs" with "The Ant and the Grasshopper" accentuates the difference between a fairy tale and a fable. The grasshopper, much like the little pigs and the child himself, is bent on playing, with little concern for the future. In both stories the child identifies with the animals (although only a hypocritical prig can identify with the nasty ant, and only a mentally sick child with the wolf); but after having identified with the grasshopper, there is no hope left for the child, according to the fable. For the grasshopper beholden to the pleasure principle, nothing but doom awaits; it is an "either/or" situation, where having made a choice once settles things forever.

10   But identification with the little pigs of the fairy tale teaches that there are developments—possibilities of progress from the pleasure principle to the reality principle, which, after all, is nothing but a modification of the former. The story of the three pigs suggests a transformation in which much pleasure is retained, because now satisfaction is sought with true respect for the demands of reality. The clever and playful third pig outwits the wolf several times: first, when the wolf tries three times to lure the pig away from the safety of home by appealing to his oral greed, proposing expeditions to where the two would get delicious food. The wolf tries to tempt the pig with turnips which may be stolen, then with apples, and finally with a visit to a fair.

11   Only after these efforts have come to naught does the wolf move in for the kill. But he has to enter the pig's house to get him, and once more the pig wins out, for the wolf falls down the chimney into the boiling water and ends up as cooked meat for the pig. Retributive justice is done: the wolf, which has devoured the other two pigs and wished to devour the third, ends up as food for the pig.

12   The child, who throughout the story has been invited to identify with one of its protagonists, is not only given hope, but is told that through developing his intelligence he can be victorious over even a much stronger opponent.

13   Since according to the primitive (and a child's) sense of justice only those who have done something really bad get destroyed, the fable seems to teach that it is wrong to enjoy life when it is good, as in summer. Even worse, the ant in this fable is a nasty animal, without compassion for the suffering of the grasshopper—and this is the figure the child is asked to take for his example.

14   The wolf, on the contrary, is obviously a bad animal, because it wants to destroy. The wolf's badness is something the young child recognizes within himself: his wish to devour, and its consequence—the anxiety about possibly suffering such a fate himself. So the wolf is an externalization, a projection of the child's badness—and the story tells how this can be dealt with constructively.

[15]The various excursions in which the oldest pig gets food in good ways are an easily neglected but significant part of the story, because they show that there is a world of difference between eating and devouring. The child subconsciously understands it as the difference between the pleasure principle uncontrolled, when one wants to devour all at once, ignoring the consequences, and the reality principle, in line with which one goes about intelligently foraging for food. The mature pig gets up in good time to bring the goodies home before the wolf appears on the scene. What better demonstration of the value of acting on the basis of the reality principle, and what it consists of, than the pig's rising very early in the morning to secure the delicious food and, in so doing, foiling the wolf's evil designs?

[16] In fairy tales it is typically the youngest child who, although at first thought little of or scorned, turns out to be victorious in the end. "The Three Little Pigs" deviates from this pattern, since it is the oldest pig who is superior to the two little pigs all along. An explanation can be found in the fact that all three pigs are "little," thus immature, as is the child himself. The child identifies with each of them in turn and recognizes the progression of identity. "The Three Little Pigs" is a fairy tale because of its happy ending, and because the wolf gets what he deserves.

[17] While the child's sense of justice is offended by the poor grasshopper having to starve although it did nothing bad, his feeling of fairness is satisfied by the punishment of the wolf. Since the three little pigs represent stages in the development of man, the disappearance of the first two little pigs is not traumatic; the child understands subconsciously that we have to shed earlier forms of existence if we wish to move on to higher ones. In talking to young children about "The Three Little Pigs," one encounters only rejoicing about the deserved punishment of the wolf and the clever victory of the oldest pig—not grief over the fate of the two little ones. Even a young child seems to understand that all three are really one and the same in different stages—which is suggested by their answering the wolf in exactly the same words: "No, no, not by the hair of my chinni-chin-chin!" If we survive in only the higher form of our identity, this is as it should be.

[18] "The Three Little Pigs" directs the child's thinking about his own development without ever telling what it ought to be, permitting the child to draw his own conclusions. This process alone makes for true maturing, while telling the child what to do just replaces the bondage of his own immaturity with a bondage of servitude to the dicta of adults.

A. Comprehension

Choose the answer that best completes each statement. Do not refer to the selection while doing this exercise.

1. "The Three Little Pigs" deals with making a choice between (a) a personality dominated by the id and one dominated by the ego; (b) thrift and wastefulness; (c) the pleasure principle and the reality principle; (d) intolerance and compassion.

2. "The Three Little Pigs" teaches children the value of (a) intelligent planning and foresight; (b) trickery and deceit; (c) indulging in momentary pleasures; (d) doing without all sensual pleasures.

3. Bettelheim states that the houses the three pigs build are symbolic of (a) various architectural styles; (b) the stages of human progress in history; (c) the three theories of human personality; (d) three schemes to outwit the wolf.

4. According to Bettelheim, fables do not have the impact on children that fairy tales do because fables are too (a) unbelievable; (b) long and tedious; (c) moralistic; (d) simple-minded.

5. The purpose of a genuine fable is to provide (a) entertainment for the listener; (b) knowledge about the real world; (c) appropriate role models for emulation; (d) moral instruction.

6. For Bettelheim, fairy tales are enjoyable primarily because (a) we may discover in them what we wish; (b) we do not have to ponder over their meanings; (c) we can enter a fantasy world, thereby escaping our own problems; (d) we can see evil—such as that personified by the big bad wolf—conquered.

7. The disadvantage, according to Bettelheim, of the fable "The Ant and the Grasshopper," is that at its end the child is faced with (a) boredom; (b) the possibility of defeat; (c) doom for the grasshopper; (d) a sense of unrealistic optimism.

8. We can accurately conclude that "The Three Little Pigs" (a) is Bettelheim's favorite fairy tale; (b) teaches children a lesson similar to that of "The Ant and the Grasshopper," only more effectively; (c) has undergone extensive revision in content and form through the ages; (d) is upsetting to very young children, who may suffer anxiety over the fate of the first two little pigs.

B. Inferences   On the basis of the evidence in the selection, mark these statements as follows: *A* for accurate inferences, *I* for inaccurate inferences, and *IE* for insufficient evidence. You may refer to the selection to answer the questions in this section, and all the remaining sections.

_____ 1. The myth of Hercules and "The Three Little Pigs" have the same theme.

_____ 2. Fables can be as effective as fairy tales for teaching moral truths if they are properly told.

_____ 3. A fable is characterized primarily by its short length.

_____ 4. "The Ant and the Grasshopper" conveys an overly drastic and possibly erroneous moral truth.

_____ 5. Children have a clear sense of justice—that evil must be punished.

_____ 6. Stories are more effective if they are told to young children rather than read.

C. Structure

1. Which of the four modes of discourse—narration, description, exposition, or persuasion—are evident in this essay? Explain with specific references to the essay. _____

   _____

2. What is the relationship between the ideas in paragraphs 3 and 4? (a) term to be defined and explanation; (b) general principle and specific illustrations; (c) cause–effect; (d) comparison and contrast.

3. In the section comprising paragraphs 7 and 8, what is being contrasted?

   _____

   What is the purpose of this contrast? _____

   _____

4. Listed below are several methods of paragraph development. Decide which method is the predominant one used in each of the paragraphs enumerated.

cause–effect	process
analysis	definition
comparison	illustration

   a. paragraph 3 _____
   b. paragraph 5 _____
   c. paragraph 7 _____
   d. paragraph 9 _____
   e. paragraph 10 _____

6. In the first sentence of paragraph 17, what does the word "while" mean?

   _____

7. Paraphrase (restate in your own words) the final sentence of the essay:

   _____

   _____

8. This essay has a clear beginning, middle, and end. The dividing line between the introduction and the body of the essay comes at the end of paragraph _____. The dividing line between the body and the conclusion comes at the end of paragraph _____.

D. Vocabulary

For each italicized word from the selection, choose the best definition according to the context in which it appears.

1. the wolf stands for the *asocial* powers [paragraph 5]: the prefix *a-* indicates (a) possessing; (b) lacking; (c) contradictory; (d) inside.
2. *overtly* moralistic fable [6]: (a) openly; (b) obviously; (c) highly; (d) cleverly.
3. beings sometimes *inanimate* [7]: (a) dead; (b) spiritless; (c) not living; (d) not real.
4. *feigned* to act [7]: (a) dared; (b) pretended; (c) decided; (d) programmed.
5. often *sanctimonious* [7]: (a) deeply religious; (b) insincere; (c) serious; (d) affectedly pious.

6. the fable *explicitly* states [7]: (a) forthrightly; (b) cautiously; (c) indirectly; (d) succinctly.

7. a hypocritical *prig* [9]: (a) thief; (b) arrogant, smug person; (c) religious zealot; (d) political conservative.

8. *beholden* to the pleasure principle [9]: (a) grateful for; (b) attracted by; (c) obliged to; bound to; (d) kept enslaved by.

9. these efforts have come to *naught* [11]: (a) a logical conclusion; (b) nothing; (c) grief; (d) a standstill.

10. *retributive* justice is done [11]: something that is done for (a) money; (b) pride; (c) a specific purpose; (d) punishment.

11. one of the story's *protagonists* [12]: (a) enemies; (b) leading characters; (c) evil spirits; (d) heroes.

12. *foiling* the wolf's evil designs [15]: (a) making fun of; (b) upsetting; (c) preventing from being successful; (d) blockading.

13. the *bondage* of his own immaturity [18]: (a) enslavement; (b) reality; (c) limitation; (d) ineffectiveness.

14. a bondage of *servitude* [18]: (a) entrapment; (b) subjection to an outside force; (c) unquestioning obedience; (d) respect for.

15. the *dicta* of adults [18—singular is *dictum*]: (a) moral lessons; (b) pieces of advice; (c) stories; fables; (d) dogmatic pronouncements.

In addition, be certain that you know the correct meanings of the terms devised by Sigmund Freud for the three motivating forces within the human personality: the *id,* the *ego,* and the *superego.*

E. Variant Word Forms   For each italicized word in parentheses, write the required form in the space provided. Add endings for plural nouns and verb tenses if necessary. You might need to consult an unabridged dictionary.

1. (*myth*—use the adjective form): Hercules was a _____ character in Greek legend.

2. (*realistic*—use the adverb form): The storyteller should always act out the story's events _____.

3. (*ferocious*—use either of the two noun forms): The wolf has traditionally been considered an animal who displays both cunning and

   _____.

4. (*gratification*—use the verb form): The first two little pigs' pleasure is quickly _____

5. (*seduce*—use a noun form): We must beware the enemy's attempts at

   _____.

6. (*explicitly*—use the adjective form): The moral truths in fables are generally quite _____.

7. (*hypocritical*—use a noun form): Only someone guilty of _____ could identify with the nasty ant.

8. (*doom*—use the verb form): The grasshopper who played all summer was _____ in the cold winter months.

9. (*retributive*—use the noun form): In tricking the wolf, the third little pig achieves _____ for the wolf's evil deeds.

10. (*deviate*—use a noun form): Some fairy tales represent a _____ from the normal pattern, in which the youngest character is victorious at the end.

F. Questions for Analysis

1. One of Bettelheim's chief purposes is to contrast fables and fairy tales in terms of their effectiveness in teaching the child about values, and he clearly feels that fairy tales are superior. Is his case convincing or not? Explain. Can you think of any fables (Aesop's or those by other writers) which do an effective job of presenting moral truths?

2. In paragraph 9, Bettelheim writes that "only a hypocritical prig can identify with the nasty ant" (in "The Ant and the Grasshopper"). First, do you accept this proposition? What unstated assumption lies behind this assertion?

3. Do you agree with Bettelheim's characterization of the wolf as "an externalization, a projection of the child's badness"? (See paragraph 14.) What else might the wolf represent to a small child?

4. Which two paragraphs in the essay would you use as a rebuttal to a critic who felt that "The Three Little Pigs" was too violent for small children?

The Story of the Three Little Pigs
From Joseph Jacobs, *English Fairy Tales*

> Once upon a time when pigs spoke rhyme
> And monkeys chewed tobacco,
> And hens took snuff to make them tough,
> And ducks went quack, quack, quack, O!

There was an old sow with three little pigs, and as she had not enough to keep them, she sent them out to seek their fortune. The first that went off met a man with a bundle of straw, and said to him,

"Please, man, give me that straw to build me a house."

Which the man did, and the little pig built a house with it. Presently came along a wolf, and knocked at the door, and said,

"Little pig, little pig, let me come in."

To which the pig answered,

"No, no, by the hair of my chiny chin chin."

The wolf then answered to that,

"Then I'll huff, and I'll puff, and I'll blow your house in."

So he huffed, and he puffed, and he blew his house in, and ate up the little pig.

The second little pig met a man with a bundle of furze and said,

"Please, man, give me that furze to build a house."

Which the man did, and the pig built his house. Then along came the wolf, and said,

"Little pig, little pig, let me come in."

"No, no, by the hair of my chiny chin chin."

"Then I'll puff, and I'll huff, and I'll blow your house in."

So he huffed, and he puffed, and he puffed and he huffed, and at last he blew the house down, and he ate up the little pig.

The third little pig met a man with a load of bricks, and said,

"Please, man, give me those bricks to build a house with."

So the man gave him the bricks, and he built his house with them. So the wolf came, as he did to the other little pigs, and said,

"Little pig, little pig, let me come in."

"No, no, by the hair on my chiny chin chin."

"Then I'll huff, and I'll puff, and I'll blow your house in."

Well, he huffed, and he puffed, and he huffed and he puffed, and he puffed and huffed; but he could *not* get the house down. When he found that he could not, with all his huffing and puffing, blow the house down, he said,

"Little pig, I know where there is a nice field of turnips."

"Where?" said the little pig.

"Oh, in Mr. Smith's home-field, and if you will be ready tomorrow morning I will call for you, and we will go together, and get some for dinner."

"Very well," said the little pig, "I will be ready. What time do you mean to go?"

"Oh, at six o'clock."

Well, the little pig got up at five and got the turnips before the wolf came (which he did about six), who said,

"Little pig, are you ready?"

The little pig said, "Ready! I have been and come back again and got a nice potful for dinner."

The wolf felt very angry at this, but thought that he would be up to the little pig somehow or other, so he said,

"Little pig, I know where there is a nice apple-tree."

"Where?" said the pig.

"Down at Merry-Garden," replied the wolf, "and if you will not deceive me, I will come for you at five o'clock tomorrow and get some apples."

Well, the little pig bustled up the next morning at four o'clock, and went off for the apples, hoping to get back before the wolf came; but he had farther to go and had to climb the tree, so that just as he was coming down from it, he saw the wolf coming, which, as you may suppose, frightened him very much. When the wolf came up he said:

"Little pig, what! are you here before me? Are they nice apples?"

"Yes, very," said the little pig. "I will throw you down one."

And he threw it so far, that, while the wolf was gone to pick it up, the little pig jumped down and ran home. The next day the wolf came again and said to the little pig,

"Little pig, there is a fair at Shanklin this afternoon; will you go?"

"Oh, yes," said the pig, "I will go; what time shall you be ready?"

"At three," said the wolf. So the little pig went off before the time as usual and got to the fair and bought a butter-churn, which he was going home with, when he saw the wolf coming. Then he could not tell what to do. So he got into the churn to hide, and by so doing turned it round, and it rolled down the hill with the pig in it, which frightened the wolf so much, that he ran home without going to the fair. He went to the little pig's house and told him how frightened he had been by a great round thing which came down the hill past him. Then the little pig said,

"Hah, I frightened you then. I had been to the fair and bought a butter-churn; and when I saw you, I got into it, and rolled down the hill."

Then the wolf was very angry indeed and declared he *would* eat up the little pig, and that he would get down the chimney after him. When the little pig saw what he was about, he hung on the pot full of water and made up a blazing fire and, just as the wolf was coming down, took off the cover and in fell the wolf; so the little pig put on the cover again in an instant, boiled him up, and ate him for supper and lived happy ever afterwards.

Selection 14   The Ordeal of Steerage
Irving Howe

Born in 1920, Irving Howe was the child of Ukrainian immigrants who settled in New York City. Howe is a professor at the City University of New York, as well as the author of many articles and books on a wide range of subjects that includes radical politics, the American labor movement, American literature, and the Jewish experience in America. World of Our Fathers, from which this selection is taken, is a comprehensive study of the immigrant in the United States that emphasizes the Eastern European Jewish experience beginning in the late nineteenth century. (Note: "steerage" refers to the section below decks where the poorer immigrants were accommodated on their journey across the Atlantic.)

1   Was the Atlantic crossing really as dreadful as memoirists and legend have made it out to be? Was the food as rotten, the treatment as harsh, the steerage as sickening? One thing seems certain: to have asked such questions of a representative portion of Jews who came to America between 1881 and 1914 would have elicited stares of disbelief, suspicions as to motive, perhaps worse. The imagery of the journey as ordeal was deeply imprinted in the Jewish folk mind–admittedly, a mind with a rich training in the imagery of ordeal.

2   Of the hundreds of published and unpublished accounts Jewish immigrants have left us, the overwhelming bulk can still communicate a shudder of dismay when they recall the journey by sea and the disembarkation at Castle Garden or Ellis Island. Only a historian sophisticated to the point of foolishness would dismiss such accounts as mere tokens of folk bewilderment before the presence of technology, or of psychic disorientation following

uprooting, journey, and resettlement. Tokens of bewilderment and disorientation there are, certainly, and these contributed to rhetorical exaggeration about the ordeal of the Atlantic crossing. But the suffering was real, it was persistent, and it has been thoroughly documented.

3 By the time they reached the Atlantic, many immigrants had been reduced to a state of helpless passivity, unable to make out what was happening to them or why. An acute description of this experience has been provided by Oscar Handlin:

a The crossing involved a startling reversal of roles, a radical shift in attitudes. The qualities that were desirable in the good peasant [and, we might add, in nonpeasant Jews also] were not those conducive to success in the transition. Neighborliness, obedience, respect, and status were valueless among the masses that struggled for space on the way. They succeeded who put aside the old preconceptions, pushed in, and took care of themselves. . . . Thus uprooted, they found themselves in a prolonged state of crisis. . . .

b As a result they reached their new homes exhausted—worn out physically by lack of rest, by poor food, by the constant strain of close, cramped quarters, worn out emotionally by the succession of new situations that had crowded in upon them. At the end was only the dead weariness of an excess of novel sensations.

4 Let us sample a few memoirists, of widely varying sensibilities, as they recall the Atlantic journey. Morris Raphael Cohen, a philosopher distinguished for acute skepticism, wrote:

a We were huddled together in the steerage [of the ship *Darmstadt*] literally like cattle—my mother, my sister and I sleeping in the middle tier, people being above us and below us. . . . We could not eat the food of the ship, since it was not kosher. We only asked for hot water into which my mother used to put a little brandy and sugar to give it a taste. Towards the end of the [fourteen-day] trip when our bread was beginning to give out we applied to the ship's steward for bread, but the kind he gave us was unbearably soggy. . . .

b More than the physical hardships, my imagination was occupied with the terrors of ships colliding, especially when the fog horn blew its plaintive note. . . . One morning we saw a ship passing at what seemed to me a considerable distance, but our neighbor said that we were lucky, that at night we escaped a crash only by a hair's breadth.

5 Here is a passage from an unpublished memoir by a barely literate woman writing in Yiddish more than fifty years after her arrival in 1891:

a The sky was blue—the stars shining. But in my heart it was dark when I went up on the ship. . . . We rode three weeks on a freight train so I had plenty of time to think things over. My future . . . where am I going? to whom? what will I do? In Grodno I was at least someone in the store. But in America, without language, with only a bit of education. . . .

Young people laughed and joked even though in my heart it was like the storm at sea. . . . And then a real storm broke out. The ship heaved and turned. People threw up, dishes fell, women screamed . . . but in my heart I didn't care what happened.

6   And here is the voice of a self-educated immigrant whose sense of life's indignities recalls the English novelist Smollett:

a   On board the ship we became utterly dejected. We were all herded together in a dark, filthy compartment in the steerage. . . . Wooden bunks had been put up in two tiers. . . . Seasickness broke out among us. Hundreds of people had vomiting fits, throwing up even their mother's milk. . . . As all were crossing the ocean for the first time, they thought their end had come. The confusion of cries became unbearable. . . . I wanted to escape from that inferno but no sooner had I thrust my head forward from the lower bunk than someone above me vomited straight upon my head. I wiped the vomit away, dragged myself onto the deck, leaned against the railing and vomited my share into the sea, and lay down half-dead upon the deck.

7   In all such recollections, the force of trauma overcomes differences of personality and cultivation. Steerage could reduce people to a common misery, and insofar as it did, their reactions were likely to be the same whether they were illiterate or students of the Talmud.* We may suspect that the shock of being uprooted led some memoirists to overstate, we may have ironic reservations about the Jewish appetite for remembered woe; but there is plenty of dispassionate evidence, ranging from government reports to accounts by journalists who themselves took the trip in steerage, that supports the dominant immigrant memory. Edward Steiner, an Iowa clergyman, wrote a book in 1906 called *On the Trail of the Immigrant,* sober in content yet full of passages like this one:

a   The steerage never changes, neither its location nor its furnishings. It lies over the stirring screws [ship's propellers], sleeps to the staccato of trembling steel railings and hawsers. Narrow, steep and slippery stairways lead to it.
b   Crowds everywhere, ill smelling bunks, uninviting washrooms—this is steerage. The odors of scattered orange peelings, tobacco, garlic and disinfectants meeting but not blending. No lounge or chairs for comfort, and a continual babel of tongues—this is steerage.
c   The food, which is miserable, is dealt out of huge kettles into the dinner pails provided by the steamship company. When it is distributed, the stronger push and crowd. . . .
d   On many ships, even drinking water is grudgingly given, and on the

*A collection of ancient Hebrew writings, which constitutes the authority for traditional Judaism.

steamship *Staatendam* . . . we had literally to steal water for the steerage from the second cabin, and that of course at night. On many journeys, particularly on the *Fürst Bismarck* . . . the bread was absolutely uneatable, and was thrown into the water by the irate emigrants.

8   By the turn of the century conditions had in some cases improved. The German lines offered a modified steerage on their newer ships, a sort of separate stateroom containing two to eight berths and with improved sanitary conditions. The lucky ones came on these ships, some of which, like the *Kaiser Wilhelm,* could now make the trip from Hamburg to New York in a bit less than six days. And even the gloomiest of accounts speak about the upsurge of hope and animal spirits among the younger immigrants: there was often music, cardplaying, even dancing when the weather eased and the decks could be used. Sometimes, the more ambitious younger emigrants brought along Russian-English dictionaries and tried to master a few words for the moment of their arrival. Above all there was talk: the Jewish immigrants' burgeoning nostalgia for the old country and curiosity about the new.

9   A congressional committee investigating steerage conditions in 1910 offered an enormously detailed report which, in bureaucratic prose, substantiates the recollections of the immigrants themselves. In the old-type steerage, it reported, "filth and stench . . . added to inadequate means of ventilation," creating an atmosphere that was "almost unendurable. . . . In many instances persons, after recovering from seasickness, continue to lie in their berths in a sort of stupor, due to breathing air whose oxygen has been mostly replaced by foul gases." A woman investigator, disguising herself as a Bohemian peasant, gave vivid details:

a   . . . one wash room, about 7 by 9 feet, contained 10 faucets of cold salt water, 5 along either of its two walls, and as many basins. . . . This same basin served as a dishpan for greasy tins, as a laundry tub for soiled handkerchiefs and clothing, and as a basin for shampoos without receiving any special cleaning. It was the only receptacle to be found for use in the case of seasickness.

b   The toilets for women were six in number. . . . They baffle description as much as they did use. Each room or space was exceedingly narrow and short, and instead of a seat there was an open trough, in front of which was an iron step and back of it a sheet of iron slanting forward. . . . The toilets were filthy and difficult of use and were apparently not cleaned at all in the first few days.

c   . . . Everything was dirty, sticky and disagreeable to the touch. Every impression was offensive. Worse than this was the general air of immorality. For 15 hours each day I witnessed all around me this . . . indecent and forced mingling of men and women who were total strangers and often did not understand a word of the same language.

10   If a certain prissiness creeps into this report, a tone we will encounter even in the most warmhearted of native responses, it does not finally matter. For about a crucial moment of the immigrant experience, this investigation offered a good portion of the truth.

A. Compre-
hension

Choose the answer that best completes each statement. Do not refer to the selection while doing this exercise.

1. The main idea of the selection is that for most Jewish immigrants, the Atlantic crossing (a) is a part of the Jewish heritage that has been passed down from generation to generation; (b) was instigated by American capitalists looking for a cheap source of labor; (c) involved mistreatment and unnecessary suffering; (d) was an unpleasant but necessary step for those immigrants who wanted to flee religious persecution.

2. One of the memoirists Howe cites states that immigrants who best survived the crossing did so because they (a) put aside traditional values such as neighborliness and respect; (b) bribed the ships' officials; (c) were strong enough to endure every kind of indignity; (d) stole from those with more ample provisions.

3. According to Howe, the effect of steerage on the immigrant was (a) a profound dislike of America; (b) many unnecessary deaths from disease or starvation; (c) a common state of misery; (d) the need for welfare once they arrived in New York.

4. Howe writes that, by the turn of the century, (a) the wave of immigration had begun to diminish; (b) conditions in steerage had begun to improve; (c) conditions in steerage had reached their lowest point; (d) the American government had decided to regulate the ships bringing immigrants to the United States.

5. Howe emphasizes that, worst of all, steerage caused (a) financial loss; (b) emotional trauma; (c) physical deprivation; (d) a breaking up of family relationships.

B. Inferences

On the basis of the evidence in the selection, mark these statements as follows: *A* for accurate inferences, *I* for inaccurate inferences, and *IE* for insufficient evidence. You may refer to the selection to answer the questions in this section, and all the remaining sections.

1. The Atlantic crossing was not as dreadful as legend has suggested.
2. Most immigrant accounts of the crossing are fairly accurate.
3. Some ships served kosher food.
4. The English novelist Smollett wrote about the Jewish immigrants' experience.
5. Rich or educated immigrants were spared the miseries of steerage.
6. Before the turn of the century, the Atlantic crossing took about two weeks.
7. The author himself made the Atlantic crossing in steerage.
8. The immigrants usually had arranged for jobs prior to their arrival in New York.

C. Structure

1. Howe's purpose is, specifically, to (a) describe the typical Jewish immigrants' experience in steerage; (b) confirm the dominant impression of

misery which immigrants experienced during the Atlantic crossing; (c) contrast the experiences of Jewish immigrants in the late nineteenth century with those who emigrated later; (d) analyze the reasons that living conditions in steerage were so bad.

2. To support the main idea, Howe relies mainly on (a) scholarly research; (b) government reports; (c) his own memories and experiences; (d) immigrants' memoirs.

3. Howe includes the remarks of Edward Steiner in paragraphs 7a–d because they represent (a) the official, or government, point of view; (b) a firsthand account by a respected journalist; (c) an objective (nonimmigrant) point of view; (d) a contrasting point of view to the other accounts cited.

4. In paragraph 7, the transitional expression "insofar as" means (a) because; (b) as a consequence of; (c) as far as one knows; (d) to the extent that.

5. Mark the *two* patterns of organization Howe uses in paragraph 8: (a) deductive; (b) chronological; (c) inductive; (d) variation of deductive; (e) spatial; (f) emphatic.

6. Howe reprints a portion of a government report, in paragraphs 9a–c, because it (a) presents a conflicting view; (b) was obtained and written under false pretenses; (c) confirms the immigrants' recollections; (d) resulted in changes aboard ships bringing immigrants.

D. Fact and Opinion

For each of the following statements from the selection, mark *F* if it represents a fact (a statement that can be verified or proved true), or *O* if it represents an opinion (a statement reflecting the author's subjective point of view).

___ 1. The Jewish mind has been imprinted strongly with the imagery of ordeal.

___ 2. The experience in steerage often caused severe emotional shock.

___ 3. Edward Steiner wrote *On the Trail of the Immigrant* in 1906.

___ 4. *On the Trail of the Immigrant* is a sober account of the ordeal of steerage.

___ 5. A congressional committee investigated steerage conditions in 1910.

___ 6. The congressional investigation offered a good portion of the truth about conditions in steerage.

E. Vocabulary

For each italicized word from the selection, choose the best definition according to the context in which it appears.

1. *elicited* stares of disbelief [paragraph 1]: (a) brought out; (b) simulated; (c) exaggerated; (d) discouraged.

2. a shudder of *dismay* [2]: (a) hopelessness; (b) memory; (c) fear; dread; (d) discouragement.

3. *tokens* of bewilderment [2]: (a) souvenirs; (b) representations; (c) examples; (d) illusions.

4. psychic *disorientation* [2]: (a) disorganization; (b) loss of self-esteem; (c) loss of one's sense of direction or location; (d) loss of will power or determination.

5. *rhetorical* exaggeration [2]: (a) concerned wtih effect; (b) deliberate; (c) inexcusable; (d) verbal.

6. an *acute* description [3]: (a) effective; (b) sharply perceptive; (c) severe; (d) crucial.

7. not those conducive to success [3a]: (a) designed for; (b) leading to; (c) committed to; (d) interested in.

8. widely varying *sensibilities* [4]: (a) abilities to be receptive to impressions; (b) abilities to think logically or critically; (c) experiences; backgrounds; (d) commonsensical attitudes.

9. distinguished for acute *skepticism* [4]: (a) intellectual achievement; (b) belief in rational thinking; (c) questioning attitude; (d) political activism.

10. the fog horn blew its *plaintive* note [4b]: (a) single; (b) complaining; (c) high-pitched; (d) mournful.

11. a sense of life's *indignities* [6]: (a) ironies; (b) offenses to self-respect; (c) sorrows; (d) unpleasantness.

12. we became utterly *dejected* [6a]: (a) detested; (b) demented; (c) depressed; (d) discouraged.

13. the force of *trauma* [7]: (a) emotional shock; (b) starvation; (c) depression; (d) violence.

14. the Jewish appetite for remembered *woe* [7]: (a) tradition; (b) intense sorrow; (c) complaints; (d) persecution.

15. there is plenty of *dispassionate* evidence [7]: (a) praiseworthy; (b) emotionally charged; (c) impartial; (d) truthful.

16. drinking water is *grudgingly* given [7d]: (a) generously; (b) rarely; (c) sparingly; (d) reluctantly.

17. *irate* immigrants [7d]: (a) starving; (b) angry; (c) insulted; (d) annoyed.

18. the Jewish immigrants' *burgeoning* nostalgia [8]: (a) developing rapidly; (b) remembering; (c) declining; (d) inquiring.

19. a report *substantiates* the recollections [9]: (a) publishes; (b) supports with evidence; (c) substitutes; (d) accepts without question.

20. a certain *prissiness* [10]: (a) hostility; (b) deliberate evasiveness; (c) prudishness; (d) doubtfulness.

Other words you should know the meaning of:
   a continual *babel* of tongues [7b—see *Babel* in the dictionary]
   immigrate/emigrate—refer to an unabridged dictionary for the difference between these two closely related words

F. Variant Word Forms

From the list of inflected forms in parentheses, choose the form that fits grammatically into the space. Add endings (-s or -ed, for example) if necessary.

1. (bewilderment, bewilder): The Atlantic crossing must have been a *bewildering* experience for East European immigrants.

2. (skepticism, skeptic, skeptical, skeptically): Until they read memoirs and other published accounts, most people view the immigrants' experiences *skeptically* –

3. (trauma, traumatize, traumatic, traumatically): There is no doubt that, for many immigrants, the Atlantic crossing *traumatized* them emotionally.

4. (grudge, begrudge, grudgingly): The ship personnel even *begrudged* the steerage passengers sufficient water to drink or wash with.

5. (woe, woeful, woefully): Howe writes that, despite the Jewish appetite for remembered *woe*, accounts of the Atlantic crossing confirm their memories.

G. Questions for Analysis

1. Howe introduces his thesis in the first two sentences of paragraph 1 by asking two questions. Why is this method appropriate in relation to the rest of the essay and in relation to his purpose in writing?

2. Handlin's account quoted in paragraph 3a mentions "a startling reversal of roles, a radical shift in attitudes" that immigrants experienced. What exactly is he referring to?

3. For what reason does Howe reprint quotations from three different memoirists (see paragraphs 4a and 6)? Since all three say essentially the same thing, wouldn't one have been sufficient?

4. What quality of Jewish writing does Howe imply exists in some immigrant accounts? What reason does Howe provide to explain this quality?

5. Certainly, the conditions aboard these ships were miserable. Why do you suppose ship companies were able to get away with such intolerable conditions for so long?

6. With the exception of Native Americans, every U.S. citizen has an immigrant background of some sort. If possible, examine the immigration experience of members of your family. How do their memories correspond to Howe's account?

Selection 15

Linguistic Chauvinism
Peter Farb

Until his recent untimely death, Peter Farb (1929–1980) was a naturalist, an anthropologist, and a writer who popularized the natural human sciences. His anthropological specialty was American Indian languages. At the time of his death, he had just completed (with George Armelagos) *Consuming Passions: The Anthropology of Eating. Word Play,* from which this selection comes, was the result of his research into the way people talk, and it remains a highly readable intro-duction to the field of linguistics.

1   When groups of people who speak different languages come into contact, any one of a number of things may happen. If their contact is only brief or occasional, they may simply dispense with speech and communicate through gestures, as in the dumb-barter of the bazaar. Or the two groups may com-municate by speaking a third language which they both know—as in India, where speakers of 14 different languages and numerous dialects find a common tongue in English. A third possibility is for members of one group to learn the language of the other, but such a solution is usually accom-plished only by conquest or domination. The fourth alternative, the one that I will discuss in this chapter, is for them to speak pidgin—a language that belongs to no one.

2   Considerable dispute exists about what a pidgin language is, for the simple reason that so many mistaken notions have been held for so long. Pidgin is not the corrupted form of a standard language—like the "broken" English spoken by an Italian tourist guide or that classic example of pseudo-pidgin, *Me Tarzan, you Jane*. Nor is it a kind of baby talk spoken by a plan-tation owner to his slaves, a master to his servants, or a merchant to his customers. And, finally, it is not a language that patronizingly makes con-cessions to the limited intelligence of "natives." A pidgin can best be de-scribed as a language which has been stripped of certain grammatical features. It is a new language that is not the mother tongue of any of its users, and it usually survives only so long as members of diverse speech communities are in contact.

3   A pidgin is a "simple" language, but this is to the credit of the pidgin rather than a condemnation. Pidgins have eliminated many of the finicky characteristics of language that contribute little to understanding what is said. Someone who speaks a pidgin French does not have to contend with masculine and feminine endings, and a speaker of pidgin English does not have to worry about the large number of irregular verbs. When it comes to the important features of language—such as the grammatical formation of questions and commands or the patterns of subordinated sentences—pidgin has rules for them just like any other language has. Pidgin is not simply a random collection of ways of putting together sentences, but rather a system that allows its speakers to constantly create new sentences they have never heard before.

4   To understand the process of pidginization, imagine that speakers of various Chinese dialects (which are not mutually intelligible) come together in a foreign place to trade or to work. Since the speakers lack a common language, they are forced to develop a new kind of language that takes its vocabulary from whatever language is dominant in their new home. If these Chinese live in a place where English is the dominant colonial language, such as Hong Kong or Singapore, they will develop what has been called Chinese Pidgin English, but which should more properly be known as English-based Chinese Pidgin. The English on which the pidgin is based is

a continuing presence while the new language is developing, and it remains available as a source from which words for the pidgin can be borrowed. If the hypothetical Chinese had instead come together in the Portuguese colony of Macao, their pidgin would then be based on Portuguese, as indeed happened when the Portuguese-based Chinese Pidgin known as Makista developed. In other words, the Chinese develop a pidgin to communicate among themselves—and only afterward will the pidgin be learned by some speakers of English, who use it to communicate with the Chinese.

5   Most pidgins are based on European languages for the simple reason that pidgins arise as by-products of colonialism, and the European powers have been notable colonizers. (Some pidgins, though, have been based on native languages. Swahili, now spoken by perhaps twenty-five million people throughout East Africa and as far west as the Republic of Congo, arose as a pidgin language based on a dialect of Zanzibar that was spread by Arab slave traders.) A pidgin language, therefore, is a strategic response to a social situation. It arises during a time of social ferment, whether the cause be military conquest, enslavement of one people by another, or trade imperialism (the very word *pidgin* is Chinese Pidgin for the English *business*). Without such ferment, no disruptions of population would have taken place to bring people from many different speech communities into contact, and to make it necessary for them to develop a pidgin language. Once a pidgin does develop, its future depends not on its intrinsic value for communication but rather on its role in the community that speaks it. Many pidgins simply die out when the need for them disappears, but some others expand when the social situation calls on the language to perform a role greater than minimal communication. It may evolve into what is known as a "creole," with an enlarged vocabulary and grammar. And it may then become the mother tongue of a speech community or even an official language of a country, as has been the case with French Creole in Haiti, Indonesian in Indonesia, and Swahili in Kenya and Tanzania.

6   A strange thing about the nearly one hundred European-based pidgin and creole languages spoken around the world is their similarity in grammar—even though no opportunity existed for many of them to come into contact and even though they are based on languages as different as English, French, Dutch, Spanish, and Portuguese. The descendants of H.M.S. *Bounty* mutineers who now live on Pitcairn Island in the South Pacific speak a creole language whose structure is not much different from the creole spoken by the descendants of African slaves in the Caribbean. The theory that seems to account best for the world-wide similarity of European-based pidgins is that they all can be traced back to a single pidgin language, a Portuguese-based one which in the fifteenth and sixteenth centuries replaced Arabic and Malay as the trade language of Africa and the Far East. During these centuries, Portugal was in the forefront of contacts with non-European peoples, and it apparently spread a pidginized version of its language to its colonies around the globe.

7   Support for this theory comes from the fact that words in many pidgin languages are derived from Portuguese even though the pidgin language as

a whole may be based on English, French, or another language. The familiar *savvy*, which is so common that it immediately indicates a pidgin language almost anywhere in the world, has been traced back to Portuguese-based Chinese Pidgin; it apparently was derived from *sabe*, the third person singular of the Portuguese verb "to know." Similarly, words from English-based Chinese Pidgin like *joss*, "god," and *mandarin*, "official," are survivals of seventeenth-century Pidgin Portuguese—derived, respectively, from Portuguese *dios*, "god," and *mandarim*, "commander." *Pickaninny* originally meant "little" in English-based Chinese Pidgin (as in *Yu kari pikanini hola?* "Do you want a little whore?"), but it has been shown to derive ultimately from the Portuguese word *pequenino*, "little."

8   The history of the word "creole" itself dates back to the slave trade. After slaves had been gathered from many parts of Africa, they were imprisoned in West African camps, euphemistically called "factories," for "processing" before being shipped out to "markets." The managers of the factories took great care to separate slaves who spoke the same tribal language, thereby lessening the danger of revolt because the slaves were prevented from communicating with one another. And further separation on the basis of language was made by the purchasers in the New World. As a result, the only tongue the slaves had in common was a pidgin that originated in West Africa and developed in the colonies to which they were sent. These pidgins became entrenched, and after a generation or two they began to expand to meet the needs of the slaves' way of life. The slaves' new language became known as *créole*, a French word meaning "native" which in turn was derived from Portuguese.

9   Nowadays "creole" refers to any language that developed from a pidgin by expansion of vocabulary and grammar and became the mother tongue for many speakers in a community. The largest center of creole languages today is undoubtedly the Caribbean area, with more than six million speakers. Several million additional people speak creoles in West Africa, South Africa, and Southeast Asia, and probably another three million people around the world use various pidgin languages. Clearly, pidgin and creole are not rare or isolated phenomena; they number more speakers today than do such languages as Dutch, Swedish, or Greek.

10   When a pidgin becomes a creole it escapes the extinction that would ordinarily result if the social conditions that brought it into being disappear. As its vocabulary and grammar expand by borrowing from the base language, the creole can become a full-fledged means of communication used in newspapers, on radio stations, even in poetry and novels. Nevertheless, if the European colonial language on which the creole was based is still widely used in their community, creole speakers usually encounter a deep-rooted prejudice. The colonial language is looked up to as the prestige one, oriented toward the white world of power and wealth, while the creole is regarded as the language of the dark-skinned masses, a reminder of their former status as slaves or exploited laborers. Whenever a creole language exists side by side with one of the European tongues in a former colony, the result is likely to be linguistic schizophrenia—technically known as "diglossia," which means "two languages" in Greek.

11 In such a situation, speakers of the creole often deny their mother tongue. Children who learn the European language in school usually are ashamed of the creole still spoken by their relatives and friends. They migrate to the cities to use their new language skill by finding employment in government or trade—and there they claim that they never learned creole or that they have forgotten any they once knew. They join the vociferous ranks of those who condemn creole as a mongrel tongue, who claim that it is an ugly language which hurts the ears just to hear it. Yet, deep down, most speakers never completely lose trust in their mother creole as the language of warmth and sincerity in contrast to the European tongues of duplicity. In Haiti, for example, a speaker says "I'm talking creole to you" when he means "I'm telling you the truth," and the expression "to talk French" means "to bribe."

12 Diglossia exists not only in areas where a creole language is spoken but also in countries that use varieties of the same language—as in some Swiss cantons where both High German and Swiss German are spoken—and in those bilingual communities that speak two or more entirely different and unrelated languages. For example, a government worker in Brussels is likely to discuss the same topics in Standard French at his office, in Standard Dutch at his club, and in a local variant of Flemish in his home. In most such cases, though, one of the two languages is accorded high prestige, the other low. In New York City, Spanish-English bilinguals of Puerto Rican descent regard English as the language of social prestige and advancement but identify Spanish with the values of friendship and intimacy. And each language performs different functions within the society, with the result that speakers must learn, as part of their speech strategies, the occasions on which the use of each language is appropriate. Who speaks what language to whom is not based on spur-of-the-moment inclinations or whims. Proper usage demands that either the high-prestige or the low-prestige language be chosen in particular speech situations.

13 The strategies of switching back and forth between languages have been closely studied in Paraguay, where considerably more than half of the entire population is fluent in both Spanish, the official language, and Guarani, the indigenous American Indian language; in the cities of Paraguay almost everyone is bilingual. Spanish is the language used for all formal occasions; it is spoken in schools, in government, in conversation with well-dressed strangers, and in the transaction of most business. Guarani is spoken with friends, servants, poorly dressed strangers, when telling a joke, when making love, and in most casual situations. Spanish is much more likely to be used in the cities, and Guarani is almost always spoken by the lower classes in rural areas.

14 These are all clear-cut speech situations in which the strategy of speaking one language instead of the other is employed, but the choice can often be much more subtle. Some parents speak Spanish to their school-age children, in that way helping them with their studies, but then switch to Guarani when the children are out of earshot. Upper-class males who are close friends usually speak to each other in Guarani, but their upper-class

wives tend much more to use Spanish in similar speech situations. Males usually speak Guarani when they have a drink or two with friends, but some in whom alcohol instills a feeling of power switch to Spanish when they become drunk. Courtship among young people begins in Spanish but changes to Guarani after a few meetings. The selection of Spanish or Guarani depends on a cluster of factors: whether the conversation takes place in the city or the country, the formality or informality of the occasion, the status of the person being addressed, the degree of intimacy between the speakers, the seriousness or levity of their conversation, and so on. All of this means that throughout the day the bilingual speaker must unerringly switch from one language to the other in response to changing speech situations.

15 Nevertheless, it is quite clear that Spanish is still the language of high prestige, and a Guarani speaker, coming to market in the city, quickly feels his inferiority. Probably all bilingual situations equally stigmatize those who use low-prestige languages. Pima Indian children in Arizona, for example, were interviewed about their beliefs regarding the English and Pima languages. Most of them had a low opinion of their own tongue. English was thought to be the best of all languages, but two other Indian languages— Navaho and Maricopa—and even Mexican and Japanese were regarded as superior to Pima by some children. The older the child, the more he considered English the superior language, presumably because he looked upon it as a passport into the affluent world of the majority culture. Nor were the Pima children impressed by their own bilingualism; the great majority of them doubted that it was a mark of intelligence.

16 Whether or not it has anything to do with intelligence, a bilingual speaker has accomplished something remarkable. By switching from one language to another, he has performed several distinct operations. He selected words from a completely different vocabulary; he used the words in different kinds of grammatical structures; and he changed the sound system to give the appropriate accent for each language. The bilingual speaker is able, in some way not yet clearly understood, to set aside one entire linguistic system and to function with a second, completely different one. Then, a moment later, he is able to switch the process and reactivate the previous system while setting aside the second language. Regardless of the lack of prestige for the minority language in most speech communities, we must admire the bilingual process. And we must also be in awe of the fact that well over half of the world's population achieves the bilingual switch from one language system to another scores of times each day.

A. Comprehension

Choose the answer that best completes each statement. Do not refer to the selection while doing this exercise.

1. Farb uses the term *pidgin* to mean (a) a corrupted form of a standard language; (b) a kind of baby talk between people of unequal status; (c) a simple language that has been stripped of its irregular grammatical features; (d) a hybrid language based on Portuguese which eventually develops into a creole language.

2. The process of pidginization occurs in the first place because (a) speakers of various dialects have no common language by which to communicate when they come together; (b) people from one community move to another and do not have the time to learn the native language well; (c) colonial governments forced native populations to learn a kind of makeshift version of the colonizers' language; (d) neither language spoken by two diverse communities has any prestige, so a pidgin language with a higher prestige develops in their place.

3. Most pidgins are based on European languages because (a) European languages are easy to learn; (b) European languages are highly prestigious; (c) Europeans were more encouraging than other cultures about contact between themselves and native populations; (d) Europeans were colonizers, and most pidgins arose as a by-product of colonialism.

4. A pidgin that becomes the mother tongue of a speech community, or even an official language of a country, is called (a) a colonial-inspired language; (b) a pseudo-pidgin; (c) a creole language; (d) a language of high prestige.

5. The worldwide similarity between European-based pidgins is explained by the fact that they can all be traced back to a single pidgin language, one based on (a) Chinese; (b) Portuguese; (c) Arabic; (d) English.

6. When a creole language exists side by side with a European language in a former colony, the result is apt to be linguistic schizophrenia, which, according to Farb, means that (a) both languages become corrupted and lose their essential grammatical features; (b) the speakers are confused about which language to use in a particular social situation; (c) the creole language becomes the language of social prestige and advancement, while the European language has inferior status; (d) the creole language is accorded an inferior status, while the European language becomes the language of social prestige and advancement.

7. Despite what its speakers say about it, a creole language is still (a) the language of trade and tourism; (b) the language used for instruction in the schools; (c) the language associated with warmth, intimacy, and honesty; (d) the superior language in a situation where two languages exist together.

8. Farb finds the bilingual speaker's ability to switch back and forth between two languages (a) admirable; (b) confusing; (c) incomprehensible; (d) remarkable.

B. Inferences   On the basis of the evidence in the selection, answer these inference questions. You may refer to the selection to answer the questions in this section, and all the remaining sections.

1. Paragraph 2: Who can you infer would be involved in a dispute about the meaning of the term "pidgin"?
   _____ linguistics _____

2. Paragraph 2: Why is "Me Tarzan, you Jane" referred to as a pseudo-pidgin? _Because of a simplified english_

3. Paragraph 3: If the "finicky characteristics" of a language" are eliminated in a pidgin language, what is left? *nouns, verbs without prep - act or adverbs*

4. Paragraph 4: Why is the term Chinese Pidgin English not as precise as English-based Chinese Pidgin? _____

5. Paragraph 5: How was the development of Swahili different from that of other pidgin languages? *Because Swahili was based on a native language*

6. Paragraph 6: What does Farb mean when he writes that Portugal was "in the forefront of contacts with non-European peoples" during the fifteenth and sixteenth centuries? _____

7. Paragraph 6: Why does Farb find it "strange" that pidgins all over the world are similar in grammar? _____

8. Paragraph 7: How do you account for the fact that the largest center of creole languages today is the Caribbean area? _____

9. Paragraph 10: What is the advantage of a pidgin language's becoming a creole language? _____

10. Paragraph 12: What is the difference in Switzerland between High German and Swiss German? _____

11. Paragraph 13: Which language—Spanish or Guarani—would most likely be used in conducting governmental business in Paraguay? _____

12. Paragraphs 12–14: What determines whether Spanish is the language of social prestige or the language of friendship and intimacy in a given culture? _____

C. Structure

1. The mode of discourse in this selection is (a) narration; (b) description; (c) exposition; (d) persuasion.

2. Specifically, Farb's purpose is to (a) explain the linguistic development of various pidgin languages; (b) define pidgin and creole languages and provide illustrations of them; (c) trace the historical events that produced pidgin and creole languages; (d) examine the causes and effects of bilingualism in a given culture.

3. Look again at paragraph 1. Explain the function of the first four sentences. *To enumerate the possibilities of what will happen* *when a group*

4. In paragraph 2, before defining a pidgin language, Farb (a) provides a historical model; (b) defines by giving examples; (c) defines by negation; (d) defines the term according to his own arbitrary personal definition.

5. The method of paragraph development in paragraph 4 is (a) process; (b) analogy; (c) comparison; (d) analysis–classification; (e) example; (f) definition.

6. The method of paragraph development in paragraph 5 is (a) cause–effect; (b) illustration; (c) analogy; (d) contrast; (e) comparison; (f) definition.

7. The purpose of paragraph 7 is to (a) define the word "creole" more specifically; (b) confirm a hypothesis by providing supporting examples; (c) provide some interesting examples of common pidgin words that are also

part of the English speaker's vocabulary; (d) offer scientific evidence for a verifiable fact.

8. The relationship between paragraphs 8 and 9 is (a) cause–effect; (b) contrast; (c) term and its definition; (d) steps in a process.

9. As it is used in paragraphs 10 and 15, "nevertheless" means (a) as a result; (b) however; (c) in addition; (d) as an illustration.

10. In paragraph 11, Farb uses a metaphor to describe a creole speaker's attitude toward his native language. What is the language compared to?

_____

Why is this metaphor appropriate?

_____

11. Which *three* methods of paragraph development are evident in paragraphs 13 and 14? (a) definition; (b) contrast; (c) analogy; (d) example; (e) comparison; (f) classification; (g) steps in a process.

12. Look again at paragraph 15. What do you suppose Farb thinks about Pima children who regard their native language as inferior to English, Japanese, and two other Indian languages, Navajo and Maricopa? (a) He thinks their attitude is correct. (b) He thinks their attitude is unfortunate. (c) He thinks their attitude is reprehensible. (d) He thinks their attitude is incomprehensible. (e) His own thoughts are not evident from the paragraph.

D. Vocabulary   For each italicized word from the selection, choose the best definition according to the context in which it appears.

1. that classic example of *pseudo*-pidgin [paragraph 2]: (a) imaginative; (b) silly; (c) fake; (d) realistic.

2. a language that *patronizingly* makes concessions [2]: describing an attitude toward people that is (a) hostile; (b) condescending; (c) infuriating; (d) exploitative economically.

3. makes *concessions* to the limited intelligence of "natives" [2]: something (a) granted as a privilege; (b) acknowledged as true; (c) permitted; (d) sold for profit.

4. the *finicky* characteristics of a language [3]: (a) unpredictable; (b) tasteful; (c) fastidious with regard to standards; (d) imprecise; vague.

5. patterns of *subordinated* sentences [3]: (a) dependent; (b) grammatically correct; (c) equal in importance; (d) combined.

6. a *strategic* response to a social situation [5]: (a) random; unpredictable; (b) effective; skillful; (c) impulsive; unplanned; (d) essential; important.

7. during a time of social *ferment* [5]: (a) excitement; (b) tension; (c) revolution; (d) unrest.

8. *savvy* indicates a pidgin language [7]: (a) practical or common sense; (b) a request for a prostitute; (c) a polite invitation; (d) intellectual knowledge; scholarship.

9. these pidgins became *entrenched* [8]: (a) popularized; (b) isolated; (c) firmly fixed; (d) limited in scope.

10. a *full-fledged* means of communication [10]: (a) having full status or rank; (b) having been fulfilled; (c) fully intelligible; (d) exhaustively thorough; complete.

11. they join the *vociferous* ranks [11]: (a) complaining; (b) revolutionary; (c) vehement; loud; (d) hostile; angry.

12. in contrast to the European tongues of *duplicity* [11]: (a) deliberate deceptiveness; (b) aggression, especially in battle; (c) warmth; sincerity; (d) complexity; difficulty.

13. one of the two languages is *accorded* high prestige [12]: (a) accompanied by; (b) brought into harmony with; (c) granted; given; (d) guaranteed.

14. who speaks what language to whom is not based on *whims* [12]: (a) logical arguments; (b) historical precedents; (c) linguistic or grammatical rules; (d) passing fancies; capricious ideas.

15. the *indigenous* American Indian language [13]: (a) native; (b) previously mentioned; (c) inferior; (d) existing only in oral form.

16. the seriousness or *levity* of their conversation [14]: (a) changeableness; inconstancy; (b) lightness of manner; frivolity; (c) gravity; weightiness; (d) subject under discussion.

17. the bilingual speaker must *unerringly* switch [14]: (a) unthinkingly; (b) unobtrusively; (c) unfortunately; (d) without making a mistake.

18. probably all bilingual situations equally *stigmatize* those who use low-prestige languages [15]: (a) brand as inferior or disgraceful; (b) praise; reward; (c) confuse; muddle; (d) characterize as remarkable or worthy of emulation.

F. Questions for Analysis

1. What evidence is there that the book from which this selection is taken is a popularization of a difficult subject?

2. Richard Rodriguez, one of the writers represented in Part 4 ("Does America Still Exist?"—Selection 18), asserts in his autobiography, *Hunger of Memory,* that bilingual instruction in schools only serves to maintain a child's separateness from the larger culture. From what you have read about bilingual communities in this selection, do you agree or disagree?

Selection 16 **Ode to Thanksgiving**
Michael J. Arlen

Michael J. Arlen (1930–   ) was born in London, England, and graduated from Harvard College in 1952. He has been a staff writer and a television critic for *The New Yorker* since 1966, and has also published several books, three of which are collections of his essays about television and American culture: *Living-Room War, The View from Highway One,* and the one from which this selection is reprinted, *The Camera Age. Passage to Ararat,* his account of his parents' early life and his journey to Armenia to learn about the country where his father was born, was nominated for a National Book Award in 1975.

1   It is time, at last, to speak the truth about Thanksgiving, and the truth is this. Thanksgiving is really not such a terrific holiday. Consider the traditional symbols of the event: Dried cornhusks hanging on the door! Terrible wine! Cranberry jelly in little bowls of extremely doubtful provenance which everyone is required to handle with the greatest of care! Consider the participants, the merrymakers: men and women (also children) who have survived passably well throughout the years, mainly as a result of living at considerable distances from their dear parents and beloved siblings, who on this feast of feasts must apparently forgather (as if beckoned by an aberrant Fairy Godmother), usually by circuitous routes, through heavy traffic, at a common meeting place, where the very moods, distempers, and obtrusive personal habits that have kept them all happily apart since adulthood are then and there encouraged to slowly ferment beneath the cornhusks, and gradually rise with the aid of the terrible wine, and finally burst forth out of control under the stimulus of the cranberry jelly! No, it is a mockery of a holiday. For instance: *Thank you, O Lord, for what we are about to receive.* This is surely not a gala concept. There are no presents, unless one counts Aunt Bertha's sweet rolls a present, which no one does. There is precious little in the way of costumery: miniature plastic turkeys and those witless Pilgrim hats. There is no sex. Indeed, Thanksgiving is the one day of the year (a fact known to everybody) when all thoughts of sex completely vanish, evaporating from apartments, houses, condominiums, and mobile homes like steam from a bathroom mirror.

2   Consider also the nowhereness of the time of year: the last week or so in November. It is obviously not yet winter: winter, with its death-dealing blizzards and its girls in tiny skirts pirouetting on the ice. On the other hand, it is certainly not much use to anyone as fall: no golden leaves or Oktoberfests, and so forth. Instead, it is a no-man's-land between the seasons. In the cold and sobersides northern half of the country, it is a vaguely unsettling interregnum of long, mournful walks beneath leafless trees: the long, mournful walks following the midday repast with the dread inevitability of pie following turkey, and the leafless trees looming or standing about like eyesores, and the ground either as hard as iron or slightly mushy, and the light snow always beginning to fall when one is halfway to the old green gate—flecks of cold, watery stuff plopping between neck and collar, for the reason that, it being not yet winter, one has forgotten or not chosen to bring along a muffler. It is a corollary to the long, mournful Thanksgiving walk that the absence of this muffler is quickly noticed and that four weeks or so later, at Christmastime, instead of the Sony Betamax one had secretly hoped the children might have chipped in to purchase, one receives another muffler: by then the thirty-third. Thirty-three mufflers! Some walk! Of course, things are more fun in the warm and loony southern part of the country. No snow there of any kind. No need of mufflers. Also, no long, mournful walks, because in the warm and loony southern part of the country everybody drives. So everybody drives over to Uncle Jasper's house to watch the Cougars play the Gators, a not entirely unimportant conflict which will determine whether the Gators get a Bowl bid or must take another post-season exhibition tour

of North Korea. But no sooner do the Cougars kick off (an astonishing end-over-end squiggly thing that floats lazily above the arena before plummeting down toward K. C. McCoy and catching him on the helmet) than Auntie Em starts hustling turkey. Soon Cousin May is slamming around the bowls and platters, and Cousin Bernice is oohing and ahing about "all the fixin's," and Uncle Bob is making low, insincere sounds of appreciation: "Yummy, yummy, Auntie Em, I'll have me some more of these delicious yams!" Delicious yams? Uncle Bob's eyes roll wildly in his head. Billy Joe Quaglino throws his long bomb in the middle of Grandpa Morris saying grace, Grandpa Morris speaking so low nobody can hear him, which is just as well, since he is reciting what he can remember of his last union contract. And then, just as J. B. (Speedy) Snood begins his ninety-two-yard punt return, Auntie Em starts dealing everyone second helpings of her famous stuffing, as if she were pushing a controlled substance, which it well might be, since there are no easily recognizable ingredients visible to the naked eye.

3   Consider for a moment the Thanksgiving meal itself. It has become a sort of refuge for endangered species of starch: cauliflower, turnips, pumpkin, mince (whatever "mince" is), those blessed yams. Bowls of luridly colored yams, with no taste at all, lying torpid under a lava flow of marshmallow! And then the sacred turkey. One might as well try to construct a holiday repast around a fish—say, a nice piece of boiled haddock. After all, turkey tastes very similar to haddock: same consistency, same quite remarkable absence of flavor. But then, if the Thanksgiving *pièce de résistance* were a nice piece of boiled haddock instead of turkey, there wouldn't be all that fun for Dad when Mom hands him the sterling-silver, bone-handled carving set (a wedding present from her parents and not sharpened since) and then everyone sits around pretending not to watch while he saws and tears away at the bird as if he were trying to burrow his way into or out of some grotesque, fowl-like prison.

4   What of the good side to Thanksgiving, you ask. There is always a good side to everything. Not to Thanksgiving. There is only a bad side and then a worse side. For instance, Grandmother's best linen tablecloth is a bad side: the fact that it is produced each year, in the manner of a red flag being produced before a bull, and then is always spilled upon by whichever child is doing poorest at school that term and so is in need of greatest reassurance. Thus: "Oh, my God, *Veronica,* you just spilled grape juice [or plum wine or tar] on Grandmother's best linen tablecloth!" But now comes worse. For at this point Cousin Bill, the one who lost all Cousin Edwina's money on the car dealership three years ago and has apparently been drinking steadily since Halloween, bizarrely chooses to say: "Seems to me those old glasses are always falling over." To which Auntie Meg is heard to add: "Somehow I don't remember receivin' any of those old glasses." To which Uncle Fred replies: "That's because you and George decided to go on vacation to Hawaii the summer Grandpa Sam was dying." Now Grandmother is sobbing, though not so uncontrollably that she can refrain from murmuring: "I think that volcano painting I threw away by mistake got sent me from Hawaii, heaven knows why." But the gods are merciful, even the Pilgrim-hatted god of

cornhusks and soggy stuffing, and there is an end to everything, even to Thanksgiving. Indeed, there is a grandeur to the feelings of finality and doom which usually settle on a house after the Thanksgiving celebration is over, for with the completion of Thanksgiving Day the year itself has been properly terminated: shot through the cranium with a high-velocity candied yam. At this calendrical nadir, all energy on the planet has gone, all fun has fled, all the terrible wine has been drunk.

5   But then, overnight, life once again begins to stir, emerging, even by the next morning, in the form of Japanese window displays and Taiwanese Christmas lighting, from the primeval ooze of the nation's department stores. Thus, a new year dawns, bringing with it immediate and cheering possibilities of extended consumer debt, office-party flirtations, good—or, at least, mediocre—wine, and visions of Supersaver excursion fares to Montego Bay. It is worth noting, perhaps, that this true new year always starts with the same mute, powerful mythic ceremony: the surreptitious tossing out, in the early morning, of all those horrid aluminum-foil packages of yams and cauliflower and stuffing and red, gummy cranberry substance which have been squeezed into the refrigerator as if a reenactment of the siege of Paris were shortly expected. Soon afterward, the phoenix of Christmas can be observed as it slowly rises, beating its drumsticks, once again goggle-eyed with hope and unrealistic expectations.

A. Compre-hension

Choose the answer that best completes each statement. Do not refer to the selection while doing this exercise.

1. According to Arlen, the truth about Thanksgiving is that it is (a) the most boring day of the year; (b) a pretentious, self-serving celebration; (c) a mockery of a holiday; (d) an outmoded way to pay a debt to the pilgrims.

2. Arlen complains that Thanksgiving is missing some features common to other holidays. Which one does he *not* mention? (a) costumes; (b) gifts; (c) sex; (d) good food; (e) a series of festive parties.

3. Arlen describes the season when Thanksgiving occurs as (a) depressing; (b) uninspiring; (c) nowhere; neither here nor there; (d) mournful.

4. An activity that competes with the Thanksgiving dinner for the diners' attention is (a) watching football games on television; (b) taking long walks in the snow; (c) playing games like Monopoly or Trivial Pursuit; (d) arguing over money.

5. For Arlen, Thanksgiving has (a) an equal number of bad and good sides; (b) more good sides than bad sides; (c) more bad sides than good; (d) a bad side and a worse side.

B. Inferences

On the basis of the evidence in the selection, mark these statements as follows: *A* for accurate inferences, *I* for inaccurate inferences, and *IE* for insufficient evidence. You may refer to the selection to answer the questions in this section, and all the remaining sections.

_____ 1. Arlen refuses to celebrate Thanksgiving with his family.

_____ 2. Thanksgiving reunions make the participants irritable.

_____ 3. Arlen lives in the Eastern part of the country.

_____ 4. Arlen thinks football is a silly game.

_____ 5. The only part of the Thanksgiving dinner that Arlen likes is the starchy dishes.

_____ 6. Arlen prefers Christmas to Thanksgiving.

C. Structure

1. The mode of discourse in this selection is (a) narration; (b) description; (c) exposition; (d) persuasion.

2. Arlen's purpose is to (a) satirize the way Americans celebrate one holiday; (b) complain about his family reunions at Thanksgiving; (c) explain why our expectations of most holidays are unrealistic; (d) poke fun at American commercialism in holidays.

3. The tone of the passage, as revealed in Arlen's attitude toward the Thanksgiving holiday, can best be described as (a) hostile; scornful; (b) silly; frivolous; (c) irreverent; derisively witty; (d) earnest; solemn.

4. In describing the football plays in paragraph 2 and the traditional Thanksgiving meal in paragraph 3, Arlen relies extensively on (a) hyperbole; deliberate exaggeration for effect; (b) restatement of the main ideas; (c) euphemisms; inoffensive phrases; (d) logical fallacies.

5. Look again at paragraph 4. Write the sentence that represents the main idea. _____

_____

6. In the same paragraph, write the sentence that acts as a transition between ideas. _____

_____

7. What do the details and the dialogue in paragraph 4 suggest about Thanksgiving? (a) that fighting and squabbling among family members are part of the traditional ritual; (b) that the celebrants drink too much and say things they don't really mean; (c) that the participants act insincere just to keep up the tradition; (d) that they are not really having any fun.

8. Look at the last sentence of paragraph 5 again. Then, if you are unsure of its meaning, look up "phoenix" in an unabridged dictionary. What is being compared to the phoenix? _____
Why is it an appropriate metaphor to end this selection? _____

_____

D. Vocabulary

For each italicized word from the selection, choose the best definition according to the context in which it appears.

1. in little bowls of doubtful *provenance* [paragraph 1]: (a) value; (b) origin; (c) quality; (d) ownership.

2. men and women who have survived *passably* well [1]: (a) outstandingly; (b) not very; (c) satisfactorily; (d) superficially.

3. their dear parents and beloved *siblings* [1]: (a) nieces and nephews; (b) aunts and uncles; (c) children; (d) brothers and sisters.

4. beckoned by an *aberrant* Fairy Godmother [1]: (a) deviating from the proper or expected; (b) physically and morally defective; (c) cruel; evil; (d) obstinate; willful.

5. by *circuitous* routes [1]: (a) well-traveled; (b) circular; (c) indirect; (d) impassable.

6. this is surely not a *gala* concept [1]: (a) festive; (b) acceptable; (c) popular; (d) satisfactory.

7. it is a vaguely unsettling *interregnum* [2]: (a) a difficult period; (b) a natural phenomenon; (c) an interval of time; (d) an interrelationship.

8. long, mournful walks following the midday *repast* [2]: (a) nap; (b) reminiscences from the past; (c) cooking; (d) meal.

9. it is a *corollary* [2]: (a) natural consequence; effect; (b) tradition; ritual; (c) amusing observation; (d) unwelcome event.

10. bowls of *luridly* colored yams [3]: (a) bizarrely; (b) beautifully; (c) repulsively; (d) glowingly.

11. lying *torpid* under a lava flow of marshmallow [3]: (a) scorching; burning; (b) stiffly; inactively; (c) garishly; gaudily; (d) invitingly; temptingly.

12. the Thanksgiving *pièce de résistance* [3–French, pronounced pyes də rā-zē-stäns']: (a) principal dish at a meal; (b) culinary disaster; (c) traditional holiday fare; (d) inedible substance.

13. there is a *grandeur* to the feelings of finality and doom [4]: (a) feeling of hopelessness; (b) greatness; splendor; (c) sense of inevitability; (d) feeling of elation.

14. at this calendrical *nadir* [4]: (a) highest point; (b) lowest point; (c) difficult time; (d) happy, festive time.

15. from the *primeval* ooze [5]: belonging to (a) the medieval period; (b) the present day; (c) the earliest period; (d) the evil, corrupt period.

16. the same *mute* ceremony [5]: (a) silly; (b) stupid; (c) absurd; (d) silent.

17. the *surreptitious* tossing out [5]: (a) secret; stealthy; (b) hurried; hasty; (c) suspicious; questionable; (d) final; conclusive.

E. Questions for Analysis

1. The *American Heritage Dictionary* defines a satire as "a literary work in which irony, derision, or wit in any form is used to expose folly or wickedness." In what way does "Ode to Thanksgiving" represent a satire?

2. As the headnote indicates, "Ode to Thanksgiving" was published in a collection of pieces about television called *The Camera Age*. Although it is really secondary to his purpose, what does Arlen suggest about the influence of television on American culture in the piece?

3. Do you find Arlen's piece funny? Why or why not? How would you characterize his brand of humor?

Selection 17   ## Acting on the Elizabethan Stage
Marchette Chute

Marchette Chute (1909–   ) attended the Minneapolis School of Art and graduated from the University of Minnesota. Recognized as an outstanding authority on
English literary history, Miss Chute has published many scholarly articles and
popular books about English poets and dramatists. Her best-known books are
Geoffrey Chaucer of England (1946), and *Shakespeare of London* (1950), from
which this selection comes.

1   Acting was not an easy profession on the Elizabethan stage or one to
be taken up lightly. An actor went through a strenuous period of training
before he could be entrusted with an important part by one of the great city
companies. He worked on a raised stage in the glare of the afternoon sun,
with none of the softening illusions that can be achieved in the modern theatre, and in plays that made strenuous demands upon his skill as a fencer, a
dancer and an acrobat.

2   Many of the men in the London companies had been "trained up from
their childhood" in the art, and an actor like Shakespeare, who entered the
profession in his twenties, had an initial handicap that could only be overcome by intelligence and rigorous discipline. Since he was a well-known actor
by 1592 and Chettle says he was an excellent one, he must have had the initial advantages of a strong body and a good voice and have taught himself
in the hard school of the Elizabethan theatre how to use them to advantage.

3   One of the most famous of the London companies, that of Lord Strange,
began its career as a company of tumblers, and a standard production like
"The Forces of Hercules" was at least half acrobatics. Training of this kind
was extremely useful to the actors, for the normal London stage consisted of
several different levels. Battles and sieges were very popular with the audiences, with the upper levels of the stage used as the town walls and turrets,
and an actor had to know how to take violent falls without damaging either
himself or his expensive costume.

4   Nearly all plays involved some kind of fighting, and in staging hand-to-
hand combats the actor's training had to be excellent. The average Lon-
doner was an expert on the subject of fencing, and he did not pay his penny
to see two professional actors make ineffectual dabs at each other with
rapiers when the script claimed they were fighting to the death. A young
actor like Shakespeare must have gone through long, gruelling hours of
practice to learn the ruthless technique of Elizabethan fencing. He had to
learn how to handle a long, heavy rapier in one hand, with a dagger for
parrying* in the other, and to make a series of savage, calculated thrusts at
close quarters from the wrist and forearm, aiming either at his opponent's
eyes or below the ribs. The actor had to achieve the brutal reality of an
actual Elizabethan duel without injuring himself or his opponent, a problem that required a high degree of training and of physical coordination.

_____

*Warding off blows.

The theatres and the inn-yards were frequently rented by the fencing socie- ties to put on exhibition matches, and on one such occasion at the Swan a fencer was run through the eye and died, an indication of the risks this sort of work involved even with trained, experienced fencers. The actors had to be extremely skilled, since they faced precisely the same audience. Richard Tarleton, a comic actor of the 80's who was the first great popular star of the Elizabethan theatre, was made Master of Fence the year before he died and this was the highest degree the fencing schools could award.

5   Not being content with savage, realistic fights in its theatre productions, the London audience also expected to see bloody deaths and mutilations; and it was necessary to find some way to run a sword through an actor's head or tear out his entrails without impairing his usefulness for the next afternoon's performance. This involved not only agility but a thorough knowledge of sleight of hand,* since the players were working close to the audience and in broad daylight. Elizabethan stage management was not slavishly interested in realism, but it was always concerned with good stage effects and when bloodshed was involved it gave the audience real blood. It had been found by experience that ox blood was too thick to run well, and sheep's blood was generally used. To stage a realistic stabbing one actor would use a knife with a hollow handle into which the blade would slip back when it was pressed home, and his fellow actor would be equipped with a bladder of blood inside his white leather jerkin, which could be painted to look like skin. When the bladder was pricked and the actor arched himself at the moment of contact, the blood spurted out in a most satisfactory man- ner. Sometimes real knives were used and a protective plate, and a juggler once staggered into St. Paul's Churchyard and died there because he had done the trick when he was drunk and forgotten his plate. In *The Battle of Alcazar* there was a disemboweling scene for which the property man sup- plied three vials of blood and the liver, heart and lungs of a sheep. Then it was up to Edward Alleyn and his two fellow actors to use skillful substitu- tion in such a way as to create the illusion, before a critical London audi- ence in broad daylight, that their organs were being torn out.

6   Another test of an actor's physical control was in dancing. Apart from the dances that were written into the actual texts of the plays, it was usual to end the performance with a dance performed by some of the members of the company. A traveller from abroad who saw Shakespeare's company act *Julius Caesar* said that "when the play was over they danced very marve- lously and gracefully together," and when the English actors travelled abroad special mention was always made of their ability as dancers. The fashion of the time was for violent, spectacular dances and the schools in London taught intricate steps like those of the galliard, the exaggerated leap called the "capriole" and the violent lifting of one's partner high into the air that was the "volte." A visitor to one of these dancing schools of

*[pronounced slīt] Tricks performed by jugglers or magicians so quickly that they cannot be observed.

London watched a performer do a galliard and noted how "wonderfully he leaped, flung and took on"; and if amateurs were talented at this kind of work, professionals on the stage were expected to be very much better.

7   ªIn addition to all this, subordinate or beginning actors were expected to handle several roles in an afternoon instead of only one. ᵇA major company seldom had more than twelve actors in it and could not afford to hire an indefinite number of extra ones for a single production. ᶜThis meant that the men who had short speaking parts or none were constantly racing about and leaping into different costumes to get onstage with a different characterization as soon as they heard their cues. ᵈIn one of Alleyn's productions a single actor played a Tartar nobleman, a spirit, an attendant, a hostage, a ghost, a child, a captain and a Persian; and while none of the parts made any special demands on his acting ability he must have had very little time to catch his breath. ᵉThe London theatre was no place for physical weaklings; and, in the same way it is safe to assume that John Shakespeare must have had a strong, well-made body or he would not have been appointed a constable in Stratford, it is safe to assume that he must have passed the inheritance on to his eldest son.

8   There was one more physical qualification an Elizabethan actor had to possess, and this was perhaps more important than any of the others. He had to have a good voice. An Elizabethan play was full of action, but in the final analysis it was not the physical activity that caught and held the emotions of the audience; it was the words. An audience was an assembly of listeners and it was through the ear, not the eye, that the audience learned the location of each of the scenes, the emotions of each of the characters and the poetry and excitement of the play as a whole. More especially, since the actors were men and boys and close physical contact could not carry the illusion of love-making, words had to be depended upon in the parts that were written for women.

9   An Elizabethan audience had become highly susceptible to the use of words, trained and alert to catch their exact meaning and full of joy if they were used well. But this meant, as the basis of any successful stage production, that all the words had to be heard clearly. The actors used a fairly rapid delivery of their lines and this meant that breath control, emphasis and enunciation had to be perfect if the link that was being forged between the emotions of the audience and the action on the stage was not to be broken. When Shakespeare first came to London, the problem of effective stage delivery was made somewhat easier by the use of a heavily end-stopped line, where the actor could draw his breath at regular intervals and proceed at a kind of jog-trot. But during the following decade this kind of writing became increasingly old-fashioned, giving way to an intricate and supple blank verse that was much more difficult to handle intelligently; and no one was more instrumental in bringing the new way of writing into general use than Shakespeare himself.

10   Even with all the assistance given him by the old way of writing, with mechanical accenting and heavy use of rhyme, an Elizabethan actor had no easy time remembering his part. A repertory system was used and no play

was given two days in succession. The actor played a different part every night and he had no opportunity to settle into a comfortable routine while the lines of the part became second nature to him. He could expect very little help from the prompter, for that overworked individual was chiefly occupied in seeing that the actors came on in proper order, that they had their properties available and that the intricate stage arrangements that controlled the pulleys from the "heavens" and the springs to the trap doors were worked with quick, accurate timing. These stage effects, which naturally had to be changed each afternoon for each new play, were extremely complicated. A single play in which Greene and Lodge collaborated required the descent of a prophet and an angel let down on a throne, a woman blackened by a thunder stroke, sailors coming in wet from the sea, a serpent devouring a vine, a hand with a burning sword emerging from a cloud and "Jonah the prophet cast out of the whale's belly upon the stage." Any production that had to wrestle with as many complications as this had no room for an actor who could not remember his lines.

11 Moreover, an actor who forgot his lines would not have lasted long in what was a highly competitive profession. There were more actors than there were parts for them, judging by the number of people who were listed as players in the parish registers. Even the actor who had achieved the position of a sharer in one of the large London companies was not secure. Richard Jones, for instance, was the owner of costumes and properties and playbooks worth nearly forty pounds, which was an enormous sum in those days, and yet three years later he was working in the theatre at whatever stray acting jobs he could get. "Sometimes I have a shilling a day and sometimes nothing," he told Edward Alleyn, asking for help in getting his suit and cloak out of pawn.

12 The usual solution for an actor who could not keep his place in the competitive London theatre was to join one of the country companies, where the standards were less exacting, or to go abroad. English actors were extravagantly admired abroad and even a second-string company with poor equipment became the hit of the Frankfort Fair, so that "both men and women flocked wonderfully" to see them. An actor like Shakespeare who maintained his position on the London stage for two decades could legitimately be praised, as Chettle praised him, for being "excellent in the quality he professes." If it had been otherwise, he would not have remained for long on the London stage.

A. Comprehension

Choose the answer that best completes each statement. Do not refer to the selection while doing this exercise.

1. The subject of this selection is (a) Elizabethan drama; (b) Shakespeare's dramatic talents; (c) the physical demands made upon Elizabethan actors; (d) the tastes of Elizabethan audiences.

2. Most Elizabethan actors began their training as (a) children; (b) teenagers; (c) university students; (d) adult apprentices.

3. Apparently, Elizabethan audiences expected to see (a) clever acrobatics and mimicry; (b) savage, realistic fights; (c) splendid costumes and elaborate sets; (d) fantasy and magic.

4. Elizabethan dramas usually ended with (a) fistfights among members of the audience; (b) singing and feasting; (c) a dance characterized by intricate steps and exaggerated leaps; (d) a rowdy party given in honor of the cast.

5. Chute emphasizes that Elizabethan actors needed to be (a) well versed in dramatic techniques and theater history; (b) physically strong and agile; (c) skilled in impromptu acting to accommodate sketchy or incomplete scripts; (d) capable of withstanding physical violence.

6. Elizabethan productions were described as being (a) unoriginal; (b) simple to execute; (c) complicated; (d) expensive to produce.

B. Inferences   On the basis of the evidence in the selection, mark these statements as follows: *A* for accurate inferences, *I* for inaccurate inferences, and *IE* for insufficient evidence. You may refer to the selection to answer the questions in this section, and all the remaining sections.

_____ 1. Shakespeare himself never became an accomplished actor.

_____ 2. Actors only pretended to fence on stage.

_____ 3. The London theater audiences approved of violence and bloodshed on the stage.

_____ 4. Most actors were skilled in only one role.

_____ 5. Blank verse was a more natural dramatic form than earlier verse forms.

_____ 6. The prompter's main role was to help actors remember their lines.

_____ 7. Women's roles were performed by men in Elizabethan dramas.

_____ 8. Elizabethan productions relied extensively on complex machinery and stage effects.

_____ 9. Acting in Shakespeare's time was a risky, occasionally dangerous occupation.

_____ 10. Shakespeare revolutionized Elizabethan drama in many ways.

C. Structure   1. The primary mode of discourse in this selection is (a) narration; (b) description; (c) exposition; (d) persuasion.

2. Write the sentence that expresses the thesis of the essay. _____

_____

3. Write the sentence that contains the controlling idea, in other words, the sentence that states the main subtopics to be developed in the body of the essay. _____

_____

4. In paragraph 2, Chute writes that Shakespeare must "have taught himself in the hard school of Elizabethan theatre how to use them [his strong body and good voice]." What does this "school" actually refer to?

_____

5. Read over paragraphs 4 through 9 again. Which pattern of organization is used? (a) inductive; (b) deductive; (c) spatial; (d) chronological; (e) emphatic.

6. Consider the structure of paragraph 7 again (the sentences have been lettered for you). Label each sentence, according to its function, as follows: *MAIN* (main idea); *MA* (major supporting statement); or *MI* (minor supporting statement).

sentence a _____   sentence d _____
sentence b _____   sentence e _____
sentence c _____

7. What is emphasized in paragraph 7? (a) the theater's intimate, relaxed environment; (b) the theater's intense, competitive atmosphere; (c) an atmosphere in the theater of continual frenzied motion; (d) John Shakespeare's legacy to his son.

8. In this essay, Chute seems primarily concerned with Shakespeare as (a) a person; (b) the greatest dramatist of all time; (c) an actor; (d) a dramatist and a poet.

D. Vocabulary

For each italicized word from the selection, choose the best definition according to the context in which it appears.

1. the *ruthless* technique [paragraph 4]: (a) relentless; (b) effective; (c) demanding; (d) cruel.

2. tear out his *entrails* [5]: (a) brains; (b) internal organs; (c) hair; (d) fingernails.

3. this involved *agility* [5]: (a) gentleness; (b) physical strength; (c) briskness; (d) nimbleness.

4. not *slavishly* interested in realism [5]: (a) blindly dependent on; (b) foolishly; (c) characteristically; (d) oppressively.

5. highly *susceptible* in the use of words [9]: (a) yielding; (b) liable to be stricken by; (c) especially sensitive to; (d) suspicious of.

6. intricate and *supple* blank verse [9]: (a) casual; (b) readily changed; (c) limber; (d) submissive.

E. Vocabulary Fill-Ins

Before you begin this exercise, be sure that you know the meaning of all the words in the list. From the list, choose a word that fits in each blank both grammatically and contextually. Use each word in the list only once, and add noun or verb endings (such as -s or -ed) if necessary. (Note that there are more words than blanks.)

succession	expert	reality	agility
realistic	competitive	weakling	since
role	grueling	qualification	intricate
illusion	instrumental	repertory	collaborate

1. Two _____ an Elizabethan actor needed were physical _____ and the capacity for long, _____ hours of practice in various skills.

2. _____ the companies used a _____ system, an actor had to play several different _____, often in quick succession.
3. A London audience expected to see _____ dueling matches; in addition, an actor had to become a(n) _____ in creating the _____ of dying a violent, bloody death.

F. Questions for Analysis

1. What are some differences between the demands made on Elizabethan actors and those made on stage, film, or television actors today?
2. What conclusion can you draw about the London theater audience of the Elizabethan period?
3. Even though you have already read the essay, you might find it instructive to practice the survey step from the SQ3R method with this selection. Read the first paragraph, the first sentence of the body paragraphs, and the last paragraph. Notice how logically constructed the essay is and how much information you can obtain from what you read. You might want to preview other selections in Part 4 in the same way.

Selection 18

Does America Still Exist?
Richard Rodriguez

Richard Rodriguez (1944–   ) was raised in Sacramento, California, the son of working-class Mexican immigrant parents. He spoke mostly Spanish until he entered a classroom and was forced to learn English, which he calls a "public" language, as opposed to Spanish, his "private" native language. *Hunger of Memory,* his 1982 autobiography, explores the years of his education, from Sacramento parochial schools to his graduate work at the University of California at Berkeley. Rodriguez is now at work on a book about Mexican culture and its influence in California.

1   For the children of immigrant parents the knowledge comes easier. America exists everywhere in the city—on billboards, frankly in the smell of French fries and popcorn. It exists in the pace: traffic lights, the assertions of neon, the mysterious bong-bong-bong through the atriums of department stores. America exists as the voice of the crowd, a menacing sound—the high nasal accent of American English.

2   When I was a boy in Sacramento (California, the fifties), people would ask me, "Where you from?" I was born in this country, but I knew the question meant to decipher my darkness, my looks.

3   My mother once instructed me to say, "I am an American of Mexican descent." By the time I was nine or ten, I wanted to say, but dared not reply, "I am an American."

4   Immigrants come to America and, against hostility or mere loneliness, they recreate a homeland in the parlor, tacking up postcards or calendars of some impossible blue—lake or sea or sky. Children of immigrant parents are supposed to perch on a hyphen between two countries. Relatives assume the achievement as much as anyone. Relatives are, in any case, surprised when

the child begins losing old ways. One day at the family picnic the boy wanders away from their spiced food and faceless stories to watch other boys play baseball in the distance.

5   There is sorrow in the American memory, guilty sorrow for having left something behind—Portugal, China, Norway. The American story is the story of immigrant children and of their children—children no longer able to speak to grandparents. The memory of exile becomes inarticulate as it passes from generation to generation, along with wedding rings and pocket watches—like some mute stone in a wad of old lace. Europe. Asia. Eden.

6   But, it needs to be said, if this is a country where one stops being Vietnamese or Italian, this is a country where one begins to be an American. America exists as a culture and a grin, a faith and a shrug. It is clasped in a handshake, called by a first name.

7   As much as the country is joined in a common culture, however, Americans are reluctant to celebrate the process of assimilation. We pledge allegiance to diversity. America was born Protestant and bred Puritan, and the notion of community we share is derived from a seventeenth-century faith. Presidents and the pages of ninth-grade civics readers yet proclaim the orthodoxy: We are gathered together—but as individuals, with separate pasts, distinct destinies. Our society is as paradoxical as a Puritan congregation: We stand together, alone.

8   Americans have traditionally defined themselves by what they refused to include. As often, however, Americans have struggled, turned in good conscience at last to assert the great Protestant virtue of tolerance. Despite outbreaks of nativist frenzy, America has remained an immigrant country, open and true to itself.

9   Against pious emblems of rural America—soda fountain, Elks hall, Protestant church, and now shopping mall—stands the cold-hearted city, crowded with races and ambitions, curious laughter, much that is odd. Nevertheless, it is the city that has most truly represented America. In the city, however, the millions of singular lives have had no richer notion of wholeness to describe them than the idea of pluralism.

10   *"Where you from?" the American asks the immigrant child. "Mexico," the boy learns to say.*

11   Mexico, the country of my blood ancestors, offers formal contrast to the American achievement. If the United States was formed by Protestant individualism, Mexico was shaped by a medieval Catholic dream of one world. The Spanish journeyed to Mexico to plunder, and they may have gone, in God's name, with an arrogance peculiar to those who intend to convert. But through the conversion, the Indian converted the Spaniard. A new race was born, the *mestizo,* wedding European to Indian. José Vasconcelos, the Mexican philosopher, has celebrated this New World creation, proclaiming it the "cosmic race."

12   Centuries later, in a San Francisco restaurant, a Mexican-American lawyer of my acquaintance says, in English, over *salade niçoise,* that he does not intend to assimilate into gringo society. His claim is echoed by a chorus of others (Italian-Americans, Greeks, Asians) in this era of ethnic pride. The

melting pot has been retired, clanking, into the museum of quaint disgrace, alongside Aunt Jemima and the Katzenjammer Kids. But resistance to assimilation is characteristically American. It only makes clear how inevitable the process of assimilation actually is.

13 For generations, this has been the pattern. Immigrant parents have sent their children to school (simply, they thought) to acquire the "skills" to survive in the city. The child returned home with a voice his parents barely recognized or understood, couldn't trust, and didn't like.

14 In Eastern cities—Philadelphia, New York, Boston, Baltimore—class after class gathered immigrant children to women (usually women) who stood in front of rooms full of children, changing children. So also for me in the 1950s. Irish-Catholic nuns. California. The old story. The hyphen tipped to the right, away from Mexico, and toward a confusing but true American identity.

15 I speak now in the chromium American accent of my grammar school classmates—Billy Reckers, Mike Bradley, Carol Schmidt, Kathy O'Grady. . . . I believe I became like my classmates, became German, Polish, and (like my teachers) Irish. And because assimilation is always reciprocal, my classmates got something of me. (I mean sad eyes; belief in the Indian Virgin; a taste for sugar skulls on the Feast of the Dead.) In the blending, we became what our parents could never have been, and we carried America one revolution further.

16 "Does America still exist?" Americans have been asking the question for so long that to ask it again only proves our continuous link. But perhaps the question deserves to be asked with urgency now. Since the black civil rights movement of the 1960s, our tenuous notion of a shared public life has deteriorated notably.

17 The struggle of black men and women did not eradicate racism, but it became the great moment in the life of America's conscience. Water hoses, bulldogs, blood—the images, rendered black, white, rectangular, passed into living rooms.

18 It is hard to look at a photograph of a crowd taken, say, in 1890 or in 1930 and not notice the absence of blacks. (It becomes an impertinence to wonder if America *still* exists.)

19 In the sixties, other groups of Americans learned to champion their rights by analogy to the black civil rights movement. But the heroic vision faded. Dr. Martin Luther King Jr. had spoken with Pauline eloquence of a nation that would unite Christian and Jew, old and young, rich and poor. Within a decade, the struggles of the 1960s were reduced to a bureaucratic competition for little more than pieces of a representational pie. The quest for a portion of power became an end in itself. The metaphor for the American city of the 1970s was a committee: one black, one woman, one person under thirty . . .

20 If the small town had sinned against America by too neatly defining who could be an American, the city's sin was a romantic secession. One noticed the romanticism in the antiwar movement—certain demonstrators who demonstrated a lack of tact or desire to persuade and seemed content to

play secular protestants. One noticed the romanticism in the competition among members of "minority groups" to claim the status of Primary Victim. To Americans unconfident of their common identity, minority standing became a way of asserting individuality. Middle-class Americans—men and women clearly not the primary victims of social oppression—brandished their suffering with exuberance.

21   The dream of a single society probably died with *The Ed Sullivan Show.* The reality of America persists. Teenagers pass through big-city high schools banded in racial groups, their collars turned up to a uniform shrug. But then they graduate to jobs at the phone company or in banks, where they end up working alongside people unlike themselves. Typists and tellers walk out together at lunchtime.

22   It is easier for us as Americans to believe the obvious fact of our separateness—easier to imagine the black and white Americas prophesied by the Kerner report (broken glass, street fires)—than to recognize the reality of a city street at lunchtime. Americans are wedded by proximity to a common culture. The panhandler at one corner is related to the pamphleteer at the next who is related to the banker who is kin to the Chinese old man wearing an MIT sweatshirt. In any true national history, Thomas Jefferson begets Martin Luther King Jr. who begets the Gray Panthers. It is because we lack a vision of ourselves entire—the city street is crowded and we are each preoccupied with finding our own way home—that we lack an appropriate hymn.

23   Under my window passes a little white girl softly rehearsing to herself a Motown obbligato.

A. Comprehension   Choose the answer that best completes each statement. Do not refer to the selection while doing this exercise.

1. According to Rodriguez, American culture is characterized by a paradoxical blend of (a) isolationism and international interests; (b) individuality and pluralism; (c) racial intolerance and pride in ethnic groups' accomplishments; (d) conservative religious values and progressive social ideals.

2. An immigrant child who begins to lose the old ways is undergoing the process of cultural (a) initiation; (b) confusion; (c) identification; (d) assimilation.

3. Paradoxically, Americans resist the inevitable joining together in a common culture because we (a) pledge allegiance to diversity; (b) are suspicious of non-Protestant or minority cultural values; (c) insist on holding on to the customs and values of the culture we left behind; (d) resent the achievements of newcomers.

4. For Rodriguez, American culture is most truly represented by (a) the shopping mall; (b) rural areas; (c) the suburbs; (d) the city.

5. When Spain attempted to conquer Mexico, Rodriguez writes, a new race was born, the *mestizo,* which refers to the union of (a) Indian and Mexican; (b) Indian and black; (c) Mexican and Spanish; (d) Indian and European.

6. Our notion of a shared public life has deteriorated in recent years, notably as a result of (a) the flight of middle-class whites from the city to the suburb; (b) the antiwar movement of the late 1960s and 1970s; (c) the black civil-rights movement of the 1960s; (d) the increasing tendency for American cities to be divided into two groups, the haves and the have-nots.

B. Inferences   On the basis of the evidence in the selection, answer these inference questions. You may refer to the selection to answer the questions in this section, and all the remaining sections.

1. Read paragraph 1 again. To whom would the accent of American English be "menacing"? _____

_____

2. Judging from paragraph 3, why would Rodriguez, as a child of eight or nine, not dare to say that he was an American? _____

_____

3. From the examples given in paragraph 6, what is Rodriguez implying about American culture? _____

_____

4. Read paragraph 7 again. What is the source of our reluctance to "celebrate the process of assimilation"? _____

_____

5. Reread paragraph 12. Why has the concept of America as a "melting pot" been retired? _____

_____

6. According to the ideas in paragraphs 13 and 14, what role does the school play in the immigrant child's life? _____

_____

7. Read paragraph 19 again. In what way were the ideals of the black civil-rights movement corrupted by the 1970s? _____

8. Read paragraph 21 again. What dream of a "single society" was suggested by "The Ed Sullivan Show" (popular during the 1950s)? _____

_____

9. Reread the beginning of paragraph 22. What discrepancy in American culture is Rodriguez referring to? _____

_____

10. On the basis of the entire essay, what is Rodriguez's answer to the question posed in the title? _____

_____

C. Structure   1. Rodriguez's purpose is to (a) explain the process of assimilation for immigrants; (b) define the essential characteristics of our common American culture as it now exists; (c) trace the concept of the "melting pot" through American history; (d) enumerate the contributions of minority groups to American culture.

2. Which of the four modes of discourse seems to predominate in the selection? (a) narration; (b) description; (c) exposition; (d) persuasion.

3. In paragraph 4, Rodriguez says, "Children of immigrant parents are supposed to perch on a hyphen between two countries." Explain the metaphor in your own words. _____

_____

Where, later in the essay, does Rodriguez refer to this metaphor?

_____

Explain what he means in your own words. _____

4. At the end of paragraph 4, Rodriguez refers to the "faceless stories" that the older generations tell at family picnics. Why does he characterize these stories in this way? _____

5. Look again at the last two sentences of paragraph 7. What is the relationship between them? (a) cause–effect; (b) term and its explanation; (c) steps in a process; (d) contrast.

6. In paragraph 11, Rodriguez contrasts America and Mexico. What, specifically, does he find different in the two cultures? _____
Why is this difference important to the understanding of both cultures today? _____

_____

7. What apparent irony does Rodriguez find in his Mexican-American lawyer friend's remarks? _____

_____

8. What method of paragraph development is most evident in paragraphs 13 and 14? (a) definition; (b) analogy; (c) classification; (d) process; (e) illustration.

9. In paragraph 15, Rodriguez says that he now speaks in the "chromium American accent" of his grammar school classmates. What does he mean by this metaphor? _____

10. What is Rodriguez's attitude toward those people who, in the 1970s, became members of "minority groups," asserted their individuality by claiming the status of "Primary Victim," and "brandished their suffering with exuberance"? (a) hostile; angry; (b) sarcastic; cynical; (c) sympathetic; favorably inclined; (d) neutral; impartial.

11. In paragraph 22, Rodriguez describes people on a city street whom he says are "related" or "kin" to one another. What is the basis of this kinship? _____
Which sentence in the paragraph explains what he means? _____

_____

12. The last paragraph contains an example: Under Rodriguez's window a little white girl passes by singing a Motown obbligato. How does this observation reinforce his main idea? (Look up "obbligato" if you are unfamiliar with the word.) _____

_____

13. Which of the following sentences from the selection *best* states its central theme? (a) "America exists as a culture and a grin, a faith and a shrug." (b) "Americans are reluctant to celebrate the process of assimilation. We pledge allegiance to diversity." (c) "Despite outbreaks of nativist frenzy, America has remained an immigrant country, open and true to itself." (d) "Americans are wedded by proximity to a common culture." Defend your choice.

14. With regard to American culture and the particular features Rodriguez outlines, his attitude can be best described as (a) positive; optimistic; (b) negative; pessimistic; (c) neutral; impartial; (d) realistic; pragmatic.

D. Vocabulary   For each italicized word from the selection, choose the best definition according to the context in which it appears.

1. the question meant to *decipher* my darkness [paragraph 2]: (a) interpret; (b) relate to; (c) accept; (d) translate.

2. the memory of *exile* [5]: (a) immigration to a new country; (b) self-imposed separation from one's country; (c) rejection of conventional values; (d) banishment from one's country by authoritative decree.

3. the memory of exile becomes *inarticulate* [5]: unable to (a) understand; (b) accept; (c) become concerned about; (d) express in words.

4. the process of *assimilation* [7]: process whereby (a) nourishment is changed into living tissue; (b) a sound is modified to make it resemble an adjacent sound; (c) a group denies its cultural heritage and system of values; (d) a group gradually adopts the characteristics of another culture.

5. presidents and civics readers proclaim the *orthodoxy* [7]: (a) a commonly accepted, or traditional, practice or belief; (b) a historical imperative; (c) an article of religious faith; (d) origin of a complex social institution.

6. our society is as *paradoxical* as a Puritan congregation [7]: describing (a) a strongly ingrained prejudice; (b) a strong religious faith; (c) an apparent contradiction; (d) a model or pattern of excellence.

7. to *assert* the great Protestant virtue of tolerance [8]: (a) reject; (b) attack; (c) agree to; (d) state positively.

8. against *pious* emblems of rural America [9]: professing an attitude that is (a) false; insincere; (b) strict; traditional in its observance of tradition; (c) unrepresentative; undemocratic; (d) marked by conspicuous religious devoutness.

9. the Spanish journeyed to Mexico to *plunder* [11]: (a) conquer; defeat; (b) bring about a religious conversion; (c) rob; pillage; (d) govern; rule by force.

10. with an arrogance *peculiar* to those who intend to convert [11]: (a) unusual; strange; (b) distinct; standing apart from others; (c) exclusive; unique; (d) limited; confined.

11. because assimilation is always *reciprocal* [15]: (a) long-lasting; (b) understandable; (c) conditional; (d) mutual.

12. our *tenuous* notion of a shared public life [16]: (a) lacking a sound basis; weak; (b) fragile; lacking firmness; (c) of little significance; flimsy; (d) stubborn; unyielding.

13. the struggle of black men and women did not *eradicate* racism [17]: (a) tear up by the roots; (b) alleviate; relieve; (c) destroy utterly; exterminate; (d) affect; cause a change in.

14. it becomes an *impertinence* to wonder [18]: quality or condition of (a) rudeness; impudence; (b) irrelevance; (c) insolence; (d) sudden compulsion.

15. the city's sin was a romantic *secession* [20]: (a) ideal; (b) withdrawal; (c) identification; (d) interlude.

16. men and women *brandished* their suffering [20]: (a) displayed ostentatiously; (b) waved menacingly; (c) discussed openly; (d) exaggerated.

17. men and women brandished their suffering with *exuberance* [20]: with (a) pain; anxiety; (b) delight; cheerfulness; (c) lavish joy; vigor; (d) engrossment in one's own interests; self-centeredness.

18. Americans are wedded by *proximity* to a common culture [22]: (a) force; (b) heritage; (c) closeness; (d) shared interest.

19. the banker who is *kin* to the Chinese old man [22]: (a) similar; (b) dissimilar; (c) related; (d) unrelated.

20. Thomas Jefferson *begets* Martin Luther King, Jr. [22]: (a) causes to exist; (b) sires; fathers; (c) reminds one of; (d) espouses the same ideas as.

E. Questions for Analysis

1. What image or definition of "America" does Rodriguez apparently have in mind in the title of his essay, "Does America Still Exist?"?

2. To what extent do you share Rodriguez's views of our common American culture as one influenced by its variety of ethnic and racial groups?

Selection 19   The End of Play
Marie Winn

Marie Winn was born in Prague, Czechoslovakia, in 1936. In 1939, she came to New York, where she was raised in a Czech neighborhood. She attended both Radcliffe College and Columbia University. The author of several children's books, Winn has also published for adults: *The Playgroup Book* (1967, with Mary Ann Porcher); *The Plug-In Drug* (1977); and *Children Without Childhood: Growing Up Too Fast in a World of Sex and Drugs* (1983), where this selection appears.

1   Of all the changes that have altered the topography of childhood, the most dramatic has been the disappearance of childhood play. Whereas a decade or two ago children were easily distinguished from the adult world by the very nature of their play, today children's occupations do not differ greatly from adult diversions.

2   Infants and toddlers, to be sure, continue to follow certain timeless patterns of manipulation and exploration; adolescents, too, have not changed

their free-time habits so very much, turning as they ever have towards adult pastimes and amusements in their drive for autonomy, self-mastery, and sexual discovery. It is among the ranks of school-age children, those six-to-twelve-year-olds who once avidly filled their free moments with childhood play, that the greatest change is evident. In the place of traditional, sometimes ancient childhood games that were still popular a generation ago, in the place of fantasy and make-believe play—"You be the mommy and I'll be the daddy"—doll play or toy-soldier play, jump-rope play, ball-bouncing play, today's children have substituted television viewing and, most recently, video games.

3   Many parents have misgivings about the influence of television. They sense that a steady and time-consuming exposure to passive entertainment might damage the ability to play imaginatively and resourcefully, or prevent this ability from developing in the first place. A mother of two school-age children recalls: "When I was growing up, we used to go out into the vacant lots and make up week-long dramas and sagas. This was during third, fourth, fifth grades. But my own kids have never done that sort of thing, and somehow it bothers me. I wish we had cut down on the TV years ago, and maybe the kids would have learned how to play."

4   The testimony of parents who eliminate television for periods of time strengthens the connection between children's television watching and changed play patterns. Many parents discover that when their children don't have television to fill their free time, they resort to the old kinds of imaginative, traditional "children's play." Moreover, these parents often observe that under such circumstances "they begin to seem more like children" or "they act more childlike." Clearly, a part of the definition of childhood, in adults' minds, resides in the nature of children's play.

5   Children themselves sometimes recognize the link between play and their own special definition as children. In an interview about children's books with four ten-year-old girls, one of them said: "I read this story about a girl my age growing up twenty years ago—you know, in 1960 or so—and she seemed so much younger than me in her behavior. Like she might be playing with dolls, or playing all sorts of children's games, or jump-roping or something." The other girls all agreed that they had noticed a similar discrepancy between themselves and fictional children in books of the past: those children seemed more like children. "So what do *you* do in your spare time, if you don't play with dolls or play make-believe games or jump rope or do things kids did twenty years ago?" they were asked. They laughed and answered, "We watch TV."

6   But perhaps other societal factors have caused children to give up play. Children's greater exposure to adult realities, their knowledge of adult sexuality, for instance, might make them more sophisticated, less likely to play like children. Evidence from the counterculture communes of the sixties and seventies adds weight to the argument that it is television above all that has eliminated children's play. Studies of children raised in a variety of such communes, all television-free, showed the little communards continuing to fill their time with those forms of play that have all but vanished

from the lives of conventionally reared American children. And yet these
counterculture kids were casually exposed to all sorts of adult matters—
drug taking, sexual intercourse. Indeed, they sometimes incorporated these
matters into their play: "We're mating," a pair of six-year-olds told a reporter
to explain their curious bumps and grinds. Nevertheless, to all observers the
commune children preserved a distinctly childlike and even innocent demeanor, an impression that was produced mainly by the fact that they spent
most of their time playing. Their play defined them as belonging to a special
world of childhood.

7   Not all children have lost the desire to engage in the old-style childhood
play. But so long as the most popular, most dominant members of the peer
group, who are often the most socially precocious, are "beyond" playing, then
a common desire to conform makes it harder for those children who still
have the drive to play to go ahead and do so. Parents often report that their
children seem ashamed of previously common forms of play and hide their
involvement with such play from their peers. "My fifth-grader still plays
with dolls," a mother tells, "but she keeps them hidden in the basement
where nobody will see them." This social check on the play instinct serves to
hasten the end of childhood for even the least advanced children.

8   What seems to have replaced play in the lives of great numbers of preadolescents these days, starting as early as fourth grade, is a burgeoning
interest in boy-girl interactions—"going out" or "going together." These
activities do not necessarily involve going anywhere or doing anything sexual, but nevertheless are the first stage of a sexual process that used to com-
mence at puberty or even later. Those more sophisticated children who are
already involved in such manifestly unchildlike interests make plain their
low opinion of their peers who still *play*. "Some of the kids in the class are
real weird," a fifth-grade boy states. "They're not interested in going out,
just in trucks and stuff, or games pretending they're monsters. Some of
them don't even *try* to be cool."

VIDEO GAMES VERSUS MARBLES

9   Is there really any great difference, one might ask, between that gang of
kids playing video games by the hour at their local candy store these days
and those small fry who used to hang around together spending equal
amounts of time playing marbles? It is easy to see a similarity between
the two activities: each requires a certain amount of manual dexterity,
each is almost as much fun to watch as to play, each is simple and yet
challenging enough for that middle-childhood age group for whom time
can be so oppressive if unfilled.

10   One significant difference between the modern pre-teen fad of video
games and the once popular but now almost extinct pastime of marbles is
economic: playing video games costs twenty-five cents for approximately
three minutes of play; playing marbles, after a small initial investment,
is free. The children who frequent video-game machines require a considerable outlay of quarters to subsidize their fun; two, three, or four dollars
is not an unusual expenditure for an eight- or nine-year-old spending an

hour or two with his friends playing Asteroids or Pac-Man or Space Invaders. For most of the children the money comes from their weekly allowance. Some augment this amount by enterprising commercial ventures—trading and selling comic books, or doing chores around the house for extra money.
11   But what difference does it make *where* the money comes from? Why should that make video games any less satisfactory as an amusement for children? In fact, having to pay for the entertainment, whatever the source of the money, and having its duration limited by one's financial resources changes the nature of the game, in a subtle way diminishing the satisfactions it offers. Money and time become intertwined, as they so often are in the adult world and as, in the past, they almost never were in the child's world. For the child playing marbles, meanwhile, time has a far more carefree quality, bounded only by the requirements to be home by suppertime or by dark.
12   But the video-game-playing child has an additional burden—a burden of choice, of knowing that the money used for playing Pac-Man could have been saved for Christmas, could have been used to buy something tangible, perhaps something "worthwhile," as his parents might say, rather than being "wasted" on video games. There is a certain sense of adultness that spending money imparts, a feeling of being a consumer, which distinguishes a game with a price from its counterparts among the traditional childhood games children once played at no cost.
13   There are other differences as well. Unlike child-initiated and child-organized games such as marbles, video games are adult-created mechanisms not entirely within the child's control, and thus less likely to impart a sense of mastery and fulfillment: the coin may get jammed, the machine may go haywire, the little blobs may stop eating the funny little dots. Then the child must go to the storekeeper to complain, to get his money back. He may be "ripped off" and simply lose his quarter, much as his parents are when they buy a faulty appliance. This possibility of disaster gives the child's play a certain weight that marbles never imposed on its light-hearted players.
14   Even if a child has a video game at home requiring no coin outlay, the play it provides is less than optimal. The noise level of the machine is high—too high, usually, for the child to conduct a conversation easily with another child. And yet, according to its enthusiasts, this very noisiness is a part of the game's attraction. The loud whizzes, crashes, and whirrs of the video-game machine "blow the mind" and create an excitement that is quite apart from the excitement generated simply by trying to win a game. A traditional childhood game such as marbles, on the other hand, has little built-in stimulation; the excitement of playing is generated entirely by the players' own actions. And while the pace of a game of marbles is close to the child's natural physiological rhythms, the frenzied activities of video games serve to "rev up" the child in an artificial way, almost in the way a stimulant or an amphetamine might. Meanwhile the perceptual impact of a video game is similar to that of watching television—the action, after all, takes place on a television screen—causing the eye to defocus slightly and creating a certain alteration in the child's natural state of consciousness.

15   Parents' instinctive reaction to their children's involvement with video games provides another clue to the difference between this contemporary form of play and the more traditional pastimes such as marbles. While parents, indeed most adults, derive open pleasure from watching children at play, most parents today are not delighted to watch their kids flicking away at the Pac-Man machine. This does not seem to them to be real play. As a mother of two school-age children anxiously explains, "We used to do real childhood sorts of things when I was a kid. We'd build forts and put on crazy plays and make up new languages, and just generally we *played*. But today my kids don't play that way at all. They like video games and of course they still go in for sports outdoors. They go roller skating and ice skating and skiing and all. But they don't seem to really *play*."

16   Some of this feeling may represent a certain nostalgia for the past and the old generation's resistance to the different ways of the new. But it is more likely that most adults have an instinctive understanding of the importance of play in their own childhood. This feeling stokes their fears that their children are being deprived of something irreplaceable when they flip the levers on the video machines to manipulate the electronic images rather than flick their fingers to send a marble shooting towards another marble.

PLAY DEPRI-VATION   17   In addition to television's influence, some parents and teachers ascribe children's diminished drive to play to recent changes in the school curriculum, especially in the early grades.

18   "Kindergarten, traditionally a playful port of entry into formal school, is becoming more academic, with children being taught specific skills, taking tests, and occasionally even having homework," begins a report on new directions in early childhood education. Since 1970, according to the United States census, the proportion of three- and four-year-olds enrolled in school has risen dramatically, from 20.5 percent to 36.7 percent in 1980, and these nursery schools have largely joined the push towards academic acceleration in the early grades. Moreover, middle-class nursery schools in recent years have introduced substantial doses of academic material into their daily programs, often using those particular devices originally intended to help culturally deprived preschoolers in compensatory programs such as Headstart to catch up with their middle-class peers. Indeed, some of the increased focus on academic skills in nursery schools and kindergartens is related to the widespread popularity among young children and their parents of *Sesame Street,* a program originally intended to help deprived children attain academic skills, but universally watched by middle-class toddlers as well.

19   Parents of the *Sesame Street* generation often demand a "serious," skill-centered program for their preschoolers in school, afraid that the old-fashioned, play-centered curriculum will bore their alphabet-spouting, number-chanting four- and five-year-olds. A few parents, especially those whose children have not attended television classes or nursery school, complain of the high-powered pace of kindergarten these days. A father whose

five-year-old daughter attends a public kindergarten declares: "There's a lot more pressure put on little kids these days than when we were kids, that's for sure. My daughter never went to nursery school and never watched *Sesame,* and she had a lot of trouble when she entered kindergarten this fall. By October, just a month and a half into the program, she was already flunking. The teacher told us our daughter couldn't keep up with the other kids. And believe me, she's a bright kid! All the other kids were getting gold stars and smiley faces for their work, and every day Emily would come home in tears because she didn't get a gold star. Remember when we were in kindergarten? We were *children* then. We were allowed just to play!"

20   A kindergarten teacher confirms the trend towards early academic pressure. "We're expected by the dictates of the school system to push a lot of curriculum," she explains. "Kids in our kindergarten can't sit around playing with blocks any more. We've just managed to squeeze in one hour of free play a week, on Fridays."

21   The diminished emphasis on fantasy and play and imaginative activities in early childhood education and the increased focus on early academic-skill acquisition have helped to change childhood from a play-centered time of life to one more closely resembling the style of adulthood: purposeful, success-centered, competitive. The likelihood is that these preschool "workers" will not metamorphose back into players when they move on to grade school. This decline in play is surely one of the reasons why so many teachers today comment that their third- or fourth-graders act like tired businessmen instead of like children.

22   What might be the consequences of this change in children's play? Children's propensity to engage in that extraordinary series of behaviors characterized as "play" is perhaps the single great dividing line between childhood and adulthood, and has probably been so throughout history. The make-believe games anthropologists have recorded of children in primitive societies around the world attest to the universality of play and to the uniqueness of this activity to the immature members of each society. But in those societies, and probably in Western society before the middle or late eighteenth century, there was always a certain similarity between children's play and adult work. The child's imaginative play took the form of imitation of various aspects of adult life, culminating in the gradual transformation of the child's play from make-believe work to *real* work. At this point, in primitive societies or in our own society of the past, the child took her or his place in the adult work world and the distinctions between adulthood and childhood virtually vanished. But in today's technologically advanced society there is no place for the child in the adult work world. There are not enough jobs, even of the most menial kind, to go around for adults, much less for children. The child must continue to be dependent on adults for many years while gaining the knowledge and skills necessary to become a working member of society.

23   This is not a new situation for children. For centuries children have endured a prolonged period of dependence long after the helplessness of early childhood is over. But until recent years children remained childlike

and playful far longer than they do today. Kept isolated from the adult world as a result of deliberate secrecy and protectiveness, they continued to find pleasure in socially sanctioned childish activities until the imperatives of adolescence led them to strike out for independence and self-sufficiency.

24   Today, however, with children's inclusion in the adult world both through the instrument of television and as a result of a deliberately preparatory, integrative style of child rearing, the old forms of play no longer seem to provide children with enough excitement and stimulation. What then are these so-called children to do for fulfillment if their desire to play has been vitiated and yet their entry into the working world of adulthood must be delayed for many years? The answer is precisely to get involved in those areas that cause contemporary parents so much distress: addictive television viewing during the school years followed, in adolescence or even before, by a search for similar oblivion via alcohol and drugs; exploration of the world of sensuality and sexuality before achieving the emotional maturity necessary for altruistic relationships.

25   Psychiatrists have observed among children in recent years a marked increase in the occurrence of depression, a state long considered antithetical to the nature of childhood. Perhaps this phenomenon is at least somewhat connected with the current sense of uselessness and alienation that children feel, a sense that play may once upon a time have kept in abeyance.

A. Compre-
hension

Choose the answer that best completes each statement. Do not refer to the selection while doing this exercise.

1. The main idea of the selection is that (a) children are now more precocious, especially in their interest in boy–girl relationships; (b) traditional games that children have played for decades are considerably more satisfying to play than video games; (c) the concept of childhood has been dramatically altered by the disappearance of childhood play; (d) addictive television viewing among children has had serious psychological and emotional consequences.

2. The age group that Winn is most concerned about in her discussion is (a) newborns; infants; (b) toddlers; one-to-three-year-olds; (c) six-to-twelve-year-olds; (d) thirteen-to-eighteen-year-olds.

3. When parents eliminate television viewing in their households, the result is (a) a complete breakdown in children's behavior; total chaos; (b) more time spent in reading and doing homework; (c) a return to the old kinds of imaginative, traditional children's play; (d) better communication between members of the family, especially at meals.

4. The pressure to hasten the end of childhood most noticeably comes from (a) one's parents; (b) one's peers; (c) one's older siblings; (d) television and other mass media.

5. Winn contrasts the phenomenon of video games with the childhood game of (a) jump rope; (b) sandlot baseball; (c) kick the can; (d) marbles.

6. In addition to television, Winn is also concerned that childhood play has changed because of another influence, specifically (a) the increased pressure for preschool and kindergarten children to acquire academic skills; (b) parents' ambitions for their children to get into good colleges; (c) the influence of television programs like *Sesame Street*; (d) a highly developed technological society that does not require children to develop manual dexterity traditionally associated with children's games.

7. In primitive societies, anthropologists have observed that children's play takes the form of (a) make-believe fantasies and staged plays; (b) make-believe work that imitates adult work; (c) sports of various kinds; (d) watching television and playing video games.

8. In her conclusion, Winn shows concern that the end of childhood play and young people's delayed entry into the adult world of work leaves them inevitably with little to do but (a) turn to crime; (b) continue watching mindless television programs; (c) turn to drugs, alcohol, and sex; (d) spend money on consumer goods.

B. Inferences   On the basis of the evidence in the selection, mark these statements as follows: *A* for accurate inferences, *I* for inaccurate inferences, and *IE* for insufficient evidence. You may refer to the selection to answer the questions in this section, and all the remaining sections.

_____ 1. Television is the sole reason today's children have turned away from traditional forms of play.

_____ 2. The change in children's play is a recent development, having begun around twenty years ago.

_____ 3. Children raised in homes without television retain their childish innocence longer than those raised in homes with television.

_____ 4. Children who wish to engage in traditionally childish pursuits, such as playing with dolls, are often teased by their peers.

_____ 5. The increase in crimes committed by preadolescents is directly attributable to their obsession with playing video games.

_____ 6. Television and video games both have the effect of altering the viewer's or user's natural state of consciousness.

_____ 7. A kindergartener who hasn't grown up watching *Sesame Street* may be academically behind those who have watched it.

_____ 8. The number of three- and four-year-olds enrolled in nursery schools has increased in the U.S. because more mothers are working outside the home.

_____ 9. So far, no studies have been done by psychiatrists to determine whether today's pressures on children have had any harmful effects.

_____ 10. Children should not be allowed to watch television at all during their formative years.

C. Structure

1. The mode of discourse in this selection is primarily (a) narration; (b) description; (c) exposition; (d) persuasion.
Defend your choice.

2. In the space, write the sentence that best states the thesis, or main idea, of the essay. *Of all childen — 1 Sentence —*

3. This essay has a clear beginning, middle, and end. The dividing line between the introduction and the body comes at the end of paragraph *1*. The dividing line between the body paragraphs and the conclusion comes at the end of paragraph *21*.

4. The essay takes up two major influences that have contributed to a radical change in childhood. Which two influences is the author concerned with? *TV Watching* and *increase presure on the youg*
At what point in the body of the essay does the author take up the second concern? Paragraph _____.

5. Look at paragraph 7 again. What is the function of the first sentence? (a) to act as a transition; (b) to offer more support for the author's observations; (c) to guard against overgeneralizing; (d) to serve as a topic sentence.

6. What method of paragraph development is used in paragraph 9? (a) example; (b) analogy; (c) comparison; (d) contrast; (e) definition.

7. What method of paragraph development predominates in the section comprised by paragraphs 10–16? (a) example; (b) definition; (c) comparison; (d) contrast; (e) cause–effect.

8. The pattern of organization most evident in the paragraphs in that same section is (a) chronological; (b) spatial; (c) deductive; (d) inductive; (e) emphatic.

9. What two methods of paragraph development are most evident in paragraph 22? (a) example; (b) definition; (c) cause–effect; (d) comparison; (e) contrast; (f) process.

10. To support her observations about the end of play, Winn relies on (a) specific children who live in New York City; (b) children who are the offspring of her friends; (c) children at the school where Winn teaches; (d) children and parents whom she interviewed for her study.

D. Fact and Opinion

For each of the following statements from the selection, mark *F* if it represents a fact (a statement that can be verified or proved true), or *O* if it represents an opinion (a statement reflecting the author's subjective point of view).

____*O* 1. Of all the changes that have altered the topography of childhood, the most dramatic has been the disappearance of childhood play.

____*O* 2. In the place of traditional, sometimes ancient, childhood games that were still popular a generation ago; in the place of fantasy and make-believe play, today's children have substituted television viewing.

_F_ 3. A mother of two school-age children says, "I wish we had cut down on the TV years ago, and maybe the kids would have learned how to play."

_F_ 4. The proportion of three- and four-year-olds enrolled in school rose from 20.5 percent in 1970, to 36.7 percent in 1980.

_O_ 5. The diminished emphasis on fantasy, play, and imaginative activities in early childhood education, and the increased focus on early academic-skill acquisition, have helped to change childhood from a play-centered time of life to one more closely resembling the style of adulthood—purposeful, success-centered, competitive.

_O_ 6. What these so-called children do for fulfillment is to get involved with addictive television viewing during the school years, followed —in adolescence or even before—by a search for a similar oblivion via alcohol, drugs, and the exploration of the world of sensuality and sexuality before they have achieved the emotional maturity necessary for altruistic relationships.

E. Vocabulary   For each italicized word from the selection, choose the best definition according to the context in which it appears.

1. patterns of *manipulation* and exploration [paragraph 2]: (a) shrewd or devious influence; management; (b) tampering with, or falsification, for personal gain; (c) operating or controlling by skilled use of the hands; (d) discovery through the senses.

2. in their drive for *autonomy* [2]: (a) independence; (b) self-discovery; (c) free activity; (d) self-awareness.

3. those six-to-twelve-year-olds who *avidly* filled their free moments [2]: (a) greedily; (b) easily; (c) eagerly; (d) appropriately.

4. make up week-long dramas and *sagas* [3]: (a) short skits; sketches; (b) comedy shows; (c) historical poems; (d) long narrative stories.

5. the other girls had noticed a similar *discrepancy* [5]: a difference between two things that (a) is major; significant; (b) should not exist; (c) is unusual; extraordinary; (d) is incapable of being reconciled.

6. their knowledge of adult sexuality might make them more *sophisticated* [6]: (a) having worldly knowledge; (b) daring; bold; (c) willing to experiment; (d) physically and emotionally mature.

7. a distinctly childlike and even innocent *demeanor* [6]: (a) façade; false front; (b) facial appearance; (c) conduct; behavior; (d) sense of wonder; awe.

8. the most socially *precocious* [7]: characterized by (a) a desire to succeed; (b) early development; (c) skill; grace; (d) awkwardness; clumsiness.

9. a *burgeoning* interest in boy–girl interactions [8]: (a) newly discovered; (b) hesitant; reluctant; (c) healthy; wholesome; (d) developing rapidly; flourishing.

10. such *manifestly* unchildlike interests [8]: (a) unpopularly; (b) clearly apparent; (c) characteristically; (d) absurdly.

11. a certain amount of manual *dexterity* [9]: (a) cleverness; (b) efficiency; (c) skill; (d) practice.

12. children who *frequent* video-game machines [10]: (a) use often; (b) buy; (c) waste time at; (d) practice at.

13. some *augment* this amount [10]: (a) subsidize; support; (b) pay for; finance; (c) increase; (d) complain about.

14. could have been used to buy something *tangible* [12]: capable of (a) being used practically; (b) being touched; (c) being appreciated; (d) increasing in value.

15. parents and teachers *ascribe* children's diminished play drive to [17]: (a) complain about; (b) assign as a cause; (c) explain; (d) describe as.

16. preschoolers in *compensatory* programs [18]: (a) advanced intellectually; (b) free; complimentary; (c) required; involuntary; (d) serving to make up for deficiencies.

17. the *dictates* of the school system [20]: (a) directives; commands; (b) autocratic rulers; (c) requirements; (d) pressures.

18. children's *propensity* to engage in "play" [22]: (a) desire; (b) inclination; (c) ability; (d) unwillingness.

19. *culminating* in the gradual transformation [22]: (a) arriving at a final stage; (b) cultivating; nurturing; (c) beginning; (d) engaging.

20. not enough jobs, even of the most *menial* kind [22]: (a) unimportant; (b) unskilled; (c) describing activities done with the hands; (d) pertaining to a servant; servile.

21. to find pleasure in socially *sanctioned* childish activities [23]: (a) respected; (b) appropriate; (c) outlawed; (d) approved.

22. the *imperatives* of adolescence [23]: (a) concerns; (b) social forces; (c) obligations; (d) protections.

23. a search for similar *oblivion* via alcohol and drugs [24]: state of (a) confusion; chaos; (b) loss of memory; forgetfulness; (c) ecstasy; pleasure; (d) good sensations; euphoria.

24. the emotional maturity necessary for *altruistic* relationships [24]: characterized by (a) selflessness; (b) selfishness; (c) friendliness; (d) competitiveness.

25. *antithetical* to the nature of childhood [25]: (a) hostile; (b) directly opposed; (c) connected; (d) unacceptable.

26. play once may have kept in *abeyance* [25]: (a) confidence; (b) captivity; (c) suspense; (d) state of suspension.

F. Questions for Analysis

1. How would you evaluate the quality of the evidence Winn cites to support her ideas?

2. Winn might be accused of indulging in generalizations in her analysis of childhood. What devices does she use to escape this charge?

3. What is the relationship between the end of childhood play, as Winn describes it, and drug or alcohol use? Does this relationship, based on your own reading and experience of the world, seem reasonable?

4. If the forces that Winn describes are as damaging as she suggests, what can parents and teachers do to counteract them?

Selection 20   ## A Republic of Insects and Grass
                      ### Jonathan Schell

Jonathan Schell (1943–   ) is a staff writer for *The New Yorker* who has written on a variety of social issues. Published in 1982, *The Fate of the Earth* was quickly perceived to be the definitive statement on nuclear war and its certain devastating effects. The opening sentences on the book's dust jacket say it best:

> *The Fate of the Earth* . . . may someday be looked back upon as a crucial event in the history of human thought. It may mark the moment at which man wrenched himself free from the psychological habits of prenuclear times, permitted the nuclear predicament to take hold in his consciousness, roused himself to confront the stark fact that his species was in imminent danger of extinguishing itself, and began to act to avert a final, absurd, irreversible, boundless calamity.

This selection explains the effects of a nuclear holocaust on the environment. (Note: Schell refers to a ten-thousand-megaton attack in this selection. For comparison, the bomb dropped on Hiroshima, at the end of World War II, was twelve and a half kilotons. Since a kiloton is one thousand tons, and a megaton is one million tons, a ten-thousand-megaton attack is incalculably greater than that used in 1945.)

1   If, in a nuclear holocaust, anyone hid himself deep enough under the earth and stayed there long enough to survive, he would emerge into a dying natural environment. The vulnerability of the environment is the last word in the argument against the usefulness of shelters: there is no hole big enough to hide all of nature in. Radioactivity penetrates the environment in many ways. The two most important components of radiation from fallout are gamma rays, which are electromagnetic radiation of the highest intensity, and beta particles, which are electrons fired at high speed from decaying nuclei. Gamma rays subject organisms to penetrating whole-body doses, and are responsible for most of the ill effects of radiation from fallout. Beta particles, which are less penetrating than gamma rays, act at short range, doing harm when they collect on the skin, or on the surface of a leaf. They are harmful to plants on whose foliage the fallout descends—producing "beta burn"—and to grazing animals, which can suffer burns as well as gastrointestinal damage from eating the foliage. Two of the most harmful radioactive isotopes present in fallout are strontium-90 (with a half-life*

---

*The time required for one half of the atoms of any given amount of a radioactive substance to disintegrate.

of twenty-eight years) and cesium-137 (with a half-life of thirty years). They are taken up into the food chain through the roots of plants or through direct ingestion by animals, and contaminate the environment from within. Strontium-90 happens to resemble calcium in its chemical composition, and therefore finds its way into the human diet through dairy products and is eventually deposited by the body in the bones, where it is thought to cause bone cancer. (Every person in the world now has in his bones a measurable deposit of strontium-90 traceable to the fallout from atmospheric nuclear testing.)

2   Over the years, agencies and departments of the government have sponsored numerous research projects in which a large variety of plants and animals were irradiated in order to ascertain the lethal or sterilizing dose for each. These findings permit the prediction of many gross ecological consequences of a nuclear attack. According to "Survival of Food Crops and Livestock in the Event of Nuclear War," the proceedings of the 1970 symposium at Brookhaven National Laboratory, the lethal doses for most mammals lie between a few hundred rads and a thousand rads of gamma radiation; a rad —for "roentgen absorbed dose"—is a roentgen of radiation that has been absorbed by an organism, and is roughly equal to a rem. For example, the lethal doses of gamma radiation for animals in pasture, where fallout would be descending on them directly and they would be eating fallout that had fallen on the grass, and would thus suffer from doses of beta radiation as well, would be one hundred and eighty rads for cattle; two hundred and forty rads for sheep; five hundred and fifty rads for swine; three hundred and fifty rads for horses; and eight hundred rads for poultry. In a ten-thousand-megaton attack, which would create levels of radiation around the country averaging more than ten thousand rads, most of the mammals of the United States would be killed off. The lethal doses for birds are in roughly the same range as those for mammals, and birds, too, would be killed off. Fish are killed at doses of between one thousand one hundred rads and about five thousand six hundred rads, but their fate is less predictable. On the one hand, water is a shield from radiation, and would afford some protection; on the other hand, fallout might concentrate in bodies of water as it ran off from the land. (Because radiation causes no pain, animals, wandering at will through the environment, would not avoid it.) The one class of animals containing a number of species quite likely to survive, at least in the short run, is the insect class, for which in most known cases the lethal doses lie between about two thousand rads and about a hundred thousand rads. Insects, therefore, would be destroyed selectively. Unfortunately for the rest of the environment, many of the phytophagous species— insects that feed directly on vegetation—which "include some of the most ravaging species on earth" (according to Dr. Vernon M. Stern, an entomologist at the University of California at Riverside, writing in "Survival of Food Crops"), have very high tolerances, and so could be expected to survive disproportionately, and then to multiply greatly in the aftermath of an attack. The demise of their natural predators the birds would enhance their success.

3   Plants in general have a higher tolerance to radioactivity than animals do. Nevertheless, according to Dr. George M. Woodwell, who supervised the irradiation with gamma rays, over several years, of a small forest at Brookhaven Laboratory, a gamma-ray dose of ten thousand rads "would devastate most vegetation" in the United States, and, as in the case of the pastured animals, when one figures in the beta radiation that would also be delivered by fallout the estimates for the lethal doses of gamma rays must be reduced —in this case, cut in half. As a general rule, Dr. Woodwell and his colleagues at Brookhaven discovered, large plants are more vulnerable to radiation than small ones. Trees are among the first to die, grasses among the last. The most sensitive trees are pines and the other conifers, for which lethal doses are in roughly the same range as those for mammals. Any survivors coming out of their shelters a few months after the attack would find that all the pine trees that were still standing were already dead. The lethal doses for most deciduous trees range from about two thousand rads of gamma-ray radiation to about ten thousand rads, with the lethal doses for eighty per cent of deciduous species falling between two thousand and eight thousand rads. Since the addition of the beta-ray burden could lower these lethal doses for gamma rays by as much as fifty per cent, the actual lethal doses in gamma rays for these trees during an attack could be from one thousand to four thousand rads, and in a full-scale attack they would die. Then, after the trees had died, forest fires would break out around the United States. (Because as much as three-quarters of the country could be subjected to incendiary levels of the thermal pulses, the sheer scorching of the land could have killed off a substantial part of the plant life in the country in the first few seconds after the detonations, before radioactive poisoning set in.) Lethal doses for grasses on which tests have been done range between six thousand and thirty-three thousand rads, and a good deal of grass would therefore survive, except where the attacks had been heaviest. Most crops, on the other hand, are killed by doses below five thousand rads, and would be eliminated. (The lethal dose for spring barley seedlings, for example, is one thousand nine hundred and ninety rads, and that for spring wheat seedlings is three thousand and ninety rads.)

4   When vegetation is killed off, the land on which it grew is degraded. And as the land eroded after an attack, life in lakes, rivers, and estuaries, already hard hit by radiation directly, would be further damaged by minerals flowing into the watercourses, causing eutrophication—a process in which an oversupply of nutrients in the water encourages the growth of algae and microscopic organisms, which, in turn, deplete the oxygen content of the water. When the soil loses its nutrients, it loses its ability to "sustain a mature community" (in Dr. Woodwell's words), and "gross simplification" of the environment occurs, in which "hardy species," such as moss and grass, replace vulnerable ones, such as trees; and "succession"—the process by which ecosystems recover lost diversity—is then "delayed or even arrested." In sum, a full-scale nuclear attack on the United States would devastate the natural environment on a scale unknown since early geological times, when, in response to natural catastrophes whose nature

has not been determined, sudden mass extinctions of species and whole eco-systems occurred all over the earth. How far this "gross simplification" of the environment would go once virtually all animal life and the greater part of plant life had been destroyed and what patterns the surviving remnants of life would arrange themselves into over the long run are imponderables; but it appears that at the outset the United States would be a republic of insects and grass.

A. Comprehension

Choose the answer that best completes each statement. Do not refer to the selection while doing this exercise.

1. The subject of this selection is (a) an explanation of the important components of radioactive materials; (b) the effects of a nuclear attack on human civilization; (c) the physical effects of radiation on the human body; (d) the effects of a nuclear holocaust on the natural environment.

2. According to Schell, which *two* of the following are the important components of radiation from fallout? (a) strontium-90; (b) gamma rays; (c) plutonium isotopes; (d) cesium-137; (e) beta particles.

3. The term "rad" (roentgen absorbed dose) refers to (a) the way nuclear megatonnage is measured; (b) the amount of gamma radiation absorbed by an organism; (c) a computerized model of the long-term effects of radiation on plant life; (d) a way of measuring the number of radioactive particles in human bone marrow.

4. Mammals would suffer not only from gamma radiation from the fallout descending on them, but also from (a) radiation in the water they drink; (b) fallout that descended on the grass they eat; (c) radiation released into the environment by trees and other large plants; (d) radiation deposited in their bones by the ingestion of strontium-90 particles.

5. Among pasture animals, those who supposedly have the highest tolerance to gamma radiation are (a) poultry; (b) horses; (c) cattle; (d) sheep.

6. According to the selection, (a) plants have a lower tolerance of radioactivity than animals; (b) large plants have a lower tolerance to radioactivity than small plants; (c) in a nuclear attack, the grasses would be killed first, and then the trees; (d) the only trees that can survive radioactive fallout are the conifers, such as pine trees.

7. Phytophagous insect species (those that feed directly on vegetation) would survive in great numbers, not only because they have a high tolerance to radioactivity, but also because (a) their natural predators would also be destroyed; (b) pesticides cannot counteract the harmful effects of radiation poisoning; (c) their external skeletons make contamination from beta particles less affecting; (d) their natural habitat, the grasses, would survive an attack.

8. Even before radioactive poisoning contaminated vegetation after a nuclear attack, three-quarters of the country's vegetation would have been destroyed by (a) thermal pulses; (b) burns from beta particles; (c) large-scale forest fires; (d) radioactivity levels in underground streams.

B. Inferences   On the basis of the evidence in the selection, answer these inference questions. You may refer to the selection to answer the questions in this section, and all the remaining sections.

1. Read paragraph 1 again. What can you infer about the feasibility of people building bomb shelters to protect themselves against the effects of nuclear fallout? _Shelters are pointless if the environment is de_ _stroyed_

2. Again from paragraph 1, which of the two components of radiation can you infer would be more harmful to humans *in the long run,* gamma rays or beta particles? _Gamma Rays enter the entire body_

3. Finally from paragraph 1, assuming that a human being was somehow not contaminated with radioactivity and had survived in a shelter, what can you infer about his chances of survival after he emerged? _there will not be any chance since environment + food_ _as can_ _eliminate_

4. Read paragraph 2 again. What can you infer about a mammal's tolerance for specific doses of gamma radiation? What seems to determine the relative doses and tolerance levels for the mammals mentioned? ___Larger animal have less resistance.___

5. From the selection as a whole, what can you infer about the chances for man to survive in a republic of insects and grass? _practically_ _Non existant._

C. Structure   1. Which of the following *best* represents the main idea of the selection? (a) "The vulnerability of the environment is the last word in the argument against the usefulness of shelters: there is no hole big enough to hide all of nature in." (b) "When vegetation is killed off, the land on which it grew is degraded." (c) "In sum, a full-scale nuclear attack on the United States would devastate the natural environment on a scale unknown since early geological times." (d) "It appears that at the outset the United States would be a republic of insects and grass."
Defend your choice. _____

_____

2. Of the four modes of discourse, which seems to represent Schell's *explicit* purpose, and which seems to represent his *implicit* purpose? Explain and defend your answers. _exposition - explicit_ _implicit persuasion_

3. Look again at paragraph 1. Which method of paragraph development predominates? (a) analogy; (b) process; (c) classification; (d) comparison; (e) contrast; (f) definition.

4. Look again at paragraph 2. Which method of paragraph development predominates? (a) analogy; (b) process; (c) example; (d) definition; (e) analysis.

5. Write the transitional phrase that helped you arrive at your answer for question 4. _For example_

6. In paragraph 2, when Schell writes parenthetically that "because radiation causes no pain, animals, wandering at will through the environment, would not avoid it," he is being (a) amusing and witty; (b) sarcastic; (c) pompous; (d) ironic.

7. Look again at paragraph 3. Write the phrase that represents the main idea. A gamma ray dose of 10 crosoked body

8. In paragraph 4, Schell includes several quotations from Dr. Woodwell at the Brookhaven National Laboratory: "gross simplification" of the environment and "succession" of the environment is "delayed or even arrested," for example. Look again at these quotations. In terms of language, they are examples of (a) sneer words; (b) figurative language; (c) words with a negative connotation; (d) irony; (e) euphemisms.

9. Throughout the selection, and especially in paragraph 2, Schell discusses the ramifications of radioactive poison on mammals, but he excludes human beings. Is this omission an oversight? Is it defensible in any way? _____

10. For the selection as a whole, what pattern of organization predominates? (a) chronological; (b) spatial; (c) deductive; (d) variation of deductive; (e) inductive; (f) emphatic. Again, defend your choice.
_____

11. The word "republic" in the title of this selection, "A Republic of Insects and Grass," seems to be a curious choice. Can you explain why Schell used it? What does the word connote? What is Schell implying?
_____

12. For what audience would you say Schell is writing? (a) pro-nuclear activists; (b) nuclear physicists or other highly trained scientists; (c) anti-nuclear activists; (d) the general public. Again, explain your choice.
_____

D. Vocabulary   For each italicized word from the selection, choose the best definition according to the context in which it appears.

1. in a nuclear *holocaust* [paragraph 1]: (a) sacrificial offering by means of fire; (b) great destruction by fire; (c) any widespread destruction; (d) the extermination of the human race.

2. the *vulnerability* of the environment [2]: (a) susceptibility to injury or danger; (b) fragile nature; (c) manipulation; (d) resuscitation; revitalization.

3. through direct *ingestion* by animals [1]: (a) inhalation; (b) absorption; (c) contamination; (d) taking in; eating.

4. a large variety of plants and animals were *irradiated* [2]: (a) contaminated because of radiation; (b) made sick from radiation poisoning; (c) exposed to radiation; (d) cured by radiation treatments.

5. in order to *ascertain* the lethal dose [2]: (a) discover; (b) publish; make known; (c) measure; (d) establish as legal.

6. in order to ascertain the *lethal* dose [2]: that which (a) is acceptable; (b) causes death; (c) is the minimal amount; (d) is legal.

7. the prediction of many *gross* ecological consequences of a nuclear attack [2]: (a) unimaginable; (b) invisible; hidden; (c) total; entire; (d) catastrophic.

8. some of the most *ravaging* species on earth [2]: (a) causing destruction; (b) physically repulsive; (c) physically attractive; handsome; (d) fertile; capable of reproducing quickly.

9. many of the insects could be expected to survive *disproportionately* [2]: out of proportion with regard to (a) their shape; (b) their size; (c) their numbers; (d) other, less harmful species.

10. the *demise* of their natural predators [2]: (a) decrease in the population; (b) change in habitat; (c) death; (d) inability to reproduce.

11. the lethal doses for most *deciduous* trees [3]: referring to trees (a) that shed their leaves at the end of the growing season; (b) that bear cones; (c) that remain green throughout the year; (d) whose leaves change colors with the seasons.

12. the country could be subjected to *incendiary* levels of thermal pulses [3]: referring to something that (a) causes fire; (b) produces contaminants; (c) is incapable of being measured; (d) is not capable of surviving.

13. the land on which the vegetation grew is *degraded* [4]: (a) worn down by erosion; (b) exposed to harmful elements; (c) exhausted; weakened; (d) deprived of crucial nutrients.

14. the growth of algae and microscopic organisms, which, in turn, *deplete* the oxygen content of the water [4]: (a) regulate; (b) restore; (c) use up; (d) cause to fluctuate.

15. *hardy* species, such as moss and grass [4]: (a) stalwart and rugged; (b) courageous; stouthearted; (c) healthy; (d) capable of surviving unfavorable conditions.

16. these effects are *imponderables* [4]: things that are incapable of (a) being thought about; (b) being measured precisely; (c) occurring; (d) being solved.

E. Questions for Analysis

1. How well has Schell succeeded in explaining the effects of nuclear attack on the environment?

2. What was your attitude toward nuclear armaments before you read this selection? Did the piece change your thinking? If so, how?

part 5 ‖ READING SHORT STORIES

Literature, Aristotle wrote, serves to delight and to instruct. Modern critics do not consider it fashionable to speak of the didactic (instructional) aspects of literature; the term has undoubtedly gotten a bad name from the sort of moralistic poetry and fiction that has been the vogue at various times throughout literary history. But Aristotle's phrase does not mean that literature should "instruct" us in the moralistic sense. It means, rather, that we read literature both for enjoyment and for its revelation of human experience and behavior. Besides providing you with a different kind of opportunity for sharpening your reading skills, short stories have been included in this book to give you enjoyment and to increase your understanding of what it is to be a human being.

ANALYZING THE SHORT STORY

The most common complaint students make about the study of literature —particularly in high school and introductory college courses—is that analysis ruins the pleasure of reading; as if examining the structure of a story (or a poem or a play) somehow destroys one's appreciation of it. Surely, literary analysis is unrewarding and meaningless when, on an exam, one must answer such questions as: What was the color of Mrs. Finch's little dog's collar? Analysis—as you know from Part 1—means breaking down a subject to see how each part functions in relation to the whole. Rather than killing one's enthusiasm or spontaneous enjoyment, analysis has—or should have —the opposite effect, to increase your understanding. The more you understand how a story or a poem works, the more likely you are to enjoy the experience of it. A car buff, for example, who has a detailed knowledge and understanding of the various internal workings of a car derives much more pleasure from it than does the sort of driver who merely knows how to make the thing go.

First, we should arrive at a broad definition of what a short story is. It is a fairly brief piece of narrative prose, and it is fictional. The length is not really important, but a rough measure for a short story is that it can be anywhere from two to three pages, to as many as thirty or forty pages, long. Stories longer than that are more apt to be classified as another form: the long short story or novella ("little novel"). More important than its length, however, is what the story accomplishes. Typically, a short story provides the reader with a series of actions or events that reveal a single aspect of a character. In contrast, a novel usually reveals many aspects of the life and experience of a character or of several characters. And, whereas a novel may describe a character's entire life, or even the lives of several generations of characters, the action of a short story is compressed, so that we see a character at a particular time in his or her life. "Miss Brill," by Katherine Mansfield, illustrates this compression well.

The action of a story is divided into two parts: rising action and falling action. During the rising action, the author provides the background or exposition, introduces the characters, describes the scene (where, when), and sets the action in motion. The main character, called the *protagonist,* encounters a conflict, a tension between himself and something else— perhaps another character, a custom or belief at odds with his own nature, an element in the physical environment, or perhaps even an element in his or her own nature. "How Much Land Does a Man Need?" by Leo Tolstoy is a good example of a story which shows us an internal conflict in the protagonist's soul—the conflict between his essentially good nature and his greed as he tries to obtain more and more land. John Updike's "Separating" shows us a conflict between characters, as a husband and wife are confronted with the task of telling their children about their imminent divorce.

The tension or conflict increases as the story progresses; that is, the action "rises" until a crisis, or turning point, is revealed. After the crisis, the action changes to a falling action, in which the character either resolves the conflict or is changed in some way. Again, Katherine Mansfield's "Miss Brill" offers a particularly skillful and sharply delineated transition from rising to falling action, as Miss Brill discovers the truth about the illusory world she has been living in. Not all stories have "happy endings"; in fact, in this group of four stories, none have. Some stories end ambiguously, so that we are not exactly sure what would happen to the characters if the action were to continue after the story ends. Again, in John Updike's "Separating," we know that Richard Jr. feels terrible anguish from his parents' impending divorce, but we cannot be certain how he will adjust to it, or even if he will adjust to it at all. The essential principle, however, is that the action, the conflict, and the crisis reveal to us something new about the character—an aspect or a truth that we were not aware of at the story's beginning.

The diagram at the top of the next page outlines the *plot*—the sequence of events—of a typical short story. (Keep in mind that not every story you read will conform exactly to this model.)

Besides plot, the second primary element in fiction is *character*—the person as he (or she) is described and revealed to us, his actions, his responses to events around him, his behavior. Out of plot and character comes the third basic element in fiction—*theme*. The theme is the underlying idea the author wishes to get across, the idea that gives rise to plot and character. In other words, the theme is embodied in the events of the story and in the way the character is shown to respond to them.

Other considerations are important, too. For example, from whose point of view do we see the events of the story? What tone do the author's words

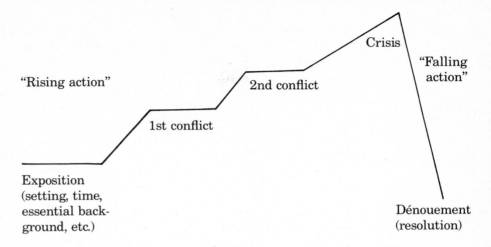

"Rising action"

Crisis

"Falling action"

2nd conflict

1st conflict

Exposition
(setting, time,
essential back-
ground, etc.)

Dénouement
(resolution)

reveal? In short stories, everything works together, and in a well-constructed story, everything counts. The reader's task is a complex one, requiring not just attention to overall structure but to little things as well. For example, in Flannery O'Connor's story, "Good Country People," the main character, whose name is Joy (ironically, given her sullen demeanor), is gradually revealed to us in a series of descriptive details. One such detail comes early in the story when we learn that Joy has legally changed her name to Hulga, which sounds to her mother (and undoubtedly to the reader, too) like "the broad blank hull of a battleship." What does this name change suggest about Joy–Hulga's self-image? The details, then, are there for a purpose: to reveal the characters and their motivations, and to provide us with clues as to what is underneath the surface.

There is a lot more to be said about the short story and its technical aspects, but these matters are probably best taken up in greater detail in a literature course.

GENERAL QUESTIONS ABOUT THE SHORT STORY

Each of the four stories in this section is followed by a set of questions. However, those questions by no means exhaust the possibilities for analysis. Here are some general questions on plot, character, and theme that you can ask yourself as you read each story.

Questions About Plot

1. How are the incidents that make up the plot related to each other? Is there a cause–effect relationship between these incidents?
2. Does the plot suggest conflict? If so, what is responsible for it?
3. Where does the crisis occur? What provokes it?
4. Is the conflict resolved, and if it is, is it resolved satisfactorily?

5. Is there any evidence of irony in the plot? (In literature, irony refers to information that is provided to the reader but that the characters are unaware of.) Does the plot suggest any additional interpretations—ones which the reader can perhaps see but the character or characters cannot?

Questions About Character

1. Define each character in terms of his or her "essence," behavior, and motivation.
2. How are the characters revealed to us?
3. Why do the characters behave as they do? Are their actions consistent with what has been revealed to us about them?
4. Do any characters change during the course of the story?
5. What is your response to each character? What is the basis for your attitude?
6. Do any of the characters stand for something greater than themselves? That is, are their actions meant to be symbolic of something outside themselves?

Questions About Theme

1. What is the theme, and how is it embodied in the story?
2. In what ways do plot and character work to convey the theme?
3. Is there more than one theme?
4. What do we learn about human existence from the story?

Short Story 1   **How Much Land Does a Man Need?**
Leo Tolstoy

Count Leo Tolstoy (1828–1910) was born in Russia at Yasnaya Polyana, his family estate. In 1847, he gave up his studies at Kazan University, and volunteered for military duty, becoming a junior officer during the Crimean War. In 1882, Tolstoy married Sophie Behrs, a marriage which turned out to be bitterly unhappy. Tolstoy was always troubled by his sexual appetites and his position as a landowner. In his fiction, as well as in his dealings with the peasants on his estate, he praised the members of the peasant class for their simplicity and forbearance. This disparity between landowners and peasant is evident in "How Much Land Does a Man Need?" (published in 1886), which is perhaps more accurately called a parable than a short story. In addition to many short stories and short novels, Tolstoy is best known for producing two of the greatest novels in Western literature: *War and Peace* (1869) and *Anna Karenina* (1877). In his later years, Tolstoy renounced all physical comforts and embarked on a new philosophy based on a simplified Christianity. After his death, Yasnaya Polyana became a mecca for his religious followers. (Note: The reference in paragraph 7 to Pahóm's lying on top of the stove is puzzling to a non-Russian. Russian stoves were the center of the main living area. They were broad devices, resembling squat beehives, on which several people could sleep to enjoy their warmth.)

1   An elder sister came to visit her younger sister in the country. The elder was married to a tradesman in town, the younger to a peasant in the village. As the sisters sat over their tea talking, the elder began to boast of the advantages of town life: saying how comfortably they lived there, how well they dressed, what fine clothes her children wore, what good things they ate and drank, and how she went to the theatre, promenades, and entertainments.

2   The younger sister was piqued, and in turn disparaged the life of a tradesman, and stood up for that of a peasant.

3   "I would not change my way of life for yours," said she. "We may live roughly, but at least we are free from anxiety. You live in better style than we do, but though you often earn more than you need, you are very likely to lose all you have. You know the proverb, 'Loss and gain are brothers twain.' It often happens that people who are wealthy one day are begging their bread the next. Our way is safer. Though a peasant's life is not a fat one, it is a long one. We shall never grow rich, but we shall always have enough to eat."

4   The elder sister said sneeringly:

5   "Enough? Yes, if you like to share with the pigs and the calves! What do you know of elegance or manners! However much your goodman may slave, you will die as you are living—on a dung heap—and your children the same."

6   "Well, what of that?" replied the younger. "Of course our work is rough and coarse. But, on the other hand, it is sure, and we need not bow down to anyone. But you, in your towns, are surrounded by temptations; to-day all may be right, but to-morrow the Evil One may tempt your husband with cards, wine, or women, and all will go to ruin. Don't such things happen often enough?"

7   Pahóm, the master of the house, was lying on the top of the stove and he listened to the women's chatter.

8   "It is perfectly true," thought he. "Busy as we are from childhood tilling mother earth, we peasants have no time to let any nonsense settle in our heads. Our only trouble is that we haven't land enough. If I had plenty of land, I shouldn't fear the Devil himself!"

9   The women finished their tea, chatted a while about dress, and then cleared away the tea-things and lay down to sleep.

10   But the Devil had been sitting behind the stove, and had heard all that was said. He was pleased that the peasant's wife had led her husband into boasting, and that he had said that if he had plenty of land he would not fear the Devil himself.

11   "All right," thought the Devil. "We will have a tussle. I'll give you land enough; and by means of that land I will get you into my power."

2

12   Close to the village there lived a lady, a small landowner who had an estate of about three hundred acres.* She had always lived on good terms

---

*120 desyatíns. The desyatína is properly 2.7 acres; but in this story round numbers are used.

with the peasants until she engaged as her steward an old soldier, who took to burdening the people with fines. However careful Pahóm tried to be, it happened again and again that now a horse of his got among the lady's oats, now a cow strayed into her garden, now his calves found their way into her meadows—and he always had to pay a fine.

13   Pahóm paid up, but grumbled and, going home in a temper, was rough with his family. All through that summer, Pahóm had much trouble because of this steward, and he was even glad when winter came and the cattle had to be stabled. Though he grudged the fodder when they could no longer graze on the pasture-land, at least he was free from anxiety about them.

14   In the winter the news got about that the lady was going to sell her land and that the keeper of the inn on the high road was bargaining for it. When the peasants heard this they were very much alarmed.

15   "Well," thought they, "if the innkeeper gets the land, he will worry us with fines worse than the lady's steward. We all depend on that estate."

16   So the peasants went on behalf of their Commune, and asked the lady not to sell the land to the innkeeper, offering her a better price for it themselves. The lady agreed to let them have it. Then the peasants tried to arrange for the Commune to buy the whole estate, so that it might be held by them all in common. They met twice to discuss it, but could not settle the matter; the Evil One sowed discord among them and they could not agree. So they decided to buy the land individually, each according to his means; and the lady agreed to this plan as she had to the other.

17   Presently Pahóm heard that a neighbor of his was buying fifty acres, and that the lady had consented to accept one half in cash and to wait a year for the other half. Pahóm felt envious.

18   "Look at that," thought he, "the land is all being sold, and I shall get none of it. So he spoke to his wife.

19   "Other people are buying," said he, "and we must also buy twenty acres or so. Life is becoming impossible. That steward is simply crushing us with his fines."

20   So they put their heads together and considered how they could manage to buy it. They had one hundred rúbles laid by. They sold a colt and one half of their bees, hired out one of their sons as a laborer and took his wages in advance; borrowed the rest from a brother-in-law, and so scraped together half the purchase money.

21   Having done this, Pahóm chose out a farm of forty acres, some of it wooded, and went to the lady to bargain for it. They came to an agreement, and he shook hands with her upon it and paid her a deposit in advance. Then they went to town and signed the deeds; he paying half the price down, and undertaking to pay the remainder within two years.

22   So now Pahóm had land of his own. He borrowed seed, and sowed it on the land he had bought. The harvest was a good one, and within a year he had managed to pay off his debts both to the lady and to his brother-in-law. So he became a landowner, ploughing and sowing his own land, making hay on his own land, cutting his own trees, and feeding his cattle on his own pasture. When he went out to plough his fields, or to look at his growing

corn, or at his grass-meadows, his heart would fill with joy. The grass that grew and the flowers that bloomed there seemed to him unlike any that grew elsewhere. Formerly, when he had passed by that land, it had appeared the same as any other land, but now it seemed quite different.

3

23   So Pahóm was well-contented, and everything would have been right if the neighboring peasants would only not have trespassed on his corn-fields and meadows. He appealed to them most civilly, but they still went on: now the Communal herdsmen would let the village cows stray into his meadows, then horses from the night pasture would get among his corn. Pahóm turned them out again and again, and forgave their owners, and for a long time he forbore to prosecute any one. But at last he lost patience and complained to the District Court. He knew it was the peasants' want of land, and no evil intent on their part, that caused the trouble, but he thought:

24   "I cannot go on overlooking it or they will destroy all I have. They must be taught a lesson."

25   So he had them up, gave them one lesson, and then another, and two or three of the peasants were fined. After a time Pahóm's neighbors began to bear him a grudge for this, and would now and then let their cattle on to his land on purpose. One peasant even got into Pahóm's wood at night and cut down five young lime trees for their bark. Pahóm passing through the wood one day noticed something white. He came nearer and saw the stripped trunks lying on the ground, and close by stood the stumps where the trees had been. Pahóm was furious.

26   "If he had only cut one here and there it would have been bad enough," thought Pahóm, "but the rascal has actually cut down a whole clump. If I could only find out who did this, I would pay him out."

27   He racked his brain as to who it could be. Finally he decided: "It must be Simon—no one else could have done it." So he went to Simon's homestead to have a look round, but he found nothing, and only had an angry scene. However, he now felt more certain than ever that Simon had done it, and he lodged a complaint. Simon was summoned. The case was tried, and retried, and at the end of it all Simon was acquitted, there being no evidence against him. Pahóm felt still more aggrieved, and let his anger loose upon the Elder and the Judges.

28   "You let thieves grease your palms," said he. "If you were honest folk yourselves you would not let a thief go free."

29   So Pahóm quarrelled with the Judges and with his neighbors. Threats to burn his building began to be uttered. So though Pahóm had more land, his place in the Commune was much worse than before.

30   About this time a rumor got about that many people were moving to new parts.

31   "There's no need for me to leave my land," thought Pahóm. "But some of the others might leave our village and then there would be more room for us. I would take over their land myself and make my estate a bit bigger. I could then live more at ease. As it is, I am still too cramped to be comfortable."

32   One day Pahóm was sitting at home when a peasant, passing through the village, happened to call in. He was allowed to stay the night, and supper was given him. Pahóm had a talk with this peasant and asked him where he came from. The stranger answered that he came from beyond the Vólga, where he had been working. One word led to another, and the man went on to say that many people were settling in those parts. He told how some people from his village had settled there. They had joined the Commune, and had had twenty-five acres per man granted them. The land was so good, he said, that the rye sown on it grew as high as a horse, and so thick that five cuts of a sickle made a sheaf. One peasant, he said, had brought nothing with him but his bare hands, and now he had six horses and two cows of his own.

33   Pahóm's heart kindled with desire. He thought:

34   "Why should I suffer in this narrow hole, if one can live so well elsewhere? I will sell my land and my homestead here, and with the money I will start afresh over there and get everything new. In this crowded place one is always having trouble. But I must first go and find out all about it myself."

35   Towards summer he got ready and started. He went down the Vólga on a steamer to Samára, then walked another three hundred miles on foot, and at last reached the place. It was just as the stranger had said. The peasants had plenty of land: every man had twenty-five acres of Communal land given him for his use, and any one who had money could buy, besides, at a rúble an acre as much good freehold land as he wanted.

36   Having found out all he wished to know, Pahóm returned home as autumn came on, and began selling off his belongings. He sold his land at a profit, sold his homestead and all his cattle, and withdrew from membership in the Commune. He only waited till the spring, and then started with his family for the new settlement.

4

37   As soon as Pahóm and his family reached their new abode, he applied for admission into the Commune of a large village. He stood treat to the Elders and obtained the necessary documents. Five shares of Communal land were given him for his own and his sons' use: that is to say 125 acres (not all together, but in different fields) besides the use of the Communal pasture. Pahóm put up the buildings he needed, and bought cattle. Of the Communal land alone he had three times as much as at his former home, and the land was good corn-land. He was ten times better off than he had been. He had plenty of arable land and pasturage, and could keep as many head of cattle as he liked.

38   At first, in the bustle of building and settling down, Pahóm was pleased with it all, but when he got used to it he began to think that even here he had not enough land. The first year, he sowed wheat on his share of the Communal land and had a good crop. He wanted to go on sowing wheat, but had not enough Communal land for the purpose, and what he had already used was not available; for in those parts wheat is only sown on virgin soil

or on fallow land. It is sown for one or two years, and then the land lies fallow till it is again overgrown with prairie grass. There were many who wanted such land and there was not enough for all; so that people quarreled about it. Those who were better off wanted it for growing wheat, and those who were poor wanted it to let to dealers, so that they might raise money to pay their taxes. Pahóm wanted to sow more wheat, so he rented land from a dealer for a year. He sowed much wheat and had a fine crop, but the land was too far from the village—the wheat had to be carted more than ten miles. After a time Pahóm noticed that some peasant-dealers were living on separate farms and were growing wealthy; and he thought:

39 "If I were to buy some freehold land and have a homestead on it, it would be a different thing altogether. Then it would all be nice and compact."

40 The question of buying freehold land recurred to him again and again.

41 He went on in the same way for three years, renting land and sowing wheat. The seasons turned out well and the crops were good, so that he began to lay money by. He might have gone on living contentedly, but he grew tired of having to rent other people's land every year, and having to scramble for it. Wherever there was good land to be had, the peasants would rush for it and it was taken up at once, so that unless you were sharp about it you got none. It happened in the third year that he and a dealer together rented a piece of pasture-land from some peasants; and they had already ploughed it up, when there was some dispute and the peasants went to law about it, and things fell out so that the labor was all lost.

42 "If it were my own land," thought Pahóm, "I should be independent, and there would not be all this unpleasantness."

43 So Pahóm began looking out for land which he could buy; and he came across a peasant who had bought thirteen hundred acres, but having got into difficulties was willing to sell again cheap. Pahóm bargained and haggled with him, and at last they settled the price at 1,500 rúbles, part in cash and part to be paid later. They had all but clinched the matter when a passing dealer happened to stop at Pahóm's one day to get a feed for his horses. He drank tea with Pahóm and they had a talk. The dealer said that he was just returning from the land of the Bashkírs, far away, where he had bought thirteen thousand acres of land, all for 1,000 rúbles. Pahóm questioned him further, and the tradesman said:

44 "All one needs do is to make friends with the chiefs. I gave away about one hundred rúbles' worth of silk robes and carpets, besides a case of tea, and I gave wine to those who would drink it; and I got the land for less than a penny an acre."* And he showed Pahóm the title-deeds, saying:

45 "The land lies near a river, and the whole prairie is virgin soil."

46 Pahóm plied him with questions, and the tradesman said:

47 "There is more land there than you could cover if you walked a year, and it all belongs to the Bashkírs. They are as simple as sheep, and land can be got almost for nothing."

---

*Five kopéks for a desyatína.

48   "There now," thought Pahóm, "with my one thousand rúbles, why should I get only thirteen hundred acres, and saddle myself with a debt besides? If I take it out there, I can get more than ten times as much for the money."

5

49   Pahóm inquired how to get to the place, and as soon as the tradesman had left him, he prepared to go there himself. He left his wife to look after the homestead, and started on his journey taking his man with him. They stopped at a town on their way and bought a case of tea, some wine, and other presents, as the tradesman had advised. On and on they went until they had gone more than three hundred miles, and on the seventh day they came to a place where the Bashkírs had pitched their tents. It was all just as the tradesman had said. The people lived on the steppes, by a river, in felt-covered tents.* They neither tilled the ground, nor ate bread. Their cattle and horses grazed in herds on the steppe. The colts were tethered behind the tents, and the mares were driven to them twice a day. The mares were milked, and from the milk kumiss† was made. It was the women who prepared kumiss, and they also made cheese. As far as the men were concerned, drinking kumiss and tea, eating mutton, and playing on their pipes, was all they cared about. They were all stout and merry, and all the summer long they never thought of doing any work. They were quite ignorant, and knew no Russian, but were good-natured enough.

50   As soon as they saw Pahóm, they came out of their tents and gathered round their visitor. An interpreter was found, and Pahóm told them he had come about some land. The Bashkírs seemed very glad; they took Pahóm and led him into one of the best tents, where they made him sit on some down cushions placed on a carpet, while they sat round him. They gave him some tea and kumiss, and had a sheep killed, and gave him mutton to eat. Pahóm took presents out of his cart and distributed them among the Bashkírs, and divided the tea amongst them. The Bashkírs were delighted. They talked a great deal among themselves, and then told the interpreter to translate.

51   "They wish to tell you," said the interpreter, "that they like you, and that it is our custom to do all we can to please a guest and to repay him for his gifts. You have given us presents, now tell us which of the things we possess please you best, that we may present them to you."

52   "What pleases me best here," answered Pahóm, "is your land. Our land is crowded and the soil is exhausted; but you have plenty of land and it is good land. I never saw the like of it."

53   The interpreter translated. The Bashkírs talked among themselves for a while. Pahóm could not understand what they were saying, but saw that

---

*A kibítka is a movable dwelling, made up of detachable wooden frames, forming a round, and covered over with felt.
†Fermented mare's milk.

they were much amused and that they shouted and laughed. Then they were silent and looked at Pahóm while the interpreter said:

54 "They wish me to tell you that in return for your presents they will gladly give you as much land as you want. You have only to point it out with your hand and it is yours."

55 The Bashkírs talked again for a while and began to dispute. Pahóm asked what they were disputing about, and the interpreter told him that some of them thought they ought to ask their Chief about the land and not act in his absence, while others thought there was no need to wait for his return.

6

56 While the Bashkírs were disputing, a man in a large fox-fur cap appeared on the scene. They all became silent and rose to their feet. The interpreter said, "This is our Chief himself."

57 Pahóm immediately fetched the best dressing-gown and five pounds of tea, and offered these to the Chief. The Chief accepted them, and seated himself in the place of honor. The Bashkírs at once began telling him something. The Chief listened for a while, then made a sign with his head for them to be silent, and addressing himself to Pahóm, said in Russian:

58 "Well, let it be so. Choose whatever piece of land you like; we have plenty of it."

59 "How can I take as much as I like?" thought Pahóm. "I must get a deed to make it secure, or else they may say, 'It is yours,' and afterwards may take it away again."

60 "Thank you for your kind words," he said aloud. "You have much land, and I only want a little. But I should like to be sure which bit is mine. Could it not be measured and made over to me? Life and death are in God's hands. You good people give it to me, but your children might wish to take it away again."

61 "You are quite right," said the Chief. "We will make it over to you."

62 "I heard that a dealer had been here," continued Pahóm, "and that you gave him a little land, too, and signed title-deeds to that effect. I should like to have it done in the same way."

63 The Chief understood.

64 "Yes," replied he, "that can be done quite easily. We have a scribe, and we will go to town with you and have the deed properly sealed."

65 "And what will be the price?" asked Pahóm.

66 "Our price is always the same: one thousand rúbles a day."

67 Pahóm did not understand.

68 "A day? What measure is that? How many acres would that be?"

69 "We do not know how to reckon it out," said the Chief. "We sell it by the day. As much as you can go round on your feet in a day is yours, and the price is one thousand rúbles a day."

70 Pahóm was surprised.

71 "But in a day you can get round a large tract of land," he said.

72 The Chief laughed.

73 "It will all be yours!" said he. "But there is one condition: If you don't return on the same day to the spot whence you started, your money is lost."

74 "But how am I to mark the way that I have gone?"

75 "Why, we shall go to any spot you like, and stay there. You must start from that spot and make your round, taking a spade with you. Wherever you think necessary, make a mark. At every turning, dig a hole and pile up the turf; then afterwards we will go round with a plough from hole to hole. You may make as large a circuit as you please, but before the sun sets you must return to the place you started from. All the land you cover will be yours."

76 Pahóm was delighted. It was decided to start early next morning. They talked a while, and after drinking some more kumiss and eating some more mutton, they had tea again, and then the night came on. They gave Pahóm a feather-bed to sleep on, and the Bashkírs dispersed for the night, promising to assemble the next morning at daybreak and ride out before sunrise to the appointed spot.

7

77 Pahóm lay on the feather-bed, but could not sleep. He kept thinking about the land.

78 "What a large tract I will mark off!" thought he. "I can easily do thirty-five miles in a day. The days are long now, and within a circuit of thirty-five miles what a lot of land there will be! I will sell the poorer land, or let it to peasants, but I'll pick out the best and farm it. I will buy two oxteams, and hire two more laborers. About a hundred and fifty acres shall be plough-land, and I will pasture cattle on the rest."

79 Pahóm lay awake all night, and dozed off only just before dawn. Hardly were his eyes closed when he had a dream. He thought he was lying in that same tent and heard somebody chuckling outside. He wondered who it could be, and rose and went out, and he saw the Bashkír Chief sitting in front of the tent holding his sides and rolling about with laughter. Going nearer to the Chief, Pahóm asked: "What are you laughing at?" But he saw that it was no longer the Chief, but the dealer who had recently stopped at his house and had told him about the land. Just as Pahóm was going to ask, "Have you been here long?" he saw that it was not the dealer, but the peasant who had come up from the Vólga, long ago, to Pahóm's old home. Then he saw that it was not the peasant either, but the Devil himself with hoofs and horns, sitting there and chuckling, and before him lay a man barefoot, prostrate on the ground, with only trousers and a shirt on. And Pahóm dreamt that he looked more attentively to see what sort of a man it was that was lying there, and he saw that the man was dead, and that it was himself! He awoke horror-struck.

80 "What things one does dream," thought he.

81 Looking round he saw through the open door that the dawn was breaking.

82 "It's time to wake them up," thought he. "We ought to be starting."

83   He got up, roused his man (who was sleeping in his cart), bade him harness; and went to call the Bashkírs.

84   "It's time to go to the steppe to measure the land," he said.

85   The Bashkírs rose and assembled, and the Chief came too. Then they began drinking kumiss again, and offered Pahóm some tea, but he would not wait.

86   "If we are to go, let us go. It is high time," said he.

8

87   The Bashkírs got ready and they all started: some mounted on horses, and some in carts. Pahóm drove in his own small cart with his servant and took a spade with him. When they reached the steppe, the morning red was beginning to kindle. They ascended a hillock (called by the Bashkírs a *shikhan*) and dismounting from their carts and their horses, gathered in one spot. The Chief came up to Pahóm and stretching out his arm towards the plain:

88   "See," said he, "all this, as far as your eye can reach, is ours. You may have any part of it you like."

89   Pahóm's eyes glistened: it was all virgin soil, as flat as the palm of your hand, as black as the seed of a poppy, and in the hollows different kinds of grasses grew breast high.

90   The Chief took off his fox-fur cap, placed it on the ground and said:

91   "This will be the mark. Start from here, and return here again. All the land you go round shall be yours."

92   Pahóm took out his money and put it on the cap. Then he took off his outer coat, remaining in his sleeveless under-coat. He unfastened his girdle and tied it tight below his stomach, put a little bag of bread into the breast of his coat, and tying a flask of water to his girdle, he drew up the tops of his boots, took the spade from his man, and stood ready to start. He considered for some moments which way he had better go—it was tempting everywhere.

93   "No matter," he concluded, "I will go towards the rising sun."

94   He turned his face to the east, stretched himself, and waited for the sun to appear above the rim.

95   "I must lose no time," he thought, "and it is easier walking while it is still cool."

96   The sun's rays had hardly flashed above the horizon, before Pahóm, carrying the spade over his shoulder, went down into the steppe.

97   Pahóm started walking neither slowly nor quickly. After having gone a thousand yards he stopped, dug a hole, and placed pieces of turf one on another to make it more visible. Then he went on; and now that he had walked off his stiffness he quickened his pace. After a while he dug another hole.

98   Pahóm looked back. The hillock could be distinctly seen in the sunlight, with the people on it, and the glittering tires of the cart-wheels. At a rough guess Pahóm concluded that he had walked three miles. It was growing warmer; he took off his under-coat, flung it across his shoulder, and went

on again. It had grown quite warm now; he looked at the sun, it was time to think of breakfast.

99   "The first shift is done, but there are four in a day, and it is too soon yet to turn. But I will just take off my boots," said he to himself.

100   He sat down, took off his boots, stuck them into his girdle, and went on. It was easy walking now.

101   "I will go on for another three miles," thought he, "and then turn to the left. This spot is so fine, that it would be a pity to lose it. The further one goes, the better the land seems."

102   He went straight on for a while, and when he looked round, the hillock was scarcely visible and the people on it looked like black ants, and he could just see something glistening there in the sun.

103   "Ah," thought Pahóm, "I have gone far enough in this direction, it is time to turn. Besides I am in a regular sweat, and very thirsty."

104   He stopped, dug a large hole, and heaped up pieces of turf. Next he untied his flask, had a drink, and then turned sharply to the left. He went on and on; the grass was high, and it was very hot.

105   Pahóm began to grow tired: he looked at the sun and saw that it was noon.

106   "Well" he thought, "I must have a rest."

107   He sat down, and ate some bread and drank some water; but he did not lie down, thinking that if he did he might fall asleep. After sitting a little while, he went on again. At first he walked easily: the food had strengthened him; but it had become terribly hot and he felt sleepy, still he went on, thinking: "An hour to suffer, a life-time to live."

108   He went a long way in this direction also, and was about to turn to the left again, when he perceived a damp hollow: "It would be a pity to leave that out," he thought. "Flax would do well there." So he went on past the hollow, and dug a hole on the other side of it before he turned the corner. Pahóm looked towards the hillock. The heat made the air hazy: it seemed to be quivering, and through the haze the people on the hillock could scarcely be seen.

109   "Ah!" thought Pahóm, "I have made the sides too long; I must make this one shorter." And he went along the third side, stepping faster. He looked at the sun: it was nearly half-way to the horizon, and he had not yet done two miles of the third side of the square. He was still ten miles from the goal.

110   "No," he thought, "though it will make my land lop-sided, I must hurry back in a straight line now. I might go too far, and as it is I have a great deal of land."

111   So Pahóm hurriedly dug a hole, and turned straight towards the hillock.

9

112   Pahóm went straight towards the hillock, but he now walked with difficulty. He was done up with the heat, his bare feet were cut and bruised, and his legs began to fail. He longed to rest, but it was impossible if he meant

to get back before sunset. The sun waits for no man, and it was sinking lower and lower.

113   "Oh dear," he thought, "if only I have not blundered trying for too much! What if I am too late?"

114   He looked towards the hillock and at the sun. He was still far from his goal, and the sun was already near the rim.

115   Pahóm walked on and on; it was very hard walking but he went quicker and quicker. He pressed on, but was still far from the place. He began running, threw away his coat, his boots, his flask, and his cap, and kept only the spade which he used as a support.

116   "What shall I do," he thought again. "I have grasped too much and ruined the whole affair. I can't get there before the sun sets."

117   And this fear made him still more breathless. Pahóm went on running, his soaking shirt and trousers stuck to him and his mouth was parched. His breast was working like a blacksmith's bellows, his heart was beating like a hammer, and his legs were giving way as if they did not belong to him. Pahóm was seized with terror lest he should die of the strain.

118   Though afraid of death, he could not stop. "After having run all that way they will call me a fool if I stop now," thought he. And he ran on and on, and drew near and heard the Bashkírs yelling and shouting to him, and their cries inflamed his heart still more. He gathered his last strength and ran on.

119   The sun was close to the rim, and cloaked in mist looked large, and red as blood. Now, yes now, it was about to set! The sun was quite low, but he was also quite near his aim. Pahóm could already see the people on the hillock waving their arms to hurry him up. He could see the fox-fur cap on the ground and the money on it, and the Chief sitting on the ground holding his sides. And Pahóm remembered his dream.

120   "There is plenty of land," thought he, "but will God let me live on it? I have lost my life, I have lost my life! I shall never reach that spot!"

121   Pahóm looked at the sun, which had reached the earth: one side of it had already disappeared. With all his remaining strength he rushed on, bending his body forward so that his legs could hardly follow fast enough to keep him from falling. Just as he reached the hillock it suddenly grew dark. He looked up—the sun had already set! He gave a cry: "All my labor has been in vain," thought he, and was about to stop, but he heard the Bashkírs still shouting, and remembered that though to him, from below, the sun seemed to have set, they on the hillock could still see it. He took a long breath and ran up the hillock. It was still light there. He reached the top and saw the cap. Before it sat the Chief laughing and holding his sides. Again Pahóm remembered his dream, and he uttered a cry: his legs gave way beneath him, he fell forward and reached the cap with his hands.

122   "Ah, that's a fine fellow!" exclaimed the Chief. "He has gained much land!"

123   Pahóm's servant came running up and tried to raise him, but he saw that blood was flowing from his mouth. Pahóm was dead!

124   The Bashkírs clicked their tongues to show their pity.

[125] His servant picked up the spade and dug a grave long enough for Pahóm to lie in, and buried him in it. Six feet from his head to his heels was all he needed.

A. Questions for Analysis

1. The theme of temptation by the Devil is archetypal in literature (Adam and Eve in the Garden of Eden and Faust are but two such legends). How important is the presence of the Evil One in Tolstoy's story? Does Pahóm have free will, or are his actions and his subsequent downfall predetermined by the Evil One's intervention? Is there any evidence that Pahóm's destruction is inevitable, with or without the Evil One's presence?

2. How many disguises does the Evil One assume throughout the story? What is the impetus for his intervention in the characters' lives?

3. How do you interpret the Bashkírs' behavior? Why isn't Pahóm suspicious of their generous (and clearly unusual) offer to take as much land as he can walk in a day? How does their presence in the story (especially the Bashkír Chief's laughing and holding his sides) influence our perception of Pahóm and his downfall?

4. Is there any evidence in the story of foreshadowing (a device by which the outcome of the story is hinted at before it occurs)?

5. "How Much Land Does a Man Need?" is a parable—a story that imparts a moral truth. How would you state the moral truth implied by the story's action?

B. Vocabulary

For each italicized word from the story, choose the best definition according to the context in which it appears.

1. the younger sister was *piqued* [paragraph 2]: (a) had her curiosity aroused; (b) felt resentment; (c) angered; (d) mildly amused.

2. in turn *disparaged* the life of a tradesman [2]: (a) praised; (b) envied; (c) questioned; (d) belittled.

3. *tilling* mother earth [8]: (a) understanding; (b) cultivating; (c) doing difficult work; (d) respecting.

4. he *grudged* the fodder [13]: (a) counted carefully; (b) gave reluctantly; (c) harbored a resentment toward; (d) was generous with.

5. the Evil One *sowed discord* among them [16]: (a) spread false rumors; (b) increased their greed; (c) encouraged dissension and disagreement; (d) dangled enticing temptations before.

6. he appealed to them most *civilly* [23]: (a) bitterly; (b) sarcastically; (c) tearfully; (d) politely.

7. he *forbore* to prosecute any one [23—past tense of *forbear*]: (a) refrained; (b) decided; (c) persisted; (d) remained indecisive.

8. Simon was *acquitted* [27]: (a) sentenced to prison; (b) found guilty; (c) cleared from blame; (d) bound over for trial.

9. Pahóm felt still more *aggrieved* [27]: (a) treated unjustly by a decision of a court; (b) saddened; (c) annoyed; (d) alarmed; distressed.

10. you let thieves *grease your palms* [28]: (a) persuade you with false testimony; (b) make a mockery of court proceedings; (c) deceive you with clever arguments; (d) bribe you.

11. Pahóm's heart *kindled* with desire [33]: (a) stirred up; lit up; (b) filled; (c) made passionate; (d) tempted.

12. he had plenty of *arable* land [37]: (a) able to be grazed on; (b) fit for cultivation; (c) cleared of obstacles; (d) suitable for grazing.

13. wheat is sown only on *virgin* soil [38]: (a) pure; in an untouched state; (b) unused; uncultivated; (c) already developed; cultivated; (d) rich; abundant in nutrients.

14. on *fallow* land [38]: describing land that is (a) cultivated year-round; (b) plowed but left unseeded during a growing season; (c) suitable only for wheat or other grains; (d) extraordinarily fertile and productive.

15. *prostrate* on the ground [79]: (a) kneeling; (b) lying face up; (c) lying face down; (d) lying in the prayer position.

Short Story 2   ## Miss Brill
Katherine Mansfield

Born in Wellington, New Zealand, Katherine Mansfield (1888–1923) published her first book of stories, *In a German Pension*, in 1911. Two more collections followed: *Bliss and Other Stories* (1920) and *The Garden Party* (1922). She died in France of tuberculosis, at the peak of her success, at the age of thirty-four.

1   Although it was so brilliantly fine—the blue sky powdered with gold and great spots of light like white wine splashed over the Jardins Publiques—Miss Brill was glad that she had decided on her fur. The air was motionless, but when you opened your mouth there was just a faint chill, like a chill from a glass of iced water before you sip, and now and again a leaf came drifting—from nowhere, from the sky. Miss Brill put up her hand and touched her fur. Dear little thing! It was nice to feel it again. She had taken it out of its box that afternoon, shaken out the moth-powder, given it a good brush, and rubbed the life back into the dim little eyes. "What has been happening to me?" said the sad little eyes. Oh, how sweet it was to see them snap at her again from the red eiderdown! . . . But the nose, which was of some black composition, wasn't at all firm. It must have had a knock, somehow. Never mind—a little dab of black sealing-wax when the time came—when it was absolutely necessary. . . . Little rogue! Yes, she really felt like that about it. Little rogue biting its tail just by her left ear. She could have taken it off and laid it on her lap and stroked it. She felt a tingling in her hands and arms, but that came from walking, she supposed. And when she breathed, something light and sad—no, not sad, exactly—something gentle seemed to move in her bosom.

2   There were a number of people out this afternoon, far more than last Sunday. And the band sounded louder and gayer. That was because the

Season had begun. For although the band played all the year round on Sundays, out of season it was never the same. It was like some one playing with only the family to listen; it didn't care how it played with only the family to listen; it didn't care how it played if there weren't any strangers present. Wasn't the conductor wearing a new coat, too? She was sure it was new. He scraped with his foot and flapped his arms like a rooster about to crow, and the bandsmen sitting in the green rotunda blew out their cheeks and glared at the music. Now there came a little "flutey" bit—very pretty!— a little chain of bright drops. She was sure it would be repeated. It was; she lifted her head and smiled.

3   Only two people shared her "special" seat: a fine old man in a velvet coat, his hands clasped over a huge carved walking-stick, and a big old woman, sitting upright, with a roll of knitting on her embroidered apron. They did not speak. This was disappointing, for Miss Brill always looked forward to the conversation. She had become really quite expert, she thought, at listening as though she didn't listen, at sitting in other people's lives just for a minute while they talked round her.

4   She glanced, sideways, at the old couple. Perhaps they would go soon. Last Sunday, too, hadn't been as interesting as usual. An Englishman and his wife, he wearing a dreadful Panama hat and she button boots. And she'd gone on the whole time about how she ought to wear spectacles; she knew she needed them; but that it was no good getting any; they'd be sure to break and they'd never keep on. And he'd been so patient. He'd suggested everything—gold rims, the kind that curved round your ears, little pads inside the bridge. No, nothing would please her. "They'll always be sliding down my nose!" Miss Brill had wanted to shake her.

5   The old people sat on the bench, still as statues. Never mind, there was always the crowd to watch. To and fro, in front of the flower-beds and the band rotunda, the couples and groups paraded, stopped to talk, to greet, to buy a handful of flowers from the old beggar who had his tray fixed to the railings. Little children ran among them, swooping and laughing; little boys with big white silk bows under their chins, little girls, little French dolls, dressed up in velvet and lace. And sometimes a tiny staggerer came suddenly rocking into the open from under the trees, stopped, stared, and suddenly sat down "flop," until its small high-stepping mother, like a young hen, rushed scolding to its rescue. Other people sat on the benches and green chairs, but they were nearly always the same, Sunday after Sunday, and—Miss Brill had often noticed—there was something funny about nearly all of them. They were odd, silent, nearly all old, and from the way they stared they looked as though they'd just come from dark little rooms or even—even cupboards!

6   Behind the rotunda the slender trees with yellow leaves down drooping, and through them just a line of sea, and beyond the blue sky with gold-veined clouds.

7   Tum-tum-tum tiddle-um! tum tiddley-um tum ta! blew the band.

8   Two young girls in red came by and two young soldiers in blue met them, and they laughed and paired and went off arm-in-arm. Two peasant

women with funny straw hats passed, gravely, leading beautiful smoke-coloured donkeys. A cold, pale nun hurried by. A beautiful woman came along and dropped her bunch of violets, and a little boy ran after to hand them to her, and she took them and threw them away as if they'd been poisoned. Dear me! Miss Brill didn't know whether to admire that or not! And now an ermine toque and a gentleman in grey met just in front of her. He was tall, stiff, dignified, and she was wearing the ermine toque she'd bought when her hair was yellow. Now everything, her hair, her face, even her eyes, was the same colour as the shabby ermine, and her hand, in its cleaned glove, lifted to dab her lips, was a tiny yellowish paw. Oh, she was so pleased to see him—delighted! She rather thought they were going to meet that afternoon. She described where she'd been—everywhere, here, there, along by the sea. The day was so charming—didn't he agree? And wouldn't he, perhaps? . . . But he shook his head, lighted a cigarette, slowly breathed a great deep puff into her face, and, even while she was still talking and laughing, flicked the match away and walked on. The ermine toque was alone; she smiled more brightly than ever. But even the band seemed to know what she was feeling and played more softly, played tenderly, and the drum beat, "The Brute! The Brute!" over and over. What would she do? What was going to happen now? But as Miss Brill wondered, the ermine toque turned, raised her hand as though she'd seen someone else, much nicer, just over there, and pattered away. And the band changed again and played more quickly, more gaily than ever, and the old couple on Miss Brill's seat got up and marched away, and such a funny old man with long whiskers hobbled along in time to the music and was nearly knocked over by four girls walking abreast.

9   Oh, how fascinating it was! How she enjoyed it! How she loved sitting here, watching it all! It was like a play. It was exactly like a play. Who could believe the sky at the back wasn't painted? But it wasn't till a little brown dog trotted on solemn and then slowly trotted off, like a little "theatre" dog, a little dog that had been drugged, that Miss Brill discovered what it was that made it so exciting. They were all on the stage. They weren't only the audience, not only looking on; they were acting. Even she had a part and came every Sunday. No doubt somebody would have noticed if she hadn't been there; she was part of the performance after all. How strange she'd never thought of it like that before! And yet it explained why she made such a point of starting from home at just the same time each week—so as not to be late for the performance—and it also explained why she had quite a queer, shy feeling at telling her English pupils how she spent her Sunday afternoons. No wonder! Miss Brill nearly laughed out loud. She was on the stage. She thought of the old invalid gentleman to whom she read the newspaper four afternoons a week while he slept in the garden. She had got quite used to the frail head on the cotton pillow, the hollowed eyes, the open mouth and the high pinched nose. If he'd been dead she mightn't have noticed for weeks; she wouldn't have minded. But suddenly he knew he was having the paper read to him by an actress! "An actress!" The old head lifted; two points of light quivered in the old eyes. "An actress—are ye?"

And Miss Brill smoothed the newspaper as though it were the manuscript of her part and said gently: "Yes, I have been an actress for a long time."

10   The band had been having a rest. Now they started again. And what they played was warm, sunny, yet there was just a faint chill—a something, what was it?—not sadness—no, not sadness—a something that made you want to sing. The tune lifted, lifted, the light shone; and it seemed to Miss Brill that in another moment all of them, all the whole company, would begin singing. The young ones, the laughing ones who were moving together, they would begin, and the men's voices, very resolute and brave, would join them. And then she too, she too, and the others on the benches—they would come in with a kind of accompaniment—something low, that scarcely rose or fell, something so beautiful—moving. . . . And Miss Brill's eyes filled with tears and she looked smiling at all the other members of the company. Yes, we understand, we understand, she thought—though what they understood she didn't know.

11   Just at that moment a boy and a girl came and sat down where the old couple had been. They were beautifully dressed; they were in love. The hero and heroine, of course, just arrived from his father's yacht. And still soundlessly singing, still with that trembling smile, Miss Brill prepared to listen.

12   "No, not now," said the girl. "Not here, I can't."

13   "But why? Because of that stupid old thing at the end there?" asked the boy. "Why does she come here at all—who wants her? Why doesn't she keep her silly old mug at home?"

14   "It's her fu-fur which is so funny," giggled the girl. "It's exactly like a fried whiting."

15   "Ah, be off with you!" said the boy in an angry whisper. Then: "Tell me, ma petite chérie—"

16   "No, not here," said the girl. "Not *yet*."

17   On her way home she usually bought a slice of honey-cake at the baker's. It was her Sunday treat. Sometimes there was an almond in her slice, sometimes not. It made a great difference. If there was an almond it was like carrying home a tiny present—a surprise—something that might very well not have been there. She hurried on the almond Sundays and struck the match for the kettle in quite a dashing way.

18   But to-day she passed the baker's by, climbed the stairs, went into the little dark room—her room like a cupboard—and sat down on the red eiderdown. She sat there for a long time. The box that the fur came out of was on the bed. She unclasped the necklet quickly; quickly, without looking, laid it inside. But when she put the lid on she thought she heard something crying.

A. Questions for Analysis

1. Who is Miss Brill? From the details Mansfield provides, what sort of life does she lead?

2. How does Miss Brill perceive herself? How does she perceive the people around her?

3. For Miss Brill, what do the Jardins Publiques (the public gardens) represent? Who are the gardens' usual occupants? In what way does Miss Brill see herself as different from them?

4. How does Miss Brill like to occupy herself on Sundays during the Season? How are we to interpret her observations about the people she watches and the conversations she overhears?

5. In paragraph 8, through whose eyes are we seeing the people? For example, look again at the exchange between the "ermine toque" and the "gentleman in grey" in paragraph 8. Who is the woman with the ermine toque, in actuality? What has really taken place between these two?

6. What is ironic about Miss Brill's interpretation of the scene in paragraph 9?

7. In what way does Miss Brill change during the course of the story? What is the impetus for that change? How are we to interpret her actions in paragraph 18? When she puts her fur back into its box, what is crying?

8. Is Miss Brill a tragic figure, or a silly, ridiculous figure? How do you think Mansfield intends us to see her? Point to details that might suggest how Mansfield intends us to respond.

B. Vocabulary   For each italicized word from the story, choose the best definition according to the context in which it appears.

1. little *rogue* [paragraph 1]: (a) beast; (b) monster; (c) scamp; (d) thief.

2. two peasant women passed, *gravely* [8]: (a) hurriedly; (b) in a dignified manner; (c) nervously; (d) importantly.

3. the men's voices, very *resolute* and brave [10]: (a) unwavering; (b) courageous; (c) full-throated; (d) loud.

Short Story 3   **Separating**
John Updike

John Updike (1932–   ) is one of America's foremost writers. Born in Shillington, Pennsylvania, he attended public schools and graduated from Harvard in 1954. He spent a year in Oxford, England, studying at the Ruskin School of Drawing and Fine Arts and, from 1955 to 1957, he was a member of the staff of *The New Yorker*. He is the author of six collections of short fiction and nine novels. Probably the best known of his novels are those in the "Rabbit" trilogy: *Rabbit, Run; Rabbit Redux;* and *Rabbit Is Rich*. "Separating," which was reissued in a collection of stories called *Problems and Other Stories*, first appeared in *The New Yorker*.

1   The day was fair. Brilliant. All that June the weather had mocked the Maples' internal misery with solid sunlight—golden shafts and cascades of green in which their conversations had wormed unseeing, their sad murmuring selves the only stain in Nature. Usually by this time of the year they had acquired tans; but when they met their elder daughter's plane on her return from a year in England they were almost as pale as

she, though Judith was too dazzled by the sunny opulent jumble of her native land to notice. They did not spoil her homecoming by telling her immediately. Wait a few days, let her recover from jet lag, had been one of their formulations, in that string of gray dialogues—over coffee, over cocktails, over Cointreau—that had shaped the strategy of their dissolution, while the earth performed its annual stunt of renewal unnoticed beyond their closed windows. Richard had thought to leave at Easter; Joan had insisted they wait until the four children were at last assembled, with all exams passed and ceremonies attended, and the bauble of summer to console them. So he had drudged away, in love, in dread, repairing screens, getting the mowers sharpened, rolling and patching their new tennis court.

2   The court, clay, had come through its first winter pitted and windswept bare of redcoat. Years ago the Maples had observed how often, among their friends, divorce followed a dramatic home improvement, as if the marriage were making one last effort to live; their own worst crisis had come amid the plaster dust and exposed plumbing of a kitchen renovation. Yet, a summer ago, as canary-yellow bulldozers gaily churned a grassy, daisy-dotted knoll into a muddy plateau, and a crew of pigtailed young men raked and tamped clay into a plane, this transformation did not strike them as ominous, but festive in its impudence; their marriage could rend the earth for fun. The next spring, waking each day at dawn to a sliding sensation as if the bed were being tipped, Richard found the barren tennis court—its net and tapes still rolled in the barn—an environment congruous with his mood of purposeful desolation, and the crumbling of handfuls of clay into cracks and holes (dogs had frolicked on the court in a thaw; rivulets had eroded trenches) an activity suitably elemental and interminable. In his sealed heart he hoped the day would never come.

3   Now it was here. A Friday. Judith was re-acclimated; all four children were assembled, before jobs and camps and visits again scattered them. Joan thought they should be told one by one. Richard was for making an announcement at the table. She said, "I think just making an announcement is a cop-out. They'll start quarrelling and playing to each other instead of focusing. They're each individuals, you know, not just some corporate obstacle to your freedom."

4   "O.K., O.K. I agree." Joan's plan was exact. That evening, they were giving Judith a belated welcome-home dinner, of lobster and champagne. Then, the party over, they, the two of them, who nineteen years before would push her in a baby carriage along Fifth Avenue to Washington Square, were to walk her out of the house, to the bridge across the salt creek, and tell her, swearing her to secrecy. Then Richard Jr., who was going directly from work to a rock concert in Boston, would be told, either late when he returned on the train or early Saturday morning before he went off to his job; he was seventeen and employed as one of a golf-course maintenance crew. Then the two younger children, John and Margaret, could, as the morning wore on, be informed.

5   "Mopped up, as it were," Richard said.

6   "Do you have any better plan? That leaves you the rest of Saturday to answer any questions, pack, and make your wonderful departure."

7   "No," he said, meaning he had no better plan, and agreed to hers, though to him it showed an edge of false order, a hidden plea for control, like Joan's long chore lists and financial accountings and, in the days when he first knew her, her too-copious lecture notes. Her plan turned one hurdle for him into four—four knife-sharp walls, each with a sheer blind drop on the other side.

8   All spring he had moved through a world of insides and outsides, of barriers and partitions. He and Joan stood as a thin barrier between the children and the truth. Each moment was a partition, with the past on one side and the future on the other, a future containing this unthinkable *now*. Beyond four knifelike walls a new life for him waited vaguely. His skull cupped a secret, a white face, a face both frightened and soothing, both strange and known, that he wanted to shield from tears, which he felt all about him, solid as the sunlight. So haunted, he had become obsessed with battening down the house against his absence, replacing screens and sash cords, hinges and latches—a Houdini making things snug before his escape.

9   The lock. He had still to replace a lock on one of the doors of the screened porch. The task, like most such, proved more difficult than he had imagined. The old lock, aluminum frozen by corrosion, had been deliberately rendered obsolete by manufacturers. Three hardware stores had nothing that even approximately matched the mortised hole its removal (surprisingly easy) left. Another hole had to be gouged, with bits too small and saws too big, and the old hole fitted with a block of wood—the chisels dull, the saw rusty, his fingers thick with lack of sleep. The sun poured down, beyond the porch, on a world of neglect. The bushes already needed pruning, the windward side of the house was shedding flakes of paint, rain would get in when he was gone, insects, rot, death. His family, all those he would lose, filtered through the edges of his awareness as he struggled with screw holes, splinters, opaque instructions, minutiae of metal.

10   Judith sat on the porch, a princess returned from exile. She regaled them with stories of fuel shortages, of bomb scares in the Underground, of Pakistani workmen loudly lusting after her as she walked past on her way to dance school. Joan came and went, in and out of the house, calmer than she should have been, praising his struggles with the lock as if this were one more and not the last of their long succession of shared chores. The younger of his sons for a few minutes held the rickety screen door while his father clumsily hammered and chiseled, each blow a kind of sob in Richard's ears. His younger daughter, having been at a slumber party, slept on the porch hammock through all the noise—heavy and pink, trusting and forsaken. Time, like the sunlight, continued relentlessly; the sunlight slowly slanted. Today was one of the longest days. The lock clicked, worked. He was through. He had a drink; he drank it on the porch, listening to his daughter. "It was so sweet," she was saying, "during the worst of it, how all the

butchers and bakery shops kept open by candlelight. They're all so plucky and cute. From the papers, things sounded so much worse here—people shooting people in gas lines, and everybody freezing."

[11]   Richard asked her, "Do you still want to live in England forever?" *Forever:* the concept, now a reality upon him, pressed and scratched at the back of his throat.

[12]   "No," Judith confessed, turning her oval face to him, its eyes still childishly far apart, but the lips set as over something succulent and satisfactory. "I was anxious to come home. I'm an American." She was a woman. They had raised her; he and Joan had endured together to raise her, alone of the four. The others had still some raising left in them. Yet it was the thought of telling Judith—the image of her, their first baby, walking between them arm in arm to the bridge—that broke him. The partition between his face and the tears broke. Richard sat down to the celebratory meal with the back of his throat aching; the champagne, the lobster seemed phases of sunshine; he saw them and tasted them through tears. He blinked, swallowed, croakily joked about hay fever. The tears would not stop leaking through; they came not through a hole that could be plugged but through a permeable spot in a membrane, steadily, purely, endlessly, fruitfully. They became, his tears, a shield for himself against these others—their faces, the fact of their assembly, a last time as innocents, at a table where he sat the last time as head. Tears dropped from his nose as he broke the lobster's back; salt flavored his champagne as he sipped it; the raw clench at the back of his throat was delicious. He culd not help himself.

[13]   His children tried to ignore his tears. Judith, on his right, lit a cigarette, gazed upward in the direction of her too energetic, too sophisticated exhalation; on her other side, John earnestly bent his face to the extraction of the last morsels—legs, tail segments—from the scarlet corpse. Joan, at the opposite end of the table, glanced at him surprised, her reproach displaced by a quick grimace, of forgiveness, or of salute to his superior gift of strategy. Between them, Margaret, no longer called Bean, thirteen and large for her age, gazed from the other side of his pane of tears as if into a shopwindow at something she coveted—at her father, a crystalline heap of splinters and memories. It was not she, however, but John who, in the kitchen, as they cleared the plates and carapaces away, asked Joan the question: *"Why is Daddy crying?"*

[14]   Richard heard the question but not the murmured answer. Then he heard Bean cry, "Oh, no-oh!"—the faintly dramatized exclamation of one who had long expected it.

[15]   John returned to the table carrying a bowl of salad. He nodded tersely at his father and his lips shaped the conspiratorial words "She told."

[16]   "Told what?" Richard asked aloud, insanely.

[17]   The boy sat down as if to rebuke his father's distraction with the example of his own good manners. He said quietly, "The separation."

[18]   Joan and Margaret returned; the child, in Richard's twisted vision, seemed diminished in size, and relieved, relieved to have had the bogieman at last proved real. He called out to her—the distances at the table

had grown immense—"You knew, you always knew," but the clenching at the back of his throat prevented him from making sense of it. From afar he heard Joan talking, levelly, sensibly, reciting what they had prepared: it was a separation for the summer, an experiment. She and Daddy both agreed it would be good for them; they needed space and time to think; they liked each other but did not make each other happy enough, somehow.

19   Judith, imitating her mother's factual tone, but in her youth off-key, too cool, said, "I think it's silly. You should either live together or get divorced."

20   Richard's crying, like a wave that has crested and crashed, had become tumultuous; but it was overtopped by another tumult, for John, who had been so reserved, now grew larger and larger at the table. Perhaps his younger sister's being credited with knowing set him off. "Why didn't you *tell* us?" he asked, in a large round voice quite unlike his own. "You should have *told* us you weren't getting along."

21   Richard was startled into attempting to force words through his tears. "We *do* get along, that's the trouble, so it doesn't show even to us—" *That we do not love each other* was the rest of the sentence; he couldn't finish it.

22   Joan finished for him, in her style. "And we've always, *especially,* loved our children."

23   John was not mollified. "What do you care about *us?*" he boomed. "We're just little things you *had.*" His sisters' laughing forced a laugh from him, which he turned hard and parodistic: "Ha ha *ha.*" Richard and Joan realized simultaneously that the child was drunk, on Judith's homecoming champagne. Feeling bound to keep the center of the stage, John took a cigarette from Judith's pack, poked it into his mouth, let it hang from his lower lip, and squinted like a gangster.

24   "You're not little things we had," Richard called to him. "You're the whole point. But you're grown. Or almost."

25   The boy was lighting matches. Instead of holding them to his cigarette (for they had never seen him smoke; being "good" had been his way of setting himself apart), he held them to his mother's face, closer and closer, for her to blow out. Then he lit the whole folder—a hiss and then a torch, held against his mother's face. Prismed by tears, the flame filled Richard's vision; he didn't know how it was extinguished. He heard Margaret say, "Oh stop showing off," and saw John, in response, break the cigarette in two and put the halves entirely into his mouth and chew, sticking out his tongue to display the shreds to his sister.

26   Joan talked to him, reasoning—a fountain of reason, unintelligible. "Talked about it for years . . . our children must help us . . . Daddy and I both want . . ." As the boy listened, he carefully wadded a paper napkin into the leaves of his salad, fashioned a ball of paper and lettuce, and popped it into his mouth, looking around the table for the expected laughter. None came. Judith said, "Be mature," and dismissed a plume of smoke.

27   Richard got up from this stifling table and led the boy outside. Though the house was in twilight, the outdoors still brimmed with light, the lovely waste light of high summer. Both laughing, he supervised John's spitting out the lettuce and paper and tobacco into the pachysandra. He took him

by the hand—a square gritty hand, but for its softness a man's. Yet, it held on. They ran together up into the field, past the tennis court. The raw banking left by the bulldozers was dotted with daisies. Past the court and a flat stretch where they used to play family baseball stood a soft green rise glorious in the sun, each weed and species of grass distinct as illumination on parchment. "I'm sorry, so sorry," Richard cried. "You were the only one who ever tried to help me with all the goddam jobs around this place."

28 Sobbing, safe within his tears and the champagne, John explained, "It's not just the separation, it's the whole crummy year, I *hate* that school, you can't make any friends, the history teacher's a scud."

29 They sat on the crest of the rise, shaking and warm from their tears but easier in their voices, and Richard tried to focus on the child's sad year— the weekdays long with homework, the weekends spent in his room with model airplanes, while his parents murmured down below, nursing their separation. How selfish, how blind, Richard thought; his eyes felt scoured. He told his son, "We'll think about getting you transferred. Life's too short to be miserable."

30 They had said what they could, but did not want the moment to heal, and talked on, about the school, about the tennis court, whether it would ever again be as good as it had been that first summer. They walked to inspect it and pressed a few more tapes more firmly down. A little stiltedly, perhaps trying now to make too much of the moment, Richard led the boy to the spot in the field where the view was best, of the metallic blue river, the emerald marsh, the scattered islands velvety with shadow in the low light, the white bits of beach far away. "See," he said. "It goes on being beautiful. It'll be here tomorrow."

31 "I know," John answered, impatiently. The moment had closed.

32 Back in the house, the others had opened some white wine, the champagne being drunk, and still sat at the table, the three females, gossiping. Where Joan sat had become the head. She turned, showing him a tearless face, and asked, "All right?"

33 "We're fine," he said, resenting it, though relieved, that the party went on without him.

34 In bed she explained, "I couldn't cry I guess because I cried so much all spring. It really wasn't fair. It's your idea, and you made it look as though I was kicking you out."

35 "I'm sorry," he said. "I couldn't stop. I wanted to but couldn't."

36 "You *didn't* want to. You loved it. You were having your way, making a general announcement."

37 "I love having it over," he admitted. "God, those kids were great. So brave and funny." John, returned to the house, had settled to a model airplane in his room, and kept shouting down to them, "I'm O.K. No sweat." "And the way," Richard went on, cozy in his relief, "they never questioned the reasons we gave. No thought of a third person. Not even Judith."

38 "That *was* touching," Joan said.

39   He gave her a hug. "You were great too. Very reassuring to everybody. Thank you." Guiltily, he realized he did not feel separated.

40   "You still have Dickie to do," she told him. These words set before him a black mountain in the darkness; its cold breath, its near weight affected his chest. Of the four children, his elder son was most nearly his conscience. Joan did not need to add, "That's one piece of your dirty work I won't do for you."

41   "I know. I'll do it. You go to sleep."

42   Within minutes, her breathing slowed, became oblivious and deep. It was quarter to midnight. Dickie's train from the concert would come in at one-fourteen. Richard set the alarm for one. He had slept atrociously for weeks. But whenever he closed his lids some glimpse of the last hours scorched them—Judith exhaling toward the ceiling in a kind of aversion, Bean's mute staring, the sunstruck growth in the field where he and John had rested. The mountain before him moved closer, moved within him; he was huge, momentous. The ache at the back of his throat felt stale. His wife slept as if slain beside him. When, exasperated by his hot lids, his crowded heart, he rose from bed and dressed, she awoke enough to turn over. He told her then, "Joan, if I could undo it all, I would."

43   "Where would you begin?" she asked. There was no place. Giving him courage, she was always giving him courage. He put on shoes without socks in the dark. The children were breathing in their rooms, the downstairs was hollow. In their confusion they had left lights burning. He turned off all but one, the kitchen overhead. The car started. He had hoped it wouldn't. He met only moonlight on the road; it seemed a diaphanous companion, flickering in the leaves along the roadside, haunting his rearview mirror like a pursuer, melting under his headlights. The center of town, not quite deserted, was eerie at this hour. A young cop in uniform kept company with a gang of T-shirted kids on the steps of the bank. Across from the railroad station, several bars kept open. Customers, mostly young, passed in and out of the warm night, savoring summer's novelty. Voices shouted from cars as they passed; an immense conversation seemed in progress. Richard parked and in his weariness put his head on the passenger seat, out of the commotion and wheeling lights. It was as when, in the movies, an assassin grimly carries his mission through the jostle of a carnival—except the movies cannot show the precipitous, palpable slope you cling to within. You cannot climb back down; you can only fall. The synthetic fabric of the car seat, warmed by his cheek, confided to him an ancient, distant scent of vanilla.

44   A train whistle caused him to lift his head. It was on time; he had hoped it would be late. The slender drawgates descended. The bell of approach tingled happily. The great metal body, horizontally fluted, rocked to a stop, and sleepy teen-agers disembarked, his son among them. Dickie did not show surprise that his father was meeting him at this terrible hour. He sauntered to the car with two friends, both taller than he. He said "Hi" to his father and took the passenger's seat with an exhausted promptness that expressed gratitude. The friends got in the back, and Richard was grateful; a few more minutes' postponement would be won by driving them home.

45   He asked, "How was the concert?"

46   "Groovy," one boy said from the back seat.

47   "It bit," the other said.

48   "It was O.K.," Dickie said, moderate by nature, so reasonable that in his childhood the unreason of the world had given him headaches, stomach aches, nausea. When the second friend had been dropped off at his dark house, the boy blurted, "Dad, my eyes are killing me with hay fever! I'm out there cutting that mothering grass all day!"

49   "Do we still have those drops?"

50   "They didn't do any good last summer."

51   "They might this." Richard swung a U-turn on the empty street. The drive home took a few minutes. The mountain was here, in his throat. "Richard," he said, and felt the boy, slumped and rubbing his eyes, go tense at his tone, "I didn't come to meet you just to make your life easier. I came because your mother and I have some news for you, and you're a hard man to get ahold of these days. It's sad news."

52   "That's O.K." The reassurance came out soft, but quick, as if released from the tip of a spring.

53   Richard had feared that his tears would return and choke him, but the boy's manliness set an example, and his voice issued forth steady and dry. "It's sad news, but it needn't be tragic news, at least for you. It should have no practical effect on your life, though it's bound to have an emotional effect. You'll work at your job, and go back to school in September. Your mother and I are really proud of what you're making of your life; we don't want that to change at all."

54   "Yeah," the boy said lightly, on the intake of his breath, holding himself up. They turned the corner; the church they went to loomed like a gutted fort. The home of the woman Richard hoped to marry stood across the green. Her bedroom light burned.

55   "Your mother and I," he said, "have decided to separate. For the summer. Nothing legal, no divorce yet. We want to see how it feels. For some years now, we haven't been doing enough for each other, making each other as happy as we should be. Have you sensed that?"

56   "No," the boy said. It was an honest, unemotional answer: true or false in a quiz.

57   Glad for factual basis, Richard pursued, even garrulously, the details. His apartment across town, his utter accessibility, the split vacation arrangements, the advantages to the children, the added mobility and variety of the summer. Dickie listened, absorbing. "Do the others know?"

58   "Yes."

59   "How did they take it?"

60   "The girls pretty calmly. John flipped out; he shouted and ate a cigarette and made a salad out of his napkin and told us how much he hated school."

61   His brother chuckled. "He did?"

62   "Yeah. The school issue was more upsetting for him than Mom and me. He seemed to feel better for having exploded."

63   "He did?" The repetition was the first sign that he was stunned.

64 "Yes. Dickie, I want to tell you something. This last hour, waiting for your train to get in, has been about the worst of my life. I hate this. *Hate* it. My father wuld have died before doing it to me." He felt immensely lighter, saying this. He had dumped the mountain on the boy. They were home. Moving swiftly as a shadow, Dickie was out of the car, through the bright kitchen. Richard called after him, "Want a glass of milk or anything?"

65 "No thanks."

66 "Want us to call the course tomorrow and say you're too sick to work?"

67 "No, that's all right." The answer was faint, delivered at the door to his room; Richard listened for the slam that went with a tantrum. The door closed normally, gently. The sound was sickening.

68 Joan had sunk into that first deep trough of sleep and was slow to awake. Richard had to repeat, "I told him."

69 "What did he say?"

70 "Nothing much. Could you go say goodnight to him? Please."

71 She left their room, without putting on a bathrobe. He sluggishly changed back into his pajamas and walked down the hall. Dickie was already in bed, Joan was sitting beside him, and the boy's bedside clock radio was murmuring music. When she stood, an inexplicable light—the moon?—outlined her body through the nightie. Richard sat on the warm place she had indented on the child's narrow mattress. He asked him, "Do you want the radio on like that?"

72 "It always is."

73 "Doesn't it keep you awake? It would me."

74 "No."

75 "Are you sleepy?"

76 "Yeah."

77 "Good. Sure you want to get up and go to work? You've had a big night."

78 "I want to."

79 Away at school this winter he had learned for the first time that you can go short of sleep and live. As an infant he had slept with an immobile, sweating intensity that had alarmed his babysitters. In adolescence he had often been the first of the four children to go to bed. Even now, he would go slack in the middle of a television show, his sprawled legs hairy and brown. "O.K. Good boy. Dickie, listen. I love you so much, I never knew how much until now. No matter how this works out, I'll always be with you. Really."

80 Richard bent to kiss an averted face but his son, sinewy, turned and with wet cheeks embraced him and gave him a kiss, on the lips, passionate as a woman's. In his father's ear he moaned one word, the crucial, intelligent word: *"Why?"*

81 *Why.* It was a whistle of wind in a crack, a knife thrust, a window thrown open on emptiness. The white face was gone, the darkness was featureless. Richard had forgotten why.

A. Questions for Analysis

1. What is this story about? Which character or characters play leading roles?

2. What has gone wrong with the Maples' marriage? Does Updike provide any clues that might explain the reason for their separation? How do Richard and Joan treat each other at this stage of their relationship?

3. How would you describe Richard's character in terms of the way he chooses to make the announcement to his children, his treatment of his wife, his behavior—especially with Richard Jr. in the car?

4. The house where the Maples have lived and raised their children is clearly symbolic in this story. What household elements does Updike emphasize? What significance do they have beyond their literal importance?

5. In paragraphs 34–40, Richard and Joan discuss the children's reaction, and it is here that we learn about the apparent existence of a "third person." Does this suggestion (later confirmed in paragraph 54) change your perception of Richard as a husband or father? If so, in what way? Look through the story again and examine your reactions to him as the events unfold.

6. Examine the reaction of the four children to the announcement. Are the three younger ones really as "brave and funny" as Richard later tells Joan? In paragraph 40, Richard suggests that his eldest son was "most nearly his conscience." How is this unspoken role borne out in the conclusion of the story?

B. Vocabulary   For each italicized word from the story, choose the best definition according to the context in which it appears.

1. the *opulent* jungle of her native land [paragraph 1]: (a) luxuriant; (b) tangled; (c) green with vegetation; (d) affluent.

2. the *bauble* of summer [1—used metaphorically]: (a) lure; temptation; (b) showy ornament; (c) frivolous enjoyment; (d) piece of expensive jewelry.

3. did not strike them as *ominous* [2]: pertaining to (a) something important; (b) something unexpected; (c) an evil omen; (d) sudden good fortune.

4. could *rend* the earth for fun [2]: (a) split; tear apart; (b) cause pain to; (c) remove forcibly; (d) poison; pollute.

5. an environment *congruous* with his mood [2]: (a) influencing; (b) in contrast; (c) joining together; (d) corresponding.

6. her too-*copious* lecture notes [7]: (a) messy; (b) incomplete; (c) abundant; (d) precise.

7. he had become obsessed with *battening* down the house [8]: (a) furnishing; (b) making prosperous; (c) fastening; (d) renovating.

8. frozen by *corrosion* [9]: the process of (a) falling into disuse or disrepair; (b) wearing away; (c) becoming immobile; (d) becoming scarred and ridged.

9. *opaque* instructions [9]: (a) unintelligible; obscure; (b) easy to follow; useful; (c) incoherent; confusing; (d) dull; tedious to read.

10. *minutiae* [9—pronounced mi-nōō′shē-ē′]: (a) a tangled mess; (b) unsuitable pieces; (c) tiny bits; (d) scraps; remnants.

11. she *regaled* them with stories [10]: (a) entertained; (b) bored; (c) over-whelmed; (d) tempted.

12. the lips *succulent* and satisfactory [12]: (a) tightly pressed together; (b) juicy; wet; (c) prim; proper; (d) full; fleshy.

13. her *reproach* displaced [13]: (a) criticism; (b) warning; (c) anger; (d) blame.

14. displaced by a quick *grimace* [13—pronounced gri mās′]: (a) expression of pain or contempt; (b) shy, secret smile; (c) sorrowful look; (d) blank, expressionless look.

15. as if to *rebuke* his father's distraction [17]: (a) ignore; (b) criticize sharply; (c) attract attention to; (d) dramatize.

16. Richard's crying had become *tumultuous* [20]: (a) violently agitated; (b) unstoppable; (c) calm; tranquil; (d) impassioned.

17. John was not *mollified* [23]: (a) fooled; deceived; (b) altered; changed; (c) placated; calmed; (d) indulged; humored.

18. a laugh, which he turned hard and *parodistic* [23]: (a) intentionally mocking; (b) nasty; bitter; (c) cruel; vindictive; (d) cynical; distrusting.

19. a little *stiltedly* [30]: (a) arrogantly; (b) uncertainly; (c) shyly; (d) stiffly; formally.

20. her breathing became *oblivious* and deep [42]: (a) labored; (b) worri-some; (c) unaware; (d) offensive.

21. a kind of *aversion* [42]: (a) escape mechanism; (b) intense dislike; (c) deviation from the normal; (d) preventive measure.

22. the moonlight seemed a *diaphanous* companion [43]: (a) transparent; allowing light to come through; (b) dark; portending evil; (c) invisible; (d) grim; uninviting.

23. the *precipitous* slope [43]: (a) rain-soaked; (b) extremely steep; (c) un-scalable; invincible; (d) anticipated; dreaded.

24. the precipitous, *palpable* slope [43]: capable of being (a) perceived; (b) heard; (c) defeated; (d) touched.

25. Richard pursued, even *garrulously,* the details [57]: (a) overly talkative; (b) eagerly; (c) dispiritedly; (d) defensively.

Short Story 4   Good Country People
Flannery O'Connor

Flannery O'Connor (1925–1964) is widely regarded as one of the most important Southern writers in modern American literature. She wrote two novels, *Wise Blood* and *The Violent Bear It Away,* and two collections of short stories, *Everything That Rises Must Converge* and *A Good Man Is Hard to Find,* from which this story comes. Stricken with lupus in her twenties, O'Connor lived quietly in Millidgeville, Georgia, until her death at the age of thirty-nine.

1   Besides the neutral expression that she wore when she was alone, Mrs. Freeman had two others, forward and reverse, that she used for all her

human dealings. Her forward expression was steady and driving like the advance of a heavy truck. Her eyes never swerved to left or right but turned as the story turned as if they followed a yellow line down the center of it. She seldom used the other expression because it was not often necessary for her to retract a statement, but when she did, her face came to a complete stop, there was an almost imperceptible movement of her black eyes, during which they seemed to be receding, and then the observer would see that Mrs. Freeman, though she might stand there as real as several grain sacks thrown on top of each other, was no longer there in spirit. As for getting anything across to her when this was the case, Mrs. Hopewell had given it up. She might talk her head off. Mrs. Freeman could never be brought to admit herself wrong on any point. She would stand there and if she could be brought to say anything, it was something like, "Well, I wouldn't of said it was and I wouldn't of said it wasn't," or letting her gaze range over the top kitchen shelf where there was an assortment of dusty bottles, she might remark, "I see you ain't ate many of them figs you put up last summer."

2   They carried on their most important business in the kitchen at breakfast. Every morning Mrs. Hopewell got up at seven o'clock and lit her gas heater and Joy's. Joy was her daughter, a large blonde girl who had an artificial leg. Mrs. Hopewell thought of her as a child though she was thirty-two years old and highly educated. Joy would get up while her mother was eating and lumber into the bathroom and slam the door, and before long, Mrs. Freeman would arrive at the back door. Joy would hear her mother call, "Come on in," and then they would talk for a while in low voices that were indistinguishable in the bathroom. By the time Joy came in, they had usually finished the weather report and were on one or the other of Mrs. Freeman's daughters, Glynese or Carramae. Joy called them Glycerin and Caramel. Glynese, a redhead, was eighteen and had many admirers; Carramae, a blonde, was only fifteen but already married and pregnant. She could not keep anything on her stomach. Every morning Mrs. Freeman told Mrs. Hopewell how many times she had vomited since the last report.

3   Mrs. Hopewell liked to tell people that Glynese and Carramae were two of the finest girls she knew and that Mrs. Freeman was a *lady* and that she was never ashamed to take her anywhere or introduce her to anybody they might meet. Then she would tell how she had happened to hire the Freemans in the first place and how they were a godsend to her and how she had had them four years. The reason for her keeping them so long was that they were not trash. They were good country people. She had telephoned the man whose name they had given as a reference and he had told her that Mr. Freeman was a good farmer but that his wife was the nosiest woman ever to walk the earth. "She's got to be into everything," the man said. "If she don't get there before the dust settles, you can bet she's dead, that's all. She'll want to know all your business. I can stand him real good," he had said, "but me nor my wife neither could have stood that woman one more minute on this place." That had put Mrs. Hopewell off for a few days.

4   She had hired them in the end because there were no other applicants

but she had made up her mind beforehand exactly how she would handle the woman. Since she was the type who had to be into everything, then, Mrs. Hopewell had decided, she would not only let her be into everything, she would *see to it* that she was into everything—she would give her the responsibility of everything, she would put her in charge. Mrs. Hopewell had no bad qualities of her own but she was able to use other people's in such a constructive way that she never felt the lack. She had hired the Freemans and she had kept them four years.

5   Nothing is perfect. This was one of Mrs. Hopewell's favorite sayings. Another was: that is life! And still another, the most important, was: well, other people have their opinions too. She would make these statements, usually at the table, in a tone of gentle insistence as if no one held them but her, and the large hulking Joy, whose constant outrage had obliterated every expression from her face, would stare just a little to the side of her, her eyes icy blue, with the look of someone who has achieved blindness by an act of will and means to keep it.

6   When Mrs. Hopewell said to Mrs. Freeman that life was like that, Mrs. Freeman would say, "I always said so myself." Nothing had been arrived at by anyone that had not first been arrived at by her. She was quicker than Mr. Freeman. When Mrs. Hopewell said to her after they had been on the place a while, "You know, you're the wheel behind the wheel," and winked, Mrs. Freeman had said, "I know it. I've always been quick. It's some that are quicker than others."

7   "Everybody is different," Mrs. Hopewell said.

8   "Yes, most people is," Mrs. Freeman said.

9   "It takes all kinds to make the world."

10   "I always said it did myself."

11   The girl was used to this kind of dialogue for breakfast and more of it for dinner; sometimes they had it for supper too. When they had no guest they ate in the kitchen because that was easier. Mrs. Freeman always managed to arrive at some point during the meal and to watch them finish it. She would stand in the doorway if it were summer but in the winter she would stand with one elbow on top of the refrigerator and look down on them, or she would stand by the gas heater, lifting the back of her skirt slightly. Occasionally she would stand against the wall and roll her head from side to side. At no time was she in any hurry to leave. All this was very trying to Mrs. Hopewell but she was a woman of great patience. She realized that nothing is perfect and that in the Freemans she had good country people and that if, in this day and age, you get good country people, you had better hang onto them.

12   She had had plenty of experience with trash. Before the Freemans she had averaged one tenant family a year. The wives of these farmers were not the kind you would want to be around you for very long. Mrs. Hopewell, who had divorced her husband long ago, needed someone to walk over the fields with her; and when Joy had to be impressed for these services, her remarks were usually so ugly and her face so glum that Mrs. Hopewell would say, "If

you can't come pleasantly, I don't want you at all," to which the girl, standing square and rigid-shouldered with her neck thrust slightly forward, would reply, "If you want me, here I am—LIKE I AM."

13 Mrs. Hopewell excused this attitude because of the leg (which had been shot off in a hunting accident when Joy was ten). It was hard for Mrs. Hopewell to realize that her child was thirty-two now and that for more than twenty years she had had only one leg. She thought of her still as a child because it tore her heart to think instead of the poor stout girl in her thirties who had never danced a step or had any *normal* good times. Her name was really Joy but as soon as she was twenty-one and away from home, she had had it legally changed. Mrs. Hopewell was certain that she had thought and thought until she had hit upon the ugliest name in any language. Then she had gone and had the beautiful name, Joy, changed without telling her mother until after she had done it. Her legal name was Hulga.

14 When Mrs. Hopewell thought the name, Hulga, she thought of the broad blank hull of a battleship. She would not use it. She continued to call her Joy to which the girl responded but in a purely mechanical way.

15 Hulga had learned to tolerate Mrs. Freeman who saved her from taking walks with her mother. Even Glynese and Carramae were useful when they occupied attention that might otherwise have been directed at her. At first she had thought she could not stand Mrs. Freeman for she had found that it was not possible to be rude to her. Mrs. Freeman would take on strange resentments and for days together she would be sullen but the source of her displeasure was always obscure; a direct attack, a positive leer, blatant ugliness to her face—these never touched her. And without warning one day, she began calling her Hulga.

16 She did not call her that in front of Mrs. Hopewell who would have been incensed but when she and the girl happened to be out of the house together, she would say something and add the name Hulga to the end of it, and the big spectacled Joy—Hulga would scowl and redden as if her privacy had been intruded upon. She considered the name her personal affair. She had arrived at it first purely on the basis of its ugly sound and then the full genius of its fitness had struck her. She had a vision of the name working like the ugly sweating Vulcan who stayed in the furnace and to whom, presumably, the goddess had to come when called. She saw it as the name of her highest creative act. One of her major triumphs was that her mother had not been able to turn her dust into Joy, but the greater one was that she had been able to turn it herself into Hulga. However, Mrs. Freeman's relish for using the name only irritated her. It was as if Mrs. Freeman's beady steel-pointed eyes had penetrated far enough behind her face to reach some secret fact. Something about her seemed to fascinate Mrs. Freeman and then one day Hulga realized that it was the artificial leg. Mrs. Freeman had a special fondness for the details of secret infections, hidden deformities, assaults upon children. Of diseases, she preferred the lingering or incurable. Hulga had heard Mrs. Hopewell give her the details of the hunting accident, how the leg had been literally blasted off, how she had never lost consciousness. Mrs. Freeman could listen to it any time as if it had happened an hour ago.

17   When Hulga stumped into the kitchen in the morning (she could walk without making the awful noise but she made it—Mrs. Hopewell was certain—because it was ugly-sounding), she glanced at them and did not speak. Mrs. Hopewell would be in her red kimono with her hair tied around her head in rags. She would be sitting at the table, finishing her breakfast and Mrs. Freeman would be hanging by her elbow outward from the refrigerator, looking down at the table. Hulga always put her eggs on the stove to boil and then stood over them with her arms folded, and Mrs. Hopewell would look at her—a kind of indirect gaze divided between her and Mrs. Freeman—and would think that if she would only keep herself up a little, she wouldn't be so bad looking. There was nothing wrong with her face that a pleasant expression wouldn't help. Mrs. Hopewell said that people who looked on the bright side of things would be beautiful even if they were not.

18   Whenever she looked at Joy this way, she could not help but feel that it would have been better if the child had not taken the Ph.D. It had certainly not brought her out any and now that she had it, there was no more excuse for her to go to school again. Mrs. Hopewell thought it was nice for girls to go to school to have a good time but Joy had "gone through." Anyhow, she would not have been strong enough to go again. The doctors had told Mrs. Hopewell that with the best of care, Joy might see forty-five. She had a weak heart. Joy had made it plain that if it had not been for this condition, she would be far from these red hills and good country people. She would be in a university lecturing to people who knew what she was talking about. And Mrs. Hopewell could very well picture her there, looking like a scarecrow and lecturing to more of the same. Here she went about all day in a six-year-old skirt and a yellow sweat shirt with a faded cowboy on a horse embossed on it. She thought this was funny; Mrs. Hopewell thought it was idiotic and showed simply that she was still a child. She was brilliant but she didn't have a grain of sense. It seemed to Mrs. Hopewell that every year she grew less like other people and more like herself—bloated, rude, and squint-eyed. And she said such strange things! To her own mother she had said—without warning, without excuse, standing up in the middle of a meal with her face purple and her mouth half full—"Woman! do you ever look inside? Do you ever look inside and see what you are *not*? God!" she had cried sinking down again and staring at her plate, "Malebranche was right: we are not our own light. We are not our own light!" Mrs. Hopewell had no idea to this day what brought that on. She had only made the remark, hoping Joy would take it in, that a smile never hurt anyone.

19   The girl had taken the Ph.D. in philosophy and this left Mrs. Hopewell at a complete loss. You could say, "My daughter is a nurse," or "My daughter is a schoolteacher," or even, "My daughter is a chemical engineer." You could not say, "My daughter is a philosopher." That was something that had ended with the Greeks and Romans. All day Joy sat on her neck in a deep chair, reading. Sometimes she went for walks but she didn't like dogs or cats or birds or flowers or nature or nice young men. She looked at nice young men as if she could smell their stupidity.

20   One day Mrs. Hopewell had picked up one of the books the girl had just put down and opening it at random, she read, "Science, on the other hand, has to assert its soberness and seriousness afresh and declare that it is concerned solely with what-is. Nothing—how can it be for science anything but a horror and a phantasm? If science is right, then one thing stands firm: science wishes to know nothing of nothing. Such is after all the strictly scientific approach to Nothing. We know it by wishing to know nothing of Nothing." These words had been underlined with a blue pencil and they worked on Mrs. Hopewell like some evil incantation in gibberish. She shut the book quickly and went out of the room as if she were having a chill.

21   This morning when the girl came in, Mrs. Freeman was on Carramae. "She thrown up four times after supper," she said, "and was up twict in the night after three o'clock. Yesterday she didn't do nothing but ramble in the bureau drawer. All she did. Stand up there and see what she could run up on."

22   "She's got to eat," Mrs. Hopewell muttered, sipping her coffee, while she watched Joy's back at the stove. She was wondering what the child had said to the Bible salesman. She could not imagine what kind of a conversation she could possibly have had with him.

23   He was a tall gaunt hatless youth who had called yesterday to sell them a Bible. He had appeared at the door, carrying a large black suitcase that weighted him so heavily on one side that he had to brace himself against the door facing. He seemed on the point of collapse but he said in a cheerful voice. "Good morning, Mrs. Cedars!" and set the suitcase down on the mat. He was not a bad-looking young man though he had on a bright blue suit and yellow socks that were not pulled up far enough. He had prominent face bones and a streak of sticky-looking brown hair falling across his forehead.

24   "I'm Mrs. Hopewell," she said.

25   "Oh!" he said, pretending to look puzzled but with his eyes sparkling, "I saw it said 'The Cedars' on the mailbox so I thought you was Mrs. Cedars!" and he burst out in a pleasant laugh. He picked up the satchel and under cover of a pant, he fell forward into her hall. It was rather as if the suitcase had moved first, jerking him after it. "Mrs. Hopewell!" he said and grabbed her hand. "I hope you are well!" and he laughed again and then all at once his face sobered completely. He paused and gave her a straight earnest look and said, "Lady, I've come to speak of serious things."

26   "Well, come in," she muttered, none too pleased because her dinner was almost ready. He came into the parlor and sat down on the edge of a straight chair and put the suitcase between his feet and glanced around the room as if he were sizing her up by it. Her silver gleamed on the two sideboards; she decided he had never been in a room as elegant as this.

27   "Mrs. Hopewell," he began, using her name in a way that sounded almost intimate, "I know you believe in Chrustian service."

28   "Well yes," she murmured.

29   "I know," he said and paused, looking very wise with his head cocked on one side, "that you're a good woman. Friends have told me."

30   Mrs. Hopewell never liked to be taken for a fool. "What are you selling?" she asked.

31   "Bibles," the young man said and his eye raced around the room before he added, "I see you have no family Bible in your parlor, I see that is the one lack you got!"

32   Mrs. Hopewell could not say, "My daughter is an atheist and won't let me keep the Bible in the parlor." She said, stiffening slightly, "I keep my Bible by my bedside." This was not the truth. It was in the attic somewhere.

33   "Lady," he said, "the word of God ought to be in the parlor."

34   "Well, I think that's a matter of taste," she began. "I think . . ."

35   "Lady," he said, "for a Chrustian, the word of God ought to be in every room in the house besides in his heart. I know you're a Chrustian because I can see it in every line of your face."

36   She stood up and said, "Well, young man, I don't want to buy a Bible and I smell my dinner burning."

37   He didn't get up. He began to twist his hands and looking down at them, he said softly, "Well lady, I'll tell you the truth—not many people want to buy one nowadays and besides, I know I'm real simple. I don't know how to say a thing but to say it. I'm just a country boy." He glanced up into her unfriendly face. "People like you don't like to fool with country people like me!"

38   "Why!" she cried, "good country people are the salt of the earth! Besides, we all have different ways of doing, it takes all kinds to make the world go 'round. That's life!"

39   "You said a mouthful," he said.

40   "Why, I think there aren't enough good country people in the world!" she said, stirred. "I think that's what's wrong with it!"

41   His face had brightened. "I didn't inraduce myself," he said. "I'm Manley Pointer from out in the country around Willohobie, not even from a place, just from near a place."

42   "You wait a minute," she said. "I have to see about my dinner." She went out to the kitchen and found Joy standing near the door where she had been listening.

43   "Get rid of the salt of the earth," she said, "and let's eat."

44   Mrs. Hopewell gave her a pained look and turned the heat down under the vegetables. "I can't be rude to anybody," she murmured and went back into the parlor.

45   He had opened the suitcase and was sitting with a Bible on each knee.

46   "You might as well put those up," she told him. "I don't want one."

47   "I appreciate your honesty," he said. "You don't see any more real honest people unless you go way out in the coutnry."

48   "I know," she said, "real genuine folks!" Through the crack in the door she heard a groan.

49   "I guess a lot of boys come telling you they're working their way through college," he said, "but I'm not going to tell you that. Somehow," he said, "I don't want to go to college. I want to devote my life to Chrustian service. See," he said, lowering his voice, "I got this heart condition. I may not live

long. When you know it's something wrong with you and you may not live long, well then, lady . . ." He paused, with his mouth open, and stared at her.

50   He and Joy had the same condition! She knew that her eyes were filling with tears but she collected herself quickly and murmured, "Won't you stay for dinner? We'd love to have you!" and was sorry the instant she heard herself say it.

51   "Yes mam," he said in an abashed voice, "I would sher love to do that!"

52   Joy had given him one look on being introduced to him and then throughout the meal had not glanced at him again. He had addressed several remarks to her, which she had pretended not to hear. Mrs. Hopewell could not understand deliberate rudeness, although she lived with it, and she felt she had always to overflow with hospitality to make up for Joy's lack of courtesy. She urged him to talk about himself and he did. He said he was the seventh child of twelve and that his father had been crushed under a tree when he himself was eight year old. He had been crushed very badly, in fact, almost cut in two and was practically not recognizable. His mother had got along the best she could by hard working and she had always seen that her children went to Sunday School and that they read the Bible every evening. He was now nineteen year old and he had been selling Bibles for four months. In that time he had sold seventy-seven Bibles and had the promise of two more sales. He wanted to become a missionary because he thought that was the way you could do most for people. "He who losest his life shall find it," he said simply and he was so sincere, so genuine and earnest that Mrs. Hopewell would not for the world have smiled. He prevented his peas from sliding onto the table by blocking them with a piece of bread which he later cleaned his plate with. She could see Joy observing sidewise how he handled his knife and fork and she saw too that every few minutes, the boy would dart a keen appraising glance at the girl as if he were trying to attract her attention.

53   After dinner Joy cleared the dishes off the table and disappeared and Mrs. Hopewell was left to talk with him. He told her again about his childhood and his father's accident and about various things that had happened to him. Every five minutes or so she would stifle a yawn. He sat for two hours until finally she told him she must go because she had an appointment in town. He packed his Bibles and thanked her and prepared to leave, but in the doorway he stopped and wrung her hand and said that not on any of his trips had he met a lady as nice as her and he asked if he could come again. She had said she would always be happy to see him.

54   Joy had been standing in the road, apparently looking at something in the distance, when he came down the steps toward her, bent to the side with his heavy valise. He stopped where she was standing and confronted her directly. Mrs. Hopewell could not hear what he said but she trembled to think what Joy would say to him. She could see that after a minute Joy said something and that then the boy began to speak again, making an excited gesture with his free hand. After a minute Joy said something else at which the boy began to speak once more. Then to her amazement, Mrs. Hopewell saw the two of them walk off together, toward the gate. Joy had walked all

the way to the gate with him and Mrs. Hopewell could not imagine what they had said to each other, and she had not yet dared to ask.

55   Mrs. Freeman was insisting upon her attention. She had moved from the refrigerator to the heater so that Mrs. Hopewell had to turn and face her in order to seem to be listening. "Glynese gone out with Harvey Hill again last night," she said. "She had this sty."

56   "Hill," Mrs. Hopewell said absently, "is that the one who works in the garage?"

57   "Nome, he's the one that goes to chiropracter school," Mrs. Freeman said. "She had this sty. Been had it two days. So she says when he brought her in the other night he says, 'Lemme get rid of that sty for you,' and she says, 'How?' and he says, 'You just lay yourself down acrost the seat of that car and I'll show you.' So she done it and he popped her neck. Kept on a-popping it several times until she made him quit. This morning," Mrs. Freeman said, "she ain't got no sty. She ain't got no traces of a sty."

58   "I never heard of that before," Mrs. Hopewell said.

59   "He ast her to marry him before the Ordinary," Mrs. Freeman went on, "and she told him she wasn't going to be married in no *office*."

60   "Well, Glynese is a fine girl," Mrs. Hopewell said. "Glynese and Carramae are both fine girls."

61   "Carramae said when her and Lyman was married Lyman said it sure felt sacred to him. She said he said he wouldn't take five hundred dollars for being married by a preacher."

62   "How much would he take?" the girl asked from the stove.

63   "He said he wouldn't take five hundred dollars," Mrs. Freeman repeated.

64   "Well we all have work to do," Mrs. Hopewell said.

65   "Lyman said it just felt more sacred to him," Mrs. Freeman said. "The doctor wants Carramae to eat prunes. Says instead of medicine. Says them cramps is coming from pressure. You know where I think it is?"

66   "She'll be better in a few weeks," Mrs. Hopewell said.

67   "In the tube," Mrs. Freeman said. "Else she wouldn't be as sick as she is."

68   Hulga had cracked her two eggs into a saucer and was bringing them to the table along with a cup of coffee that she had filled too full. She sat down carefully and began to eat, meaning to keep Mrs. Freeman there by questions if for any reason she showed an inclination to leave. She could perceive her mother's eye on her. The first round-about question would be about the Bible salesman and she did not wish to bring it on. "How did he pop her neck?" she asked.

69   Mrs. Freeman went into a description of how he had popped her neck. She said he owned a '55 Mercury but that Glynese said she would rather marry a man with only a '36 Plymouth who would be married by a preacher. The girl asked what if he had a '32 Plymouth and Mrs. Freeman said what Glynese had said was a '36 Plymouth.

70   Mrs. Hopewell said there were not many girls with Glynese's common sense. She said what she admired in those girls was their common sense. She said that reminded her that they had had a nice visitor yesterday, a

young man selling Bibles. "Lord," she said, "he bored me to death but he was so sincere and genuine I couldn't be rude to him. He was just good country people, you know," she said, "—just the salt of the earth."

71   "I seen him walk up," Mrs. Freeman said, "and then later—I seen him walk off," and Hulga could feel the slight shift in her voice, the slight insinuation, that he had not walked off alone, had he? Her face remained expressionless but the color rose into her neck and she seemed to swallow it down with the next spoonful of egg. Mrs. Freeman was looking at her as if they had a secret together.

72   "Well, it takes all kinds of people to make the world go 'round," Mrs. Hopewell said. "It's very good we aren't all alike."

73   "Some people are more alike than others," Mrs. Freeman said.

74   Hulga got up and stumped, with about twice the noise that was necessary, into her room and locked the door. She was to meet the Bible salesman at ten o'clock at the gate. She had thought about it half the night. She had started thinking of it as a great joke and then she had begun to see profound implications in it. She had lain in bed imagining dialogues for them that were insane on the surface but that reached below to depths that no Bible salesman would be aware of. Their conversation yesterday had been of this kind.

75   He had stopped in front of her and had simply stood there. His face was bony and sweaty and bright, with a little pointed nose in the center of it, and his look was different from what it had been at the dinner table. He was gazing at her with open curiosity, with fascination, like a child watching a new fantastic animal at the zoo, and he was breathing as if he had run a great distance to reach her. His gaze seemed somehow familiar but she could not think where she had been regarded with it before. For almost a minute he didn't say anything. Then on what seemed an insuck of breath, he whispered, "You ever ate a chicken that was two days old?"

76   The girl looked at him stonily. He might have just put this question up for consideration at the meeting of a philosophical association. "Yes," she presently replied as if she had considered it from all angles.

77   "It must have been mighty small!" he said triumphantly and shook all over with little nervous giggles, getting very red in the face, and subsiding finally into his gaze of complete admiration, while the girl's expression remained exactly the same.

78   "How old are you?" he asked softly.

79   She waited some time before she answered. Then in a flat voice she said, "Seventeen."

80   His smiles came in succession like waves breaking on the surface of a little lake. "I see you got a wooden leg," he said. "I think you're brave. I think you're real sweet."

81   The girl stood blank and solid and silent.

82   "Walk to the gate with me," he said. "You're a brave sweet little thing and I liked you the minute I seen you walk in the door."

83   Hulga began to move forward.

84   "What's your name?" he asked, smiling down on the top of her head.

85   "Hulga," she said.

86   "Hulga," he murmured, "Hulga. Hulga. I never heard of anybody name Hulga before. You're shy, aren't you, Hulga?" he asked.

87   She nodded, watching his large red hand on the handle of the giant valise.

88   "I like girls that wear glasses," he said. "I think a lot. I'm not like these people that a serious thought don't ever enter their heads. It's because I may die."

89   "I may die too," she said suddenly and looked up at him. His eyes were very small and brown, glittering feverishly.

90   "Listen," he said, "don't you think some people was meant to meet on account of what all they got in common and all? Like they both think serious thoughts and all?" He shifted the valise to his other hand so that the hand nearest her was free. He caught hold of her elbow and shook it a little. "I don't work on Saturday," he said. "I like to walk in the woods and see what Mother Nature is wearing. O'er the hills and far away. Pic-nics and things. Couldn't we go on a pic-nic tomorrow? Say yes, Hulga," he said and gave her a dying look as if he felt his insides about to drop out of him. He had even seemed to sway slightly toward her.

91   During the night she had imagined that she seduced him. She imagined that the two of them walked on the place until they came to the storage barn beyond the two back fields and there, she imagined, that things came to such a pass that she very easily seduced him and that then, of course, she had to reckon with his remorse. True genius can get an idea across even to an inferior mind. She imagined that she took his remorse in hand and changed it into a deeper understanding of life. She took all his shame away and turned it into something useful.

92   She set off for the gate at exactly ten o'clock, escaping without drawing Mrs. Hopewell's attention. She didn't take anything to eat, forgetting that food is usually taken on a picnic. She wore a pair of slacks and a dirty white shirt, and as an afterthought, she had put some Vapex on the collar of it since she did not own any perfume. When she reached the gate no one was there.

93   She looked up and down the empty highway and had the furious feeling that she had been tricked, that he had only meant to make her walk to the gate after the idea of him. Then suddenly he stood up, very tall, from behind a bush on the opposite embankment. Smiling, he lifted his hat which was new and wide-brimmed. He had not worn it yesterday and she wondered if he had bought it for the occasion. It was toast-colored with a red and white band around it and was slightly too large for him. He stepped from behind the bush still carrying the black valise. He had on the same suit and the same yellow socks sucked down in his shoes from walking. He crossed the highway and said, "I knew you'd come!"

94   The girl wondered acidly how he had known this. She pointed to the valise and asked, "Why did you bring your Bibles?"

95   He took her elbow, smiling down on her as if he could not stop. "You can never tell when you'll need the word of God, Hulga," he said. She had a

moment in which she doubted that this was actually happening and then they began to climb the embankment. They went down into the pasture toward the woods. The boy walked lightly by her side, bouncing on his toes. The valise did not seem to be heavy today; he even swung it. They crossed half the pasture without saying anything and then, putting his hand easily on the small of her back, he asked softly, "Where does your wooden leg join on?"

96   She turned an ugly red and glared at him and for an instant the boy looked abashed. "I didn't mean you no harm," he said. "I only meant you're so brave and all. I guess God takes care of you."

97   "No," she said, looking forward and walking fast, "I don't even believe in God."

98   At this he stopped and whistled. "No!" he exclaimed as if he were too astonished to say anything else.

99   She walked on and in a second he was bouncing at her side, fanning with his hat. "That's very unusual for a girl," he remarked, watching her out of the corner of his eye. When they reached the edge of the wood, he put his hand on her back again and drew her against him without a word and kissed her heavily.

100   The kiss, which had more pressure than feeling behind it, produced that extra surge of adrenalin in the girl that enables one to carry a packed trunk out of a burning house, but in her, the power went at once to the brain. Even before he released her, her mind, clear and detached and ironic anyway, was regarding him from a great distance, with amusement but with pity. She had never been kissed before and she was pleased to discover that it was an unexceptional experience and all a matter of the mind's control. Some people might enjoy drain water if they were told it was vodka. When the boy, looking expectant but uncertain, pushed her gently away, she turned and walked on, saying nothing as if such business, for her, were common enough.

101   He came along panting at her side, trying to help her when he saw a root that she might trip over. He caught and held back the long swaying blades of thorn vine until she had passed beyond them. She led the way and he came breathing heavily behind her. Then they came out on a sunlit hillside, sloping softly into another one a little smaller. Beyond, they could see the rusted top of the old barn where the extra hay was stored.

102   The hill was sprinkled with small pink weeds. "Then you ain't saved?" he asked suddenly, stopping.

103   The girl smiled. It was the first time she had smiled at him at all. "In my economy," she said, "I'm saved and you are damned but I told you I didn't believe in God."

104   Nothing seemed to destroy the boy's look of admiration. He gazed at her now as if the fantastic animal at the zoo had put its paw through the bars and given him a loving poke. She thought he looked as if he wanted to kiss her again and she walked on before he had the chance.

105   "Ain't there somewheres we can sit down sometime?" he murmured, his voice softening toward the end of the sentence.

106 "In that barn," she said.

107 They made for it rapidly as if it might slide away like a train. It was a large two-story barn, cool and dark inside. The boy pointed up the ladder that led into the loft and said, "It's too bad we can't go up there."

108 "Why can't we?" she asked.

109 "Your leg," he said reverently.

110 The girl gave him a contemptuous look and putting both hands on the ladder, she climbed it while he stood below, apparently awe-struck. She pulled herself expertly through the opening and then looked down at him and said, "Well, come on if you're coming," and he began to climb the ladder, awkwardly bringing the suitcase with him.

111 "We won't need the Bible," she observed.

112 "You never can tell," he said, panting. After he had got into the loft, he was a few seconds catching his breath. She had sat down in a pile of straw. A wide sheath of sunlight, filled with dust particles, slanted over her. She lay back against a bale, her face turned away, looking out the front opening of the barn where hay was thrown from a wagon into the loft. The two pink-speckled hillsides lay back against a dark ridge of woods. The sky was cloudless and cold blue. The boy dropped down by her side and put one arm under her and the other over her and began methodically kissing her face, making little noises like a fish. He did not remove his hat but it was pushed far enough back not to interfere. When her glasses got in his way, he took them off of her and slipped them into his pocket.

113 The girl at first did not return any of the kisses but presently she began to and after she had put several on his cheek, she reached his lips and remained there, kissing him again and again as if she were trying to draw all the breath out of him. His breath was clear and sweet like a child's and the kisses were sticky like a child's. He mumbled about loving her and about knowing when he first seen her that he loved her, but the mumbling was like the sleepy fretting of a child being put to sleep by his mother. Her mind, throughout this, never stopped or lost itself for a second to her feelings. "You ain't said you loved me none," he whispered finally, pulling back from her. "You got to say that."

114 She looked away from him off into the hollow sky and then down at a black ridge and then down farther into what appeared to be two green swelling lakes. She didn't realize he had taken her glasses but this landscape could not seem exceptional to her for she seldom paid any close attention to her surroundings.

115 "You got to say it," he repeated. "You got to say you love me."

116 She was always careful how she committed herself. "In a sense," she began, "if you use the word loosely, you might say that. But it's not a word I use. I don't have illusions. I'm one of those people who see *through* to nothing."

117 The boy was frowning. "You got to say it. I said it and you got to say it," he said.

118 The girl looked at him almost tenderly. "You poor baby," she murmured. "It's just as well you don't understand," and she pulled him by the

neck, face-down, against her. "We are all damned," she said, "but some of us have taken off our blindfolds and see that there's nothing to see. It's a kind of salvation."

119 The boy's astonished eyes looked blankly through the ends of her hair. "Okay," he almost whined, "but do you love me or don'tcher?"

120 "Yes," she said and added, "in a sense. But I must tell you something. There mustn't be anything dishonest between us." She lifted his head and looked him in the eye. "I am thirty years old," she said. "I have a number of degrees."

121 The boy's look was irritated but dogged. "I don't care," he said. "I don't care a thing about what all you done. I just want to know if you love me or don'tcher?" and he caught her to him and wildly planted her face with kisses until she said, "Yes, yes."

122 "Okay then," he said, letting her go. "Prove it."

123 She smiled, looking dreamily out on the shifty landscape. She had seduced him without even making up her mind to try. "How?" she asked, feeling that he should be delayed a little.

124 He leaned over and put his lips to her ear. "Show me where your wooden leg joins on," he whispered.

125 The girl uttered a sharp little cry and her face instantly drained of color. The obscenity of the suggestion was not what shocked her. As a child she had sometimes been subject to feelings of shame but education had removed the last traces of that as a good surgeon scrapes for cancer; she would no more have felt it over what he was asking than she would have believed in his Bible. But she was as sensitive about the artificial leg as a peacock about his tail. No one ever touched it but her. She took care of it as someone else would his soul, in private and almost with her own eyes turned away. "No," she said.

126 "I known it," he muttered, sitting up. "You're just playing me for a sucker."

127 "Oh no no!" she cried. "It joins on at the knee. Only at the knee. Why do you want to see it?"

128 The boy gave her a long penetrating look. "Because," he said, "it's what makes you different. You ain't like anybody else."

129 She sat staring at him. There was nothing about her face or her round freezing-blue eyes to indicate that this had moved her; but she felt as if her heart had stopped and left her mind to pump her blood. She decided that for the first time in her life she was face to face with real innocence. This boy, with an instinct that came from beyond wisdom, had touched the truth about her. When after a minute, she said in a hoarse high voice, "All right," it was like surrendering to him completely. It was like losing her own life and finding it again, miraculously, in his.

130 Very gently he began to roll the slack leg up. The artificial limb, in a white sock and brown flat shoe, was bound in a heavy material like canvas and ended in an ugly jointure where it was attached to the stump. The boy's face and his voice were entirely reverent as he uncovered it and said, "Now show me how to take it off and on."

131　She took it off for him and put it back on again and then he took it off himself, handling it as tenderly as if it were a real one. "See!" he said with a delighted child's face. "Now I can do it myself!"

132　"Put it back on," she said. She was thinking that she would run away with him and that every night he would take the leg off and every morning put it back on again. "Put it back on," she said.

133　"Not yet," he murmured, setting it on its foot out of her reach. "Leave it off for a while. You got me instead."

134　She gave a little cry of alarm but he pushed her down and began to kiss her again. Without the leg she felt entirely dependent on him. Her brain seemed to have stopped thinking altogether and to be about some other function that it was not very good at. Different expressions raced back and forth over her face. Every now and then the boy, his eyes like two steel spikes, would glance behind him where the leg stood. Finally she pushed him off and said, "Put it back on me now."

135　"Wait," he said. He leaned the other way and pulled the valise toward him and opened it. It had a pale blue spotted lining and there were only two Bibles in it. He took one of these out and opened the cover of it. It was hollow and contained a pocket flask of whiskey, a pack of cards, and a small blue box with printing on it. He laid these out in front of her one at a time in an evenly-spaced row, like one presenting offerings at the shrine of a goddess. He put the blue box in her hand. THIS PRODUCT TO BE USED ONLY FOR THE PREVENTION OF DISEASE, she read, and dropped it. The boy was unscrewing the top of the flask. He stopped and pointed, with a smile, to the deck of cards. It was not an ordinary deck but one with an obscene picture on the back of each card. "Take a swig," he said, offering her the bottle first. He held it in front of her, but like one mesmerized, she did not move.

136　Her voice when she spoke had an almost pleading sound. "Aren't you," she murmured, "aren't you just good country people?"

137　The boy cocked his head. He looked as if he were just beginning to understand that she might be trying to insult him. "Yeah," he said, curling his lip slightly, "but it ain't held me back none. I'm as good as you any day in the week."

138　"Give me my leg," she said.

139　He pushed it farther away with his foot. "Come on now, let's begin to have us a good time," he said coaxingly. "We ain't got to know one another good yet."

140　"Give me my leg!" she screamed and tried to lunge for it but he pushed her down easily.

141　"What's the matter with you all of a sudden?" he asked, frowning as he screwed the top on the flask and put it quickly back inside the Bible. "You just a while ago said you didn't believe in nothing. I thought you was some girl!"

142　Her face was almost purple. "You're a Christian!" she hissed. "You're a fine Christian! You're just like them all—say one thing and do another. You're a perfect Christian, you're . . ."

143   The boy's mouth was set angrily. "I hope you don't think," he said in a lofty indignant tone, "that I believe in that crap! I may sell Bibles but I know which end is up and I wasn't born yesterday and I know where I'm going!"

144   "Give me my leg!" she screeched. He jumped up so quickly that she barely saw him sweep the cards and the blue box into the Bible and throw the Bible into the valise. She saw him grab the leg and then she saw it for an instant slanted forlornly across the inside of the suitcase with a Bible at either side of its opposite ends. He slammed the lid shut and snatched up the valise and swung it down the hole and then stepped through himself.

145   When all of him had passed but his head, he turned and regarded her with a look that no longer had any admiration in it. "I've gotten a lot of interesting things," he said. "One time I got a woman's glass eye this way. And you needn't to think you'll catch me because Pointer ain't really my name. I use a different name at every house I call at and don't stay nowhere long. And I'll tell you another thing, Hulga," he said, using the name as if he didn't think much of it, "you ain't so smart. I been believing in nothing ever since I was born!" and then the toast-colored hat disappeared down the hole and the girl was left, sitting on the straw in the dusty sunlight. When she turned her churning face toward the opening, she saw his blue figure struggling successfully over the green speckled lake.

146   Mrs. Hopewell and Mrs. Freeman, who were in the back pasture digging up onions, saw him emerge a little later from the woods and head across the meadow toward the highway. "Why, that looks like that nice dull young man that tried to sell me a Bible yesterday," Mrs. Hopewell said, squinting. "He must have been selling them to the Negroes back in there. He was so simple," she said, "But I guess the world would be better off if we were all that simple."

147   Mrs. Freeman's gaze drove forward and just touched him before he disappeared under the hill. Then she returned her attention to the evil-smelling onion shoot she was lifting from the ground. "Some can't be that simple," she said. "I know I never could."

A. Questions for Analysis

1. It is almost always impossible to describe why something is funny, since dissecting humor seems to have the effect of ruining it. Nonetheless, can you describe O'Connor's brand of humor in "Good Country People" and point to some examples that reflect it?

2. The title, "Good Country People," and other clichés are significant in this story. Who uses them? What use does O'Connor make of them?

3. What purpose does Mrs. Freeman serve?

4. What is Hulga's conception of herself? How does O'Connor reveal it?

5. Study the images O'Connor uses in paragraphs 1, 14, and 16. What do they have in common?

6. In what way are Hulga's degree in philosophy and her artificial leg symbolic?

7. This story might be interpreted as showing the discrepancy between appearance and reality. In what ways is this discrepancy shown in the story?

8. Reread the sequence in which the Bible salesman makes his first appearance. How does O'Connor manage to convey that the young man and his sales pitch are phony?

B. Vocabulary   For each italicized word from the story, choose the best definition according to the context in which it appears.

1. whose constant *outrage* [paragraph 5]: feeling of (a) exploitation; (b) disgrace; (c) resentful anger; (d) shame.

2. *obliterated* every expression [5]: (a) mashed; (b) destroyed completely; (c) altered slightly; (d) disrupted.

3. her face so *glum* [12]: (a) severe; (b) gloomy; (c) offensive; (d) sorrowful.

4. for days she would be *sullen* [15]: showing (a) brooding ill humor; (b) boredom; indifference; (c) arrogance; haughtiness; (d) loneliness; alienation.

5. the source of her displeasure was always *obscure* [15]: (a) unnoticed; (b) inconspicuous; (c) undisguised; humble; (d) hidden.

6. a positive *leer* [15]: (a) insult; (b) threat; (c) malicious look; (d) suggestive; sexual look.

7. some evil *incantation* [20]: (a) message; (b) mysterious code; (c) slogan; (d) magical spell; charm.

8. a tall, *gaunt* youth [23]: (a) decrepit; (b) thin and bony; (c) gray; ashen; (d) physically weak.

9. he said in an *abashed* voice [51]: (a) embarrassed; (b) alarmed; (c) puzzled; (d) ashamed.

10. the slight *insinuation* [71]: (a) interrogation; (b) inference; (c) indirect suggestion; (d) accusation.

11. she had to reckon with his *remorse* [91]: (a) compassion; (b) anxiety; (c) confusion; (d) regret.

12. he stood below, apparently *awe-struck* [110]: filled with (a) dread; (b) wonder; (c) confusion; (d) anticipation.

13. the boy's look was irritated but *dogged* [121—pronounced dog'id]: (a) surly; (b) submissive; (c) stubborn; (d) inflexible.

14. like one *mesmerized* [135]: (a) astounded; (b) anesthetized; (c) enchanted; (d) hypnotized. (Note: look up the etymology of this word in an unabridged dictionary.)

15. in a *lofty* indignant tone [143]: (a) pompous; (b) obstinate; (c) nasty; (d) sublime.

INDEX